About the Author

Thomas Christie has a life-long fascination with films and the people who make them. Currently reading for a PhD in Scottish literature, he lives in Scotland with his family.
He holds a first-class Honours degree in Literature and a Masters degree in Humanities, specialising with distinction in British Cinema History, from the Open University in Milton Keynes.
Books by Thomas Christie include *Liv Tyler, Star in Ascendance: Her First Decade in Film* (2007), *John Hughes and Eighties Cinema* (2009), *Ferris Bueller's Day Off: Pocket Movie Guide* (2010) and *The Cinema of Richard Linklater* (2011). Available from Crescent Moon Publishing.
For more information about Tom and his books, visit his website at: http://www.tomchristiebooks.co.uk

Julia Kristeva: Art, Love, Melancholy, Philosophy, Semiotics
by Kelly Ives

Luce Irigaray: Lips, Kissing, and the Politics of Sexual Difference
by Kelly Ives

Helene Cixous I Love You: The Jouissance of Writing
by Kelly Ives

THE CHRISTMAS MOVIE BOOK

TIM BURTON'S
THE
NIGHTMARE
BEFORE
CHRISTMAS

TOUCHSTONE PICTURES presents TIM BURTON'S "THE NIGHTMARE BEFORE CHRISTMAS" A BURTON/DINOVI Production
Music, Lyrics and Score by DANNY ELFMAN Based on a Story and Characters by TIM BURTON Adaptation by MICHAEL McDOWELL Animation Screenplay by CAROLINE THOMPSON
Produced by TIM BURTON and DENISE DINOVI Directed by HENRY SELICK

Thomas A. Christie

The Christmas Movie Book

CRESCENT MOON

First edition 2011. © Thomas A. Christie 2011.
Printed and bound in the U.S.A.

Set in Baskerville 10pt.
Designed by Radiance Graphics.

British Library Cataloguing in Publication data available for
this title.

ISBN-13 9781861713346

Crescent Moon Publishing
P.O. Box 1312
Maidstone
Kent
ME14 5XU, Great Britain
www.crmoon.com

contents

ACKNOWLEDGEMENTS

This book will always hold a very special significance to me. While in the process of writing it, thoroughly embroiled in my analysis of the jollity and good cheer of the festive season as I was, my dear mother Sandra passed away unexpectedly as the result of a short illness.

When my mother died, I didn't just lose a parent. I also lost my best friend. There is no way of measuring how many happy times we shared together, or all of the many different experiences that she encouraged and supported me through as we lived our lives together. From my first words all the way through to the launch of my first book, we were never far from each other's side. Her infectious zest for life, her thoughtfulness, her endless compassion and all of her little kindnesses will live with me for as long as I walk this earth.

But if there's one thing that could be said about Alexandra Christie, it's that she was a woman who truly loved Christmas. Mum had an enthusiasm for the festive season that could be matched by few others; nobody had their gifts stashed away earlier, or chosen with as much careful consideration. Even before the calendar had turned over to December, she would be planning out all of her decorations, making (very) early preparations for Christmas dinner, and counting down the days until the double issue of the *Radio Times* hit the shelves of the local newsagents.

It seems strangely appropriate that her passing should happen to coincide with me writing a book that focused on her favourite time of the year. I knew without doubt that there could be no greater tribute to her than to complete the work that I had begun, and to celebrate the Christmas spirit that she had loved so very much.

Mum's favourite Christmas movie was *The Bishop's Wife* – a film which is, at heart, an unabashed celebration of faith, family and community. These were all things which played a huge part in her life, and I would like to think that – just like Cary Grant's character, the angel Dudley – she left the world a better place for having passed through it, due to the positive and cheering effect that she'd had on so many lives over the years. Of all people, she knew that the Christmas spirit isn't just something that makes a guest appearance during a few days at the end of the year... although all too often, due to the demands and stresses of everyday life, that's exactly what we let it become. Mum showed me that the Christmas spirit is something that can – and should – be maintained throughout every day and every month of our lives, shown in common humanity, in support and concern for those around us. Altruism is never a weakness, and always a strength.

Until we meet again, mum, thank you so much for being the person that you were, and for forging me into the person that I have become. You taught me that there is always goodness and optimism to be found in a hard-edged and uncompromising world, if we only keep looking hard enough. It is so often the case that when life appears to be at its bleakest, the most surprising of things can lie just around the corner, and you showed me that hope – true hope – is a force that never ceases to surprise.

So rest in peace, mum, and know that I will always love you. You will be missed, but you will never be forgotten.

This book is dedicated to the memory of
my mother and father,
and to anyone else who has ever loved Christmas.

"I will honour Christmas in my heart, and try to keep it all the year."

A Christmas Carol (1843), Charles Dickens (1812–70)

"Christmas is not a date. It is a state of mind."

Mary Ellen Chase (1887–1973)

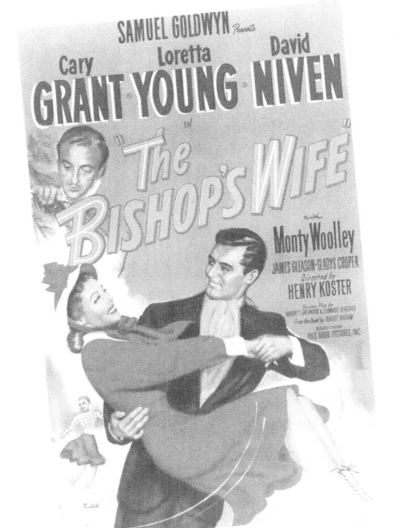

THIS HOLIDAY, DISCOVER YOUR INNER ELF.

INTRODUCTION

The festive season has enjoyed an unusual and surprisingly dynamic relationship with the international film industry over the years. Christmas, after all, is a time of year which has become increasingly well-known for the traditions that have developed around it, as much as for its religious (and, more recently, commercial) significance. It is a month of the year that has brought us everything from annual greetings cards to plastic fir trees propped up in living rooms across the Western world. Yet for all the deeply traditional conventions that have come to be associated with this fondly-anticipated season of the year, the Christmas film has come to prove every bit as adaptive as other cinematic genres during the rapid social changes of the twentieth century, and movies in this category can still command formidable returns at the box-office even in the present day. As the decades have passed by, so too have the themes and styles of these festively-themed motion pictures continued to develop – radically so in some periods – in order to remain relevant to contemporary audiences. Sometimes the premise of modern takes on the Christmas film will be inventive, sometimes they are distinctly offbeat, but more often than not they can still be seen to retain some distant reflection of the optimistic, life-affirming foundations of the genre which were laid down during its golden age in the 1940s and 50s.

This book covers some of the most significant movies from sixty years of the Christmas film genre, from the period immediately following World War II up to the turn of the new millennium and beyond. Although there had been numerous other films with a festive theme before this date – most memorably Gus Meins's and Charles Rogers's *Babes in Toyland* (1934), Edwin L. Marin's *A Christmas Carol* (1938), Mark Sandrich's *Holiday Inn* (1942), Vincente Minnelli's *Meet Me in St Louis* (1944) and Robert Siodmak's *Christmas Holiday* (1944) – I would be inclined to argue that the distinct category of the Christmas film as it has come to be recognised today began to take shape in the post-War years, largely due to the long-term artistic influence of the films in this formative genre which were being produced at that time. To this end, it may perhaps be of use to explain the use of the term 'Christmas film' as it appears in the context of the analysis to come. It is now generally considered that there are three discrete categories of Christmas motion picture. First, and most pertinent to this study, is the film that deals with the theme of Christmas as its central subject matter, considers issues deriving from the festive season, or which somehow examines the social, cultural or religious conventions of Christmas. The second category, which is also referred to occasionally throughout the book, is the film which is set at Christmas, either principally or in part, but which may or may not directly address topics directly related to Christmas. These include comedies and dramas set during the festive period but which lack a specific Christmas theme, such as Frank Capra's *Pocketful of Miracles* (1961), Nora Ephron's *Mixed Nuts* (1994) and Doug Liman's *Go* (1999), but at the more extreme end of the spectrum may also encompass features such as Richard Donner's seasonally-aligned *Lethal Weapon* (1987) or even John McTiernan's *Die Hard* (1988), where the action takes place entirely on Christmas Eve (not that the terrorist-infested Nakatomi Tower ever seemed to be in much danger of an impromptu visit from Santa Claus). The third category, which is not covered by the remit of this book, refers to the films which are regularly shown by television networks over the course of the festive period (especially in the United Kingdom), but which otherwise have no direct connection with Christmas. Features in this category typically include cinematic classics and epic blockbusters such as John Sturges's *The Great Escape* (1963) and Victor Fleming's *The Wizard of Oz* (1939), popular musicals like Robert Wise's *The Sound of Music* (1965) and Ken Hughes's *Chitty Chitty Bang Bang* (1968), and the appearance of at least one entry from Eon Productions' perennially successful James Bond film series.

It must also be noted that this book discusses films which have been produced for, and screened on, the big screen only. There is no examination of features which have been produced by television networks over the years, largely because to do so would necessitate another volume of analysis entirely – the 1960s and 70s in particular saw the production of some highly memorable Christmas TV movies featuring big-name actors, among them Paul Bogart's *A House Without a Christmas Tree* (1972) and Eric Till's *An American Christmas Carol* (1979), while cinematic output in the genre during the same period was notably sparse. Indeed, the Christmas TV movie has continued to go from strength to strength over the past few decades, meaning that entries in this category have become entirely too plentiful for this survey to address in any kind of satisfactory way. For this reason, the great many direct-to-video releases of recent years are also not included within the confines of this study.

Naturally, no discussion of Christmas films can possibly avoid featuring Charles Dickens' famous novella *A Christmas Carol* (1843) at some point in the proceedings. This story, perhaps the most prominent among all tales of the festive season in English literature, has been adapted many times for television and the cinema, both in the form of straightforward period adaptations of the Dickens text and in reinterpretations which have updated the central premise for contemporary audiences. Indeed, anything approaching a full appraisal of cinematic versions of *A Christmas Carol* could easily have filled this book many times over, but to do so would have presented only a partial and fractional analysis of a filmic genre which is, as we will see, deeply multifaceted in nature. For this reason, within this book I have limited discussion of film adaptations of *A Christmas Carol* to no more than one per decade, which gives some indication of how this one well-known story – which admittedly bestrides the genre like a colossus – fits into the broader canvas of the Christmas film. Anyone seeking a fuller examination of the many ways in which Dickens's festive tale has been reinvented and reinterpreted over the course of past decades need look no further than Fred Guida's excellent resource *'A Christmas Carol' and Its Adaptations: A Critical Examination of Dickens' Story and Its Productions on Stage, Screen and Television* (2000), which offers a detailed and comprehensive overview of Ebenezer Scrooge's tribulations in their many varied cinematic forms.[1]

The collection of specific films which I have chosen for discussion in this book may seem mildly controversial to some, but they have been carefully selected in order to give the broadest possible analysis of the different themes addressed by directors and screenwriters in Christmas motion pictures over the course of the chronological period that is under examination. Apologies if some of your personal favourites haven't been included in the coming chapters, but I hope that you will find that elements of the full gamut of Christmas films can be glimpsed throughout the following pages, from the good (*It's a Wonderful Life*) to the bad (*Santa Claus Conquers the Martians*) via the classic (*White Christmas*) and the unconventional (*Black Christmas*).

Taken together, the choice of films in this book has been employed as a springboard for a broader assessment of how they have come to fit into the wider tapestry of Christmas movie subgenres, and to discuss the range of conventions and themes that have been established as time has passed. Although recent years have borne witness to the well-received publication of comprehensive surveys of Christmas films, including Frank Thompson's acclaimed *American Movie Classics' Great Christmas Movies* (1998)[2] and Gary and Susan Svehla's excellent *It's Christmas Time at the Movies* (1998)[3], this book takes a slightly different approach to the subject. By employing a chronological frame of reference, the evolution of the canon of Christmas films will be charted from 1945 onwards, and the changing styles and attitudes of audiences will be addressed as well as universal themes which have remained constant within the genre across the passing years. Christmas films have not only been enjoyed by vast audiences over the decades, but have also proven to be deeply influential, inspiring directors and screenwriters in profound and occasionally unusual ways. Sometimes these films are intended to promote seasonal themes of peace, mutual understanding and goodwill, while others slyly provide satirical comment on culture and society at the time of their production. On more than a few occasions both approaches have been employed at once, and to great effect. So pour a glass of mulled wine, help yourself to a mince pie, and get ready to discover the way that Christmas Past came to develop into Christmas Present as well, perhaps, as taking a glimpse into what Christmas Future may yet have to offer us.

PROLOGUE:
EARLY CHRISTMAS FILMS

It is no exaggeration to say that Christmas films have been with us, in one form or another, since the birth of cinema itself. The development of the genre which we have come to identify as the Christmas film, however, has been a gradual one which took form over a number of decades. Although the foundations of what we now recognise as archetypes of Christmas film-making were laid down in the genre's golden age in the period immediately following the Second World War, movies with a Christmas setting had been made as far back as the end of the nineteenth century, with many silent films and early 'talkies' being situated in a festive locale or incorporating Christmas iconography into their narratives.

There is growing consensus amongst commentators that the first Christmas film to be exhibited to the general public was the American Mutoscope Company's *Night Before Christmas* (1897), a short feature which centred upon a group of children hanging up stockings in their family home on Christmas Eve before heading for bed in anticipation of a visit from Santa Claus. The directorial credit for this film is generally attributed to American Mutoscope's famous founder, William Kennedy Dickson, and it was to form the first instalment of a cycle of four interrelated Christmas features, all of which were released in the same year. (The other short films in the cycle, in order, were *Santa Claus Filling Stockings*, *Christmas Morning*, and *The Christmas Tree Party*). American Mutoscope's famous cycle has also come to be known collectively by the title *Christmas Eve* (1897) and also *The Visit of St Nicholas* (1897), though perhaps the most significant other Christmas film of the late nineteenth century was a British feature, *Santa Claus* (1898), which had a running time of around one minute in duration and was produced by George Albert Smith Films. Directed by Smith himself, this feature was remarkable in a number of ways: it was one of the first films to include an opening title screen which contained alphabetic lettering, it used iris-masking of the camera lens in order to produce a fantasy sequence which played out over the main action, and it was also to utilise some pioneering visual effects (for the time) such as stop-motion jump-cuts. It, like Dickson's film, featured a brief appearance from Santa Claus as he visits a family home on Christmas Eve.

The dawn of the twentieth century brought with it a boom in silent features, with an eager public appetite for new works in all kinds of different genres. The Christmas film was no exception, and the opening decades of the new century were to bring a wide variety of entries in this incipient category of moviemaking. Amongst the most prominent works to see release in this period included the heart-warming family scenes of *A Holiday Pageant at Home* (1901), Edwin S. Porter's *The Night Before Christmas* (1905) (which included some inventive effects work), and D.W. Griffith's spirited *A Winter Straw Ride* (1906). Rather more serious in tone was *A Trap for Santa* (1909), which dealt with themes of alcoholism and petty crime over the festive season, and Harold M. Shaw and Bannister Merwin's *A Christmas Accident* (1912), an early tale of yuletide redemption. Burglary and mistaken identity featured in *The Adventure of the Wrong Santa Claus* (1914), where an opportunistic felon receives his comeuppance when caught during some Christmas Eve thievery, while Will Louis's *Santa Claus Versus Cupid* (1915) shares the theme of criminality but concludes its narrative positively thanks to the timely intervention of Father Christmas himself. Mr and Mrs F.E. Kleinschmidt released their independent production *Santa Claus* (1925) some years later, where Jolly Old Saint Nick recounts his numerous activities outwith his annual Christmas Eve travels around the globe, while shortly afterwards popular comedian Charley Chase was to star in *There Ain't No Santa Claus* (1926), an offbeat tale of romantic gestures, Christmas gifts and overdue rent money.

By far the most prominent yuletide feature in the cinema of these decades was, perhaps not surprisingly, a string of adaptations of Charles Dickens's *A Christmas Carol*. Among the best-remembered of these early festive outings was Walter R. Booth's *Scrooge, or, Marley's Ghost* (1901), a five-minute silent British feature which is generally considered to be the earliest surviving filmed version of the story. This was followed by Essanay Studios' *A Christmas Carol* (1908), filmed in Chicago with Thomas Ricketts as Scrooge, and another silent version, J. Searle Dawley's *A Christmas Carol* (1910), produced for Edison Studios and starring Marc Dermott as the famous Dickensian miser. The short film *Scrooge* (1913) (also known as *Old Scrooge* from the time of its American screening some years later) starred Sir Seymour Hicks, who had played Ebenezer to great acclaim in stage productions in years gone by, while 1916 was to see the release of Rupert Julian's famous *The Right to Be Happy* (1916), featuring Julian himself in the role of Scrooge, which was the first adaptation of *A Christmas Carol* to run to feature length. Also held in critical esteem was Edwin Greenwood's *A Christmas Carol* (1923), a British production which presented Russell Thorndike as the penny-pinching Victorian anti-hero.

Another recurrent staple of this early period of Christmas film-making were the many adaptations of Peter B. Kyne's 1913 novel *The Three Godfathers*, which proved to be almost as popular a source of inspiration as Dickens's novella had been. Cinematic versions of the tale began with Edward LeSaint's *The Three Godfathers* (1916), which was remade a few years later by John Ford under the title *Marked Men* (1919). Both films starred Harry Carey, and featured a story which centred upon three bank robbers who accidentally stumble upon a newly-born infant child in the desert - a scenario with obvious overtones of the Nativity. The film was remade by William Wyler as *Hell's Heroes* (1930), the first film that he had directed which was to feature a sound track, and then it was to be adapted again by Richard Boleslawski in 1936 (once more with the title *The Three Godfathers*) before John Ford returned to the story to create what has become widely regarded as the definitive version in 1948, starring John Wayne, Pedro Armendáriz and Harry Carey Jr.

The era of the talkies brought with them a new wave of Christmas-related features, albeit with a very broad range of subject matter which meant that some dealt with the themes of the festive season more closely than others. Tom Walls's *Turkey Time* (1933), an adaptation of Ben Travers's stage play, was a Christmas-situated comic family farce, while Charles Rogers and Gus Meins's *Babes in Toyland* (1934) (sometimes known in later years by the alternative title *March of the Wooden Soldiers*), was a comic fantasy which made good use of its legendary stars Stan Laurel and Oliver Hardy. Based on Victor Herbert's 1903 operetta of the same name, *Babes in Toyland* is one of the few films of this vintage which remains readily available on the commercial market; it has been colourised more than once, and was remade by Jack Donohue for the Walt Disney Company in 1961. Henry Edwards's *Scrooge* (1935) was a British feature-length version of Dickens's story, with Sir Seymour Hicks reprising his role as Ebenezer Scrooge following his appearance in the 1913 silent adaptation. Edwards's version is considered to be the first version of the tale to feature sound, but its reputation has been dwarfed in subsequent years by Edwin L. Marin's *A Christmas Carol* (1938), a glossy MGM production which starred Reginald Owen as Scrooge. The Marin version is perhaps the best-known feature-length adaptation of the Dickens text prior to Brian Desmond Hurst's legendary 1951 film which introduced Alastair Sim in the title role. George B. Seitz's (now rather obscure) comic crime fantasy *The Three Wise Guys* (1936) also made its debut in this decade, as did Garson Kanin's *Bachelor Mother* (1939), a well-received comedy of manners set around the festive season which starred David Niven and Ginger Rogers.

The war years were to bring about a modest boom in Christmas films, the comforting conventions and warm assurance of the nascent genre proving to be a welcome departure from the horrors that were affecting Europe and, later, the Pacific at the time of production. Steve Sekely's *A Miracle on Main Street* (1940) and Mitchell Leisen's *Remember the Night* (1940) were both melodramas set at Christmas, the latter more romantically-oriented than the former, whereas love and affection were to form the basis of Edward Sutherland's *Beyond Tomorrow* (1940), a festive fantasy with an appealing line in whimsy. Preston Sturges's *Christmas in July* (1940) is a warm-hearted tale of goodwill, but perhaps the best-known feature of the year came in the form of Ernst Lubitsch's *The Shop Around the Corner* (1940), which starred a youthful James Stewart and Margaret Sullavan. Lubitsch's film, a romantic comedy set in Budapest, won praise for the performances of its two accomplished leads and was later adapted into a Broadway musical in 1963. Frank Capra's scathing social satire *Meet John Doe* (1941) also made effective use of the Christmas period, as did Mark Sandrich's *Holiday Inn* (1942). Although the latter film only features one short section which takes place over the festive season, it was memorable enough - particularly when coupled with the big-screen debut of Irving Berlin's hugely successful song 'White Christmas' (performed by the inimitable Bing Crosby), which would find even greater fame in later years - that it has latterly become something of a yuletide staple. William Keighley's *The Man Who Came to Dinner* (1942) was an adaptation of Moss Hart and George S. Kaufman's successful 1939 comedy stage play of the same name, and was to feature a delightful turn from stage veteran Monty Woolley as the protagonist Sheridan Whiteside. Woolley would return to festive cinema some years later, with arguably even greater success, in Henry Koster's *The Bishop's Wife* (1947). With the war nearing its conclusion, William Dieterle's romantic comedy *I'll Be Seeing You* (1944) was joined on cinema screens by Robert Siodmak's distinctive film noir *Christmas Holiday* (1944), an adaptation of a W. Somerset Maugham novel which was a rather downbeat take on crime and domestic unhappiness set against the backdrop of Christmas. But perhaps the most noteworthy festive feature of the period immediately before the cessation of World War II was Vincente Minnelli's *Meet Me in St Louis* (1944), a triumph of musical wistfulness which celebrated times gone by as well as, though expressed by rather more subtle means, encouraging optimism for the years to come.

As the above summation demonstrates, a reasonable number of films had been released between the turn of the century and the end of the Second World War which had made use of a Christmas setting, but relatively few of them had dealt directly with the nature of the festive season itself. Although producers, directors and screenwriters had employed Christmas to achieve a variety of functions - from providing an atmospheric backdrop for domestic dramas to framing comic situations - not many were inclined to consider the season in depth, in order to examine (as Dickens had done with such panache) exactly what it was about that fateful, wintry period in December that wielded the power to transform attitudes and mould new hope and optimism from despair and broken dreams. All of that was to change with the end of the war, as the West entered a period of intense self-consideration and cultural reflection which was to touch every part of society. The Christmas film was about to enter its golden age: an era which would define the themes of the genre, and forever change expectations about this most unique time of year.

†

THE BELLS OF ST MARY'S (1945)

Rainbow Productions

Director: Leo McCarey
Producer: Leo McCarey
Screenwriter: Dudley Nichols, from a story by Leo McCarey

MAIN CAST

Bing Crosby	-	Father Chuck O'Malley
Ingrid Bergman	-	Sister Mary Benedict
Henry Travers	-	Horace P. Bogardus
William Gargan	-	Joe Gallagher
Ruth Donnelly	-	Sister Michael
Joan Carroll	-	Patricia 'Patsy' Gallagher
Martha Sleeper	-	Mary Gallagher
Rhys Williams	-	Dr McKay

The Bells of St Mary's may seem like a slightly contentious choice to begin a survey of Christmas films. Although it has come to be comfortably embedded within the genre over the years, and indeed is now one of the most regularly cited Christmas features of the period immediately following the Second World War, on first glance the film actually appears to spend very little time centring upon the festive season itself. However, with its prominent messages of faith and goodwill, *The Bells of St Mary's* was to present the viewer with many of the themes which have come to be associated with the pantheon of Christmas films in general. Nor indeed should we allow the film's comparatively short dalliance with the festive season to distract us from its underlying purpose: when Scrooge asserts at the end of *A Christmas Carol* that he promises to keep Christmas in his heart the whole of the year round, he could do far worse than look to *The Bells of St Mary's* for a blueprint of how to do exactly that.

The film, in its depiction of organised religion, actually proves to be something of a peculiarity in the broader canon of Christmas films. On the face of it, this may seem like an unusual fact given the historical origin of Christmas celebrations. Although later features would occasionally dip into traditional religious iconography, calling upon elements ranging from angels to the Virgin Birth, *The Bells of St Mary's* centres upon people of faith and the manner in which their belief in a supreme being can bring about events which would otherwise seem impossible. While many other subsequent Christmas films would draw upon the vital importance of having faith in one's fellow human being, few others – even during this period which preceded multi-faith (and now secularist) Western society – were to deal with the perceived significance of religious belief quite so directly. This interesting clash between the spiritual and the practical would later be explored by Henry Koster in *The Bishop's Wife* (1947), and of course in George More O'Ferrall's *The Holly and the Ivy* (1952).

The Bells of St Mary's was directed by long-time industry veteran Leo McCarey, who also acted as producer as well as providing the storyline for the film's screenplay. McCarey had been active as a director since 1921, having helmed a wide variety of features including *Let's Go Native* (1930), *The Awful Truth* (1937), *Make Way for Tomorrow* (1937) and *Love Affair* (1939). Throughout his distinguished career, he had worked with such legends of early Hollywood as Harold Lloyd, Laurel and Hardy, Mae West and Eddie Cantor, in addition to directing one of the Marx Brothers' best-known films, *Duck Soup* (1933). His characteristic blend of subtle, understated comedy and sentimental human observation was to reach its apex with *Going My Way* (1944), the film which was to introduce audiences to the popular character of Father Charles 'Chuck' O'Malley, played with much verve by Bing Crosby. The plot centred upon the arrival of O'Malley at the parish of St Dominic's, where he energetically attempts to modernise the church's appeal to the wider neighbourhood in order to better serve the community in which it is based. The film was a huge hit at the box-office and did exceptionally well with critics, going on to win seven Academy Awards (including Best Picture, Best Director and Best Actor) and being nominated for a further three.[1] The massive success of *Going My Way* would lead to a much-anticipated sequel the following year, a production which was to reunite McCarey and Crosby: *The Bells of St Mary's*.

Father O'Malley has been assigned by the church to support the nuns who administrate a ramshackle inner-city parochial school named St Mary's. The building is dilapidated and, in spite of recent structural repairs, is heading towards dereliction. O'Malley learns that the children face a cross-town journey to another school if St Mary's is condemned, though the sisters of the school – led by the devoted Sister Mary Benedict (Ingrid Bergman) – are adamant that the power of prayer will solve their problems.

A modern office building is being constructed next to the school, on the playing fields which have had to be sold in order to fund the repairs to St Mary's. Sister Benedict believes that they must all put their trust in God to persuade the new building's owner, curmudgeonly businessman Horace P. Bogardus (Henry Travers), to donate it to the church so that it can be used as a new school with modern facilities. However, she greatly underestimates Bogardus's stubbornness: the crotchety mogul is determined to buy St Mary's itself for a token sum so that he can demolish it and turn the area into a car park for his new workforce. If the church refuses to sell the school, Bogardus is fully prepared to use his influence with the city's planning council to close it down compulsorily.

As the film progresses, the viewer follows Father O'Malley and Sister Benedict through a year of trials and tribulations at St Mary's. In that time, the staid Sister Benedict must instruct one of her bullied young students in the noble art of boxing, and Father O'Malley manages to repair the ailing marriage of estranged couple Joe and Mary Gallagher (William Gargan and Martha Sleeper) while helping to buoy the self-confidence of their daughter Patsy (Joan Carroll). The staff even manage to squeeze in a heavily improvised Nativity play, enacted by the infant members of St Mary's, which culminates in a rousing rendition of 'Happy Birthday to You' as the baby Jesus makes His way into the world.

As the end-of-term graduation nears, time is beginning to run out for St Mary's. O'Malley attempts to talk Bogardus into giving St Mary's a reprieve, but he simply won't hear of it. However, upon later discovering that the older man is suffering from a heart complaint, O'Malley succeeds in convincing Bogardus's doctor (and, eventually, Bogardus himself) that by performing selfless deeds he has the potential to improve his physical wellbeing as well as his spiritual welfare. This message takes a while to filter through to Bogardus, but eventually he begins to consider O'Malley's instruction more seriously. After a period of prayer at his local chapel, Bogardus takes into account the many benefits that his new building could bring to the children who attend St Mary's. He tells Sister Benedict that – in spite of the considerable cost of the office block's construction – he has decided to donate it to the church in order to allow the students to have access to modern facilities. The sisters are overjoyed that their prayers have been answered in the nick of time.

While the new school is outfitted with up-to-the-minute equipment, Dr McKay (Rhys Williams) informs O'Malley that he has discovered during a routine chest X-ray that Sister Benedict is suffering from the early stages of tuberculosis. He implores O'Malley to keep the news from Sister Benedict, in the hope that her generally optimistic outlook will speed a recovery if she is unaware of the potential seriousness of her condition. O'Malley arranges with the church to transfer her across the country to a warmer, drier climate in the expectation that her health will improve, but Sister Benedict is devastated by the news that she will no longer be able to head up the new St Mary's when it opens for the first time. She initially believes that O'Malley has recommended her removal, given that they had disagreed over a number of issues during their time working together, and although she leaves her post without complaint she is distraught at having to do so. Just as she is set to depart the premises, however, O'Malley finds that he is unable to let her go without a frank explanation of her situation, and relates the circumstances more fully. Now seeing the full picture, Sister Benedict is elated – not only does she realise that there is no bad blood between O'Malley and herself, but there is also a real possibility that she can return to St Mary's once the condition of her health picks up. Satisfied with the direction of her life once more, she leaves the school willingly and contentedly.

The Bells of St Mary's presents a disarmingly idealised depiction of contemporary life, where it seems that all problems can be overcome with little more than a kind heart and unwavering faith in a higher authority. Any naïveté that this may imply to modern eyes must be considered in the context of the general moral climate of the time. As Bruce Babington and Peter William Evans note in their book Biblical Epics: Sacred Narrative in the Hollywood Cinema (1993), the effectiveness by which the film achieves its aims can be seen to lie in the fact that no matter how lofty the issue of spirituality may seem, the characters' goals are inevitably practical and functional, benefiting ordinary people and working to the advantage of the community at large.[2] It is testament to McCarey's breezy direction that the film does not linger overduly upon incidents which, though unashamedly sentimental, always stop short of having a quality of out-and-out saccharine. While the requisite bullying and needling takes place between the schoolkids of St Mary's from time to time, everyone always somehow manages to achieve rapprochement in the end with their heads held high. Horace Bogardus, the hardest of hard-nosed businessmen, has no time for the intrinsic value that the sisters of St Mary's place on their school, and yet is somehow able to be persuaded by a combination of divine intervention and O'Malley's smooth-talking. And, of course, the gentle differences of opinion between the earnest but demure Sister Benedict and the progressive, cheery Father O'Malley are fully resolved by the film's conclusion, where the best of all possible resolutions has been established.

It is easy to see why The Bells of St Mary's became so popular with the audiences of the time. The film's optimistic conviction must have seemed particularly welcome to cinemagoers after the intense dramas and propaganda features which had populated theatres during the war years. Although its actual Christmas content extends only so far as the brief sequence where the school's infants enact a (somewhat radically adapted) stage version of the Nativity, the film's December release in cinemas did seem appropriate. This is a feature which exudes goodwill and mutual understanding, such that it transcends its underlying message of the power of religious faith to extend into a rather more broadly encompassing narrative which centres on considering the common good over one's own personal goals. Though the film is not entirely without concession to material needs, this materialism is largely passive in nature. The desire for a new school building, for instance, not only saves the children from a long journey to another facility elsewhere in the city, but also retains the sisters' sense of purpose and pride in their instructive and developmental roles. (It is also strongly hinted that Bogardus is rich enough to avoid financial ruin by donating his prized office block – and, indeed, he receives a valuable trade-off in the greater feeling of self-worth and generosity of spirit that his altruistic benevolence achieves.)

Slightly more contentious is Father O'Malley's proactive behaviour in reconciling Joe and Mary Gallagher. Although separated for many years (though not actually divorced), O'Malley tracks down wayward musician Joe who eventually recognises the need to reconcile with his estranged wife and start afresh. O'Malley's actions are in part motivated by a desire to recreate a stable home life for the couple's daughter, Patsy, a bright student whose emotional turbulence is causing her to fail at school. The importance of the family unit is a perennial theme that runs through many Christmas films, but rarely is its significance quite so profoundly indicated as it is throughout *The Bells of St Mary's*. However, credibility is stretched to near breaking point by the way in which the couple instantly reintegrate into each other's lives, striking up a largely-effortless reconciliation in spite of being separated for so long that their daughter doesn't even recognise her father. Yet this in turn provides additional drama when the sensitive Patsy – who through a misunderstanding believes that her mother is seeing another man – is thrown into such turmoil that she fails her end of year exams. Patsy's poor performance in class leads to a standoff between Sister Benedict, who believes that standards must be maintained at all costs, and Father O'Malley, who suggests that perhaps bending the rules might be admissible in order to avoid the crippling effect on Patsy's self-esteem if she isn't somehow allowed to pass. That both characters' views seem so reasonable is laudable even although, in the serendipitous tradition of the rest of the film, a mutually-agreeable resolution is eventually arrived at.

McCarey makes full use of his star cast, with Bing Crosby, Ingrid Bergman and Henry Travers all delivering excellent performances. Crosby was of course a highly successful performer by the mid-1940s, his vocal talents and likeable acting style ensuring that he quickly became well-known for his appearances in popular musical features including Norman Z. McLeod's *Pennies from Heaven* (1936), Victor Schertzinger's *Rhythm on the River* (1940) and Mark Sandrich's festive *Holiday Inn* (1942), as well as appearances in the hugely successful *The Road To* film series (1940-62) where he appeared alongside Bob Hope and Dorothy Lamour, and his Oscar-winning role in *Going My Way* in 1944. Crosby's performance as Chuck O'Malley allows ample opportunity to display his renowned aptitude for singing throughout the course of the film, and his effortless charm works well in emphasising the on-screen chemistry he shares with Ingrid Bergman's Sister Mary

Benedict. Bergman, who had appeared in films in her native Sweden from 1932, shot to fame in Gustaf Molander's *Intermezzo* (1936), later remade by Gregory Ratoff in 1939 as *Intermezzo: A Love Story*. Although she had enjoyed great success for performances in films as diverse as Sam Wood's *For Whom the Bell Tolls* (1943), George Cukor's *Gaslight* (1944) and Alfred Hitchcock's *Spellbound* (1945), it is almost certainly her appearance as Ilsa Lund in Michael Curtiz's *Casablanca* (1942) that had gained her a full measure of cinematic immortality. Bergman creates a multi-faceted character which belies Sister Benedict's prim and slightly stolid exterior; whether teaching a bullied student the refinements of pugilism or reviving her youthful passion for baseball, the viewer is left in little doubt that this nun is a character who seeks to embrace society and improve the lives of others, rather than simply shy away from the world that lies outside her cloistered existence.

Bergman and Crosby create a fascinating on-screen duo, a pairing made all the more interesting by the fact that – due to their characters' devout religious faith – there is never any clichéd reliance on romantic tension, but rather the development of a professional friendship which, in spite of their frequent differences of opinion, endures the ups and downs of their rarefied situation.[3] Their central roles are well supported by a talented cast of supporting actors, including Ruth Donnelly as a quietly refined Sister Michael and Rhys Williams as the jocular Dr McKay, but particular praise is due for Henry Travers as the bewildered Horace Bogardus. A British-born character actor who had been active in film since 1933, usually playing amiable or eccentric parts in films such as Richard Thorpe's *Wyoming* (1940), Raoul Walsh's *High Sierra* (1941) and perhaps most notably William Wyler's *Mrs Miniver* (1942), Travers brings dignity and more than a touch of humour to Bogardus, managing to make his improbable transformation of character appear as plausible as the narrative will allow. Evolving from a pitiless capitalist into a slightly baffled philanthropist throughout the course of the film, the dextrous Travers works hard to imbue Bogardus with a kind of credible internal motivation as the befuddled businessman tries to rationalise the unconventional logic that O'Malley sets loose upon him. Yet of course, Travers's role as Bogardus was not his most prominent performance in a Christmas film, for only a year later he would make his famous appearance (possibly the best-known of his career) as the affable angel Clarence Oddbody in Frank Capra's *It's a Wonderful Life*.

The Bells of St Mary's was a smash hit at the box-office, and its success was reflected in its performance at awards ceremonies. Although it failed to replicate the massive achievement of *Going My Way* at the Academy Awards, the film nonetheless received an impressive seven nominations for Oscars (including Best Actor in a Leading Role, Best Actress in a Leading Role, Best Director and Best Picture), and won an award for Best Sound Recording. The film also won a Gold Medal at the 1946 Photoplay Awards, while Ingrid Bergman's performance as Sister Mary Benedict earned her a Golden Globe Award and a New York Film Critics Circle Award in the same year. The film's enduring resonance with audiences at the time led Crosby and Bergman to reprise their roles for two separate radio adaptations of *The Bells of St Mary's*, which were broadcast in August 1946 and October 1947.[4] Additionally, a television remake was produced by CBS in 1959; directed by Tom Donovan, it starred Robert Preston as Father O'Malley, Claudette Colbert as Sister Benedict, and Charles Ruggles as Horace Bogardus. Although *The Bells of St Mary's* contained a number of songs, the rendition of the title song has become far and away the best-known. Composed by A. Emmett Adams with lyrics by Douglas Furber, it was first published in 1917 but became greatly popularised by the success of the McCarey's film. It has since been re-recorded many times by artists as diverse as Perry Como, the Drifters, Andy Williams, Connie Francis, Vera Lynn, Jimmy Preston and Sheryl Crow.

In *The Bells of St Mary's*, Father O'Malley makes mention of the generosity of spirit that comes from Christmas, and indeed the film's rapid succession through one particular period in the school's life shows clearly how McCarey is suggesting that the values and goodwill of the festive season can be applied to wider existence outside of a single week in December. As mentioned earlier, the film is among the most overtly spiritual of films associated with Christmas, its status challenged only perhaps by Henry Koster's *The Bishop's Wife* (1947) and Milton H. Lehr's *The Juggler of Notre Dame* (1970), and yet for a film about religious faith it undoubtedly manages to be secular enough to satisfy mainstream tastes. Indeed, so wide-ranging is the human scope of McCarey's canvas that we are left in no doubt that irrespective of the viewer's own religious beliefs (or even lack of them), this film articulates with unwavering precision the director's message that every member of society carries within themselves the capacity to improve the lives of others; irrespective of the scale of these efforts, we are shown that all are significant in their own way and always have the potential to encourage the most profound of transformations.

Historical Context

The Bells of St. Mary's premiered in the United States on 6 December 1945, in New York City, going on national release on 27 December that year. Other films making their first appearance on the same release date were Edwin L. Marin's *Johnny Angel*, D. Ross Lederman's *Out of the Depths*, Harry Edwards's *Spook to Me*, Phil Rosen's *The Red Dragon* and Humphrey Jennings's *A Diary for Timothy*. Topping the Billboard chart of Best Sellers in Stores that week was Harry James with 'It's Been a Long, Long Time'. In the news during the week of *The Bells of St. Mary's* cinematic release was the formal foundation of the World Bank and the establishment of the International Monetary Fund, while the United States Congress made official its recognition of the Pledge of Allegiance.

2

IT'S A WONDERFUL LIFE (1946)

Liberty Films

Director: Frank Capra
Producer: Frank Capra
Screenwriter: Frances Goodrich, Albert Hackett and Frank Capra, with additional scenes by Jo Swerling, from a story by Philip Van Doren Stern

MAIN CAST

James Stewart	-	George Bailey
Donna Reed	-	Mary Hatch Bailey
Henry Travers	-	Clarence Oddbody
Lionel Barrymore	-	Mr Potter
Thomas Mitchell	-	Uncle Billy
Beulah Bondi	-	Mrs Bailey
Frank Faylen	-	Ernie
Ward Bond	-	Bert

What can possibly be said about Frank Capra's *It's a Wonderful Life* that hasn't already been considered many, many times before? Almost certainly the most recognisable of all modern Christmas stories, the film has become a true classic of modern cinema: a motion picture which has genuinely stood the test of time, being faithfully screened every festive season around the world, it has come to epitomise everything that is heart-warming about the Christmas spirit. And yet it is indisputably true to say that *It's a Wonderful Life* has become much more than simply a festive cinematic favourite. Beloved of academics and media commentators for decades, Capra's complex narrative and multiple layers of subtext have ensured that the movie has become one of the most thoroughly discussed American films of the post-War period.

In many ways, *It's a Wonderful Life* is the quintessential Christmas film. Its enduring popularity over the years is testament to the universal nature of its key themes and its evocation of the positive effects of community spirit and human kindness. Although it faced a relatively lukewarm critical and commercial reception on its initial release in 1946,[1] the film has now come to be regarded as an all-time classic ever since its unexpected revival on television networks throughout the 1970s. Released repeatedly on VHS video, DVD and now Blu-Ray, including a number of attempts to colourise the film (with varying degrees of success), *It's a Wonderful Life* has now entered into the public consciousness so profoundly that for generations it has become synonymous with Christmas at the movies.

It's a Wonderful Life marked an interesting point in the careers of both its director, Frank Capra, and its star James Stewart. For the multiple Academy Award winner Capra, the film's lack of pulling power at the box-office dealt his career an unfortunate blow, meaning that he was never again to reach the dizzying heights of his earlier successes with acclaimed films such as *It Happened One Night* (1934), *Mr Deeds Goes to Town* (1936), *You Can't Take It With You* (1939), *Mr Smith Goes to Washington* (1939) and *Arsenic and Old Lace* (1944). Yet it must be emphasised that the film was not the crippling box-office failure that urban myth has come to suggest: its commercial performance saw it do more than break even within a year of its release, and it is difficult to reconcile any tales of a universal critical panning with the fact that *It's a Wonderful Life* won Capra a Golden Globe for Best Director in 1947, and the same year was to see the film being nominated for five Academy Awards in prominent categories (including Best Picture, Best Director, Best Actor in a Leading Role, Best Sound Recording and Best Film Editing).[2] One of these nominations, the Best Actor Award, was reserved for James Stewart, and though he did not win in the 1947 Awards (he had earlier been the recipient of an Oscar for his part in George Cukor's *The Philadelphia Story*, 1940), the role had been among his best-regarded since his appearance in W.S. Van Dyke II's *It's a Wonderful World* (1939) and his earlier pre-War collaborations with Capra, most notably in the title role of *Mr Smith Goes to Washington*. Prior to his War service, Stewart had risen through a variety of supporting and leading roles from the early thirties to become one of the pre-eminent acting talents in Hollywood, and following his remarkable performance in *It's a Wonderful Life* he cemented a post-War return to acting with great aplomb, paving the way for a glittering future career that would see him headlining several prominent Westerns, occupying the starring role in a number of Alfred Hitchcock's best-regarded thrillers, and – perhaps most memorably – appearing as the lovable eccentric Elwood P. Dowd in Henry Koster's *Harvey* (1950), an adaptation of Mary Chase's Pulitzer Prize-winning play.

The inspired plot of *It's a Wonderful Life* has long since passed into the annals of cinematic legend. In the small American town of Bedford Falls on the Christmas Eve of 1946, the family of George Bailey are praying for him, sensing that he is upset and in a turbulent state of mind. In the heavens, angels hear the prayers that have been offered up and decide to despatch Clarence Oddbody (Angel, Second Class) to visit Earth and convince George that his life is worth living. If Clarence is successful, not only will he have saved George and answered his family's prayers, but he will also have earned his angel wings in the process.

Through the briefing which Clarence (Henry Travers) receives prior to his arrival on Earth, we are led through the life of George Bailey (James Stewart) from his youth until the present day. Starting in a wintry 1919, where young George (Bobbie Anderson) saves the life of his little brother Harry (Georgie Nokes) who is drowning in an icy pond – even though George subsequently loses part of his hearing due to a resulting ear infection – we see the beginning of a life of sacrifice which is endured for the benefit of other people. After returning to his part-time job as a delivery boy at the town druggists, George discovers that pharmacist Mr Gower (H.B. Warner), racked with grief and remorse over the recent death of his son from flu, has accidentally given a sick child the wrong prescription. In so doing, he saves Gower from a potential manslaughter charge.

George graduates from high school in 1928 and regales an admirer, his childhood sweetheart Mary Hatch (Donna Reed), with his dreams of travelling widely and becoming an architect, designing structures all over the country. However, his ambitious plans are derailed by the impact of other events. He decides to assist with the family business, Bailey Building and Loan, until Harry (Todd Karns) has completed high school, following which George will attend college to gain his required qualifications. However, nobody foresees the sudden stroke which is later suffered by his father, which leaves George unexpectedly in charge of the building and loan company – an act of altruism made all the more necessary by the scheming of local property developer Mr Potter (Lionel Barrymore), who is determined to persuade the organisation's board of directors that their provision of home loans for low-income earners is financial folly.

George decides to gift the savings he had put aside for his education to his brother Harry, so that at least one of them can attend college. However, his belief that Harry will take over the reins of the building and loan company following his graduation – thus allowing George a late opportunity at further education – is sunk when Harry returns with a new wife, and the news that his father-in-law has offered him a good post in his business. George is disappointed that his ambitions have once again been curtailed, but doesn't have the heart to persuade Harry to turn down the offer of employment because he knows that his brother's future prosperity will likely rest upon it. George resignedly begins to realise that his own fate is unavoidably intertwined with that of his building and loan business.

Marrying Mary, George and his new bride are in the process of leaving town to go on honeymoon when there is an entirely unanticipated run on the local bank, which leaves the building and loan company teetering on the brink. In order to ward off Potter's attempts to extort money from those who can least afford it through crippling loans, George agrees with Mary to use their $2000 honeymoon fund to lend the people of Bedford Falls the money they need to get by. The crisis thus passes with the building and loan company still intact, but Potter is infuriated that George's self-sacrifice has once again won the day. He is no happier with George's later formation of the Bailey Park housing project, which entices residents away from the chronically high rate of rent they had to pay in order to live in Potter's properties. Desperately trying to disrupt George's plans, Potter offers him a job with a drastically higher salary. However, George firmly declines Potter's proposal, remaining contemptuous of the older man's obvious derision towards the people of the town.

Years later, the Second World War breaks out. George, who now has a family with Mary, is unable to enlist in the war effort on account of being deaf in one ear following his childhood rescue of Harry. He has no choice but to remain in Bedford Falls as an air raid warden while Harry serves his country with distinction, becoming a fighter pilot in the U.S. Air Force. His bravery is recognised by the government, and Harry is awarded the Medal of Honor for his military service. Back in Bedford Falls, George and Harry's jovial Uncle Billy (Thomas Mitchell) is on his way to the bank on Christmas Eve with savings from the building and loan when he meets Potter. Full of pride and satisfaction that his nephew's courage in the defence of the United States is to be recognised by the authorities, Billy shows Potter a newspaper article outlining Harry's achievements, but is so caught up in the moment that he accidentally misplaces the $8000 that he was due to deposit. The amount is later discovered in full by Potter, but he decides to keep the money for himself rather than alerting George and Billy to its whereabouts.

George is driven to distraction by Billy's carelessness; a banking inspector is due to visit the building and loan company later, and the vast shortfall in funds will mean a certain end to the business. He frantically hunts around the town in search of the missing $8000 but, as Billy clearly has no idea of its whereabouts, he is at a loss as to where he should even start to look. George becomes unbalanced with the worry he feels, upsetting his family and a number of the townsfolk in the process. Eventually, he is compelled – as a final act of utter hopelessness – to approach Potter for a loan to make up the deficit facing the building and loan company. Never letting on that he is in possession of the missing funds, Potter smugly berates George before denying him a loan with the greatest of self-satisfaction.

Now totally despondent, George drives out to a remote bridge on the outskirts of town. Crashing his car into a tree, he staggers over to the bridge with the intention of committing suicide. This, he reasons, will solve the problem, as he has a $15,000 life insurance policy that will be paid out in the event of his death. However, as he is set to jump into the icy water he is shocked to see a stranger drowning in the river beneath him – Clarence. Diving in to save him, George is bewildered when Clarence introduces himself as George's guardian angel. George finds it difficult to take this revelation seriously. Deeply resentful at the impending demise of the building and loan, he indignantly tells Clarence that the world would likely have been a better place if he had never been born in the first place. Calling his bluff, Clarence decides to show George exactly what the town would look like if this had in fact been the case.

In an instant, George finds himself in an alternate reality where he soon discovers that he has, in fact, never been born. The warmly inviting Bedford Falls has long since ceased to be, and is now a grim collection of slums named Pottersville. In this town, without George's philanthropy to act as a brake on Potter's greed, the inhabitants are dark and twisted shadows of their true selves. At every turn, he finds himself faced with suspicion and hostility in a world where generosity and altruism seem to be virtually non-existent. Mary, having never met George, is now an unmarried librarian who is deeply distrustful of the world around her. The pharmacist Mr Gower was arrested for his accidental poisoning of a young boy – the tragic error which George wasn't around to stop – and after a lengthy spell in prison he is reduced to alcoholism and begging in order to survive. Bailey Park was never built and is now a graveyard, while the Bailey Building and Loan is a run-down dance hall. Things go from bad to worse when George realises that as he hadn't existed to save Harry, not only did his brother drown in youth, but as a result the many people who Harry had saved during the war have also died on account of the young man's early demise. Even the easy-going Uncle Billy has been declared medically unable to function in society, and is now confined to a mental institution.

George is stunned at how one single man's actions – his own – could have such a vastly transformative effect on the community in which he lives. Appalled at the horrifying state of Bedford Falls in his absence, he begs God to return him to life again so that his actions will once more have consequence. His prayer granted, George finds himself back at the exact point in time that he had met Clarence on the bridge. Racing home, now jubilant at his newly-found sense of worth and purpose, George is elated to discover that the town has returned to normal. Of course, this inevitably also means that the banking inspector is present and seeking answers with regard to the missing funds from the building and loan company. However, before George can be prosecuted for fraud, the townsfolk and his family – including the recently-returned Harry – rally around and reveal that they have raised the necessary funds to rescue George from being taken into custody, as well as saving the building and loan from collapse. George is stunned that, after so many years of selfless concern for his neighbourhood, the community have now come to his own aid instead. As the gathered assembly break into a rendition of 'Auld Lang Syne', George hears a bell ringing on his Christmas tree and remembers Clarence's earlier revelation that whenever a bell rings, an angel is being granted his or her wings. Mindful of all that his guardian angel has done for him, George realises that – in spite of the difficulties that have faced him over the years – he really has had a wonderful life after all.

It's a Wonderful Life seems so firmly and centrally embedded in the framework of the cinematic Christmas experience that it is difficult to believe that throughout the fifties and sixties it had drifted into near-total obscurity. Only with its lapse into the public domain in the seventies, which led to many subsequent screenings on American television, did the film achieve cult notoriety and – soon after – mass appeal. In an ironic twist, what had been considered one of Capra's less successful films has turned into his most iconic, and today it is almost certainly his best-remembered. Yet as mentioned earlier, the film has become much more than a fondly regarded seasonal classic, for it contains themes both subtle and bold which have led to it being studied and discussed at great detail over the past few decades. Most contentious among these, inevitably, was the film's depiction of the unscrupulous banker Potter and his unabashed theft of funds from George's Building and Loan which is the central cause of conflict in *It's a Wonderful Life*. There was alarm in some quarters of officialdom at the time that Bedford Falls' most prominent banker, who would have been considered one of the archetypal pillars of society at the time, should be considered as an antagonist – particularly one so ruthlessly venal and immoral.[3] However, Lionel Barrymore's gleefully malevolent performance is one of such skill and distinction that we are left in little doubt that Potter's actions are borne more of malice than simple capital gain – his antipathy towards George (and the citizens of Bedford Falls in general) has less to do with commercial competitiveness than it does with spite towards the town's nominal philosophy of mutual co-operation. Indeed, it is even more difficult to consider the film as being generally negative towards capitalism when the protagonist himself, with all of his virtue and altruism, also works in the banking industry.[4]

Instead, there is much more to be said about the film's evocation of small-town life, and Capra's staunch defence of the self-determination of individuals, than its admittedly ambiguous approach to politics.[5] Whereas *The Bells of St Mary's* had depicted a specifically (and traditionally) Christian approach to social responsibility and working towards the common good of the community, the moral thrust of *It's a Wonderful Life* appears much more secular, quite in spite of its memorable evocation of angels and divine intervention. The film displays a more universal approach to its subject than McCarey's film had done, stipulating clearly the need for individuals to support each other for the greater good of their neighbourhood and, by extension, society at large. As Clarence so memorably observes, nobody who has friends around them can truly be called a failure in life, and it is this simple but all-encompassing promotion of mutual support which has really become the film's lasting legacy to later Christmas films. George Bailey's unstinting selflessness echoes all the way down his life, from the sacrifice of his hearing to save his brother through to the abrogation of his wanderlust in order to support his family business, but it takes the goodwill of the festive season (and the near-tragedy which occurs during it) to highlight just how much his community appreciate him and the way in which he has forfeited his dreams in order to support the town he loves so much.

In the film's fantasy sequence set in the dystopian slum of Pottersville, we see first-hand the nightmarish social drudgery which thrives in a world where George had never been on hand to aid the lives of those around him. The lurid excesses of Potter's corrosively negative effects on the community are made all the more immediate given Capra's painstaking build-up to their depiction, showing the audience detailed snapshots of George's interactions with the denizens of Bedford Falls during his life up until that point in order to heighten the emotional impact when we are introduced to the same characters in the harsh neon light of Pottersville. (The same technique was later used to great effect in the creation of the bleak, uncompromisingly grim parallel version of Hill Valley, corrupted by the spiteful manipulations of the Biff Tannen character, in the second act of Robert Zemeckis's *Back to the Future: Part II*, 1989.) But just as we are given a bitter taste of hopelessness in viewing the direct consequences of a world without George, where greed and exploitation have been allowed to predominate unchecked in Bedford Falls, so too can we share in George's elation at his return to normality and – in his beatific realisation that his life has not been lived in vain after all – savour the film's triumphant conclusion.

Some have considered Capra's preoccupation with the dark mirror-image of Bedford Falls to be a wider comment on the potential dangers facing America in a time of rapid social and cultural flux. This may, in fact, be part of the reason why he labours George's virtues so extensively, for the voracious covetousness represented by Potter is so potentially all-embracing that Capra seems eager to delineate just how acute the underlying danger of unrestricted acquisitiveness can be to the fabric of society, if it is not continually constrained by the bulwark of personal responsibility. Capra's intent to demonstrate the transformative effects of just one life on the condition and development of a community is absolutely at the heart of the film, for just as George's self-sacrifice comes to unite Bedford Falls, so too does Potter's overly-materialistic malevolence threaten to destroy it.[6] Unlike Horace Bogardus in *The Bells of St Mary*'s, no Damascene conversion is possible for Potter – he cannot be manipulated or reasoned with, and thus he seems incapable of any kind of constructive development with regard to his moral outlook. And yet, as Brian Geoffrey Rose has observed, *It's a Wonderful Life* is so intensely concerned with small-town life – and those who make it what it is – that the film actually marked a comparative departure from Capra's earlier deep anxieties with contemporary social developments in films such as *Mr Deeds Goes to Town*.[7]

It is worth noting that Capra entirely manages to avoid allowing the film to descend into the Manicheanism of an overt morality tale; while the audience can remain in no doubt of his social and cultural concerns, *It's a Wonderful Life* is every bit as focused on the small, everyday joys of life in a close-knit community as it is with the fragility of such an existence.[8] It is here that the film's supporting cast is allowed to shine, both in their Bedford Falls and Pottersville guises. Donna Reed sets the screen alight as the spirited Mary Hatch, later to become the supportive, family-oriented Mrs Bailey. Yet while her energetic performance as George's independent-minded soul-mate stays in the memory, so too does her portrayal of Mary's nervy, withdrawn alter-ego, cast adrift in a dystopian existence where she met neither George nor any other romantic partner. Whether depicting members of George's family like Thomas Mitchell's Uncle Billy and Beulah Bondi's Mrs Bailey, or town characters such as Frank Faylen's taxi driver Ernie and Ward Bond's Bert the policeman, Capra's film succeeds like few others in weaving a tapestry of a neighbourhood where all individuals have worth and meaning, and then subverting that same diorama to lay bare just how delicate the status of their largely-contented existence actually is. Affably overseeing proceedings is the genial angel Clarence, unforgettably played by Henry Travers. The diametric opposite of his earlier portrayal of Horace Bogardus, Travers invests much warmth and wistfulness in his depiction of this trainee guardian angel, and it is of little surprise that the character – appearing as he did in the twilight of Travers's career – would come to be regarded as the most recognisable of his entire filmography. Clarence is unwaveringly certain of the positivity and purposefulness of George's existence, and will stop at nothing to convince the beleaguered banker that he must not throw away the potential that the rest of his life may still afford him. So profound is the pathos of Clarence's success in his task that it is hard to imagine anyone in the audience who does not share, to some extent, in the satisfaction of his achievement.

For all the multitude of memorable performances in *It's a Wonderful Life*, the film belongs primarily to James Stewart. The most remarkable thing about George Bailey is that for all of his unstinting selflessness, he remains an identifiable figure. He is virtuous, yet he is not saintly. He may be honourable, undoubtedly, but he is also vulnerable. And while he is just and unselfish, he is also all too human – when pushed to the furthest of extremes, we see him come close to the ultimate breaking point. Yet it says a great deal for Capra, and the distinctive character he creates, that George's would-be suicide on the bridge is not depicted as the last desperate attempt of a broken man to escape the consequences which face him, but rather as an act of supreme sacrifice: we are left in no doubt that George's genuine intention is to willingly give his life in exchange for the life insurance that could secure the futures of those close to him. The amiable Jimmy Stewart appears absolutely tailor-made for the role of the folksy, well-intentioned George Bailey, and it is little surprise that he repeatedly named the role as his favourite performance among all of his many cinematic appearances.

It is almost impossible to overstate the cultural influence of *It's a Wonderful Life*.[9] There are few now who would argue that it is near-impossible to find fault with any element of the film, from Dimitri Tiomkin's unforgettable score to Emile Kuri's brilliant set decoration, which brings alive the comforting charm of Bedford Falls just as effectively as it underscores the nightmarish wantonness of Pottersville. In 2006, the American Film Institute cited the film as the most inspirational motion picture ever to be produced,[10] and indeed this auspicious legacy now seems to be safely cemented within the annals of popular cinema. With the singular exception of *A Christmas Carol*, it has become the most regularly parodied and pastiched of all festive stories. Many long-running television series across the world have used the film's memorable premise of the conflict between altruism and individualism as the basis for one of their episodes (often, but not exclusively, set at Christmas), and throughout the passing years the warm sentimentality of the original has occasionally been subverted into a thinly-veiled attempt to satirise the issues of the day. Effective spoofs have ranged from sophisticated political farces such as the 'It's a Soaraway Life' sketch from the BBC's *A Bit of Fry and Laurie*[11] all the way through to Mike Judge's darkly humorous (and predictably surreal) 'It's a Miserable Life' Christmas special of MTV's infamous *Beavis and Butthead*.[12]

The film was remade for television by Donald Wrye in 1977, as *It Happened One Christmas*.[13] Although it has become a rather obscure feature in recent years, this TV movie – based, as *It's a Wonderful Life* had been, on Philip Van Doren Stern's short story 'The Greatest Gift' – was nominated for two Primetime Emmy Awards in its day, and featured none other than the legendary Orson Welles as the nefarious Henry Potter. Starring Marlo Thomas as Mary Bailey Hatch and Wayne Rogers as George Hatch, *It Happened One Christmas* relates a gender-reversed version of the original film's events, complete with an affable female angel named Clara Oddbody, played by Cloris Leachman. In spite of its talented cast and decent production values, *It Happened One Christmas* has now largely vanished into a state of relative anonymity, but as a curiosity it remains of general interest to film enthusiasts. Additionally, elements of *It's a Wonderful Life*'s parallel universe storyline – comparing the world of the everyday against an altered reality where the protagonist has not had the chance to affect the community around themselves – have emerged in numerous cinema releases over the years, most recently including films such as James Orr's *Mr Destiny* (1990), John Murlowski's *Richie Rich's Christmas Wish* (1998), Brett Ratner's *The Family Man* (2000) and, at the extreme end of the spectrum, Peter Capaldi's influential and supremely surreal Academy Award-winning short film *Franz Kafka's It's a Wonderful Life* (1993).

There have been numerous stage adaptations of *It's a Wonderful Life*, and James Stewart was to reprise the role of George Bailey on 8 May 1949, for a radio adaptation of the film on NBC's Screen Director's Playhouse. Additionally, Stewart and Donna Reed were to be reunited in their roles as George and Mary Bailey for radio adaptations of *It's a Wonderful Life* on Lux Radio Theatre (10 March 1947) and The Screen Guild Theatre (29 December 1947 and 15 March 1951). Although Stewart would forever be immortalised in the modern cultural consciousness as George Bailey, he did make other interesting contributions to the world of Christmas features, first with his appearance in Richard Quine's whimsically offbeat *Bell, Book and Candle* (1958) and then later with his heart-rending performance as elderly widower Willy Kreuger in Kieth Merrill's short but memorable TV movie *Mr Kreuger's Christmas* (1980).[14] A deeply touching evocation of disheartening loneliness over the festive season, Stewart delivers an extraordinary performance throughout Merrill's feature, his portrayal of the kindly but deeply despondent Mr Kreuger culminating in an uplifting and life-affirming climax which makes this hidden gem well worth seeking out.

Although most cinemagoing audiences of the 1940s were unlikely to have realised it at the time, the release of *It's a Wonderful Life* had not only raised the bar for Christmas films for the rest of the decade, but it had set the course for this formative genre for all time. To this day, Capra's masterpiece remains the film to beat in terms of heart-warming human drama, the encouragement of festive community spirit, and triumph over adversity. With its eternal charm and intertwined messages of seasonal goodwill and social responsibility, *It's a Wonderful Life* has more than earned its classic status in the world of cinema, and its reputation is unlikely to be seriously challenged either now or in the foreseeable future.

Historical Context

It's a Wonderful Life was first screened to the American public on Friday 20 December 1946 in New York City's Globe Theatre, with a national release the following day. Also released in cinemas on this date were Eddie Donnelly's *Beanstalk Jack*, Jean Yarbrough's *A Buckaroo Broadcast*, Jack Hannah's *Double Dribble* and John Brahm's *The Locket*. Kay Kyser's song 'Old Buttermilk Sky' was at the top of the Best Sellers in Stores chart compiled by Billboard. That week was also to see the commencement of the First Indochina War, Léon Blum becoming the Prime Minister of France, and the General Assembly of the United Nations voting to establish its headquarters in New York City.

3

MIRACLE ON 34TH STREET (1947)

Twentieth Century-Fox Film Corporation

Director: George Seaton
Producer: William Perlberg
Screenwriter: George Seaton, from a story by Valentine Davies

MAIN CAST

Maureen O'Hara	-	Doris Walker
John Payne	-	Fred Gailey
Edmund Gwenn	-	Kris Kringle
Gene Lockhart	-	Judge Henry X. Harper
Natalie Wood	-	Susan Walker
Philip Tonge	-	Julian Shellhammer
Porter Hall	-	Granville Sawyer
Jerome Cowan	-	District Attorney Thomas Mara

If *It's a Wonderful Life* has become a kind of perennial declaration of the virtues of the small town, a bygone age of the American community that has been immortalised on celluloid, then *Miracle on 34ᵗʰ Street* has become just as nostalgic an examination of the spirit of Christmas past, albeit one which offers a very different kind of wistful reminiscence from that which had been offered by Frank Capra. Yet like Capra's classic, it was – at the original time of its release – a thoroughly contemporary take on American lives and social conventions which would have seemed wholly relevant to most post-War audiences. The film offers up a surprising duality of purpose, celebrating the commoditisation of Christmas – the energetic cultural dissemination of festive mores through the mass-market – at the same time as it presents anxieties about the aggressive encroachment of commercialism into the season of giving, which saw the inclusiveness of the traditional Christmas challenged by the demands of materialistic individualism.

Miracle on 34ᵗʰ Street has, of course, become especially well-known as one of the first truly prominent portrayals in film of what has now become the archetypal characterisation of Santa Claus, complete with white-fur-trimmed red suit, large black belt, bobble-hat and heart-warmingly avuncular laugh. This modern depiction of Father Christmas in a vibrant red outfit was popularised largely through the imagery of cartoonist Thomas Nast in the late nineteenth century, which had differed from the earlier depictions of St Nicholas in ecclesiastical robes (though Nast's character wore a tan costume in his earliest incarnations, his clothing later becoming red with the passing of the years). However, the red-suited Santa who has become so firmly embedded in today's cultural psyche owes much to Coca-Cola's widespread Christmas advertising campaigns, featuring artwork by graphic designer Haddon Sundblom, between 1931 and 1964. Sundblom's characterisation of Santa appeared considerably more jovial and buoyant than Nast's had been, and was much more recognisable as the jolly gift-bearing figure that we know today. Santa had also made prominent appearances in what have come to be considered the very first Christmas motion pictures, namely the American Mutoscope Company's *Santa Claus* cycle (1897), a series of four interrelated short films which are generally believed to have been directed by American Mutoscope's famous founder, William Kennedy Dickson. Thus while Father Christmas had appeared on film before *Miracle on 34ᵗʰ Street* (a recognisably ebullient Santa, played by Ferdinand Munier, had appeared in Gus Meins's and Charles Rogers's *Babes in Toyland* in 1934, for instance), this movie has comfortably established itself as one of the earliest and most popular cinematic evocations of the character – a fact underscored by the interesting detail that it remains the only film to date which features an actor who was awarded an Oscar for his portrayal of Santa Claus.

By the 1940s, director George Seaton had earned a firm reputation as a talented screenwriter in Hollywood, having provided the scripts for films such as Sam Wood's *A Day at the Races* (1937), Alexander Hall's *This Thing Called Love* (1940) and Irving Cummings's *That Night in Rio* (1941). His directorial career at the time included features such as *Diamond Horseshoe* (1945), *Junior Miss* (1945) and *The Shocking Miss Pilgrim* (1947), and he would later go on to direct films including

Williamsburg: The Story of a Patriot (1957), *Airport* (1970) and – perhaps most prominently – *The Country Girl* (1954), for which he won an Academy Award for Best Writing (Screenplay) in 1955 and was also nominated at the same ceremony for the Best Director Oscar. Seaton had previously been Academy Award-nominated for his screenplay for *The Song of Bernadette* (1943) at the 1944 Oscar ceremonies, and would later be nominated for the script he had adapted for *Airport*. But *Miracle on 34th Street* was to prove one of the crowning glories of his career, and one which would bring him no small degree of success at the Academy Awards and elsewhere.

While on a leisurely saunter through New York City in November, a kindly old gentleman named Kris Kringle (Edmund Gwenn) wanders across the elaborate Macy's parade for the Thanksgiving season. Kris is alarmed when he discovers that the Santa Claus hired by Macy's to head up the parade (Percy Helton) is decidedly inebriated, and chastises the man for intending to appear drunk in front of hundreds of adoring children. He voices his concerns to the parade's organiser, Doris Walker (Maureen O'Hara), who is shocked at the intoxicated Santa's condition. However, as Doris has severe doubts about the possibility of getting him sobered up in time for the parade starting, she manages to cajole the reluctant Kris into agreeing to take the man's place. As Kris's appearance fits the bill perfectly – he is pleasantly avuncular, festively plump and sports a neatly groomed white beard – the elderly gent appears impeccably suited to the part, and proves hugely popular with the crowd when the parade gets underway.

Kris's appearance impresses Macy's, and the company decide to recruit him for their annual Santa Claus display which is situated at their store on 34th Street. There he befriends a kind-hearted young cleaner named Alfred (Alvin Greenman), who he discovers also has an annual role as Santa at his local YMCA every Christmas. Before Kris's first appearance, toy department manager Julian Shellhammer (Philip Tonge) instructs him that if he should come across any children who are undecided about what gifts they would like for Christmas, he should recommend a variety of toys that Macy's are currently overstocked with. Indignant, Kris tears up Shellhammer's list, asserting that children should always have the chance to make up their own minds about their choice of Christmas presents.

Meanwhile, Doris finds herself the object of the affections of an attorney living in a neighbouring apartment in her apartment block. Fred Gailey (John Payne) has befriended Doris's young daughter Susan (Natalie Wood), but is disappointed in the little girl's lack of imagination or sense of fun. Doris explains that she has raised Susan to understand that childhood fantasies are pointless and should not be indulged, in order to avoid disappointment in later life. Fred is particularly saddened by Susan's inability to believe in Santa Claus, so when the opportunity arises he surreptitiously decides to take her along to see Kris at Macy's Christmas display. She is initially sceptical about Kris's claims that he is the real Santa Claus, but later sneaks back into the grotto to overhear him speaking to a war orphan from the Netherlands (Marlene Lyden) in fluent Dutch, much to the little girl's delight, which makes Susan begin to question her disbelief.

Kris is having an impact on more than Susan, however. When he meets a little boy who wants a toy fire engine for Christmas, which his mother assures him has proven impossible to find at any store in town, Kris is quick to recommend another shop in the area that he knows will have the item in stock. Shellhammer is thunderstruck by Kris's honesty, which he feels is certain to be losing sales for Macy's, and is particularly appalled to discover that Kris has recommended that one parent should visit rival department store Gimbel's for a better quality of ice skate. But Shellhammer's disapproval quickly turns to puzzlement when he receives a barrage of positive feedback from overjoyed shoppers, grateful for Kris's recommendations. Thanks to Kris, many have managed to track down gifts that they had thought impossible to obtain, leading them to hail Macy's for the company's apparent support of the Christmas spirit.

Doris is frustrated that Susan has become so captivated by Kris, quite in spite of her efforts to drum out any vestige of the fantastic from her mind. Growing increasingly exasperated, she calls Kris into her office and beseeches him to explain to Susan that he is not the real Santa Claus, but merely playing a part for the benefit of commercial interest. However, Kris shocks her by refusing to do so – he insists that he is, in fact, the genuine article. This leads Doris to doubt his sanity, especially when she notes that his company employment record corroborates Kris's deliberate insistence that he is the true Santa. She is on the cusp of dismissing Kris from the firm's employ, coming up with an elaborate cover story that a previous employee is to be appointed in his place, when she is suddenly called to the office of company owner R.H. Macy (Harry Antrim). She and Shellhammer appear slightly in awe when Macy congratulates them for the huge success of what he believes to be a co-ordinated marketing campaign that has been generated by the toy department. Though mildly annoyed that neither he nor his advertising section had been consulted first, Macy is over the moon at the massive amount of positive publicity that has been generated by Kris's strategy of ensuring that customers get the best deal – particularly as it has meant that Macy's have pulled well ahead of the competition. Elated, Macy promises Doris and Shellhammer a sizeable Christmas bonus.

As they leave Macy's office, Doris explains to Shellhammer that she is in the process of firing Kris. Stunned, Shellhammer insists that she reinstate him, but Doris voices her concerns over his mental fitness for the job. Willing to compromise, and anxious not to upset Macy, Shellhammer suggests that they ask Kris to undergo psychological tests conducted by company specialist Granville Sawyer (Porter Hall). If Kris passes, Shellhammer reasons, then he must surely be of no danger to the public. Though slightly puzzled at the request, Kris readily agrees to undergo the tests when asked. He completes the assessment effortlessly, but inadvertently irritates the self-important Sawyer when he becomes concerned about the man's own mental wellbeing. Sawyer angrily dismisses Kris from his office, all the while exhibiting signs of stress and anxiety such as exaggerated nervous tics and general tetchiness.

Infuriated by Kris's questioning of his psychological health, Sawyer strongly recommends to Doris that he be dismissed from employment at Macy's with immediate effect. But as luck would have it, Doris has invited Dr Pierce (James Seay) – a resident practitioner at the nursing home where Kris lives – to her office to give his own professional opinion. Pierce insists that Kris is not dangerous to either staff members or the public, and that although he obviously harbours delusions of being Santa Claus, there is no reason why he cannot be a productive and effective member of society. Shellhammer readily agrees with his assessment, being mindful of the huge benefits that Kris continues to bring to the store. Sawyer is miffed at perceiving that his professional recommendation has been snubbed, but Doris remains deeply sceptical, knowing that she will be held personally responsible if Kris should commit an indiscretion during his duties. Pierce suggests that perhaps it would be beneficial if Kris was to live closer to his place of employment in the lead-up to Christmas, thus meaning that a member of the Macy's staff could accompany him to and from work. Shellhammer plots a way to convince his wife (Lela Bliss) to allow Kris to live at their home for the next few weeks, but Fred agrees instead that Kris can stay at his apartment instead. Delighted, Kris agrees with Fred that if he will encourage the embittered Doris to see the good in life, Kris will concentrate on helping Susan to experience the wonder of Christmas for the first time.

During a meal break, Kris is aghast when he discovers that the usually-upbeat Alfred in a deep depression; Sawyer has convinced the teenager that he is psychologically unwell, based on the evidence that as he enjoys distributing presents in his annual role as the YMCA Santa Claus, he must be compensating for the guilt of earlier misdeeds. Assuring his young friend that his mental state is entirely unimpaired, Kris storms off to challenge Sawyer in his office. Demanding an explanation of Sawyer's misdiagnosis, Kris angrily questions the validity of his professional qualifications. Sawyer indignantly blusters his way through Kris's accusations, but his arrogance infuriates Kris to the point where he raps Sawyer over the head with his cane. Kris leaves the office just as Shellhammer and Doris arrive. Sawyer greatly overplays the extent of his injury, and blatantly lies about the cause of Kris's attack. As Kris isn't present to give his own side of the story, they have no choice but to take Sawyer's account at face value.

No longer satisfied with simply having Kris fired, Sawyer quickly hatches an elaborate scheme to have him admitted to a mental hospital. Saddened because he believes Doris to have been complicit in the scheme (even although she knows nothing about it), Kris intentionally fails the psychological examination and is confined to a secure ward. Fred is called at his office to bring some of Kris's personal effects, and while visiting is alarmed to discover that his friend has been assessed for permanent residence at the hospital.

Urging Kris to fight back against the injustice that has been perpetrated against him, Fred petitions Judge Henry X. Harper (Gene Lockhart) to hold a hearing at the Supreme Court in New York over the issue of Kris's sanity. This decision is met with disdain by District Attorney Thomas Mara (Jerome Cowan), and outright alarm by Sawyer, who has been instructed by Macy in no uncertain terms to have the case dropped in order to avoid a public relations disaster for the store. However, events have already proceeded too far to derail the hearing, and when Sawyer attempts to persuade Fred to pull the plug on his case because of the potential for bad publicity, Fred instead decides to ensure that Kris's court appearance gains the maximum possible exposure.

The hearing causes a number of problems for those involved. Harper is seeking re-election the following year, and is desperate to find a way of resolving the proceedings without damaging his prospects in the process (even his wife and grandchildren are giving him the cold shoulder at the fact that he is calling Kris's probity into question). The judge is all too aware that any official who makes a public declaration to the effect that Santa Claus doesn't exist – particularly at a trial which is taking place at Christmas – will face certain electoral suicide. Fred, meanwhile, having accepted this most unusual of cases, finds that his position has become untenable at the law firm where he works. He resigns in order to defend Kris, which brings him into conflict with Doris who berates him for having sacrificed his long-term security in order to chase after a whimsical fantasy. Fred is maddened by her hard-headed cynicism, and fires back that she may eventually learn that the fantastic can matter more than any number of mundane certainties.

The hearing arrives, and Mara wastes no time in calling Kris to the stand and asking him – under oath – to confirm his belief that he is Santa Claus. Kris agrees wholeheartedly that he is, which leads Mara to the natural conclusion that he is insane. However, Fred shocks Harper and Mara – to say nothing of the court at large – when he asserts that while Mara cannot *disprove* that Kris really is Santa, he can and will establish that Kris and Santa are one in the same. Harper is alarmed, knowing that he faces a public backlash that will cripple his re-election campaign if he rules that Santa Claus does not exist, and therefore agrees to let Mara and Fred present evidence to give him an opportunity to devise an impartial way out of his predicament.

R.H. Macy is called to the stand by Fred, who asks him whether he is willing to testify under oath that he believes that Kris really is Santa Claus. Macy is deeply conflicted, considering the publicity disaster – and the disappointment of so many children – which would result if he should say the wrong thing. Reluctantly, he states for the record that he does indeed believe that Kris and Santa Claus are the same person. However, once he has given his testimony he angrily dismisses Sawyer from the company's employ. Fred then surprises the court by calling Mara's own son, Thomas Mara Jr. (Robert Hyatt) as a witness. Mara Jr. asserts that he believes that Santa does exist, as his father had told him so – and he believes that his father is an honest man who would not lie to him about something so important. He also confirms that, to his mind, Santa *is* real and present in the form of Kris. This leaves Mara with little room for tactics of his own, and he is grudgingly forced to admit that Santa Claus does exist – but not that he necessarily exists in the form of Kris Kringle.

Fred finds himself desperately racking his brains in an attempt to prove that Kris is the genuine, original and unique Santa Claus. In the hope that she can cheer Kris up, Susan writes him a note of encouragement which (unknown to her) is countersigned by Doris. They address it to the Supreme Court building and post it. At a sorting office in the city, a mail worker (Jack Albertson) discovers the letter and calls over his supervisor, Lou (Guy Thomajan), to present him with an idea. The post office are in receipt of a great many letters to Santa, most of them unaddressed or simply directed to 'The North Pole'. As the Kringle hearing is currently taking place at an actual geographical location, the sorter suggests that the vast number of letters in the dead letter office be cleared out and delivered to Kris while he is there in person.

Back at the courtroom, it is now Christmas Eve. Kris is overjoyed to receive the letter – it proves to him not only that Susan has put her faith in him, but also that Doris has some belief of her own to offer. Fred begins the latest round of his defence by getting the court to acknowledge that the United States Post Office is an official organ of the American federal government. This is accepted. He then presents Harper with three letters which have been processed by the post office, addressed simply to 'Santa Claus'. This, Fred claims, is proof that the government acknowledges the existence of Santa Claus, and that he must be present in the form of Kris as he was the person to whom the letters were delivered. Harper asks Fred if he can present further evidence to this effect and place them on his desk. Fred then calls a small army of postal delivery men into the court, who empty bag after bag of letters in front of Harper. Swamped under many thousands of letters addressed to Santa, Harper is left with no option but to rule in favour of Kris. Everyone in the court (with the possible exception of Mara) is elated with the verdict, and Kris warmly thanks Harper for having reached the right decision.

Kris reluctantly has to turn down Doris's offer of dinner – it is, after all, Christmas Eve, and he has other business to attend to. The next morning, he meets up with Fred, Doris and Susan – along with Macy and Alfred, whose character has returned to its cheerful norm. Susan appears downcast that she didn't receive the special gift that she had asked Kris for – a new home out in the suburbs, away from the inner-city apartment that she had grown up in. She thus resolves that Kris isn't really Santa Claus at all, but just a friendly old man. However, Susan soon changes her mind when Kris suggests a new route to Fred when driving home which will present lighter traffic, only to discover the perfect home that she has always dreamed about. The house is currently empty, a 'For Sale' notice standing outside. Susan is entranced to find that the house is exactly as she imagined it, right down to a swing in the back garden. Overjoyed at the realisation that Doris had encouraged Susan to believe in Kris, even although she appeared at first to have been disappointed, Fred suggests that he should purchase the house and move into it with Doris (his offer couching an implicit proposal of marriage). He initially appears slightly conceited, believing that he has somehow achieved an unlikely success against all the odds. However, Fred's vanity doesn't last for long: he and Doris soon discover a cane in the living room which looks identical to the one used by Kris, which leads Fred to admit that perhaps it wasn't he who had made their Christmas dreams come true after all.

At its heart, *Miracle on 34th Street* is a film about faith. Not religious faith, as in *The Bells of St Mary's*, or the faith in a common humanity that is shown throughout *It's a Wonderful Life*, but rather a simple, robust belief in the Christmas spirit and the positive effects which can derive from it. Kris repeatedly makes the point that it is human nature to put our faith in some things which may appear indefinable or intangible, and that we should never give up hope even when the odds are stacked against us. But he also emphasises that it is important to choose carefully what it is that we put our faith in, because those beliefs will ultimately shape and define us. We see this optimistic outlook at work not just in Susan, whose natural youthful exuberance has been stymied by hard-hearted pragmatism, but also in the staid matter-of-factness evident in Doris's world view, her glacial temperament eventually thawing as a result of Kris's wistful encouragement and the idealistic Fred's romantic advances. No-one, it seems, can stand in the way of Kris's irrepressible festive spirit. Sawyer's deceit eventually leads to his own downfall, while the wily attorney Mara is smart enough to know when he's playing a game that he can't win. But Kris has no interest in gaining the upper hand over those who oppose his message of goodwill; his only goal appears to be propagating a universal message of benevolence to all, typified by Christmas but relevant the whole year through.

In an America that was only just beginning to emerge from the austerity of the war years, the film's note of caution over the commercialisation of Christmas would doubtless have seemed timely. Kris states quite emphatically his concern that the festive season is ceasing to focus on the importance of giving, being more concerned with materialism and self-interest. His scheme of conveying parents to stores other than Macy's, in order to track down hard-to-find gifts or better quality presents, baffles the corporate top-brass with its simplicity and ability to generate public support for the company (even though they risk losing some Christmas revenue, many customers pledge to become loyal shoppers there throughout the year). Yet even here Kris's altruism is impeccable; presented with a sizeable bonus by R.H. Macy, Kris determines to spend it on a new X-ray machine in order to aid the diagnoses of his old friend Dr Pierce. When it becomes apparent that Macy's cheque won't quite cover the cost, Macy's arch-rival Mr Gimbel (Herbert Heyes) – present for a publicity photoshoot – not only offers to make up the difference, but to sell the machine to Kris at cost price.

Even as early as the forties, themes deriving from commercialism at Christmas felt like a perfect fit; films such as Ernst Lubitsch's *The Shop Around the Corner* (1940), Don Hartman's *Holiday Affair* (1949) and Robert Z. Leonard's *In the Good Old Summertime* (1949) had all – in different and sometimes subtle ways – touched upon the intersection between the festive season and the retail business. *Miracle on 34th Street* remains one of the best-known early exponents of the need to recognise the importance of unselfishness and philanthropy at Christmas, and yet rather than appearing preachy the film actually blurs the boundaries between commercial trade and individual generosity quite profoundly. Kris seems perfectly happy to enter the employ of Macy's, and though he is an unconventional staff member (to say the least) he has few qualms about jumping through any and all corporate hoops that are presented to him. While he is keen to encourage parents to seek out the best bargains when purchasing gifts for their children, he has no difficulty in accepting the fact that mass-production is the most expedient way of ensuring that as many toys as possible are available to satisfy the present-buying public. And as the media storm surrounding Kris's trial proves ample testimony, effective marketing and publicity was increasingly becoming key to ensuring brisk business – a fact that is far from lost on R.H. Macy.

Central to the film, even although his character is technically a supporting one, is Edmund Gwenn's warm and affable interpretation of Father Christmas. Giving one of the best-known and most accomplished performances of his cinematic career, Gwenn's portrayal owes much more to the grandfatherly jollity of the Sundblom incarnation of Santa Claus than it does to the comparatively schoolmasterly portrayal depicted by Nast during the American Civil War and later. Active in cinema since appearing as Rupert K. Thunder in L.C. MacBean's *The Real Thing at Last* (1916), Gwenn made many appearances over the years in features as diverse as Walter Forde's *Condemned to Death* (1932), Guy Newall's *The Admiral's Secret* (1934), Ewald André Dupont's *The Bishop Misbehaves* (1935), Jack Conway's *A Yank at Oxford* (1938) and Fred M. Wilcox's *Lassie Come Home* (1943). Gwenn is exceptional as the compassionate old man with a not-so-secret identity, and he impresses not only as the kind-hearted figure of legend but also (especially in the film's third act) in reflecting the deep disillusionment and occasional flicker of hopelessness that Kris feels when he comes to believe that Doris and Susan – and, by extension, the world at large – have abandoned their trust in him. The ongoing question of Kris's sanity, and the effectiveness of psychological assessment in categorising him, becomes a compelling one throughout the course of the film. Having passed the mental fitness tests with flying colours, Kris angrily berates Sawyer's unrealistically high opinion of his psychiatric talents when he is found making baseless and sweeping analytical assumptions.[1] Contrasted with the even-minded physician Pierce, who is certain that Kris poses no threat to either himself or to others, and Shellhammer, desperately weighing the vague possibility of Kris becoming unbalanced against the vast benefits that he brings to Macy's, Sawyer becomes a memorable antagonist, petty and spiteful but riddled with insecurities and sporting an impressive range of anxieties. Porter Hall plays the part to the hilt, milking the character for every ounce of malicious self-importance to great effect.

Of the main characters, Maureen O'Hara's performance as the straight-laced but occasionally resentful Doris stays in the mind, as does John Payne's stoic turn as the independently-minded Fred, determined to keep the Christmas spirit alive even in the cool detachment of an inner-city courthouse. O'Hara was well-known to audiences at the time for performances in Alfred Hitchcock's *Jamaica Inn* (1939), William Dieterle's *The Hunchback of Notre Dame* (1939) and William A. Wellman's *Buffalo Bill* (1944), while Payne would readily have been recognised by audiences for appearances in films such as Henry King's *Maryland* (1940), Walter Lang's *Tin Pan Alley* (1940) and H. Bruce Humberstone's *Iceland* (1942). Just as believable as the budding romance between Fred and Doris, and as touching as the gradual warming of Doris's affection towards the festive spirit, is Natalie Wood's portrayal of Susan's first embrace of the world of her imagination. Wood had previously appeared in Irving Pichel's films *Tomorrow is Forever* (1946) and *The Bride Wore Boots*

(1946), but her appearance in *Miracle on 34th Street* remains easily the most prominent of her early career as a child actor.

There are many other memorable performances throughout the film, from Philip Tonge's dryly obsequious Julian Shellhammer to a nicely drawn appearance by William Frawley as savvy political advisor Charlie Halloran. In particular, Gene Lockhart creates a skilfully multi-layered portrayal of Judge Harper, presenting a man who is conflicted between his approval ratings with the public and his desire to ensure that some semblance of justice is done – a tall order, under the circumstances. Both a doting grandfather and a political realist, Harper is forced to rely on his many years of legal experience to derive a satisfactory conclusion to Kris's case that won't render him permanently unelectable (and would also guarantee that his family will never speak to him again). The solution which eventually presents itself proves to be as inspired as it is strangely rational, its validity emphasising that sometimes logic can wrap itself in unusual and unexpected forms – especially where Kris Kringle is concerned.[2]

Regardless of the fact that the studio took the unusual step of releasing *Miracle on 34th Street* in the May of 1947, quite in spite of its festive theme, the film performed well with audiences and also at the Academy Awards, winning Oscars for Valentine Davies's original story and George Seaton's screenplay in 1948, in addition to the Best Actor in a Supporting Role Award for Edmund Gwenn. The film was additionally nominated for Best Picture. However, the Academy Awards were not to be the only recognition that the film was to receive in 1948: it also won Seaton a Best Adapted Screenplay award at the Locarno Film Festival, as well as Golden Globe Awards for both Seaton's screenplay and Gwenn's supporting performance.

Miracle on 34th Street has been remade several times for television, including Robert Stevenson's 1955 remake (also later known as *Meet Mr Kringle*), screened on CBS as part of The 20th Century-Fox Hour,[3] William Corrigan's 1959 version for NBC,[4] and Fielder Cook's 1973 version for CBS.[5] The film also inspired a Broadway musical version in 1963, *Here's Love*, which was written by Meredith Willson. Additionally, a number of radio adaptations were broadcast, the first being in 1948.[6] However, more prominent in recent years has been Les Mayfield's cinematic updating of the story in 1994, starring Richard Attenborough as 'Kriss' Kringle, which featured a screenplay by eighties film legend John Hughes (who also acted as the film's producer). Mayfield's remake updated the story in order to enhance its relevance for audiences of the mid-nineties, with Hughes deftly reworking Seaton's original screenplay to take account of the social and cultural changes which had occurred in the intervening decades.[7] Elizabeth Perkins and Dylan McDermott make appealing leads, with Mara Wilson's Susan appearing suitably starstruck by old Mr Kringle's effortless invocation of the wonder of Christmas. Simon Jones also delivers a wonderfully tongue-in-cheek performance as Shellhammer. However, the film offers many narrative changes from Seaton's original; the psychologist Sawyer is eliminated from the plot, while Kringle's downfall is engineered instead by a rival department store. (Just as prominently, Macy's department store is replaced by the fictional 'Cole's'.) However, at its core the film retains the same message of remembering the vital importance of belief, substituting the original's mailbag-festooned conclusion for a rather more low-key climax which contains an understated subtext concerning religious faith, drawing parallels between belief in the spirit of Christmas and trust in a higher power. The remake of *Miracle on 34th Street* split critical opinion at the time of its release, largely given the difficulty inherent in following the timelessly iconic original, and it remains to be seen how the longevity of Mayfield's film will compare to the classic which inspired it.[8]

Even today, *Miracle on 34th Street* remains one of the best-loved of all Christmas movies. There are very few films of any genre which encapsulate so vividly the excitement of childhood expectation at the festive season, or which underscore with such panache the need to retain a daily faith in the indefinable, irrespective of one's ideological, philosophical or religious background.[9] But the film is also crucially significant in the fact that although it was released in late springtime, such was its commercial viability that it still remained popular in cinemas by the time that the festive season itself had arrived.[10] Faced with the success of this archetypal Christmas film, there were few in the studios who were now willing to deny that this newly-emerging genre had definite artistic and economic potential.

Historical Context

Miracle on 34th Street received its cinematic release in the United States on Friday 2 May 1947. Other films released on that day were John Farrow's *Blaze of Noon*, Eugene Forde's *Jewels of Brandenburg*, Frederick De Cordova's *Love and Learn*, André De Toth's *Ramrod* and Robert Carlisle's *Unusual Occupations: The Stunt Girl*. Topping Billboard's Best Sellers in Stores chart that week was 'Heartaches' by Ted Weems. In the news on the same week, the Boulder Dam in Nevada was officially renamed the Hoover Dam, and Thor Heyerdahl's expedition on the raft Kon-Tiki departed from the coast of Peru in an attempt to prove that Polynesia could have originally been settled by Peruvian natives.

4

THE BISHOP'S WIFE (1947)

The Samuel Goldwyn Company

Director: Henry Koster
Producer: Samuel Goldwyn
Screenwriter: Leonardo Bercovici and Robert E. Sherwood, from a novel by Robert Nathan

MAIN CAST

Cary Grant	-	Dudley
Loretta Young	-	Julia Brougham
David Niven	-	Bishop Henry Brougham
Monty Woolley	-	Professor Wutheridge
James Gleason	-	Sylvester
Gladys Cooper	-	Mrs Hamilton
Sara Haden	-	Mildred Cassaway
Karolyn Grimes	-	Debby Brougham

The Bishop's Wife has become one of the great treasures of the post-War era of Christmas films, and yet for some reason its reputation has never quite rivalled those of its better-known contemporaries. Though it may seem like a too-often-forgotten jewel of festive movie-making, it is probably fair to say that rather than being intentionally disregarded by modern audiences *The Bishop's Wife* instead tends to be unfairly overlooked on account of its proximity to films from the same period which have acquired greater stature over the course of the passing decades.

Demonstrating an interesting distillation of themes that had manifested themselves earlier in the decade, *The Bishop's Wife* exhibits a complex melange of sentimentalism and faith issues blended into a gently idiosyncratic comedy-drama format. Like *It's a Wonderful Life* and *Miracle on 34th Street*, it is a film where Christmas – and themes deriving from the festive season – are central to the storyline rather than merely ancillary to it. Yet it also shares *The Bells of St Mary's* concern with matters of religious belief (albeit that this subject matter is treated in a markedly different way) to delineate exactly why Christmas is significant not just as an annual celebration, but as an opportunity to engage with society at large and consequently to improve lives. As *The Bishop's Wife* makes clear throughout its narrative, this is not solely an opportunity presented to followers of a religion; it is accessible to everyone who seeks to make the world a better place irrespective of whether they choose to follow a spiritual belief or not.

The film had a problematic genesis, with legendary producer Samuel Goldwyn rejecting an original cut which had been directed by William A. Seiter and then contracting a new director, Henry Koster, to begin shooting from scratch.[1] Koster had been active in the film industry since the early thirties as both a director and screenwriter; the early features that he had been involved with in his native Germany were credited to his name at birth, Hermann Kösterlitz. After moving to the United States in the late thirties, Koster continued to build a solid reputation in the film world, directing features such as *The Rage of Paris* (1938), *First Love* (1939), *Spring Parade* (1940) and *Music for Millions* (1944) before starting work on *The Bishop's Wife*. Adapted by Robert E. Sherwood and Leonardo Bercovici from a novel by Robert Nathan, the film was to feature a stellar cast of youthful actors including Cary Grant, Loretta Young and David Niven. Though the product of much effort and negotiation behind the scenes (most especially including Grant's request that Goldwyn reverse his original casting decision and grant him the role of the angel rather than the bishop)[2], the end result of Goldwyn and Koster's labours is one of the most unconventional – and impressive – Christmas films of the late forties.

Snow is falling and Christmas carols are being sung in an American city as a genial, well-dressed man named Dudley (Cary Grant) makes an appearance seemingly out of the blue. Dudley seems entranced by the public's high spirits as they approach the festive season, and manages to narrowly avert disaster when he helps a man with impaired sight (David Leonard) to cross the road, only just saving him from being struck by a passing car. He then saves a little girl in a runaway pram by stepping in at the exact moment that a truck is on a collision course with her. But Dudley's timely acts of goodwill appear to be almost a secondary consideration to him; the true purpose of his presence in town seems to centre on Julia Brougham (Loretta Young), a young lady who he is revealed to be following at a distance.

Julia is on her way to buy a Christmas tree from florist Mr Maggenti (Tito Vuolo), who she finds engaged in a lively but essentially good-natured argument with ageing intellectual Professor Wutheridge (Monty Woolley). Julia is puzzled to find that the professor is also in the process of buying a slightly dishevelled Christmas tree of his own, given that he is an atheist, but he explains that he is more interested in the nostalgia offered by the festive season than he is in its religious significance. Remembering Julia from when she lived in the area, back when her husband Henry was the minister of a local church there, Wutheridge asks how Henry's campaign to build a new cathedral is proceeding. Julia responds that the funding problems are endless, and that her husband – now a bishop – is tired and worried about the uphill struggle that he faces. A historian by discipline, the professor hands Julia a lucky Roman coin that he had bought many years ago in Brindisi, asking her to consider it a donation to Henry's fundraising drive. Julia thanks him, voicing her regret that she no longer lives in the neighbourhood with all of her old friends and parishioners.

As soon as Julia has departed, Dudley intercepts Wutheridge and pretends (much to the professor's prolonged suspicion) to have known him in Vienna when the old academic had been lecturing on Roman history there. With some gentle questioning, he informs Dudley that nobody in the area sees Henry Brougham now that he has been made a bishop; instead, Henry spends his time courting financial contributions from wealthy benefactors while his old church is impoverished and barely surviving.

Julia returns home to discover that she is late for a planning meeting being held between Henry (David Niven), architect Mr Perry (Ben Erway) and the formidable Mrs Hamilton (Gladys Cooper). As they study the blueprints of the new cathedral, major friction is readily apparent due to Mrs Hamilton's obvious desire to turn the building into a monument to her late husband, while Henry feels it is inappropriate to glorify any one individual in a house dedicated to the worship of God. Mrs Hamilton is infuriated by Henry's unwillingness to bend to her will, dressing him down and reminding him that she was responsible for his promotion to bishop in the first place. She makes it clear that the building will be constructed to her specification, and that she is completely unwilling to compromise.

Following Mrs Hamilton's departure, Henry voices his frustration at her intractability. He is keen to build a cathedral that will be for the use of everyone, not just the wealthy elite. Julia is concerned that Henry has become so worn-out by the ongoing struggle to raise capital for the construction effort that he has lost sight of what is really important – his family, his friends and his wellbeing, to say nothing of his faith. But with regret, Henry tells her that he will have no choice but to continue his incessant fundraising drive over the Christmas holidays in order to tap into any potential for generosity in the season of festive goodwill. She gives Henry the professor's coin, but is saddened when he casually discards it, believing it to be worthless and pouring disdain on his old friend. Julia is further dismayed by how short-tempered and irritable that Henry has become, knowing how carefree and good-natured he had been prior to his promotion.

Over dinner Henry makes an attempt at rapprochement and asks Julia if she would like to spend the afternoon with him the following day, just enjoying each other's company and putting the worries of the cathedral to one side for a while. However, he soon discovers that he has other commitments and will be unable to make good on his arrangements with his wife. Frustrated at how he no longer seems to be in control of his own life, Henry prays desperately for help only for Dudley to appear out of thin air in his study. Explaining that he has been sent in response to Henry's prayers, Dudley reveals that he is an angel. Even although he is a man of faith, this revelation stretches Henry's credulity to the limit; he begins to wonder if his exhaustion is making him hallucinate. Dudley explains that he has been assigned to lend a hand in Henry's efforts to build the cathedral, much to the bishop's obvious scepticism. However, when Julia enters the room unexpectedly, Dudley conceals his true identity and tells her that he has just signed up as Henry's new personal assistant. When he adds that he intends to give the bishop the chance to relax a little by shouldering some of his burden, Julia is overjoyed – this is exactly what she has been praying for. Henry is now thoroughly bamboozled, but before he can question Dudley any further he discovers that the angel has vanished as quickly as he appeared.

Henry is so shocked by this turn of events that, after a sleepless night, he seems to have convinced himself that it was all an illusion. This is soon disproved, however, when Dudley arrives bright and early the next morning, effortlessly charming Henry's frosty but efficient secretary Mildred Cassaway (Sara Haden) and housekeeper Matilda (Elsa Lanchester). He tries in vain to convince Henry to allow him to attend the various planning and funding meetings that are scheduled for the day, thus allowing Henry the opportunity to spend time with Julia and their daughter Debby, but the bishop refuses point-blank to even consider it. Henry leaves Dudley to reorganise his study's extensive card index, but – as soon as he has departed – Dudley wastes no time in using his supernatural powers to order the card-files in no time at all. This leaves him free to meet Julia and Debby (Karolyn Grimes) in the nearby park, where he first gives the bishop's daughter a crash-course in throwing snowballs before arranging to have lunch with Julia at her favourite restaurant, Michel's. Over some French cuisine presented enthusiastically by the owner (Eugene Borden), Julia explains that she and Henry have fond memories of the place given that they became engaged there. Dudley reassures her that she has a happy and full life ahead of her, and that she has no need to worry about the future.

On the way back home, Julia is pointing out a bonnet that she admires when she and Dudley again encounter Professor Wutheridge. By now the professor has determined that he has no recollection of Dudley, but when Julia identifies him as Henry's new assistant Wutheridge invites them both back to his home for a glass of wine. They agree, and the professor explains his regret that in years of planning to write an epic history of Rome to rival that of Edward Gibbon, he has never actually put pen to paper due to a chronic lack of inspiration. Dudley produces Wutheridge's Roman coin, retrieved from Henry's study, and explains to the professor that it is an incredibly rare piece – one of only a hundred of its kind to be minted by Julius Caesar. Enraptured by Dudley's account of history, Wutheridge finds that he has renewed enthusiasm for his project. Dudley assures him that, in spite of his advancing years, he still has time to complete it.

Back in his office, Henry grows annoyed as the hours advance with no sign of either Dudley or Julia. When they do finally arrive, he is nonplussed by Julia's sudden cheerfulness and confronts Dudley. Once Julia has gone to check on Debby, Henry challenges Dudley to prove that he is an angel once and for all by performing a miracle. Dudley gently censures the bishop, telling him that he is there to help his efforts, not perform parlour tricks. He then leaves the room through a door, which – when Henry attempts to open it – turns out to have been locked all along.

Henry begins to grow jealous of Dudley when he realises what a positive impact that he is having on Julia's disposition. His own mood is far from improved when, soon after, he discovers Dudley entertaining Debby with stories from the Bible. Henry arranges an appointment with the formidable Mrs Hamilton, but directly afterwards realises that he has double-booked himself with a recital that is being held for him at his old church. Although far from pleased with the arrangement, Henry allows Dudley to accompany Julia to the performance instead, while he visits Mrs Hamilton alone. The bishop meekly apologises to Mrs Hamilton for his earlier opposition to her plans for the cathedral, reasoning that it is better to bite his tongue and express contrition than to risk losing her financial support. When she accepts his apology, and secures Henry's assurance that her husband's memorial notice will be on prominent display in the new cathedral (to say nothing of an appearance in one of the stained glass windows), Henry attempts to make a speedy withdrawal in an attempt to join Julia and Dudley. However, some divine intervention leaves him trapped in one of Mrs Hamilton's chairs; nothing seems able to dislodge him from it.

At St Timothy's, Henry's old church, Dudley is introduced to the new vicar Mr Miller (Regis Toomey) and his organist Mrs Duffy (Sarah Edwards). Miller is disappointed that Henry is not present, but accepts that the demands of his new role mean that his time is limited. Julia voices regret that things have changed so much since Henry's departure; the church, though homely and comfortable, is clearly very basic, while Henry has become distant from the parishioners who had held him in such high esteem. Miller seems embarrassed that only a couple of choirboys have turned up for the recital, given the diversion of the rapidly-approaching festive season, but once Dudley coaxes one of the boys into singing Miller looks on amazed as the rest of the choir begin to file into the church as if by magic. Julia is saddened that Henry is unable to join them for any of the performance, little realising that he is still trapped in Mrs Hamilton's chair.

After the recital is over, Dudley hails a cab while Julia – much to her dismay – notices that someone is on the verge of buying the bonnet that she has so admired from the milliner's shop. With a little fast thinking from Dudley, the potential purchaser is soon dissuaded from her new acquisition, meaning that Julia becomes the proud owner of the hat after all. They take a scenic route home, asking curmudgeonly taxi driver Sylvester (James Gleason) to drive them back via the park. On doing so, Dudley is enthused to discover that people are skating on an iced-over pond. Asking Sylvester to pull over, he treats Julia to a dazzling display of ice-skating, soon encouraging her to get in on the act. Even Sylvester is persuaded to join in, the three of them eventually combining to perform an intricate synchronised routine. The whole situation has a profound effect on Sylvester, who feels so moved and energised by Dudley's involvement in his life that not only does he rediscover his faith in human nature, but – even more extraordinarily for him – he also agrees to waive his taxi fee.

Julia and Dudley arrive home later, where Henry – now released from Mrs Hamilton's chair – is infuriated by their lack of punctuality. Noticing how elated Julia seems after her wonderful evening, Henry rails against Dudley, suspecting him of being attracted to his wife. But Dudley is more concerned that Henry has ignored his principles in order to kow-tow to Mrs Hamilton and encourage her vanity. He explains to the bishop that the money required to construct the grand building in question could be used to support the poor instead. But Henry is disinterested in the noble purpose that Dudley outlines, not least because he knows that Mrs Hamilton will never accept it. He prays that Dudley be relieved of his duties in his parish and return to heaven but Dudley appears to have other ideas. Julia is upset when Henry explains that he has dismissed Dudley from his service. However, she holds out hope of his return, assuring Debby that he will keep his promise to tell her stories of his friendship with Santa Claus.

The approach of Christmas Eve does little to improve Henry's demeanour. As he and Julia depart on a gruelling trip around the homes of wealthy parishioners, the bishop asks Miss Cassaway to type up his Christmas Eve sermon. However, Dudley arrives soon after Henry leaves and offers to save Mildred the trouble: he will type the sermon for her, freeing her from a long stint of overtime. Once she has gone, Dudley burns Henry's original text and composes a new one, the typewriter recording his every word while he dictates the sermon. He also saves Matilda the trouble of decorating the newly-arrived Christmas tree, using his miraculous powers to embellish it with tinsel, ornaments and fairy-lights in an instant.

But Dudley's work doesn't stop at Henry's residence. He pays an unscheduled visit to Mrs Hamilton, charming his way past her butler Stevens (Erville Alderson) into her drawing room. There, he discovers a handwritten musical composition dedicated to Mrs Hamilton and proceeds to play it on her beautiful ornamental harp. Hearing the music, Mrs Hamilton is dumbstruck and immediately tries to determine its source. On discovering Dudley, she explains that the piece was written for her by the only man that she had ever loved, a penniless young musician who had died four decades beforehand. Dudley coaxes her into telling him more, and she explains that although she had never truly loved her wealthy late husband, she was too terrified of poverty to marry her soul mate. By the time that Henry and Julia arrive for their scheduled visit, Mrs Hamilton is a woman transformed; her usual cold-hearted demeanour has given way to warmth and understanding as a result of her spiritual encounter with Dudley. She tells Henry that she has seen the error of her ways, and wishes to donate all of the resources that she had intended for the cathedral fund to be distributed to the poor. The bishop is so nonplussed by this incredible turn of events that he finds himself forced to withdraw, much to the surprise of Julia and Mrs Hamilton.

In reflective mood, Henry goes wandering past his old church, and eventually makes his way to the apartment of Professor Wutheridge. The professor is delighted to see his old friend after so long, and even Henry's relentlessly standoffish manner can't dampen the warmth of Wutheridge's welcome. He explains to the bishop that since Dudley's visit, he has inexplicably developed the power to decipher ancient Roman texts which have thus far baffled the talents of modern Latin scholars. The professor is elated that his book is finally underway after so many years of inaction, and in spite of his avowedly non-religious mindset he is forced to admit that Dudley is not a normal human being, reasoning that he must have been sent by a higher power. But Henry cannot share his good cheer, feeling that Dudley has poisoned Julia against him. Wutheridge scoffs at this explanation, explaining that Dudley's only action has been to make Julia happy, but Henry feels that perhaps the angel's true intention was to prove to him that his marriage has faltered. The professor assures him that the love that is shared between Henry and Julia is unlikely to be threatened by someone who is not of this earth; all that Dudley has done is to emphasise how vital it is that Henry realise the importance of the love that he shares with Julia. Wutheridge also insists on returning the rare Roman coin to the bishop, explaining its true value to him.

Back home, Julia is admiring the newly-decorated Christmas tree when Dudley arrives. He explains that he will be leaving soon, much to his regret. With a little reluctance, he explains that he has formed an attachment to her, and as such she will never see her again. Julia knows that the attraction between them can never come to fruition and, deeply upset, wishes Dudley gone from her life. She races from the room just as Henry arrives. Fuming at Dudley, who he perceives more than ever as attempting to steal his wife from him, he demands that the angel be gone. But Dudley explains that he is already on his way, his work in the parish now done. Henry asks how this can be, given that the cathedral's construction is as remote a possibility now as it was in the beginning. Dudley replies that Henry didn't pray for a cathedral, but for guidance – and that is exactly what he received. Telling the bishop that when he leaves, there will be no recollection of his visit by anyone who had encountered him, Dudley departs for the last time.

Just as Dudley had warned, Henry and Julia have retained no memory of his actions over the past days or even his existence. They are puzzled by the unexplained arrival of a striking angel doll in Debby's room, an enigmatic gift from an unknown benefactor, but have little time to ponder it before Henry is due to give his Christmas Eve sermon at St Timothy's. The little church is packed that night with a full congregation which includes Professor Wutheridge (who appears slightly bemused at his attendance). A rather melancholic Dudley watches from a distance, though he is now invisible to the eyes of the others. Henry is puzzled when he starts to deliver his sermon and discovers that the text is very different from the one that he had written. However, the people attending worship seem enraptured by the sentiment, which is that no-one should forget the reason why Christmas has endured for so long. Satisfied, although a little wistful, Dudley walks away from the church, his work done.

For a film which is so acutely concerned with religious faith, it is surprising to note just how inclusive *The Bishop's Wife* actually is. Although it shares a common theme with *The Bells of St Mary's*, namely that faith can achieve remarkable ends, its rather original take on the notion of divine intervention and lack of orthodox sermonising (apart from Dudley's quotation of Psalm 23, there is little direct reference to the Bible) mean that in spite of the film's concern with the clergy, its central message of reaching out to lend a helping hand to others is as secular and all-encompassing as *It's a Wonderful Life* had proven to be. Indeed, at no point throughout the film is Henry's denomination ever mentioned, though some commentators have ventured the opinion that *The Bishop's Wife* presents, at heart, a distinctively Episcopal variation on the topics presented in *The Bell's of St Mary's*.[3] *The Bishop's Wife* marked a high water mark in the subgenre of religiously-themed Christmas films, and yet it was also to herald the beginning of a sharp decline in the production of such features; although angels and the Virgin Birth would continue to be regularly referenced in later festive film-making, movies which actively linked the historical event of Christ's birth with social issues in the everyday were to become much more sporadic in later years. That said, from George More O'Ferrall's *The Holly and the Ivy* (1952) all the way through to Catherine Hardwicke's *The Nativity Story* (2006), the undeniable Biblical underpinnings of the Christmas story have determined that no matter how secularised and commercialised that festive film-making has become, religion has never been entirely eliminated from the genre.

Key to the success of *The Bishop's Wife* is its range of winning performances. The central love triangle is played with nuanced subtlety by Cary Grant and Loretta Young, while a cast-against-type David Niven works hard to turn the embattled Henry Brougham from priggish killjoy into the very acme of incredulous bewilderment. Whether Niven entirely succeeds in this task is less due to any defect in his performance than the fact that the character of Henry is so difficult for the viewer to actually grow fond of. The bishop's stuffed-shirt manner and cut-glass Received Pronunciation delivery – to say nothing of his apparent single-minded obsession with cathedral-building to the detriment of his family, friends and parishioners – undeniably makes him problematic to engage with, much less warm to. When, at the film's conclusion, we see the newly re-energised Henry – his priorities realigned by Dudley's now-forgotten spiritual influence in his life – his continued mannerly decorum makes it almost impossible to know exactly how far-reaching the change in his character will really prove to be. Niven was already a prolific performer by the time of *The Bishop's Wife*, having made many appearances in films since the early 1930s including Michael Curtiz's *The Charge of the Light Brigade* (1936), John Cromwell's *The Prisoner of Zenda* (1937),

William Wyler's *Wuthering Heights* (1939), Sam Wood's *Raffles* (1939), and perhaps most famously Michael Powell and Emeric Pressburger's sublime *A Matter of Life and Death* (1946). He would, of course, continue to be active in film until his death in 1983, winning an Academy Award for his performance in Delbert Mann's *Separate Tables* (1958). His performance in *The Bishop's Wife* is perhaps most remarkable for his excellent comic timing and subtly ironic delivery, particularly when trapped in Mrs Hamilton's drawing room chair (a visual gag which could have been decidedly laboured in lesser hands), and his exquisitely fussy, hidebound way of dealing with a manifested agent of God – something that Henry has supreme difficulty dealing with, even after having spent his entire adult life preaching about just such encounters.

If the film belongs to anyone, however, it is Cary Grant and Loretta Young. The suave and sophisticated Grant, an actor for whom the term 'screen legend' could have been personally designed, oozes charm from every pore, investing the dapper Dudley with warmth and charisma in every frame. Grant, who had already been nominated for two Academy Awards by the time that he appeared as Dudley (for performances in George Stevens's *Penny Serenade*, 1941, and *None But the Lonely Heart*, 1944), was most certainly hot property in the world of film during the late forties. Making his film debut in Frank Tuttle's *This Is the Night* (1932), he had made many appearances throughout the thirties and forties, with roles in films such as Marion Gering's *Madame Butterfly* (1932), Howard Hawks's *Bringing Up Baby* (1938), George Cukor's *The Philadelphia Story* (1940), Frank Capra's *Arsenic and Old Lace* (1944), and Alfred Hitchcock's *Notorious* (1946), to name only a few. Grant very effectively combines his dry wit and comedic skills with his dramatic strengths to create, in Dudley, a character who is both sympathetic and appealing. From his kindly interactions with Henry's daughter Debby through to his far-reaching effects on virtually all of the supporting cast, the role seems perfectly suited to Grant's unique style of onscreen magnetism, and his beautifully understated pseudo-romance with Julia is all the more credible as a result of it. Both Dudley and Julia are fully aware that their mutual attraction can never be allowed to flourish, a fact that neither wishes to recognise but which clearly pains them grievously. Some critics have noted the thematic awkwardness of an implied romantic attraction between a married woman and a spiritual being – who, based on his actions throughout the film, is ethically above reproach and exclusively concerned with enriching moral actions.[4] It says a great deal for the skill of Grant's performance that, when all of Dudley's miracles have been performed and his life-affirming tenets imparted, we are able to catch a tantalising glimpse of the fatigued, disillusioned being behind the sharp suit and ready grin, weary of checking the excesses of humanity. As Julia, Loretta Young shines as the disenchanted but loyal bishop's wife of the title, unquestioningly dedicated to her husband and faithful to her beliefs while simultaneously enraptured by the dashing, captivating newcomer who has swept into her life. Young made her first cinematic appearance as a child actor in 1917, and grew increasingly prolific throughout the 1920s and 30s. Her many performances included films as diverse as George Fitzmaurice's *The Devil to Pay* (1930), Henry King's *Ramona* (1936) and

Richard Wallace's *A Night to Remember* (1942), before winning an Academy Award for her performance in H.C. Potter's *The Farmer's Daughter* (1947).

The supporting cast of *The Bishop's Wife* is uniformly strong, particularly veteran actor/ screenwriter James Gleason as Sylvester, the plain-speaking taxi driver who is reawakened to the joys of living by Dudley's intervention in his life, and Gladys Cooper as the excruciatingly frosty Mrs Hamilton, whose transfiguration seems all the more touching when the audience become aware of the reason behind her domineering nature. Yet special mention is due to Monty Woolley's scene-stealing performance as the brilliant, eccentric and mildly cantankerous Professor Wutheridge. Woolley, who ironically enough had been a Yale University academic before becoming a highly successful actor and director on Broadway,[5] is utterly convincing as the jaded atheist who is forced to confront his deeply ingrained frustration at life's disappointments. By turns comic and moving, Wutheridge is a fully rounded supporting character of the best type, and Woolley's multifaceted performance is worthy of recollection long after the film has concluded.

The Bishop's Wife had an uneven response from critics at the time of its release,[6] but went on to perform well at the 1948 Academy Awards, winning Gordon Sawyer the Oscar for Best Sound Recording and receiving nominations for Best Film Editing, Best Music, Best Picture, and Best Director for Henry Koster. Like many other films of the forties, the film was later to be adapted for radio. Grant, Young and Niven all reprised their original roles for a Screen Guild Theater production in 1948.[7] Niven later returned to the bishop's role for radio in 1949,[8] acting against Tyrone Power in a Lux Radio Theater production, while Grant was to join actress Phyllis Thaxter for two other radio performances in 1953[9] and 1955,[10] both productions also for the Lux Radio Theater.

The film was remade in the nineties by Penny Marshall as *The Preacher's Wife* (1996), which provided a contemporary setting for the story as well as a starry cast which included Courtney B. Vance, Denzel Washington and Whitney Houston. Marshall's film was less overtly festive than *The Bishop's Wife*, though many Christmas-related themes do remain within it. *The Preacher's Wife* does, however, feature an impressive number of musical numbers throughout, including many Gospel hymns, and received a well-deserved Academy Award nomination for Best Music (Original Musical or Comedy Score).

By the end of the 1940s, some of the most prominent themes in the Christmas film genre had been firmly established. *The Bells of St Mary's* had emphasised that the Christmas spirit can – and should – be preserved all the year round, to the benefit of all. *It's a Wonderful Life* had stressed the fact that Christmas presents us with a chance to give something back to our community and value our family, while *Miracle on 34th Street* underscored the point that society shouldn't allow commercialism to distract itself from the true meaning of Christmas. And finally, *The Bishop's Wife* had shown that those who celebrate Christmas should never forget the true reason which lies behind the power and influence of the festive season, irrespective of one's religious or cultural belief. Indeed, *The Bishop's Wife* in particular had shown that the Christmas film had begun to take on a life of its own, the holiday's widening cultural embrace meaning that the festive season was becoming a more widely-encompassing phenomenon which was overlapping the confines of its Christian heritage to incorporate secular society. The film also shared a common thread with the other aforementioned movies, in that it featured a genial outsider who – through spiritual or supernatural means – makes use of the Christmas spirit in order to change people for the better.

Many other festively-themed films saw release in the late 1940s, some of them featuring high-profile stars. To name but a few, these movies included Peter Godfrey's *Christmas in Connecticut* (1945), starring Barbara Stanwyck and Sydney Greenstreet; Joseph Kane's *The Cheaters* (1945); Edwin L. Marin's *Christmas Eve* (1947); John Ford's *Three Godfathers* (1948), featuring John Wayne, and Don Hartman's *Holiday Affair* (1949), which starred Robert Mitchum and Janet Leigh. The inclusion of big name actors in these well-received and widely circulated films had led to considerable audience familiarity with this new emerging genre of the Christmas film, and indeed this success was reflected in recognition at awards ceremonies throughout the decade. Because of the critical and commercial success of Christmas films in the immediate post-War period, it seemed certain that the genre was now destined to become a new fixture of film-making in the years to come.

Historical Context

The Bishop's Wife was first released in America on Tuesday 9 December 1947, and was the only major motion picture to be released in the United States on that particular date. At the top of the Billboard Best Sellers in Stores Chart on this day was Francis Craig's song 'Near You'. Featuring in the news around this time was the dedication of Florida's Everglades National Park by President Harry S. Truman, and the withdrawal of the United Mine Workers Union from the American Federation of Labor.

5

SCROOGE: A CHRISTMAS CAROL (1951)

George Minter Productions

Director: Brian Desmond Hurst
Producer: Brian Desmond Hurst
Screenwriter: Noel Langley, from the novella by Charles Dickens

MAIN CAST

Alastair Sim	-	Ebenezer Scrooge
Michael Hordern	-	Jacob Marley/ Marley's Ghost
Mervyn Johns	-	Bob Cratchit
Hermione Baddeley	-	Mrs Cratchit
John Charlesworth	-	Peter Cratchit
Kathleen Harrison	-	Mrs Dilber
Brian Worth	-	Fred
George Cole	-	Young Ebenezer Scrooge

If the late forties had presented films with a common theme of the transfigurative power of Christmas, the early fifties would serve up a film which typified the ability of the festive season to transform attitudes and lives for the better. This film was, of course, *Scrooge*: the first of many adaptations of Charles Dickens's *A Christmas Carol* to grace cinema screens in the post-War period. It has also become, for many people, one of the very finest versions of the story ever to be committed to celluloid, in no small part due to the bravura performance of Alastair Sim who, in one of his best-known roles, came to set the standard by which future evocations of the Ebenezer Scrooge character would be judged.

Although Brian Desmond Hurst's *Scrooge* has come to be considered one of the most successful of all adaptations of Dickens's festive tale, it was by no means the first to appear in cinemas. Earlier decades had seen the release of film versions of *A Christmas Carol* which had included Harold M. Shaw's *A Christmas Carol* (1914), Rupert Julian's *The Right to Be Happy* (1916), Henry Edwards's *Scrooge* (1935), and – perhaps most notably – Edwin L. Marin's *A Christmas Carol* (1938), which featured a memorable turn from Reginald Owen as Dickens's famously short-tempered miser. Yet Hurst's rendering of *Scrooge* was a very far-reaching and detailed adaptation, one which added layers of dimension to the character of Dickens's legendary skinflint in a way that so few other variations on the tale have ever managed to equal either before or since. Also active as a producer, Brian Desmond Hurst began his directorial career in 1934 with *The Tell-Tale Heart*, and was a prolific film-maker throughout the thirties and forties, creating popular features including *Riders to the Sea* (1935), *Prison Without Bars* (1938), *The Lion Has Wings* (1939), *Dangerous Moonlight* (1941) and *Theirs is the Glory* (1946). He remained involved in the world of film until the early sixties, but to many commentators *Scrooge* would always remain his finest hour.

The story of *A Christmas Carol* has become arguably the best-known of all festive tales not related to the actual Nativity, and has become so readily recognised through its many appearances in film and on television (to say nothing of radio, audiobooks and even computer games) that to attempt any but the most brief of synopses seems like a rather redundant endeavour. There can be only a few who are unaware of the details of Dickens's account, published by Chapman and Hall in 1843, of the covetous, tight-fisted businessman Ebenezer Scrooge. Single-mindedly obsessed with the pursuit of wealth while simultaneously contemptuous of the poor and needy, Scrooge's fixation on commerce at the expense of human concerns has made him cold-hearted and disdainful towards even the faintest notion of joy and charity. But as he prepares to retire to bed on Christmas Eve, Scrooge is visited by the tortured spirit of his long-dead business partner, Jacob Marley, who beseeches him to change his miserly and ruthless outlook on life for the sake of his eternal soul. Scrooge is unconvinced, believing that he is hallucinating, but Marley warns him that three spirits will visit his home – each representing a different aspect of Christmas – in the hope that he can avoid the same tormented afterlife that Marley himself is suffering. Sure enough, Scrooge is called upon by three separate spectres who reveal – in turn – the formative influences (good and bad) of his past, the mistakes of his present, and the consequences of his future if he does not mend his ways. His character profoundly altered by the revelations that the spirits have brought to him, Scrooge finds himself a completely changed man, baffling his peers as he exhibits new tendencies of generosity, cheerfulness and empathy with those around him. The revolution in Scrooge's attitudes, we are told, is as enduring as it is comprehensive, and Dickens leaves us in no doubt by the story's conclusion that the Christmas spirit has changed Scrooge in a way that nothing else could have done.

There are two main factors which set Hurst's *Scrooge* apart from previous adaptations of *A Christmas Carol*: the immense quality of Alastair Sim's lead performance, and the way in which Dickens's story is developed by screenwriter Noel Langley in order to deepen the viewer's understanding of Scrooge's motivations. As Fred Guida noted in his landmark study of the many adaptations of *A Christmas Carol*, Hurst's *Scrooge* is particularly noteworthy in the fact that it goes to great lengths to examine the seminal influences which came to define Scrooge's character[1] and, in turn, observes the way in which his driving force comes to be shaped by this formative stimulus. Much of this is detailed in subtle deviations from, and embellishments to, the original source material. Langley's screenplay provides an explanation of Scrooge's departure from his employment with the jovial Mr Fezziwig, introducing a new scenario which describes his corruption by another businessman who – working together with Marley – Scrooge eventually proceeds to usurp. The details of Scrooge's birth are also changed, with his sister Fan - originally his younger sibling in the novella – now becoming older than Ebenezer, while it is explained that Scrooge's mother had died during his birth, providing motivation for the antipathy between Scrooge and his father. Also, the breakdown of Scrooge's romance with his fiancée Alice (named Belle in Dickens's book) is made all the more poignant by revealing that, after she ends their engagement due to Scrooge's increasingly unmanageable greed, she devotes her life to caring for the destitute.

In the hands of a less able screenwriter, any changes to Dickens's eminently well-known story may have led to disaster, but taken collectively the embellishments added by Langley enhance the already compelling nature of a narrative which is so intimately concerned with redemption and transformation.[2] Few other adaptations of *A Christmas Carol* have gone to such lengths to present Jacob Marley as a living, breathing human being – complete with dimensions of character and malign, avaricious purpose – as well as a wailing, chain-rattling spectre. Indeed, while Scrooge has naturally always been the central figure of any adaptation of Dickens's tale, Hurst's film is at pains to develop supporting characters such as Fred, Fan and even Fezziwig with greater clarity than has been offered by many later variations on the story. The result is that Scrooge's character is fleshed out in a much more persuasive way, making his eventual conversion to moral behaviour all the more convincing.

The success of any adaptation of *A Christmas Carol* rests almost entirely upon the strength of its lead actor, and in the opinion of many critics – both now and at the time of release – Alastair Sim was to establish quite simply the most convincing evocation of Ebenezer Scrooge ever to be committed to film.[3] From his short-tempered, cantankerous first appearance all the way through to Scrooge's joyous realisation that he has achieved a redemption he would never have believed possible (and would never before have considered seeking), Sim throws himself completely into the performance of a lifetime, and it is no surprise that – in the eyes of commentators such as Kate Carnell Watt and Kathleen C. Lonsdale – his presentation of the character has become the benchmark by which all subsequent performances have been judged.[4] Sim had been known to British cinemagoing audiences since the mid-thirties, and by the time of *Scrooge* he was a much-loved performer throughout the United Kingdom. He was cast in a wide variety of comedic and dramatic roles throughout the thirties and forties, among them Henry Edwards's *The Private Secretary* (1935), Sonnie Hale's *Gangway* (1937), Sidney Gilliat's *Waterloo Road* (1945) and, appearing with Gordon Harker, the Inspector Hornleigh series (starting with Eugene Forde's *Inspector Hornleigh*, 1939). Sim would, of course, go on to further success with films such as Guy Hamilton's *An Inspector Calls* (1954) and Frank Launder's *The Belles of St. Trinian's* (1954), and was nominated for a BAFTA Award for his appearance as army chaplain Captain William Paris in Frank Launder's *Folly to Be Wise* (1953). He also reprised the role of Ebenezer Scrooge some two decades later in Richard Williams's well-regarded animated adaptation of *A Christmas Carol* (1971), which was transmitted by the American Broadcasting Company. Also featuring Sim's *Scrooge* cast-mates Michael Hordern as Jacob Marley and Melvyn Hayes as Bob Cratchit, the film won Richard Williams the Academy Award in the Best Short Subject: Animated Films category at the 1973 Oscar ceremony.

It was not only Sim's acting prowess which elevated his performance as Scrooge above those of his predecessors. His outward appearance, gestures and distinctive delivery all combined to create a kind of definitive depiction of the character; Dickens's bewildered miser, misplaced within the experiences of his own life as his cynicism gradually begins to erode, has rarely seemed like such a tangibly human character than when entrusted into the hands of Hurst and Sim. After such a strong run throughout the forties of American films dealing with the ability of Christmas to reshape attitudes and alter lives for the better, a return to Dickens's story – arguably among the most prominent exponents of this theme in Western film and literature – needed to be robust in its presentation of the transformative power residing within the festive season. Fortunately Hurst was able to meet this challenge with such success that it has not only become one of the best-known Christmas films of the 1950s, but is also among the most-watched of all British motion pictures originating from that decade.

The supporting cast of *Scrooge* is also consistently solid. Mervyn Johns's cinematic career started in 1934, following which he quickly built a prolific body of work as a character actor in a wide variety of films such as Alfred Hitchcock's *Jamaica Inn* (1939), Walter Forde's *Saloon Bar* (1940), Basil Dearden's *The Halfway House* (1944), Paul L. Stein's *Counterblast* (1948), and George Cukor's *Edward, My Son* (1949). As a memorable Bob Cratchit, meek but honourable, he enjoys good on-screen chemistry with Hermione Baddeley, Hurst's choice for Mrs Cratchit. Baddeley, who had been appearing on cinema screens since the late 1920s, had built a successful career with performances in films which included John Boulting's *Brighton Rock* (1947), Daniel Birt's *No Room at the Inn* (1948), and Henry Cornelius's *Passport to Pimlico* (1949). She would later go on to widespread critical acclaim for her appearance as Elspeth in Jack Clayton's *Room at the Top* (1959), which earned her nominations at both the Academy Awards and the BAFTA Awards. Yet perhaps most prominent of all the supporting players is Michael Hordern's impressive Jacob Marley, a character who proves to be merciless in life but tortured in death. Hordern, an esteemed stage actor whose cinematic career began with Carol Reed's *A Girl Must Live* (1939), had appeared in films as diverse as Peter Ustinov's *School for Secrets* (1946), Fergus McDonell's *The Small Voice* (1948), Terence Fisher's *Portrait from Life* (1948), Antony Darnborough and Terence Fisher's *The Astonished Heart* (1950) and Anthony Kimmins's *Flesh & Blood* (1951) before his performance in *Scrooge*. His later appearance as the King in Bryan Forbes's *The Slipper and the Rose* (1976) was to earn him a nomination for Best Supporting Actor at the 1977 BAFTA Awards.

The film's incidental cast is every bit as remarkable, and features a veritable roll-call of British character actors of the time including George Cole, Hattie Jacques, Patrick Macnee and Jack Warner. Yet particular praise must go to Kathleen Harrison for her impeccably well-judged comic performance as Mrs Dilber, Scrooge's charlady. (The character is actually a composite of the laundress in Dickens's novella and the hitherto-unnamed house cleaner of the original book.) Her humorous interactions with Sim's Scrooge, particularly her shock at his levity on Christmas Day, still raise a smile after all these years.

The film also benefits from Richard Addinsell's dynamic musical score, which is restrained when necessary but able to convey the emotional resonance of Scrooge's journey of personal self-discovery with finely-honed precision. Worthy of note too is the sumptuous set design by an uncredited Freda Pearson, which perfectly captures the finer points of life in the mid-nineteenth century. This is especially true of Scrooge's joyless offices and austere living quarters, but also in the many rewarding little details which present themselves in the Cratchits' modest home and in Fred's warmly welcoming abode.

Scrooge performed well at the British box-office at the time of its release,[5] and also received a generally favourable response from reviewers. However, its American release was less approvingly regarded, with a decidedly lukewarm critical reception.[6] However, within a few years the film began to appear on television in the United States, and – as would later be the case with *It's a Wonderful Life* – it eventually developed a growing and affectionate reputation amongst the viewing public. Today, it is commonly regarded amongst many reviewers as one of the finest Christmas films ever made.[7] Indeed, its influence extends far beyond other adaptations of *A Christmas Carol*, succeeding as a fine costume drama just as much as a sentimental fable of the festive season.

In many ways, *Scrooge* was a mélange of the traditional and the modern, mixing the perennial key themes of Dickens's classic story with the more progressive, contemporary viewpoints that had been advanced by American Christmas films in the late forties. Whereas films like *The Bells of St Mary's* and *Miracle on 34th Street* had embedded a long-established assemblage of cultural attitudes towards the Christmas spirit into a modern-day framework, *Scrooge* instead emphasised the universality of Dickens's subject matter – benevolence, social concern and compassion furthered by Yuletide good will – as being relevant to any cultural setting, past or present. This *modus operandi* is advanced by a screenplay which is acutely concerned with fleshing out Scrooge's motivation, elevating him from a cipher for greed and self-interest into a tragic, misguided everyman and emphasising that by selecting the wrong life choices, his unfortunate fate could so easily by repeated by anyone.

Scrooge was emblematic of a gear change in Christmas films, continuing the theme of the festive season's power to reform and improve both outlooks and lives while paving the way for new approaches later in the decade. While the angels popular in the Christmas movies of the forties behaved quite differently to the ghosts encountered by Scrooge,[8] their purpose was more or less the same: to encourage their earthly charges to recognise the error of their ways and alter their conduct, for the betterment of both themselves and those around them. Yet as the austerity of the immediate post-War era was beginning to give way to a new age of optimism and confidence, so too would Christmas films begin to change as the decade continued. *Scrooge*, with its timeless appeal and engaging performances, had typified all that was attractive about the most traditional of Christmas tales, related in a way that was relevant and pleasing to contemporary audiences. But as audiences advanced further into the fifties, there was an appetite for new and exciting approaches to festive film-making to manifest themselves; a hunger which was soon to be appeased in the most memorable of ways.

Historical Context

A Christmas Carol went on release in the United States on 2 December 1951, following an earlier British premiere on 31 October of that year. Coinciding with the film's American release were the premieres of André De Toth's *Man in the Saddle* and Lewis D. Collins's *Texas Lawmen*. At number one on Billboard's Best Sellers in Stores Chart that week was 'Cold, Cold Heart', performed by Tony Bennett. The same week was also to see the television premiere of NBC's famous detective series *Dragnet*, and the news that lethal gases emanating from an eruption of the Philippines's Mount Hibok-Hibok (also known as Mount Catarman) had brought about the tragic loss of five hundred lives.

6

WHITE CHRISTMAS (1954)

Paramount Pictures

Director: Michael Curtiz
Producer: Robert Emmett Dolan
Screenwriters: Norman Krasna, Norman Panama and Melvin Frank

MAIN CAST

Bing Crosby	-	Bob Wallace
Danny Kaye	-	Phil Davis
Rosemary Clooney	-	Betty Haynes
Vera Ellen	-	Judy Haynes
Dean Jagger	-	Major General Thomas F. Waverly
Mary Wickes	-	Emma Allen
Anne Whitfield	-	Susan Waverly
John Brascia	-	John

White Christmas is almost certainly the best-known of all American festive films produced in the 1950s. It also proved to be one of that decade's most successful musicals. With its lavish song-and-dance numbers, extravagant sets and winning charm, the film marked a huge break from other Christmas films which had immediately preceded it. Filmed in Technicolor with the VistaVision process – the first film to use the then-pioneering technique[1] – *White Christmas* largely eschews the character-changing profundities common to the festive movies of the late forties, instead focusing on the festive season as a time of exuberant joy and celebration. The result is a film with an infectious sense of fun and goodwill; a Christmas movie that it is almost impossible to dislike.

It is fair to say that with *White Christmas*, films of the festive season underwent a dramatic shift in momentum when compared to what had come before. The vibrant colour, and also the fine detail of the VistaVision process, saw the Christmas movie edging away from the austerity of the post-War years – a fact made all the more explicit due to *White Christmas*'s unabashed patriotism. It is a film which celebrates America and the innate power of showbusiness as much as it does the holiday season, bringing together the finest elements of the United States' famous 'can do' attitude to emphasise exactly what it is about Christmas that has the ability to fire the imagination.

Although popular legend has come to regard the film as an ostensible remake of Mark Sandrich's *Holiday Inn* (1942), which had also starred Bing Crosby and featured many popular Irving Berlin songs, in truth *White Christmas* bears little more than a superficial similarity to the earlier film, which had featured a rural inn that opened for business exclusively on public holidays (of which Christmas was but one). Also starring Fred Astaire and Marjorie Reynolds, *Holiday Inn* has become famous as the first film to feature Berlin's song 'White Christmas' and, though it is a fact that is often overlooked in recent years, Crosby also performed it to great acclaim in Stuart Heisler's *Blue Skies* (1946).[2] The *Holiday Inn* version of 'White Christmas' won Berlin the Academy Award for Best Music in an Original Song, though he would be nominated for a further seven Oscars throughout his long career. Bing Crosby's performance of the song subsequently became so popular, both from its use in films and from its widespread general release, that it is now by far the single best-selling Christmas song of all time.[3]

Helming *White Christmas* was celebrated Hungarian director Michael Curtiz, who was well-known to the filmgoing public by the mid-fifties for his prolific and high-profile output, most famously including the now-legendary *Casablanca* (1942) for which he won an Academy Award. Highly active in European filmmaking (as Mihály Kertész) prior to a move to America in the 1920s, he was responsible for many successful films from the late twenties onwards and was primarily known at the time for his work with Warners, including features such as *The Mystery of the Wax Museum* (1933), *British Agent* (1934), *Captain Blood* (1935), *The Charge of the Light Brigade* (1936), *Four Daughters* (1938), *Angels with Dirty Faces* (1938), *The Sea Wolf* (1941), *Yankee Doodle Dandy* (1942) and *Mildred Pierce* (1945), amongst a great many others. The sentimental musical entertainment of *White Christmas* was a somewhat atypical film for Curtiz, who had become known for his skilful cinematic explorations of complex moral ambiguity. However, upon its release the movie achieved immediate popularity at the box-office, becoming one of the best-known and most financially successful films of his later career.[4]

The narrative of *White Christmas* opens on the Christmas Eve night of 1944, where a division of American soldiers are camped in war-torn Europe. Two entertainers, Captain Bob Wallace (Bing Crosby) and Private First Class Phil Davis (Danny Kaye) are putting on a song and dance show to boost troop morale while enemy bombs burst around them. The division's commanding officer, Major General Thomas Waverly (Dean Jagger) is about to be relieved by a hard-nosed replacement, General Harold Coughlan (Gavin Gordon). Waverly has obvious affection for the soldiers under his command, and makes use of Wallace and Davis's show to bid them all farewell before Coughlan takes over. As he departs by jeep, the camp is bombarded by the Nazis, causing chaos as ruined buildings begin to topple in the surrounding area. Davis's fast reflexes are all that save Wallace from being crushed under falling debris, though at the cost of a wound to his arm.

Later, Wallace visits Davis in a field hospital to thank him for saving his life. He adds that if he can ever do anything to help Davis in the future, that he shouldn't hesitate to ask. Davis wastes no time in proposing that he and Wallace become a double act after the war is over and, although Wallace is highly reluctant (being a successful entertainer in his own right), Davis plays on his sympathy in order to persuade him to agree.

Sure enough, once V-E Day has come about and their division is disbanded, Wallace and Davis return to the United States and make a huge success of their entertainment careers. They soon catch the eye of trade papers such as *Variety*, and after continuing triumph with their stage performances they decide to move into production. They put on a Broadway musical, *Playing Around*, to great acclaim for a two year run, and eventually the production moves to Florida. There, Davis voices his concern that since he and Wallace became producers, Wallace has become a single-minded workaholic, so focused on the success of their careers that he has allowed himself little time for leisure or romance. Wallace responds that he will only entertain the notion of a relationship when the right woman comes into this life; he is unwilling to settle for just any potential partner who might happen by.

Before they are due to leave Florida, Wallace reveals that he has received a letter from a sergeant who they served with in the War, requesting that he and Davis go to a club named Novello's to see a musical performance by his sisters. Davis is highly sceptical about the whole affair, knowing that the letter is inviting them to an audition in all but name, but nevertheless he agrees to go along. The two entertainers in question, Judy (Vera Ellen) and Betty (Rosemary Clooney) are surprised to discover that Wallace and Davis have actually come to the club; in the dressing room, Betty is amazed that their brother would have written such a letter – he has accepted a job in Alaska and should have been unaware that Davis and Wallace's show would have been taking place in the same area of Florida that the sisters' revue is currently ongoing. Sheepishly, Judy reveals that she had written the letter herself, hoping that their brother's old acquaintances would be able to help them with their careers.

Both Wallace and Davis are impressed with the Haynes Sisters' performance, a song and dance number named – fittingly enough – 'Sisters'. After the show, they meet for a drink and an immediate attraction becomes obvious between Davis and Judy. Betty seems rather disappointed that Wallace is unable to offer them any advice. Later, feeling slightly guilty, she tells him the truth about the letter that brought him there. Wallace laughs, telling her that everyone in showbusiness always has an ulterior motive, but she is indignant in the face of his cynicism. Meanwhile on the dancefloor, Judy tells Davis that they will be leaving for Vermont the next day. He is disappointed, knowing that he and Wallace are due to leave Florida themselves later that night.

Davis and Judy enjoy a long dance, which is eventually interrupted by an agitated Betty who reminds her that they must prepare for their next routine. Novello (Herb Vigran), the club's owner, rushes up to the sisters to inform them that a sheriff (James Parnell) has arrived with a warrant for their arrest. It transpires that the pair have been accused by their landlord (Sig Ruman) of causing accidental damage to an expensive rug, but have refused to pay the $200 that has been demanded in recompense. In a convoluted scheme, Davis convinces the sisters to take the train tickets that he and Wallace had intended to use later that night. Smuggling the women out of their apartment with their suitcases, he convinces Novello to stall the sheriff while he and Wallace mime the sister's closing act (using a vinyl record that Davis finds in the pair's apartment) to a puzzled but enraptured audience. As the routine comes to an end, the sheriff and the landlord smell a rat and set off in pursuit of the two beleaguered entertainers. Fortunately the men are able to get their belongings together and escape the club through Judy and Betty's apartment window, boarding a taxi before the sheriff can catch up with them.

Wallace and Davis only just manage to catch the northbound train on time, though Wallace is suspicious when Davis seems unable to find their tickets, forcing him to purchase space on a draughty club car instead. Wallace looks forward to getting back to New York, but Davis tries to persuade him (much to Wallace's confusion) to go to Vermont instead. Eventually the penny drops and Wallace realises that Davis has given away their train tickets to the Haynes sisters. However, before he has the opportunity to confront them the two women come down to the club car to thank Wallace for having agreed to give them the tickets (Davis having convinced them that it had been Wallace's idea in the first place). Judy reveals that they are headed to Vermont for the holidays, causing Wallace to recognise exactly why Davis has been trying so hard to persuade him to go there. Betty also attempts to convince him to come along, and Wallace soon realises that resistance to the idea is pointless.

Some time later, the train pulls in to Pine Tree, Vermont. In spite of much expectation of blizzards and skiing, Davis is disappointed to discover that the temperature seems rather more clement than he'd anticipated – not a flake of snow has fallen since Thanksgiving. Wallace, Davis and the sisters head for the cosy Columbia Inn, which they soon discover to be owned by none other than their old commanding officer, Major General Waverly. The general is pleased to see his old military subordinates, though it becomes obvious that his inn has been facing hard times due to a lack of custom – guests have been reluctant to visit due to the chronic lack of snow, especially so close to Christmas. The sisters, who have been booked to perform at the inn over the holidays, give their opening show to an audience of barely a dozen people. The inn's housekeeper, Emma Allen (Mary Wickes), reveals that Waverly has invested everything he owns into the business. If the inn should go into decline, as appears to be its fate, then the general will be bankrupt. Wallace immediately springs into action, getting on the phone to New York and having all the sets and costumes from his Broadway show shipped up to Vermont. In spite of the logistical expense, Wallace hopes that their famous act will be able to draw public attention to the Columbia Inn and reverse the general's ailing fortunes.

The general appears baffled as the vast amounts of equipment required to put on the show starts arriving at his inn. Knowing Waverly to be a proud man, Davis and Wallace conceal their true intentions from him, telling the general instead that they merely plan to rehearse new elements of their show and are keen to do so in a location other than their usual inner-city venue for once. He is similarly nonplussed when they explain that the change of scene will allow them to try out their new material on a different audience, but seems to take them on their word – especially once he sees them in action with a set-piece full of elaborate costumes and intricately-detailed props and staging.

At night, Judy and Davis hatch a plan to get Wallace and Betty to spend more time together. As Betty is unable to sleep, Judy advises her to help herself to a midnight snack, but when Betty heads down into the inn's bar area she finds Wallace playing the piano there. Both unaware that their meeting has been engineered, Wallace offers Betty a variety of refreshments from the bar, and they begin to talk. Betty tells Wallace how much she admires his plan to keep the general's business afloat, and they enjoy a brief romantic tryst before Waverly – oblivious to their presence – interrupts the encounter when he enters the room in search of a midnight snack of his own.

The next day, Wallace arrives back from town when he meets the general sitting outside the inn. He shows him the newly-printed show-bills for the show, but Waverly indicates that he's on to the ruse – he assures Wallace that there is no need to worry about the financial health of his business, as he has applied to rejoin the Army. As it happens, Wallace has just visited the Post Office to pick up the day's mail, and the general's reply from Washington D.C. has already arrived. However, the response makes it clear – in the most diplomatic of terms – that the post-War armed forces no longer have any need for him. Waverly is clearly deflated but puts on a brave face, though his subterfuge is totally wasted on Wallace. Knowing that his old commanding officer has been crushed by the rejection, Wallace catches up with Davis at one of the rehearsals and suggests that they round up as many of their old division as possible. If they were to attend the show in honour of the general, it would show him unequivocally that he remains respected and needed.

Wallace calls Ed Harrison (Johnny Grant), a high-profile television host in New York City, and asks if he can use his top-rated show to broadcast an appeal in order to encourage as many of the general's old troops as possible to come to Vermont to join him at the inn. Harrison is so enthused by the idea that he tries to encourage Wallace to have the entire show broadcast as a Christmas Eve TV special, and outlines a cynical plan to exploit Waverly's financial woes to gain sympathy with the public. It would also, he suggests, mean thousands of dollars' worth of free advertising for Wallace and Davis. Wallace is not impressed by this plan, rejecting any attempt to take advantage of the general's plight, but neither he nor Harrison are aware that Emma is listening in to the conversation on an extension line. As she is interrupted, however, she only hears a fragment of their discussion and mistakenly comes to believe that Wallace is attempting to exploit the general's situation for his own ends. Disgusted by this apparent turn of events, she makes plain her disdain to Betty. At first Betty does not believe that Wallace would be capable of such a selfish act, but soon even she begins to doubt his good intentions.

Appalled by what she has learned from Emma, Betty angrily rounds on Wallace at a rehearsal. She makes it clear that she regrets getting closer to him the previous night, and tells him that she wants to withdraw from the show. Wallace is hurt and confused by her complete change of heart, particularly as she offers no explanation for it, but he is unable to talk her around. Davis and Judy watch as Betty angrily storms out of the building. As they are also unaware of the reason for her ire, they presume that she is resisting the prospect of a relationship with Wallace due to the fact that she is so protective towards her sister; Judy reasons that until she is engaged, her older sister will never consider settling down herself. Davis is then taken aback when Judy suggests that they should announce their own engagement, in the hope that it will convince Betty that she is free to consider romance with Wallace more seriously. Judy assures Davis that he shouldn't be daunted at the prospect of this union; it is only a temporary measure, she promises him, and agrees to keep the whole thing as low-key as possible.

Waverly organises a cast party at the inn that night, which everyone seems to enjoy with the exception of Betty. Noticing that her sister is still unhappy, Judy hatches a plan with Davis to get her up onto the dancefloor – and into the arms of Wallace. However, at the first opportunity she breaks away and heads off into the furthest corner of the room. Frustrated at Betty's evasiveness, Judy decides that there can only be one thing for it: she persuades Davis to announce their engagement in front of the assembled cast. Everybody is delighted at their happy news, but Betty is horrified and unable to disguise her unease even from Judy. After Wallace has congratulated his long-time friend, Davis suggests that he approach Betty and attempt to reconnect with her. However, Wallace is concerned when it becomes obvious that she can barely stand to be in the same room as him; unwilling even to converse with Wallace, she leaves the party abruptly. Later that night, Judy enthusiastically tells Betty that she is now free of responsibility for her younger sister, meaning that she is free to do what she wants in life. Betty offers no reply, Judy believing that she is asleep but unaware that she is actually too upset to answer.

The following morning, Betty asks the general to drive her to the Pine Tree train station, where she is due to board a train to New York. She hands him a letter to pass on to Judy, but Waverly advises her to stay, sensing ambivalence in her manner. Betty beseeches the general not to interfere and heads for the train just as it begins to pull away from the platform. As it happens, Wallace is also there, making arrangements with the stationmaster (I. Stanford Jolley) for the arrival of the large number of people that he anticipates will respond to his televised appeal over the holiday season. Wallace spots Betty as the train starts to leave and makes one last attempt to ascertain why she has experienced such a total change in attitude. However, she remains silent on the issue, leaving Wallace upset and confused in her wake.

Back at the inn, Judy receives Betty's letter and is stunned to discover that she has gone to perform at the Carousel Club in New York. Judy is dismayed that her sister would leave her side so unexpectedly, not least because there had been no discussion of the matter beforehand. Sheepishly, she and Davis approach Wallace and explain their engagement ploy to him. Wallace is annoyed that they would pull such a stunt as a means to bring him closer to Betty, but secretly seems quite touched by their plan. He is also heading for New York, where is due to appear on that evening's edition of the Ed Harrison Show. Before he leaves, he tells Davis that he must – at all costs – ensure that the general does not watch the broadcast, so that he remains unaware of the appeal. Davis realises that this is a taller order than it sounds, knowing the Ed Harrison Show to be one of Waverly's favourite programmes.

As it happens, Wallace is due to meet with Harrison at the Carousel Club, and arrives just in time to catch Betty's act. Betty notices Wallace and becomes reluctant to perform, but after she has delivered her song she decides to bite the bullet and join him at his table. Wallace explains that Judy and Davis had faked their engagement in order to draw the two of them closer together, and Betty appears to reconsider his sincerity when he emphasises that there is no reason to let the matter upset her. However, her attitude turns aloof again when Harrison arrives in a rush and pulls Wallace away so that they will arrive at the studio in good time for the evening broadcast. Wallace tries to arrange a later meeting with Betty, but she is having none of it – dismissively, she brushes off his attempts.

Wallace makes his appeal on national TV as scheduled while, back in Vermont, Davis distracts the general by pretending to have broken his leg. As Wallace asks everyone connected with Waverly's old division to make their way to Pine Tree on Christmas Eve, he stresses that no-one will be making any financial benefit from the event. Elsewhere in New York, Betty is watching the show on television and becomes tearful as she realises that Wallace's intentions have been altruistic all along.

Sure enough, when the time comes dozens upon dozens of former soldiers descend upon Pine Tree train station and make their way to the inn. But Judy is relieved most of all by one particular arrival – Betty, who returns just in time for the evening's performance. Waverly, meanwhile, is frustrated to discover that Emma has sent away both of his suits to be dry-cleaned, leaving him with no alternative but to wear his old general's uniform to the show. However, when he enters the inn's function room he is stunned to discover so many of his old officers and troops lining up for his personal inspection. Almost overcome with emotion, he warmly greets them before blowing out the candles on a special ceremonial cake to mark ten years since that fateful night back in 1944 when he handed over command of the division.

Waverly sits at the central table as Wallace and Davis perform a complex routine dedicated to their nostalgic memories of army life. Wallace is somewhat taken aback when he discovers Betty's surprise return – the first he knows of her change of heart is when she arrives on stage. After the number is over, one of the general's old aides informs him that it has started to snow. Sure enough, by the time Waverly reaches the inn's front doorway there is already a generous covering on the ground, with flakes continuing to fall heavily. The general is overjoyed, knowing that it is the best possible news for his business.

Wallace and Davis, together with Betty and Judy, then perform their final act of the evening – a lively rendition of 'White Christmas'. Dressed as Santa Claus, Wallace is surprised to discover a gift from Betty in his bag; a model of a knight in shining armour. They embrace, knowing that they have finally overcome the misunderstanding between them. The stage's background scenery is pulled away to reveal snow continuing to fall outside as Davis invites the audience to join him in a toast to the festive season.

White Christmas is a deeply patriotic film: one which celebrates the work of the armed forces without ever glorifying war, and which rejoices in the virtues of traditional community spirit while also recognising the challenges manifested in a world which was in the throes of radical change. Although the film contains few of the stylistic touches that had come to characterise Curtiz's highly distinctive work in the thirties and forties,[5] the glitz and the glamour of *White Christmas* heralded a vital sea-change in the way that Christmas films were perceived from that point onward. The silver screen charm of *Miracle on 34th Street*'s department store displays and the folksy small-town appeal of Bedford Falls in *It's a Wonderful Life* had been superseded by a new kind of Christmas narrative – one which was vibrant, larger than life and ready to embrace the developing tastes of a country which had hurtled through a multifarious social and cultural transformation since the end of the War.[6]

The film creates an effective contrast between the fates of Wallace and Davis and their old commanding officer, General Waverly. The younger men, both fresh and energetic professionals, use their ambition, drive and flawless work ethic to rapidly climb the ladder of showbusiness after their army division is demobilised. For the general, however, life is decidedly less benevolent. Considered surplus to requirements at the Pentagon, he is cast adrift into a country that has changed drastically since he had entered the service. With his business facing closure, and having to deal with the humiliation of being rejected by his old colleagues in Washington D.C., it falls to Wallace and Davis to ensure that Waverly is aware that he has not been forgotten by his old comrades – and, by extension, that his exemplary war service has not been allowed to slip out of the grasp of the national consciousness. The selflessness of Wallace and Davis's gesture, further underscored by the resolution of Betty and Emma's misunderstanding of their philanthropic intentions, is suggestive of a wider concern within the film: the way in which long-standing tradition was being challenged by the modernity of the post-War era. To this end, *White Christmas* presents itself as a film which is more secular in nature of many of the Christmas films which had preceded it; there are no particular religious undertones in evidence at all, largely because the narrative is concerned more with the ease of access between Americans and a holiday season which is inclusive enough for everyone, irrespective of the nature of their personal beliefs.[7] Whereas some Christmas films, such as *The Bishop's Wife*, had stressed the comprehensive nature of Christmas in terms of the religion which had been responsible for the celebration's genesis, the narrative of *White Christmas* instead expressed the view that the festive season was one which had embedded itself firmly within the American psyche precisely because it was a shared celebration of goodwill and mutual understanding, regardless of whether one expressed any faith in the Christian underpinnings of the event.[8] Given the film's key theme of family, specifically the notion that the family unit extends beyond blood ties, the salute to Waverly's military service by his old division – long since disbanded – accentuates the sense that the common purpose of war, which has so profoundly united these men in collective fellowship, has also forged a new America in its wake: an optimistic, hopeful country with both determination and confidence.

A film like *White Christmas* ultimately proves hugely reliant upon the quality of its central performances, and fortunately Bing Crosby and Danny Kaye's onscreen chemistry meant that the friendship between the two likeable protagonists remains believable and engaging throughout. Crosby's easygoing charm contrasts nicely with Kaye's impeccable comic timing and well-regarded physical comedy, evident most clearly in Davis's constant mischievous manipulation of Wallace by means of his old war wound, and of course his entertainingly amusing affectation of a broken leg while trying desperately to distract Waverly's attention. Crosby had remained highly active in film since his appearance as Father O'Malley in *The Bell's of St Mary's*, making prominent appearances in films as diverse as Norman Z. McLeod's *Road to Rio* (1947), Billy Wilder's *The Emperor Waltz* (1948), Frank Capra's *Riding High* (1950), Hal Walker's *Road to Bali* (1952) and George Seaton's *Little Boy Lost* (1953), amongst many others. He was nominated for the Academy Award for Best Actor in 1955 shortly after the release of *White Christmas*, in recognition of his performance in George Seaton's *The Country Girl* (1954). Danny Kaye had been working in the film industry since his appearance in Al Christie's 1935 comedy short *Moon Over Manhattan*. Also a well-regarded actor on the stage, he had given a number of increasingly high-profile performances throughout the forties and fifties which had included Elliott Nugent's *Up in Arms* (1944), Norman Z. McLeod's *The Secret Life of Walter Mitty* (1947), Henry Koster's *The Inspector General* (1949), Walter Lang's *On* the *Riviera* (1951), and in the title role of Charles Vidor's *Hans Christian Andersen* (1952). In 1955 Kaye was to receive a huge honour in the form of an Honorary Academy Award for his services to the American film industry.

If the rapport between the two leads was effective, so too was their onscreen relationship with their new-found female companions, the adventurous Judy and feisty, independent Betty. *White Christmas* gave both Vera Ellen and Rosemary Clooney a golden opportunity to shine, and they match their male counterparts every step – and song – of the way. Indeed, the film has become known as one of the best-known features in the filmographies of both actresses. Vera Ellen's Hollywood career began alongside Danny Kaye in H. Bruce Humberstone's *Wonder Man* (1945), and from there she went from strength to strength with appearances in films such as Gregory Ratoff's *Carnival in Costa Rica* (1947), Stanley Donen and Gene Kelly's *On the Town* (1949), Richard Thorpe's *Three Little Words* (1950) and Charles Walters's *The Belle of New York* (1952). Rosemary Clooney had made her first appearance in the film world in the early fifties, and prior to her performance in *White Christmas* she had become known for her work in films including Norman Taurog's *The Stars Are Singing* (1953), Claude Binyon's *Here Come the Girls* (1953) and George Marshall's *Red Garters* (1954).

The film's supporting performances, though in actuality they are relatively few in number, are also solid throughout. Dean Jagger excels as the retired general, nostalgic for the past glories of his career but suffering from his perceived lack of purpose since retirement. His barely-contained emotion at the film's climax is truly touching to behold, and is perfectly attuned to the sentiment of the occasion. Mary Wickes also gives a nicely-judged performance as well-meaning busybody Emma Allen, her fussing over the inn generally – and Waverly's affairs specifically – slowly being derailed by the arrival of ever more New York stage hands and theatrical paraphernalia as the film unfolds.

White Christmas opened to great critical anticipation in the October of 1954,[9] and went on to become the biggest box-office success of the year.[10] Indeed, it became such a commercial success that it eventually went on to become the fifth highest-grossing cinematic musical of the decade.[11] Many reviewers, then and now, have praised the film for everything from Irving Berlin's winning selection of songs – including 'Sisters', 'Snow', '(We'll Follow) The Old Man', 'What Can You Do with a General?', 'Love, You Didn't Do Right By Me', and of course the already-famous title song – to Sam Comer and Grace Gregory's wonderful set design. Although some commentators have in recent years voiced scepticism over the film's perceived virtues,[12] others have made the point that to disapprove of *White Christmas* in narrative terms is pointless, as such censure would surely involve observing the same apparent imperfections that existed in other musicals of the same genre which were popular at the time: namely that plot and characterisation are elements that prove to be subordinate to the musical numbers and dance sequences which make up the bulk of the running time and are, in the eyes of many, what is responsible for making the film's content so popular in the first place.[13]

Irving Berlin received an Oscar nomination for his song 'Count Your Blessings

Instead of Sheep' in the Best Music: Original Song category at the 1955 Academy Award ceremony, just one of the memorable pieces of music which had been responsible for making *White Christmas* a lasting success amongst audiences. With its unashamed razzmatazz and obvious affection for both America and the entertainment industry, Curtiz's flm had made an immediate impact on audiences in the United States and beyond. The cobwebs of post-wartime asceticism now blown away, from now on the Christmas film would be concerned with more than social commentary or issues of spirituality and character transformation; *White Christmas* had shown that motion pictures made for the festive season could boast high-end production values to rival entries in any other genre, and that the commercial interest in this category of flm had only continued to grow amongst audiences since its golden age in the 1940s.

Historical Context

White Christmas received its American release on 14 October 1954. The only other film to make a new appearance in movie theatres on that day was a re-release of Edward Bernds's *Billie Gets Her Man*, following its original cinematic premiere on 9 September 1948. Topping the Billboard Best Sellers in Stores Chart during that week was, ironically enough, Rosemary Clooney with her song 'Hey There'. In world news that week, Hurricane Hazel struck North America, causing a total of 348 deaths, and Ho Chi Minh entered Hanoi following the pull-out of French troops.

7

WE'RE NO ANGELS (1955)

Paramount Pictures

Director: Michael Curtiz
Producer: Pat Duggan
Screenwriter: Ranald MacDougall, from a play by Albert Husson

MAIN CAST

Humphrey Bogart	-	Joseph
Aldo Ray	-	Albert
Peter Ustinov	-	Jules
Leo G. Carroll	-	Felix Ducotel
Joan Bennett	-	Amelie Ducotel
Gloria Talbott	-	Isabelle Ducotel
Basil Rathbone	-	Andre Trochard
John Baer	-	Paul Trochard

Affectionately known to many film buffs as 'Michael Curtiz's other Christmas movie', the style and focus of *We're No Angels* is just about as far removed as it is possible to be from *White Christmas* while still remaining in the same genre of film. The extravagant set-pieces and elaborate song and dance acts were gone in favour of a tongue-in-cheek stage adaptation, full of witty dialogue and skilfully depicted characterisation. The film deviated sharply from *White Christmas*'s subtext, which had subtly expounded upon the way in which the meaning of the festive season was beginning to be usurped by more commercial concerns – namely, the many different ways in which notions of Christmas (if not the spirit of Christmas) could be packaged and marketed. With *We're No Angels*, Curtiz returned to the more traditional theme of Christmas as a means of renewal and personal redemption, using a starry cast of actors to advance an age-old premise in the most entertainingly unconventional of ways.

The film, an adaptation of Samuel and Bella Spewack's 1953 stage play *My Three Angels* (which, in turn, was adapted from Albert Husson's earlier play *La Cuisine Des Anges*), was an unusual departure for Curtiz, but even more so for lead actor Humphrey Bogart – a man who had played heroes and villains to great acclaim for almost three decades, but who was very rarely to be found cast in comedy roles. Curtiz had, of course, famously worked with Bogart on *Casablanca* in 1942, but the pair had also collaborated on many other features over the years including *Kid Galahad* (1937), *Angels with Dirty Faces* (1938), *Virginia City* (1940) and *Passage to Marseille* (1944).

We're No Angels also marked a different approach for Curtiz in the sense that it combined the technical advances of *White Christmas* with something of the earlier conventions that had typified earlier Christmas films. The vibrant colour remained, as did the innovative VistaVision process, but *We're No Angels* signified a return to the transformational power of the festive season, examining the ways in which behaviour could be modified and improved through interaction (indirect or otherwise) with the Christmas spirit. This said, Curtiz's film is no mere collection of sentimental clichés mixed with a helping of festive good cheer. Just as the sub-tropical setting of *We're No Angel* is an undeniably refreshing change from the conventional tinsel-bedecked domestic backdrop that had been so popular in Christmas movies of the time, so too were the wry wit and humorously macabre moments which differentiated it from many of the narratives which had begun to establish themselves in the genre.

Christmas has come to the infamous Devil's Island penal colony in the winter of 1895. Hiding patiently in the island's harbour are confidence trickster Joseph (Humphrey Bogart) and murderers Albert (Aldo Ray) and Jules (Peter Ustinov), who have recently escaped from the prison complex and are biding their time in the civilian colony until they can board an outbound ship. They encounter Arnaud (John Smith), a medical officer from a ship anchored off the coast, and pick his pockets when he asks them for directions. Among their ill-gotten gains is a letter addressed to Felix Ducotel, who runs a general store on the island. The men decide to deliver it to him personally, in the hope that he may reward them.

The convicts find Ducotel (Leo G. Carroll) to be a friendly, mild-mannered gent of advancing years. Believing the men to be prisoners on parole rather than escapees, he offers them each a cigar to thank them for taking the trouble of delivering the letter to him, little realising that they have already been helping themselves liberally to his stock. Noticing that the roof of the store is leaking, Joseph suggests that to Ducotel that he and his colleagues could repair it for him. Ducotel informs him that business is so poor that he would be unable to pay the men for their efforts, but Joseph – knowing that they will have free access to pilfer from the shop's supplies – assures him that this is no problem. Once the three criminals have made their way to the roof, however, Joseph explains that he intends to raid the shop during the night in order to forge the required documents that they will need to stow themselves aboard the soon-to-depart ship on the coast. He assures them that by the very next day, with a bit of luck, they will all be headed for Paris.

Using the building's roof-level windows as a means to eavesdrop, the convicts listen in on a conversation between Ducotel and his wife Amelie (Joan Bennett). Amelie is concerned for the business, not least as Ducotel's position as manager is contingent on its financial success. Ducotel tries to calm her fears, but Amelie persists, warning that the conniving Andre Trochard (Basil Rathbone) will soon be arriving to inspect the accounts. She cautions him that Trochard has taken advantage of him in the past, and that although Ducotel and Trochard are cousins Andre will think nothing of casting him aside if it is expedient to do so. Later, a throwaway remark from a customer, Madame Parole (Lea Penman), about the marital status of the Ducotels' daughter Isabelle (Gloria Talbott) stings Amelie; she dislikes being reminded that her offspring remains unmarried at eighteen years of age. Having read Isabelle's diary, however, Amelie is vexed that her daughter is in love with Paul Trochard (John Baer), knowing that Paul's uncle Andre is unlikely to consent to a union between the affluent Trochards and the less upwardly-mobile Ducotels.

Isabelle returns from church and tells her mother how much she misses Paris; she wishes that she was back in France, where she has so many happy memories. She also confesses her love for Paul, to which Amelie responds with an unconvincing affectation of amazement. Amelie asks her daughter how she can be certain that Paul returns her affections when he is thousands of miles away, but Isabelle replies that she and Paul had agreed not to correspond by letter, preferring instead to wait for a year to see if their feelings for each other remained. Meanwhile, Ducotel finally opens the letter that the convicts delivered to him and reacts with shock; his cousin Andre has arrived at the colony earlier than he had expected, and is currently aboard the ship berthed off the island's harbour. It also transpires that Andre's nephew Paul has accompanied him on the journey. As quarantine control prohibits Andre from disembarking, Amelie pleads with Ducotel to leave Andre on the ship until Christmas is over. However, Ducotel resignedly heads for the dock to make arrangements for Andre and Paul's release; after all, the letter states that Andre intends to spend Christmas with the Ducotels, which will give him ample time to inspect their accounts.

Isabelle is elated when she discovers that Paul will be joining her family for the festive season, but becomes so upset when she reads the remainder of Andre's letter that she promptly faints. Joseph, Albert and Jules, who have witnessed the whole episode from the roof, make their way back down into the shop to ascertain the cause of her upset, and discover from the letter that Andre has arranged a marriage between Paul and the daughter of a prosperous shipbuilder. Amelie is initially wary when she finds the convicts surrounding her unconscious daughter, especially on hearing a throwaway remark about Jules having earlier murdered his wife, but she discovers that their intentions are honourable when Albert carefully carries Isabelle through the shop to her bedroom in order to allow her to revive. She is also bewildered when Joseph deals with a rare customer to the shop; a highly gifted swindler, he wastes no time in selling him a silver brush and comb set, in spite of the fact that the man is quite clearly bald.

Ducotel arrives back at the shop with news that the port authorities will be unable to release Andre until the following day. He is confused to discover Joseph poring over his financial ledgers; the convict is appalled that the accounts are so badly audited. Before he can explain himself to Ducotel, another customer arrives, to which Joseph promptly sells a jacket that is much too small for the man's girth. He advises Ducotel to put the cash from the sale in his deposit box, the suggestion being that he later intends to raid it before the convicts leave. As Joseph heads back onto the roof, continuing the pretence of repair work, Ducotel tells him that he is so grateful to the three men for their help that he would like to invite them to Christmas dinner. Touched by the older man's sincerity, the convicts readily agree. Joseph even says that he plans to 'acquire' a turkey especially for the occasion.

Later that day, Jules heads off to the governor's garden to steal some flowers to arrange while Joseph smuggles a live turkey into the kitchen, getting ready to prepare it for dinner. Albert is hanging Christmas decorations when he discovers Isabelle surreptitiously trying to escape the house. Awkwardly, she explains that she intends to run away and commit suicide due to the news of Paul's engagement. Albert tells her not to be so rash in her intentions; Paul, he points out, would hardly have travelled thousands of miles to tell her that he wanted nothing to do with her when he could so easily have communicated this fact by letter. Instead, he believes that it is more likely that Paul plans to elope with her against Andre's wishes. Isabelle brightens when she hears this alternative viewpoint, even although she considers it highly unlikely. A shy woman, she is further intrigued when Albert tells her how attractive he finds her. Even his low-key revelation of how he ended up in prison for murdering his uncle, who had refused to lend him money, does little to temper her fascination with Albert's motivations.

Amelie is puzzled to discover her daughter's greatly brightened mood. Heading into the kitchen, she finds Joseph busy preparing the turkey. She quizzes him about how he came to be incarcerated on Devil's Island, and he tells her about his incredible talent for deception and fraud. Totally unrepentant, Joseph assures her that – given the chance – the only thing that he would do differently in his life would be to avoid having been captured. Joseph realises that they will need a bottle of fine wine to accompany the turkey, and sets off to find one. As he does so, he brings the Ducotel's Christmas tree – little more than a glorified twig with some modest decorations – through to the dining area. There, Isabelle places a shabby ornament on the top of the tree: three angels, which she explains had belonged to her ever since she had been given her first Christmas tree many years ago. The convicts note that the angels look rather scruffy and unimpressive, but the beaming Isabelle assures them that to her, they look just perfect: their presence is a gift from heaven. The men look stunned as, in turn, she kisses each of them on the cheek.

The Ducotel family are all dressed in their best finery as the convicts invite them to take their places at the Christmas table. Felix, Amelie and Isabelle are righteously impressed by the beautiful flowers, perfectly-prepared turkey and gramophone music as the men unveil a full-size fir tree which has been lavishly decorated. They seem entranced as Joseph, Jules and Albert regale them with a hearty Christmas carol. However, they are all unaware that Andre and Paul have arrived early at the dock and are already making their way to the shop. Following the meal, the three convicts are toasting a fruitful new year when they hear Amelie's beautiful voice as she sings while playing the piano. Entranced, they all stop to listen.

Before they turn in for the night, Ducotel thanks the convicts for having gone to such extreme efforts to create the perfect Christmas dinner for his family. He hands Joseph an envelope stuffed with banknotes as a token of their gratitude, even in spite of their straitened financial circumstances, and the whole family voice their thanks as they head for bed. This presents the three criminals with a huge crisis of conscience; how can they steal from such inherently kind and decent people? However, Joseph is still determined that they must escape the colony at all costs – one way or another. While the convicts wash the dishes, Andre and Paul arrive at the front of the shop and noisily demand entry. Just as anticipated, Andre is conceited and arrogant, while Paul is similarly starchy with a haughty, superior attitude. Furious at having been left waiting for so long on the ship, Andre commands Ducotel to tell him why rooms haven't yet been prepared for his arrival. Ducotel hurriedly moves his family out of their bedrooms to make space for his disagreeable relatives during their visit. Andre is also unimpressed to discover that convicts are being employed on the premises. The three criminals, by contrast, are overjoyed by the new arrivals; Andre's luggage contains everything that they need to gain admission to the ship that remains offshore, including all of the required official documentation.

Noticing that Paul and Isabelle appear pleased to see each other, Andre demands that his nephew immediately go to his room and stay there. Firmly, Andre explains to Ducotel that he will not tolerate any relationship between the pair, believing that Isabelle is scheming her way into a wealthier branch of the family. Instead, he insists that Paul's engagement to the shipbuilder's daughter must go ahead for the sake of his own long-term fortunes. While Andre continues to harangue his cousin, Jules is rifling through his suitcase unnoticed. Andre confronts Ducotel on the issue of why the business is continually performing at a loss, but Joseph unexpectedly steps in to help, producing receipts to prove that for the past few months they have actually been in profit. Andre appears temporarily placated, but as he heads off to bed he warns Ducotel that they will spend the next day – Christmas Day – going through the ledgers.

When Ducotel realises that Joseph plans to doctor the books, he refuses to collaborate on the grounds that he is an honest man and will not be party to a criminal action. However, Jules easily breaks into his safe, allowing Joseph to massage the figures to suit himself. Just as he is in the process of setting to work, Andre emerges from his room, suddenly deciding to check over the ledgers before he goes to sleep in advance of his full inspection the next day. Joseph is frustrated by this unexpected turn of events, but Ducotel is relieved; he would rather be judged wanting by honourable means than attempt to be saved through trickery and deception.

Deciding that there is now little to be done to help Ducotel escape his fate, the convicts decide that they will assist Isabelle and Paul with their romance before they leave. Joseph forges a note to Isabelle, pretending to be Paul, urging her to meet with the young man that night. As Albert heads off to deliver it, Jules and Joseph persuade Paul that he must attend this impromptu rendezvous. Paul is very reluctant, pointing out that he does not love Isabelle and is unwilling to feign affection for her. However, with some not-so-gentle persuasion they manage to smuggle Paul out of his room just as Amelie arrives at the door in search of Isabelle. Joseph explains to her about the secret tryst that has been arranged, causing Amelie to voice her trepidation; she knows that Paul is not the right partner for her daughter. Joseph agrees, but tells her that Isabelle must discover this fact for herself. Relieved, Amelie apologises for having ever doubted the intentions of Joseph and his two acquaintances. As she points out, how could she ever have believed them capable of robbing her family when they have acted so honourably? Joseph is silently chastened by her comment.

In the garden, Isabelle makes an impassioned declaration of her love for Paul, who seems supremely uncomfortable. She suggests to him that he could leave France and join her in the colony, making a living there without any need of marrying a financially-convenient partner of Andre's preference. However, they are interrupted by none other than Andre himself, who – discovering the young couple together – angrily demands that Paul return to his room immediately. Isabelle beseeches Paul to make a stand against his dictatorial uncle, but much to her disappointment he meekly acquiesces to Andre's wishes and withdraws. As Paul is leaving, Andre hands him Ducotel's ledgers and advises him to check over them before the morning. Rounding on Isabelle, Andre demands that she make no further romantic overtures to his nephew; he is so obsessed by financial gain that he has convinced himself that everyone is determined to rob him of his fortune by any means, including marital ties. Isabelle angrily responds that Andre's greed and cynicism has left him with a terminally necrotic view of life, but he brushes off her insults, telling her that she should be more concerned with her father's fate – he has noted irregularities in Ducatel's finances which could lead to his own incarceration on Devil's Island.

As Andre moves to return to the house, his path is blocked by Jules, Joseph and Albert. Intimidated, he threatens to have their parole revoked by the authorities the next day, but is clearly cowed by their casually threatening behaviour towards him. However, Andre is unexpectedly saved when Paul bursts through a nearby door, momentarily distracting the convicts. Paul insists that his uncle take a look at some details that he has flagged up in the ledgers, which provides Andre with just the opening he needs to escape the fate that the criminals have in store for him. Blustering that he will soon uncover evidence that Ducotel has been leeching cash from his business interests, Andre withdraws into the house (and relative safety) with Paul. Thoughtfully, Joseph considers that one further option is left open to them: Andre can still be eliminated, which would give Ducotel a reprieve from a very difficult future. The three criminals discuss the issue, trying to devise a foolproof way of sealing Andre's fate. Joseph suggests that he gain employment with Andre's business when he returns to France, with the goal of bankrupting him within the year. However, Albert has a rather more immediate plan – unleashing his poisonous pet snake, Adolph, on Andre instead.

As the convicts make their way back into Ducotel's home, Joseph has a pang of conscience. While Andre is certainly an objectionable character, his sudden death would seem overly convenient given Ducotel's current financial woes. Furthermore, it would be upsetting for Amelie and Isabelle, particularly as none of the men particularly feel like lying through their teeth to them if awkward questions are asked. As they wring their hands over the morality of the issue, Andre bursts into the room, fuming at the missing stock that has been catalogued in the ledger. Noticing Albert's wicker cage on the table, currently containing Adolph, Andre decides that it must be stolen stock from the shop and seizes it from him. The criminals warn him that a snake is inside the cage, but Andre refuses to believe them, considering their protestations to be a ruse. Now convinced that something of value is inside, he takes the cage into his room, determined to get to the bottom of the issue. Joseph, Albert and Jules prevaricate in a supremely flippant manner before eventually electing (much later) to warn Andre that the snake is real – and lethal. But to no-one's surprise, Joseph finds that Andre has already discovered this fact for himself rather too late.

The next morning, Joseph forges a Will for Andre – in the deceased cousin's perfectly replicated handwriting – which divides his estate equally between Paul and Ducotel. Jules smuggles it into Andre's briefcase, which is then carefully placed back into his room. Madame Parole unexpectedly appears in the shop, wishing to complain about a bottle of wine that she has purchased, and Joseph sees the chance to encourage an uninvolved bystander to 'stumble upon' Andre's corpse. However, when it becomes clear that she won't budge from the main shopping area, Joseph instead uses the encounter to recover the funds for her long-unpaid store account. Outraged, she departs the shop seething, but Joseph puts the cash aside for Ducotel instead of pocketing it for himself.

Jules and Albert are concerned – Adolph the snake is still on the loose after biting Andre. The three men search feverishly, but are interrupted by Isabelle who is on the way to early morning mass at the church. The convicts try to persuade her to ask Andre if he will accompany her to the service, intending for her to discover the body and thus making them seem blameless, but she remains upset at his attitude from the previous night and refuses to speak to him. After she leaves the shop, the criminals continue their search, but they have barely started looking again when Ducotel appears. Joseph tries to convince him to call on Andre in his room, given their failure with Isabelle, but Ducotel is so relieved that his cousin hasn't yet awakened that he decides not to tempt fate and thus elects to go for a walk instead.

The next person that Joseph encounters is Amelie, but when he is unable to influence her to enter Andre's room, on the pretence of making his bed, he becomes frustrated. While Amelie talks with Joseph, Jules discovers that Paul is now up and about. Paul demands to know why his uncle isn't yet awake, and Jules jubilantly invites him to visit Andre's room and find out. Sure enough, Paul emerges soon after with the announcement that Andre has died during the night. The convicts pretend to be shocked by this declaration, while Amelie is genuinely stunned. Paul, on the other hand, can barely contain his glee – on returning to his own room, he can't stop himself from laughing at his obnoxious uncle's fate, although he quickly sobers up when he discovers that Jules and Albert are observing him. Jules suggests that Paul look through his uncle's papers, just in case he had left any instructions to be enacted after his death – such as, for instance, a Last Will and Testament.

Ducotel arrives back at the house and is staggered by the news of his cousin's death. Amelie suggests that they head for the Board of Health in order to obtain a death certificate for Andre. Just as the Ducotels are leaving, Joseph overhears Madame Parole talking to a gendarme, discussing the convicts' presence at the shop. As the gendarme suggests that she give a statement to the commandant, Joseph realises that his game is almost up. He heads back into Ducotel's home and tells Jules and Albert that they need to depart as quickly as possible. Meanwhile, Paul is burning the Will that Joseph had forged, realising that as his uncle's next of kin he will inherit Andre's entire fortune if there is no legal evidence to the contrary. Paul goes looking for Ducotel but, when he discovers that Felix is not at home, he attempts to make vague arrangements for Andre's funeral with the convicts. He repeatedly denies any knowledge of Andre having a Will, and makes it clear that he will stand by his uncle's position regarding Ducotel – Felix and his family will only be allowed to continue trading on the island if his stock and accounts are found to be in order.

Livid at Paul's callous treachery, Joseph immediately starts work on forging another Will. However, before he can begin in earnest Paul returns to the room with the news that he has just been bitten by a snake that he accidentally discovered hiding in Andre's coat pocket. The criminals' mirth is tangible. Realising that he doesn't have long to live, the increasingly delirious Paul is dragged out to the summer house by the convicts and dies soon after. No sooner has Albert safely recovered Adolph, someone enters the shop's main door – Isabelle, on her return from church. Joseph explains to her that Andre has passed away, and she voices concern over the effect that this development will have on

Paul. The convicts choose not to inform her of Paul's demise, but instead try to convince her that Paul really did love her in spite of his earlier protestations to the contrary. She thanks them for their kindness, but tells them that she realises that Paul never had any feelings for her – and, indeed, she knows now, with new maturity, that she wouldn't have returned them in any respect.

The three men opine that although Isabelle may seem downcast at the realisation that no romance will be possible with Paul, she will surely find a more deserving love in the future. Albert voices his regret that he can't be the right man for her, and they reflect on the issue of who might take Paul's place in Isabelle's affections. Right on cue, Arnaud the medical officer arrives in the shop and tells the convicts that he has been sent to catalogue Andre's death. He meets Isabelle, and the two show early signs of mutual attraction. Shortly afterwards, Isabelle discovers Paul's corpse in the garden and screams; Arnaud heads to her aid and finds that she has fainted. As the convicts direct Arnaud to take Isabelle to her room, they consider that their work at the Ducotel's home is now done.

A quick change of clothing later, the now-smartly attired trio are just leaving the shop when they meet Ducotel and Amelie on their way back home. Ducotel asks if they are leaving, and the convicts reply to the effect that they have mended more than the roof for Felix and his family. They make their way to the docks, knowing that they need only take a short trip across the water to make it to the anchored ship and freedom. But at the last minute they have a collective change of heart. Deciding that prison life wasn't so bad after all, they determine that they don't want or need the added complication of going on the run. At least, the convicts reason, they always knew exactly where they were during their incarceration. Besides, Joseph thinks aloud as they begin to head back to the penal complex, if things don't work out for them then they can always try the same scheme again during the following year's festive season.

We're No Angels features two prominent qualities which are immediately apparent throughout the whole of the film: the witty dexterity of the script, and the appealing charm of all the performances – most especially those of the three leads. In spite of Curtiz's renowned gift for visual flair, the film never entirely manages to evade its obviously stage-based foundations.[1] The narrative takes place almost entirely in one location – Ducotel's shop, which is also his home – but such are the quality and range of the performances (both main and supporting) that the action is never allowed to feel claustrophobic. The story itself is among the most deliciously unorthodox of all Christmas tales, with everything from the exotically unfamiliar setting to the quirky range of characters combining to create a very memorable modern fable that features an eccentric but oddly effective three wise men. Ranald MacDougall's sharp, drolly amusing screenplay actually deviates very little from Samuel and Bella Spewack's original play for the stage, *My Three Angels*; the only noteworthy difference is that the three convicts are formally on parole from prison in the play, whereas the jailbreak aspect of MacDougall's screenplay contributes a modicum of additional dramatic urgency and suspense to the criminals' motivations throughout the film.

What really cements *We're No Angels* as a true Christmas classic is the sheer charisma of the three talented misfit protagonists, brought to life perfectly by Humphrey Bogart, Aldo Ray and Peter Ustinov. Each of the trio bring different skills to the team – Joseph's silver-tongued hoaxing and light-fingered agility, Jules's amiable charm and safecracking skills, and Albert's winning mixture of good humour and intimidating muscle. Taken together, their well-observed performances are second to none, both in terms of the comic timing of their delivery and their skilfully-rendered physical slapstick. There is much humorous glee in Ray and Ustinov's recurrent 'accidental' battering of the self-important cousin Andre with his own luggage, to say nothing of the gloriously whimsical sequence where the convicts extensively draw out the process of warning Andre about the snake that he has unknowingly wrested from Albert (a course of action which becomes so vastly prolonged that they end up cutting cards to find their nominee, all the while fully aware that Andre has almost certainly been bitten already). There is much wry amusement to be found in the early establishment of Albert's pet snake Adolph, a kind of peculiar twist on the Chekhov's Gun principle, while the halos which appear over the heads of the three convicts in the closing sequence – along with the single, prominent star high in the night sky – proves that although the men may claim to be no angels, and have retained the essence of their jovial criminality even at the end of the play, there is no doubt that their actions have changed the lives of one family infinitely for the better during that eventful Christmas.

Humphrey Bogart was, of course, a solid gold star name in cinemas by the time of *We're No Angels*, due to his legendary performances in films such as John Huston's *The Maltese Falcon* (1941) and *The African Queen* (1951), Curtiz's own *Casablanca* (1942), Howard Hawks's *The Big Sleep* (1946), and Edward Dmytryk's *The Caine Mutiny* (1954). He had been nominated for Academy Awards as Best Actor in a Leading Role for *Casablanca* and *The Caine Mutiny*, winning an Oscar for his performance as Charlie Allnut in *The African Queen*. However, he had appeared in a great many other roles besides; having started his career in Edmund Lawrence's short film *The Dancing Town* (1928), he went on to build himself a prolific and diverse career with appearances in films such as William Keighley's *Bullets or Ballots* (1936), William Dieterle's *The Great O'Malley* (1937), Edmund Goulding's *Dark Victory* (1939), Zoltan Korda's *Sahara* (1943), and John Huston's *The Treasure of the Sierra Madre* (1948). Bogart's deadpan delivery had been well established in many of his earlier roles, but rarely did he have such an opportunity to exhibit his full range of comedic skills as he was afforded in *We're No Angels*, or indeed the chance to demonstrate his surprisingly impressive singing voice. Cast against type to great effect, the heady blend of jocular charm and under-the-surface coercion that Bogart brings to Joseph is also mirrored in the complex fusion of sophistication and unruly intensity that comprises Albert's character. Aldo Ray had been active in film since the beginning of the decade, first appearing in Mickey Rooney's romantic crime drama *My True Story* (1951). He had continued to perform regularly in films throughout the fifties, with roles in a diverse range of films such as David Miller's *Idols in the Dust* (1951), George Cukor's *The Marrying Kind* (1952), Curtis Bernhardt's *Miss Sadie Thompson* (1953), and Raoul Walsh's *Battle Cry* (1955). He had been nominated for the Golden Globe Award for Most Promising Newcomer in 1953, for his performance as Davie Hucko in George Cukor's *Pat and Mike* (1952). Rounding off the trio was Peter Ustinov's Jules, a character whose beguiling sense of well-spoken refinement offset a hint of danger and ruthless criminal efficiency. Ustinov was, at the time, only at the beginning of a massively successful career as an actor, director, producer and writer, one that had begun in the early forties and which would extend into the early twenty-first century. A true polymath in every sense of the word, he had first appeared in Michael Powell and Emeric Pressburger's *One of Our Aircraft is Missing* (1942), and built on this well-regarded early performance with roles in films such as Basil Dearden and Will Hay's *The Goose Steps Out* (1942), *Private Angelo* (1949), which Ustinov co-directed with Michael Anderson, and Michael Curtiz's *The Egyptian* (1954). Ustinov's cinematic credentials also extended to a directorial career, which included films like *School for Secrets* (1946) and *Vice Versa* (1948). He was perhaps best-known at the time for his well-regarded performance as the Roman Emperor Nero in Mervyn LeRoy's *Quo Vadis* (1951), which had gained him an Academy Award nomination for Best Actor in a Supporting Role. Ustinov would later win Academy Awards in the same category for his appearances in Stanley Kubrick's *Spartacus* (1960) and Jules Dassin's *Topkapi* (1964), with a further nomination (along with co-writer Ira Wallach) in recognition of his screenplay for Eric Till's *Hot Millions* (1968).

With such strong performances at the centre of the film, it would have been easy for the supporting players to be overshadowed by the sheer wealth of charm on display. However, quite the opposite is true – all of the film's characters are given ample time to shine, with performers such as Joan Bennett, Gloria Talbott and John Baer all rising admirably to the occasion. Particular note, however, is due to veteran actors Basil Rathbone and Leo G. Carroll for their captivating appearances. Rathbone, who had enjoyed a highly successful career in the cinema, was perhaps best known for his performances as Arthur Conan Doyle's Sherlock Holmes in the long-running cycle of popular films which had begun with Sidney Lanfield's *The Hound of the Baskervilles* (1939) and Alfred L. Werker's *Sherlock Holmes* (1939). A two-time Academy Award nominee for Best Actor in a Supporting Role (as Tybalt in George Cukor's *Romeo and Juliet*, 1936, and King Louis XI in Frank Lloyd's *If I Were King*, 1938), Rathbone delivers a mesmerising masterclass in creating an unsympathetic character for the screen, accentuating Andre's overweening arrogance and oppressive, bullying demeanour with a haughty, aloof physicality. The reverse side of Andre's coin, of course, is the kindly, bumbling Felix Ducotel, played to the hilt with shambling benevolence by Leo G. Carroll. Known at the time for prolific appearances in such films as Sidney Franklin's *The Barretts of Wimpole Street* (1934), William Wyler's *Wuthering Heights* (1939) and Alfred Hitchcock's *Spellbound* (1945), Carroll's Christmas film credentials had already been established by his appearance as Marley's Ghost in Edwin L. Marin's *A Christmas Carol* (1938). The blundering kind-heartedness of Ducotel, a man so clearly adored by his wife and daughter, forms the emotional nucleus of the film, with Carroll's adroit performance communicating the character's noble qualities very ably.

There are many other factors to recommend *We're No Angels*, from Sam Comer and Grace Gregory's excellently observed set decoration (especially evident in the vast array of period knick-knacks on sale in Ducotel's shop) to Mary Grant's first-rate costume design. However, the film has been given only a lukewarm response from reviewers in the intervening years,[2] with some commentators noting that in their opinion, the comedic elements of the feature tended to succeed better than its overall presentation.[3] But in spite of these critical caveats, the film did well at the box-office at the time of its release,[4] and its profusion of star names from the time have meant that *We're No Angels* has retained interest from film enthusiasts ever since its production date. The film was loosely remade by Neil Jordan in 1989, also entitled *We're No Angels*, starring Robert De Niro, Sean Penn and James Russo. Concerning three convicts on the run in 1930s who become mistaken for priests as they desperately attempt to escape over the Canadian border, the film had little more than a superficial thematic resemblance to the 1950s original and in general it did not perform particularly well with critics at the time of its release.[5]

We're No Angels was released at a point in the fifties when, in spite of continued audience interest, the Christmas film was on the cusp of going out of fashion with film-makers and studios. Although the decade had seen other features which dealt specifically with Christmas themes, including George More O'Ferrall's *The Holly and the Ivy* (1952), Frank Tashlin's *Susan Slept Here* (1954) and Richard Quine's *Bell, Book and Candle* (1958), or which had featured prominent Christmas settings, such as Sidney Lanfield's *The Lemon Drop Kid* (1951), Billy Wilder's *Stalag 17* (1953) and Morton da Costa's *Auntie Mame* (1958), the following two decades would see the genre fade almost to the point of obscurity in cinemas. But just as the golden age of the traditional Christmas film in the forties had exhibited a rapid evolution into the glamorous modernity of *White Christmas*, this highly adaptive film genre still had more than a few surprises in store for the years which lay ahead.

Historical Context

We're No Angels was first released in the United States on 7 July 1955. Also to be released on that date was Charles Lamont's *Lay That Rifle Down* and José Ferrer's *The Shrike*. At number one in Billboard's Best Sellers in Stores Chart over the course of that week was Pérez Prado with 'Cherry Pink (and Apple Blossom White)'. Featuring that week in current affairs was the news of E. Frederic Morrow becoming the first African-American executive on the White House staff, the conclusion of the English harbour strike, and Beverly Hanson winning the first Ladies Professional Golf Association Championship.

8

THE APARTMENT (1960)

The Mirisch Corporation

Director: Billy Wilder
Producer: Billy Wilder
Screenwriter: Billy Wilder and I.A.L. Diamond

MAIN CAST

Jack Lemmon	-	Calvin Clifford 'Bud' Baxter
Shirley MacLaine	-	Fran Kubelik
Fred MacMurray	-	Jeff D. Sheldrake
Ray Walston	-	Joe Dobisch
David Lewis	-	Al Kirkeby
Jack Kruschen	-	Dr Dreyfuss
Naomi Stevens	-	Mrs Mildred Dreyfuss
Joan Shawlee	-	Sylvia

As we have seen, the 1950s were witness to a transitional phase in the early life of the Christmas movie, where themes such as the festive season's perennial capacity for character transformation were retained while others, including specific explorations of spirituality and the religious origins of Christmas, started to be downplayed by film-makers. The key feature of the decade was the development and repackaging of traditional Christmas themes in order to keep pace with the increasing social change of the post-War era. By the sixties, however, Christmas cinema was entering a kind of wilderness era from which it would not fully re-emerge until the genre's major revival in the early 1980s. Although sixties television provided fertile ground for the emergence of many well-regarded Christmas features, including Kizo Nagashima and Larry Roemer's *Rudolph the Red-Nosed Reindeer* (1964), Bill Melendez's *A Charlie Brown Christmas* (1965), Chuck Jones and Ben Washam's *How the Grinch Stole Christmas* (1966) and Jules Bass and Arthur Rankin Jnr's *Frosty the Snowman* (1969), film theatres were to be largely devoid of festive fare throughout the course of the decade.

As mentioned in the introduction, some films concern themselves specifically with the meaning and the effects of Christmas, whereas others tend to be situated within the Christmas period but offer a rather more muted appraisal of themes related to the inspiration of the festive season and the influence of the Christmas spirit. *The Apartment*, it is fair to say, falls squarely into the latter category of festive movie. Yet it has nonetheless come to be regarded as one of the central Christmas films of the 1960s, its prominence assured by its touching, warm-hearted exploration of the holiday season's ability to turn around even the most bleak of circumstances. A lasting story of hope in the face of corporate detachment, it is often easy to forget that most of the film's narrative takes place between Christmas and the New Year. But by its conclusion, *The Apartment* leaves the audience in no doubt that it is among the most life-affirming of festive tales; one that firmly elevates the optimism of the human spirit over mundane drudgery, allowing a ray of hopefulness to shine into the struggle of everyday life

The Apartment was the brainchild of celebrated writer, producer and director Billy Wilder. A massively talented and prolific film-maker, Wilder had become particularly well-known for producing features with dealt uncompromisingly with complex moral subject matter and complicated social issues. He often explored these topics within a comedic framework, but always proved to be resolutely unafraid in courting controversy with the investigation of his chosen themes. Especially well-known at the time for his winning romantic comedy-dramas *Sabrina* (1954), *The Seven Year Itch* (1955) and *Some Like It Hot* (1959), *The Apartment* was a hotly anticipated film on its release, with much media speculation centring on Wilder's new production.[1] Wilder chose as his charismatic lead performer Jack Lemmon, an actor who was eminently well-qualified for an appearance in a Christmas film following his critically successful and good-natured performance in Richard Quine's *Bell, Book and Candle* (1958) alongside James Stewart. However, as we shall see, *The Apartment* was to be anything but a typical Christmas film.

It's the first of November 1959 in New York City, and office worker Calvin Clifford 'Bud' Baxter (Jack Lemmon) is at his desk on the nineteenth floor of the headquarters of Consolidated Life, a big-city insurance firm. Bud often works late at his office, not because of any undue diligence on his part, but because he has come to an arrangement with his superiors at the same workplace to make use of his apartment as a venue to conduct extra-marital affairs outwith the knowledge of their wives. He does this in the hope of currying favour with his bosses, including managers such as Al Kirkeby (David Lewis), who is conducting an affair with company telephonist Sylvia (Joan Shawlee). However, Bud's efforts do not even engender in Kirkeby the basic courtesy of remembering his name. The arrangement works out well for his superiors, but less so for Bud who is often left waiting around in the cold before he can regain access to his own home if (or, rather, when) his bosses' liaisons should over-run. The pact is also raising the suspicions of Bud's neighbours, especially Mildred Dreyfuss (Naomi Stevens), who are apprehensive about the suspicious noises emanating from his apartment while he is apparently away at work.

When Kirkeby discovers that Sylvia has left her galoshes at Bud's apartment, he returns later that evening to retrieve them. Bud meekly asks him if he would consider being more punctual in future, given that he has had to hang around outside in the freezing winter weather. In a facile attempt to salve his conscience, Kirkeby assures Bud that he has put in a good word for him with Jeff Sheldrake (Fred MacMurray), director of the company's personnel department, and that Bud is sure to be in line for a promotion in the near future. However, he follows this up with requests for Bud to stock the apartment with more alcohol and snacks, even though it becomes obvious that Bud has been having to fund these demands out of his own pocket. Later, as he deposits a bin full of empty bottles outside his apartment, Bud meets his well-meaning neighbour Dr Dreyfuss (Jack Kruschen), who – on sight of the contents of Bud's trash – believes him to be an alcoholic. Without much subtlety, the doctor advises Bud to take more care of himself: having heard the endless succession of liaisons going on from the next apartment, he obviously suspects that Bud is also massively promiscuous.

Bud has retired to bed when he is startled by a late phone call. Joe Dobisch (Ray Walston), one of the office's administration managers, has met a beautiful and rather inebriated blonde woman (Joyce Jameson) at a bar nearby, and requires urgent use of Bud's apartment. This does not sit well with Bud, who is exhausted and does not exactly relish waiting around outside in the middle of the night. However, Dobisch makes it clear that he is unwilling to take no for an answer, giving Bud his assurance that he will make sure that his name will be on the efficiency rating top ten if he should help him out. Bud soon realises that he has no choice, and reluctantly departs his home to make way for Dobisch and his new acquaintance. Pausing only to leave a warning note on his record player (the late night music has been causing his neighbours to protest), he departs from the building just as Dobisch's cab arrives.

While Dobisch makes himself at home, telling the blonde lady that the apartment belongs to his mother, the fatigued Bud is left with no option but to wander the streets of New York. The next morning he arrives at work with a heavy cold, looking rather the worse for wear. While waiting for the elevator, he attempts to engage Kirkeby in conversation, but is indifferently brushed off. However, his spirits brighten when he sees the beautiful Fran Kubelik (Shirley MacLaine) who operates one of the building's elevators. His attraction to her is obvious, not least from his lively flirting. Once he reaches his floor, Kirkeby voices his disdain at the fact that no man in the firm appears able to win Fran over with their charms.

Later that day, Bud's cold appears to be getting worse. He calls up Dobisch on an internal line and tells him that because he had left the wrong key under the welcome mat, Bud was unable to regain access to his apartment and thus had to wake his landlady in the middle of the night. Dobisch assures him that the correct key will soon be on its way in the internal mail, and that he is in the process of sending a report to Sheldrake which will recommend Bud's efficiency. As Bud's fever continues to become inflamed, he calls Mr Vanderhoff (Willard Waterman) of the public relations department; Vanderhoff was due to use the apartment that night, but Bud is forced to cancel due to the state of his health. Vanderhoff is reluctant to agree, but eventually is left with no alternative and rearranges his 'appointment' instead. This encroaches onto another booking by Mr Eichelberger (David White), who is forced to rearrange in turn, clashing with yet another arrangement – this time with Kirkeby. Fortunately Kirkeby is amenable to the change, meaning that Bud's heavily-packed diary of apartment reservations is finally rebalanced.

Bud is called to Sheldrake's office in personnel. Taking Fran's elevator, he tries to gently talk her into a date, but she offers no reply. However, his tangible enthusiasm at the prospect of promotion means that even this subtle rebuff can't make a dent in his excitement. Sheldrake's secretary Miss Olsen (Edie Adams) frostily orders Bud into the office. There, Sheldrake congratulates Bud on his efficiency and popularity within the company. Several executives have personally requested that Bud be transferred to their own departments. However, Sheldrake is suspicious of Bud's merits, having already deduced the source of the young man's high esteem. He offers Bud the chance to explain himself. Bud tells Sheldrake that about a year ago, while attending a night-school class in advanced accounting, he had offered an employee the use of his apartment in order to change his clothing prior to an appointment. However, little realising the true motives at hand, he was soon receiving requests from other high-up members of staff to similarly make use of his home, and the situation escalated into its current state. Bud fully expects to receive at least a reprimand from Sheldrake, but instead he offers him two theatre tickets to see *The Music Man* on Broadway – he too wants the use of Bud's apartment. Left with no real option but to comply, Bud accedes to Sheldrake's request. In return, Sheldrake promises Bud that he considers him to be a worthy candidate for promotion when the company's next personnel shake-up takes place the following month.

More out of hope than expectation, Bud hangs around the building after work in the hope of catching Fran when she leaves. On meeting her, he asks if she will join him at the theatre. At first she declines, telling him that she is due to meet someone that evening, but sensing his eagerness she relents and tells him that although she has business to attend to first, she will meet him at the theatre just before the show starts. Bud is overjoyed, though Fran seems more reserved in her affections. Once they have parted company, Fran heads for a restaurant nearby. There, she meets a supremely furtive Sheldrake – her unnamed date for the evening. It soon becomes apparent that she and Sheldrake had been engaged in a rather intense affair during the summer, but that Fran had broken it off when she realised that it was not sustainable – Sheldrake would never have voluntarily left his wife and children. However, Sheldrake emphasises that his feelings for her continue to run deep. Fran is resistant to the force of his personality, assuring him that a break between them was for the best, but Sheldrake seems unable to contemplate that there is no hope of rekindling their romance. He tells her that he has been in contact with his lawyer about a divorce from his wife, and that he will set the legal proceedings in motion if Fran will admit that she is still in love with him. Fran tells him that she does, having never believed that he would actually go ahead with a divorce. They leave the restaurant when it starts to become crowded; one of the newcomers is Miss Olsen, who observes the fact that Sheldrake and Fran have been at the same table together. Fran tells Sheldrake that she must head off for her other date (although he is unaware that she plans to meet Bud). Sheldrake instead persuades her to join him at the apartment, calling a cab for this purpose. Unknown to either of them, Bud has been left out in the cold again – he is waiting patiently outside the theatre, even although the show has started, in the vain hope that Fran will still show up to meet him.

Bud's exasperation eventually pays off when, some time later, he is given a promotion to Second Administrative Assistant. He has barely enough time to relish having an office of his own, however, before he is visited by Dobisch, Kirkeby, Vanderhoff and Eichelberger. They have come, ostensibly, to offer their congratulations on his promotion, but it soon becomes apparent that they are displeased that Bud has been making his apartment less available to them. Unable to tell them about Sheldrake's use of his home, he tries to fob them off by telling them that he appreciates his own personal space from time to time. They are unhappy with his attitude, however, and warn him that just as they have made possible the elevation of his position within the company, so too can they diminish him as they see fit. Their thinly-veiled threats are interrupted by the arrival of Sheldrake; Bud quickly encourages the other men to leave when the personnel director comes into the office, keen to keep their new arrangement private. Sheldrake asks Bud to have a second key to the apartment cut for his own personal use, and books it for Thursday night. Bud agrees to both of Sheldrake's demands, little realising that the affair that he is conducting is with Fran. He also returns a compact to Sheldrake that he had found in his apartment, assuming that it belongs to the woman that he had been entertaining. He points out that it has a cracked mirror, but that he found it that way. Sheldrake admits that it broke when his companion for the evening threw it at him in a fit of anger.

Christmas Eve arrives at Consolidated Life, and a rowdy party is taking place on the nineteenth floor. As the water cooler is being merrily augmented by copious amounts of liquor, Bud decides to take a drink to Fran, who is still operating one of the elevators in spite of the ongoing festive hijinx. Fran is surprised to see him, given that he has been avoiding her for weeks, but he tells her that in spite of initially being hurt at the way that she stood him up at the theatre in November, he forgives her, understanding that she must have had good reason not to have made the date. He whisks her out of the elevator and into the partying crowd. Promising to get more drinks, he leaves Fran on the periphery of the multitude, where she is accosted by the tipsy Miss Olsen. Olsen needles Fran, telling her that she knows about her surreptitious affair with Sheldrake and admitting that a few years ago he had conducted a similar liaison with her. Indeed, she goes on to reveal that Sheldrake has been something of a serial womaniser within the company, and that Fran should eventually expect to be treated no differently than any of his many other previous conquests.

Unaware of the conversation between Fran and Miss Olsen, the still-merry Bud returns with more drinks. The now very uncomfortable Fran tells him that she feels a little claustrophobic in the crowd, so he ushers her into his office and promptly shows off his new bowler hat – a status symbol that he has purchased to celebrate his new position as a junior executive. He tries again to ask Fran out on a date, but – not unkindly – she turns him down once more. He tells her that he has growing influence with Sheldrake and will put in a good word on her behalf, in the hope of assuring her promotion within the company. She seems reluctant about him doing so, however, but doesn't divulge her own relationship with Sheldrake. However, when Bud jokily rearranges his hat to a more jaunty angle, she produces her compact to give him an idea of how he looks; on seeing the cracked mirror, he immediately puts two and two together. Bud is shocked by the discovery, but doesn't confront Fran with his knowledge. Instead, their meeting is interrupted by a call from Sheldrake, who asks Bud if he has made all the necessary arrangements for his next meeting at the apartment – including a Christmas tree. Still stunned by the revelation of Fran's affair with Sheldrake, Bud leaves the office while the raucous party continues to rage around him.

Bud is drowning his sorrows in a busy bar. He is so miserable, and indeed so inebriated, that even a visit from Santa Claus (Hal Smith) is unable to raise a smile. A woman in a fur coat, Margie MacDougall (Hope Holiday), tries to attract Bud's attention with all the subtlety of a breeze-block through a plate glass window. After much cajoling, she eventually leaves him with no option but to buy her a drink, while she plays a song on the bar's jukebox and strikes up a conversation about the Cuban Revolution. As they chat, Bud explains that he is unmarried and has no family, but unfortunately for him that doesn't mean that his home is vacant. Meanwhile, back at that very apartment, Sheldrake is growing frustrated by Fran's behaviour; she is deeply upset and can't stop crying. Believing that her distress is borne out of his constant delay over instigating her divorce, Sheldrake assures her that the time isn't right – he'll start the ball rolling with his lawyers only once the conditions are favourable for him. Fran then tells him about her conversation with Miss Olsen, and rings off the names of some of the women in the company that he has previously conducted affairs with. He brushes off her concerns with glib platitudes, but his furtive glances at his watch give the lie to his obvious awkwardness. She gives him a vinyl record album as a Christmas gift, though he elects to leave it in the apartment to avoid having to explain it to his wife. In return, he gives her a hundred dollar bill and tells her to buy something nice with it, though she is too thoroughly disillusioned to bother making her distaste at his shoddy gesture apparent. Sheldrake then sets off, knowing that he has already missed his train, though he seems to be growing impatient with Fran's genuine emotional upset. Before he departs, he tells her that their relationship will not always be composed of clandestine meetings; one day the love he feels for her will win out. But Fran clearly no longer believes him. With a parting wish for a Merry Christmas, Sheldrake leaves, but Fran decides to stay a while longer in the apartment. She puts on the album that she had given Sheldrake, and – now that she is alone – finally vents her pent-up feelings of anger and hurt. Crying, she heads for the bathroom to freshen up. There, she discovers Bud's well-stocked supply of sleeping tablets and appears to consider them very closely.

Back at the bar, Bud and Mrs MacDougall are ejected by Charlie the bartender (Benny Burt) due to the lateness of the hour. Margie asks Bud if he'd like to come back to her home, but Bud remarks that they may as well return to his – after all, it's a popular enough venue. Once they arrive at the apartment, Bud asks Margie to get the drinks while he puts on some music. He is surprised to discover Fran's album on the turntable, but soon exchanges it for something a little more up-tempo. He then finds Fran's gloves lying on his coffee table, which perplexes him even more. But his confusion reaches a crescendo when he puts the gloves into his bedroom and discovers Fran lying unconscious on his bed. At first, believing her to be asleep, he angrily tells her to get out of his apartment. But on discovering the empty bottle of sleeping tablets next to her prone form, he soon realises that she has attempted to commit suicide. Quickly sobering up, he races next door to Dr Dreyfuss and begs him to revive Fran, then unceremoniously ejects a confused Mrs MacDougall.

Dr Dreyfuss checks out Fran's condition and takes her into the bathroom in the hope of clearing the tablets from her system. Sure enough, Bud soon hears vomiting and realises that the doctor has got to her just in time. Taking her back through to the living room, Dreyfuss administers some medication to stabilise her condition. Unaware of the (rather complicated) truth behind the situation, the doctor voices disdain at what he perceives to be Bud's loose morals; his assumption is that following an argument with Fran, which had prompted her to overdose on the tablets, Bud had obviously gone to a bar with the goal of picking up another woman as quickly as possible. Telling Bud to fetch some coffee, he adds that another half hour would have made all the difference between them saving Fran and her suicide attempt being successful. Eventually they manage to revive her to the point where she regains semi-consciousness, but Dreyfuss warns that they must keep her awake for a few hours until the sleeping tablets lose their effectiveness. After this has passed, and Fran is safely back in Bud's bed, the doctor again warns Bud that it's time for him to stop behaving so irresponsibly. The next time such an incident happens, he cautions, it may be too late to turn things around.

On Christmas morning, Bud finds his livid landlady Mrs Lieberman (Frances Weintraub Lax) demanding to know the source of the previous evening's commotion. Bud manages to assure her that it won't happen again, though her temper is at breaking point. However, his own anger – with regard to Fran's narrow escape from death – is barely held in check. He rings up Sheldrake, who is at home playing with his children and their Christmas presents. Bud explains the situation to Sheldrake, but he makes it perfectly clear that he wants nothing to do with Fran's recovery – only that it is essential that his name be kept out of any subsequent investigations. Bud is clearly disgusted by Sheldrake's complete lack of regard for Fran's predicament, but has little recourse but to accede to his office superior's desire to avoid any engagement with the situation.

Fran tries to get up, but Bud discovers her stumbling around just in time to save her from collapsing. She wants to brush her teeth, so Bud finds her a new toothbrush while surreptitiously sweeping the bathroom for any razorblades and other potentially dangerous items. While Fran freshens up, Bud tries to persuade a hostile Mrs Dreyfuss to let him borrow some coffee. Concerned at Fran's condition, Mrs Dreyfuss instead brings her over a meal, although Fran is in no mood to eat it. Bud tries to entertain Fran with conversation and, eventually, card games. But she is so deeply depressed with her current situation that she responds poorly to both. Fran explains that although she knows Sheldrake to be a cold and unfeeling liar, she still loves him in spite of his multitude of failings. Over a game of gin rummy, she tells Bud that she feels doomed to never find a suitable partner; every romance she has had has ended in disappointment. Bud attempts to assure Fran that Sheldrake was anxious about her health when they spoke on the phone, but she knows that he is lying to spare her feelings.

Bud is aware that he must keep Fran safe at the apartment for a few days until she has fully recuperated. However, he has completely forgotten that his apartment has been booked for an afternoon appointment by Kirkeby, who arrives unannounced with Sylvia. Kirkeby is initially angered by Bud's presence, particularly when he is ordered to leave, but his attitude softens slightly when he realises that Bud has female company. Glancing through to the bedroom and seeing Fran asleep in Bud's bed, Kirkeby is righteously impressed that Bud has managed to romance the one woman in the company whose affections have always been considered unwinnable. He promises to keep this knowledge a secret, though Bud seems to be long past caring about the tiresome office politics of Consolidated Life.

Once Christmas has passed, Sheldrake returns to his office and wastes no time in unceremoniously firing Miss Olsen. He tells her that he will not tolerate her interference in his private life; she is too contemptuous of his behaviour to argue with him. Sheldrake calls Bud at home and asks about Fran's condition, again reiterating his desire to be kept out of things. However, Bud encourages Sheldrake to speak with Fran on the phone and encourage her recovery. Fran is extremely reluctant to join the conversation, but eventually finds the courage. Sheldrake is distant and condescending towards her, insisting that they put the incident behind them and effectively profess that it had never happened. Fran's disgust is evident.

Neither of them are aware that Miss Olsen is silently listening in on the conversation using her internal phone. Once Sheldrake has rung off, the vengeful Olsen calls up his wife and arranges to meet her in the near future.

Bud has gone out for some groceries when he returns to find an anxious Mrs Lieberman at the apartment door. Having smelt gas, she was all set to find the pass key. Alarmed that Fran may be trying to gas herself with his oven, Bud races into the apartment to discover that she was using the hob and had simply forgotten to light it. Fran is eager to return to her family, who are presumably worried sick about her, but Bud encourages her to remain there for one more day – Dr Dreyfuss had recommended 48 hours of rest before her health was likely to return to normal. He promises her that he will make dinner for her that evening, as a parting gift before she leaves the next day.

Back at Consolidated Life, a concerned Karl Matuschka (Johnny Seven) arrives in search of Fran. Eventually directed to Dobisch's office, he explains that he is Fran's brother-in-law, and that his wife has been concerned about her sister's unexplained whereabouts over the past couple of days. Kirkeby is also present in the office, and is still smarting about having been ejected by Bud the previous day. He and Dobisch are also clearly envious of Bud's success in romancing Fran, so they decide to hand over his details to Karl as an act of spite.

With the aid of a tennis racquet, Bud is preparing a rather unconventional spaghetti dinner for Fran. However, the candles on the table have barely been lit before a furious Karl turns up and demands to know what is going on. Fran manages to keep his anger under control until she can get dressed, but the situation becomes complicated when Dr Dreyfuss arrives and asks how the patient is doing. When the situation with the sleeping tablets is brought up, Karl insists on knowing what had happened to his sister-in-law. Bud lies to spare Fran's feelings and claims that he was responsible for her malady, which earns him a beating from Karl but saves Fran from explaining what had happened with Sheldrake. Karl marches Fran out of the apartment while a melancholic but blissfully oblivious Dreyfuss tells Bud that he probably had it coming all along.

The next morning, sporting an impressive black eye, Bud returns to work. He arranges to meet with Sheldrake in the hope of persuading him that he will take the 'problem' of Fran out of his hands – that is to say, that by entering into a relationship with her, Bud will save any embarrassment from bleeding into Sheldrake's private life. But he is caught flat-footed when he arrives in Sheldrake's office and discovers that it is full of luggage; Miss Olsen had carried out her plan to inform Mrs Sheldrake of her husband's many affairs, meaning that he really is now heading for a divorce whether he wants to or not. Thus Sheldrake still plans to pursue Fran, though he makes it clear to Bud that he also intends to enjoy the single life before he thinks of settling down with anyone. Sheldrake has a further surprise for Bud: his assistant has been transferred to Consolidated Life's Denver office, meaning that he has a vacancy for an assistant director in the personnel department. Sheldrake shows Bud through to his plush new office and reels off the many new perks of the executive experience that he can enjoy, but is puzzled by the younger man's apparent lack of enthusiasm. Later that night, Bud meets

Fran in the building's foyer. She seems to find the encounter awkward, but tells Bud that she is happy that Sheldrake's divorce has finally been set in motion; the two of them are planning to keep their relationship quiet until the legal proceedings are underway. Bud is clearly crushed by her gullibility, but puts on a brave face.

On New Year's Eve, Sheldrake calls Bud into his office and asks him for the use of his apartment – he's planning a romantic tête-à-tête with Fran, but his temporary accommodation is too public. But for once, Bud stands up to him, refusing to give up his home when he knows how hollow Sheldrake's intentions towards Fran really are. Sheldrake makes the choice clear to Bud: either he hands over the key to his apartment, or he will be fired with immediate effect. Disgusted, Bud hands over a key, but Sheldrake quickly realises that it is the key to the executive washroom. Bud explains to him that he has decided to take Dr Dreyfuss's advice and start behaving like a human being rather than the corporate drone that he is in danger of becoming. In short, Bud has realised that it's time to put the petty machinations of Consolidated Life behind him.

Bud decides to pack up his things at the apartment. Dr Dreyfuss arrives to borrow some ice-cubes for his New Year's party, and is surprised to see that all of Bud's possessions are in boxes. Bud tells him that although he is unsure of his destination, he needs to make a clean break from the apartment. The doctor invites him to join his family and friends at the party, but Bud politely declines, feeling in no mood to celebrate. He doesn't realise that at the same time, Fran is at another party – Sheldrake has taken her to their usual restaurant to ring in the new year of 1960. He tells her that he has had to arrange a hotel room in Atlantic City, due to everywhere in town being booked up. Disdainfully, he explains that there was no way that he could use the apartment due to Bud's defiance of him, and seems completely bewildered at how Bud could be so ungrateful (completely unmindful of the many sacrifices that Bud had previously made for him). It is clear that Sheldrake regards adultery as one of the perks of his job; like access to the executive canteen, he feels that it is his right to use and abuse people as he sees fit, and cannot understand Bud's objection to his behaviour. Fran brightens when she hears of the way that Bud had stood up to Sheldrake's moral misbehaviour, particularly when she deduces the true depth of Bud's feelings toward her. The restaurant's patrons perform a boisterous rendition of 'Auld Lang Syne' as the midnight bells approach. Sheldrake joins in but, upon turning to join Fran in a toast to the year ahead, discovers that his companion has gone.

Fran races along the street towards Bud's apartment. On entering the building she hears what sounds like a gunshot and, believing that Bud has decided to end it all, desperately hammers at his door. Puzzled, Bud appears in the doorway with a newly-opened bottle of champagne – much to Fran's relief. Entering the apartment, she asks where he's headed now that he has packed up and ready to go. When Bud replies that he isn't sure, she responds that she feels exactly the same way; indirectly, she confirms that her relationship with Sheldrake is over. Deciding to complete their unfinished game of gin rummy, she cuts the cards just as Bud tells her with absolute determination how he feels about her. Smiling, and knowing that she feels exactly the same way, she tells him that it's time to stop talking and just deal a fresh new hand of cards.

The Apartment is, to say the least, far removed from typical Christmas cinema. A mature film with distinctly adult themes, withering in its social commentary and articulate disdain for the spiteful, shallow nature of office politics, on the surface it appears to engage only sporadically with the festive season. Yet the classic Christmas theme of the holiday season's power to improve the lives of individuals and communities is still very much at the core of *The Apartment*. Wilder uses the Christmas parties and New Year festivities of the film as more than a backdrop; Bud and Fran's low-key engagement with the festive season, celebrating at work but privately discontented, contrasts very effectively with Sheldrake's perfunctory acknowledgement of the holidays, whether playing half-heartedly with his young children, ordering Bud to decorate his apartment with a tree at a specific time, or giving Fran – almost as an afterthought – a trivial monetary gift that requires no thought whatsoever. So too is Bud's domestic misery over his superiors' misuse of his home accentuated by the bumptious Kirkeby thinking nothing of using the apartment on, of all times, Christmas Day. The intoxication of the office party gives Sheldrake's secretary Miss Olsen the perfect opportunity that she has been seeking to attempt to sabotage his fling with Fran, while the film's New Year's Eve conclusion seems like just the right point for Bud and Fran to celebrate the end of their old lives and the start of a blossoming new romance.

The film was controversial at the time due to its depiction of Consolidated Life's executives as flawed, essentially corrupt individuals, a ragtag collection of immoral cowards who are only too willing to abuse their subordinates professionally and domestically in order to get what they want.[2] The notion that the dynamics of office life can behave like a naturally occurring soup – that is to say that it is scum, not cream, which has a tendency to rise to the top – was one which created no small amount of contention at the time, and Wilder's depiction has remained fresh and germane even half a century later.[3] Although the screenplay, a collaboration between Wilder and his long-time writing partner I.A.L. Diamond, is fecund in its elaboration of moral concerns, they never allow the film to become overtly preachy or didactic.[4] In fact, the narrative does at times seem to be at pains to emphasise that although Bud eventually takes up a more principled position than his supposed superiors, he too is an imperfect individual and certainly no saint. Much time is invested in his moral hand-wringing over the ethical considerations of allowing his bosses to make use of his home for their illicit affairs, and indeed this contrasts perfectly with Fran's conscience-wrestling as she balances her feelings for Sheldrake against the knowledge that their romance will, if successful, eventually destroy the cohesion of his family.

Moral tales are relatively common in the genre of the Christmas film, but rarely had audiences been exposed to quite such a cutting interpretation of executive machinations as Wilder had presented in *The Apartment*. Far from a Manichean construal of the managerial mind, the film focused not on corporate corruption but rather the dishonest nature of mendacious individuals who were entirely willing to abuse their positions of power to achieve profligate ends.

Indeed, Wilder's use of the holiday season becomes particularly relevant in this regard; the traditional virtues of family and friendship that Christmas promotes are either neglected or rejected by Consolidated Life's managers (Sheldrake is barely interested in keeping his sons entertained with their new toys on Christmas morning, and Kirkeby uses Christmas Day as nothing more than a vehicle for yet another extramarital tryst), while Bud and Fran both crave the comfort and solace that are offered by the ideals of the festive season. The main difference between the protagonists and their superiors at Consolidated Life is that whereas Sheldrake and his ilk have already sold their souls to the corporate machine, and seem to have no issue in having done so, Bud and Fran are both seeking something indefinable that cannot be provided by the prestige of a promotion or the prospect of a better office. By the end of the film, both Fran and Bud have realised that they define their jobs, not the other way around. But for the likes of Kirkeby and Dobisch, this distinction will probably always seem meaningless.[5]

The Apartment has a very great deal to recommend it, from Wilder's celebrated ability for skilful frame composition[6] to Adolph Deutsch's powerful score, and especially Edward G. Boyle's fantastic set design, contrasting the stark and clinical corporate interiors of Consolidated Life with the comfortable homeliness (and endearing clutter) of Bud's apartment. However, the film's greatest success is dependent upon the two remarkable central performances which drive it. Jack Lemmon has rarely been so memorable as in the role of the hapless, basically decent Bud, a man whose ambition is tempered with humility, and who desires success through merit rather than by dishonest means. Lemmon's acting career started in television in the late 1940s. His performances on American TV were also prolific throughout the early fifties, and he made his first appearance on film in George Cukor's *It Should Happen to You* (1954) soon after. His film career throughout the 1950s included roles in movies such as Mark Robson's *Phffft* (1954), John Ford and Mervyn LeRoy's *Mister Roberts* (1955), Robert Parrish's *Fire Down Below* (1957), Delmer Daves's *Cowboy* (1958), Richard Quine's *Bell Book and Candle* (1958), and - perhaps most memorably - Billy Wilder's *Some Like It Hot* (1959). No stranger to industry recognition of his talents, Lemmon had won an Academy Award for Best Actor in a Supporting Role in 1956 for his performance in *Mister Roberts*, and had been nominated for Best Actor in a Leading Role for *Some Like It Hot*. He won the Best Actor in a Leading Role Academy Award again some years later for his appearance in John G. Avildsen's *Save the Tiger* (1973), and was nominated for the award on a staggering five further occasions; as well as his Oscar nomination for *The Apartment*, he was also nominated for performances in Blake Edwards's *Days of Wine and Roses* (1962), James Bridges's *The China Syndrome* (1979), Bob Clark's *Tribute* (1980) and Costa-Gavras's *Missing* (1982). Lemmon would collaborate with Wilder many times in the future, in films which included *Meet Whiplash Willie* (1966), *Avanti!* (1972), *The Front Page* (1974) and *Buddy Buddy* (1981). He and Shirley MacLaine would both, of course, famously work again with Wilder a few years later in *Irma la Douce* (1963), an adaptation of the Alexandre Breffort play, which also claimed its own success at the Academy Awards.

Shirley MacLaine was the perfect foil for Lemmon's likeable, slightly neurotic protagonist. Fran Kubelik is smart and sassy, but also sensitive and vulnerable. Her deep hurt at Sheldrake's malign machinations is tangible, as is her growing sense of disaffection, which mirrors Bud's own dawning realisation and disillusionment at the way that he has been treated by his superiors. MacLaine made her cinematic debut in Alfred Hitchcock's *The Trouble with Harry* (1955), and later went on to perform in a wide variety of films which included Michael Anderson's *Around the World in Eighty Days* (1956), Joseph Anthony's *The Matchmaker* (1958), George Marshall's *Stranger with a Gun* (1958) and Walter Lang's *Can-Can* (1960) before appearing in *The Apartment*. MacLaine later won the Best Actress in a Leading Role Academy Award for her performance in James L. Brooks's *Terms of Endearment* (1983). She received numerous nominations for Best Actress in a Leading Role over the years, for performances in films including Vincente Minnelli's *Some Came Running* (1958) and Herbert Ross's *The Turning Point* (1977), as well as for her appearances in *The Apartment* and Wilder's aforementioned *Irma la Douce*. Additionally, she received an Academy Award nomination for her documentary film *The Other Half of the Sky: A China Memoir* (1975), co-directed with Claudia Weill.

The Apartment also benefits from an absolutely faultless supporting cast. The film is packed with excellent performances, including Edie Adams's turn as the bitterly aloof Miss Olsen; Jack Kruschen as the concerned, neighbourly Dr Dreyfuss, and Naomi Stevens as Mildred, his compassionate but formidable wife. However, it is Bud's selection of sleazy, philandering bosses who tend to linger longest in the memory. David Lewis is superb as the sordid Al Kirkeby, while Ray Walston – who was perhaps best known at the time for his performance as Luther Billis in Joshua Logan's *South Pacific* (1958) – is similarly impressive as the seedy, malicious admin manager Joe Dobisch. Central among this catalogue of grotesque corporate characters is, of course, the notorious Jeff D. Sheldrake. Screen veteran Fred MacMurray would have been a well-known face to audiences by the time of *The Apartment* due to his high-profile appearances in films such as George Stevens's *Alice Adams* (1935), Henry Hathaway's *The Trail of the Lonesome Pine* (1936) and Wesley Ruggles's *True Confession* (1937). MacMurray excels in creating a multifaceted scoundrel, projecting Sheldrake as a craven adulterer whose professional veneer and abuse of power do little to make the character seem any less pitiful or insincere in the eyes of the audience.

The Apartment performed incredibly well with both critics and the public, quickly becoming a solid box-office success.[7] Reviewers at the time praised the film for its strong lead performances, particularly in Jack Lemmon's strong evocation of a troubled central character which managed to convey empathy and pathos without allowing the weight of the role to detract from the implementation of his robust comic skills.[8] This appreciation for the film's impeccable acting has continued to be expressed in the writing of modern commentators, many of whom have emphasised the strong on-screen chemistry between Lemmon and MacLaine,[9] and the highly effective ensemble cast.[10]

Wilder's film went on to do extremely well at awards ceremonies, not least at the Academy Awards where it won five Oscars and was nominated for five more. In all, *The Apartment* won the Academy Award for Best Picture; Best Director; Best Film Editing; Best Writing (Story and Screenplay: Written Directly for the Screen), and Best Art Direction/ Set Decoration (Black and White). Jack Lemmon was nominated for Best Actor in a Leading Role, Shirley MacLaine for Best Actress in a Leading Role, and Jack Kruschen for Best Actor in a Supporting Role. The film was also nominated for Best Cinematography (Black and White), and Best Sound. *The Apartment* achieved recognition at many other awards ceremonies, including wins at the Golden Globes and the BAFTA Awards.

Not only has *The Apartment* remained one of Billy Wilder's best-regarded and most commonly screened films, but its already-assured longevity has been enhanced by the release of *Promises, Promises*, a musical comedy production which premiered on Broadway in 1968 and then on the West End in 1969. It has more recently been revived as a Broadway production in 2010. With music written by Burt Bacharach, lyrics by Hal David and the book by Neil Simon, the play follows the tribulations of hapless employee Chuck Baxter (played by Jerry Orbach in the original production) and adheres to the plot of the original film fairly closely.[11]

The Apartment has come to be regarded as one of the high points of Billy Wilder's stellar directorial career, and the film provided Jack Lemmon with one of his most celebrated roles. With its highly impressive array of awards, its commercial success and critical acclaim, Wilder's movie had established that the Christmas film (or, at the very least, films with a prominent festive setting) remained relevant in the fast-moving new world of the 1960s. The film reflected the rapidly changing culture of an increasingly liberated society, highlighting new developments in professional living, sexual behaviour and moral attitudes while simultaneously emphasising that the traditional virtues of Christmas had not been forgotten or rendered obsolete by the relentless march of progress.

Historical Context

The Apartment received its American premiere in New York City on 15 June 1960, going on general release the following week, 21 June. It was the only major film to be released on that particular date. The Everly Brothers were topping the Billboard Charts at the time with 'Cathy's Clown'. In the headlines during the course of that week, Madagascar and the Federation of Mali and Senegal became independent from France, Japan agreed upon a security treaty with the United States, and a major earthquake was to strike Belgium.

9

SANTA CLAUS CONQUERS THE MARTIANS (1964)

Jalor Productions

Director: Nicholas Webster
Producer: Paul L. Jacobson
Screenwriter: Glenville Mareth, based on a story by Paul L. Jacobson

MAIN CAST

John Call	-	Santa Claus
Leonard Hicks	-	Kimar
Vincent Beck	-	Voldar
Bill McCutcheon	-	Dropo
Victor Stiles	-	Billy
Donna Conforti	-	Betty
Chris Month	-	Bomar
Pia Zadora	-	Gimar

There are some Christmas films which seem to be perfectly in tune with the cultural zeitgeist of their production; movies which, in their fruitful engagement with the themes and spirit of the festive season, perfectly chime in with the public mood in such a way that they quickly establish a reputation as a holiday favourite amongst audiences. *Santa Claus Conquers the Martians* is, to put it bluntly, not one of those films.

As anyone with even a passing interest in Christmas films is sure to know, *Santa Claus Conquers the Martians* has acquired a reputation as the worst festive movie ever committed to celluloid. Although opinions have differed over the years, very few commentators have seen fit to rush to its defence; while some may venture that the film isn't quite as comprehensively awful as urban legend would suggest, virtually no-one has been brave enough to claim it as a must-see cinematic treat.

So if *Santa Claus Conquers the Martians* is such a poor example of festive film-making, why should it be included in a history of the genre? The answer, quite simply, is that in spite of the film's relative obscurity, the sheer lack of Christmas films appearing on the big screen in the 1960s has meant that – like it or not – this unremitting kitsch-fest of holiday tackiness has become one of the decade's most prominent exponents of the festive movie. Films such as Rene Cardona's surreal *Santa Claus* (1960) and Terence Young's *The Christmas Tree* (1969) have rarely been seen on television in recent years, whereas Anthony Harvey's superlative *The Lion in Winter* (1968), an adaptation of James Goldman's celebrated play chronicling the power struggles within the family of King Henry II during a particularly fraught December in 1183, is generally regarded more as a *tour de force* of character-based historical drama than a straightforward Christmas film. So in truth, the real question is not why a cinematic disaster like *Santa Claus Conquers the Martians* has come to be remembered all these years down the line, but rather how such a seemingly innocuous family movie could possibly have gone so horribly wrong as to merit its ignominious critical reputation.

On the planet Mars, two green-skinned alien children – Bomar (Chris Month) and Gimar (Pia Zadora) are avidly watching a television interview being broadcast direct from Santa Claus's workshop at the North Pole by a presenter from KID-TV (Ned Wertimer). Andy Henderson (though puzzlingly he is also later addressed as Andy Anderson) has been given exclusive access to meet with Santa (John Call) not long before his annual Christmas Eve trip to deliver gifts to children all around the world. Santa explains his busy schedule and emphasises that he and his elves can get toys distributed to everyone on time, though he flatly denies any plans to use a rocket-fuelled sled for extra efficiency. After a brief meeting with Mrs Claus (Doris Rich), Santa shows Andy some of the new toys that the elves have been working on. Winky (Ivor Bodin), the space specialist at Santa's workshop, has developed a toy rocket, but Andy is most interested in a Martian action figure that he has also recently invented. Andy wonders aloud if there are children on Mars, and hopes – if this is the case – that they too have their own version of Santa Claus to spread joy and goodwill.

However, unknown to anyone on Earth, all is not well on the Red Planet. Martian patriarch Kimar (Leonard Hicks) is explaining to his goofy servant

Dropo (Bill McCutcheon) the concerns he has over the wellbeing of his children. They are so fixated by Earth television programmes that their appetite is suffering, and yet they seem to have no interest in anything else. Unable to fathom their fascination with Earth culture, Kimar sends his son and daughter, Bomar and Gimar, to bed. He remains troubled, and tells his wife Momar (Leila Martin) that apparently the problem is the same all across Mars – Martian children have become entranced by the idea of Santa Claus and Christmas presents. Momar suggests that Kimar consults the wisdom of Chochem (Carl Don), an ancient Martian whose many centuries of life have afforded him the intelligence and judgement of the ages.

After confirming his course of action with the Martian ruling council, Kimar makes his way out into a primordial forest to seek out Chochem. The eight-hundred year old sage appears, quite literally in a puff of smoke, and listens patiently to Kimar's concerns. Chochem then explains that although the Martians do not realise it, it is currently early December on Earth and the planet is eagerly anticipating the arrival of Christmas. As Martian children are technologically augmented from infancy to receive knowledge and understanding, meaning that they learn and mature at a dramatically increased rate, they have forgotten how to play and have fun. Chochem urges Kimar that in order to resolve the problem of the children's restlessness, they must rediscover the joy of games and laughter. In short, he says in parting, Mars needs a Santa Claus of its own.

Kimar consults the council and tells them that Earth has had the monopoly on Santa Claus for long enough – it's time to kidnap Santa and set him to work on Mars. Kimar's rival on the council, Voldar (Vincent Beck), is dead against this course of action: he believes that the last thing Mars needs is the distraction of happy, recreation-loving children. But Kimar is resolved on the matter; he orders a spacecraft made ready for immediate departure.

Arriving in orbit around Earth, Voldar uses the ship's scanner to home in on New York City. Voldar scoffs that the Martians could lay waste to the planet easily, though Kimar admonishes him for his bloodthirstiness; they are there for one reason only, and that is to kidnap Santa Claus. As the scanner's magnification is increased, the Martians are confused when they find a large number of different men in Santa Claus outfits, most of whom appear to be conducting street collections for charity. Kimar is buoyed by this discovery – surely with so many different Santa Clauses to choose from, the people of the Earth won't notice that one of them has gone missing?

American tracking stations detect the Martian spacecraft in order, causing an alert to be issued. Kimar orders the ship's radar shield to be raised, but is surprised when he is informed that it is malfunctioning. Soon after, it is discovered that Dropo has been hiding inside the radar control box; the shield begins to function again once he has been extracted. Angrily telling Dropo that he will be dealt with later, Kimar lands the ship near a lake in the United States. There he meets a couple of American kids, Billy (Victor Stiles) and Betty Foster (Donna Conforti). At first, the youngsters are shocked at the aliens' unexpected arrival, but quickly recover. Kimar asks why there are so many Santa Clauses spread across the country, and Billy replies that there is only one real Santa Claus – the rest are just his helpers, there only for the holiday season. Billy also explains that Santa will be resident in his workshop at the North Pole, so Kimar determines that they must make haste for that destination at once. Voldar insists on bringing Billy and Betty along with them, to avoid any chance that they might inform the authorities of the Martians' presence.

Once on the ship, the kids are soon befriended by Dropo, who takes them on an unofficial guided tour of the control room. However, he is interrupted when Kimar and Voldar return early, and is forced to store Billy and Betty in the radar control box to avoid their detection. Kimar manoeuvres the ship to the North Pole, where the Martians – together with their robot, Torg – set off to bring Santa to Mars by fair means or foul. Before they leave, Voldar suggests that they should also bring the children with them to the Red Planet, thus leaving the details of Santa's disappearance a mystery as no witnesses will be left to tell of the Martian incursion. Kimar tells Dropo that he must guard the children at all costs until he gets back. But as soon as the Martians have departed from the control room, Billy wastes no time in sabotaging the ship's radar shield, knowing that the Martians will now be tracked whenever they try to leave Earth.

Billy and Betty make a break for freedom, racing into the snowy wastes of the North Pole just before the Martians emerge from the ship. An increasingly insubordinate Voldar has discovered that the children have escaped and, noticing their footprints leading away into the snow, Kimar resolves that they must catch up with the fugitive kids before they have an opportunity to warn Santa of the Martian plans. Betty and Billy prove to be more resourceful than the Martians give them credit, evading a rampaging polar bear (Gene Lindsey) before eventually being accosted by the lumbering Torg. However, the robot ignores Voldar's demand that it should crush the children to death, having been programmed by Kimar to obey only his own commands. He releases the two Foster kids, but warns them not to attempt another escape – the next time, they may not live to tell the tale.

The Martians move on to Santa's workshop, where Torg storms the building and causes pandemonium among the elf workers. Santa confuses him for a giant clockwork toy, which perplexes the Martians and makes Kimar decide to move his team in on the workshop themselves. Once there, they use a freeze ray to put Mrs Claus and several of the elves into suspended animation. Santa soon realises that he has no choice but to accompany the Martians back to their ship. Kimar is surprised to discover that Torg will no longer obey his voice commands, and so – believing it now to be functionally useless – decides to leave the robot on Earth.

With the eyes of the world now on Mars (one newspaper reports that Santa has been 'kidnaped' [sic] by the Martians), America's top rocket scientist Dr Werner Von Green (Carl Don again) outlines a plan to send astronauts into space on a rescue mission to bring Old Saint Nick back to Earth in time for Christmas. But as they make their getaway, the Martians are initially oblivious to any attention from the Earth. Santa wastes no time in trying to cheer up Billy and Betty, but they are homesick and worried about what awaits them on Mars. Trying to cheer them up, Santa tells them that he's always wanted to visit Mars, but his attempts at merriment fall on deaf ears. Even Dropo, who arrives at their cell with some nutritious food pills, is unable to raise a smile.

Back at the control room, the Martians discover that the radar shield is inoperative. Voldar inspects the equipment and discovers the damage that has been caused by Billy. Kimar is impressed with the boy's inventiveness and orders that the shield be repaired. However, Voldar vows revenge and heads for the cell. There, he offers Santa, Billy and Betty a tour of the ship – his first destination of choice is the airlock. Voldar locks the oblivious trio into the room and starts the depressurisation countdown; after sixty seconds, Santa and the children will be pulled into the depths of space when the airlock opens. Billy realises what is going to happen and panics, but Santa manages to keep a cooler head and discovers a nearby ventilation pipe near the main airlock door. In the airlock control area, Kimar is furious to hear of Voldar's nefarious scheme and gets involved in a prolonged fist-fight with him. Just as Kimar gets the upper hand, Santa and the kids arrive out of the blue, having escaped through the air duct. Kimar is amazed that Santa could fit through such a tiny passageway, but Santa replies that all his years of climbing up and down chimneys had come in handy at just the right time.

Determining that Voldar should stand trial for his treachery, Kimar orders the ship to land back on Mars. But before they even have the opportunity to set down on Martian soil, Voldar manages to escape his cell. Kimar recommends that Santa and the children be given round-the-clock protection, as he is certain that his vengeful adversary will strike again. Santa is introduced to Kimar's family, and – seemingly unfazed by his alien abduction – promises Momar that he will do his best to bring the Christmas spirit to her children, and to all the youngsters of Mars. Kimar encourages Santa to meet his children, and in no time he effortlessly encourages Bomar and Gimar into a fit of laughter. The Martian children also befriend the Foster kids, who they discover are the same age as themselves. Kimar, Momar and Dropo are all amazed to hear the guffawing coming from Bomar and Gimar's room, knowing that the children have never expressed amusement before.

Some time later, Shim (Joe Elic) gives a reconnaissance report to Voldar, who is now a fugitive hiding out in a remote Martian cave. He tells Voldar that Santa's new toy factory, which has recently been set up, is operating at full capacity. Unlike the North Pole workshop, Kimar has given Santa access to a mechanised assembly line, meaning that toys will soon be flowing freely to children all over Mars. Voldar is incensed, believing that Santa and Kimar will sentimentalise Martian life and sabotage their culture's long history of dispassionate efficiency. He decides to hatch a scheme that will derail Santa's seasonal cheer and goodwill once and for all.

At the factory, the Martian conveyor belt is churning out toys faster than Santa's helpers (Bomar, Gimar, Betty and Billy) can handle them. Dropo is particularly impressed by the sheer proficiency of the enterprise. Letters to Santa are flooding in from all over Mars, as the excited alien children want their own present from Father Christmas. Santa wistfully considers how, after all his centuries of painstakingly crafting toys for the children of Earth, he ended up pushing buttons on a control console to produce his gifts. Closing up proceedings for the day, Santa unveils a new suit which has been specially tailored for him by Momar. Dropo is keen to try it on, but Santa tells him that he'd need to dramatically increase his girth before it would even come close to fitting him.

Returning to Kimar's home, Santa decides to turn in for the night. Kimar becomes concerned that Billy and Betty seem unhappy and withdrawn; his wife tells him that they are obviously homesick, and that it is imperative that he returns them to their family on Earth. This leaves Kimar with a crisis of conscience, knowing that the children must be returned but similarly aware that he can't risk revealing his kidnap plan to the other humans. Meanwhile, Dropo is gorging on food pills in the hope of being able to fit into Santa's costume. Realising that overeating will take too long to fatten him up, he resorts to using a pillow to increase his waistline. He is elated that he can now fit into the suit (albeit that he has some problems fitting Santa's hat over his antennae), and decides to go back to the factory to produce more toys while the real Santa is asleep.

Dropo doesn't realise that someone else is already at the production line – Voldar and his henchmen, attempting to sabotage the conveyor belt's control mechanism. They are interrupted by the sudden appearance of the hapless Dropo and, confusing him for Santa Claus when they see his red suit and false beard, they seize him and take him back to their cave hideout. The next morning, Momar discovers that Dropo is missing. Santa tells her that, as his new suit has also been misplaced, it is likely that Dropo is out having fun pretending to be Santa Claus somewhere. Believing that he is most likely at the toy factory, Santa and the children head there in search of their errant Martian friend. However, on arrival they discover that Dropo is nowhere to be found, and that the machine is producing defective toys.

Santa suggests that Kimar come to the factory and inspect the control box. Kimar determines that the machine has been deliberately rewired, and he and Santa come to the conclusion that Voldar is responsible for both the sabotage and the abduction of Dropo. Determining to find the renegade, Kimar steps out of the factory only to meet none other than Voldar himself. Voldar tells Kimar that he has Santa hostage, and will release him only on the condition that the factory be deactivated, the Foster kids returned to Earth, and no further attempt made to transplant Christmas to Mars. Kimar appears to agree, only to reveal that the real Santa is currently hard at work in the factory. As Voldar realises that he has kidnapped an impostor, Kimar orders that the accomplices be hunted down and a search be conducted to free Dropo. However, neither Martian realises that Dropo has already made good his escape from the cave and is on his way back.

A struggle breaks out in the storage room where Kimar is holding Voldar. Billy, who is heading for the room to pick up a tin of red paint, overhears Voldar threatening to come after Santa. He quickly reports this news, and Santa hatches a plan to throw a spanner in the works. Shortly afterwards, Voldar appears with a ray-gun and tries to intimidate Santa, only to be ambushed by Bomar, Gimar and the Fosters, who attack him with a wide variety of toys from the factory. Santa reacts with hilarity as Voldar is brought down by a nothing more than an avalanche of festive playthings and wind-up models. The newly-escaped Dropo arrives on the scene only to be held at gunpoint by Voldar's ally Stobo (Al Nesor), but the villain is soon disarmed by a newly-emerged Kimar, who has now regained consciousness. Santa is impressed by the suitably festive Dropo, who has clearly taken the Christmas spirit to heart. As Voldar and his henchmen are taken into custody, Santa suggests to Kimar that Mars doesn't need him at all – it already has a perfectly good Santa Claus in the form of Dropo.

Realising that it's time to leave, Santa bids farewell to Kimar and his family. Billy and Betty exchange gifts with their new friends Bomar and Gimar while Kimar thanks Santa for having brought the Christmas spirit to Mars, changing the planet forever as a result. Even Dropo gets in on the act, now tubbier than ever thanks to some strategically-placed balloons, as the assembled Martians give Santa a heartfelt send-off. The Fosters then head off into space on the Martian ship as Santa assures them that, if they hurry, they should be able to get back to Earth just in time for Christmas Eve.

With some films it can be difficult to find fault with their production, whereas in others a single flaw can fatally undermine a movie's artistic integrity. With *Santa Claus Conquers the Martians*, however, the most difficult issue is to ponder exactly where to start in the veritable catalogue of production gaffes and deficiencies that are so proudly on display. From the badly-animated title sequence (which frankly displays crew credits such as the 'custume' designer) to the washed-out colour and jarring edits, the film starts poorly and still manages to go sharply downhill. Among the many oddities to mull over are the Martians' bizarre, never-explained headgear and their hair-dryer ray-guns, to say nothing of their squeezy-bottle spacecraft (complete with a radar control box that looks like it has been made out of balsa wood) and indigenous forest which appears to be composed of twigs draped in polythene. This is not to say that Earth fares any better, with the North Pole's copious Styrofoam rocks and an actor burdened with the least realistic polar bear costume in film history as he 'terrorises' the region near Santa's workshop. Then there is the unconvincingly-shoehorned military stock footage scattered around the first act of the film (whether it is required or not), the amazingly bad fight choreography between Voldar and Kimar, and a killer robot which appears to have been constructed almost entirely from cardboard and tinfoil. And this is just for starters.

Although John Call gives an appealingly warm central performance as Santa, unassailably jolly and seemingly unruffled by the prospect of alien abduction from start to finish, his is one of the few displays of acting in the film which is actually watchable for any length of time. Leonard Hicks's Kimar is enjoyably grave and stoical, while a game Bill McCutcheon tries hard – indeed, some might say a little too hard – to wring every ounce of humour out of the never-knowingly-funny Dropo. Otherwise, the overacting ranges from the entertaining (Vincent Beck as Voldar) to the grin-inducing (Al Nesor as Stobo), by way of the downright painful (Doris Rich as Mrs Claus), whereas Donna Conforti deserves a mention for delivering one of cinema's single most astonishing displays of wooden acting in the role of Betty.

The plot of Glenville Mareth's gleefully demented script is peppered with more holes than an entire year's supply of Swiss cheese. Exactly how does a ten-year old boy know how to disable the advanced alien technology of a Martian radar shield? Why does Kimar, so desperate to evade the attention of the Earth authorities that he is willing to kidnap small children in order to conceal his visit to the planet, then decide to leave a massive Martian robot behind? For what reason is Dr Von Green's plan to send an astronautic rescue party to Mars given such prominence when, once it has been outlined, it is never mentioned again for the rest of the film? And, perhaps most inexplicably of all, how can Voldar possibly confuse Dropo with Santa Claus when – given that he is bright green, has half his body mass and boasts metal antennae protruding from his head – they don't look even remotely alike? These glaring inconsistencies cannot even be excused by the fact that the film is so blatantly aimed at children, given that younger audiences are often the most alert and discerning of all moviegoers.

One of the single most puzzling aspects of *Santa Claus Conquers the Martians* is how the film could have developed into such a nightmare production when so many talented people were involved in its creation. Director Nicholas Webster was a respected and experienced film-maker; initially a film-cutter for Metro-Goldwyn-Mayer, he worked as a cinematographer for the United States Army during World War II and, after the conclusion of the conflict in 1945, was responsible for creating documentaries for the Department of Agriculture.[1] Webster had previously helmed documentaries and features for television including *The Violent World of Sam Huff* (1960) and the Emmy Award-nominated *Walk in My Shoes* (1961). For the cinema, he had been responsible for films such as *Dead to the World* (1961) and *Gone Are the Days!* (1963), before taking a rather more conventional science fiction approach to the exploration of the Red Planet in *Mission Mars* (1968) some years later. His later directorial career, primarily television-based, continued until the early 1980s and included episodes of popular series including *Get Smart* (1970), *Bonanza* (1970 and 1972), and *The Waltons* (1974). It is fair to say that, in spite of the widespread notoriety of *Santa Claus Conquers the Martians*, the film's quality is not representative of Webster's wider career, and nor should it distract commentators from an otherwise skilled and well-crafted body of work.

Likewise, the film's cast contained a number of well-established performers. John Call's acting career had included thirty years in Broadway productions and numerous appearances on television and in film (many of them uncredited), including Roy Huggins's *Hangman's Knot* (1952), Harmon Jones's *The Kid from Left Field* (1953) and David Miller's *Happy Anniversary* (1959). Bill McCutcheon likewise enjoyed a long film career, one which extended into the 1990s, and would later win a Tony Award for his performance as Moonface Martin in the Broadway revival of *Anything Goes* in 1988. Perhaps most notably, the film marked the debut appearance of Pia Zadora. Active later on stage and in films such as Peter Sasdy's *The Lonely Lady* (1983) and John Waters's *Hairspray* (1988), she won a Golden Globe Award for New Star of the Year in a Motion Picture for her performance in Matt Cimber's *Butterfly* (1982), starring alongside Orson Welles and Stacy Keach.

Santa Claus Conquers the Martians is quite unique in the sense that it doesn't really work as a Christmas film in anything but name, is too dull to be a successful children's film (in spite of its occasional moments of cheery juvenility), and certainly has little currency as a science fiction film. By the 1960s, the golden age of flying saucers, Martian invasions and ray-guns was starting to give way to a much more sophisticated approach to cinematic sci-fi – lest we forget, this was the same decade which brought audiences features such as Jean-Luc Godard's *Alphaville* (1965), Francois Truffaut's *Fahrenheit 451* (1966), Franklin J. Schaffner's *Planet of the Apes* (1968) and Stanley Kubrick's *Dr Strangelove* (1964) and *2001: A Space Odyssey* (1968). Yet despite the fact that the film has more in common with the visual and narrative style of Ed Wood's infamous *Plan 9 From Outer Space* (1959) than the more challenging, thought-provoking movies which were featuring in the sci-fi genre at the time, *Santa Claus Conquers the Martians* was actually treated fairly humanely by reviewers at the time of its release,[2] and had vanished into relative obscurity until its revival some years later. After being featured in *The Monster Times* and, on television, on *The Canned Film Festival* (1986), the cult reputation of *Santa Claus Conquers the Martians* was firmly cemented into popular culture following its appearance in a special Christmas episode of the offbeat TV series *Mystery Science Theater 3000* in 1991.[3] *MST3K*'s massively entertaining critical demolition of the film was to greatly raise its profile, and was responsible for bringing it to the attention of a whole new, hitherto-unsuspecting generation of moviegoers.

It is difficult to find consensus among commentators as to what exactly makes *Santa Claus Conquers the Martians* such a uniquely bad movie. While its reputation as a stalwart example of chronically bad film-making is often mentioned by critics,[4] opinion is divided as to which specific factor was most responsible for its failure. Some draw attention to the laughable production values,[5] whereas others instead pinpoint the exasperatingly hammy performances – usually with the hapless Dropo gaining particular mention in this regard.[6] One perceptive analysis in recent years has been that whereas the sheer ineptitude of *Santa Claus Conquers the Martians* could have lent itself quite adequately to an out-and-out parody, the deadly sincerity of the narrative naturally means that audiences are inevitably laughing at the film rather than with it.[7] It has also been noted that the film's sugary sentimentality, which is laid on by the shovel, has made it unpalatable in the harsh light of today's ingrained cynicism.[8]

But in spite of all this, *Santa Claus Conquers the Martians* has not been entirely without its supporters, especially in recent years. Some commentators, such as Richard Crouse, have noted that the film's cheesy sense of charm – ripe as it is with an inimitably shabby form of tackiness – can make it great fun to watch if the viewer is in the right mindset (albeit for rather different reasons than the creators had intended).[9] Crouse appears to be of the opinion that *Santa Claus Conquers the Martians* has acquired an unfair reputation over the years since its release, and that even although it is far removed from any notion of a cinematic work of genius, it is somewhat undeserving of the universal critical pillorying that it has been subjected to. This view was not shared by Stephen D. Hales, who seems in much closer accord with the accepted critical consensus over the film's multitude of flaws, but he does raise the interesting fact that – quite in spite of the vast catalogue of faults and drawbacks in both the production and the screenplay – *Santa Claus Conquers the Martians* nevertheless emphasises the universality, the righteousness and the benefits of the Christmas spirit.[10] And this, perhaps, is the most benevolent thing that can be said about the film: that its heart is always in the right place, even although virtually nothing else is.

Santa Claus Conquers the Martians continues to live on in the popular cultural consciousness, and as long as there are lists of bad movies it is difficult to imagine a time that the film won't be lodged somewhere in the top ten. Its cult status now assured, it is often shown on cult TV channels and has been released internationally on DVD. Al Hirt's theme song 'Hooray For Santa Claus', which plays over the opening and closing credits, has also proven to be surprisingly enduring. Either annoyingly catchy or simply annoying depending on individual opinion, the song was written by Milton DeLugg and Roy Alfred and was released as a single in November 1964 (a version of 'White Christmas' was on the B-side).[11] An additional noteworthy oddity has been the belated release of a novelisation when, in September 2005, author Lou Harry composed a distinctly ironic account of the film's events – abundant with knowing whimsy – which was published by Chamberlain Brothers. Talk of a remake of *Santa Claus Conquers the Martians* has surfaced and resurfaced from time to time, and some essence of the film's madcap legacy – albeit in a rather tongue-in-cheek form – has lived on in more recent films such as George Bonilla's *Santa Claus Versus the Zombies* (2010).

It seems fair to say that *Santa Claus Conquers the Martians* formed something of a nadir for the Christmas movie, and indeed for sixties film-making in general. Like *The Apartment* before it, though for very different reasons, it marked a break from the festive movie's golden age of the forties and fifties; whereas Billy Wilder's film had highlighted the major social and cultural changes that were sweeping across America at the time, *Santa Claus Conquers the Martians* instead sets itself the rather more modest goal of presaging the mass production era of toy-making which had already taken hold of the country. Just as Santa voices regret at the impersonal nature of push-button manufacturing, much preferring the care which goes into the hand-made toys that he constructs at the North Pole, so too are we continually reminded that these technological advancements should never make Santa himself obsolete: the Christmas spirit, after all, is comprised of much more than simply gifts and playthings. But as the sixties came to a close and a new decade was about to dawn, the innocent artlessness of *Santa Claus Conquers the Martians* would soon seem a world away from what was still to come for the Christmas film genre.

Historical Context

Santa Claus Conquers the Martians was released for the first time in the United States on 14 November 1964, and was the only box-office debut on that date. 'Baby Love' by The Supremes was at the top of the Billboard Hot 100 during that week. In the news during the week of the film's release, Eisaku Sato became the new Japanese premier, and Paula Murphy made the headlines by smashing the female land speed record.

10

SCROOGE (1970)

Waterbury Films / Cinema Center Films

Director: Ronald Neame
Producer: Robert H. Solo
Screenwriter: Leslie Bricusse, from a story by Charles Dickens

MAIN CAST

Albert Finney	-	Ebenezer Scrooge
Alec Guinness	-	Jacob Marley's Ghost
Edith Evans	-	Ghost of Christmas Past
Kenneth More	-	Ghost of Christmas Present
Paddy Stone	-	Ghost of Christmas Yet to Come
Laurence Naismith	-	Mr Fezziwig
David Collings	-	Bob Cratchit
Richard Beaumont	-	Tiny Tim

The sixties, it is fair to say, had not been a vintage decade for Christmas films, but its peculiar blend of the traditional and the experimental was set to continue for some years to come. The 1970s would witness a continuation of Christmas cinema's long wilderness period, with even fewer well-known movies in the genre appearing on the big screen during the course of the decade. That said, and as had been the case in the sixties, the Christmas film did continue to thrive in the form of made-for-television productions, with many high-quality features being broadcast throughout the whole of this ten-year period. These included TV movies featuring some prominent star names, such as Donald Wrye's *It Happened One Christmas* (1977), with Orson Welles and Cloris Leachman; Paul Bogart's *The House Without a Christmas Tree* (1972) and George Englund's *A Christmas to Remember* (1978), both of which starred Jason Robards; Randal Kleiser's *The Gathering* (1977), with Edward Asner; Eric Till's *An American Christmas Carol* (1979), which featured an excellent central performance from Henry Winkler, and Fielder Cook's *The Homecoming: A Christmas Story* (1971), which was the precursor to the popular television series *The Waltons* (1972-81).

Scrooge arrived at the very beginning of this new decade, and in creative terms the film was to face an uphill struggle on two fronts. Firstly, the shadow of Alastair Sim's portrayal – considered by many to be the definitive cinematic Ebenezer Scrooge – continued to loom large in the public consciousness. Any new interpretation of Charles Dickens's story would therefore need to break entirely new ground for itself in order to justify its existence when Brian Desmond Hurst's 1951 adaptation still remained a firm favourite amongst moviegoers, particularly in Britain. Secondly, because it was to be a musical version of Dickens's tale the film would need to raise the bar considerably in order to meet the requirements of public expectation. The 1960s had seen a very large number of incredibly popular screen musicals, many of which had performed impressively both at the box-office and with the critics. These films had included Jerome Robbins and Robert Wise's *West Side Story* (1961), George Cukor's *My Fair Lady* (1964), Robert Wise's *The Sound of Music* (1965), Richard Lester's *A Funny Thing Happened on the Way to the Forum* (1966), Joshua Logan's *Camelot* (1967), George Roy Hill's *Thoroughly Modern Millie* (1967) and Richard Fleischer's *Doctor Dolittle* (1967), to name only a few of the most prominent in the genre. However, most relevant to the production of Scrooge was the massive acclaim that had been afforded to Carol Reed's *Oliver!* (1968), which had starred Mark Lester and Ron Moody. With a plethora of memorable songs penned by Lionel Bart, *Oliver!* had proven without doubt that while Dickens was a novelist who had engaged with the most weighty of social issues during his lifetime, his unique skill in creating characters and his gift for spellbinding dialogue continued to lend his work perfectly to adaptation for the big screen.

Helming this new version of *Scrooge* was director Ronald Neame. Nominated three times for Academy Awards in his lifetime, Neame was a true stalwart of British cinema by the time of Scrooge's production. Active in the film industry from the late 1920s, he became a cinematographer in the thirties and made his debut as a director with *Take My Life* (1947). Also a producer, occasional actor and award-winning screenwriter, the many films that he directed included *The Million Pound Note* (1954), *The Chalk Garden* (1964), *The Prime of Miss Jean Brodie* (1969) and, following the release of *Scrooge*, *The Odessa File* (1974), *Meteor* (1979) and *First Monday in October* (1981). He will of course always be fondly remembered amongst cineastes for popularising the disaster movie genre with his hugely successful *The Poseidon Adventure* (1972), produced by Irwin Allen.

Contributing *Scrooge*'s screenplay, as well as its all-important music and lyrics, was composer Leslie Bricusse. Also an established producer as well as a musician and screenwriter, Bricusse has been nominated for Academy Awards on no less than eight occasions, and has won twice (in the Best Music, Original Song Score category for Richard Fleischer's *Doctor Dolittle*, 1967, and Blake Edwards's *Victor/Victoria*, 1982). At the time, Bricusse had become especially well-known for the score that he had provided for Herbert Ross's *Goodbye Mr Chips* (1969), a musical remake of Sam Wood's 1939 classic of the same name. Bricusse had also composed the music and lyrics for many stage musicals, and his Dickensian credentials were especially apparent from his work on *Pickwick* in 1963, which he had written in collaboration with Cyril Ornadel.

Neame was to court controversy in his casting of his protagonist; the elderly miser Scrooge was to be played by accomplished actor Albert Finney, a performer who was only in his early thirties at the time of filming. Rather than allowing his comparatively young age to be a hindrance, however, Finney made for an effective and very distinctive Ebenezer Scrooge. Though make-up was carefully applied to make him appear much older than his thirty-four years, he wisely avoids any caricature of Sim's earlier performance – or, indeed, any other cinematic Scrooge which had come before him. Though his bitter, snappish miser makes for a compelling central character throughout, it is in the film's closing stages – where Ebenezer takes on a youthful energy and vigour as he realises that he has quite literally been given a new lease of life – that Finney's portrayal really shines. An actor of considerable distinction, Finney had been active in television and theatre, including the Royal Shakespeare Company, from the mid-1950s. He made his cinematic debut as Mick Rice in Tony Richardson's *The Entertainer* (1960), and soon after was to enjoy many high-profile, critically successful roles in films such as Karel Reisz's *Saturday Night and Sunday Morning* (1960), Tony Richardson's *Tom Jones* (1963), Carl Foreman's *The Victors* (1963), Stanley Donen's *Two for the Road* (1967), Serge Bourguignon and Robert Sallin's *The Picasso Summer* (1969), and *Charlie Bubbles* (1967), which Finney was also to direct. He has been nominated for Academy Awards on five occasions, and has also received three Golden Globe Awards (Most Promising Newcomer: Male, for *Tom Jones*; Best Motion Picture Actor in a Musical or Comedy for *Scrooge*, and Best Performance by an Actor in a Mini-Series or a Motion Picture Made for Television for Richard Loncraine's *The Gathering Storm*, 2002), as well as nominations for six other Golden Globes. At the BAFTAs he has been nominated for twelve awards over the years, winning two of them (Most Promising Newcomer to Leading Film Roles for *Saturday Night and Sunday Morning*, and Best Actor for *The Gathering Storm*) as well as receiving the prestigious BAFTA Academy Fellowship Award in 2001 in recognition of his outstanding achievement in cinematic productions.

Fundamental to the success of any musical, of course, is the quality of its songs, and Bricusse was to pepper *Scrooge* with a wide variety of different forms and styles which suited the diverse group of performers well. Finney impresses with pieces such as 'I Hate People' (Scrooge's anthem, more or less), 'You You' (as he voices his heartbreak over the loss of his one true love), and the concluding 'I'll Begin Again'. But there are many other enjoyable songs, including Suzanne Neve's performance of 'Happiness', as Isabel rejoices in her love for the young Scrooge, and 'The Beautiful Day', delivered by Richard Beaumont's Tiny Tim. Most well-known of all, of course, was 'Thank You Very Much', the lively ensemble piece near the film's conclusion which was nominated for Best Original Song at the Academy Awards.

As had been the case with Brian Desmond Hurst's 1951 adaptation, there were a number of variations between the narrative of *Scrooge* and the original source material. Some are fairly innocuous, such as Scrooge's nephew being named Harry rather than the traditional Fred, or the revelation that Scrooge's one-time fiancée (now Isabel instead of Belle) had been the daughter of his old employer Fezziwig. But other differences are much more pronounced, such as the extended sequence in Hell where Scrooge is forced to face the consequences of his life's choices, and also in the film's closing musical number where the rehabilitated penny-pincher famously dresses in a Father Christmas outfit to underscore the profound transformation of his character.

Like the Alastair Sim film before it, Neame's *Scrooge* was to form an impressive who's-who of British acting luminaries. Though many are obvious, such as stage legend Dame Edith Evans and *Reach for the Sky*'s Kenneth More, one of Britain's most popular screen performers at the time, the film also featured a great many character actors who were familiar to UK film and television audiences. These included Roy Kinnear, Gordon Jackson, Molly Weir, Anton Rogers, David Collings, Kay Walsh, Derek Francis, Laurence Naismith and – in a particularly entertaining appearance – Geoffrey Bayldon, who will forever be remembered by a whole generation of children as London Weekend International's eccentric mediaeval wizard *Catweazle* (1970-71). Yet foremost among this extensive list of performance talent was none other than Alec Guinness, a man often regarded as one of the greatest British acting talents of the twentieth century. A multiple winner and nominee at the Academy Awards, Golden Globes, BAFTAs and Emmy Awards, amongst many others, by the time of *Scrooge* he was already a towering figure in British cinema, known to the viewing public for his many roles which had included David Lean's *Great Expectations* (1946), *The Bridge on the River Kwai* (1957), *Doctor Zhivago* (1965) and *Lawrence of Arabia* (1962); Robert Hamer's *Kind Hearts and Coronets* (1949); Charles Crichton's *The Lavender Hill Mob* (1951); Alexander Mackendrick's *The Ladykillers* (1955); Anthony Mann's *The Fall of the Roman Empire* (1964), Ken Hughes's *Cromwell* (1970) and, with Ronald Neame, *The Card* (1952), *The Horse's Mouth* (1958) and *Tunes of Glory* (1960). And all this before the world had even heard the name Obi-Wan Kenobi. Guinness makes a memorable Marley; ironically flippant at times and yet implacably serious at others, he brings a simultaneous sense of both wrath and pity to the role, along with an almost painful sense of belated compassion. When Marley says that he has not a single word of comfort to bring Scrooge, it seems impossible not to believe him, and Guinness makes full use of the film's supplementary scenes in Hell to flesh out the character, making him seem much more than the wailing spectre of foreboding that audiences had come to expect from some previous screen versions of the tale. The result, as Fred Guida notes in his pioneering study of adaptations of *A Christmas Carol*, is one of the most innovative and exceptional renderings of Marley's character to have appeared on cinema screens thus far.[1]

Key to any new version of *A Christmas Carol* is the extent to which the film presents an innovative angle on Dickens's often-told story, and additionally the way in which it makes itself relevant to its contemporary audience. In the case of *Scrooge*, Neame and Bricusse work hard – just as Finney does – to represent a different take on the well-established tale by emphasising the aspects of Ebenezer's psychology which have been affected by the protagonist's shifting goals and sense of self-worth. This was a particularly challenging remit, given that the Hurst version of the film had been widely praised for the manner in which it had sketched out the dark foundations of Scrooge's later self-interest and material avarice. However, Bricusse's script is effective in the way that it subtly shifts the emphasis onto the young Ebenezer's betrayal of his benefactor Fezziwig, first rejecting the older man's compassion and benevolence, and then callously breaking the heart of his daughter. Finney very effectively conveys the bitterness of Scrooge over both his lost love and his missed opportunities in life, giving a restrained but telling glimpse into the emotional turmoil that is fuelling Ebenezer's angry, objectionable exterior. Like the earlier version of *Scrooge*, the production benefits from some lavish period costumes[2], courtesy of Margaret Furse, and also Terry Marsh's skilled costume design – along with Bob Cartwright's art direction – which creates a suitably distinctive Dickensian London, albeit one which sometimes seems darker and slightly more foreboding than the version which had been offered up by Hurst back in the early fifties.

Neame's film received a mixed response from reviewers at the time of its release. Some were critical of Bricusse's songs, considering them lacklustre and at times even tedious,[3] while others felt that the impressive visual effects masked an otherwise tired production.[4] However, it was also noted that Dickens's common themes of personal redemption and the reforming power of Christmas remained so persuasive that *Scrooge* was greatly enhanced by their articulation,[5] and indeed this is an observation which has also been made in the present day by advocates of the film's effective expression of individual responsibility and the value of community spirit.[6] In recent years, opinion has remained sharply divided between commentators who believe that Finney was miscast as the film's protagonist and that the songs were largely unmemorable,[7] and others who felt exactly the opposite, praising the central performance and considering the music and lyrics to be so enjoyable that they have made *Scrooge* the most successful and well-rounded musical version of *A Christmas Carol* to date.[8]

No matter how divergent critical opinion had proven to be over the perceived merits of *Scrooge*, there was no doubting its achievement at awards ceremonies. The film received four Academy Award nominations in 1971: for Terence Marsh, Robert Cartwright and Pamela Cornell in the Best Art Direction/ Set Decoration category; for Margaret Furse's costume design; for Leslie Bricusse's song 'Thank You Very Much' in the Best Music: Original Song category, and for Leslie Bricusse, Ian Fraser and Herbert W. Spencer in the Best Music: Original Song Score category. Additionally, Albert Finney was to win a Golden Globe Award for Best Motion Picture Actor (Musical/ Comedy) for his performance as Scrooge, with further nominations for Leslie Bricusse (for Best Screenplay as well as Best Original Song), and Ian Fraser, Herbert W. Spencer and Leslie Bricusse for Best Original Score. His work on the film was also to see Terence Marsh nominated for the Best Art Direction Award at the 1971 BAFTA Awards Ceremony.

One indication of *Scrooge*'s enduring popularity has been the success of its stage version, featuring Bricusse's songs from the film, which premiered in November 1992. Originally starring Anthony Newley in the title role, the show premiered at the Alexandra Theatre in Birmingham. It has continued to be well-attended by audiences, being revived for a British national tour by Tommy Steele in 2003 and, in the United States, opening in Chicago in October 2004 with Richard Chamberlain as Scrooge.

Although the film has generally not been regarded as the finest of Neame's filmography,[9] it was commercially successful and has remained popular amongst audiences since the time of its release. Just as importantly, it had proved that it was entirely possible to create new and accomplished iterations of *A Christmas Carol* even when the fond memories of Alastair Sim's definitive performance continued to set a particularly high watermark for any subsequent adaptation to meet. Although it was imparting one of the most traditional of all Christmas tales, *Scrooge* had nonetheless shown that the cinema of the festive season still had room for innovation and creative ingenuity. And yet, as we shall soon see, this only marked the beginning of the inventiveness at work in the genre that was to come later in the 1970s.

Historical Context

Scrooge debuted to American audiences on 5 November 1970, the only major film to do so on that day. Topping the Billboard Hot 100 that week were the Jackson Five with 'I'll Be There'. Making the headlines at the time was the news that Chile had a new president in the form of Salvador Allende, American President Richard Nixon had announced the beginning of troop withdrawal from Vietnam, and the formation of Andrei Sakharov's new Human Rights Committee was unveiled to the public.

BLACK CHRISTMAS (1974)

Film Funding/ Vision IV

Director: Bob Clark
Producer: Bob Clark
Screenwriter: Roy Moore

MAIN CAST

Olivia Hussey	-	Jess Bradford
Keir Dullea	-	Peter Smythe
Andrea Martin	-	Phyl Carlson
Margot Kidder	-	Barb Coard
John Saxon	-	Lieutenant Ken Fuller
Douglas McGrath	-	Sergeant Nash
Marian Waldman	-	Mrs Mac
James Edmond	-	Mr Harrison

Although the seventies were hardly a boom-time for Christmas films, this is not to say that the period was without its innovations, and *Black Christmas* stands as one of the bravest experiments with the genre of its time. As its title so aptly suggests, the film is an inversion of everything that had come to be associated with the Christmas movie: the warm celebration of the family unit was replaced by the pain of dysfunctional relationships, comfort and joy were substituted for fear and suspense, and there was most certainly no happy ending on offer. In short, *Black Christmas* is one of the darkest representations of the festive period ever to be presented on the big screen, a startling tale of horror which would make Ronald Neame's visions of a Dickensian Hell seem like Santa's grotto by comparison.

Black Christmas is significant for two reasons. Firstly, it was responsible for the genesis of the Christmas horror film, a subgenre which would be particularly prevalent in the eighties but which has continued to retain popularity in recent years. Secondly, it was a seminal entry in the field of 'slasher' horror films – some commentators have even come to consider it the first of its kind, though (as we will see) there is some contention amongst critics on this point. One thing remains certain, however: *Black Christmas* was a mould-breaking, highly original piece of film-making, and one which has garnered a considerable cult following since the time of its release.

An inventive director, Bob Clark was also a producer, actor and accomplished screenwriter. By the time of *Black Christmas*, he had helmed films such as fantasy *The Emperor's New Clothes* (1966), comedy *She-Man* (1967), light-hearted horror *Children Shouldn't Play with Dead Things* (1973) and the dark suspense movie *Dead of Night* (1974). Clark also wrote three of these four films, acted as producer on one of them, and made an uncredited cameo on another. His prior experience in the horror genre was to serve him well in the production of *Black Christmas*: not only has it come to be considered one of the best-regarded of his early films, but it has ultimately established itself as among the most prominent of his entire filmography.

The film opens with a shot of a festively-decorated sorority house at night. The building, with its brightly lit windows, looks warm and inviting while 'Silent Night' plays through the opening credits. But as students are making themselves comfortable inside, the camera switches to a subjective viewpoint: an unknown figure is watching the house's inhabitants from the cold outdoors. Barb (Margot Kidder), one of the people inside, seems surprised that the front door has been left open and closes it. The mysterious prowler, still unseen, backs off momentarily. After a few moments he then begins trying to find another way of gaining entry to the building.

A low-key party is taking place in the sorority house. Arrangements are being made for hosting a children's party on campus the next day. The telephone rings and student Jess (Olivia Hussey) answers it. Discovering that it is a long-distance call for Barb, she passes on the message, causing Barb to withdraw from the room in order to take the call on another line. Meanwhile, the prowler has succeeded in gaining access to the house via an open window, clambering into a darkened attic. Downstairs, Barb is trying hard to have a conversation with her mother on the phone, in spite of interference on the line and the noise of the party in the next room. She is completely oblivious to the fact that she is being watched by the silent stalker.

Another student, Clare (Lynne Griffin), arrives at the house just as Barb is ringing off. They begin to chat in the main room when the telephone rings once again. Jess picks up the receiver and hears heavy breathing on the other end. As this has become a regular occurrence, the others come through to hear what 'the moaner' has to say for himself. What follows is a bizarre collection of animalistic noises, screams and yelps, peppered with graphic profanity. As the caller's taunts become more obscene in nature, Barb takes the receiver from Jess and derides the anonymous pervert for his unwanted verbal deviance. Apparently angered at being insulted, the voice on the other end of the line states matter-of-factly that Barb will soon be dead and then hangs up.

Barb seems unaffected by this mysterious threat, but the others are rattled by the menacing call. Barb assures them that she has received several such calls while living in the city, and that the threats are nothing to worry about – they are merely the delusional fantasies of a sick mind. Clare warns her that another student was sexually assaulted on the campus recently, and that she cannot be too careful, but Barb casually brushes off her words of caution. Upset by her friend's cavalier attitude, Clare withdraws to pack before she leaves for the holidays. As Jess chides Barb for having been so blunt with Clare, brassy house mother Mrs Mac (Marian Waldman) arrives at the door with a bundle of presents. Though Barb is unimpressed by her appearance, the other students are pleased to see the matriarchal figure and are quick to usher her into the warmth of the lounge.

Upstairs, Clare is packing in her room. She is happy to be reunited with Claude, the house cat who has been missing for the past few days but who has now taken up residence on her bed. Clare removes some neatly-stored clothes from her closet to put them in her suitcase, completely oblivious to the fact that the prowler is watching her through a sheet of dress protection plastic at the back of the cupboard. When she hears the cat mewling in distress, Clare heads back to the closet and is shocked to see a vague figure there. Before she has any time to react, the plastic sheeting is forced over her face, suffocating her.

Clare's screams cannot be heard downstairs, however, where the students are persuading a reluctant Mrs Mac to put on a floral night-dress that they have bought her for Christmas. In the hallway, the shadow of a misshapen profile can be seen shuffling away; the sound of bestial grunting can be heard in the figure's wake. As the party is winding down, the telephone rings once again – in spite of some trepidation, it turns out to be Jess's musician boyfriend Peter (Keir Dullea). Jess is keen to talk to Peter face-to-face about a matter that she considers to be of the utmost importance. But Peter has been practicing a particularly challenging piano composition around the clock for the past three days, hence his absence from the party. With a performance examination pending, he is reluctant to come over so late at night. Obviously anxious to speak with him, yet bristling at his lack of enthusiasm to discuss things, Jess arranges to meet with Peter the following afternoon.

While the eccentric Mrs Mac becomes ever more inebriated, thanks to a variety of concealed bottles of alcohol, Jess knocks on the door of Clare's room and is surprised when her friend doesn't answer. Unknown to her or any of the other students, however, Clare's body has been deposited on a rocking chair in the loft, the plastic sheet still wrapped around her now-lifeless face.

The next day, Clare's father Mr Harrison (James Edmond) is becoming worried; he had arranged to meet her at a quadrangle on the university grounds but is concerned that she hasn't appeared on schedule. He meets the inscrutable Peter, who directs him to the sorority house, but after enquiring with Mrs Mac it becomes clear that she hasn't seen Clare either. The house mother suggests that they try the common area where the children's Christmas party is being held.

Over at the main campus, Jess explains to Peter that she is pregnant with their child. Peter is delighted to hear the news, but Jess makes it plain that she wants to have an abortion; indeed, she hadn't initially intended to tell Peter of the conception at all, and has only recently decided to. Troubled by her apparent disregard for his own feelings on the matter, Peter asks her if she has entirely thought through all of the ramifications of this monumental decision. However, Jess has her own reasons and doesn't want to discuss the issue any further: she emphasises to Peter that he has no chance of changing her mind. Dismayed at how aloof and clinical she seems over this most emotional of matters, he sends her away, but relents before she leaves the room and asks if she will meet him that night to talk further about the situation.

Mr Harrison is still drawing a blank with regard to Clare's whereabouts. When it becomes apparent that none of the other students have seen her, he heads to the police station and reports her missing. The desk sergeant, Nash (Douglas McGrath), tells Harrison that he is probably worrying over nothing; there's a good chance that there is an innocent explanation, such as Clare having a secret tryst with a boyfriend.

Back at the sorority house, Jess takes another call from the prowler. It is even stranger than his previous one, with a woman's voice calling for someone named Billy followed by sundry brutish grunting noises. Jess is shaken up by this most unusual of communications, though she can make no sense of it. Later, she heads for an ice hockey arena where Clare's boyfriend Chris (Art Hindle) is practicing with his team. She explains about Clare's disappearance, and together they head for the police station where he demands an explanation from Lieutenant Fuller (John Saxon) as to why Clare's case is not being taken seriously.

At night, Mr Harrison remains at the sorority house, where Mrs Mac continues to reassure him that his daughter is probably safe wherever she might be. But he remains troubled by her lack of communication, to say nothing of being perplexed by the off-the-wall ramblings of Barb, who has become seriously drunk after the children's party. The increasingly paranoid Barb begins ranting that because she had upset Clare the night before, everyone is certain to blame her if Clare is later discovered to have fled the house and has somehow been killed as a result. Phyl (Andrea Martin), one of her sorority sisters, eventually manages to persuade Barb to retire to bed before she can upset Mr Harrison any further. As soon as Barb has departed, however, Jess and Chris arrive and tell Mr Harrison that the police have instigated a search for the missing Clare. Together with Phyl, they depart to assist in the hunt, leaving Mrs Mac alone in the building with Barb.

The search party is gathered at a local park, where a young girl – Janice Quaife – had gone missing earlier that day. Lieutenant Fuller explains the procedures to the assembled crowd; they are to spread out and comb the area for any evidence that may lead to the girl's discovery. It is hoped that anything that can pinpoint Janice's location may also assist in finding Clare. However, Mr Harrison and Janice's mother, Mrs Quaife (Martha Gibson), seem to be losing hope of finding their respective daughters alive.

Mrs Mac is busy getting packed to leave for the holidays, little realising that the prowler remains focused on the sorority house. Her taxi waits outside, the driver blowing his horn impatiently. Almost ready to leave, Mrs Mac hears the distressed meowing of Claude the cat and decides to check on him before she heads off. Tracing the cat to the attic, she is horrified when she discovers Clare's suffocated corpse, but has little time to ponder the situation before she, too, is murdered by the prowler. The taxi driver (Gerry Arbeid) grows increasingly intolerant at the fact that his fare still hasn't shown up, unaware that she has been throttled to death inside the house. The mysterious figure watches as the taxi eventually drives away and then becomes caught up in a frenzied tantrum, throwing objects around the loft in an inexplicable fit of rage.

Back at the park, a grisly discovery is made when Janice's body is finally found in the undergrowth. The assembled searchers are horrified with what has been uncovered – all, that is, apart from Jess, who has returned to the sorority house for her scheduled meeting with Peter. As soon as he has entered, however, the telephone rings – more strangulated yelps and the usual range of discordant voices, only this time crying for help and repeatedly calling for Billy. Jess pleads with the enigmatic caller to stop ringing the house, but eventually is left with no choice but to hang up. She searches for Mrs Mac but, knowing that she intended to leave for Christmas, finds nothing unusual in her absence.

Jess rings the police to report the string of obscene phone calls, and is shocked to discover that Peter is there; when she was late for their rendezvous, he let himself into the house to wait for her return. Peter is not in the best of moods, however: distracted by her news earlier in the day, his recital had gone badly with his examiners, later causing him to destroy his Steinway piano in fury. He tells Jess that he intends to leave the university's conservatory and asks her to marry him. Jess is startled but resolute: she tells Peter that she still has many ambitions that she intends to fulfil, and that it is unreasonable of him to expect her to abandon them in order to get married, even if his own vision of the future has changed. Disappointed, but willing to accept that his proposal has been snubbed, Peter then pushes Jess on the issue of the abortion. He remains resentful over both her dispassionate detachment from the issue and her reluctance to involve him in the decision. Peter insists that she reconsider, but Jess will not be dictated to and demands that he leave. He does so, though he is insistent that if she has an abortion she will regret the consequences. The threatening tone of his parting words is not lost on Jess.

At the police station, Fuller discovers the report about the obscene phone calls and puts two and two together – the address is the same one where Clare is resident during term-time. Fuller heads to the sorority house with Phyl and a technical specialist, Bill Graham (Les Carlson), arriving at the building just as the agitated Peter is leaving. Graham puts a tap on the phone line in an attempt to trace the mystery caller, while Fuller heads for Clare's room to search it for any hint as to her whereabouts. Fuller's low-key interrogation of Jess and Phyl turns up nothing new, but he gives the remaining sorority sisters the reassurance that an unmarked police car is waiting outside; the officers inside are ready to act at a moment's notice. As Fuller and Graham leave the house, however, Peter can be seen waiting among the trees nearby, his expression intense.

Back inside the house, Phyl becomes upset as the events of the day start to catch up with her. She is certain that Clare is dead, but Jess reassures her that they shouldn't jump to conclusions. Tired out by everything that has happened, an exhausted Phyl retires to bed, leaving Jess alone downstairs. Neither of them are aware that the muttering, increasingly deranged killer is still in the attic, gently swinging Clare's body back and forth on the rocking chair.

Apprehensive, Jess waits by the phone for the next call to come. But the prowler is on the move once again, descending from the loft. He makes his way into Barb's darkened room, where she lies sleeping. A few moments later, Jess hears Barb making sounds of distress and rushes to her aid. She discovers that Barb is having an asthma attack, and quickly gives her access to an inhaler. Barb quickly recovers and puts her symptoms down to a nightmare she was having – she had merely dreamed that the intruder was coming for her. Neither of them notices that the prowler is silently backing away from the room and retreating into the hallway.

The sound of carol singers can be heard from outside the building, and Jess withdraws from Barb's room to investigate. Still drowsy from her earlier heavy drinking, Barb appears to fall back into slumber. Jess opens the front door and discovers the child choir to be an oddly emotionless collection of carollers, technically proficient but singularly lacking in seasonal spirit. While they sing, the murderer sees his chance and returns to Barb's room. Telling the sleeping Barb that 'it's me, Billy,' he grabs a glass ornament of a unicorn from a nearby table and repeatedly stabs her with its horn. Barb only recovers consciousness as the attack is delivered, and is thus too shocked to cry out as she is brutally killed by the unseen assailant.

As soon as their carol is over the children are shooed away from the door by an attendant, who informs Jess that due to the murder of Janice Quaife earlier in the day they are unwilling to risk the safety of the carollers by leaving them unsupervised. Their conversation is interrupted when the house's phone rings. Full of trepidation, Jess heads back to answer it, while Graham and Fuller wait patiently to track the call. Lifting the receiver, Jess is met with another bizarre exchange, with a child's voice crying out to 'Billy' in pleading tones to cease attacking, while adult voices respond cryptically. With a woman's assurance that something will be 'just like having a wart removed', which reminds Jess of the words used by Peter during their earlier argument about her forthcoming abortion, the line goes dead. Jess is once again disturbed by the alarming concatenation of exclamations from the phone, but is especially worried about the caller having used the exact same expression as Peter had done. A few moments later, Fuller rings Jess to tell her that Graham was unable to trace the call – the next time the prowler phones the house, he reiterates the fact that she will have to keep him on the line for longer. Puzzled at the way that the mystery caller is apparently able to shift between different voices, Fuller asks Jess about Peter, who he saw leaving the house. Before he is able to continue the conversation, a disturbance in the police station causes him to ring off abruptly, but he promises to call her back soon.

Phyl has awakened due to all the commotion of Barb's asthma attack, and discusses with Jess the possibility that Peter may have been the one involved in Clare's disappearance. The unseen prowler is watching them from a crack in a nearby doorway. Phyl is unconvinced that Peter would be capable of such an act, but Jess is unconvinced: the caller's words seem to be too much of a coincidence. Almost on cue, the phone rings; this time it's Peter, sobbing uncontrollably. His words almost unintelligible due to his distress, Peter desperately begs Jess once again to reconsider aborting the baby. Jess pleads with him to calm down and discuss things rationally, but Peter proves to be anything but coherent. Before the police can get a trace on his location, he hangs up. Highly suspicious at Peter's distraught state of mind, Fuller calls up Jess and demands to know what the conversation was about. Reluctantly, Jess explains about her abortion plans, leading Fuller to suspect that Peter could indeed be the same person who is behind the obscene calls. However, Jess remembers that Peter had been present earlier in the evening when one of the calls was made, which appears to exonerate him. Unconvinced, Fuller resolves to question Peter and asks about his likely whereabouts. Thinking ahead, he also requests Peter's administrative records from the dean of admissions.

One of Fuller's aides explains that a full search of the campus has revealed no trace of Clare. Left with no option, Fuller instructs him to start a house-to-house search of all residences in the adjacent area. A couple of search party members (Jack Van Evera and Les Rubie) arrive at the sorority house and scare Phyl and Jess with their unexpected appearance. They urge the two students to keep the house securely locked to avoid encountering the abductor, which Jess assures them that they will. She and Phyl laugh at the searchers' apparent ineptitude as they leave, but Jess seems less amused when she suddenly realises that the back door is currently the only entrance to the house that is actually locked. They quickly set about securing all of the windows (pointedly neglecting to visit the attic) when Phyl enters Barb's room to check on its safety. Just as soon as she has stepped into the darkened area, however, the door slams closed on her.

Downstairs, Jess has finished a sweep of the doors and windows and is confused when Phyl doesn't respond to her repeated calls. She is cut short when the phone rings. Answering it with customary trepidation, she is met with a succession of mewling animal noises, more fevered pleas to 'Billy', and another barrage of sinister grunting. This time, however, the conversation is intercut with shots of another room in the sorority house, making it clear that the obscene caller is ringing from the same location as Jess. The exchange becomes more and more heated, with an agitated adult male demanding to know 'where the baby is'. Jess seems as baffled as she is uneasy by this chaotic and disturbing commotion.

Fuller is examining the wreckage of Peter's piano at the conservatory, noting that the troubled musician is not present in the building, when one of his officers informs the lieutenant that a trace has finally been made on the mystery caller. Returning to his car, he contacts Nash at the station only to be told the one thing that he didn't expect to hear: the prowler is calling from the very same building that his victims are located in. Frantically, he radios Jennings (Julian Reed), the detective that he had positioned on a stakeout near the sorority house. Fuller is frustrated when he doesn't respond, unaware that Jennings is slumped dead in his car, his throat slashed.

Realising that it is imperative that he reach the sorority house as quickly as possible, Fuller orders Nash to call Jess and persuade her to leave the building as quickly as possible. However, the tactless Nash lets slip that the prowler is in the same building as Jess, making her unwilling to leave without her friends Phyl and Barb. Retrieving a poker from the common room's coal fire, she creeps upstairs to Barb's room. Finding that the door is trapped shut, Jess forces it open, only to be met with the sight of Barb and Phyl's bloodied corpses. Shocked by this horrific scene, she notices the killer's eye peeking through a gap in Barb's closet. 'It's me, Billy,' he whispers, beseeching her to keep quiet about what he has done. Jess slams the door against him, causing the prowler to cry out in uncontrollable rage. Racing downstairs, she almost reaches the front door when the prowler grips her, dragging her backwards. Narrowly escaping his grasp, she hides in a nearby room as he yells furiously and flails around like a trapped animal. Then, suddenly, he stops. Jess listens as his footsteps fade away into the distance, a door closing behind him.

Still armed with the poker, Jess silently stalks through the house and eventually descends into the basement. Hearing some muttering and scuffling noises accompanied by the dark profile of a shadow, she locks herself in and withdraws into the darkness just as Peter arrives at the door. Calling out for Jess, Peter breaks the door's glass pane and gains entry to the basement. Searching through the darkness, Peter appears relieved when he finally finds her hiding against a wall, gripping the poker tightly. Calmly, Peter asks her why she didn't respond to his calls, but Jess offers no answer.

Outside the house, Fuller arrives with backup and discovers Jennings's dead body. A sudden scream from the building causes the officers to come running to its source. Heading down into the basement, the police discover Jess pinned under Peter's corpse; it is obvious from his injuries that she has attacked him with the poker. Jess is clearly in shock, so the officers sedate her and return her to her room. Fuller is keen to question her, but the medical specialist on site explains that due to her condition she will most likely be unresponsive to conversation until the next day. The bodies are removed from the premises, and Fuller is keen to deflect the sudden press and media interest away from the sorority house over to the police station, which will give the soon-to-arrive forensic teams some breathing room. Believing that Jess will be safe in her bed now that Peter has been dealt with, the police withdraw from the house, leaving her asleep.

But Jess is far from safe, and certainly not alone. Panning through the empty house, including views Barb's blood-spattered mattress and Clare's poignantly half-packed suitcase, the camera centres on the accessway into the attic where ominous humming can be heard. 'Agnes? It's me, Billy,' says the enigmatic voice, as the viewpoint edges away from the still-undiscovered corpses of Mrs Mac and Clare to leave the house through the loft window. Pulling out to a wider shot of the house, an unsuspecting police officer stands guard at the sorority house's doorway as, eerily breaking the silence, the telephone begins to ring for one last time as the end credits roll.

Black Christmas is a film which has few pretensions beyond telling a suspenseful story well, and in that it exceeds brilliantly. To his credit, Clark makes an artistic decision to limit the amount of blood and gore on display in favour of building an atmosphere of tangible foreboding,[1] and both he and screenwriter Roy Moore are highly successful in ratcheting up the tension and air of apprehension as the film progresses. Yet although it can seem easy to forget the fact, this is also a Christmas film though in many ways, it almost feels like an anti-Christmas film. Clark and Moore create a deft subversion of many traditional Christmas themes as the foundation of the film's sinister ambience. Bright fairy-lights and festive decorations adorn the sorority house all the way throughout the evening's butchery – it is heavily implied that the massacre takes place on Christmas Eve – while church bells ring out traditional carols at the same time as Peter and Jess are discussing the implications of her pending abortion. This latter point is particularly noteworthy, for the central religious significance of Christmas – namely the Virgin Birth – is here being juxtaposed with an unwanted pregnancy which is almost certainly going to end with a termination (presuming that the foetus survived the violent struggle between Peter and Jess in the basement). Yet Christian ethics prove to be neither a help nor a hindrance in the ensuing slaughter: the staid, morally-upright Clare is dealt with just as decisively as the hard-nosed, foul-mouthed Barb.

The effectiveness of the prowler is a vital ingredient to the film's success and, as some commentators have noted, it should not be forgotten that *Black Christmas* was one of the very first slasher horrors to use subjective camera angles to articulate the murderer's first-person viewpoint.[2] Director Bob Clark himself was one of the anonymous figures behind the prowler's shadow, and also one of the uncredited voices who made up the unfathomable but deeply disturbing phone calls. The evolution of the calls' mounting danger, beginning with random obscene abuse and then edging towards a very real sense of imminent peril, manages to be genuinely disturbing. Yet for all the violent depravity that is in evidence, Clark infuses his film with a very wry sense of humour which is obvious from the ironically cosy opening sequence, which – with its picture-book decorated house and comforting carols – is evocative of much more traditional family Christmas fare. To the eyes of modern audiences, the film appears strangely bloodless in comparison to later entries in the field, with Clark allowing dramatic tension to triumph over superfluous gore, while an effective measure of macabre humour is injected into the narrative without the dark wit ever seeming strained or jarring. This is particularly true of the dim-witted Sergeant Nash's incessant bumbling, and also the guilty secret of Mrs Mac's many hidden bottles of booze (they are found, throughout the film, in locations which include toilet cisterns, shoeboxes and hollowed-out books). But there is also a more subtle type of drollness in evidence, such as the eerie concurrence of a (slightly creepy) children's choir singing 'O Come All Ye Faithful' with Barb's brutal murder, and the revelation (from the police cars' bodywork decals) that the murders are taking place in the fictional university town of Bedford, surely a subversion of the security and contentment brought to mind by *It's a Wonderful Life*'s Bedford Falls.

One of the most mysterious aspects of the film – or unsatisfying, depending on one's point of view – is the ambiguous question of who *Black Christmas*'s murderer actually was.[3] Certainly Peter appears to be responsible for at least some of the killings. His early displays of violent temper, destroying his piano in reaction to Jess's pregnancy news and his subsequent poor performance at the recital, coupled with his surprise early appearance at the house when Jess returns from the search party at the park, initially makes him appear to be little more than a red herring. His likely culpability seems to be too heavily emphasised to be plausible. Yet there is no reason why he could not have been responsible for most of the obscene phone calls, with the singular exception of the one which takes place after his death. Although he does make an appearance in person when Jess is on the phone, appearing to exonerate him, at the time she is actually calling the police to report the calls after the event, leaving Peter ample time to have rung her anonymously from an extension line before coming downstairs. It appears to be Peter who drags Jess away from the front door when she is frantically trying to escape the house after discovering Phyl and Barb's butchered bodies, and yet the wild animal noises are coming from upstairs at the same time as Peter is struggling with her downstairs. And perhaps most tellingly of all, after Peter's emotional, grief-choked phone conversation (quite different from the obscene calls that have been plaguing Jess), his cold, distant mode of address in the basement – followed by the manner and distribution of his wounds when the police discover his body – make it appear that Jess has acted in self-defence rather than attacking pre-emptively. Yet the closing shots, which suggest that the deranged, muttering prowler has managed to escape the house (unseen by the police) from his attic lair, raises profound questions. Was Peter the only killer? The eye peeking at Jess through the crack in Barb's closet door doesn't appear to match either of Peter's, and the prowler's wild commotion appears to be independent of Peter's endgame attack on Jess while occurring simultaneously with it. But did Peter act alone, with another murderer working in the house autonomously, or were they both involved in the carnage together? Were either of them responsible for the murder of Janice, the schoolgirl found dead in the park nearby? And who exactly *are* Agnes and Billy? Clark and Moore seem dogged in their determination to present no easy answers and, as commentators such as Adam Rockoff have noted, we are left with no choice but to accept that the killer has no logical purpose behind his actions at all: he is, quite simply, mad.[4]

Black Christmas's central performances were strong, with the actors appearing to fit in seamlessly with the authentic seventies pop art and student paraphernalia of the sorority house just as effectively as they were to blend into the ominous darkness of the shadows. As Jess, Olivia Hussey presents an unconventional heroine for the time; the character's absolute sense of independence and self-determination makes her very different from the 'scream queens' of horror movies past. Hussey had been active on television since the mid-sixties, appearing in the cinema in films such as Delmer Daves's *The Battle of the Villa Fiorita* (1965) and David Bracknell's *Cup Fever* (1965). Her big break came when Franco Zeffirelli cast her as Juliet in his beautifully-shot adaptation of William Shakespeare's *Romeo and Juliet* (1968). Her performance in Zeffirelli's film was to win her the Most Promising Newcomer (Female) Award at the Golden Globes in 1969. Following that, her profile as an actress continued to remain visible due to appearances in a variety of features such as Gerry O'Hara's domestic drama *All the Right Noises* (1971), Antonio Isasi-Isasmendi's crime thriller *Summertime Killer* (1972), and *Lost Horizon* (1973), Charles Jarrott's adaptation of the James Hilton novel.

Keir Dullea is both chilling and enigmatic as Peter, the temperamental musician who appears glacially cool one moment and emotionally charged the next. His performance excels in presenting a disturbed and troubled character whose actions, in spite of screen time which is actually quite brief, manages to instil the film's third act with genuine menace. Dullea was a well-established film star by the time of his appearance in *Black Christmas*. He had performed regularly on television and on the big screen since the early sixties, with prominent roles in Irvin Kershner's *Hoodlum Priest* (1961) and also Frank Perry's *David and Lisa* (1962), for which he received a BAFTA Film Award Nomination for Most Promising Newcomer to Leading Film Roles. Having also won the Golden Globe for Most Promising Newcomer (Male) in 1963, Dullea's career grew in stature with a continued and prolific television career interspersed with performances in films ranging from Marco Vicario's *Le Ore Nude* (1964), an adaptation of Alberto Moravia's novel *Appuntamento al Mare*; Burt Kennedy's Old West comedy *West of Montana* (1964); Andrew Marton's war drama *The Thin Red Line* (1964), and David Lowell Rich's thriller *Madame X* (1966). He then was to take up what has become, in the eyes of many commentators, his most famous role in the form of Dr David Bowman, the central character in Stanley Kubrick's groundbreaking *2001: A Space Odyssey* (1968). (He would reprise this role many years later, in Peter Hyams's *2010: The Year We Made Contact*, 1984, which was similarly based upon an Arthur C. Clarke novel.) He then continued to alternate between challenging film roles, starring in Cy Endfield's *De Sade* (1969) and Lewis Gilbert's *Paul and Michelle* (1974), as well as television features such as Alan Landsburg's *Black Water Gold* (1970) and David Friedkin's *Montserrat* (1971).

The film also benefits from a wide and rather diverse range of solid supporting performances, many of them memorable. James Edmond's dignified but slowly traumatised Mr Harrison, Marian Waldman's coarsely amusing Mrs Mac, John Saxon's stoically professional Lieutenant Fuller and Andrea Martin's sweet-natured Phyl are all impressively-drawn characters. But Margot Kidder's larger-than-life appearance as the hard-drinking, straight-talking Barb made her the standout supporting actor in the views of many reviewers.[5] Kidder had been active on television since the late sixties, making her film debut in Norman Jewison's *Chicago, Chicago* (1969). In the 1970s she continued to develop her television career while also starring in cinematic releases including Waris Hussein's *Quackser Fortune Has a Cousin in the Bronx* (1970), Brian De Palma's *Blood Sisters* (1973) and Jack Starrett's *The Gravy Train* (1974). She would, of course, become instantly recognisable soon after for her performance as Lois Lane in Richard Donner's celebrated comic-book adaptation *Superman: The Movie* (1978), a role that she was to reprise in the film's three sequels throughout the eighties.

Black Christmas received cautious praise from many critics at the time of its release,[6] but its pioneering inventiveness with the genre to which it belongs and an almost-immediate cult following has seen its reputation grow extensively over the intervening years.[7] The film was nominated for the Golden Scroll Award for Best Horror Film at the 1976 Academy of Science Fiction, Fantasy and Horror Films Awards, and Roy Moore's screenplay was also nominated for an Edgar Award for Best Motion Picture at the Edgar Allan Poe Awards the same year. Additionally, Margot Kidder won the Best Performance by a Lead Actress Award at the 1975 Canadian Film Awards, while Kenneth Heeley-Ray won the Best Sound Editing (Feature) Award at the same ceremony.

The film was remade in 2006 by director Glen Wong. Also entitled *Black Christmas* (though abbreviated to *Black X-Mas* in the film's publicity posters), Wong's movie took a dramatically different approach to Clark's original, not only identifying the killer but giving him a detailed (and somewhat convoluted) backstory. The film also beefed up the Christmas connection to the murders; in Wong's remake, the festive season is not simply the backdrop to the killings, but actually responsible (in a roundabout way) for the prowler's motivation. Andrea Martin is recast as house mother Mrs Mac, but otherwise the remake featured an entirely new cast of actors which included Michelle Trachtenberg, Katie Cassidy, Lacey Chabert and Oliver Hudson. The remake did, however, also raise the unavoidable question as to whether it may have been better for Billy and Agnes's identities to have remained an enigmatic mystery: the additional information about the killer's *modus operandi* seems to greatly lessen the impact of the film's suspense rather than enhancing it. Reviews of the remake were very uneven at the time of its release, ranging from the lukewarm[8] to the decidedly unsympathetic.[9]

For an overwhelming majority of viewers, however, Bob Clark's original *Black Christmas* is forever likely to be the definitive version of the story, due to the film's popularity amongst horror fans and the continuing interest being generated via its influential website *It's Me, Billy*.[10] Today the film's significance to the slasher horror subgenre cannot be overstated, and it is viewed by many commentators as the evolutionary link between proto-slasher films such as Michael Powell's *Peeping Tom*

(1959), Alfred Hitchcock's *Psycho* (1960) and Mario Bava's *Bay of Blood* (1971) and the many later entries in this category of movie including Sean S. Cunningham's *Friday the 13th* (1980), Paul Lynch's *Prom Night* (1980), and Wes Craven's *A Nightmare on Elm Street* (1984).[11] Others have cited John Carpenter's famous cult hit *Halloween* (1978) as being stylistically influenced to a degree by the format and conventions established by *Black Christmas*.[12] But of course, the film's impact goes even further than that in terms of the Christmas horror movie subgenre. *Black Christmas* was to have a major bearing upon this field, influencing many later films such as Lewis Jackson's *Christmas Evil* (1980), David Hess's *To All a Good Night* (1980), Charles E. Sellier's *Silent Night, Deadly Night* (1984), Edmund Purdom's *Don't Open Till Christmas* (1984), David Steiman's *Santa's Slay* (2005) and, perhaps most notably of all, Joe Dante's *Gremlins* (1984).

There is no doubting that *Black Christmas* is a film that demands attention. The iconic poster image of the suffocated Clare, plastic wrapped around her face as she lies slumped in a rocking chair, was a striking precursor to later horror imagery such as the blood-stained hockey mask of *Friday the 13th* and Freddy Kreuger's infamously lethal metal glove in *A Nightmare on Elm Street*. Not only was the film to spawn dozens of imitations and spark inspiration for many other directors and screenwriters in the coming years, but it had proven to be the most ingenious and unconventional Christmas film of the 1970s. It must be said, however, that in spite of the movie's numerous merits, the population of the field during this period was not particularly dense – aside from Ronald Neame's *Scrooge*, the only other two major cinematically-released Christmas films of the decade were Milton H. Lehr's contemplative historical tale *The Juggler of Notre Dame* (1970) and Joan Rivers's *Rabbit Test* (1978), a satire on the Virgin Birth which starred Billy Crystal. But as the seventies drew to a close, so too did the Christmas film's long wilderness period. With the beginning of the 1980s, the genre would return with a vengeance – and this time, its pace was to show no signs of slowing down.

Historical Context

Black Christmas was released to American audiences on 20 December 1974. Earl Bellamy's film *Seven Alone* was also debuting in cinemas that day. At number one in the Billboard Hot 100 chart was Carl Douglas with 'Kung Fu Fighting'. In current affairs that week, Nelson A. Rockefeller was sworn in as the 41st Vice President of the United States, the San Francisco Visitors' Centre was formally opened at San Francisco City Hall, and nuclear tests were carried out by America at the Nevada Test Site and also by the Soviet Union at Semipalitinsk.

12

TRADING PLACES (1983)

Paramount Pictures/ Cinema Group Ventures

Director: John Landis
Producer: Aaron Russo
Screenwriters: Timothy Harris and Herschel Weingrod

MAIN CAST

Dan Aykroyd	-	Louis Winthorpe III
Eddie Murphy	-	Billy Ray Valentine
Jamie Lee Curtis	-	Ophelia
Denholm Elliott	-	Coleman
Ralph Bellamy	-	Randolph Duke
Don Ameche	-	Mortimer Duke
Kristin Holby	-	Penelope Witherspoon
Paul Gleason	-	Clarence Beeks

With the arrival of the 1980s, the Christmas movie was suddenly back in vogue again. But after two decades of relative obscurity on the big screen, the genre had swiftly attained new relevance in the era of high capitalism and conspicuous consumption. Over the course of the next ten years, the Christmas film would be dominated by depictions of the battle between the altruism of the festive season and the emergent glorification of greed and materialism. The avaricious spirit of *It's a Wonderful Life*'s Mr Potter, it seemed, had returned with a vengeance, and a whole new generation of George Baileys would be required to counter the influence of the soulless, insatiable encroachment of the coolly corporate mindset.

Trading Places was one of the first Christmas films of the new decade, and although it has come to be regarded as one of the most original and ingenious of entries in the genre over the course of the eighties,[1] it is also noteworthy in the sheer restraint with which the film engages with the festive season. The central plotline of the film has often been considered as having more in common with Mark Twain's novel *The Prince and the Pauper* (1881) than it has with any form of conventional Christmas narrative. And yet, with its very obvious Yuletide setting, the film is nonetheless imbued with a distinctly festive spirit of humanity and fair-play, where philanthropy wins out against covetousness and malice thanks to a heady mix of scheming ingenuity and the exultant spirit of the season.

A gifted screenwriter, producer and actor as well as an internationally successful director, *Trading Places*'s John Landis began his film-making career with the comedic horror *Schlock* (1973), a well-received feature which he was also to write and star in. His filmography then went from strength to strength as he helmed chaotic comedies *The Kentucky Fried Movie* (1977) and the monumentally successful *National Lampoon's Animal House* (1978), before directing one of the most acclaimed of all his films, *The Blues Brothers* (1980), an action-packed musical comedy which would prove to be a lasting contribution to eighties popular culture. He followed this up with the atmospheric horror *An American Werewolf in London* (1981), cinema documentary *Coming Soon* (1982), a segment of anthology film *Twilight Zone: The Movie* (1983), and one of the best-known music videos of all time, the thirteen-minute epic *Thriller* (1983) which accompanied Michael Jackson's record-breaking song of the same name.

Trading Places begins, with a stirring performance of Mozart's famous *Marriage of Figaro* overture, in downtown Philadelphia. A montage of shots, showing everything from historical landmarks to busy shoppers, indicates that Thanksgiving is passing and that Christmas is now well on its way. Focusing on an upmarket town house, dapper butler Coleman (Denholm Elliott) is retrieving a freshly-delivered newspaper from the front step, the shot juxtaposed with a homeless man who is sheltering under an old newspaper in a vain attempt to retain some of his body heat. Coleman is preparing a lavish breakfast on a silver tray for his employer, Louis Winthorpe III (Dan Aykroyd), a wealthy broker. After assisting him to prepare for work, Coleman chauffeurs Winthorpe to his place of employ, prosperous commodities brokerage Duke and Duke. There, he makes his way past similarly expensively-suited colleagues to reach his oak-panelled private office, where he discovers with satisfaction that an earlier hunch on the price of pork bellies has paid off. Winthorpe clearly has a keen instinct for the market, even although he appears detached and aloof when interacting with other people.

Moving to an opulent mansion house situated in expansive, snow-covered grounds, brothers Randolph and Mortimer Duke (Ralph Bellamy and Don Ameche), the owners of Duke and Duke, are also leaving home – in their case, in a chauffeur-driven Rolls Royce. Watching the stock market from their car's onboard computer, they are impressed to discover that Winthorpe's tip for pork belly shares has paid off, netting them a tidy sum. They telephone Winthorpe to congratulate him, and arrange to meet him later at the exclusive Heritage Club.

As their car arrives at the club, the Dukes are appalled when they are accosted by penniless beggar Billy Ray Valentine (Eddie Murphy). Claiming to be a Vietnam War veteran with no use of his legs due to a combat injury, Valentine pleads with Randolph and Mortimer for anything they are willing to give, but ends up being dragged away by the club's doorman (P. Jay Sidney). Once inside, Mortimer reads with enthusiasm a newspaper report which appears to bode well for Duke and Duke's forthcoming trading in orange juice. But Randolph seems indifferent to the news, being more concerned with an article on the subject of natural selection. Randolph is convinced that an individual's environment shapes their character and potential, while Mortimer is equally certain that one's capabilities and aptitudes are entirely a matter of genetics. As they debate, Winthorpe arrives with the monthly paycheques for the Dukes to sign. He is puzzled by one cheque, made out to a Clarence Beeks, when no employee is listed under that name. However, Mortimer is alarmed at Winthorpe's attention having been attracted to the matter, assuring him that Beeks is employed in a research capacity and should be considered off the record. To get him off the subject, the Dukes ask Winthorpe how preparations are going for his impending marriage to their grand-niece, Penelope Witherspoon (Kristin Holby). But they have no real interest in his personal affairs, and dismiss him curtly as soon as their business is complete. After Winthorpe's departure, Mortimer reflects that they are fortunate to have the younger man as a steady hand on their company's tiller. Randolph responds that this is no real surprise, given Winthorpe's expensive Ivy League education, but Mortimer retorts that with Winthorpe's impeccable breeding he would have been certain to succeed irrespective of his social background.

Outside in a snowy park, Valentine is approached by two police officers (Robert E. Lee and Peter Hock) who are suspicious of his purported blindness and inability to walk. Being Vietnam War veterans themselves, they know after a few questions that his cover story is bogus, and when they rumble his scam he affects amazement, claiming that his sudden 'recovery' is a miracle from God. Keen to put as much distance as he can between himself and the policemen, he hurriedly moves away from them only to accidentally bump into Winthorpe, who is in the process of leaving the club. Unintentionally knocking Winthorpe's briefcase out of his hand, Valentine quickly attempts to return it, but Winthorpe believes he is being mugged and calls the police. Panicking, Valentine races into the club hoping to escape custody but, as he is still holding the briefcase, Winthorpe remains convinced that he is attempting to abscond with the company payroll. The police need little time to catch Valentine, and Winthorpe – believing nothing of Valentine's account that the whole encounter has been an unfortunate accident – presses full charges. Before Valentine is taken into custody, Randolph asks him a few questions about his background and determines that he is the product of his deficient upbringing and an impoverished environment. But the unabashedly racist Mortimer disagrees, believing that genetics is the key issue.

The scheming Duke brothers hatch a plan which will prove once and for all whether nature or nurture is the deciding factor in life. They propose that they should ruin Winthorpe, stripping him of his wealth, influence and prestige, in the belief that he will then immediately turn to a life of crime. In order to do this, however, they believe that he will have to lose everything – his home, his job, his fiancée, and his friends. After all, the Dukes reflect, they have utterly destroyed enemies in the past, so it makes little difference to them if they decide to do the same thing to an innocent man in the name of intellectual curiosity. That night, while Winthorpe is having a romantic evening with Penelope, the Dukes telephone Coleman and explain their plans to him. Being in their employ (Winthorpe's home is owned by the brothers), Coleman has no choice but to agree to make the necessary arrangements.

The next morning, Valentine is entertaining the other incumbents of his jail cell with hilariously overblown tall tales of his purported attack on Winthorpe. He is amazed to discover that he has been bailed, and has barely left the confines of the police station before the Dukes' Rolls Royce pulls up alongside him. Explaining that they were responsible for putting up his bail money, Randolph and Mortimer tell Valentine that they operate a philanthropic organisation which assists people in need. Although the penniless Valentine is deeply suspicious of their ambiguous motivations, they assure him that their concern for his wellbeing is genuine. They will provide him with an $80,000-a-year post at their firm, a car, a house, and anything else that he requires. Valentine decides to play along, but is clearly uneasy about the indistinct basis of their generosity. The Dukes waste no time in moving Valentine into Winthorpe's home, introducing him to Coleman and assuring him repeatedly that the house, and everything that is in it, is now Valentine's own private property. But once he is out of earshot, Mortimer makes it clear to Randolph that as soon as their bet has been settled – one way or another – Valentine will be thrown back out onto the streets again at the earliest possible opportunity.

Soon after, a blissfully-unaware Winthorpe is making his way to the Heritage Club as normal. He is oblivious to the fact that he is being tailed by Clarence Beeks (Paul Gleason), the Dukes' private operative. The club's members have been summoned by its president (Gwyllum Evans) due to an accusation of theft. Beeks is called as a security expert and pinpoints Winthorpe as the perpetrator; his wallet is shown to contain three marked $50 bills which have allegedly been stolen from a jacket in the club's cloakroom. In reality, Beeks has planted them on the stunned Winthorpe, who is forcibly removed from the club and taken to a nearby police station. Unknown to Winthorpe, Beeks follows him and has a word with a corrupt cop named Clements (Frank Oz), who 'discovers' an illegal bag of phencyclidine that has been stashed in Winthorpe's suit, meaning that he is charged with narcotics offences above and beyond the original accusations that have been made against him.

Still somewhat in awe of the good fortune that has been bestowed upon him, Valentine hooks up with some old acquaintances and takes them back to his house for a raucous party. However, he soon tires of their company, realising that they have no respect for him or his home. Dismayed by the contempt with which they are treating the house, he orders them to leave. Coleman, noticing a change in Valentine's attitude already (he is starting to appear increasingly protective of his new property and belongings), suggests that he have an early night before starting his new job in the morning; he will take care of the mess that is left behind.

A mess is exactly what Winthorpe is in; now thoroughly roughed up by his fellow inmates, he is released from his police cell when Penelope arrives to bail him out. Disgusted by his unkempt appearance, she tells him that he has been fired by Duke and Duke following allegations of embezzlement. Winthorpe is shocked, knowing that this new revelation is as untrue as all the other accusations that have been made against him. Penelope is convinced that Winthorpe has been leading a double-life as a drugs dealer, a claim that he strenuously denies. But just as Penelope appears to be on the cusp of believing him, Ophelia (Jamie Lee Curtis), a prostitute who has been bribed by Beeks, arrives and begs Winthorpe for a quick fix of angel dust. Now certain that Winthorpe has been dealing in narcotics, Penelope rounds on him furiously, telling him that she never wants to see him again and then swiftly departing in her car

Bewildered by this latest inexplicable incident, Winthorpe asks Ophelia why she had interjected when she is clearly a stranger to him. Ophelia replies that she had been paid by one of his friends to do it, but Beeks has already disappeared when she points in his general direction, leaving Winthorpe baffled. Now desperate, he persuades her to pay for a taxi to his house on the proviso that he will repay her in full when they get there. However, the locks on the doors have all been changed, and Coleman pretends not to recognise him. The butler, though looking rather guilty at his employers' subterfuge, threatens to call the police if Winthorpe doesn't depart from the doorstep immediately. Growing ever more mystified, Winthorpe's next stop is at the bank, where he tries to make a cash withdrawal only to be told that tax inspectors have frozen his account. He is forcibly ejected from the premises before he can attempt to negotiate.

Winthorpe is now left with literally nowhere to turn. Realising that he is telling the truth about his inexplicable fall from grace, as far-fetched as it seems, Ophelia takes pity on Winthorpe and agrees to take him home with her until he can get back on his feet. As their taxi departs, Winthorpe is staggered when he sees Valentine passing in his own private limousine, particularly when he notices that it is being driven by Coleman. Valentine is equally shocked when he sees the bedraggled Winthorpe, remembering him from his earlier encounter, and becomes apprehensive when an uncomfortable Coleman evades the subject. The limousine arrives at the headquarters of Duke and Duke, where Valentine is arriving for his first day in Randolph and Mortimer's employ. There, he is treated to an absurdly patronising explanation of commodities brokerage by the brothers, but it is clear that the savvy Valentine is already taking to the business like a duck to water.

Ophelia arrives with Winthorpe at her apartment in a rough area of the city. Still enraged by Coleman's betrayal and unable to deduce exactly what has caused his downfall, Winthorpe vows revenge. But the level-headed Ophelia explains that he has no time to plot retribution; there is the far more pressing issue of making ends meet. Winthorpe is speechless when she reveals to him the details of her line of work in prostitution, but she is entirely too level-headed to engage with his apparent disapproval. Instead, Ophelia explains that her willingness to put a roof over his head comes at a price: she plans to retire within the next few years, and will be expecting a five-figure sum from Winthorpe in return for her current benevolence.

Back at Duke and Duke, Valentine impresses Randolph when he shows a clear aptitude for reading the market, making the Dukes a substantial profit when he correctly predicts the falling price of pork bellies. This irritates Mortimer, who can see that Randolph is gleeful over this early evidence that his theory of the pre-eminence of environment over genetic factors is a valid one: Valentine may lack Winthorpe's expensive education and privileged upbringing, but he has a keen insight into the behaviour of the general public that is entirely alien to the elitist Duke brothers. Mortimer secretly deposits Randolph's money clip on the ground in an obvious attempt to test Valentine's loyalty as they depart. However, the younger man immediately returns it to its owner as soon as he notices it, lending further credence to Randolph's premise of nurture triumphing over nature. Mortimer, who clearly expected Valentine to steal the money, is not happy.

Winthorpe makes an unexpected – and deeply unwelcome – appearance at an exclusive sports club, where he remains a member. He approaches a group of his old friends, including Penelope, in the hope that they will support him as character witnesses as he fights the charges that have been brought against him. Aghast, the snobbish acquaintances are clearly embarrassed by his presence and ask him to leave, leading Winthorpe to realise how insubstantial their bonds of friendship really were. Next, he heads for a pawnbroker's store in an attempt to trade in his expensive watch. Unimpressed, the shop's owner (Bo Diddley) believes the item to be stolen and offers Winthorpe a comparatively paltry $50 in return for it. Winthorpe is dismayed, but realises that he has little choice but to comply. As he is in the process of transacting with the pawnbroker, he notices a handgun on sale in the shop and appears to take a keen interest in it.

On the way back to Ophelia's apartment, Winthorpe passes the window of a high-class restaurant and is flabbergasted to discover the Duke Brothers and a collection of upper class business associates enjoying dinner with Valentine. The whole room appears to be hanging on Valentine's every word, leading Winthorpe into an even greater state of puzzlement. As he stands outside the window in the pouring rain, watching his former employers lionising a total stranger while he becomes drenched, Winthorpe cannot seem to believe how far he has fallen so quickly. By the time he returns to the apartment, he is running a fever. Ophelia puts him to bed, cancelling an appointment with one of her clients in order to give Winthorpe a decent night's sleep.

The next morning is Christmas Eve. In spite of Winthorpe's protestations that he is becoming a nuisance, Ophelia tells him to stay in bed until he is fully recovered. Heading out for some Christmas shopping, she promises that she will return later to cook him a quiet dinner. Before she leaves, she gives him a copy of the day's *Financial Journal*, leading Winthorpe to boggle at a front-page headline which states that the Dukes' surprise appointment of Valentine is thrilling the market. Furious, Winthorpe vows revenge before the festive season has passed.

A lavish Christmas party is being held at the headquarters of Duke and Duke. The brothers are presiding over a punchbowl while their employees mill around, but no-one appears to realise that Winthorpe is also present in the room, disguised in a decidedly tatty Santa Claus outfit. As Winthorpe helps himself to the sumptuous buffet, stuffing his pockets with expensive hors d'oeuvres, Valentine is in his office puzzling over the monthly payroll. In particular, he is confused by a $10,000 cheque made out to Clarence Beeks. He approaches the Dukes to ask for an explanation, but Mortimer hurriedly pockets the cheque and fobs him off by telling him that Beeks has recently left the firm. Valentine becomes suspicious when Mortimer lets slip some vague information about his bet with Randolph.

On returning to his office, Valentine discovers Winthorpe desperately concealing a range of narcotics in one of his desk drawers. Winthorpe, believing that Valentine was responsible for the drugs which were planted on him earlier, is keen to repay the favour and calls the Dukes into the office with the hope of framing Valentine. But the brothers are quick to take Valentine's side, leading Winthorpe to produce the handgun that he had procured from the pawn shop as soon as Valentine calls security. The Dukes try to encourage Winthorpe to put the gun away, but are interrupted with the arrival of a security officer. Shouting threats of vengeance, Winthorpe manages to escape the building, but the incident has left Valentine mystified. Mortimer and Randolph tell Valentine the cover story of Winthorpe's alleged misdemeanours, but their astute new employee is clearly beginning to smell a rat.

Later, Valentine is in a stall in the company's gents' toilets when the Dukes enter the washroom. Unaware that Valentine is either present or within earshot, Mortimer tells his brother that he accepts the fact that environment has proven to be a more potent motivator than genetics where Winthorpe and Valentine have been concerned. Admitting defeat, he hands over a $1 bill to Randolph – their agreed bet. Valentine is appalled as he overhears the conversation, particularly when he learns that Winthorpe's personal and professional reputation has been destroyed solely for the Dukes' private amusement. Mortimer is unwilling to rehire Winthorpe after his recent conduct, and they also both plan to unceremoniously return Valentine to the streets after the New Year. However, they agree to wait until the Secretary of Agriculture releases the annual crop reports at the beginning of January – providing that Beeks fulfils a mysterious task that they claim to have set him.

Deeply inebriated and clutching a bottle of whisky, Winthorpe is staggering out of the Duke and Duke building. Valentine, also leaving, catches sight of the bedraggled figure and tries to speak with him, but Winthorpe assumes that the other man has an ulterior motive and hurries off, quickly catching a bus to the other side of town. On arrival, he believes that he has reached his lowest ebb when a dog urinates against his leg mere moments before a torrential thunderstorm. Withdrawing his gun, he tries to blow his brains out only to discover that the empty chamber is clicking harmlessly. Expressionless, he throws the gun away only for it to discharge into a shop window as soon as it hits the sidewalk. Shortly afterwards, Valentine arrives by taxi and follows Winthorpe to Ophelia's apartment, where he finds that the soggy Santa has passed out in the bathtub.

Winthorpe awakes in his old bed on Christmas Day, back in his opulent town house and believing that his whole predicament has simply been a bad dream. He becomes outraged by Valentine's presence, but the Dukes' treachery is soon explained to him and corroborated by Coleman, who was privy to their bet from the start. Winthorpe immediately plans to assault Randolph and Mortimer with a shotgun, ending their duplicity once and for all, but Valentine suggests instead that they give the brothers a taste of their own medicine and ruin their fortunes. A chance news bulletin on television shows Clarence Beeks, an operative for a private security firm, ferrying the crop reports on behalf of the government prior to their announcement in January. Immediately recognising the name, Winthorpe and Valentine both realise that the Dukes plan to intercept the reports prior to their official release, illegally gaining inside knowledge which would allow them to gain supremacy in the lucrative frozen orange juice market.

Back at the Duke and Duke building, Valentine intercepts a phone call between Beeks and the Duke brothers where the security man arranges a rendezvous in an exclusive New York hotel so that he can relay his top-secret information. Sure enough, on New Year's Eve Beeks is boarding a train from Washington D.C. en-route to Philadelphia. The train is packed with costumed revellers; among the many passengers are Harvey (James Belushi), a party-loving man in a gorilla suit, and an actual gorilla (Don McLeod) which is being transported to the city in a cage. Much to Beeks's irritation, Valentine appears unexpectedly in his train compartment impersonating a Cameroonian student, followed shortly after by Coleman, dressed as a priest and sporting an Irish accent. Next comes Ophelia, affecting a Swedish accent but dressed in a traditional Austrian national costume (including lederhosen). While Beeks is – at Ophelia's request – storing her backpack on a luggage shelf, Valentine swipes his briefcase and substitutes it for an identical replacement. He then smuggles the case out of the compartment and passes it to Winthorpe, who is hiding further along the carriage.

Just when things look as though they can't possibly become any more convoluted, Winthorpe arrives in the compartment – dressed as a Rastafarian. With some further subterfuge, he attempts to return Beeks's case without him noticing. But the canny security agent reveals that he is only too aware what has been going on, pulling a gun on Ophelia and threatening to shoot if they don't do exactly as he says. Beeks orders them to leave the compartment, and the group weaves through a drunken party in the buffet carriage before ending up in a cargo container next to the caged gorilla. It is clear that Beeks plans to execute Winthorpe, Valentine and their associates, but he is momentarily distracted by the sudden appearance of the costumed Harvey. Sidetracked, he is then knocked unconscious by the nearby gorilla. Wasting no time, the group strip Beeks of his clothing and put him into the gorilla suit, then lock him in the cage while they make their getaway.

In a darkened multi-storey hotel car park, Mortimer and Randolph are awaiting the arrival of Beeks with their advance copy of the crop report. Sure enough, a shadowy figure in a hat and trench-coat appears, seemingly out of nowhere, and accepts from the brothers a briefcase packed with banknotes. In return, he throws them a manila envelope; its contents delight the Dukes no end. They thank Beeks for a job well done, but the shady individual has already departed. At no point to the brothers realise that the man they have been dealing with was actually Valentine, disguised in Beeks's stolen clothing.

Armed with the predictions of the real crop reports, Valentine and Winthorpe head for the New York Stock Exchange with every penny they have, together with the collective life savings of Coleman and Ophelia. Believing, from the false report that they have obtained, that orange production has been adversely affected by the harsh winter, the Dukes attempt to corner the market, driving up the price. But once this figure has peaked, Winthorpe begins to sell instead, sending the price back down again. Bewildered, Mortimer and Randolph realise to their horror that the crop reports have been falsified. They frantically head down to the trading floor in a vain attempt to reverse the instructions they had given for their dealings. They are interrupted by the scheduled statement from the U.S. Secretary of Agriculture (Maurice D. Copeland), which confirms that the winter weather has had no discernible effect on orange production. Stunned, the Dukes have no alternative but to look on as they are financially ruined. They seem totally amazed at the inventive way in which Winthorpe has betrayed them, though Valentine reveals that he had made his own $1 bet with Winthorpe – that the two of them could ruin the Duke brothers and make a fortune in the process. Winthorpe and Valentine leave the stock exchange wealthier than in their wildest dreams, while Randolph and Mortimer – who had thrown every penny they owned into their scheme – face insolvency and humiliation. Thus Winthorpe, Valentine, Ophelia and Coleman enjoy their new-found riches from the comfort of a paradisiacal Caribbean hideaway, knowing that the Dukes will no longer be in a position to ruin the lives of anyone else.

As many commentators have noted, *Trading Places* is a film which very much wears its heart upon its sleeve in terms of the moral message that it seeks to convey.[2] Landis presents a film where altruism is clearly the victor over self-interest, unambiguously marking out the boundary lines between Randolph and Mortimer (cold, distant, snobbish, uncaring, racist and egocentric) and the majority of the less wealthy characters (who are generally selfless, inventive, warm and inclusive). Yet the film does contain some surprisingly mixed messages in this regard. The film's opening shots, cutting between scenes of luxurious opulence and grinding poverty, are suggestive of a much starker depiction of free market excesses than that the central scenario which Landis actually sets up. Clearly we are shown that unfettered capitalism has an ugly side which contains the potential to create grotesques such as the Duke brothers, but it is that same system of capitalistic freedom which gives Valentine and Winthorpe the capability to turn the tables on their adversaries in the most devastatingly effective of ways. So it is perhaps more correct to say that the film's primary concern is not capitalism at all, but rather cultural attitudes towards wealth and the way that society had come to regard economic prosperity as an end in itself. The standoffish Winthorpe comes to realise that his wealth was no guarantor of a satisfying life, and finds that poverty has a humanising effect – he has no choice to engage with society when his circumstances change, forcing him to deal with people directly rather than through proxies such as Coleman or his subordinates at Duke and Duke. Likewise, Valentine clearly finds within himself hitherto-undiscovered reserves of business acumen, but he retains the ability to realise that cash is far from the all-encompassing panacea that he had so long presumed it to be when he was still impoverished and homeless. Winthorpe is faced with the unpalatable realisation that money attracts fair-weather friends who exhibit no lasting loyalty (even Winthorpe's engagement is shown to be little more than a social imperative – his fiancée is even more obsessed with prestige and position than he was), while Valentine becomes increasingly aware that the Dukes are treating him as little more than one of the commodities that they trade in, lifting him out of poverty with every intention of plunging him back into it again just to satisfy their whims.

And yet, for all its multifaceted engagement with socio-economic issues – Western society's relationship with free market capitalism was, after all, one of the key topics of eighties American filmmaking – *Trading Places* is also indisputably a Christmas film at heart. Winthorpe's suffering appears particularly poignant when reflected against the light of tinsel and festive decorations, while the snowy Philadelphia streets provide an atmospheric backdrop to events. There is an interesting visual contrast between Ophelia's homely but endearingly low-key Christmas tree and the opulent but singularly characterless corporate celebrations taking place at Duke and Duke, but most notable is the way in which the festive season once again weaves its transformational powers upon a film's characters, improving the lives of Winthorpe and Valentine (albeit through respective baptisms of fire) while eventually consigning Mortimer and Randolph to a deserving fate. If Winthorpe is the Scrooge of the tale, an avaricious snob turned responsive egalitarian, then the Duke brothers are surely the latter-day corporeal incarnations of Jacob Marley, unavoidably destined for ruin due to the short-sightedness of their own materialism.

However, if we consider the central issue of *Trading Places* to be the corrupting influence of excessive wealth then it is interesting to see how Timothy Harris and Herschel Weingrod's screenplay deals with the topic in a broader context. There is no doubt that the Duke brothers are the villains of the piece, their 'old money' background and towering social influence shielding them from censure to such an extent that they seem thoroughly jaded with their ability to buy and sell whatever (and whomever) they please. Yet there seems to be precious little of the Christmas spirit in evidence throughout the film's final act, for Winthorpe and Valentine find that they can only succeed by turning the Dukes' dishonest scheme against them – not by reporting Beeks' duplicity to the authorities, but by using the very same chicanery to benefit them financially.[3] This does raise the rather immediate issue of whether two wrongs can make a right: the money raised from Valentine and Winthorpe's frantic dealing at the New York Stock Exchange not only assures their own long-term wealth, but also that of the hard-working Coleman and Ophelia into the bargain, while the Dukes are condemned to ruination. So while it does seem clear that it is the greed and excess which can thrive in the shadow of unchecked capitalism that are being criticised, rather than the mechanics of the free market system itself, the ultimate fate of the protagonists remains unclear at the film's conclusion. When all is said and done, it is left to the viewer to ascertain whether their new-found riches will truly be able to secure happiness for any of them in the long term (Ophelia's love for Winthorpe is, after all, something that was born in poverty and remains beyond price), or whether any of the beneficiaries of Randolph and Mortimer's misfortune will be fated to tread the same road of detached ennui that had corrupted the Duke brothers so thoroughly, thus repeating the same entropic cycle.[4]

The film's appeal is due in large part to the quality of its two charismatic lead performers. Dan Aykroyd impresses as the priggish Louis Winthorpe, a man who is forced to go from riches to rags (and then back to riches again) in the course of less than a month. From his pampered preening and smug self-satisfaction through to his slow-motion meltdown as his life collapses around him, Aykroyd takes his time to gradually build an impression of likeability around Winthorpe as the film progresses, allowing audience sympathy to grow in a way that lends a very immediate sense of the character's complicated emotional journey. (His whisky-soaked, suicidal variation on Old Saint Nick also must rank as one of the most melancholic appearances of Santa Claus in living memory.) At the time of *Trading Places*'s release, Dan Aykroyd was well-known for being one of the writing staff on television's popular *Saturday Night Live* between 1976 and 1979. He and his co-writers won the Emmy Award for Outstanding Writing in a Comedy/ Variety or Music Series in 1977, and were nominated for Emmys again in 1978 and 1979. In terms of performance, Aykroyd was active in television from the mid-seventies, making his big-screen debut in Rex Bromfield's romantic comedy *Love at First Sight* (1977). He appeared in a number of memorable TV features at the time, including Eric Idle and Gary Weis's *The Rutles: All You Need Is Cash* (1978) and Gary Weis's *Things We Did Last Summer* (1978), before hitting the big time as Sergeant Frank Tree in Steven Spielberg's *1941* (1979) and, most especially, as Elwood Blues in John Landis's *The Blues Brothers* (1980), which featured a screenplay written by both Aykroyd and Landis. Aykroyd continued to appear in comedies such as John G. Avildsen's *Neighbors* (1981) and Michael Pressman's *Doctor Detroit* (1983) before being cast as Louis Winthorpe and, the following year, would deliver what was perhaps his best-remembered performance of the decade as Dr Ray Stantz in Ivan Reitman's *Ghostbusters* (1984), which he co-wrote with

Harold Ramis. In 1990, Aykroyd was nominated for the Academy Award for Best Actor in a Supporting Role in recognition of his performance as Boolie Werthan in Bruce Beresford's *Driving Miss Daisy* (1989).

Aykroyd is matched step for step by Eddie Murphy's barnstorming performance as the cunning Billy Ray Valentine. Murphy throws his all into the role, producing an intelligent, high-energy rendering of a very distinctive character. Valentine's development curve is every bit as dramatic as Winthorpe's proves to be, allowing Murphy's charm and skill for character development to shine through from every scene. Like Aykroyd, Murphy was a writer for *Saturday Night Live* – in his case, between 1982 and 1984 – as well as making appearances as a performer on the show from 1980 until 1984. Also a talented and controversial stand-up comedian, and later a producer and screenwriter, he made an explosive cinematic debut as Reggie Hammond in Walter Hill's *48 Hrs* (1982) (a role which he would later reprise in Hill's sequel, *Another 48 Hrs*, in 1990). Murphy's acting career continued to be highly successful throughout the eighties, with lead performances in films such as Martin Brest's *Beverly Hills Cop* (1984), Michael Ritchie's *The Golden Child* (1986) and John Landis's *Coming to America* (1988). In recent years, Murphy has been nominated for the Best Performance by an Actor in a Supporting Role Academy Award for his appearance in Bill Condon's well-received musical drama *Dreamgirls* (2006).

Trading Places was not to be the last time that these actors would collaborate with John Landis. Aykroyd and Landis worked together again on Landis's films *Spies Like Us* (1985) and *Susan's Plan* (1998), as well as the prologue of *Twilight Zone: The Movie* (1983), which was also directed by Landis. Murphy and Landis would join forces in later years when Murphy was headlining *Coming to America*, and also when he reprised his famous role as Axel Foley in Landis's *Beverly Hills Cop III* (1994).

Screen veterans Don Ameche and Ralph Bellamy lead an excellent supporting cast with their scene-stealing performances as the two Machiavellian Duke brothers. The film also benefits from the ever-classy Denholm Elliott at his most reserved as the compassionate butler Coleman, and Paul Gleason's enjoyably sleazy turn as the larger-than-life Clarence Beeks. Jamie Lee Curtis also impresses in an early role as the streetwise, gum-chewing Ophelia. Curtis had made appearances in many successful horror films from the time of her cinematic debut in John Carpenter's cult classic *Halloween* (1978), including Carpenter's *The Fog* (1980), Paul Lynch's *Prom Night* (1980), Roger Spottiswoode's *Terror Train* (1980) and Rick Rosenthal's *Halloween II* (1981), but her award-winning performance in *Trading Places* marked a shift in gear for her acting career which would see her attain a much higher profile as the decade continued.

Trading Places also features an interesting range of cameo appearances from actors and performers such as Alfred Drake, Bo Diddley, Al Franken, Tom Davis, Frank Oz and, perhaps most notably, James Belushi, the brother of Dan Ackroyd's co-star in Landis's *The Blues Brothers*. Indeed, this was just one connection between *Trading Places* and Landis's earlier film. The prison number which is assigned to Winthorpe is exactly the same number that is given to Jake

Blues, played by John Belushi, in *The Blues Brothers*. Landis would repeatedly prove himself to be no stranger to clever in-jokes: Don Ameche and Ralph Bellamy would later reprise their roles as a (now destitute) Randolph and Mortimer Duke in Landis's later film *Coming to America*, also starring Eddie Murphy, where a bizarre twist of fate allows the elderly brothers to discover that they have been presented with one last chance at redemption.

Trading Places did well at the box-office, and also met with a warm reception from reviewers. Critics took particular note of the fact that the film works hard to present an engaging (rather than preachy) social message,[5] while others praised the film's deftly-employed comedy due to the fact that it is allowed to develop organically rather than ever appearing forced or stilted.[6] A number of commentators were fulsome in their approval of Eddie Murphy's energetic performance as Billy Ray Valentine, which they perceived as being vital to the film's success,[7] and indeed more recent appraisals of the film have come to consider *Trading Places* as being one of the early catalysts which would propel Murphy into the A-list, eventually making him one of the most successful actors in eighties cinema.[8]

The film performed well at awards ceremonies, being nominated for the Best Music: Original Song Score Oscar at the Academy Awards in 1984 for Elmer Bernstein's soundtrack. Eddie Murphy was nominated for a Golden Globe Award in the Best Performance by an Actor in a Motion Picture (Comedy/ Musical) category, while the film itself was nominated for the Best Motion Picture (Comedy/ Musical) award at the same ceremony. At the BAFTA Awards, Denholm Elliott won the Best Supporting Actor Award and Jamie Lee Curtis was awarded Best Supporting Actress, while Timothy Harris and Herschel Weingrod's script was nominated for the award for Best Screenplay: Original.

With its overarchingly benign tone and its upbeat central message of common humanity overcoming dishonourable greed, *Trading Places* had set the prevailing agenda for many later Christmas films of the eighties. Although the movie is situated largely within the hard-faced world of finance, there is a real sense of warmth at its heart, and Landis's inventively unconventional approach to the festive season leaves a lasting impression that Christmas miracles still had a place in a the modern world, even one that was filled with divisive politics and fiscal woes. *Trading Places* was right at the vanguard of the Christmas film's return to prominence – and relevance – among cinematic audiences after the genre's long period of relative neglect, and its success with the critics and at the box-office augured well for the fortunes of this ever-versatile category of film in the years to come.

Historical Context

Trading Places debuted in cinemas across the United States on 8 June 1983, the only major new film release to appear on that day. Irene Cara's song 'Flashdance (What a Feeling)' was at the top of the Billboard Hot 100 that week. Appearing in the news at the time was Margaret Thatcher's Conservative Party achieving a second landslide victory in the British general election, Li Xiannian being declared President of the People's Republic of China, and Alice Miller's triumph at the West Virginia LPGA Golf Classic competition.

13

A CHRISTMAS STORY (1983)

Metro-Goldwyn-Mayer/ Christmas Tree Films

Director: Bob Clark
Producers: Bob Clark and René Dupont
Screenwriters: Jean Shepherd, Leigh Brown and Bob Clark, from a novel by Jean Shepherd

MAIN CAST

Peter Billingsley	-	Ralphie Parker
Melinda Dillon	-	Mrs Parker
Darren McGavin	-	The Old Man/ Mr Parker
Ian Petrella	-	Randy Parker
Tedde Moore	-	Miss Shields
Scott Schwartz	-	Flick
R.D. Robb	-	Schwartz
Yano Anaya	-	Grover Dill

Trading Places had underscored the fact that the world of the 1980s was changing rapidly, and the public perception of Christmas with it. Following in a similar vein, *A Christmas Story* was to juxtapose the mores of modern society with that of America's then-recent past, an affectionate love-letter to a bygone golden age of the festive season. The eighties, after all, were to see social and cultural attitudes shifting in a number of ways, and the Christmas movie was just one genre which was to be challenged and reconfigured in the light of this new age of cynicism and aggressive individuality. Thus while *A Christmas Story* was warmly nostalgic with regard to its subject matter, it stopped short of idealising the era of its setting any more than it sentimentalised Christmas itself. Instead, the film was part of a broader re-examination of the festive season which was taking place throughout the decade, contrasting sympathetically-rendered Yuletide reminiscences with some of the stark emotional realities of growing from childhood into adolescence.

A Christmas Story was adapted from the novels of actor and writer Jean Shepherd, with primary reference to *In God We Trust, Others Pay Cash* (1966) though with other incidents from the film having appeared in his later work *Wanda Hickey's Night of Golden Memories and Other Disasters* (1971). Popular for his wry observations and down-to-earth humour, he was a recognisable name to audiences thanks to well-received features such as his TV documentary series *Jean Shepherd's America* (1971) and his many radio broadcasts over the years. His long career established him as one of the most prominent American humorists of the late twentieth century, and a true multimedia personality before the term had even been popularised. Shepherd was to act as the narrator of *A Christmas Story* in addition to collaborating on its screenplay, and also appeared in a number of different roles throughout the film – some of them unexpected.

It seemed slightly ironic that this cheerful slice of wistful nostalgia should have been brought to the big screen by Bob Clark, the same man who had been responsible for presenting one of the darkest, most edgy depictions of the festive season in the previous decade's *Black Christmas*. Yet *A Christmas Story* has come to be regarded as one of Clark's best-known features, and the vast stylistic disparities between it and his earlier film were to fit surprisingly comfortably into what was an increasingly versatile filmography. Following *Black Christmas*'s appearance in 1974, Clark had gone on to direct tense thriller *Breaking Point* (1976), Sherlock Holmes mystery *Murder by Decree* (1979) and the moving theatre-based drama *Tribute* (1980) before he released one of his most commercially successful films, the infamous teen comedy *Porky's* (1982). This was followed soon after by the equally raucous *Porky's II: The Next Day* (1983), establishing him as an inventive director who was unafraid to experiment with wildly different genres and approaches to his craft. With *A Christmas Story*, however, he was to engage with a type of film which was quite different in tone and content from any of his previous movies. The end result would ultimately be one of the most enduringly successful of eighties Christmas films.

December has arrived in the snowy Indianan town of Hammond. It's the 1940s and, in a house in Cleveland Street, nine-year-old Ralphie Parker (Peter Billingsley) is eagerly awaiting the approach of the festive season. Having recently been transfixed by the annual window display in one of the town's department stores, he has become obsessed with the prospect of receiving a Red Ryder BB gun for Christmas. Coming to the swift conclusion that this is the dream gift that he has always wanted, Ralphie becomes totally focused on convincing his parents to buy one for him before it is too late.

Ralphie's initial efforts to gain the attention of his mother (Melinda Dillon) and father (Darren McGavin) are far from successful. Trying desperately to drop hints wherever possible, he is crushed when his mother tells him that there is no way that she will consider buying him a gift that will run the risk of him losing an eye. Ralphie can see no easy way of circumventing her parental concern, but remains absolutely fixated on having a BB gun of his own. He crafts a fanciful daydream where he defends his home from a pack of nefarious burglars, but is soon brought down to earth when his father enters one of his regular battles with the house's temperamental furnace.

Once his mother has bundled up Ralphie's younger brother Randy (Ian Petrella) to face the winter cold, the two boys head for school. After an English lesson, two of Ralphie's friends – who have been having a protracted argument about whether someone's tongue will stick to ice-frosted metal – enter an elaborate exchange of dares and double-dares until Flick (Scott Schwartz) accedes to Schwartz's (R.D. Robb) taunting and plants his tongue on the school's frozen flagpole. Unfortunately for Flick, who had long ridiculed Schwartz's warnings, he soon finds himself stuck fast to the frigid metal pole, leading soon after to an embarrassing visit from the police and fire brigade. The boys' teacher, Miss Shields (Tedde Moore) is dismayed by Flick's fate, but Ralphie's amusement at his headstrong friend's fortunes soon turns to joy when he discovers that the class has been set an essay-writing assignment, the topic being what gift the students would most like to receive for Christmas. Surely, he reasons, this may present him with another opportunity to emphasise his desire for the much-wanted BB gun.

On their way home after school, Ralphie, Randy, Schwartz and Flick (now vehemently attesting that he'd felt no pain at all during his encounter with the flagpole in a hopeless attempt to save face) are accosted by school bully Skut Farkus (Zack Ward) and his dim-witted sidekick Grover Dill (Yano Anaya). They manage to escape with only their pride damaged, racing in the opposite direction as Farkus and Dill sneer at their retreat. Once he is safely ensconced in the warmth of his home, Ralphie quickly puts pencil to paper as he scribbles out an impassioned treatise on the essential nature of BB guns and why they make such uniquely good Christmas presents. As he marvels at his finished work, his father arrives back from work with exciting news – he has received a telegram with the news that he has will soon be the recipient of a major prize that he has won in a competition. Mr Parker is convinced that this ambiguous treasure will be delivered later that evening, and much speculation takes place over what it might actually turn out to be.

Sure enough, as the family eat dinner there is a knock at their front door. A delivery man (Jim Hunter) has arrived with a mysterious wooden crate. Mr Parker can barely contain his excitement as it is wheeled into the living room, and he wastes no time in opening it with a crowbar and hammer only to reveal, through seemingly endless piles of sawdust, a lamp-stand in the shape of a woman's leg, complete with stocking and high-heeled shoe. Mr Parker is delighted by his new acquisition, but his wife is appalled and Ralphie is just plain confused. But nobody will be allowed to dampen Mr Parker's spirits: he is so delighted by this unexpected bounty that he proudly displays it right in the centre of his living-room window, then rushes outside to see what it looks like from the street. Mrs Parker is mortified as many of her neighbours and other passers-by stop on the sidewalk to peer with curiosity at the bizarre lamp. However, she manages to distract any awkward questions from Ralphie by directing him and his brother with their favourite radio programme (*Radio Orphan Annie*) which, as luck would have it, is just starting its broadcast.

The next day, Ralphie and his friends race to school, keen to avoid another confrontation with Farkus and Dill. Ralphie hands over his assignment to Miss Shields, confident that his literary genius will be richly rewarded by a good grade. After he has returned home, his father takes the whole family to a rather shabby Christmas tree emporium, where a silver-tongued salesman (Les Carlson) tries to convince him of the virtues of his stock. It quickly becomes apparent that many of the trees have seen better days, but Mr Parker nevertheless strikes a bargain and has one of the better specimens tied to his car. On the drive home, however, a flat tyre forces him to pull over and affect repairs. Mrs Parker suggests that Ralphie go out and help his father, but following a mishap the boy is heard swearing, causing his parents to later punish him by sucking on a bar of soap until he confesses the source of the profanity. Ralphie knows full well that he had heard it from his father, who is no stranger to a curse-word, but believing discretion to be the better part of valour he blames his friend Schwartz instead. Mrs Parker calls Schwartz's mother to complain (resulting in a quick clip round the ear for Ralphie's hapless acquaintance), following which she promptly sends Ralphie to bed, where he dreams of his family's remorse when they discover that he has gone blind – not from an accident with a BB gun, but from soap poisoning.

Morning brings a flotilla of Christmas gifts for Mrs Shields as her students await the grades from their essays. Many of the children have brought her trinkets or little potted plants, but – not to be outdone – Ralphie presents her with an ostentatious wicker basket filled with fruit, hoping to unsubtly entice her into giving him a favourable mark for his essay. He gets home after school to the exciting discovery that his *Radio Orphan Annie* decoder pin has arrived in the mail – his long-awaited reward for collecting tokens from malted beverage jars. Ralphie's exhilaration continues until the radio programme broadcasts its secret message and, armed with his decoder, he avidly decrypts the series of numbers only to be faced with an advertisement for the self-same malted drink which sponsors the show. Feeling betrayed by this blatant marketing ploy, Ralphie's disappointment is tangible.

Later, his father is once again fighting the house's furnace down in the basement when the infamous leg lamp is unexpectedly shattered while, by total coincidence, Mrs Parker is watering plants nearby. Mr Parker is distraught at the loss of his beloved prize, blaming his wife for deliberately breaking it just to get it away from the living room window. He accuses her of being envious of his affection for his hard-won reward, but Mrs Parker denies having been responsible for damaging it, eventually blurting out that it was the most egregiously-designed lamp that she'd ever had the misfortune to set eyes upon. Undeterred, Mr Parker tries desperately to repair it with glue, but fails miserably. Still fuming, though appearing genuinely saddened by the loss of his treasured trophy, he silently takes the remains of the lamp into the garden and buries it like a much-loved pet. Ralphie seems nonplussed at the loss of his father's 'major award', though the new sense of ill-feeling that now permeates the house doesn't bode well for his increasingly desperate attempts at hinting for his perfect gift.

Narrowly avoiding another skirmish with Farkus and Dill (the hapless Flick is not so lucky), Ralphie makes it back to school with high hopes of achieving a top grade for his BB gun essay. But he is crushed when Miss Shields returns his exercise book with a mark of C+, adding as an afterthought that he is sure to shoot out his eye if he ever gets his hands on the aforementioned air rifle. Any hope Ralphie has of presenting his parents with a top-graded piece of writing, thus advancing his aim of impressing the virtues of the Red Ryder BB gun in the process, has been cruelly dashed. Disenchanted by his bad fortune, he makes his way home only to be snowballed by Farkus, which finally tips him over into an incoherent rage. He furiously barrels into the mocking bully, walloping him for all that he is worth. Farkus's sidekick Dill is likewise no match for the outpouring of Ralphie's pent-up wrath, and is reduced to running for his father while the onslaught continues. Only the arrival of Mrs Parker, summoned by the anxious Randy, can break up the fight – a tearful Ralphie is led away as Farkus, now thoroughly bloodied, shakes himself out of his dazed disbelief.

Back home, Ralphie is full of apprehension over his father's reaction to the news of the fight. However, Mrs Parker tactfully skirts around the issue and skilfully manages to get her husband onto his favourite subject of baseball instead, saving Ralphie from near-certain punishment. Ralphie is grateful to his mother for her thoughtfulness, and later – once the air has cleared – wonders what his next step should be on the path to the BB gun. He decides to ask Santa Claus to provide the gift, in the hope that jolly old Saint Nick will intercede on his behalf. Fortunately for Ralphie, Santa is currently to be found not at the North Pole, but at the rather more conveniently-located Higbees Department Store in town. Following the family's visit to the annual Christmas parade, and after much cajoling, Mr and Mrs Parker finally relent and allow Ralphie and Randy the chance to visit Santa with their requests for presents. But the queue is impossibly long, meaning that by the time the boys finally reach Santa the store is almost ready to close. Frogmarched over by some rather belligerent elves, Ralphie is overawed when he meets Santa (Jeff Gillen, voice of Jean Shepherd) and is then too tongue-tied to ask for the BB gun. But the store is operating a kind of high-pressure production line for the grotto, meaning that each individual child's time on Santa's knee is at a premium. Just as he is being whisked away by one of Santa's surly helpers, Ralphie suddenly recovers his voice and makes clear his plea to Father Christmas, only to be told – to his despair – that he'd be in danger of taking his eye out. By the time his parents return, Ralphie is thoroughly miserable.

On the night of Christmas Eve, Mr Parker is struggling gamely with the family Christmas tree – nothing is allowed to deter his enthusiasm for his impressive array of electric fairy-lights, including the occasional blown fuse. Soon it is time for the brothers to turn in for the evening, hastened by their mother's warning that Santa will soon be delivering their presents. Sure enough, the next morning has brought the freshly-fallen snow of a white Christmas, though Ralphie and Randy scarcely have time to notice before thundering downstairs to their presents. Alongside patterned socks and a toy zeppelin, Ralphie is aghast to discover that his Aunt Clara has gifted him a bright pink bunny costume which his mother forces him – despite his vocal protestations – to try on. But as luck would have it, this indignity is only prelude to a last-minute Christmas surprise for Ralphie; after all of the gifts have been opened, his father casually draws his attention to a solitary, unopened and thus-far unnoticed box which contains none other than a Red Ryder BB gun

Euphoric, Ralphie can barely suppress his excitement as he races outdoors to make full use of his treasured new possession. But underestimating the recoil of the air rifle, he accidentally knocks his glasses from his face. In a fevered attempt to find them, Ralphie tramples over them, shattering both lenses. He rapidly concocts a tall story to avoid antagonising his mother, but neither notices that the house's back door has been left open, allowing their neighbour's dogs into the kitchen. The intruding hounds quickly wreak havoc, toppling the kitchen table and devouring the family's Christmas turkey. Mrs Parker is distraught at the scene of canine carnage, but her husband – practical as ever – decides that the family need not go hungry because of this unexpected disaster. He drags everyone across town to the Chop Suey Palace, where the manager (John Wong) and his team of waiters (Johan Sebastian Wong, Fred Lee and Dan Ma) serenade the Parkers with an upbeat selection of Christmas carols as they get ready for their meal. Quite in spite of all the stumbling blocks that have faced them, the family find themselves in high spirits and – knowing that the most important thing is that they are safe, well and together – are fully able to enjoy their meal.

Later that night, Mr and Mrs Parker toast the passing of another Christmas by the electric light of their tree, watching a new fall of snow from their living room window. Tucked up in bed, his BB gun lovingly nestled in his arms, Ralphie reflects on the ultimate success of his efforts to receive this most valued of gifts, knowing somehow that there would never be another Christmas present quite like it ever again.

It would take a hard heart indeed not to be touched in some way by the invitingly nostalgic whimsy of *A Christmas Story*. From Ralphie's daydreaming flights of fancy to the low-key, mildly bizarre family conflicts which surface throughout the film (quarrels so surreal that they will inevitably strike a chord with almost any real-life family), Bob Clark weaves a skilful narrative tapestry which quickly builds emotional sympathy between the audience and his range of likeable characters. His use of period detail is impeccable throughout, from the vintage automobiles on the streets of Hammond through to the wonderful array of forties-era toys on display under the Parkers' Christmas tree. So too does Clark exhibit a keen eye for the rituals and traditions of childhood, from the legendary frozen flagpole incident to the ongoing territorial skirmishes between Ralphie and his younger brother Randy. Even Ralphie's encounters with paper-tiger bully Skut Farkus are transformed into a clash of the titans, the mundanity of this everyday schoolyard conflict seeming like a monumental struggle from the viewpoint of youth. Jean Shepherd's voice drips with reminiscent zeal as he so very effectively narrates the film's action from the point of view of an adult Ralphie, who is affectionately looking back upon his bygone childhood with the benefit of wistful hindsight (an analogous approach, similarly combined with colourful daydream scenes, was later used to great effect in television's highly successful series *The Wonder Years*, 1988-93). Yet perhaps most immediate impression of all is the tangible sense that everyone involved in the film seems to be having a lot of fun, most especially in the delightfully whimsical fantasy sequences.

Clark appears intent on presenting the flipside of the festive season that he had brought to audiences in the darkly threatening *Black Christmas*, and indeed the fond collection of memories presented in *A Christmas Story* is deeply evocative of a time and a place that contemporary audiences were all too aware had passed into memory, albeit the memory of the collective national consciousness. He is careful never to allow the film to sink into a quagmire of treacly sentimentalism, peppering the narrative with bittersweet reminders that for young Ralphie, childhood is on the cusp of passing (as we see in his bitter disillusionment over the decoder key which can be used only to decrypt commercial advertisements, and the realisation that his much-sought-after BB gun is the absolute pinnacle of Christmas gifts, as though acknowledging that it's likely to be all downhill from hereon in). This kind of unconventional, welcomingly cheerful nostalgia was the perfect antidote for audiences who had been facing the grim realities of resurgent Cold War tensions and the economic turbulence of the early eighties. Like *Trading Places*, released in the same year, *A Christmas Story* faced the difficulty of appearing in cinemas at a time when Christmas films had been out of vogue for over two decades, and thus Clark works hard to articulate a kind of national longing for a bygone golden age in much the same way that *Trading Places* had succeeded in presenting a timely commentary on the nature and distribution of wealth in a modern context. The two films had radically different themes and approaches, and yet both are acutely concerned with making the Christmas film relevant for contemporary cinemagoing audiences.

Another topic which was raised by *A Christmas Story*, and one that would be revisited by other films later in the decade, was the commoditisation of Christmas. Although this had become a staple theme of many Christmas films since the late forties, *A Christmas Story* seems intently focused on emphasising that the commercialisation of the festive season had been a long-ongoing process, and that it was unfair to situate any criticism that Christmas was being subverted into a protracted marketing campaign solely upon the doorstep of the 1980s. As had been the case with *Trading Places*, Clark chooses to do this not by criticising the mechanics of the free market, but rather by stressing the ambivalence of its social effects upon cultural attitudes. While it is true that Ralphie's desires seem entirely focused upon a mass-marketed toy, its commercial value is less relevant to him than is the intrinsic need to possess what is, in his eyes, the very acme of gifts. Whether his parents or Santa Claus (or even the Easter Bunny) are ultimately responsible for its acquisition is neither here nor there: his intense yet innocent focus on his goal is what is paramount. And yet the audience are left in no doubt that the love and approval of Ralphie's family appears to matter at least as much to him as any materialistic desire: his gratitude and firm acknowledgement that there would never be another present quite like it seems to underscore the fact that the adored BB gun would not be casually cast aside in favour of the next year's favoured craze, but his affection for his parents and brother – with all of their many foibles – is expressed more or less all the way throughout the film. Likewise, the commercial sector is depicted as more than simply an arbiter of skilfully-marketed Christmas goods; it is portrayed as something which typifies convenience just as much as it symbolises acquisitiveness or materialism. Whereas on one hand we see the encroachment of corporate insincerity towards the meaning of Christmas in the form of the cheerless department store Santa's grotto (staffed by stroppy employees who are working strictly to rule, and without much in the way of festive cheer), the other extreme is that of the expediency of service provision: when the Parkers' turkey dinner is ruined, a trip to a nearby restaurant quickly resolves the problem. In this sense, screenwriters Clark, Brown and Shepherd adroitly make the point that in spite of whatever warm glow may be reflected from the memories of our respective childhoods, there never really was a golden age of Christmas – the festive season is, and always has been, exactly what each of us chooses to make it.[1]

Peter Billingsley makes for an agreeable Ralphie Parker, never allowing his performance to stray into mawkishness or excess. His admirable restraint in the role is a key factor in the film's success, for he creates an affable and relatable character who was relevant to child audiences watching in the eighties just as much as he was relatable to mature audiences who were more closely acquainted with the historical period that was being depicted throughout the film's narrative. Billingsley would have been familiar to audiences at the time due to his portrayal of Messy Marvin, the star of Hershey's Chocolate Syrup advertisements throughout the early eighties.[2] He had made his cinematic debut in Joseph Brooks's romantic drama *If Ever I See You Again* (1978), and he continued to build an impressive early filmography with appearances in films such as John Schlesinger's *Honky Tonk Freeway* (1981), David Steinberg's *Paternity* (1981) and Dick Richards's *Death Valley* (1982) before his appearance in *A Christmas Story*. Billingsley was nominated no less than four times for Young Artist Awards, winning in 1987 for his starring role in Hoite C. Caston's *The Dirt Bike Kid* (1985). In later years, he has been a successful screenwriter, director and producer in addition to his continuing acting career.

Just as important to the effectiveness of *A Christmas Story* was the depiction of Ralphie's appealingly offbeat parents. As Mrs Parker, Melinda Dillon creates a engaging and eminently practical home-maker, someone who cares for her young family just as much as she despairs for her husband's oddball schemes. Dillon, who had been active on American television since the early 1960s, was best-known for playing Jillian Guiler in Steven Spielberg's *Close Encounters of the Third Kind* (1977), although she had also appeared in a diverse range of other movies which included Stuart Rosenberg's *The April Fools* (1969), Hal Ashby's *Bound for Glory* (1976) and George Roy Hill's *Slap Shot* (1977). She was nominated for the Best Actress in a Supporting Role Academy Award for her appearance in *Close Encounters of the Third Kind*, and also for her performance in Sydney Pollack's *Absence of Malice* (1981). Additionally, in terms of her connection with Christmas features, she was to play Dulcy in Michael Ray Rhodes's modernised television version of *The Juggler of Notre Dame* (1982), a remake of Milton H. Lehr's 1970 cinematic original. Dillon's down-to-earth approach throughout *A Christmas Story* contrasts perfectly with Darren McGavin's pleasingly eccentric turn as Ralphie's father. A mass of preposterous ideas cloaked beneath a cloud of mild profanity, Mr Parker is one of the most remarkable characters in the film. A gruff but devoted family man with a heart of gold, even his ongoing battle with his wife over the infamous 'leg lamp' does little to dampen his insatiable enthusiasm for the approaching Christmas celebrations. McGavin had been active in film and on television since the mid-1940s. Perhaps best-known to viewers as investigator Carl Kolchak in the memorable but short-lived TV series *Kolchak: The Night Stalker* (1974-75) and its two preceding TV movies (1972, 1973), he had a prolific career as an actor which saw him appearing in episodes from dozens of well-known television series including *Alfred Hitchcock Presents* (1955), *Rawhide* (1961), *Dr Kildare* (1965), *Police Story* (1974), *The Martian Chronicles* (1980), and in the title role of all 79 episodes of *Mike Hammer* (1958-59), a series based upon Mickey Spillane's detective novels. In 1990 he was nominated for an Emmy Award for Outstanding Guest Actor in a Comedy Series for his appearance as Bill Brown in TV series *Murphy Brown* (1988).

A Christmas Story also features many enjoyable supporting performances, including *Black Christmas*'s Les Carlson as the shady Christmas tree salesman and Tedde Moore as Ralphie's slightly prissy schoolteacher, Miss Shields. There is a cameo appearance from Jean Shepherd who, along with the voice of the narrator (the adult Ralphie) and the department store Santa Claus, also appears as a well-dressed man waiting in the queue for Santa's grotto. Bob Clark also appears in an entertaining cameo as Mr Swede, the Parkers' pleasant but rather obtuse neighbour, who is in awe of Mr Parker's overblown account of his 'major award' as the notoriously tacky novelty lamp shines proudly from the family's living room window.

A mixed response from the reviewers of the time awaited *A Christmas Story* on its release. While some praised the film for its skilful evocation of nostalgia surrounding its forties setting,[3] others considered Clark's direction to be leaden, believing that it struggled to convey the subtleties of Shepherd's shrewd sense of humour.[4] However, the film's critical reputation has been greatly enhanced over time. More recent appraisals have praised the universality of the film's appeal, which have enabled it to reach out to audiences of all ages.[5] Some have remarked upon the charming way in which the film examines how the Christmas spirit is able to reveal itself in everyday life,[6] whereas other commentators have singled out Clark's skill in presenting a level-headed depiction of his chosen period, venerating the cultural charm of the time without viewing either youth or the festive season through rose-tinted glasses.[7]

Although *A Christmas Story* was only a moderate box-office success at the time of its cinematic release, it soon followed the likes of *It's a Wonderful Life* and the Alastair Sim version of *Scrooge* onto cable television channels where it rapidly developed a rock-solid cult following. The film's heady mix of humour and nostalgia has proven to be a lasting success with audiences, and it has become so immortalised in festive lore that it is now something of a tradition for it to be broadcast on American cable TV in 24-hour marathons during December.[8] *A Christmas Story* also did well at the awards ceremonies of the time. This was particularly true of the Genie Awards, where the film won the Best Achievement in Direction award for Bob Clark (the accolade was tied with David Cronenberg, who also won that year for his film *Videodrome*, 1983), and also the Best Screenplay award. Additionally, at the same ceremony *A Christmas Story* was nominated for awards in no less than seven other areas: Best Motion Picture, Best Performance by an Actress in a Supporting Role (for Tedde Moore), Best Achievement in Cinematography, Best Achievement in Film Editing, Best Achievement in Costume Design, Best Achievement in Overall Sound, and Best Achievement in Sound Editing. The film's screenplay was nominated for a Writers Guild of America Award for Best Comedy Adapted from Another Medium, while at the Young Artist Awards there were nominations for Peter Billingsley (Best Young Actor in a Motion Picture: Musical, Comedy, Adventure or Drama) and Ian Petrella (Best Young Supporting Actor in a Motion Picture: Musical, Comedy, Adventure or Drama).

In addition to the film's ongoing appeal with audiences, a stage adaptation of *A Christmas Story* was written by Philip Grecian in 2000 and immediately became popular with theatregoers, being performed annually in a variety of venues since its debut. Additionally, Bob Clark was to revisit the same characters in 1994 with his film *It Runs in the Family* (also occasionally known by the title *My Summer Story*). Starring Charles Grodin as Mr Parker, Mary Steenburgen as Mrs Parker and Kieran Culkin as Ralphie, the sequel retained only Tedde Moore from the original cast (again playing Miss Shields) along with the voice of Jean Shepherd, narrating once more in the guise of the adult Ralphie. Although the film has some degree of similarity to the original film, not least in its poignant recollections of childhood experiences, it performed poorly at the box-office and was not a critical success.[9]

With *A Christmas Story*, Bob Clark had presented eighties cinema with one of its most unique, heart-warming depictions of the festive season and, although the scale of his achievement was not immediately obvious at the time of its release, it has remained one of the most perennially successful films in the genre to be produced in that decade. Because of the sheer timelessness of the film's backwards-looking fascination with the customs of yesteryear, it is still regularly entertaining audiences more than a quarter of a century after its cinematic debut. At a time when the very thematic apparatus of the Christmas film was being examined and reconsidered, *A Christmas Story* was a breath of fresh air, its blend of the traditional and the innovative ultimately helping to pave the way for the re-emergence of festive movie-making as a means of commercial and critical interest amongst commentators and audiences.

Historical Context

A Christmas Story was released on 18 November 1983 in the United States. It was only one of a great many films debuting on this day; others included John G. Avildsen's *A Night in Heaven*, Jackie Kong's *The Being*, Paul Lynch's *Cross Country*, Ferdinand Fairfax's *Nate and Hayes*, Richard Fleischer's *Amityville 3-D*, Robert Hiltzik's *Sleepaway Camp*, and - perhaps most noteworthy of all - Barbra Streisand's *Yentl*. Lionel Richie was headlining the Billboard Hot 100 that week with 'All Night Long (All Night)'. In the news headlines at the time, the first cruise missile was sited at Greenham Common in England, and the Turkish Republic of Northern Cyprus was declared.

14

SANTA CLAUS: THE MOVIE (1985)

TriStar Pictures/ Calash Corporation/ GGG/ Santa Claus Ltd.

Director: Jeannot Szwarc
Producers: Ilya Salkind and Pierre Spengler
Screenwriters: David Newman, from a story by Leslie Newman and David Newman

MAIN CAST

David Huddleston	-	Santa Claus
Dudley Moore	-	Patch
John Lithgow	-	B.Z.
Judy Cornwell	-	Mrs Anya Claus
Burgess Meredith	-	The Ancient One
Jeffrey Kramer	-	Dr Eric Towzer
Christian Fitzpatrick	-	Joe
Carrie Kei Heim	-	Cornelia

If Christmas movies in the early eighties had expressed a degree of ambivalence between the conflict that was being established between the mass consumption of the modern age and the altruistic notions of the Christmas spirit, then *Santa Claus: The Movie* was instead to nail its colours firmly to the mast. A stirring clarion call to never forget the simple joy of giving, the film formed the most comprehensive origin story for Santa Claus that had appeared in cinemas up until that point. But ultimately it would prove to be a movie that did not simply focus upon the character of Santa Claus, but one which would examine precisely what it was that this mythic figure has come to stand for in popular culture.

While it is true that *Santa Claus: The Movie* had one of the highest profiles of all Christmas films in the 1980s, it has also become infamous as one of the decade's costliest box-office failures – in terms of its performance in American cinemas, at least. The film was a production of the famous Paris-based Alexander and Ilya Salkind, the father and son team who had so successfully brought comic book hero Superman to the screen in 1978 with Richard Donner's well-received adaptation of the same name. Thus with audience expectations running high, the stage was set for a truly epic interpretation of the life story of a true icon of the festive season.

Santa Claus: The Movie was directed by Jeannot Szwarc, who had been active in television and film since the late 1960s. Szwarc had helmed episodes from popular TV series such as *Ironside* (1968 and 1969), *Alias Smith and Jones* (1971), *Columbo* (1973), *The Six Million Dollar Man* (1974), *Kojak* (thirteen episodes between 1973-77), and no less than nineteen episodes of *Rod Serling's Night Gallery* from 1970 until 1973. His cinematic work in the seventies had included science fiction horror *Bug* (1975) and maritime thriller sequel *Jaws 2* (1978), but it was the early eighties in which his features for the big screen were to become more fully established: time travel adaptation *Somewhere in Time* (1980), spy thriller *Enigma* (1983) and comic book adventure *Supergirl* (1984) had all been reasonably well-received by audiences and many critics, while these films had also featured a prominent range of star names such as Christopher Reeve, Martin Sheen and Peter O'Toole.

Santa Claus: The Movie begins on a Christmas Eve of many centuries ago, in a setting that suggests a period in the early Middle Ages. A large group of enraptured children are listening to an elderly lady (Aimée Delamain), mesmerised by her tales of mythical elves who live at the very top of the world at the North Pole. They are huddled together in a warm log cabin, safe from the harsh blizzard that is blowing outside. Some of the older children are growing listless, however; they are awaiting the arrival of Claus (David Huddleston), a kindly woodcutter who lives nearby with his wife Anya (Judy Cornwell). Sure enough, a sleigh soon arrives outside drawn by reindeer: Claus has made his annual appearance, and is soon joyfully handing out hand-carved wooden toys to the jubilant boys and girls. The villagers are amazed that Claus can find the time to make such beautiful gifts when he works so many long hard hours at his chosen profession, but his wife explains that making Christmas special for the little ones is important to her husband, encouraging him to put in as much effort as is necessary.

Claus is keen to depart, as he has made more toys for children in another village nearby. The villagers urge him to reconsider, given the harshness of the weather, but he protests that his reindeer Donner and Blitzen will be able to get through the snow to their destination. However, their warnings soon transpire to be prescient indeed; some time after departing, the snowfall grows so heavy that Claus eventually loses his way. The reindeer, unable to draw the sleigh through such treacherous conditions, collapse from the cold. With no way of leaving, Claus and Anya are trapped in the sleigh, the freezing temperatures eventually making them succumb to unconsciousness as the snow falls even heavier.

When they awake, the forest around them has disappeared. In its place are the icy plains of the North Pole, where a huge, spectral building takes form in front of their astounded eyes. They are further dumbfounded when a group of diminutive, brightly-clothed people approach their sleigh. The head of the little band introduces himself as Dooley (John Barrard), who explains that Claus and Anya's arrival has long been expected. Dooley tells the couple that he and his colleagues are from a race known as elves – not the fanciful legend that the old storyteller had spoken of, but real, flesh-and-blood creatures. The elves introduce Claus to what is to be a new home for Anya and himself – a vast workshop at the very top of the world, which is shrouded from the naked eye.

Inside, Claus is impressed by the elves' expansive toy-making facilities, and is given a guided tour by Dooley and another of the elf supervisors, Puffy (Anthony O'Donnell). The couple watch in wonder as they witness the painstaking creation of many painted wooden toys of all shapes and sizes. Claus also becomes bemused by Patch (Dudley Moore), an elf with a seemingly unquenchable interest in science and technology who seems determined to impress the new arrivals. Eventually, the elves lead Claus and Anya to a gargantuan storeroom which is packed from floor to ceiling with immaculately-built wooden toys of all shapes and sizes. Dooley explains that Claus has been set the task of delivering all of these many gifts to children all across the world. Awestruck, Claus responds that there is no way that he could possibly live long enough to perform such a task, but Dooley is amused by his doubt. Claus and Anya, he clarifies, will both live eternally – their lifespan is now as infinite as that of the elves.

Taken aback by these miraculous events, neither Claus nor Anya are able to sleep at night. Claus decides to pay a visit to his reindeer, only to discover Patch talking to them kindly in an attempt to persuade them to eat. Like Claus himself, Donner and Blitzen are a little stunned by their circumstances and feel reluctant to consume much. Pleased at Patch's gentle manner, Claus asks to meet the many other reindeer in the stables and is soon introduced to Prancer and Dancer, Comet and Cupid, and so on. He is baffled at why the workshop would require so many reindeer, but Patch remains tight-lipped on the details, instead telling Claus that all will be revealed in the fullness of time.

As time passes, Claus becomes overjoyed as he watches the creation of so many wonderful new toys for the world's children. The elves run an incredibly efficient operation which is administered with clockwork precision, and yet each and every gift is made with painstaking care and attention. Meanwhile, some elves are treating the reindeers' food with a mysterious magic dust, and Anya is enthusiastically overseeing the creation of a new fur-trimmed suit for Claus which is being created by elf tailor Goober (Melvyn Hayes). Claus can only observe with wonder and astonishment as he sees simple blocks of wood rapidly turned into beautifully crafted toys, which are then flawlessly gift-wrapped and placed into large parcel sacks.

Soon Christmas is approaching, and Claus – now decked out in his freshly-tailored red suit, and standing by a grand sleigh drawn by all of the workshop's reindeer – is addressed by the Ancient One (Burgess Meredith), the oldest and wisest of all the elves. He tells Claus that his appointment to his new role is the fulfilment of a prophecy that one day a skilled craftsman and artist, having no son or daughter of his own, would come to distribute gifts to every child on Earth. Claus is sceptical of how he will be able to visit the home of each and every boy and girl in just one night, much less have the ability to do so on an annual basis, but the elderly elf explains that time will effectively stand still for the period of Claus's travels, allowing him to take as long as is necessary to deliver presents to everyone across the globe. Elated that Claus will be taking up the mantle of distributing Christmas gifts from that point onwards, the Ancient One proudly proclaims that the jolly, red-suited toymaker will be known henceforth as Santa Claus. Taking up his seat in the majestic new sleigh, Claus watches as the elves feed the reindeer from plates of victuals treated with magical dust. The reindeers' antlers then convulse with a golden light, the animals appearing mystically energised. Before he knows it, Claus's sleigh is flying out of the workshop and into the air, leading him on his long journey.

As the centuries pass, the legend of Santa Claus begins to spread. Children all across the globe, delighted with their gifts, start writing letters to Santa, thanking him for his generosity and giving suggestions of what they would like him to bring them in the coming year. Soon the elves are inundated with correspondence, which is magically whisked out of the homes of each child when they aren't looking and sent through the skies all the way to the North Pole workshop. After many years have gone by, Claus receives a letter from a little girl who is upset at the way her brother is mistreating her beloved kitten in the lead up to Christmas. Infuriated by this cruelty, Anya suggests that Claus should only deliver presents to children who have behaved themselves throughout the year. Albeit with some reluctance, Claus agrees to her proposal and tells Dooley to compile an annual list of which children have been naughty, and which have been nice.

As the years pass and he eventually reaches the modern day, Claus is slowly becoming worn out by all of the requests from the children of the world. Their Christmas wishes have led to an increasingly packed schedule, making it difficult for Claus to get everything done in time for each following year. Anya recommends that he think about employing an assistant to ease his burden, but Claus is hesitant, feeling that nobody would want all of the hard work that would accompany such a position. Dooley disagrees, however: he can think of two elves who would be only too happy to be considered for the post.

Meanwhile, in a cold and snowy New York City, the homeless Joe (Christian

Fitzpatrick) is struggling against the freezing conditions. The fact that everyone around him is so full of the Christmas spirit does little to help his general mood of despondency, particularly as he is trying hard to keep out of view from any passing police patrols. He watches with disdain as a street corner Santa (Walter Goodman), who claims to be collecting for charity, pockets the donation money for himself. But Joe is unaware that he too is being watched; a little girl named Cornelia (Carrie Kei Heim) is looking out at him from an opulent town house across the street. They catch each other's gaze momentarily, but Cornelia is soon called away by her guardian with a warning to concentrate on her homework instead of idle distractions. It seems that for all her luxurious surroundings, Cornelia is almost as unhappy as the chilly, penniless Joe.

At the North Pole, Claus is unsure whether to choose the technologically-minded Patch as his assistant, or the reliable traditionalist Puffy. He tells both elves to apply themselves to their own method of toy production; the one who is able to yield the best results will be awarded the job. Patch immediately goes to work on an elaborate production-line system, which initially proves able to construct and paint complex toys with precision. However, when Patch steps up manufacturing to a hazardous rate of production, the toys quickly become unsafe – steps in the process are missed out in error, leading to the toys ending up in a dangerous condition. Claus is unaware of this fact, as is Patch, so when he sees the prodigious output of Patch's manufacturing – which appears to be much greater than the respectable amount produced by the old-school toymaker Puffy – he has no hesitation in awarding the innovative elf with the treasured assistant's role.

On Christmas Eve, a miserable Joe is forced to watch from the street as families gather together for meals in the warmth. Cornelia is not oblivious to his plight, however – when the opportunity arises, she sneaks some food and drink outside for him to collect, though the two never actually have the chance to meet. As Claus flies over the city on his annual rounds, he spots Joe warming himself near a brazier and takes pity on him. Claus decides to take the youngster for a ride on his sleigh, an experience which takes Joe aback – until that night, he had never believed that Santa Claus even existed. Claus brings Joe along on his travels as he distributes gifts to children throughout the city, and eventually they arrive at Cornelia's house. The young girl is amazed to discover Santa himself delivering presents to her home, though Claus feels a little self-conscious at having been caught in person. Joe and Cornelia recognise each other and quickly strike up a friendship. Cornelia offers to prepare some food for him while Claus chooses to depart, allowing the two acquaintances to get to know each other better. As he leaves via the building's chimney, he promises Joe that they will meet again.

After Christmas has passed, Dooley and Claus are dismayed when dozens of Patch's wooden tricycles and carts are returned to the North Pole as defective goods. Never in all the centuries of Claus's gift distribution has any child been compelled to return a faulty present. A deeply saddened Claus is forced to dismiss Patch from his post as assistant, but the elf is so ashamed at his lack of quality control that he saves Claus the trouble and resigns instead, handing over his cherished assistant's apron. As Puffy is awarded the position in his stead, Patch becomes so miserable that he decides to leave the workshop in search of pastures new. Stopping only to wish the reindeer a mournful farewell, Patch departs without telling anyone of his plans, taking with him only a bag of the elves' magic dust.

At the same time, in Washington D.C., a Senate hearing has been convened to investigate the unsafe toys that are being manufactured by shady businessman B.Z. (John Lithgow). The panel's chairman (Jerry Harte) is appalled when the lack of safety involved in the construction of B.Z.'s toys becomes apparent – a cheap doll made from a highly flammable material easily bursts into flame when in brief contact with a cigarette lighter, while another is shown to be stuffed with broken glass, nails and sawdust. Trying hard not to appear ruffled, B.Z. assures the investigating panel that he will look into the matter and ensure that these dangerous exhibits are simply a couple of isolated, defective units. But the chairman is wholly unconvinced by these assurances, and demands that every B.Z. toy on the market is withdrawn from sale immediately, threatening the revocation of B.Z.'s licence to manufacture and trade if he does not comply.

Brushing his way past the press, B.Z. is clearly flustered behind his cool façade. His chief of staff, Dr Eric Towzer (Jeffrey Kramer) informs him that the company's sales have suffered badly through the bad publicity surrounding their manufacturing issues, and that things will need to turn around rapidly to save the company from disaster. But B.Z.'s fate takes an unexpected turn when, returning to his office, he finds Patch. The elf seems to have appeared there out of thin air, much to B.Z.'s bewilderment. On his arrival in New York, Patch has come across an elaborate shop window display showcasing B.Z.'s toys, and – believing the disreputable manufacturer to be a modern-day equivalent of Santa Claus – is keen to offer his services to him. As altruism is an entirely foreign concept to B.Z., he is suspicious of Patch's motives, but the elf explains that he has conceived of a way to deliver an exciting new toy to children through B.Z.'s manufacturing facilities, delighting the planet's youth while restoring his tarnished reputation with Claus and the other elves. B.Z. initially believes Patch to be an escaped lunatic, but soon warms to his idea when the diminutive new arrival professes to have no knowledge of money, thus making him eminently vulnerable to being swindled. Patch suggests that he uses his magic elf dust to create special lollipops which will be advertised on television all across the world, but which will be distributed for free. Scandalised by the notion of giving anything away for nothing, B.Z. eventually realises that if he does share out the lollipops at no cost, he has a unique chance to restore his company's badly-damaged standing with the public. Furthermore, if Patch's treats are as successful as he believes they will be, customers will be potentially willing to pay huge amounts to try them again. His curiosity (and business acumen) well and truly piqued, B.Z. agrees to turn over the use of his company's factories to Patch.

Back at the workshop, Claus is worried about the whereabouts of his old friend. Anya and the elves are also concerned about Patch, but Claus feels particularly guilty, worrying about his own culpability in his former assistant's departure. He tries to take his mind off of things by carving a wooden figure, just as he did in the olden days, but Anya soon notices that Claus has unconsciously modelled the toy on Patch. As Christmas once again approaches, however, B.Z. airs a cheesy commercial which features Patch publicising his new lollipops. The elves pick up the transmission, and are dismayed to find their lost friend working for a rival organisation. Aggrieved by Patch's involvement with a toy company, Claus nonetheless voices relief that they now know that the wayward elf is safe. But he has little time to ponder the situation: Christmas Eve has arrived, and he has presents to deliver once again.

This Christmas, however, Santa's sleigh has a competitor in the skies: in New York, Patch is launching the Patchmobile, a futuristic car (albeit one which appears to be made from painted wood) which runs on magic elf dust. Launching into the air with great excitement, Patch sets to work delivering a magic lollipop into the home of every child. Claus soon discovers one of the sparkling sweetmeats under the Christmas tree of every home as he makes his rounds, making him question whether he still has relevance to the world's boys and girls. But he is soon cheered when he discovers his friend Joe and presents him with a gift of his own – the handmade wooden model of Patch. Claus seems touched that the sceptical young man has come to trust him, particularly when the rest of the planet seems to have lost faith in his purpose.

On Christmas morning, curious young children unwrap Patch's lollipops and discover that they have the short-lived ability to float in mid-air. Everyone is entranced by the unique sweets, with the exception of Cornelia: she has little time for the greedy B.Z., who has by now been revealed as her step-uncle and usually-absent guardian. But the company's magical gifts soon cause a media sensation, with journalists from press and television swarming into B.Z's boardroom seeking further details. B.Z. is evasive, but leads the reporters to believe that another, even more incredible product will soon be on the way. Rapidly making his departure when the questions start becoming more awkward, B.Z. tries to persuade Patch to manufacture a new successor to the lollipops – a candy cane which contains an even more concentrated formula of elf dust. Patch is reluctant; believing that he has now proven his worth as an innovator to Claus, he is now ready to return to his friends at the North Pole. But B.Z. remains persistent, assuring Patch that this is just one last favour to bring lasting joy to children all around the world. Privately, he knows that the product will enable anyone who consumes it to fly rather than simply hover; an unmatchable piece of merchandise that will net him a fortune in revenue. Somewhat unenthusiastically, Patch tells him that such an item could theoretically be ready by the following December, but B.Z. is disinclined to wait for Christmas to come around again – he wants to strike while the iron is hot, and maximise on the intense media interest. To this end, he declares that the candy canes should be ready for distribution on March the 25th, exactly three months afterwards: a date which he proudly designates Christmas II.

Claus is deeply despairing at the rise of B.Z.'s gimmicks, feeling certain that the world no longer has any place for him. He laments the fact that society has changed so much since he started delivering presents that he has become a relic of a bygone age. The festive season has become so commercially-oriented, he feels, that no-one seems to take delight in the simple act of giving any longer. The elves try to cheer him up with innovative new toys, but nothing seems to stir up any enthusiasm in him. For the first time in his life, Claus feels aimless in his calling.

B.Z. is awakened early in the morning by Towzer, who is the bearer of grim news. Patch's candy canes, which are based upon a very condensed recipe of magic elf dust, are also proving to be extremely volatile; when they are placed near a source of heat, they cause a violent explosion. But B.Z. is unconcerned with what he considers to be a trifling detail; his plan is to pocket as much as he can in advance payments for the new product, and then leave the country for Brazil before the canes' lethal nature is uncovered. This way he will be safely free from any punishment or threat of extradition while Patch, who is blissfully unaware of the sweets' instability, will be forced to face the consequences. B.Z. is outraged when he discovers that his conversation has been overheard; Cornelia has smuggled Joe into the basement due to him suffering a bad cold, and a random sneeze tips off the corrupt toymaker to the boy's presence. He has Joe forcibly restrained and taken to his factory, where he will be kept incarcerated in order to avoid leaking the news of the canes' explosive nature.

However, B.Z. is blissfully unaware that Cornelia has also been eavesdropping on his nefarious plans. She quickly composes a letter to Claus, which instantaneously arrives at the North Pole – much to the surprise of Dooley, who isn't expecting any Christmas requests so early in the year. On learning that Joe is in danger, Claus quickly gets his sleigh ready, but the elves inform him that two of the reindeer are ill with the flu. Knowing that he will be forced to enact his rescue with only six reindeer instead of the usual eight, Claus heads straight to New York and retrieves Cornelia from her home. Together, they rush off to rescue Joe, but discover that Patch has beaten them to it – having stumbled across the captured youth in the factory, the homesick elf has released him and offered passage to the North Pole, where Patch intends to give his supply of candy canes to Claus. This will not only restore his tarnished reputation, he feels, but should also give Santa the year off from making new toys. But Patch is unconscious of the canes' instability in the presence of heat, and has stashed a huge amount of them into the storage compartment of the Patchmobile.

A tense chase ensues, where Claus and Cornelia pursue the errant Patch and his new friend Joe. As the Patchmobile races towards the Arctic, its lethal cargo begins to heat up, and Claus – seeing a plume of smoke rising from the flying car – realises that time is of the essence. Persuading his reindeer to perform an intricate 360° loop, Claus is only just able to manoeuvre his sleigh under the Patchmobile in time to retrieve Joe and Patch as the car explodes into a sensational fireball. The old friends are overjoyed to see each other safe and well once again.

Returning to the workshop, the elves seem jubilant at the return of the long-lost Patch. Amazed to see Santa's residence in person, Cornelia and Joe beg Claus to allow them to stay there until the following Christmas. Laughing, Dooley remarks that he will now need to add the title of schoolteacher to his list of duties. Cornelia seems unconcerned at what her step-uncle's reaction to her apparent disappearance may be, though: unbeknown to her or the others, B.Z. has performed a vanishing act of his own. As the police storm his factory and take Towzer into custody, the malevolent businessman stuffs himself with Patch's candy canes, allowing him to fly out of his office and evade justice. But unfortunately for B.Z., the canes have a rather more extreme effect on his physiology than he had intended – while Claus and his friends celebrate at the North Pole, the crooked industrialist is left floating in orbit around the Earth with no idea how to return home.

Santa Claus: The Movie is very much a film of two halves. The beginning of the movie is a very effective exploration of the genesis of the Santa Claus figure, charting his transformation from a selfless, kind-hearted woodcutter to the bringer of joy and happiness to all the children of the world. This presents a clear break from traditional depictions of Santa Claus as a derivation of the Christian St Nicholas,[1] offering instead an alternative interpretation where Claus's powers are magical rather than spiritual in origin. That said, more or less everything else which surrounds the Santa Claus mythos in popular culture is present and correct throughout the film – the elaborate elf-run workshop at the North Pole, the cookies and milk on the mantelpiece, the 'naughty and nice' list, and even an airing of Clement Clarke Moore's poem *A Visit from St Nicholas* (better known today as *'Twas the Night Before Christmas*).

However, the film's latter half often appears rushed and, in many ways, is an awkward fit with what has preceded it. With such a charming and elaborate setup of Claus's new home, including the affable elves' mystical motivations and the amazing scale of the North Pole workshop, the narrative's abrupt collision with the present day can't help but leave much of the second and third acts seeming a little flat by comparison. Having clearly established Claus's altruistic kindness, the film's later sections set up the ruthless manufacturer B.Z. as the very embodiment of self-interest and monetary greed: the absolute antithesis of everything that Santa and the Christmas spirit seek to represent. The over-the-top, cigar-chewing industrialist, complete with expensive suit and spats, is the scheming architect of Christmas II: a superficial corporate monstrosity which makes a mockery of the very nature of the festive season. While previous entrepreneurial nemeses of the festive season such as Mr Potter and the Duke Brothers may have considered Christmas to be an irrelevance at best, or an inconvenience at worst, the disreputable B.Z. wants nothing less but to stamp out Santa (and, by extension, Christmas) altogether, all in the name of profit.

This, perhaps, best highlights one of the core thematic tensions within *Santa Claus: The Movie*: in spite of the film's strong defence of generosity and munificence, opposing the corporate mentality and excessive individual materialism, it is clearly itself a commercial endeavour – a feature which has been carefully structured to appeal to the broadest possible demographic and the largest possible audience.[2] David Newman's screenplay expresses concerns about the corrosive effect of a deconstructed postmodern culture on long-established Christmas traditions, best articulated through Claus's soul-searching with regard to how he can possibly find a role for himself in today's aggressively consumer-oriented society. Yet the North Pole workshop's output is shown to be entirely isolated from any kind of market system, emphasising the virtue of the elves' generosity in stark contrast to B.Z.'s uncompromising covetousness.[3] Although it presents a narrative which is cautionary in its view of modernity, the film nonetheless seems so eager to appear relevant to contemporary secular audiences that it is at pains to dissociate its protagonist from the pre-existing religious legend of St Nicholas, instead creating a new identity for him which is based entirely around the expectations of popular culture.[4] For B.Z., however, even the redemptive qualities of Christmas cannot provide him with a lifeline. Having squandered any potential for goodwill during his initial partnership with Patch, B.Z.'s greed eventually destroys him, underpinning the damaging nature of excessive (and insatiable) materialism. Thus the point is made that even although rabid profit-making has become synonymous with the modern age, sometimes even at the expense of authenticity or quality (as B.Z.'s dubious goods so emphatically demonstrate), no amount of acquisitiveness can ever replace the lasting satisfaction that comes from philanthropy.[5]

There is much to recommend the production of *Santa Claus: The Movie*, not least Stephanie McMillan's outstanding set decoration and Bob Ringwood's innovative costume design. Szwarc conjures up a workshop for Santa Claus which is surely the stuff of dreams for any young viewer, with a painstaking attention to detail that quickly builds a tangible sense of wonder. This is especially true of the wonderfully expressive Animatronic reindeer, which brighten up every scene that they appear in. Henry Mancini provides a dynamic and emotionally moving score, blending many styles and supplementing the soundtrack with the music of many well-known Christmas carols as well as effective contributions from artists such as Aled Jones, Sheena Easton and The Ambrosian Children's Chorus. The film also benefits from many pleasing supporting performances and cameo appearances from veteran actors such as Burgess Meredith, John Barrard, Jeffrey Kramer, Don Estelle, Judy Cornwell and Melvyn Hayes.

It seems obvious to note that any film entitled *Santa Claus: The Movie* is almost certain to live or die based upon the skill of its lead actor, and in David Huddleston the role was occupied by a performer who truly looked the part, successfully embodying the humanity and compassion of the festive spirit. Huddleston's Santa was more kindly than jolly, however, and his interpretation of the character feels slightly uneven at times – warm and affable for the most part, but also oddly self-contained at times. Yet Huddleston proves himself more than worthy of the famous red bobble-hat, and it is of little surprise that for many members of the MTV Generation who grew up with the film, his portrayal of Santa Claus has become the definitive one. Huddleston had been acting on television and in film since the early sixties, and was perhaps best known for his prolific appearances in Westerns such as Howard Hawks's *Rio Lobo* (1970), Robert Benton's *Bad Company* (1972) and Ted Kotcheff's *Billy Two Hats* (1974). He parodied his Western character actor persona magnificently in Mel Brooks's anarchic comedy *Blazing Saddles* (1974) as the patriarchal Olson Johnson. A versatile actor, he continued to be active on television throughout the seventies and eighties while also appearing in a wide variety of different film genres in the cinema – his performances included roles in Jack Conrad's crime drama *Country Blue* (1973), John Sturges's police action movie *McQ* (1974), Peter Hyams's science fiction conspiracy thriller *Capricorn One* (1977), Enzo Barboni's action spoof *Go For It* (1983), and Sig Shore's tongue-in-cheek comedy *The Act* (1984). In 1990 he was nominated for an Emmy Award in the Outstanding Guest Actor in a Comedy Series category for his appearance as Grandpa Arnold in TV's *The Wonder Years* (1988).

Dudley Moore shines as Patch, the elf inventor who is so keen to assist Claus that his ambition clouds his judgement, leading him into a journey of self-discovery that defines the second and third acts of the film. One of the film's true masterstrokes lay in the casting of the charismatic Moore spectacularly against type – he was far better known to audiences of the time for his sophisticated wit and devilish charm – and he makes the most of his character's appealing naiveté to create a likeable eccentric, a kind of *idiot savant* who is simultaneously brilliant and blundering. In spite of Patch's rather overwrought punning (hardly a scene passes without mention of 'elf-confidence', 'elf-control', 'elf-awareness', etc.), some of the film's most memorable sequences feature his marvellous Heath Robinson-style inventions, breathing new life into both the timeless traditionalism of the North Pole and the bleak, impersonal B.Z. factories. Moore was recognisable to a generation of British viewers for his television series *Not Only But Also* (1965-70), in collaboration with Peter Cook, and for films such as Bryan Forbes's *The Wrong Box* (1966), Stanley Donen's *Bedazzled* (1967) and Richard Lester's *The Bed Sitting Room* (1969). He continued to be highly active both on television and in the cinema throughout the 1970s, appearing in films including William Sterling's *Alice's Adventures in Wonderland* (1972), Colin Higgins's *Foul Play* (1978) and Paul Morrissey's *The Hound of the Baskervilles* (1978) before achieving major success in Blake Edwards's *10* (1979) and most especially Steve Gordon's *Arthur* (1981), his performance in the latter gaining him an Academy Award nomination for Best Actor in a Leading Role. He was nominated for Golden Globe Awards five times in his career, winning on two occasions - for his lead role in *Arthur*, and for his performance in Blake Edwards's *Micki + Maude* (1984). Featuring alongside Moore in the pivotal role of B.Z. was the always-watchable John Lithgow. Making the most of his every appearance, Lithgow appears to take great delight in embellishing the disreputable character's palpable greed and moral laxity, giving a scene-stealing performance which becomes so over the top that it is one of the most entertaining aspects of the whole film. A highly successful character actor, Lithgow's cinematic career began in the early 1970s when he appeared in Paul Williams's comedy drama *Dealing: Or the Berkeley-to-Boston Forty-Brick Lost-Bag Blues* (1972). He made appearances in films such as Jeremy Kagan's *The Big Fix* (1978), Robert M. Young's *Rich Kids* (1979) and Bob Fosse's *All That Jazz* (1979) before going on to even greater success in the eighties. His profile was considerably enhanced following performances in a variety of features which included George Roy Hill's *The World According to Garp* (1982), George Miller's segment of *Twilight Zone: The Movie* (1983), James L. Brooks's

Terms of Endearment (1983), Herbert Ross's *Footloose* (1984) and Peter Hyams's *2010* (1984). He has been nominated twice for Academy Awards, for his supporting performances in *The World According to Garp* and *Terms of Endearment*. Later in his career, he was to be nominated on four occasions for Golden Globe Awards for his television work, winning twice (for appearances in *3rd Rock from the Sun* in 1997 and *Dexter* in 2010), and his TV performances also led to him being nominated for an astonishing eleven Emmy Awards throughout his career, winning on four occasions to date (in 1986, 1996, 1997 and 1999).

Upon its release, *Santa Claus: The Movie* met with a critical response that could only be described as lukewarm at best. While some reviews praised the entertainment value of Lithgow's enthusiastically exaggerated performance,[6] others felt that the film suffered from the fact that the antagonism generated by the boggling B.Z. was altogether too muted and is introduced into proceedings too late, meaning that the narrative ultimately lacked the excitement that should have been generated by the tension and dispute between Claus's guileless generosity and B.Z.'s profit-driven avarice.[7] A common response amongst commentators was that the opening scenes of the film were very effectively staged, engendering a sense of awe and wonder, but that the epic tone that these sequences suggest is soon squandered by the remainder of the narrative, which appears somewhat bland and directionless by comparison.[8] This criticism has continued into the present day, with retrospective reviews commending the film for the beauty and grandeur of the early scenes at the North Pole,[9] but censuring it for the way in which the transition between the mythic splendour of Santa's workshop and the lacklustre urban setting of the present day sequences clashes so awkwardly.[10]

Some recent reviews have drawn attention to the irony of the fact that *Santa Claus: The Movie*'s condemnation of unchecked commercialism was ultimately to coincide with the film becoming one of the greatest box-office calamities of the eighties – at least with audiences in the United States.[11] Having been produced on an estimated budget of $50,000,000,[12] the film's domestic gross in the U.S. would prove to be only $23,717,291.[13] Given the copious publicity for *Santa Claus: The Movie* on the build-up to its release, its failure with American audiences couldn't possibly have been anything other than a huge disappointment to the film-makers involved. Even although the film's fortunes were very different in Britain and continental Europe, where *Santa Claus: The Movie* performed favourably with audiences and actually became a commercial smash hit overall, doing much more than simply breaking even, the lack of interest in the crucially important North American market precluded the possibility of any cinematic sequels or spin-offs going into production. That said, the film has remained popular enough in recent years to have achieved releases on both DVD and Blu-Ray, and it has also become a regular staple of festive television schedules.

In the end, it seems that the cause of the critical indifference surrounding *Santa Claus: The Movie* may stem not from any one particular deficiency in the film's production, but rather that it tries a little too hard to be all things to all audiences. On one hand, it strives to be a captivating account of how one of the most prominent emblems of Christmas came into being (in terms of modern interpretation, at least), while on the other it seeks to become a moral tale in a contemporary setting that has relevance to modern audiences. Although the film's uneven structure and occasionally disjointed narrative doesn't quite succeed in its attempt to fulfil every aspiration that it sets itself, its peculiar mix of fable and contemporaneity – along with the undeniable quality and intricacy of the production – combine to make *Santa Claus: The Movie* a striking curiosity which, even today, seems quite arresting amongst Christmas films.

Historical Context

Santa Claus: The Movie made its American cinematic debut on 29 November 1985. It was the only major release of a film in the United States on that day. Starship's song 'We Built This City' was at the number one spot on the Billboard Hot 100 during that week. In current affairs at the time, a nuclear test was performed by France at Muruora Island, and Random House famously purchased the rights to publish the memoirs of former U.S. President Richard M. Nixon.

15

SCROOGED (1988)

Paramount Pictures / Mirage Productions

Director: Richard Donner
Producers: Richard Donner and Art Linson
Screenwriters: Mitch Glazer and Michael O'Donoghue

MAIN CAST

Bill Murray	-	Frank Cross
Karen Allen	-	Claire Phillips
John Forsythe	-	Lew Hayward
John Glover	-	Brice Cummings
Bobcat Goldthwait	-	Eliot Loudermilk
David Johansen	-	The Ghost of Christmas Past
Carol Kane	-	The Ghost of Christmas Present
Robert Mitchum	-	Preston Rhinelander

By the time of the late eighties, the central theme of Christmas films in this decade – that is, that the corporate over-commercialisation of Christmas was actively presenting itself as threat to the meaning and spirit of the season – had become so well-established in the public consciousness that it had almost reached a point of over-familiarity. Films such as *Trading Places* and *Santa Claus: The Movie*, together (to a lesser extent) with other entries in the genre such as Phillip Borsos's *One Magic Christmas* (1985) and John R. Cherry III's *Ernest Saves Christmas* (1988), had emphasised the need to value and protect the Christmas spirit at all costs, lest that its importance and central significance to the festive season risk becoming lost in a neverending torrent of economic commoditisation and trendy toy advertisements.

Scrooged, however, was to take a slightly different tack. Whereas other Christmas films of the eighties had presented a stream of contemporary corporate villains as their antagonists – characters who exhibited neither conscience nor virtue, such as B.Z. and the Duke Brothers – *Scrooged* was instead to turn the tables by examining in detail the nature and motivations of just such an over-ambitious, business-focused scoundrel. With its protagonist Frank Cross, *Scrooged* would not only follow the traditional path of moral transformation that had been typical of so many Christmas films, but – in the process of his redemption – also illuminated something of the cynical, merchandise-focused and marketing-obsessed culture of consumption that had taken root throughout the course of the 1980s.

Although a contemporary updating of *A Christmas Carol* had been attempted before (most notably in the case of Eric Till's *An American Christmas Carol*, which had been broadcast on television by ABC in 1979), *Scrooged*'s finely tuned sense of modern-day edginess and the scathing bite of the screenplay's supremely sardonic wit meant that the film seemed tailor-made for the time of its production. The intense aura of cynicism which is evoked lent *Scrooged* a different kind of relevance to audiences than the other, much more traditional adaptation of Dickens's tale that had been released earlier in the decade. Clive Donner's *A Christmas Carol* (1984) had aired on the CBS television network in the United States, but had gone on to receive a cinematic release in the UK. With a starry cast that had included George C. Scott as Ebenezer Scrooge, David Warner as Bob Cratchit and Frank Finlay as the Ghost of Jacob Marley, this atmospheric film had received an amenable reception from critics on both sides of the Atlantic. But *Scrooged*, with its relentless sense of world-weary modernity and a complex metanarrative, was in no danger of being mistaken for the customary Victoriana established in most filmic variations on Dickens's tale.

Responsible for bringing the project to the big screen was industry veteran Richard Donner. A long-time stalwart of film and television, Donner had helmed episodes of some of America's best-known TV series throughout the 1960s and 70s. His filmography reads like a veritable who's-who of classic American TV: Donner's early career included work on series such as *Have Gun, Will Travel* (1961-62), *The Twilight Zone* (1963-64), *The Man from U.N.C.L.E.* (1964), *Gilligan's Island* (1964-65), *Get Smart* (1965), *The Fugitive* (1966), *The Wild Wild West* (1966), *Ironside* (1972), *Kojak* (1973-74) and *The Streets of San Francisco* (1974), amongst a great many others. He had also directed films for the cinema at that time, such as crime farce *Salt and Pepper* (1968) and romantic comedy-drama *Lola* (1970), but he shot to prominence soon afterwards with supernatural horror *The Omen* (1976) and then the vastly successful, all-star comic book adaptation *Superman: The Movie* (1978). Throughout the early eighties, he directed features in a wide variety of genres including emotional drama (*Inside Moves*, 1980), controversial comedy (*The Toy*, 1982), romantic fantasy (*Ladyhawke*, 1985), family adventure (*The Goonies*, 1985) and crime thriller (*Lethal Weapon*, 1987). Also a producer and occasional screenwriter, Donner has also become known for the many cameo appearances that he has made in his films. In 2000 he was conferred the Hollywood Film Award for Outstanding Achievement in Directing at the Hollywood Film Festival.

It's the lead-up to Christmas in the New York City of the late eighties, and TV network president Frank Cross (Bill Murray) is far from the epitome of festive cheer. He seems to have little enthusiasm for the festive line-up that's been presented by his production panel, which includes promos for *The Night the Reindeer Died*, an action thriller which sees Santa's workshop stormed by terrorists only to be defended by a machine-gun-toting Lee Majors, and *Bob Goulet's Cajun Christmas*, where singer-actor Robert Goulet sings a cheerful selection of carols aboard a rowing boat while simultaneously attempting to dodge a pursuing alligator. Unimpressed, Cross asks to see the promo for the network's forthcoming TV movie *Scrooge*, an international production of *A Christmas Carol* which is due to be broadcast live to air on Christmas Eve. *Scrooge* has cost his network (the fictional IBC) an eye-watering $40million to produce, and Cross is livid when he discovers that the promo reel presents a rather cosy, traditional showcase for the feature which includes its wide range of stars (such as Buddy Hackett as Scrooge, John Houseman as the narrator and gymnast Mary Lou Retton as Tiny Tim).

The assembled executives are either too sycophantic or too spineless to disagree with Cross's acidic derision towards their efforts, but one of them – Eliot Loudermilk (Bobcat Goldthwait) – decides to buck the trend. He bravely tells Cross that, in spite of whatever personal misgivings he may have about the promo, the feedback from the public has generally been good. But Cross is not satisfied, saying that it isn't enough that the audience *want* to see the programme: they need to be filled with terror at the very prospect of missing it. He then runs an alternative promo that he has produced himself, full of unsettling imagery and ending on an apocalyptic note that suggests that *Scrooge* is essential viewing: neglecting to watch the broadcast could put the viewer's very life at risk, according to the closing slogan. The executives are stunned at Cross's single-mindedly merciless pursuit of ratings, and most can't leave the room fast enough as soon as the meeting is over. But Loudermilk feels that he has a moral responsibility to speak out, and approaches Cross quietly to recommend that his substituted promo should not be screened due to its inappropriately distressing nature. Cross is outraged that his judgement is being questioned, and promptly has Loudermilk fired from his post before ordering that he be immediately ejected from the building for good measure.

Watching with ill-disguised glee from his palatial office as, many floors below,

Loudermilk is handed the contents of his desk and is shoved off the premises, Cross begins dictating a list of Christmas presents to his secretary Grace Cooley (Alfre Woodard). It soon becomes apparent that almost everyone he knows is being gifted a bath towel monogrammed with the company emblem for the holidays, with the exception of the handful of people that he wants to impress or keep on-side (who will be receiving a state of the art VHS videotape recorder instead). His distinctly grudging roll-call of festive offerings is interrupted by the unexpected arrival of the network's chairman, the powerful but rather eccentric Preston Rhinelander (Robert Mitchum). Rhinelander has discovered some new research which claims that dogs and cats are beginning to take an interest in television programming, and suggests that IBC should start to include gimmicks which will appeal to household pets who may be watching. Knowing how much expectation has been placed on *Scrooge*'s potential for success among the viewing public, Rhinelander suggests that dormice should be featured as a part of the production to attract the feline viewership. Cross is staggered at the bizarre nature of Rhinelander's request, but – as he is one of the very few people in the company that he has no authority to dismiss – he has no alternative but to acquiesce to the older man's peculiar suggestions.

As Rhinelander returns to the upper echelons of the building, Cross becomes disconcerted when he meets the ambitious, smooth-talking Brice Cummings (John Glover), an impeccably-groomed Californian who tells Cross that he had gone to school with Rhinelander's son and is clearly on good terms with the company's top-brass. Anxious at the prospect of his position as network president coming under threat, Cross quickly retreats back to his office and demands that Grace dig up every piece of available information about Cummings so that he can formulate a defence against being usurped. Grace has an appointment to take her ill son to a medical specialist (an engagement which had to be made months previously), but the hard-hearted Cross couldn't care less about her predicament; he tells her in no uncertain terms that his professional requirements supersede any personal arrangements of her own.

Cross's brother James (John Murray) has been waiting patiently in the network president's office. They head out onto the street after work, and James tries in vain to persuade Cross to join him and his family for Christmas dinner. However, it soon becomes apparent to James that his brother hates the festive season almost as much as he hates people. Cross quickly precludes any further discussion of the matter by deftly stealing a taxi from under the nose of an elderly lady although, ironically, his intended destination is the annual Humanitarian of the Year Awards ceremony. There, he receives the prestigious statue with insincerely-delivered platitudes and barely disguised contempt. But the disdain that Cross holds for the award is made evident when he carelessly leaves it in the back seat of a cab after returning to the IBC headquarters.

Working late in his office, Cross is surprised to hear a knock at the door. A quick examination of the hallway outside reveals nothing, but he has scarcely had time to return to his desk before the insistent thumping begins again. The heavy doors to his office splintering apart, Cross is greeted with an otherworldly sight:

the gruesome ghost of his old boss Lew Hayward (John Forsythe), his body now badly decomposed and still wearing a decayed golf outfit from when he had died of a heart attack on the fairway seven years earlier. Frank, who has retrieved a revolver from his desk drawer, fires several rounds into Hayward, but firearms prove to have little effect on a target who is already dead. Unimpressed by his old subordinate's attempts at bravado, Hayward explains to Cross that he is now suffering in the hereafter as a result of his pitiless, cold-hearted actions in life. He beseeches Cross to reform his ways and be considerate of his fellow human beings before time runs out for him, too. Believing the whole encounter to be hallucinatory, Cross is dismissive of Hayward's warning, pointing out that his now-deceased predecessor was a legend in the world of TV during his lifetime and that he didn't get there by playing by the rules. But Hayward is insistent. Picking Cross up by the throat, he thrusts him through the glass of his office window, leaving him to dangle in midair many storeys above street level. Warning Cross that he will be visited by three spirits – the first to arrive at noon the next day – Hayward laughs as his rotting arm shears off at the elbow, leaving Cross to plunge to his apparent death. Just before he can make impact on the ground, however, Cross realises that he is back in his office. As he struggles to come to terms with what he has just witnessed, the telephone on his desk mysteriously calls up his old girlfriend Claire Phillips (Karen Allen), who he hasn't seen or spoken to in fifteen years. That the keypad should do this of its own accord is deeply bewildering to Cross. Leaving her a confused (and confusing) message on her answering machine, Cross begs for Claire to get in touch as soon as possible, hoping that she may know something about the bizarre events that are currently playing out. With Hayward gone and no evidence of his explosive visit in sight (even the office doors are back to normal), Cross seems to momentarily question whether the encounter had been a figment of his imagination after all. But he is forced to put his doubts aside when he takes a swig from a shotglass and discovers a decrepit-looking golf ball in his mouth.

Across town, Grace and her family are discussing the curious condition of her young son Calvin (Nicholas Phillips). Unable to speak, Calvin has baffled the various doctors that Grace has consulted, but the medical bills are piling up and she is concerned about how to meet the rising costs – not least as her 'Christmas bonus' from Cross has taken the form of an IBC bath-towel. A single mother of several children, it is clear that Grace is anxious that the meagre salary she receives from the network is presenting her with difficulty in making ends meet. She is momentarily shaken from her worries when she discovers that, as the family (Damon Hines, Tamika McCollum, Koren McCollum and Reina King) lack the money for a Christmas tree, they have taken the iniative and decorated little Calvin instead, complete with electric fairy-lights.

The next morning, Cross can barely contain his merriment when he discovers that an eighty-year-old TV viewer has died while watching his disturbing *Scrooge* promo. Clearly believing that there is no such thing as bad publicity, Cross is elated that the network's advertising has raised the profile of the broadcast to the point that it has become front-page news. His gloating is interrupted when he is needed on the set of *Scrooge*, where frantic preparatory work is still ongoing. A television censor (Kate McGregor-Stewart) is protesting at the revealing costumes that are being worn by some of the dancers, but Cross is unwilling to take her concerns seriously – he is happy to court controversy, and sees no reason to downplay risqué elements of the production given his obsession with chasing ratings. A stage-hand accidentally knocks the censor unconscious with a prop from the set, requiring medical attention, but before help can arrive he is surprised by an entirely unexpected appearance – his old girlfriend Claire. He seems amazed to see her, the previous evening's fevered events seeming little more than a blur now. Now the director of a charitable organisation that provides support for the homeless, Claire seems dismayed to discover how irritable and bitter her one-time sweetheart has become. She watches in quiet contemplation as he roughly manhandles the injured censor around so that she can see the dancers in action (the dazed woman is now too stupefied to argue), and then argues with one of the production's animal handlers (Ralph Gervais) who is refusing – on animal cruelty grounds – to staple a set of antlers onto a mouse for dramatic effect. Claire is astonished by Cross's callousness and general insensitivity, but he is flippant towards her concerns and sneers at her compassion. When she asks why he decided to call her out of the blue the previous night, he dodges the question, but there remains an obvious spark of attraction between the two – not least when he discovers that, like himself, she is currently single. However, their unexpected reunion is derailed following Cross's ill-tempered discovery of Calvin on the set (Grace has brought him to work as a special pre-Christmas treat) and a construction disaster with the set's elaborate backdrop of Victorian building exteriors. Watching his growing sense of furious exasperation with quiet pity, the gentle Claire withdraws before he can notice.

Soon after, Cross meets with Rhinelander for a pre-arranged business lunch at an upmarket city restaurant. As Cross explains some of the elaborate events that will be taking place during the transmission of *Scrooge*, including live footage of a mural being painted on the Berlin Wall, Rhinelander drops the bombshell that he has hired a consultant to collaborate with Cross to avoid any chance of him becoming unable to cope with his current weighty workload. Cross, naturally, is livid – particularly when he discovers that the consultant in question is none other than the ultra-ambitious Cummings, who has also been invited to lunch by Rhinelander. As the unbearably smug Cummings tells Cross (in a staggering display of insincerity) not to consider him a threat to his position at the network, the clock strikes twelve. Now that noon has arrived, the events foretold by Hayward start to spring into action. Cross becomes increasingly hysterical, discovering an eyeball in his glass of water and then witnessing a waiter being set on fire. None of the others are witnessing his hallucinations, however, and Rhinelander assumes that Cross's inexplicable delirium has been brought on by stress and overwork.

Unable to cope with the succession of nightmare visions, Cross excuses himself from the table and staggers out of the restaurant. He hails a taxi, but upon entering finds that the driver is unwilling to accept his directions. Worse still, he discovers that he is trapped inside, both doors of the cab securely trapped shut.

Cackling sinisterly, the unkempt driver reveals himself to be the Ghost of Christmas Past (David Johansen). Slowing down only to steal a bottle of liquor from the hapless Loudermilk, now destitute and looking rather the worse for wear, the Ghost speeds into a dense mist. When the taxi emerges, the year is 1955. Cross is baffled at the apparent shift in time, not least as a head-on collision with a truck soon proves that the cab and its inhabitants are now both invisible and incorporeal. The Ghost drives to the grim house that the young Cross had grown up in, which – given that it is Christmas Eve – shows no sign of any festive cheer whatsoever. Cross is scornful, telling the Ghost that he has no intention of being affected by the apparitions of times gone by. Moving inside, they discover a four-year-old Frank (Ryan Todd) sitting in front of a black-and-white television set, totally engrossed in the programming. Cross's heavily pregnant mother Doris (Lisa Mende) sits quietly nearby, but peace is soon shattered by the appearance of his gruff father Earl (Brian Doyle Murray). Young Frank soon discovers that his dad, a butcher, has an unexpected Christmas surprise for him – five pounds of veal. When he responds that he had asked Santa Claus for a toy train, the bitter Earl responds that if he isn't happy with his festive fare, he should get a job and earn enough money to buy a train set for himself, reasoning that his son needs to learn that life is unfair by nature. As his mother heads out of the room with the parting words that Frank should be careful of spending too much time with the TV, the adult Cross is crying in despondency over a long-gone past.

After leaving the house, Cross tries to conceal the depth of his regret, but the Ghost presses him on his wasted childhood – Frank was to spend all of his adolescence and teenage years glued to a television screen. Cross retorts that he had many enriching experiences in his youth, but the Ghost quickly notices that all of them have been pilfered from the popular programming of the time, including *Little House on the Prairie*. Frustrated, Cross asks to be returned to the IBC office, and the Ghost is happy to oblige. When they arrive, however, Cross discovers that it is 1968. A boisterous Christmas party is being held by the network executives (a tradition that Cross soon put a stop to once he had become president), but a youthful Frank – still a junior employee at the time – is stubbornly refusing to take part in the frivolities. The present-day Cross is dismayed to note how his younger self seems totally oblivious to the affections of the bubbly Tina (Rebeca Arthur), one of his colleagues back in the sixties. But the Ghost is more concerned with another acquaintance that he made that Christmas – Claire, who he shows meeting Cross for the first time outside a convenience store. The pair immediately fall in love, and a year later they are living in an inner-city apartment together. The Ghost conjures up scenes from a happy Christmas Eve that they spent in each other's company, where the ever-romantic Cross proudly presents Claire with a gift of kitchen knifes, and receives an illustrated copy of the *Kama Sutra* in return. Fast-forwarding a couple of years, the young Frank is now in his early twenties and in costume for the *Frisbee the Dog* show. Having impressed the president of the network, Hayward (still very much alive at this point) invites him and Claire to dinner during a short break in the show's filming. Cross knows that this is the break that his career has been waiting for. But when Claire arrives soon after, she is unhappy with the idea of dining out with Hayward – they already have a long-standing arrangement to visit friends that night. Cross is staggered by her refusal, knowing that pleasing Hayward is essential to his chances of progress in the company. Claire is upset at how cold and distant Cross is becoming towards her, and – as she starts to become aware that he now values his career more than his relationship with her – she suggests that they separate. Still totally focused on dinner with the network president, Cross tacitly agrees, thus ending their relationship. The Ghost is stunned at Cross's foolhardiness at having put his professional life ahead of the love of his soul-mate. He berates Cross for having such a skewed idea of his priorities in life, but Cross tries hard to laugh off the criticism.

Disappearing as rapidly as he had first appeared, the Ghost leaves Frank back in the present day, on the set of *Scrooge*. Still shaken by his recent experiences, Frank causes a minor disturbance during the dress rehearsal before heading off to find Claire. Using the business card that she had left him during their previous meeting, he soon tracks her down at Operation Outreach, the homeless shelter that she runs on 9th Street. After initially being mistaken for Richard Burton (implausible though it may sound), Cross is reunited with Claire and tells her how much he regrets the choices he had made in his earlier life. She is delighted at his apparent change of heart, leading Cross to suggest that they go out to dinner there and then – just like the meal they shared on the Christmas Eve of their first meeting back in '68. But a couple of administrative hitches at the shelter lead to some unexpected setbacks; Claire asks Cross to wait momentarily until she can resolve the problems, but Cross becomes angry, adamant that Claire's assistants should iron out the issues instead. When she refuses, he insists that she fires them, but cannot seem to comprehend the fact that volunteers can't be struck from a payroll that doesn't exist. Confused by his irritation, Claire tells Cross that she will gladly accompany him if he will just wait momentarily, but by now he has had enough. Storming off, Cross tells her that he has made a mistake and – in a parting shot – suggests that she should concentrate on her own self-interest for a change, rather than constantly looking out for the wellbeing of others.

Arriving back at the final rehearsal for *Scrooge*, Cross's mood doesn't improve when he discovers that Cummings has stepped in to assume directorial duties in his absence. Worse still, he is effortlessly charming the cast and crew, much to Cross's chagrin. Feigning concern for the inexplicably-missing Cross, Cummings makes clear his willingness to take the reins of the high-profile broadcast and then departs rapidly before Cross has the chance to talk with him at any length. Left alone on the empty set, Cross is more than taken aback when he discovers a life-sized fairy – the Ghost of Christmas Present (Carol Kane). Discovering that her apparently sweet nature masks outbursts of inexplicable physical violence, Cross is swept across the city by the fairy and soon finds himself at Grace's home in Harlem just as she arrives home from work. Her family are excited that Christmas Eve has arrived and, in spite of their relative poverty, they are determined to make the most of the holiday season. While his siblings laugh and joke around, little Calvin remains silent and detached from all the festive merriment. The fairy explains that Calvin hasn't spoken a word since he witnessed the death of his father in a shooting some five years beforehand. This comes as a surprise to Cross, who is so self-obsessed that he hadn't even noticed that Grace's husband had died.

Leaving the Cooley family to their Christmas, the fairy next whisks Cross downtown to the home of James and his wife Wendie (Wendie Malick). Cross discovers that his brother is also enjoying festive cheer; a group of friends have been invited round for drinks and a game of Trivial Pursuit. Wendie remembers that James still hasn't opened Cross's Christmas present, and with a mixture of eagerness and trepidation brings over a large wrapped box. Mindful that their gift the previous year had been a shower curtain, James tears open the decorative paper to reveal a top-quality video recorder and promptly reasons that Cross must've accidentally mixed it up with something else. Cross fumes at the fact that Grace has obviously decided to put James's name down for the VCR instead of his intended bath-towel, but mellows slightly when he remembers that the gifts are all tax-deductible anyway. He is chastened somewhat when James voices regret that Cross never joins them for Christmas dinner, especially when his brother resolves to keep asking every year until he finally concedes.

The next stop is a freezing cold recess beneath the streets of the city. As pedestrians pass over the metal grille overhead, Cross discovers one of the regulars of Claire's homeless shelter – a man named Herman (Michael J. Pollard), now dead from hypothermia. He rages at the pointlessness of the man's death, but knows that his regret is ultimately pointless; nothing can be done to help this dispossessed acquaintance now. Breaking down a door in an attempt to get out, Cross bizarrely finds himself back on the set of *Scrooge* once again. This time, however, the production is mere minutes away from broadcast. Cummings is initially angered by the appearance of what he believes to be a practical joker but, on discovering that the intruder is Cross, quickly suggests that the seemingly-unhinged network president retire to his office and oversee things from a safe distance. Cross appears to be on the verge of an all-out nervous breakdown when he discovers the Ghost of Christmas Future in the elevator, but feels foolish when he discovers that it is only an actor in costume (Chaz Conner Jr.).

Minutes later, the broadcast is in full swing. Cummings oversees the production with clockwork precision, but Cross remains in his office with considerable trepidation about what he knows is yet to come. While Rhinelander watches at home with great satisfaction as his pet cats take an interest in the antler-wearing dormice which belong to Scrooge's nephew Fred (a hastily-inserted addition to Dickens's story, made at his earlier suggestion), Cross opens a Christmas gift from his brother – a framed photograph of the two of them taken in childhood. For once he seems genuinely moved due to James's obvious fraternal affection. As the narrative of IBC's *Scrooge* reaches the encounter with the Ghost of Christmas Yet to Come, a gigantic skeletal hand reaches out of a bank of television monitors behind Cross's back. Before it can tap him on the shoulder, however, Loudermilk bursts into the office without warning and starts firing indiscriminately at Cross with a shotgun. The furious former employee explains to Cross that since losing his job, his wife has left him – taking his infant daughter – and since then he has been roughed up, robbed, and has spent much of his remaining time blind drunk. But Cross has now reached a point where virtually nothing can surprise him, and thus is able to evade the gunfire long enough to reach the safety of an elevator.

Sadly for Cross, however, this particular elevator is far from secure. Inside is a horrific, Grim Reaper-esque being which holds the screaming husks of tortured souls beneath the folds of its dark cloak. The Ghost of Christmas Future has no discernible face: only a television screen where its head should be, which continually shows a disjointed series of rapid, bizarre imagery. The elevator plunges downward, and the doors slide open to reveal a corridor with an observation window. Cross looks through it to discover a padded cell with an adolescent Calvin (Raphael Harris) inside. He learns that even in the future, Calvin will never speak, and subsequently is admitted to a mental institution. The young man looks up at Cross accusatorily.

Next, the Ghost takes Cross to an upmarket future restaurant, where an expensively-dressed Claire is dining with a couple of similarly nouveau-riche friends (Susan Barnes and Lynne Randall). Upon noticing a group of penniless urchins begging near their table, a newly-snobbish Claire orders the waiter (Gilles Savard) to chase them from the establishment. At her acquaintances' protests, Claire snaps back that she had once wasted her time with the penniless and the destitute, but that she had reconsidered her generosity of spirit after Frank had advised her to put her own interests first. Now she has no time for the under-privileged, determined instead to look out for herself.

Finally, the elevator hits the bottom of the shaft though, as Cross soon discovers, its final destination also has no relation to the building that the lift carriage actually belongs to. He is now in an austere crematorium, watching in horror as his own funeral is taking place. Only his brother and sister-in-law have bothered to attend the service; the rest of the hall is empty. As a priest (Michael O'Donoghue) recites from the Book of Psalms, a middle-aged James and Wendie watch impassively as Cross's coffin edges towards the crematorium's furnace. Desperately hanging on to the coffin's handles in a doomed attempt to halt its motion, Cross suddenly finds himself inside it just as the wooden exterior begins to catch fire. Screaming frenziedly as the flames begin to lick around him, Cross knows that he has reached the end of his life

Only to find himself back in the IBC headquarters again. Racing around his office with jubilation, knowing that he has only escaped death by a whisker, Cross finds himself once again at the end of Loudermilk's shotgun. But rather than choosing to run this time, Cross decides that his new approach to life will start there and then. He promises to rehire Loudermilk at twice his original rate of salary, and to promote him to the position of vice-president of programming at IBC. Loudermilk is amazed at this complete change of character in Cross, but the transformed network president has no time to debate the finer points of his redemption. He races for the elevator with a new purpose in his step.

As the broadcast of *Scrooge* nears its end, Cross bursts onto the set unexpectedly – interrupting the actors – and addresses the camera directly. He apologises for having been such an inconsiderate character, arranging for a huge live show to be produced on Christmas Eve when most of the people involved would much rather have been doing anything other than working. In the control room, Cummings is ecstatic, knowing that Cross's unscripted appearance has almost certainly ended his career. But his glee is short-lived; Loudermilk bursts into the room, still armed with his shotgun, to ensure that Cross's transmission isn't taken off the air. A furious Rhinelander calls up with the singular purpose of firing Cross, but Loudermilk answers the phone and places the blame for Frank's TV appearance squarely on the now-bound and gagged Cummings, ensuring that the pushy usurper will take the flak for putting Cross on live television. But as Cummings is a little tied up by now, there is little that he can do except sit back and watch.

Cross soon whips up a party atmosphere on the set, expressing his regret for the way he has treated his brother and his colleagues over the years. He also declares his undying love for Claire, causing her to race out of the shelter on 9th Street and catch a taxi to the studio. As Cross's monologue to camera continues, other executives and members of the crew begin to creep into shot, as do many of the actors. He extols the virtues of kindness and generosity, and tells the world that if people really put their faith in the Christmas spirit, they can change everything for the better. All they need to do is believe, and the planet can become a much-improved place for everyone. Cross is awestruck when little Calvin wanders up to him and utters his first words in years (a Tiny Tim-esque 'God bless us, everyone'), much to the joyful amazement of his mother who is watching nearby. As Claire joins him for a celebratory kiss, their love rekindled at last, Cross notices his old boss – the still-decomposing Hayward, on the edge of the set but unseen by the others – who now appears to be satisfied that his work of reforming Cross's character is complete.

Scrooged is quite possibly the least conventional version of *A Christmas Carol* ever committed to film. Not only is it a thoroughly contemporised take on Dickens's story (though there is admittedly a scattering of cultural references which have badly dated it), but it manages to successfully employ a risky strategy of planting a fictional production of *A Christmas Carol* at the heart of the narrative, which is – of course – itself a loose adaptation of the very same novella. It is much to the credit of screenwriters Mitch Glazer and Michael O'Donoghue that they are able to pull off this potentially hazardous approach so ably; the Dickens tale is so familiar to Cross that he immediately recognises the *modus operandi* of the Ghosts of Christmas, for instance, but he still remains unable to resist the allure of their transformative power. The network's cheesy production of *Scrooge* is the source of much of the film's best satire, not least in its outrageous gimmicks (such as the hilariously crowbarred-in appearance of the antlered dormice, obviously added by the IBC production team at the very last minute) and improbable casting which includes Buddy Hackett as a somewhat implausible Ebenezer Scrooge, the charismatic Jamie Farr as the ghost of Jacob Marley, and Mary Lou Retton as a surprisingly acrobatic Tiny Tim Cratchit.

Some commentators have argued that the film's relentless cynicism and generally flippant sense of irony does lend its purpose more readily to parodying the extremes of the modern Christmas (and the media's embellished interpretation of it) than it does to promoting Dickens's original theme of extolling the values of Christmas throughout the year.[1] Indeed, others such as Fred Guida have raised the important point that because the film spends so long lampooning the clichéd ethos of *A Christmas Carol* in the form of IBC's production of *Scrooge*, it becomes difficult to consider its own closing scenes of a rehabilitated Cross with any degree of genuine earnestness.[2] This view was echoed by James Chapman, who has argued that *Scrooged* is situated within the very same category and niche of media convention as the kind of productions that it aims to send up.[3] Interestingly, other critical observers have noted that the journey of redemption that Frank Cross undergoes, coupled with the film's combination of ethical concerns and modern anxieties, closely mirrored the moral struggle articulated in Bill Murray's later role as TV presenter Phil Connors in Harold Ramis's well-received fantasy film *Groundhog Day* (1993).[4]

Richard Donner creates a memorable evocation of a chilly New York throughout *Scrooged*, capturing not only the icy ambience but also the city's distinctively dynamic character. He also ensures that the film works well in balancing its satirical criticism of network television (most noticeable in Rhinelander's crackpot schemes to chase ratings, and the smiling ruthlessness of Cross and Cummings's brinkmanship) with rather less subtle wit such as the perpetually-injured censor and the ongoing tribulations of the hapless Loudermilk. Wayne Finkelman's costume design is noteworthy, particularly in the flashback sequences set in the late sixties and early seventies where some righteously groovy fashion styles are in evidence. Danny Elfman's score also aids the production, lending both energy and atmosphere, and there is a great deal to enjoy in the triumphant rendition of Jackie De Shannon, Randy Myers and Jimmy Holiday's 'Put a Little Love in Your Heart', the film's climactic song which is performed to good effect by Annie Lennox and Al Green.

The term 'star vehicle' is often overused when discussing the movies, but there is no question that *Scrooged* is a film which is absolutely dominated by Bill Murray's laconic, no-holds-barred central performance. While this prompted some critics to note that the film's success with individuals would likely depend on the degree to which they appreciated Murray's acting style,[5] there is no doubting that he throws everything – up to and including the kitchen sink – into the role of Frank Cross. From the character's snarling, subordinate-persecuting tyranny to his underplayed, moving moments of emotional awakening (all the more powerful due to his admirable dramatic restraint), every frame of *Scrooged* belongs entirely to Murray from start to finish. Well-known to American audiences for his appearances on TV's *Saturday Night Live* between 1975 and 1980, Murray quickly established himself as a prominent performance talent in eighties cinema due to appearances in films such as Harold Ramis's *Caddyshack* (1980), and Ivan Reitman's *Meatballs* (1979) and *Stripes* (1981). His star climbed even higher after his roles in Sydney Pollack's *Tootsie* (1982) and most especially Ivan Reitman's massively successful *Ghostbusters* (1984), and he had also performed in Tom Schiller's fantasy *Nothing Lasts Forever* (1984) and John Byrum's romantic drama *The Razor's Edge* (1984), an adaptation of the W. Somerset Maugham novel.

Additionally, he made a short but memorable cameo appearance as masochistic dental patient Arthur Denton in Frank Oz's musical comedy *Little Shop of Horrors* (1986). (There is a subtle reference to this film in *Scrooged* where, right at the film's conclusion, Cross can be heard shouting Audrey II's famous catchphrase 'Feed me, Seymour!') Murray was nominated for the Golden Globe Award for Performance by an Actor in a Motion Picture for his performance as Dr Peter Venkman in *Ghostbusters* (1984) and, later in his career, for his appearance in Wes Anderson's satire *Rushmore* (1998). He won a Golden Globe (again, in the Best Performance by an Actor in a Motion Picture: Comedy/ Musical category) for his standout performance in Sofia Coppola's romantic comedy-drama *Lost in Translation* (2003), and was also to be nominated for an Academy Award for the same role.

Balancing the misanthropic excesses of Cross's bullying, self-centred persona is his first and only true love, the beautiful Claire Phillips. Clearly fulfilling Belle's function from *A Christmas Carol* just as plainly as Lew Hayward is a substitute for Jacob Marley, Claire's natural compassion and generosity of spirit is very ably articulated by Karen Allen, who enjoys an excellent on-screen chemistry with Bill Murray to present a memorably sanguine, breezy foil to Cross's unrelenting scorn and pessimism. (Unlike Dickens's Belle, however, Claire discovers that she and Cross have one last chance at reconciliation – an opportunity that was forever denied to Scrooge.) Allen's cinematic career started on a high note thanks to an impressive and likeable performance in John Landis's hugely successful *National Lampoon's Animal House* (1978). After a small role in Woody Allen's *Manhattan* (1979), she went on to higher-profile appearances in films such as Philip Kaufman's *The Wanderers* (1979), William Friedkin's *Cruising* (1980) and Rob Cohen's *A Small Circle of Friends* (1980). Much greater fame came in 1981 with the role of feisty adventurer Marion Ravenwood in Steven Spielberg's *Raiders of the Lost Ark* (a role which she would reprise many years later in Spielberg's *Indiana Jones and the Kingdom of the Crystal Skull*, 2008). In the years leading up to *Scrooged*, she continued to build her reputation as a performer through a diverse range of roles in films including Alan Parker's domestic drama *Shoot the Moon* (1982), Ted Kotcheff's mind control thriller *Split Image* (1982), John Carpenter's science fiction adventure *Starman* (1984), and Gilbert Cates's murder mystery *Backfire* (1988). She was also nominated for an Independent Spirit Award for her supporting performance in Paul Newman's *The Glass Menagerie* (1987), adapted from the perennially popular drama by Tennessee Williams.

Scrooged was also remarkable in its quirky but effectively wide-ranging ensemble of supporting actors. Hollywood legend Robert Mitchum is exceptional as the addlepated network chief Preston Rhinelander, and actor and standup comedian Bobcat Goldthwait also impresses, cast against type as the meek but independently-minded junior executive Eliot Loudermilk. John Forsythe, Alfre Woodard and David Johansen all deliver solid performances, as does John Glover as the joyfully slimy Brice Cummings, but perhaps the standout supporting appearance comes from Carol Kane as the Ghost of Christmas Present, almost certainly the most brazenly pugilistic fairy ever to appear in a Christmas film.

There are also many cameo appearances throughout *Scrooged*, including several of Bill Murray's brothers who also worked in the acting profession: John Murray features as Cross's despairing brother James, Brian Doyle Murray as his crotchety father Earl, and Joel Murray as a guest at James's Christmas Eve party. There were also brief appearances by the film's screenwriters, both veterans of *Saturday Night Live* (as Murray had been). Michael O'Donoghue features as the priest who presides over Cross's future funeral, while Mitch Glazer can be seen as another of the family friends who are attending the party of James and Wendie.

To say that *Scrooged* split the opinions of reviewers at the time of its release would be a gross understatement; it proved to be perhaps the most critically divisive Christmas film of the entire decade, provoking some strong reactions. While some commentators favoured the high-quality production values and the humorous, carefully selected cameos,[6] others found that film's cynicism became so all-encompassing that it permeated the whole production, deadening the comedy and rendering the conclusion ineffective.[7] A few critics praised *Scrooged* for its genuine embrace of the festive spirit as it nears its climax[8] and lauded its distinctively acerbic humour,[9] but on the other side of the argument there was criticism of the film's perceived lack of emotional impact[10], censure of the alleged stage-management of the audience's psychological response to the film,[11] and the fact that – for a comedy – some reviewers simply found the jokes to be unfunny.[12] In recent years, the film's critical stature has grown substantially, with modern commentators approving of Bill Murray's wildly entertaining central performance,[13] Richard Donner's highly innovative approach to the well-known original material,[14] and the film's well-observed, droll approach to its comedic situations.[15]

Scrooged was not forgotten at awards ceremonies following its release. Thomas R. Burman and Bari Dreiband-Burman were nominated for the Academy Award for Best Makeup in 1989, and Eric Brevig and Allen Hall's special effect work was nominated for a Saturn Award in 1990. Also at the Saturn Awards, the film was nominated in the Best Fantasy Film category, while Bill Murray was nominated for Best Actor. *Scrooged* also fared well at the BMI Film Music Awards, where Danny Elfman's original score was to win a coveted BMI Award.

Scrooged was a significant entry in the pantheon of eighties Christmas films: although it emphasised the potential corrosiveness that could result from assuming high office within a corporate environment without a responsible mindset, it also highlighted the redemptive ability of the Christmas spirit to turn around the attitudes of even the most ruthless and self-infatuated of individuals. The film's tacit suggestion appears to be that even if an organisation driven purely by unchecked commercial gain had by now moved beyond any possibility of moral redemption, liberation from self-interest still remained an attainable prospect for individual people within those organisations: a freedom to which they may still aspire. The redemptive expectation of reaching beyond selfishness and egocentricity in order to improve the lives of others is a compelling motivation, and one which would also remain relevant to Christmas film-making in more recent years.

Historical Context

Scrooged made its first appearance in American cinemas on 23 November 1988. Also making their debuts in film theatres on that day were Daniel Petrie's *Cocoon: The Return* and Peter Masterson's *Full Moon in Blue Water*. Bon Jovi were at number one on the Billboard Hot 100 that week with 'Bad Medicine'. In the news at the time of the film's release, a convention on the extraction of Antarctic mineral resources was agreed upon, a large earthquake struck the northern United States and Canada, and Soviet Chess Grandmaster Elena Akhmilovskaya married American International Master of Chess William John Donaldson at the World Chess Olympiad in Thessaloniki, Greece.

16

NATIONAL LAMPOON'S CHRISTMAS VACATION (1989)

Hughes Entertainment/ Warner Brothers

Director: Jeremiah Chechik
Producers: John Hughes and Tom Jacobson
Screenwriter: John Hughes

MAIN CAST

Chevy Chase	-	Clark Griswold
Beverly D'Angelo	-	Ellen Griswold
Juliette Lewis	-	Audrey Griswold
Johnny Galecki	-	Russell 'Rusty' Griswold
Randy Quaid	-	Cousin Eddie Johnson
Miriam Flynn	-	Cousin Catherine Johnson
William Hickey	-	Uncle Lewis
Mae Questel	-	Aunt Bethany

National Lampoon's Christmas Vacation performs an important transitional function for the Christmas film. While it engages with the customary eighties theme of the philanthropic nature of the festive spirit conflicting with commercial self-interest, it also laid the foundations for what would become the predominant concern of Christmas films in the nineties, namely the unchanging value of the family unit. The film was also the third instalment in the popular *National Lampoon's Vacation* series, which had started in 1983 with Harold Ramis's *National Lampoon's Vacation* and continued with Amy Heckerling's *National Lampoon's European Vacation* in 1985. Featuring Chevy Chase as the well-meaning but hugely accident-prone Clark W. Griswold and Beverly D'Angelo as his long-suffering wife Ellen, the cycle had followed the Griswolds' holiday travels with their teenage son and daughter, and quickly attained a cult following amongst audiences. In *National Lampoon's Christmas Vacation*, however, the Griswolds would not be causing havoc across the United States or in continental Europe while on vacation, but would instead be bringing the holiday season into their home as they enjoyed festive celebrations with their many eccentric relations. While the film marked a more family-oriented turn for the *Vacation* series in comparison to the first two ribald entries in the cycle, care is taken to ensure that the yuletide theme and staunch emphasis on domestic merriment would not compromise laughs for the sake of emotional sentiment.

In the eyes of many commentators, the lasting success of the *National Lampoon's Vacation* series amongst audiences is largely accredited to the knowing, well-structured screenplays which were penned for the films by writer-director John Hughes. Achieving widespread success throughout the eighties for the cycle of teen movies that he directed (including *Sixteen Candles*, 1984; *The Breakfast Club*, 1985, and *Ferris Bueller's Day Off*, 1986) and those for which he had provided the screenplay (*Pretty in Pink*, 1986, and *Some Kind of Wonderful*, 1987), the original *National Lampoon's Vacation* was one of Hughes's earliest scripts for the cinema, and also one of his most enduringly popular. The screenplay was based upon his short story 'Vacation '58' which had been published in the satirical *National Lampoon* magazine, the seminal journal which went on to spawn a variety of spin-offs in many different media, including films under the *National Lampoon* banner from the late seventies onwards. The darkly satirical tale of an overly enthusiastic father's determination to have the perfect holiday road trip – only to meet with disaster at every turn – struck a chord with many, due in large part to Chevy Chase's impeccable comic performance. This was followed a few years later with *National Lampoon's European Vacation*, which Hughes co-wrote with screenwriter Robert Klane. That first sequel had seen the Griswolds winning a family package tour of Europe which, to put it mildly, does not go to plan. Hughes would return to solo screenwriting duties for the third *Vacation* film, as well as acting as one of the film's producers, and he appeared to take great delight in demonstrating that the Griswolds had no need to travel in order to cause mayhem; they were quite able to instigate utter chaos while staying in the comfort of their own home.

National Lampoon's Christmas Vacation was the first cinematic outing for director Jeremiah Chechik, who would later go on to direct films including *Benny and Joon* (1993), *Tall Tale* (1995) and *Diabolique* (1996) as well as a number of features for television. The film was also to see the return of not just the central cast regulars Chevy Chase and Beverly D'Angelo as Clark and Ellen Griswold, but also Randy Quaid and Miriam Flynn who were to reprise their roles as the ever-entertaining Johnson cousins (Ellen's relatives from Kansas) who had appeared in the original *Vacation* movie.

It's December in Chicago, and devoted dad Clark W. Griswold (Chevy Chase) has taken his resigned but endlessly-patient wife Ellen (Beverly D'Angelo) and kids Audrey (Juliette Lewis) and Rusty (Johnny Galecki) on a long drive out of the suburbs to find their family Christmas tree – a vital element in marking the start of the year's festivities. Clark is absolutely determined to make the most of Christmas, whereas his long-suffering family seem reconciled to the notion of simply trying to survive it.

After a few close shaves with other drivers on the way into the wilderness, Clark eventually discovers the one flawless tree that he knows that will look perfect in the family's living room. There's only one problem: it's absolutely gargantuan. Having forgotten to take his saw with him on the journey, Clark and company are forced to dig out the huge tree (roots and all) and bring it home atop their car. The outsized tree's massive scale leads to smug derision from Clark's stuck-up yuppie neighbours, Todd and Margo Chester (Nicholas Guest and Julia Louis-Dreyfus), though he wastes no time in giving as good as he gets in response. Ultimately, however, Todd and Margo's reservations may not have been entirely misplaced, as Clark discovers to his detriment when he unties the tree only to watch its unfettered branches shoot out and shatter his living room windows.

In bed at night, Ellen voices her concern about Clark's determination to host a large family gathering over the Christmas period, which will include her parents as well as his own. She points out that they all inevitably end up bickering over the most meaningless of small details whenever they meet, which will put a strain on the festivities. Clark nevertheless assures her that everything will be fine, due to the unique ability of Christmas to reconcile misunderstandings. Ellen is far from convinced by his optimistic take on the situation.

At his office in the city the next day, Clark is looking forward to the lucrative Christmas bonus that he is due to receive from his work in food additive design. He reveals to one of his colleagues, Bill (Sam McMurray), that he has put down a hefty deposit on a new pool that he intends to have installed in his back yard. Even the cantankerousness of his irritable boss Frank Shirley (Brian Doyle Murray) does nothing to dampen his festive spirit. After work, he goes shopping for some lingerie for Ellen at a large department store, though he quickly becomes tongue-tied when he finds himself being served by a beautiful sales assistant (Nicolette Scorsese).

Later, the family are each making their own individual preparations for Christmas when an ominous doorbell sounds, signalling that their relatives have arrived: Clark's parents Nora and Clark Senior (Diane Ladd and John Randolph) and Ellen's father and mother, Arthur and Frances Smith (E.G. Marshall and Doris Roberts). Even before the front door has been opened, they have already started arguing in earnest. Audrey, on the other hand, is more concerned by the unedifying prospect of them sleeping in her room during their stay.

Clark commandeers Rusty into helping him festoon the house with external Christmas lights. As ever, he goes completely overboard and enshrines every inch of the house's exterior with cabling and bulbs, though he suffers a number of minor injuries as he does so. At one point, Clark misses his footing on the ladder and clings to the house's guttering for dear life. As he does so, a sharp-edged length of ice is fired from a now-detached segment of gutter and smashes through the Chesters' bedroom window, destroying their expensive-looking stereo system. However, as the 'evidence' quickly melts in their central-heating of their home, they have no clue on their return as to what can have caused the damage (though of course, their suspicions quickly fall in the general direction of their hapless neighbour).

His work now complete, Clark insists on his relatives joining him outside in the freezing cold – in their pyjamas and dressing gowns – as he attempts to build their collective anticipation for the activation of the lights. However, much to Clark's dismay the big switch-on proves to be a damp squib when he throws the switch and nothing happens. His relatives are far from impressed by this non-event, leaving Clark frustrated. He resolves to keep checking every single light in the system until he can uncover the source of the hitch.

Having worked late into the night to find the fault in the lighting (though ultimately to no effect), Clark is late getting up the next morning. Still in his nightclothes, he sneaks up into the loft to hide away some Christmas presents. Frances, unaware of Clark's whereabouts, sees the open loft hatch and closes it to keep out the cold air. This leaves Clark trapped in the attic while all of his relatives go out shopping for the day. Fortunately, he soon finds some warm clothing in a dusty trunk, and in the process uncovers a bundle of home movies from the fifties and sixties on old film reels. He then whiles away the rest of the day watching scenes of his childhood Christmases on a projector, though the warmth of his nostalgia is rapidly dissipated when Ellen – unaware of his position – pulls open the loft hatch and sends both Clark and the projector clattering down onto the first floor landing.

In the evening, Clark is still fastidiously checking every bulb on the exterior of the house – though still to no avail. As his aggravation mounts, Ellen eventually realises that he hasn't properly connected the power extension, and soon remedies the situation. Clark is stunned by the spectacle before him, which draws so much electricity that the nearby power station has to switch over to auxiliary nuclear reserves just to keep the rest of the city's lights on. The family are belatedly amazed by Clark's triumph, though it goes down less well with the Chesters who find themselves momentarily blinded by the intensity of the lights (especially as they were enjoying a romantic night in at the time of the switch-on).

The exhilaration of Clark's accomplishment is short-lived, however, as he unexpectedly finds himself face-to-face with the dreaded Cousin Eddie (Randy Quaid), who has driven up from Kansas in his ancient RV to spend the festive season with him. Eddie has brought along his wife Catherine (Miriam Flynn) and a few of his extensive family, Ruby Sue (Ellen Hamilton Latzen) and Rocky (Cody

Burger), along with his overly-familiar dog Snots. Clark is both startled and dismayed to see Eddie and his brood, not least as no-one had actually invited them. However, Eddie soon makes it clear that he's planning to stick around for a while, much to Clark's consternation.

Resigned to the fact that Eddie and his family are there to stay for the holidays, and possibly a little longer besides, Clark takes them along with his own kids to a night of sledging. Clark intends to make use of a secret weapon – a prototype kitchen lubricant that his company has been developing. He treats the base of his sledge with the potent lotion in the hope of reducing its friction against the ground. However, it works rather too well, and he ends up careening through the air at a worryingly fast rate. Tearing into a forest and then along a busy road at a rate of knots, Clark is fortunate to get through the encounter in one piece.

At work, just before he and his colleagues leave for the Christmas season, Clark is worrying about the fact that he still hasn't received his bonus. Bill assures him that he has just heard that an envelope has been delivered to his home by courier, and that surely Clark's own notification letter can't be far behind it. Back home, Clark stares out of the kitchen window and daydreams about his family enjoying themselves in the still-to-be-installed pool. He then lets his imagination run riot, picturing the stunning lingerie saleswoman from the department store frolicking on the springboard, before he is interrupted by Ruby Sue. His little niece is concerned that she and her brother won't be receiving any Christmas gifts – the previous year, even although they had both been on their best behaviour, no presents had been forthcoming on Christmas Day. Clark feels humbled by Ruby Sue's obvious gratitude at being allowed to stay at his family's house, and makes her a promise that he'll prove to her not only that Santa Claus is real, but also that jolly old Saint Nick will bring presents for her and Rocky.

The next morning, after Clark and Ellen watch dumbfounded as Eddie empties the contents of his RV's chemical toilet into the street's sewerage drain, they jointly decide to lend Eddie and Catherine some financial aid in order to give their children some Christmas presents. When Clark later broaches the subject with Eddie, however, he is surprised to find not only that he readily accepts the idea, but that he already has a list made out – including gifts for Catherine – which he promptly hands over to the flabbergasted Clark.

Christmas Eve arrives, and with it comes the elderly Uncle Lewis and Aunt Bethany (William Hickey and Mae Questel). Lewis is tetchy and argumentative, while Bethany is cheerful but permenantly bewildered. Clark and Ellen are taken aback to discover that Lewis and Bethany have (accidentally or otherwise) wrapped up their pet cat as a Christmas gift, and discreetly let it loose. Combined with the pressures of all their other guests, Lewis's irascibility taxes even Clark's good nature to the absolute limit.

Christmas dinner then follows, though it quickly transpires that the turkey has been grossly overcooked and is now little more than a desiccated husk. However, as Catherine was responsible for cooking it, the family chew their way through the remnants in order to spare her feelings. In the meantime, Lewis and Bethany's cat is gnawing on the power cord of the Christmas tree's lights and inadvertently electrocutes itself underneath one of the living room chairs. Clark and Eddie circumspectly remove the evidence from the house, during which Clark notices a worrying gaseous vapour starting to emanate from the sewer where Eddie had emptied his chemical toilet earlier.

Clark has barely rejoined the dinner table when he spots an unusual flash from the living room – Lewis has accidentally burnt down the Christmas tree with his omnipresent cigar. Just as Rusty begins to worry that Clark is heading for one of his legendary meltdowns, a knock at the door signals the late arrival of the envelope containing Clark's bonus. However, upon opening it – amongst much fevered expectation from the rest of the family – he is astonished to discover that rather than a cash windfall, the envelope actually contains an annual membership to the Jelly of the Month Club. This proves to be the final straw, causing Clark to fly into a hysterical rage. He angrily proclaims that all he wants for Christmas is his boss, Frank Shirley, brought from his affluent home to account for his miserliness in depriving all of his employees of their expected cash bonus. Eddie begins to look thoughtful, and slips away soon afterwards.

Still slightly unhinged, Clark promptly goes into the garden and cuts down a conveniently-placed tree with a chainsaw, in order to provide a replacement for the char-grilled original. In the process, he manages to smash the Chesters' dining room window, though he shows little sign of remorse at this (or even awareness of it happening). As Clark embellishes the tree with hastily-sourced replacement decorations, he quickly discovers a hyperkinetic squirrel hiding amongst the branches. A panicked frenzy ensues as the family try to evade the squirrel while it races through the house, a chase which culminates when the front door is thrown open and the interloping rodent jumps onto Margo, who has arrived to confront Clark about her broken window. The squirrel is soon followed by the frantic Snots, who dives onto Margo in order to attack the fleeing animal. Now bruised and tattered, the livid Margo eventually withdraws before she can be injured any further.

With the ground floor of the house now virtually in ruins thanks to the squirrel debacle, Clark and Ellen's parents all decide that they want to leave. But Clark, now nearing a full-fledged state of mania, is having none of it. For a quiet life, everyone settles down in front of the fire while Clark recites '*Twas the Night Before Christmas* for the benefit of the younger members of the family. But before he can complete the story, Eddie returns with a surprise guest – Frank Shirley, in his pyjamas, gagged and tied up with ribbon. Shirley is initially incensed, threatening to fire Clark and have Eddie jailed. However, when Clark elaborates on how cheated he feels at having been unexpectedly deprived of his bonus – which he has relied upon for years – Shirley relents and decides to reinstate it with a generous additional increase of 20%. Clark is stunned at this unexpected turnaround in fortune. However, his elation is merely transitory, for immediately afterwards a police SWAT team arrives – having been called by Shirley's concerned wife Helen (Natalia Nogulich) – and hold Clark and his family at gunpoint. When Helen discovers the extent of her husband's penny-pinching, however, she sides with the Griswolds – as do the police. The charges are soon dropped against Eddie and the rest of the family, much to everyone's relief. As the unexpected guests leave, Clark reflects wistfully that in spite of everything that has gone wrong – and the fact that his home now looks like a warzone – he still feels fortunate to be spending Christmas with his extended family.

With its all-encompassing festive spirit and pervasive sense of geniality, *National Lampoon's Christmas Vacation* was an effective deviation from the earlier bawdy entries in the series, relying on the comic strengths of Clark's infectious enthusiasm to deliver the perfect holiday season while also providing plenty of keen observational insight into the delights (and potential pitfalls) of Christmas. Hughes's well-judged visual device of a traditional Advent calendar counting down towards Christmas Eve is highly effective in leading the audience towards the apex of the festivities – and the height of Clark's ever-building hysteria. Yet in spite of the film's sense of warmth and good nature, Hughes and Chechik provide more than enough touches of the requisite *Vacation* anarchy to save the film from ever risking a headlong dive into sentimentality. Just as Clark and Eddie drink egg-nog from a pair of matching Marty Moose mugs (Marty having been the mascot of Walley World in the original *Vacation* film), the audience is provided with plenty of evidence – from Clark's manic sleigh-ride to the later slapstick of the squirrel infiltrator – that this is undisputedly Christmas the way that only a *National Lampoon* movie could depict it.

Although the film centres upon Clark's single-minded obsession to ensure that everyone staying at his home is treated to the perfect festive holiday – whether they want one or not – the main source of conflict comes from the heartless Frank Shirley (a brilliantly aloof performance from Brian Doyle Murray). Like so many other corporate figures in eighties Christmas films, Shirley considers the holiday season nothing more than an inconvenience at best, and his tight-fisted betrayal of the workforce is foreshadowed just enough throughout the film that, when it is eventually revealed, the audience is aware of just how much the bonus meant to Clark and how deceived he feels at his self-important boss's muted dishonesty. The treachery is compounded, of course, by the fact that Clark was relying on the expected cash injection not solely for his own ends, but – once again – to provide selflessly for his whole family. The film does not seek to make any weighty point about corporate exploitation of employees or the encroachment of commercialism into the festive season: the Griswolds were much too seasoned a family of consumers to generate much scepticism concerning the growing role of the free market in determining the way that the modern Christmas is packaged for the buying public. However, it does firmly elevate the importance of the family unit over the expediency of business or profit. When Shirley is kidnapped, it is not just Eddie who is held accountable, but rather the whole family which stands united behind Clark and his benevolent (but dim-witted) cousin. Likewise, when it becomes apparent that even Shirley's own wife is appalled at his short-changing of his personnel, it is suggested that there are some things – such as the much-prized tradition of the Christmas bonus – which must be considered sacrosanct even in the face of the seemingly-unstoppable march of corporate self-interest. As Shirley is grudgingly forced to admit, the world of business may be concerned with profit and domination of the market, but it is ultimately made possible by the individual workers – a labour force which is easy to regard as a faceless conglomeration, but less regularly as distinct people with their own hopes and dreams. Thus Shirley must face up to the inescapable truth of his actions' results when it is reflected in the light of Christmas: that his budgetary reductions may have looked appealing on the pages of a ledger, but they have caused dismay for employees, their families, and anyone who was reliant on the expected December payout. Fortunately for the Griswolds and their relatives, Shirley proves capable of enlightenment with an immediacy that had so often evaded the other corporate antagonists of Christmas films in the eighties (and even beforehand).

Chevy Chase once again slips effortlessly back into the role of the good-hearted but mania-tinged Clark Griswold. Delivering a pitch-perfect performance as the perpetually unlucky father who just wants to deliver a wonderful holiday season (no matter how ill-fated his attempts may be), Chase is on top form throughout. From the running gag with the tree sap – Clark's hands end up sticking to everyone and everything after he arranges his new Christmas tree – to his exquisitely ham-fisted delivery as he falteringly tries to buy lingerie for Ellen from a strikingly attractive department store attendant, Chase's portrayal of the character constantly impresses with a continuously witty, astute delivery and in his endless capacity for physical comedy. Chase, who had achieved enormous popularity for his appearances and writing for NBC television's *Saturday Night Live* throughout the seventies, was well established as one of the comedy icons of 1980s American film, having appeared in films which included Harold Ramis's *Caddyshack* (1980), John Landis's *Spies Like Us* (1985), and Michael Ritchie's *Fletch* (1985) and *Fletch Lives* (1989). He had also been nominated for the Best Motion Picture Acting Debut (Male) Award at the Golden Globes for his performance in Colin Higgins's comedy thriller *Foul Play* (1978).

There is no weak link in the supporting cast either, starting with Beverly D'Angelo as the ever-accommodating Ellen. Having appeared in prominent roles in Woody Allen's *Annie Hall* (1977), Milos Forman's *Hair* (1979), Richard Lester's *Finders Keepers* (1984), and Neil Jordan's *High Spirits* (1988), D'Angelo had been nominated for an Emmy Award in the Outstanding Supporting Actress category for her performance as Stella DuBois Kowalski in John Erman's television adaptation of Tennessee Williams's *A Streetcar Named Desire* (1984). She again makes the most of Ellen's drollness and silent despair at Clark's well-intentioned exploits, though it could be argued that she has less to do in this film when compared to other entries in the series. Johnny Galecki and Juliette Lewis are both effective as the long-suffering Griswold kids, articulating well the frustration of warring siblings faced with the unwelcome intrusion of older relatives. (Lewis, who would later be nominated for an Academy Award, Emmy and Golden Globe, was at the time best known for appearances in Richard Benjamin's *My Stepmother Is an Alien*, 1988, and Max Tash's *The Runnin' Kind*, 1989.) William Hickey and Mae Questel are memorable as the crotchety, cigar-chomping uncle and affably ditzy aunt respectively, but the film's standout performance is from Randy Quaid, who comes close to stealing the show as Cousin Eddie. If anything,

Eddie is even more unhygienically off-putting than on his appearance in the first *Vacation*, and Quaid makes full use of his character's greatly-expanded screen time, brilliantly articulating both sponging guile and ingenuous charm. Managing to tread an impossibly fine line which allows his character to appear both repellent and oddly endearing at the same time, he encourages a smile in just about every scene that he appears in.

Although the film takes place almost exclusively in one snowy suburban locale, Chechik is skilled in making full use of every situation for well-timed comedy effect. This is true from Clark's high-wire stunts as he staples Christmas lights to his roof all the way through to the slow-motion demolition of the Chesters' upmarket but pretentiously-decorated home. Hughes's script makes good use of the intermittent interludes away from the house, be they at Clark's inner-city office or the area's pleasant woodland regions, and employs them efficiently in a way that enhances the film's festive flavour instead of diminishing it. Angelo Badalamenti provides a dynamic score which nicely accompanies *Christmas Vacation*'s sense of manic action, as well as providing the obligatory holiday atmosphere whenever required. (Badalamenti was later to achieve huge success with his haunting theme music for David Lynch's *Twin Peaks* television series, 1990-91.) Given the static nature of the family Christmas celebrations, Lindsay Buckingham's 'Holiday Road' – a song which became so prominent in early Griswold outings – is nowhere to be heard this time around. In its place, however, is the film's lively title song, 'Christmas Vacation', which is performed by Mavis Staples.

Although *National Lampoon's Christmas Vacation* exudes seasonal charm, not all contemporary critics were convinced of the film's merits. At the time of its release, some reviewers believed that the film was not fully the sum of its parts[1], suffering from uneven humour and a few flaccid performances.[2] Yet others were to praise the film's entertaining evocation of the potential drawbacks of the holiday season[3], and were warmly approving of its likeable ensemble cast.[4] Modern commentators have generally tended towards favourable criticism of *Christmas Vacation*. While a few have claimed that the film is unable to endure close scrutiny outside of its festive context[5], others have admired the nostalgia value of its distinctively eighties take on the traditional concerns of the Christmas movie.[6] Some have singled out Hughes's witty dialogue and the emotional warmth of the script for particular approval[7], while others believed it to be one of the best films in the *Vacation* series, presaging much of the slapstick physical comedy that would appear in many of Hughes's later scripts throughout the course of the nineties.[8]

Christmas Vacation was also followed by a belated made-for-television spin-off, Nick Marck's *National Lampoon's Christmas Vacation 2: Cousin Eddie's Island Adventure* (2003), written by Matty Simmons. Although Chase and D'Angelo did not feature this time around, the TV movie did star Randy Quaid and Miriam Flynn, once again reprising their roles as Eddie and Catherine Johnson, as well as Dana Barron as Audrey Griswold. There was also a fourth and final film in the main *Vacation* series, Stephen Kessler's *Vegas Vacation* (1997), which was an entertaining but critically under-rated return to the traditional holiday format of the original film. Although the film was not to carry the *National Lampoon* brand name, it did retain key cast members of the *Vacation* series including Chevy Chase, Beverly D'Angelo, Randy Quaid and Miriam Flynn.

Hughes and Chechik's wryly-observed take on the traditional family Christmas, with all of its irritations as well as its many pleasures, was an inspired one which has proven to stand the test of time since its release; the film has been released many times on VHS, on DVD both as a standalone release and as part of various compilation packs, and more recently on Blu-Ray. With its entertaining medley of eccentric relatives and chaotic comedy situations, the film's continual emphasis on the importance of the family marked a turning point for Christmas films. With a new decade dawning, so too was there to be a shift in focus for festive film-making – a change in emphasis which would have new and sweeping ramifications for the genre.

Historical Context

National Lampoon's Christmas Vacation made its first appearance in American cinemas on 1 December 1989. Also appearing on that date was Ted Mather's drama *Dance to Win*, and Andrei Konchalovsky's crime comedy *Homer and Eddie*, starring Whoopi Goldberg and James Belushi. Another significant feature making its debut was Deborah Shaffer's musical documentary *Dance of Hope*, which would later be nominated for the Grand Jury Prize at the Sundance Film Festival. Milli Vanilli were at number one in the Billboard Charts that week with 'Blame It on the Rain'. In the news at the time, Soviet President Mikhail Gorbachev met with Pope John Paul II at the Vatican, Vishwanath Pratap Singh was sworn in as India's new President following the resignation of Rajiv Gandhi, and Luis Alberto Lacelle was elected as the President of Uruguay.

17

HOME ALONE (1990)

Hughes Entertainment/ Twentieth Century Fox Film Corporation

Director: Chris Columbus
Producer: John Hughes
Screenwriter: John Hughes

MAIN CAST

Macaulay Culkin	-	Kevin McCallister
Joe Pesci	-	Harry Lyme
Daniel Stern	-	Marv Merchants
John Heard	-	Peter McCallister
Catherine O'Hara	-	Kate McCallister
Roberts Blossom	-	Marley
Angela Goethals	-	Linnie
Devin Ratray	-	Buzz

By the early 1990s, the world was changing. The Berlin Wall had fallen, the Soviet Union was on the verge of collapse, and U.S. President George H.W. Bush was speaking of the emergence of a New World Order. So too were cultural attitudes beginning to shift, with the 'greed is good' ethos of the eighties giving way to concerns beyond the economic factors which had dominated much of the social commentary during the decade. Just as these far-reaching changes would affect the world of cinema in general, so too would the Christmas film adapt to reflect the newly developing domestic and international outlook. The energetic defence of the Christmas spirit in the face of corporate excess was to fade, gradually being replaced by a move towards a greater celebration of the family and the community as well as the re-emergence of a another traditional theme – the need for a sense of belonging in a world that seemed to be changing more rapidly than ever before.

Home Alone marked the return of John Hughes to the Christmas film after the previous year's *National Lampoon's Christmas Vacation*, and the movie would further develop the themes of the importance of familial love and affection to the festive season that he had established throughout his earlier feature. Yet although the two films shared some common factors – an inviting home in the Chicago suburbs, and Christmas plans that go drastically awry – the approach that Hughes would adopt for his screenplay was to prove drastically different the second time around. *Home Alone* was also to feature child actor Macaulay Culkin, with whom Hughes had worked during his earlier family comedy *Uncle Buck* (1989). Culkin's wryly mature performance in that film had been favourably received by the critics of the time, but few could possibly have predicted the meteoric box-office success that was soon to come.

Home Alone came relatively early in the flmography of director Chris Columbus. Prior to the film's release, he was best-known for helming the cult comedy *Adventures in Babysitting* (1987) (also known as *A Night on the Town*), and nostalgic comedy-drama *Heartbreak Hotel* (1988). Subsequently a producer of note, he is also a well-regarded screenwriter, having composed scripts throughout the eighties for films such as Joe Dante's *Gremlins* (1984), James Foley's *Reckless* (1984) and Barry Levinson's *Young Sherlock Holmes* (1985). Later to direct features including *Mrs Doubtfire* (1993), *Stepmom* (1998) and *Bicentennial Man* (1999), his profile has been raised even further in more recent years due to the success of *Harry Potter and the Philosopher's Stone* (2001) and its sequel *Harry Potter and the Chamber of Secrets* (2002). But in the view of many commentators, *Home Alone* seems likely to remain one of the most instantly recognisable of all his films.

Chaos reigns in a cosy, upmarket home near Chicago; decorated for Christmas, its peaceful exterior gives little hint of the pandemonium that is taking place inside. Members of the McCallister family are frantically busying themselves with last-minute holiday packing before they head off on a vacation to Paris the next day. The extended group of family members have gathered together at the house to share the flight out. Nobody seems to notice seemingly-affable policeman Harry Lime (Joe Pesci), who is fruitlessly trying to catch the attention of a member of the family. His unexpected presence in the front hall has escaped the attention of the house's owners, Peter (John Heard) and Kate McCallister (Catherine O'Hara), who are busy getting packed upstairs. Their son, eight-year-old Kevin (Macaulay Culkin), is puzzling over what to put in his own suitcase, though he receives neither help nor sympathy from the plethora of siblings and cousins who are weaving their way through the house. Frustrated at being virtually ignored in his own home, Kevin exasperatedly cries out that as soon as he's old enough to move out, he plans to live alone. But his self-pity is interrupted when he glances out of the window and spots his neighbour, old man Marley (Roberts Blossom), clearing snow from his driveway. Kevin's brother Buzz (Devin Ratray) spins him a yarn that Marley had been a notorious serial killer in the late fifties, having murdered his victims with a snow-shovel very similar to the one that he is currently using. Kevin looks on with a new sense of awe as the seemingly-innocuous elderly gent continues to grit the road outside.

Aided by the opportune arrival of a pizza delivery man, Harry eventually manages to get hold of Peter and explains that he is doing a spot-check of houses in the area to ensure that everyone is aware of the dangers posed by burglars in the run up to Christmas. Peter gives him a rough outline of his home's defences, but is drawn away before Harry can finish pumping him for information. The cop continues to wander the ground floor until he encounters Kate, who tells him that the family will be departing early the next morning for France. Seeming unusually satisfied by this news, Harry departs with a promise that the McCallisters should rest assured that their house will be watched carefully while they are out of the country. Meanwhile, Kevin starts a fight with Buzz in the kitchen and accidentally drenches everyone's passport when he spills milk over them. As his tantrum is the last thing that the already-frenetic family need to deal with, Kate orders him to go up into the house's loft conversion and stay out of trouble. Aggrieved at this perceived injustice (he only attacked Buzz because his older brother had deliberately eaten his takeaway pizza), Kevin fires back that he would be much happier if he had no family at all.

During the night, a storm knocks out power to the house, resetting all of the alarm clocks. Thus the McCallisters are awakened by the arrival of airport courier minibuses at eight o'clock, which is when they were expected to be prepared to leave. A frantic dash takes place as they desperately try to get ready on time. As the luggage is loaded onto the minibuses parked outside, a head-count accidentally includes Mitch Murphy (Jeffrey Wiseman), a nosey kid from across the street who is rummaging through the McCallisters' bags. Thus when the family depart, even more flustered than before, they are completely unaware that they are one person short – particularly as their attention is diverted by a last minute warning from an electrical company lineman (Peter Siragusa) that although power has been restored to the house, the phone lines will be out of operation for the foreseeable future. Racing through the airport, the family are relieved when they manage to check in for their flight with mere moments to spare.

Back at the house, Kevin is bewildered when he wakes up and emerges from the attic to discover that his home is empty. He drifts from room to room, not quite believing the house to be vacant and completely oblivious to the fact that his family are now heading over the Atlantic towards their Parisian destination. Growing increasingly concerned, he heads over to the garage and discovers that his parents' cars are still parked there. As Kevin had never seen the long-departed airport minibuses, having been asleep when they had arrived, he begins to wonder whether his continual desire to see the back of his bickering family has finally paid off: from his point of view, they seem to have simply disappeared into thin air. At first, he seems mildly troubled by this prospect, but after remembering their harsh words to him the night before he soon decides that the solitary life may not be so bad at all.

Deciding to make the most of his new situation, Kevin is soon eating popcorn while jumping on his parents' bed and taking potshots at the laundry chute with Buzz's prized air rifle. He settles down in front of the TV with a massive bowl of ice-cream and marshmallows to watch an old forties gangster movie, blissfully unaware that his parents are only now realising that he is absent from their flight. But as the rest of the McCallister clan continue to head to Paris, full of guilt and unable to contact the house by phone, a carefree Kevin is having the time of his life careening down the stairs on a wooden sledge.

That night, two burglars are parked in a plumbers' van at the end of Kevin's street. One of them is none other than Harry, now revealed to be no policeman – he has been impersonating a cop prior to the holiday season, using his scam home security checks in order to trick householders into revealing if they will be away from their homes over Christmas. He is even able to tell when electric timers are set to activate, meaning that lit-up windows and doors are no deterrent: Harry is fully aware of which houses are fair game for a raid. This impresses his enthusiastic but slow-witted partner in crime, Marv Merchants (Daniel Stern), who is more than ready to put his crowbar to good use. Knowing that the McCallisters' home contains particularly rich pickings, they decide to make it their first stop on the street. But Kevin sees their shadows passing the lounge window as they head for the entry to the basement, giving him enough time to switch on as many lights as possible before they are able to force entry. Startled by the sudden activity – Harry had expected the house to be empty after his earlier discussion with Peter and Kate – the pair waste no time in departing. Petrified by the prospect of the house being broken into, Kevin cowers under his parents' bed until he can hear that the burglars' van has gone. Once they have left the street, he chastises himself for having been scared and heads out of the house proudly proclaiming that he will no longer be made to feel afraid. A few moments later, however, he runs into Marley and – not dissuaded by the elderly man's kind smile – promptly takes to his heels, screaming in terror until he is safe in his parents' bedroom once again.

At an airport in Paris, Kate and Peter are becoming increasingly frustrated at their inability to contact Kevin. With the phone lines still not restored to their street, they are unable to contact any of their neighbours, and the rest of their contacts are either away for the holidays or otherwise out of reach. Eventually they manage to persuade the local police force to send an officer to the house in order to check that Kevin is safe. But as Kevin refuses to answer the door, the police assume that the call has been a hoax. The earliest flight back to Chicago is still two days away, so Kate elects to stay at the airport in the hope that a cancellation will become available beforehand. Peter and the rest of the family head for the home of his brother, who has moved to Paris for work some years beforehand, in the hope of getting in contact with Kevin by telephone one way or another.

The next morning, Kevin discovers that he can't find his toothbrush and decides to head out to buy a new one. In search of money, he decides to raid Buzz's savings box but as it is placed on the topmost point of a set of wall-mounted shelves, he inadvertently brings the whole lot crashing down when he tries to climb them to retrieve the cash. As Kevin gathers together the purloined dollar bills, he is oblivious to the fact that the collapsing shelves have shattered Buzz's tarantula tank, setting loose his brother's cherished pet spider. Heading out onto the snowy street, he is confused to discover a van parked in the Murphys' driveway across the street. Little does Kevin realise that it belongs to Harry and Marv, who are currently clearing out the Murphys' home. While the pair are gathering valuables into swag bags, the answering machine kicks in — Peter is leaving a message, stating that he is still in Paris and asking if the Murphys will ring him back. Realising that the McCallisters' house is vacant after all, the burglars are ecstatic; they resolve to target it again as soon as night falls.

Kevin goes into a pharmacy to buy a toothbrush, but is shocked when Marley enters the shop and — gripped with fear — races away without paying. Believing him to be a shoplifter, the store's clerks (Jim Ortlieb and Ann Whitney) send the stock boy (Jim Ryan) to catch him. But Kevin is too hysterical with panic to see sense, and makes a break for it across a crowded park, losing his pursuers by skidding across a frozen pond filled with ice-skaters. When he eventually calms down, he becomes ashamed at having stolen property from the drugstore and wanders along the street in a daze. Meanwhile, Harry and Marv are leaving the Murphys' house, their efforts at breaking and entering quite superbly unsubtle. Determined to leave a calling card, Marv blocks the Murphys' drains and leaves the taps running, thus fostering their professional reputation as 'the Wet Bandits'. As they draw their van out of the driveway, they narrowly avoid hitting Kevin, who is still a little stupefied at the earlier events. Kevin immediately recognises Harry from the older man's earlier visit to his home while dressed as a policeman, now realising with shock what has been going on. Harry does not reciprocate Kevin's recollection, but notices his shocked expression nonetheless. Suspicious, he and Marv decide to follow Kevin in their van to see which house he enters, but Kevin diverts the burglars by ducking into a nearby church, causing them to lose his trail.

True to form, the Wet Bandits return to the street that night, and are stunned to discover that a party appears to be in full swing at the McCallisters' house. Puzzled at this latest development, and yet knowing that the family couldn't have returned from France so quickly, neither of them can fathom what is going on. But inside the house, Kevin has rigged up some mannequins with a series of ropes and pulleys, along with employing a variety of other improvised gadgets including cardboard cut-outs and an electric train set, to throw the burglars off the scent. Now totally baffled, Harry determines that they should return the following night in the hope that the 'guests' will have departed by then. Marv fires up the van's engine and heads off before they can be recognised; Kevin watches with immense satisfaction as they recede from view.

Over in Paris, a frustrated Peter continues without success to reach someone in Chicago who can get in contact with Kevin. While he continues to worry, the kids are resolutely unimpressed by their status quo – especially Buzz, who believes that Kevin richly deserves his current predicament. But he has no idea that back home, Kevin is currently ordering up his favourite pizza via home delivery, appearing to revel in the fact that he is using his irascible older brother's money to pay for it. At the airport, Kate has had some success of her own; with a mixture of smooth-talking and blatant bribery, she has managed to trade her two first-class seats on a later flight in order to board a plane back to the United States that same night.

Kevin is starting to miss his family, but keeps himself busy with housework to distract himself from his situation. Harry and Marv are once again casing the house, and are surprised that it should look so quiet in the daylight after having been so busy during the 'party'. Marv decides to head to the back of the house for a closer look, but Kevin pre-empts him by playing his favourite gangster movie on the kitchen TV set; the obtuse burglar believes the dialogue to be a conversation that is going on inside the house, and makes a run for it when he hears gunfire (actually Kevin setting off some firecrackers). Racing back to the van, he advises Harry that they should leave quickly, but his partner is not so sure. Keen to see exactly who else is in the house, and therefore giving them valuable evidence if the police should make enquiries into any crimes in the area (thus providing convenient cover for their own criminal activities), Harry decides that they should stay put for the time being.

Kate is back in the United States at last, though she has been forced to take a number of domestic flights in the hope of returning to Chicago by any means necessary. She is now trapped in Scranton with no available flights and, as it is now Christmas Eve, the airline ticket agent (Alan Wilder) is not hopeful that she will have any luck finding a way home any time soon. Physically exhausted and emotionally drained, Kate seems to be on the cusp of psychological meltdown when help comes in the most unlikely of forms. Gus Polinski (John Candy), a musical performer and self-proclaimed 'Polka King of the Midwest', has been forced to hire a truck to take his band to Milwaukee after their flight has been cancelled. As their route will take them through Chicago, Gus offers to take Kate along and return her to Kevin as soon as is possible.

The Wet Bandits are shaken out of their stakeout slumber when an oblivious Kevin emerges from the house, intent on chopping down a fir tree in his garden so that he can decorate it in time for Christmas. Recognising him, Harry realises that he and Marv have been tricked – Kevin has been the house's only occupant all along. Marv is reluctant to break into a house with a child living in it, but Harry is determined: the McCallisters' house is a burglar's paradise, and he is hell-bent on stripping it bare. Neither of them realise that Kevin can overhear their exchange, including their plan to return and force entry at nine o'clock that night.

Knowing now what his timetable for the rest of the day must be, Kevin is able to squeeze in a visit to a local Santa Claus (Ken Hudson Campbell), who is en-route to a party now that his grotto has been locked up for the season. Kevin asks Santa if he will consider giving him no presents the following day, on the condition that he return his family to their home instead. Baffled at the boy's deadly earnestness, 'Santa' tells him that he will do what he can. Making his way home, Kevin finds it difficult to watch other families gathering together in warm, cosy homes when he knows that he will have to return to an empty house once again. He stops by at his local church, where a choir are practicing for a Christmas Eve service later that night. Kevin takes a seat on a pew, only to be joined soon afterwards by Marley. Much to his amazement, the old man is friendly and conversational; he assures Kevin that although many tall tales are told about him, there is no need to be afraid. Slowly, the boy comes to realise that his mortal fear of the kindly gent has been based entirely upon fabrication. Marley explains that his grand-daughter is singing in the choir that night, and that he is attending the rehearsal to hear her sing as he is keen to avoid his son, who will be attending the later service. In response to Kevin's further questioning, Marley reveals that he and his son have been estranged following a raging argument many years beforehand, and although he has become keen for rapprochement he is wary of extending an olive branch for fear that it may be rejected. Kevin advises him to make the attempt anyway; if his hand of friendship is rebuffed, Marley will have lost nothing. In return, Marley emphasises the importance of family, telling Kevin that no matter what comes between him and his parents or siblings, the bonds of love will still remain.

Realising that time grows short, Kevin runs home and gets ready to defend his home from Harry and Marv's intended burglary. Devising a highly elaborate series of booby-traps, Kevin moves at breakneck speed to get all of his snares into position before the Wet Bandits can arrive. Sure enough, the van pulls up right on time, and Kevin knows that the game is on. After their attempt to gain entry through the back door leads to a painful encounter with Buzz's air rifle, the Bandits decide to divide their efforts – Marv heads for the basement, while Harry goes to the front door. Only just managing to gain entry to the house (though accruing many bumps and bruises along the way), the burglars soon find themselves victim to an overabundance of jury-rigged, damage-inducing devices which include irons, tar, nails, a blowtorch, glue, feathers, model cars, red-hot metal, paint pots, tripwires and even Christmas tree ornaments. Even Buzz's escaped tarantula manages to save Kevin from potential disaster when it makes an opportune appearance. After a prolonged game of cat and mouse, Kevin leads the Bandits away from his home and across the street to the Murphys' house – now flooded, due to Marv's earlier calling-card intervention. Once there, Kevin seems to have been outwitted at the last minute, but he is saved by the surprise appearance of Marley, who knocks the two burglars unconscious with his snow shovel. Concerned for Kevin's wellbeing, he returns the boy to his home, where Kevin watches in comfort as the police (responding to his own tip-off) arrive at the Murphy's home and take Harry and Marv into custody. Thanks to Marv's watery trademark, the officers know each and every property that the Bandits have broken into, and they are determined that the pair will face appropriate justice.

Now safe, Kevin quickly returns his home to normality, anticipating the arrival of Christmas. But all the festive embellishment and comfortable warmth of the house can do nothing to assuage his loneliness. The next morning, he awakes to a white Christmas and races downstairs in the hope that his family will have returned to him. He is deeply disappointed when he discovers that everything is exactly as he had left it the previous night, but his regret soon turns to delight when his mother arrives at the front door almost immediately afterwards (courtesy of Polinski and his rental truck). Kate and Kevin enjoy a tearful reunion, but neither is prepared for the sight of Peter and the rest of the McCallister kids, who pile in after having returned home on the scheduled early-morning flight from Paris. (Because of all the hitches with her domestic flights, Kate has – in real terms – only beaten them home by a matter of minutes.) The family are overjoyed to be back together again; even Buzz is grudgingly pleased to see that Kevin is safe and well. While Peter puzzles over the discovery of Harry's gold tooth, which is lying dislodged on the living room floor, Kevin looks out of the window and sees a jubilant Marley warmly embracing his son, their differences now settled. Satisfied that all has turned out well in the end, Kevin takes a moment to marvel at the unifying power of the Christmas spirit that is, until Buzz discovers what remains of his room.

Home Alone is a stirring tribute to the nuclear family, and one which appears unerringly traditional in comparison to later nineties films with similar themes of domestic relationships and reconciliation at Christmas. Like Robert Lieberman's *All I Want For Christmas* (1991), the film promotes the benefits of marriage and the stable family unit, whereas the decade's later offerings became significantly more inclusive, emphasising that term family can encompass a very diverse range of relationships which transcend mere blood relations. But Hughes seems much more interested in ensuring that his audience are being entertained than he is with making any profound socio-political point, and indeed he and director Columbus work hard to maintain a warm, festive atmosphere throughout. The McCallisters' luxurious home in an affluent suburb offers Kevin the widest possible range of opportunities to defend his property against the Wet Bandits, and indeed his inspired range of improvised security countermeasures are a joy to behold.

While the film has, of course, become most affectionately regarded for its climactic sequence where Kevin repels the burglars from his home, it is also notable for the poignancy of its emotional heart, which emphasises the need to belong and feel wanted (especially at Christmas) without drifting into over-sentimentality. Certainly Hughes is careful to take a decisively light-hearted approach to the film's events as they unfold, providing a kind of ironclad internal logic which belies the relative implausibility of much of the narrative. Although the conceit of he disconnected telephone line works well in the days immediately prior to the omnipresence of cellphones, it would otherwise seem overly convenient that absolutely no family acquaintances are left in the Chicago area to check on Kevin, or that – terrified by the prospect of being completely alone for so long – even the most independent of adolescents would be able to resist the temptation to call on one of the few remaining non-vacationing neighbours for help (or even to find a call-box and phone the police). Hughes somehow manages to keep the tone so blithe and upbeat, largely due to Culkin's captivating lead performance, that the audience is never allowed time to consider the grave implications that so easily could have befallen a child who had really been left in Kevin's situation.

Typical of a John Hughes production, *Home Alone* also contains many witty references to classic films, and to popular culture in general. Joe Pesci's hapless burglar Harry Lyme, of course, shares his name with Orson Welles's famous character in Carol Reed's seminal Graham Greene adaptation *The Third Man* (1949). Kevin's much-loved gangster movie, *Angels with Filthy Souls*, is an obvious pastiche of Michael Curtiz's *Angels with Dirty Faces* (1938), which had starred James Cagney and Humphrey Bogart. While killing time in Paris waiting for their flight home, the McCallisters wind up watching *It's a Wonderful Life* dubbed into French (a fact which is particularly apposite given that *Washington Times* critic Hal Hinson was later to describe *Home Alone* as a filmic collision between the emotional sentimentality of Frank Capra and the cartoon mayhem of animator Chuck Jones).[1] And perhaps most noteworthy of all, the posters and promotional material for the film demonstrated Hughes's keen interest in artwork, featuring Culkin screaming with his hands on either side of his face in a gesture which closely imitated Edvard Munch's famous painting *The Scream*.[2]

Columbus's direction is efficient and capable, nicely contrasting the frantic, accelerated mayhem of the bustling McCallister house in the early scenes with Kevin's later escapades alone in his deserted home. There are additionally many pleasing sight gags which recur, such as the McCallisters' constantly-capsized garden statue which appears to be in the line of every car or van that approaches it, and also wry humour such as Santa's gift of lime-favoured Tic-Tacs (being the night of Christmas Eve, he had given all of the remaining candy-canes to his assistant before closing up for the evening). The film features a number of nicely understated supporting performances such as Gerry Bamman's memorably crass Uncle Frank, moaning snidely one minute and then shamelessly pilfering complimentary airline goodies the next, and John Candy's warm-hearted cameo appearance, heavily influenced by his earlier role as travelling shower curtain-ring salesman Del Griffith in Hughes's *Planes, Trains and Automobiles* (1987). *Home Alone* also benefits greatly from a sweeping score by legendary film composer John Williams. Moving effortlessly between tender contemplation and frenetic action, the soundtrack is uniformly impressive, though the atmospheric title theme and up-tempo 'Holiday Flight' are standout pieces. The film also features the song 'Somewhere in My Memory', with music by Williams and lyrics by *Scrooge*'s Leslie Bricusse, which is performed as a melancholy Kevin watches other families in the neighbourhood getting ready for Christmas as he dejectedly faces returning to an empty house.

Though still only ten years old at the time of *Home Alone*'s release, Macaulay Culkin was already an established actor, having made his screen debut in Jack Bender's TV horror movie *The Midnight Hour* (1985). Following this was an episode of television series *The Equalizer* in 1988, and appearances in Daniel Petrie's moving family drama *Rocket Gibraltar* (1988) and Alan J. Pakula's romance *See You in the Morning* (1989). His profile was considerably enhanced with his performance in John Hughes's comedy hit *Uncle Buck* (1989), in which he was to appear with his later *Home Alone* co-star John Candy. Although *Home Alone* is by far his most recognisable cinematic role to date, Culkin has remained active in theatre, television and cinema over the past two decades; most prominent amongst his film work has been Chris Columbus's *Only the Lonely* (1991), Howard Zieff's *My Girl* (1991), Emile Ardolino's *The Nutcracker* (1993), Donald Petrie's *Ri¢hie Ri¢h* (1994), and – more recently – in four episodes of Seth Green's avidly-followed cult TV series *Robot Chicken* (between 2005 and 2006).

Almost as central to the film's success as Culkin's winning performance were the two ill-fated antagonists, an appealing portrayal of quite possibly the least-competent burglars ever to terrorise a suburban street. Joe Pesci had appeared occasionally on film and television since the early 1960s before making an indelible impression on audiences with his performance in Ralph De Vito's *The Death Collector* (1976). He achieved considerable critical acclaim throughout the early 1980s due to his high-profile appearances in films including Martin Scorsese's *Raging Bull* (1980), James Signorelli's *Easy Money* (1983), and Sergio Leone's *Once Upon a Time in America* (1984), as well as the short-lived but well-received TV series *Half Nelson* (1985). Later in the eighties he continued to diversify, with performances in movies such as Elie Chouraqui's action thriller *Man on Fire* (1987), Jerry Kramer and Jim Blashfield's musical fantasy *Moonwalker* (1988), and Richard Donner's crime comedy sequel *Lethal Weapon 2* (1989). Pesci was nominated for an Academy Award in the Best Actor in a Supporting Role category for his performance in *Raging Bull*, and would later go on to win an Oscar in the same category for his role as Tommy DeVito in Martin Scorsese's *Goodfellas* (1990). Among his many other awards and nominations were a BAFTA win in 1982 for Most Outstanding Newcomer to Leading Film Roles (for his appearance in *Raging Bull*), and Golden Globe nominations in 1981 and 1991 (for *Raging Bull* and *Goodfellas*). Casting a heavyweight actor like Pesci as the stooge in a family comedy may have seemed like a recipe for disaster, given that he had become so well known for playing emotionally complex characters and borderline-sociopathic organised crime operatives, but it would ultimately reveal itself to be a masterstroke: his Harry Lyme was to prove the most congenial of rogues, happy to clear out someone's house one minute and then advise wandering kids about road safety the next.

It is much to Pesci's credit that we feel every little indignity and burst of pain that his character is exposed to during the film's climax (his one-man battle with a flight of icy steps is singularly unforgettable), and he shares this skill with his co-star Daniel Stern: the two actors' performances complement each other perfectly. Similarly known for serious dramatic roles throughout the eighties, often as eccentrics or intellectuals, Stern transformed himself for the part into a wide-eyed, zealous but ultimately rather dense character. Marv seems more concerned with the adrenaline rush of burglary than the value of his ill-gotten gains, and his doomed desire to establish Harry and himself as a legendary criminal duo ultimately proves to be their downfall. Stern had made his cinematic debut in the late seventies with his performance as Cyril in Peter Yates's sporting comedy drama *Breaking Away* (1979). In the eighties he combined roles in prominent films such as John Schlesinger's *Honky Tonk Freeway* (1981) and Barry Levinson's *Diner* (1982) with quirkier cult movies such as Douglas Cheek's *C.H.U.D.* (1984) and Tim Burton's *Frankenweenie* (1984). Following a stint as Joey Nathan in TV series *Hometown* (1985), Stern's success had continued in many diverse features which included Woody Allen's *Hannah and Her Sisters* (1986), Annabel Jankel and Rocky Morton's *D.O.A.* (1988), George P. Cosmatos's *Leviathan* (1989) and Herbert Ross's *My Blue Heaven* (1990).

Although Hughes's stellar reputation as a producer and film-maker had been well established in the eighties, no-one could have predicted just how well *Home Alone* would go on to perform at the box-office when it was released in November 1990. With an estimated budget of $15,000,000, the film had made back $17,081,997 by the end of its opening weekend alone.[3] It enjoyed a long run in cinemas, eventually grossing $285,761,243 in the domestic market and a further $190,923,432 in foreign territories: an incredible combined worldwide gross of $476,684,675.[4] This meant that *Home Alone* not only became the top-grossing film of 1990, but would also earn a place as one of the twenty most profitable movies in film history.[5]

The film's meteoric commercial success has meant that its decidedly uneven critical reception is often forgotten today. While some reviewers applauded *Home Alone*'s dry sense of humour and its embrace of 'anti-sentiment' (noting that it followed through on its unconventional premise rather than abandoning it late in the day, as *Scrooged* had done),[6] others felt that the slapstick elements were unamusing and the central situation unengaging, with some expressing the somewhat radical view that it was one of the worst films that Hughes had ever been involved with.[7] Most reviews tended to fall between these two extremes, however, with Culkin's strikingly mature performance often singled out for special praise by commentators.[8] More recent appraisals of the film have been considerably more receptive, with critics of the past few years noting the film's universal appeal to audiences young and old,[9] its deft application of clowning physical comedy,[10] and the congruence with Hughes's earlier output, sharing many of the concerns he had expressed throughout the eighties concerning the intrinsic value of the individual.[11]

Home Alone performed well at a number of award ceremonies following its release. It received two Academy Award nominations in 1991: one for John Williams's original score, and the other for Williams and Leslie Bricusse in the Best Original Song category for 'Somewhere in My Memory'. Williams's music was also successful at other ceremonies: his score won a BMI Film Music Award in 1991, and 'Somewhere in My Memory' was also nominated for a Grammy Award in the category of Best Song Written Specifically for a Motion Picture or for Television in 1992. *Home Alone* was nominated for a Golden Globe Award for Best Motion Picture: Comedy/ Musical, with Macaulay Culkin also nominated for Best Performance by an Actor in a Motion Picture: Comedy/ Musical at the same ceremony. Culkin was to win a Young Artist Award for Best Young Actor Starring in a Motion Picture in 1991 with the film winning in the Most Entertaining Family Youth Motion Picture: Comedy/ Action category, while Angela Goethals was nominated for the Best Young Actress Supporting Role in a Motion Picture Award. The Casting Society of America was also to present Jane Jenkins and Janet Hirshenson with an Artios Award for Best Casting for Feature Film: Comedy.

Given the film's massive box-office success, a sequel seemed inevitable, and sure enough the main cast and production team were to reunite soon after to create *Home Alone 2: Lost in New York* (1992). Once again directed by Chris Columbus and featuring a John Hughes screenplay, the similarly Christmas-situated *Home Alone 2* centres upon a mishap which sees Kevin separated from his family on the way to a family holiday to Miami and eventually winding up (as the title suggests) in New York City. Once there, he manages to trick his way into renting a well-appointed room at an upmarket hotel, and is then faced with the twin difficulties of reuniting with his family while simultaneously thwarting an attempt by the recently-escaped Wet Bandits (now rechristened the Sticky Bandits) to burgle a vast toy store in the city over the holidays. As well as Macaulay Culkin, all of the central characters are portrayed by the original actors, including John Heard and Catherine O'Hara as Kevin's beleaguered parents and Joe Pesci and Daniel Stern as the increasingly browbeaten two-man burglary team. The film also featured excellent supporting performances by the ever-charismatic Tim Curry as a snooty hotel concierge and Irish actress Brenda Fricker, who portrays a character with a very similar function to Roberts Blossom's Marley in the original film. Although the film was a huge financial success, it was unable to replicate the monumental box-office achievement of the first *Home Alone*, and the many similarities between the sequel's narrative and incidents which had taken place in the original were not lost on critics, who gave *Lost in New York* an emphatically mixed response at the time of its release.

Following this was another sequel, *Home Alone 3* (1997), which retained Hughes as screenwriter but was to see the directorial duties taken up by Raja Gosnell (who had been the editor of the first two films). Starring Alex D. Linz as eight-year-old Alex Pruitt, the film features an entirely different cast of characters with none of the original performers returning. Featuring a convoluted plot which centres on a smuggled computer chip that has accidentally fallen into the hands of a young boy (who must subsequently defend his home from a team of terrorists that are determined to retrieve it at any cost), the film featured a similarly wintry atmosphere to the first two *Home Alone* movies but otherwise had little in common with its considerably more profitable predecessors. In spite of general critical hostility to *Home Alone 3*, a further sequel – this time a made-for-TV movie – was broadcast on ABC in 2002. Returning to the story of young Kevin McCallister, now portrayed by Mike Weinberg, Rod Daniel's *Home Alone 4: Taking Back the House* featured a rematch between Kevin and burglar Marv Merchants (French Stewart), now joined by his wife and partner-in-crime Vera (Missi Pyle). The only *Home Alone* film not to feature a John Hughes screenplay (the script was penned by Debra Frank and Steve L. Hayes), the narrative focuses in part on Kevin coming to terms with his parents' recent divorce, but by now the novelty of the cycle's madcap home-defence slapstick had worn decidedly thin.

The immense commercial success of *Home Alone* in cinemas heralded a new boom-time for Christmas-themed films. Although it has been noted that the film contained a faint whiff of criticism towards upper-middle class lifestyles, calling attention to the fact that the value placed on materialistic pursuits and pursuing a comfortable quality of life was simultaneously underscoring the need for parents to ensure that they adequately prioritised their offspring,[12] *Home Alone* nonetheless signified a move away from the manifest cultural commentary that had been so conspicuous in the Christmas movies of the eighties. By emphasising traditional values in a manner that was relevant to – and popular with – contemporary audiences, the influence of Columbus's film was to be far-reaching enough to set the pace for later family-oriented features in the Christmas genre. Just as it had drastically raised the bar at the box-office, so too would the style and approach of *Home Alone* cast a long shadow over the festive film-making of the decade to come.

Historical Context

Home Alone made its nationwide film debut across America on 16 November 1990 (following a debut screening in Chicago on 10 November). Also making their first appearances in cinemas that day were John G. Avildsen's *Rocky V*, Mike Gabriel and Hendel Butoy's *The Rescuers Down Under*, and Marleen Gorris's *The Last Island*. 'Love Takes Time' by Mariah Carey was at the top of the Billboard Hot 100 chart that week. In current affairs, President George H.W. Bush signed the Clear Air Act of 1990, Michael Heseltine contested Margaret Thatcher's leadership of the Conservative Party in the UK, and the Philippines were struck by a major typhoon.

18

THE MUPPET CHRISTMAS CAROL
(1992)

Jim Henson Productions/ The Jim Henson Company/ Walt Disney Pictures

Director: Brian Henson
Producers: Brian Henson and Martin G. Baker
Screenwriter: Jerry Juhl, based on the novella by Charles Dickens

MAIN CAST

Michael Caine	-	Ebenezer Scrooge
Dave Goelz	-	The Great Gonzo (as Charles Dickens)
Steve Whitmire	-	Kermit the Frog (as Bob Cratchit)
Frank Oz	-	Miss Piggy (as Emily Cratchit)
Steven Mackintosh	-	Fred, Scrooge's Nephew
Robin Weaver	-	Clara
Meredith Braun	-	Belle
Louise Gold	-	Mrs Dilber

If *Home Alone* had determined a new tone for Christmas films, indicating a sort of back-to-basics approach for the genre as the nineties progressed, then *The Muppet Christmas Carol* was to fit snugly into this new remit of rediscovered traditionalism. A determinedly family-oriented take on Dickens's acutely well-known tale, the warm and charming approach of the Jim Henson Company towards the source material was to seem far removed indeed from the contemporary cynicism that had been on display in *Scrooged*. Yet for all its emphasis on fidelity to the original text, this treatment of *A Christmas Carol* was certainly to prove anything but conventional, and would firmly establish itself as an adaptation that only the Muppets Studio could have achieved.

Devised by celebrated puppet creator and performer Jim Henson, the Muppets are characters who are operated by means of an amalgamation of marionette and puppet technology. Their colourful felt bodies and expressive features made them immediately popular with audiences when they first appeared on American television on the *Sam and Friends* series (1955-61). After numerous appearances on national TV, Henson's work achieved mass exposure with the debut of acclaimed educational series *Sesame Street* in 1969. Following this in the seventies was the television phenomenon that, in the minds of many viewers, will always be Henson's crowning achievement: *The Muppet Show* (1976-81). Using its variety show premise to full effect over the course of five seasons, the show's massive success with audiences led to the Muppets becoming firmly established in popular culture on both sides of the Atlantic. By the time that James Frawley's *The Muppet Movie* was released in 1979, the characters had become so well-known amongst the general public that they had largely ceased to be considered as manually operated marionette-puppets, but rather as autonomous celebrities in their own right. Kermit the Frog's long-running flirtations with Miss Piggy, Fozzie Bear's doomed ambitions to become a comedy legend and the Great Gonzo's generally bizarre behaviour had all passed into the cultural consciousness, with different generations finding entertainment in the frenetic hijinks of Henson's characters. Throughout the eighties Jim Henson Productions were to release a further two well-received Muppet movies, Jim Henson's *The Great Muppet Caper* (1981) and Frank Oz's *The Muppets Take Manhattan* (1984), along with many other TV series and specials which included *Fraggle Rock* (1983-87) and *The Storyteller* (1988). Although Henson died in 1990, his artistic legacy his lived on and has continued to flourish. His creations have remained perennially popular with audiences throughout the world, with Muppets appearing on television and in film productions regularly up until the present day.

The Muppets have a long and fruitful relationship with the festive season, with TV highlights over the years having included Jon Stone's *Christmas Eve on Sesame Street* (1978), Tony Charmoli's *John Denver and the Muppets: A Christmas Together* (1979), Eric Till's *The Christmas Toy* (1986), Peter Harris and Eric Till's *A Muppet Family Christmas* (1987) and, in more recent years, Kirk R. Thatcher's *It's a Very Merry Muppet Christmas Movie* (2002) and *A Muppets Christmas: Letters to Santa* (2008). *The Muppet Christmas Carol*, however, remains their only cinematic outing to date which has featured the festive season. Helmed by Jim Henson's son, Brian

Henson, the film was to follow in the tradition of the preceding three Muppet movies in that it would present a variety of musical numbers to punctuate the action. Furthermore, this unique adaptation of Dickens's story would blend together a variety of Muppet characters who would, in turn, be portraying characters from the original text. Thus audiences were, for instance, presented with performer Steve Whitmire operating Kermit the Frog, who in turn is playing Bob Cratchit.

Brian Henson's association with Muppetry is a long one which stretches back to an appearance in Jim Henson's short film *Wheels That Go* (1967) as well as the first episode of *Sesame Street* back in 1969. His performances throughout the eighties included puppet operation in Jim Henson's *The Great Muppet Caper* (1981) and *Labyrinth* (1986), Frank Oz's *The Muppets Take Manhattan* (1984) and Walter Murch's *Return to Oz* (1985), while he contributed special effects for episodes of TV's *Fraggle Rock* in 1984 as well as on *The Muppets Take Manhattan*. Active as a producer since 1991, his directorial career began with the TV series *Jim Henson Presents Mother Goose Stories* (1987-88). His work as a director, writer and producer has continued since then, and he has since helmed *Muppet Treasure Island* (1996) and episodes of TV's *Muppets Tonight* (1996-98), as well as acclaimed TV science fiction drama *Farscape: The Peacekeeper Wars* (2004). In 1992 he was to win the Scientific and Engineering Award, along with co-nominees Faz Fazakas, Dave Housman, Peter Miller and John Stephenson, at the Academy Awards.

Given that the overwhelming majority of the characters in Henson's adaptation of *A Christmas Carol* are being portrayed by the madcap Muppets, it is suprising – and commendable – to note how loyal the film remains to the spirit and nature of the original text. So profoundly integrated are the Muppet characters in the popular cultural psyche that at no point are the audience inclined to think of them as human-operated devices: they appear, quite simply, to be nothing less individual actors in their own right. And it is precisely because of this notion of the Muppets as autonomous performers that the film works so well: like *The Muppet Show* before it, the film toys with a kind of teasing postmodernity, creating a film which is wholly a Muppet feature just as much as it is wholly a faithful adaptation of a Dickensian novella.[1] Perhaps the most apparent proponent of this strategy is the use of The Great Gonzo (Dave Goelz), among the most eccentric of all Muppet characters, in the role of Charles Dickens. Accompanied by his friend, a laconic rat with a New Jersey accent named Rizzo (Steve Whitmire), Gonzo is acutely aware of the fact that he is playing the part of Dickens largely in order to act as the film's narrator. Rather than approaching the role in a direct way, as a conventional narrator might be inclined to, Gonzo playfully utilises his portrayal of Dickens throughout the film to explore the range and reach of its narrative function. The fourth wall is regularly broken when Rizzo continually calls into question the plausibility of Gonzo's depiction of the nineteenth century literary genius (considering, for instance, the likelihood of the real Dickens being blue and furry, or having a talking rat as a friend), and also when the pair regularly discover that they have difficulty keeping up with the action – a narrator may be omniscient, after all, but omnipresence is discovered to be another matter entirely. The latter factor leads to numerous scrapes throughout the film, where Gonzo discovers that he has been temporarily (and inadvertently) cut off from the main focus of the film and must employ devices such as grappling hooks to get back into spotlight when necessary.

Gonzo and Rizzo's continual commentary on the film's cultural relevance and faithfulness to the source material is highly entertaining, and is one factor of the film which makes it a unique and distinctive adaptation of such a familiar tale. (Gonzo is so dedicated to the furtherance of the novella, in fact, that his closing words are an entreatment to the viewers to get hold of their own copy of Dickens's book if they have enjoyed watching the film.) Commentators such as Hugh H. Davis have favourably considered the skill of screenwriter Jerry Juhl in employing this technique to engage audiences with the characters – as Muppets, familiar from previous televisual and cinematic outings – while simultaneously offering an accurate depiction of Dickens's characters from the original source text.[2] There is also the fact, as James Chapman has noted, that the film simultaneously calls upon audience awareness of the individual Muppet characters and their behaviour as well as preconceptions about the story and presentation of *A Christmas Carol* in popular media, thus making it a filmic experience that is acutely concerned with its own textual identity.[3]

Certainly a working knowledge of *The Muppet Show* adds an extra dimension to the film, though it is certainly not essential to the enjoyment of *The Muppet Christmas Carol*. Statler and Waldorf, the two senior citizens who were forever scoffing at the performance talents of the other Muppets in the TV show, appear in the twin roles of Jacob and Robert Marley: because the two characters are inseparable within the Muppet universe, their function with audiences who are familiar with their earlier appearances would seem impaired (or at least unusual) if only one were present, and for this reason the story's *dramatis personae* is amended accordingly. Likewise Scrooge's old employer Fezziwig becomes 'Fozziwig', the owner of a rubber chicken factory, referencing one of the props used by Fozzie Bear in his (perpetually ill-fated) attempts to become a successful stand-up comedian in earlier Muppet appearances. Sam the Eagle, a proud patriot who always espouses the virtues of truth, justice and the American way, needs to be reminded at the last minute that he is supposed to be British – or, at least, playing a character who is British – for the purposes of fulfilling his role as Scrooge's old schoolmaster. (In a nice touch, an elderly version of Sam/ the schoolmaster and Fozzie/ Fozziwig can be seen at the end of the film when Scrooge momentarily visits their retirement home.) Other minor roles, such as that of Bob Cratchit's wife, are expanded and embellished to accommodate the relative prominence of their Muppet actor (in this case, the glamorous but infamously capricious Miss Piggy, cast somewhat against type as the pragmatic Emily). It almost seems strange, then, that no amount of augmentation to fit Dickens's story into a Muppet-oriented framework ever seems to compromise the film's truthfulness to the textual source, or even threaten the suspense of disbelief – and considering that the production calls for singing fruit and vegetables at one point, this is no mean feat. There are other minor deviations from the original, such as the elimination of Scrooge's sister Fan from the Christmas Past sequences, and the considerable curtailing of the climactic scenes at the home of his nephew, Fred. But generally, the tale is related with such close consideration to the original novella that even the film's subtle visual in-jokes are in no danger of overstaying their welcome: later scenes reveal a store named 'Statler and Waldorf', whereas another shop bears the name 'Micklewhite's' – a reference to Maurice Micklewhite, the real name of the film's human star, Michael Caine.

The necessity for human actors in the film is summed up perfectly by Ginger Stelle, who observes that as Scrooge is characterised by a capacity for fundamental change in his very nature (leading to the emergence of an entirely different temperament and disposition), the use of a Muppet character/performer for the part would be inappropriate precisely because the audience had become so familiar with each of their particular personalities.[4] Therefore any of the more prominent Muppets, known to behave and react in a certain way, would not be plausible in the role of Scrooge due to the fact that many viewers would have a preconceived notion of their likely actions and conduct, thus potentially damaging the film's dramatic credibility. As Scrooge is human, of course, his earlier selves are also played by humans, as are his fiancée and also his nephew. Yet it is much to the credit of Brian Henson's direction that the human actors and Muppet performers mix so seamlessly on screen: not even the final scenes around the Christmas dinner table appear jarring, where scores of Muppets prepare themselves for a turkey dinner in immediate proximity to the human cast members, due to the film's innate balance of unconventional internal logic and sheer festive charm.

Michael Caine makes for a very restrained Scrooge: judiciously, he chooses to make no attempt to compete with his furry co-stars when it comes to dominating the screen, instead presenting a nuanced performance of great subtlety. His transformation during his three spiritual visitations is carefully underplayed, and even his display of reformed character on Christmas Day is delicately drawn while remaining warmly sincere. There may be no dancing in the street as with Albert Finney's Scrooge, nor even the barely-contained glee of Alastair Sim, but Caine's evocation of Ebenezer is touching precisely because of its suggestion of wistful regret over wasted opportunity rather than the customary display of joy and merriment that had become so common to other big screen versions of Dickens's famous miser. One of the most successful British actors of the post-War era, Caine began appearing in films and on television in the early fifties. His breakthrough role came in 1964 as the aristocratic army officer Lieutenant Gonville Bromhead in Cy Endfield's *Zulu*, following which Caine went on to make some of his best-known appearances in films such as Sidney J. Furie's *The Ipcress File* (1965), the title role in Lewis Gilbert's *Alfie* (1966), and Guy Hamilton's *Battle of Britain* (1969), quickly establishing himself as a household name in British cinema. Beginning the seventies with his masterful portrayal of Jack Carter in Mike Hodges's *Get Carter* (1971), his acclaimed performances included roles in John Huston's *The Man Who Would Be King* (1975), John Sturges's *The Eagle Has Landed* (1976), and Richard Attenborough's *A Bridge Too Far* (1977). He remained highly active throughout the eighties, starring in Lewis Gilbert's *Educating Rita* (1983), Woody Allen's *Hannah and Her Sisters* (1986), John Mackenzie's *The Fourth Protocol* (1987) and Frank Oz's *Dirty Rotten Scoundrels* (1988). His long and distinguished acting career has been recognised many times at awards ceremonies, including his presentation with the prestigious Academy Fellowship Award at the 2000 BAFTA Awards. He has been nominated for BAFTAs on some eight occasions, winning in the Best Actor category for his performance in *Educating Rita*. Additionally nominated for twelve Golden Globe Awards (winning for appearances in *Educating Rita*, David Wickes's TV drama *Jack the Ripper*, 1988, and Mark Herman's *Little Voice*, 1998), he has also received three Emmy nominations. At the Academy Awards he has been nominated six times, receiving the Best Actor in a Supporting Role Award for *Hannah and Her Sisters* as well as his performance in Lasse Hallström's *The Cider House Rules* (1999). Caine remains a highly-visible actor today, most notably with recent appearances as butler Alfred Pennyworth in Christopher Nolan's box-office smashes *Batman Begins* (2005) and *The Dark Knight* (2008), which have won him a whole new generation of fans.

The other human performers are well-employed, even if their appearance generally amounts to little more than an extended cameo. Most notable are Steven Mackintosh as Scrooge's nephew Fred, Robin Weaver as the bubbly, cheerful Clara, and Meredith Braun as a beautiful and suitably melancholic Belle. The sets are flawless throughout, with decorator Michael Ford creating a highly detailed environment which conveys aspects of Victorian style and warm touches of larger-than-life Muppet character in a combination which is as classy as it is seamless. Special note is also due to the detailed costume design by Ann Hollowood and Polly Smith, particularly in their work on Scrooge's meticulously-crafted attire which helps to make Michael Caine's appearance one of the most dapper versions of all cinematic iterations of Dickens's curmudgeonly old skinflint. Miles Goodman provides a likeable, atmospheric score and, like almost all of the Muppets' cinematic outings, the film also includes a variety of musical numbers, in this case featuring music and lyrics composed by Paul Williams. Standout pieces include the opening song 'Scrooge', where the protagonist is introduced as he makes his way briskly through the streets of Victorian London; 'Marley and Marley', the introduction of Scrooge's old partners in their spectral form, and 'Thankful Heart', where the reformed Ebenezer voices thanks for his change in character. Perhaps the best-known song from the film, 'When Love is Gone', is performed by Scrooge and Belle at the cusp of their separation (a scene which was excised from the original cinematic release of the film, but later reinstated for VHS and DVD releases), and is mirrored by the later 'When Love is Found', sung by the assembled cast at the conclusion. Singer Martina McBride also performs a reprise of 'When Love is Gone' during the film's end credits sequence.

A somewhat lopsided critical reception awaited *The Muppet Christmas Carol* at the time of its release. Some reviewers applauded the way that Henson and his team had evoked a sense of timelessness throughout the film, incorporating the Muppets faultlessly into a particular place and era which were quite different from their usual contemporary adventures,[5] while others found that the adaptation was lacking in much of the drive and energy that had been typical of *The Muppet Show*.[6] Although many reviews were lukewarm, finding that the film was technically competent but had brought little that was new to the telling of Dickens's oft-told moral fable,[7] even the more hostile critics spared Gonzo's cleverly self-aware narrative abilities from their analytical censure.[8] Retrospective reviews of the film in more recent times have remained fairly polarised. While commentators have praised the emotionally moving power and subtlety of Caine's central performance,[9] others have criticised it for being rather too sedate to fully convince, particularly following the character's seismic change of heart at the end of the film.[10] Some reviewers have echoed earlier criticism that *The Muppet Christmas Carol* was deficient in presenting a consistent sense of vigour or liveliness throughout its narrative's proceedings,[11] but balancing the argument are commentators who have praised the film's irresistible charm and the dexterity of Brian Henson's direction.[12]

The Muppet Christmas Carol's commercial performance at the box-office, though respectable, was adversely affected on account of the fact that it was released into cinemas at the same time as a number of other high-profile features, most notably the blockbuster *Home Alone 2: Lost in New York*. Nonetheless, the film has achieved lasting cult success due to its place in the pantheon of Muppet features, and its profile has been further enhanced by its repeated releases on video and DVD over the years. *The Muppet Christmas Carol* was also to win Brian Henson the Best Direction Award at the Fantafestival Awards in 1993.

Today, *The Muppet Christmas Carol* remains almost certainly the most prominent adaptation of Dickens' story to have been produced in the 1990s. Although there were other versions released throughout the decade, some of them highly acclaimed, they were generally broadcast on television rather than released into cinemas. Foremost among these was Patrick Stewart's strikingly austere Ebenezer Scrooge in David Hugh Jones's *A Christmas Carol* (1999), shown on TV's Hallmark Entertainment channel. This followed Stewart's hugely successful one-man performance of Dickens's novella in 1991, where he was to play every character from the book to great critical acclaim and was later nominated for the Drama Desk Award for Outstanding One-Person Show for his efforts. Other noteworthy Scrooges of the nineties included Jack Palance in Ken Jubenvill's TV movie *Ebenezer* (1997), an interesting Wild West interpretation of the story where the story of Scrooge is transplanted to nineteenth-century America.

One of the most family-friendly live action versions of the tale, *The Muppet Christmas Carol* had treated the style and content of Dickens's work with respect while also introducing original new angles to the story in order to retain contemporary interest. While it contains plenty to entertain younger viewers, adults (particularly those who grew up with *The Muppet Show*) will no doubt appreciate the film's loyalty to the distinctive characters of the Muppet players, as well as the knowing narrative ingenuity of Charles Dickens in the guise of Gonzo. But the film also suggested a retreat from the darkness of eighties adaptations of the tale, lacking both the commanding soberness of the George C. Scott version and the sardonic bite of *Scrooged*. There is also, in the closing scenes where Scrooge acknowledges the importance of his family and new-found friends, a warm appreciation of personal responsibility and the benefits of mutual co-operation: surely amongst the most traditional of all Christmas messages. But as we shall see, Scrooge was far from the least conventional character to seek a sense of belonging in the Christmas films of the nineties.

Historical Context

The Muppet Christmas Carol first appeared in American cinemas on 11 December 1992. Two other films were also making their debuts in theatres on that day: Jonathan Kaplan's *Love Field* and Steve Miner's *Forever Young*. Whitney Houston's 'I Will Always Love You' was at number one on the Billboard Hot 100 chart during that week. Appearing in the news at the time, United States Marines landed in Somalia as part of Operation Restore Hope, Japanese Crown Prince Naruhito announced his engagement to Masaka Owada, and an earthquake struck Flores Island, triggering a tsunami which was to kill some three thousand people.

19

THE NIGHTMARE BEFORE CHRISTMAS
(1993)

Touchstone Pictures/ Skellington Productions Inc.

Director: Henry Selick
Producers: Tim Burton and Denise Di Novi
Screenwriter: Caroline Thompson, based on a story and characters by Tim Burton

MAIN CAST

Chris Sarandon	-	Voice of Jack Skellington
Danny Elfman	-	Singing Voice of Jack Skellington/ Voice of Barrel/ Voice of Clown with the Tear Away Face
Catherine O'Hara	-	Voice of Sally/ Voice of Shock
William Hickey	-	Voice of Dr Finklestein
Glenn Shadix	-	Voice of Mayor
Paul Reubens	-	Voice of Lock
Ken Page	-	Voice of Oogie Boogie
Ed Ivory	-	Voice of Santa

Like *The Muppet Christmas Carol*, the subtly-employed postmodernism of *The Nightmare Before Christmas* was to foreshadow the rather more amorphous, deconstructed approach to the festive season that was fast approaching with the turn of the century. Although the film's deft employment of stop-motion techniques was to lend it a highly distinctive aspect which remains instantly recognisable even today, at its heart is an ebulliently vibrant collision of two diametrically opposed worlds: a narrative of playful juxtaposition which, for all its lack of convention, nonetheless remains acutely involved with the traditional concerns which underpin Christmas.

Just as *Home Alone* had introduced one of the predominant themes of 1990s Christmas film-making, namely the issue of the centrality of the family unit within the traditional Christmas narrative, *The Nightmare Before Christmas* was to concern itself more with the other prevalent topic to emerge in that decade: the importance of belonging. Although viewers had by now become well accustomed to festive narratives which stressed the significance of community and striving to have a positive effect upon the lives of those around us, the nineties came to lay new emphasis upon this familiar theme by instead examining the way that Christmas's unique seasonal blend of goodwill and altruism could help individuals to consider and redefine themselves, even if this meant challenging long-held perceptions about their lives. *The Nightmare Before Christmas* was to establish itself as the very epitome of this premise, and its appealingly outlandish approach to its subject matter has meant that it has since become one of the most prominent festive films of the nineties.

The Nightmare Before Christmas was directed by Henry Selick, a talented animator and stop-motion expert who had worked for Walt Disney Studios and in a freelance capacity before beginning work on this, his debut feature film. Known for his earlier short works which included *Seepage* (1982) and, for television, *Slow Bob in the Lower Dimensions* (1991), *The Nightmare Before Christmas* remains one of the greatest triumphs of his career, winning him critical acclaim as well as recognition at awards ceremonies. The film has, however, come to be associated even more with the inimitable visual style of its producer, Tim Burton, upon whose story and characters it came to be based. Burton had, by the early nineties, achieved great fame and the approval of commentators due to a well-regarded string of high-profile features which had included *Pee-Wee's Big Adventure* (1985), the monumentally successful superhero blockbuster *Batman* (1989), and its sequel *Batman Returns* (1992), the latter being a film which had demonstrated its own unique take on the festive season. *The Nightmare Before Christmas*, however, owed the approach of its design more to the eccentric look of Burton's macabre *Beetle Juice* (1988) and the similarly off-the-wall peculiarities of *Edward Scissorhands* (1990), but few would deny that the finished product was a work of visual art which proved to be entirely original, a filmic experience which was charmingly offbeat and yet breathlessly inventive.

In a strange land where every holiday season has its own dimensional reality, Jack Skellington (voice of Chris Sarandon/ singing voice of Danny Elfman), the Pumpkin King, rules over Halloween Town, a moody realm of vampires, witches, werewolves, and monsters under the stairs. The skeletal, good-natured Jack is the very epitome of Halloween, being full of enthusiasm for the morbid and ghoulish. The denizens of the town, including the Mayor (voice of Glenn Shadix) offer their heartfelt gratitude to their leader for another successfully scary season, glad that they have fulfilled their purpose of frightening and generally being ghastly for another year. Jack has a particular secret admirer in Sally (voice of Catherine O'Hara), the Frankensteinian creation of the grisly scientific genius Dr Finklestein (voice of William Hickey). But unbeknownst to the townsfolk, Jack is secretly becoming disenchanted with conjuring up the same old terrors every year. Saddened at his growing lack of contentment, he sneaks away from the throng to find space for contemplation, little realising that he is silently being followed by Sally, who shares his sense of dissatisfaction.

The next morning, the Mayor arrives at Jack's house with the plans which have been drawn up for the following year's Halloween, but is confused when he discovers that the Pumpkin King is not at home. He doesn't realise that Jack has been walking all night in the forests outside the town. But the situation has become confusing to Jack too, for meanwhile he is discovering that he has walked so far that he has left Halloween Town altogether. Arriving at an intersection point between different seasonal worlds, he finds unfamiliar markers on trees in a clearing which indicate a range of holiday seasons that seem new and strange to him, including Easter, Thanksgiving and Valentine's Day. Becoming entranced by a particular symbol which looks like a decorated fir tree, Jack soon finds himself drawn into a curious vortex and whisked away from the familiarity of the dark woodland.

Jack is eventually deposited in an ice-covered wonderland, full of snowmen, elves, skating penguins and colourful toys as far as the eye can see. He is stunned by this bizarre sight of comfort and joy, as the ways of Christmas Town are completely foreign concepts to him. Amazed by the strange sense of goodwill that he senses, Jack watches in astonishment as he sees the many different customs of Christmas played out in front of him: elves making toys, trees being decorated, mistletoe being hung, and electric fairy-lights being draped everywhere. Yet he is also puzzled by the complete absence of things that he has taken for granted in his native land, such as abundant creepy-crawlies and night terrors.

Back in Halloween Town, panic is beginning to grip the residents. Everyone has searched high and low for Jack, but to no avail. Then, just as they are beginning to lose hope, the Pumpkin King himself makes a triumphant return on a snowmobile, a large and suspicious-looking sackcloth bag tied up beside him. Jack hurriedly arranges a town meeting, where he explains all the wondrous things that he had seen in the land of Christmas. However, he soon finds that he has difficulty explaining the notion behind festive gifts and Christmas stockings to the assembled gathering of ghosts and monsters, all of whom expect every newly-presented idea to have a more sinister undertone than that which actually exists. Disappointed that they do not share his zeal for the wonders of this new season that he has discovered, Jack enthrals them with an account of the terrifying ruler of Christmas Town: a horrifying, dark-hearted fiend in a red suit who he calls

Sandy Claws.

Back in his home, Jack is voraciously reading through every literary exploration of the festive season that he can lay his bony hands on, including Dickens's *A Christmas Carol*. He is growing increasingly exasperated at his inability to rationalise the goodwill and happiness of Christmas with his macabre, horror-centric mindset. Jack eventually decides to pay a visit to Dr Finklestein's laboratory to borrow some scientific equipment, and is soon setting up off-the-wall experiments with sprigs of holly, cuddly toys and candy canes in a last-ditch attempt to unlock the secrets of Christmas. But no amount of research is sufficient to allow Jack to reduce festive cheer into a simple equation, no matter how hard he tries. Even a surprise visit from Sally, who has temporarily slipped from the notice of her over-protective creator Dr Finklestein, can entirely brighten Jack's mood.

The next morning, the townsfolk are beginning to voice concern for Jack's single-minded obsession with fathoming the Christmas spirit when he proudly proclaims that he has had a moment of enlightenment: surely it isn't necessary to fully understand Christmas in order to enjoy it. To this end, he decides that Halloween Town will launch its own, rather unique version of Christmas with some 'improvements' along the way. Jack enlists Dr Finklestein to create some Halloween-style flying reindeer, while the mischievous trick-or-treaters Lock, Shock and Barrel (voices of Paul Reubens, Catherine O'Hara and Danny Elfman) are given a secret task to which they are all sworn to secrecy: they must kidnap Santa Claus himself and bring him to Jack. But the impish trio are also henchmen of the spectral Oogie Boogie (Ken Page), who has his own rather more malign plans for Santa, to say nothing of Christmas in general.

Jack is holding auditions for Christmas acts (with rather mixed success) when Sally arrives and tells him that she has received a grim premonition of disaster arising from his attempts to construct a new kind of festive season from elements of Halloween. But her warning falls on deaf ears, as Jack is far more concerned with asking her to tailor him a Santa Claus outfit in time for Christmas. Sally's concerns are soon interrupted with the arrival of Lock, Shock and Barrel who, to Jack's manifest disdain, have kidnapped the Easter Bunny by mistake. This is but a temporary setback in Jack's plans, however, as he watches in satisfaction as his fellow townspeople work tirelessly to get ready for the imminent arrival of the festive season, busily constructing gifts which add a little deathly peril to the usual Christmas cheer. Even Dr Finklestein's efforts have come to fruition, with a set of levitating skeletal reindeer newly-constructed just in time to pull Jack's sleigh.

Back over in Christmas Town, everyone is blissfully aware of Jack's ill-conceived intentions as Christmas Eve arrives. Santa Claus (voice of Ed Ivory) is just in the process of checking his 'naughty and nice' list when his doorbell rings unexpectedly. Answering it, he discovers three diminutive trick-or-treaters who promptly capture him in an oversized bag and take him to Halloween Town. Once there, Santa is shocked at the grim sight that meets him: a bizarre hotchpotch of the grim and the ghastly, all engaged in an effort to bring Christmas to life by the ghoulish power of Halloween. He demands to know why he has been kidnapped, but Jack seems content to simply tell him that he can consider this a well-earned vacation from his usual duties; this year, Christmas will be taken care of by his neighbours in Halloween Town. Pausing only to steal Santa's hat, Jack tells Lock, Shock and Barrel to keep jolly old Saint Nick comfortable until the festive season is over, little realising that they plan to take him to Oogie Boogie's lair. Sally, meanwhile, pleads with Jack to reconsider his ill-intentioned plans, telling him that he is not being true to himself or even to the spirit of Halloween. But once again, Jack is too wrapped up in his plans to take heed of her warning.

The night of Christmas Eve comes at last, and Jack rises from what appears to be a coffin (actually his sleigh), resplendent in his somewhat avant-garde Santa Claus suit and ready to spread his own special brand of festive cheer. In an eleventh-hour attempt to force him to come to his senses, Sally creates a chemically-induced fog to impede the skeletal reindeers' take-off. Jack is momentarily devastated, his Christmas plans seemingly ruined, until he discovers that his ghostly pet dog Zero's nose is able to glow brightly enough to lead the way through the mist. Sally watches in dismay as the gruesome sleigh lurches into the night, Jack and the reindeers careening off into the sky.

Jack quickly sets about distributing his gifts in characteristically enthusiastic fashion, but his range of chilling presents – which include deadly snakes and shrunken heads – don't exactly go down well with their recipients, who react with universal terror. The police are soon inundated with complaints about Jack's actions, which leads to a public service broadcast advising everyone that an impostor has ruined Christmas (an announcement which meets with widespread glee when it is heard in Halloween Town). The broadcaster explains that the U.S. Armed Forces are preparing to take action against this malign impersonator, a statement which spurs Sally to seek out the real Santa Claus in order to release him before Jack's sleigh is shot out of the sky.

While Jack dodges fire from anti-aircraft batteries (mistakenly thinking that the people of the Earth are thanking him with fireworks for his efforts), Sally makes her way to Oogie-Boogie's hideout where Santa is being held against his will. There, she launches an audacious attempt to spring the hapless hostage from the villainous ghost's clutches, but is ultimately defeated when her ruse is uncovered. Meanwhile, Jack discovers too late that the military are trying to bring an end to his distinctive strain of festive cheer when a surface-to-air missile launcher scores a direct strike on his sleigh. Tumbling to the ground, the flaming wreckage eventually lands in an inner-city graveyard, where a bewildered Jack – his Santa suit now decidedly singed – wonders where it all went wrong. Finally realising the error of his ways, he reverts to his original persona as the Pumpkin King of Halloween and resolves to set things right while there's still time.

Back in Halloween Town, Oogie-Boogie is preparing to drown Santa and Sally in a vat of molten lead. Before he is able to do so, however, Jack returns in the nick of time and confronts his ghostly nemesis. Oogie-Boogie subjects Jack to a variety of mechanical defences, all of which he narrowly manages to overcome, before the malicious spectre eventually falls foul of his own bubbling vat. Jack sets

Santa free with an apology, beseeching him to correct the terrible mistake that has been made. Now seriously miffed, Santa tells Jack that he will do his best, but suggests that in future Jack should listen to Sally's advice rather than arbitrarily wresting control of other holidays for no reason other than pure caprice.

As Jack finally begins to realise the true extent of Sally's feelings for him, Santa makes good on his promise and travels around the world faster than ever before, not just delivering 'real' Christmas gifts but efficiently removing all of Jack's horrifying presents into the bargain. He even makes the time for an impromptu visit to the skies above Halloween Town, delivering its first fall of snow (and deeply confusing the residents as a result). While the townsfolk come to terms with the night's tumultuous events, Jack meets Sally in the graveyard where he declares his love for her, all thoughts of his bungled attempts to take over Christmas now far from his mind.

If there is one thing that can be said for *The Nightmare Before Christmas*, it is that Tim Burton's stylistic imprimatur is clearly stamped upon each and every frame of the film.[1] His inimitable sense of the innovative and the macabre come to the fore in very rewarding ways, not least in the film's wealth of acutely-observed small details, and the celebration of traditional Halloween frights would strongly foreshadow many of Burton's later features, such as *Sleepy Hollow* (1999) and – most especially – *The Corpse Bride* (2005). Yet the keen eye of director Henry Selick is very much in evidence too,[2] giving a foretaste of his later critical acclaim with films such as *James and the Giant Peach* (1996) and *Coraline* (2009). The film is positively brimming with entertainingly gruesome facets, from Jack's bizarrely ill-conceived experiments to deduce the meaning of Christmas through to the extensive raft of inventive character designs which include the trick-or-treaters' walking bathtub, the changing expressions of the Mayor's swivelling head, and the often-mystified Dr Finklestein who, when confused, scratches not his head but his exposed brain (thanks to a convenient flip-top scalp). The hapless inventor is the brunt of much of the film's darkest humour, not least during Sally's many resourceful attempts to poison her domineering creator (as everyone in Halloween Town is already dead, otherwise lethal concoctions have little more than a soporific effect on him). Even the title is wickedly well-judged, the film's style and narrative being as far removed from Clement Clarke Moore's vision of the night before Christmas as it is possible to achieve.

Aside from the film's gleefully sinister wit and visual flair, screenwriter Caroline Thompson manages to weave engaging emotional observation into the narrative without her efforts ever relying on the traditional sentimentality of conventional Christmas storytelling. As his festive plans turn awry, Jack's woes stem from the fact that he is trying to be someone that he is not, and is therefore neglecting who he truly is. Jack is so keen to evade the tedium of yet another Halloween that he is willing to do anything to usurp Christmas, even if – by his own admission – he has next to no understanding of the indefinable alchemy that actually makes the season tick. In so doing, he not only feels compelled to forcibly remove Santa from his traditional role, but his obsessive focus on his plans to give Christmas a radical make-over allows the genuinely malign Oogie-Boogie the opportunity to hatch his own, rather less altruistic scheme. Through misfortune Jack eventually learns the importance of being true to himself, and just in time to restore Christmas to normality. The ethereal Oogie-Boogie is vanquished, Santa released back to his annual duties, and – in finally recognising Sally's affections – Jack appears to accept that sometimes common sense and a realistic recognition of one's own limitations can be positive, self-enhancing factors rather than the symptom of a humdrum, stagnant mundanity as he had originally believed.

Much of what makes *The Nightmare Before Christmas* unique amongst festive films lies in the proficiently-articulated chaos of the anarchic, ghoulish Halloween Town encroaching upon the ordered jollity of Christmas.[3] There is a great deal of gentle pathos in Jack's near-total inability to understand why the very things that make Halloween so unique are anathema to the diametrically-different festive season. Even by the film's conclusion, there is a nagging sense that Jack probably still can't comprehend why it would be inappropriate to leave a man-eating snake beneath someone's Christmas tree, but – we seem to be assured – he is now content to leave Santa to get on with the job of delivering comfort and joy to the children of the world, and will instead remain satisfied with rallying his kinsmen in the land of talking pumpkins and vampire bats.

It is difficult to overstate the skill by which the animated figures are able to articulate a full range of emotional expressions; Selick's work, particularly with the lead character, is near-faultless in its capacity to express the broadest extent of feelings and sentiments. Yet the ground-breaking character design is only one part of the film's artistic success. Danny Elfman provides not just a characteristically lively score but also a full range of songs throughout the film, the most memorable of them almost certainly proving to be 'What's This?', performed by Jack upon being confronted with the many bewildering sights of Christmas Town when he first arrives there. Nominated for Academy Awards on four separate occasions (including two in the same year in 1997), Elfman has been a long-term collaborator with Burton on a wide range of cinematic projects, having provided the original score for many of his projects which, at the time, had included *Pee-wee's Big Adventure* (1985), *Beetle Juice* (1988), *Batman* (1989), *Edward Scissorhands* (1990) and *Batman Returns* (1992), as well as a diverse range of other feature films such as Richard Donner's *Scrooged* (1988), Martin Brest's *Midnight Run* (1988), Warren Beatty's *Dick Tracy* (1990) and Clive Barker's *Nightbreed* (1990). Additionally, Elfman was to provide Jack Skellington's singing voice throughout the film, while the character's general dialogue was performed by Hollywood veteran Chris Sarandon.

For a film with such distinctive model-work, where every expression is so faithfully reproduced, it only stands to reason that the quality of the voice acting for *The Nightmare Before Christmas* would prove essential to the film's success. It is fortunate, then, that the film benefits from such a wide range of well-delivered performances, key among them being Sarandon's astonishingly varied portrayal of Jack. Able to bring the spindly figure alive with great aplomb, Sarandon manages to wring every possible emotion from the conflicted skeleton, conjuring up ennui and dissatisfaction just as ably as he evokes the character's sense of wonder and single-mindedness. The result is a performance that is both charming and accessible throughout, no matter how outlandish Jack's environment may happen to be. Sarandon was well-known to audiences from the seventies onwards, when he had been nominated for the Best Actor in a Supporting Role Academy Award for his extraordinary performance as Leon Shermer in Sidney Lumet's *Dog Day Afternoon* (1975). Later to appear in films as varied as Michael Winner's *The Sentinel* (1977), Sam Peckinpah's *The Osterman Weekend* (1983) and Rob Reiner's *The Princess Bride* (1987), he had already ably proven his horror credentials with prominent roles in films such as Tom Holland's *Fright Night* (1985) and *Child's Play* (1988). Sarandon is proficiently supported in *The Nightmare Before Christmas* by Catherine O'Hara, well established in the public consciousness at the time for having played ill-fated suburban mother Kate McCallister in the first two entries in the *Home Alone* series. In the role of Sally, the kindly, detachable-limbed creation of Dr Finklestein, O'Hara crafts a likeable character who is full of empathy and compassion but who is not above a little poisoning and deception where necessary (all in the best traditions of Halloween Town, of course). A veteran of television's *Second City TV* between 1976-79 and 1981-84, O'Hara had made cinematic appearances in films throughout the eighties which had included Martin Scorsese's *After Hours* (1985), Mike Nichols's *Heartburn* (1986), and Tim Burton's own *Beetle Juice*, as well as a range of nineties features such as Alan Alda's *Betsy's Wedding* (1990) and *Dick Tracy*. In 2010, O'Hara was awarded an Emmy Award in the category of Outstanding Supporting Actress in a Miniseries or Movie for her performance in HBO's *Temple Grandin* (2010).

The film benefits from an impeccable range of supporting voice performances, delivered by an extremely varied range of actors. These included *National Lampoon's Christmas Vacation* veteran William Hickey, best remembered by many as ageing Mafia Don Corrado Prizzi in John Huston's *Prizzi's Honor* (1985); Paul Reubens, well-known at the time for his screen guise as the madcap Pee-Wee Herman, and talented improvisational comedian and voice actor Greg Proops. Glenn Shadix impresses as the nervy, indecisive Mayor of Halloween Town, as does Edward Ivory as the permanently bewildered Santa Claus. Particular mention, however, must go to Ken Page for a no-holds-barred performance as the playfully malevolent Oogie-Boogie. Able to perfectly meld the frivolous and the genuinely sinister, Page ensures that his character becomes a memorable villain for the most unconventional of films.

The Nightmare Before Christmas performed very well with critics at the time of its release, with an overwhelmingly positive response from most commentators. While many were effusive in their praise of the film's pioneering visual style,[4] others commended the skilful subversion of recognised Christmas tropes into something entirely new and original.[5] A number of reviewers singled out Danny Elfman's scores and songs for approval,[6] with some paying tribute to Tim Burton and Henry Selick's care in presenting an inventive world of gothic scares which never alienates its youthful audience.[7] The film remained popular in the years after its release, soon accumulating cult credibility and maintaining a lasting high regard amongst other Christmas features of the same vintage.[8] Re-released in cinemas during October 2006, this time being issued in Disney Digital 3D, *The Nightmare Before Christmas* has continued to uphold its critical reputation in recent years. Modern commentators have continued to pay homage to the film's winning performances[9] and its unique, moody sense of the fantastic[10], with very few dissenting voices in the general chorus of approval amongst reviewers.[11]

The Nightmare Before Christmas was nominated for the Best Visual Effects Award at the 1994 Academy Awards, the nomination shared between effects team members Pete Kozachik, Eric Leighton, Ariel Velasco-Shaw and Gordon Baker. Danny Elfman's score for the film was nominated for the Best Original Score (Motion Picture) Award at the Golden Globes in the same year, and he was to win the Saturn Award for Best Music, while the film itself picked up the Best Fantasy Film Award at the same ceremony. There were also Saturn nominations for Best Director for Henry Selick, and in the Best Special Effects category. The film was also nominated for the Best Dramatic Presentation Award at the Hugo Awards, and the Outstanding Family Motion Picture Award at the Young Artist Awards ceremony. There was further success at the Annie Awards, where Henry Selick was honoured with the Best Individual Achievement for Creative Supervision in the Field of Animation Award, and art director Deane Taylor was conferred the Best Individual Achievement for Artistic Excellence in the Field of Animation Award. *The Nightmare Before Christmas* itself was nominated for the Best Animated Film Award at the same year's Annie Awards ceremony.

Even after almost two decades, no other Christmas film has managed to come close to recapturing the dark gothic charm of Burton and Selick's unique festive caper. It is perhaps for this reason that it has remained so popular with audiences, reissued again and again on DVD and Blu-Ray as well as, in recent years, making seasonal appearances in cinemas (both in its original 2D and new 3D incarnations). *The Nightmare Before Christmas* has proven to be the perfect blend of seasonal charm and creative innovation, conjuring up a hugely distinctive world where the cosy and the macabre collide in a way which seems simultaneously energising and eye-catching. Yet its core theme, which speaks so clearly about the importance of recognising the authenticity of our individual character, is counterbalanced by an exploration of Jack's reliance on – and the support provided by – his honorary 'family', the citizens of Halloween Town. These topics, which proved to be so prominent in nineties festive film-making, would also come to the fore later in the decade, where they would emerge in quite strikingly different ways.

Historical Context

The Nightmare Before Christmas received a nationwide release in the United States on 29 October 1993, following a premiere showing at the New York Film Festival on 9 October. It was the only major film to premiere in America on the date of its national cinematic release. Mariah Carey's song 'Dream Lover' was headlining the Billboard Hot 100 that week. In current affairs, the Canada Liberal Party/ Bloc Quebecois won power in the Canadian general election, and an aviation emergency was announced when an Air Nigeria Airbus A310 was hijacked in mid-flight.

20

THE SANTA CLAUSE (1994)

Walt Disney Pictures/ Hollywood Pictures/ Outlaw Productions

Director: John Pasquin
Producers: Robert Newmyer, Brian Reilly and Jeffrey Silver
Screenwriters: Leo Benvenuti and Steve Rudnick

MAIN CAST

Tim Allen	-	Scott Calvin/ Santa Claus
Judge Reinhold	-	Dr Neil Miller
Wendy Crewson	-	Laura Calvin Miller
Eric Lloyd	-	Charlie Calvin
David Krumholtz	-	Bernard the Elf
Larry Brandenburg	-	Detective Nunzio
Mary Gross	-	Miss Daniels
Peter Boyle	-	Mr Whittle

The Santa Clause quickly earned a reputation as one of the most high-profile of nineties Christmas films at the time of its release, and today it remains amongst the most enduring festive movies to emerge during that decade. While the engaging performance of its popular star was to greatly enhance its reputation during the time of its release, its continued esteem amongst audiences in recent years can perhaps be seen to have stemmed more from the lasting charm of its central premise: that of the transposition of a contemporary everyman onto the captivating canvas of popular Christmas mythology.[1] With its themes of family relations proving more complex than in many previous festive features (especially in contrast to the forthright celebration of the nuclear family which is depicted in *Home Alone*), and its fish-out-of-water concept perfectly encapsulating the prominent topic of fitting in which had been explored by other films of the time, *The Santa Clause* would ultimately prove to be, in many ways, one of the quintessential Christmas movies of the 1990s.

Bringing this slice of modern Christmas folklore to life was John Pasquin, a director and producer (as well as an occasional screenwriter) whose career had begun in television in the early eighties; his work behind the camera spanned the entire decade, helming episodes of popular series including *Family Ties* (1983-88), *Newhart* (1985-86) and *Thirtysomething* (1987). *The Santa Clause* was to form his cinematic debut, though he has returned to the world of film numerous times in recent years, developing movies such as *Jungle 2 Jungle* (1997), *Joe Somebody* (2001) and *Miss Congeniality 2: Armed and Fabulous* (2005), as well as continuing to remain very active in television.

In the American town of Lakeside, toy corporation owner Mr Whittle (Peter Boyle) is hosting a lavish Christmas Eve event in celebration of the company's best ever sales. He singles out marketing executives Scott Calvin (Tim Allen) and Susan Perry (Judith Scott) for special praise due to their efforts in promoting the firm's products. Scott takes great delight basking in his boss's congratulations, but gets so carried away with the office festivities that he ends up leaving much later than intended. This causes friction with his ex-wife Laura (Wendy Crewson) and her new husband, psychologist Dr Neil Miller (Judge Reinhold), as Scott had agreed to look after his son Charlie (Eric Lloyd) – who normally lives with Laura and Neil – overnight while they stay with Neil's parents. Scott's home is notably lacking in festive appeal, however, and Charlie is less than keen on the idea of staying with his slick but cynical father. However, Scott proves to have more of a festive spark than anyone expected when he discovers that Neil has been advising Charlie that Santa Claus is more of an allegorical expression of festive cheer than he is an actual being. Infuriated that Laura should have allowed such cold emotional detachment to put their son's faith in Santa at risk, Scott assures Charlie that jolly old Saint Nick is most definitely alive and well – after all, he is an adult and still fervently believes in him. Laura is indignant that Scott should question Neil's judgement and her own parenting skills.

Scott's noble but ultimately doomed attempts to cook his son a traditional turkey dinner do little to impress Charlie, who seems resigned to a joyless Christmas Eve. After a largely-fruitless tour of the town's restaurants, they eventually wind up at their local branch of Denny's, which is currently populated by office workers from a multinational corporation and also, more germanely to Scott and Charlie, single fathers and their children (who have also, it seems, had major troubles with their own respective turkey dinners). Charlie is singularly unimpressed at the prospect of eating his Christmas Eve meal in such clinically impersonal surroundings, especially when it becomes obvious that the restaurant have already run out of most of the items on their festive menu.

Back home, Scott is reading from Clement Clarke Moore's *A Visit from St. Nicholas* while Charlie lies in bed. Sensing that his son is close to falling asleep (even if his evening has made Charlie unlikely to be entertaining any visions of sugar plums dancing in his head), Scott tries to withdraw from the room quietly but the suddenly-awake Charlie has other ideas. Soon Scott is being bombarded by awkward questions about the plausibility of Santa's annual gift-bearing visits. How did his reindeer acquire the ability to fly? How does Santa manage to fit down a house's chimney and, in a modern world which has so few open fireplaces, how is he able to deliver presents to homes without them? Scott does his best to answer his son's questions to the best of his ability and, though he is saddened by Charlie's dispassionate doubtfulness, finds himself secretly cheered when he receives a request to leave out some milk and cookies by the tree – just in case.

Later that night, Charlie is amazed when he hears heavy footfalls on the roof above his head. Believing that Santa is in the process of paying his regular Christmas Eve visit, he races through to Scott's bedroom. Scott, however, comes to the immediate conclusion that the house is being burgled, and races outside to confront the apparent intruder. Sure enough, he soon spots a man on his roof, but in calling out he startles the trespasser and causes him to fall to the ground. Charlie is initially awestruck, until he realises the uncomfortable truth – Scott appears to have killed Santa Claus (John Pasquin). Confident that he is only dealing with an interloper in fancy dress, Scott frisks the body for identification, finding a calling card (marked 'Santa Claus, North Pole') which instructs him to put on Santa's red suit and trust the reindeer to do the rest. Scott is initially contemptuous of these grandiose directions until he happens to notice a magic sleigh and full compliment of reindeer perched on the roof of his house.

Scott tries and fails to come to terms with this strange turn of events, but discovers that he is unable to check the body for any further documents because it has disappeared into thin air – only Santa's empty suit remains on the snowy ground. Before he can make any further attempt to rationalise the situation, however, Scott finds that Charlie has ascended a ladder which has mysteriously appeared at the front of the house, and is now firmly ensconced at the reins of Santa's sleigh. Still believing the whole thing to be an elaborate hoax, Scott orders his son to move, but the reindeer mistakenly believe that he is talking to them and fly off into the starry night, whisking along Scott and Charlie in the sleigh behind them.

It soon becomes apparent that the reindeer expect Scott to assume Santa's duties for the night: they deposit the sleigh on top of a nearby house, where he is persuaded by Charlie to don the red suit and deliver presents to the children inside. Scott only does so only with the utmost reluctance (not least as the suit is several sizes too big for him), but soon discovers that he has developed the unexpected personal ability to fly – and, what's more, to fit down any size of chimney stack. His first effort is less than successful, as he is harassed by a family dog, sets off the house's burglar alarm and then wakes the inhabitants. However, he soon begins to get the knack of the job, which is just as well given that the reindeer have a long night planned.

Finding that Santa's toy-sack magically refills after every visit, Scott realises that he has his work cut out for him. But apart from a few ill-tempered moments (he eventually tries to rationalise his situation by deducing that he is hallucinating, or at the very least having a very strange dream), by dawn all of the gifts have been delivered. Scott orders the reindeer to take him home, but Lakeside isn't where they have in mind. They whisk the sleigh off to the North Pole and then detach themselves and wander off into the distance, leaving a rather confused Scott and Charlie in the icy wilderness. A few moments later, however, an elf arrives (apparently from nowhere) and causes a literal North Pole to rise from the snow-covered ground. Keying in a code sequence, the elf watches as the sleigh descends into a vast underground workshop.

Scott is stunned by the seemingly miraculous sight that awaits him. The workshop is staffed entirely by elves; although the beings are impossibly ancient, in physical terms they appear just like small children. Charlie is amazed by the astonishing marvels that are on display, but Scott is still more concerned about the fact that he can make neither head nor tail of their peculiar situation. In his search for answers he comes across Bernard (David Krumholtz), a senior elf, who finally explains what is going on. When the previous incumbent of the role fell from the roof of Scott's house, the role of Santa Claus became vacant, and Scott has now formally assumed Santa's identity by wearing his suit. (This, stated in impossibly small print on the calling card that Scott discovered, is the eponymous Santa Clause.) Scott now has eleven months to tie up any outstanding affairs from his existing life before he must return to the North Pole and take over Santa's duties the following December. Still finding the whole state of affairs rather difficult to swallow, Scott asks Bernard what would happen if he simply refused to accept that he was Santa Claus. This horrifies the elves, and a deeply sombre Bernard explains that if there is no Santa, there would – in turn – be no Christmas.

Bernard gives Charlie a special gift – a very old, magical snowglobe – while he charges Judy the elf (Paige Tamada) to sort out Scott's ill-fitting red suit. Charlie is overjoyed to be visiting the legendary workshop at the North Pole, but Scott is troubled at the prospect that, rather than being a visitor, he may soon be a permanent resident there. The kind-hearted Judy explains that it is not surprising that he finds it difficult to believe what is happening to him. After all, she tells Scott, children have no difficulty having faith in Santa because they instinctively know that he is there for them, even although there is no empirical proof of his existence. For adults, no amount of evidence would ever be sufficient, and so they quickly grow out of their youthful trust in the magic of Christmas. This simple statement gives Scott pause for thought.

The next morning, Scott awakens at home in bed and tries to rationalise the previous evening's events as nothing more than a strange dream. However, this notion is immediately challenged by the fact that he is wearing a pair of red silk pyjamas, embroidered with S.C. on the breast pocket, which had been given to him by Judy at the North Pole. Frantically, he races outside to see if he can find any evidence of the fallen Santa or the sleigh which had been on the roof, but eventually comes up with nothing. Charlie, on the other hand, is still entranced by his Christmas experiences – a fact which doesn't go down well with Neil and Laura when they arrive to collect him later. Laura is unhappy that Scott appears to have filled Charlie's head with fanciful notions when she and Neil have been trying to instil him with a sense of rationality and common sense. Scott, for his part, is no longer sure what to think.

Some time later, Charlie's class are giving presentations about the work of their parents. Charlie, who has brought along both Scott and Neil, decides that he wants Scott to give the first presentation. Scott begins to explain about his work in toy production, but Charlie immediately butts in and tells the class that his father is, in fact, Santa Claus. No amount of counter-explanation from Scott will satisfy Charlie to the contrary, which alarms Neil and Laura as much as it does the class's teacher, Miss Daniels (Mary Gross). This leads to a meeting with the school's headteacher, irritable Principal Compton (Joyce Guy), where Scott tries desperately to convince everyone that Charlie is merely explaining the events of a vivid dream that he'd had on Christmas Eve. Nobody is convinced by this account of events, however.

Scott takes Charlie to the zoo and, as they watch polar bears swimming, tries to convince him that the events of Christmas Eve were nothing more than the product of his imagination. But Charlie, who still carries Bernard's snowglobe around with him wherever he goes, is having nothing to do with Scott's attempts to rationalise what happened at the North Pole. He tells his father that he is simply in denial, but that the truth will eventually establish itself. Scott assures him that this is not the case, but is blissfully unaware that a procession of reindeer has begun to follow him as he heads out of the zoo.

Neil and Laura become increasingly concerned with Charlie's fixation on Christmas, especially as he seems to be spending most of his time role-playing as Santa. When Scott comes to visit his son, Neil explains that he is worried about the effect that he is having on Charlie; he questions whether Scott's continued presence in Charlie's life is becoming counter-productive to his personal development. Laura also begins to wonder if Scott is trying to assume the larger-than-life role of Santa in an attempt to compensate for the time that he has so far failed to spend with his son. Fearing for the future of his access to Charlie, Scott implores him to keep his North Pole experiences a secret from Neil, his mother and everyone at the school. Charlie can't understand why this should be, but is eventually persuaded to remain quiet about the strange incident at Christmas.

Yet as it should happen, Charlie's behaviour is not the only problem that Scott encounters. He awakens one morning to discover that he has grown a full beard and, more worryingly, has put on a large amount of weight. This is greeted by bewilderment at his office, where the other executives are stunned at his greatly-altered appearance. Scott tries to explain away his rapid increase in body mass by telling them that he has suffered a massive allergic reaction to a bee sting, but it is clear that nobody believes him. His colleagues are further concerned when, during an office meal, he orders a large number of different items from the dessert menu and unashamedly wolves them down, one after the other. Later, during a presentation based on advertising strategies for a toy armoured tank, Scott becomes indignant that the company's proposed promotion exploits the image of Santa Claus, portraying the figure in a bad light by neglecting the true spirit and traditions of Christmas. Eventually the CEO, Mr Whittle, loses his patience and orders Scott out of the conference room. Privately, Whittle tells Scott that he is concerned about his appearance, his behaviour, and his general state of mind. Scott tries to excuse his actions, but Whittle demands that he gets himself sorted out at the earliest possible opportunity.

Increasingly worried about his health, Scott books an appointment with medical doctor Pete Novos (Steve Vinovich) who gives him a full checkup. After a vigorous physical, Dr Novos is baffled to discover that Scott's health is perfect even although he is continuing to gain weight. His hair is also greying, his beard now having turned almost completely white. The doctor suggests that the unexpectedly rapid growth in Scott's facial hair (although he shaves regularly, his beard grows back completely within hours) can probably be explained away by a hormonal imbalance, and that his greying hair is a natural part of the approach to middle age. However, even he is unable to clarify the reason why Scott's heart, though strong, is beating to the tune of Christmas carols.

Scott goes along to spectate at one of Charlie's school soccer games. While there, he is vexed to discover that many of the children instinctively know that he is Santa Claus. They line up so that they can each, in turn, tell him what they want for Christmas. This does not play at all well with Neil and Laura, who arrive to watch Charlie's game but are so stunned at Scott's appearance that they decide to leave instead, taking Charlie with them. Laura is appalled that Scott should have chosen to change his appearance to win the favour of his son, which she sees as a desperate attempt to capitalise on Charlie's affection. As neither of them realise that Scott has little choice in the state of his current appearance, Neil also recommends that Scott should attend a therapy session at his practice in order to get to the root of his apparent identity crisis. Scott becomes dismayed as it becomes increasingly clear that he is now in real danger of losing access rights to his son.

Things continue to grow ever stranger for Scott. First a fleet of delivery vans deposit a vast array of neatly-packaged red boxes at his home, inside which he finds the gargantuan 'naughty and nice' list (which he is under strict instructions to check twice). Then he discovers that no matter how regularly he should decide to shave or apply hair dye, he immediately reverts to having a full white beard and completely white hair. Neil urges Laura to consider a court injunction to suspend Scott's visitation rights to meet with Charlie. Although initially reluctant, Laura goes along with the plan, and when Charlie is interviewed by the examining judge (Ron Hartmann) he explains about Scott's secret life as Santa in great detail. Considering Neil and Laura's concerns about Charlie's wellbeing and Scott's mental fitness, the judge decides to revoke Scott's right to maintain access to his son.

Along with his other woes, Scott is devastated to be apart from his son just as their relationship was starting to improve. He decides to pay a visit to Neil and Laura's home in order to say one last goodbye to Charlie now that his visitation rights have been suspended. Neil is highly resistant to the notion, particularly as they are currently sharing a Thanksgiving turkey dinner, but eventually Laura concedes and allows them a moment in private together. Charlie is desperately unhappy at the prospect of being apart from Scott, and tells his father that he wants to be with him – even in spite of Scott's attempts to tell him that it's far better that he stay with Laura and Neil for the time being. Before Scott can try to reason any further with Charlie, Bernard appears out of nowhere: the time has come for Scott to return to the North Pole. What Scott doesn't realise, however, is that Charlie is coming with them.

When Neil and Laura discover that Charlie is missing, they immediately assume that Scott has abducted him. This triggers a large-scale police manhunt to apprehend Scott, led by Detective Nunzio (Larry Brandenburg). The police are, to put it mildly, bemused at an assignment to find Santa Claus and take him into custody. Charlie telephones Laura from the North Pole and explains that he is safe and well, but hangs up before the call can be traced. Desperate to track Scott down, the police form a ring of steel around the Miller family home, while every passer-by who happens to be wearing a Santa suit is stopped for interrogation – not an easy task, given that Christmas is fast approaching.

At the North Pole, meanwhile, Scott is busily getting ready for his annual Christmas Eve delivery. Now entirely reconciled to his new role in life, he looks on with enthusiasm as Quintin (Nic Knight), the elf in charge of research and development, unveils a new Santa suit which is flame retardant and entirely resistant to even the most scorching of fireplaces. Charlie is equally excited about the impending delivery of gifts, unveiling with great gusto the range of new technical innovations that have been built into Santa's (now suddenly rather high-tech) sleigh.

At first, Scott's Christmas sleigh-ride goes perfectly, with presents delivered right on schedule and much consumption of milk and cookies. However, things take a more problematic turn when Charlie suggests that they visit Neil and Laura's house to deliver their gifts. A squad of police officers are lying in wait in the Millers' living room, ready to arrest Scott for child abduction. The children of the area are upset to see Santa handcuffed and taken into custody in the back of a police patrol car. But in spite of Scott's protestations that Charlie is safe and well in his sleigh, his son goes unnoticed up on the roof of the Millers' home.

Realising that something has happened to Scott, Bernard and Quintin deploy the Effective Liberating Flight Squad (ELFS), who immediately engage in a rescue mission. This jet-packed cadre of elite elves set off for the Miller residence, baffling the inhabitants of a nearby police car as they rescue Charlie from the roof and speed off into the night to save Scott. After circumventing a hapless desk sergeant (Gordon Masten), the ELFS break into the cells of the local police station and rescue Santa. Scott then wastes no time in returning Charlie to Neil and Laura, finally putting an end to their agonising vigil. The Millers are so relieved to see Charlie again that, rather than immediately calling for Scott's re-arrest, they are willing to hear him out. At first, he tells Charlie that it is for the best that he remain with his mother and Neil, though he does ask Laura if she will allow him to spend time with Charlie every Christmas Eve. Finally realising that Scott is not delusional, but really has genuinely become Santa Claus, Laura burns the injunction papers and tells Scott that he is free to visit his son whenever he pleases. Furthermore, Bernard arrives (once again, out of thin air) and informs Charlie that he can visit his father at any time of his choosing – all he needs to do is give the magic snowglobe a shake, and Scott will join him.

Neil, who still believes that Scott is unhinged, is becoming concerned that he and Laura are allowing themselves to be caught up in Scott's complex web of illusion and hallucination. But this time, Laura won't be swayed: she is convinced that Santa Claus is real, and in the form of her ex-husband. A police SWAT team storm into the house in an attempt to apprehend Scott for a second time, but they are too late – he has returned up the chimney to his sleigh before they can reach him. Faced with the sight of Santa hovering above the ground with a sleigh pulled by flying reindeer, Neil too is forced to face the fact that even the most sophisticated of delusions could not be fooling everyone simultaneously, including the growing crowd of bystanders outside. As he leaves, Scott parachutes gifts to Laura and Neil – a board game and toy whistle respectively, which they had wanted for Christmas as children but had never received. It was that experience which had convinced them both that Santa Claus didn't exist; now that Scott has rectified this omission, they are both left in no doubt. Satisfied with Scott's efforts, a group of elves (who have been watching unseen from the crowd) depart at the same time as Santa's sleigh leaves to return on its Christmas Eve journey. Keen to test the effectiveness of his snowglobe, Charlie calls Scott shortly afterwards and joins his father as he begins his new job in earnest, spreading joy and goodwill across the world.

The Santa Clause has an interesting significance amongst the Christmas films of the nineties, in the sense that it is a family drama which features divorced parents rather than the traditional nuclear family setting that had become so conventional within the genre. The theme of divorce – and how parental bonds could survive it – had established itself in a number of family films throughout the early nineties, most notably in Chris Columbus's *Mrs Doubtfire* (1993) and Robert Lieberman's festively-situated *All I Want for Christmas* (1991), while the theme of a cynic rediscovering the wonder of the festive season was also a recognisable trope, having surfaced prominently in films including Phillip Borsos's *One Magic Christmas* (1985). Yet what is especially striking is the way in which the film's drama, centring on the threat of Scott becoming legally estranged from his son Charlie, often seems largely subordinate to the main theme: the transfigurative influence of

Christmas. The result is that Laura and Neil are often allowed to come across as rather stolid and mean-spirited (as Scott had been, prior to his transformation), which can make it difficult to warm to their characters even given the validity of their concerns over Scott's apparent identity crisis. Fortunately, Judge Reinhold and Wendy Crewson both give appealing enough performances to take the edge of their characters' apparent lack of sympathy, but there is no arguing that the legal and emotional drama of the film does tend to bog down the narrative momentum just at the exact moment that it should ideally be picking up pace.

The film does, however, give a scrupulously modern take on the Santa mythology, in stark contrast to other evocations that had come before it. Whereas *Santa Claus: The Movie* had taken care to craft an ancient, pagan mythology for Father Christmas, albeit one which was at odds with established traditions surrounding the character, *The Santa Clause* takes great relish in forging another direction entirely, bringing some progressive zest to an overly-familiar concept. In particular, the elves of the North Pole are nicely realised as children and young teenagers with an upbeat, seen-it-all attitude, rather than the diminutive bearded men of tradition. The reindeer also boast dynamic, expressive features, easily proving to be the equal of their counterparts in *Santa Claus: The Movie*.

The film's director, John Pasquin, appears to be having no small amount of fun in his brief cameo, where he plays Scott's ill-fated predecessor in the role of Santa. This is but one of the film's many mischievous features, for there are also a number of nods to Christmas movies of years past. *Miracle on 34ᵗʰ Street* is about to be screened on Scott's TV on the night of Christmas Eve, while a little girl – upset at seeing a handcuffed Scott led away by the police – delivers the famous 'Let Santa go!' line from George Seaton's classic movie. Additionally, Scott's eventual decision to share Christmas dinner with Charlie at a chain restaurant has distinct echoes of the concluding scenes from *A Christmas Story*.

It is difficult to describe any festive film which kicks off with the death of Santa Claus as being anything other than daring, no matter how tastefully the aforementioned incident is handled by the script. It is therefore quite fascinating, in this sense, to consider the way in which so many of the more problematic aspects of Scott's gradually changing identity are played down by Pasquin and screenwriters Leo Benvenuti and Steve Rudnick. We gain a tantalising glimpse of Scott, the archetypal corporate go-getter, losing the respect of his colleagues due to his irrational behaviour, but the long-term effects of this transformation on his personal lifestyle are never fully explored. Nor, indeed, do we visit with any degree of clarity the issue of Scott becoming increasingly aware of the fact that his drastically altered appearance has made him cease to be attractive to the opposite sex, and the profound effect that this presumably would have on his self-esteem. It would be all too simple to explain these issues away with the fact that *The Santa Clause* is, essentially, a light-hearted family film which would do well to avoid such issues of self-awareness and psychological integrity. But the repeated significance attached to Neil and Laura's questioning of Scott's sanity, culminating in the legal separation of father and son, does rather leave the issue open to further and deeper interpretation. It is of note, therefore, that the film was originally intended to be much darker in tone, and interesting to consider exactly what the final product may have looked like with only a few deviations from the established narrative.[2]

As might be expected in a film which focuses on its central character to the extent that it does, much of the success of *The Santa Clause* hinges on Tim Allen's captivating lead performance as Scott Calvin, the man who would be Santa. It is fortunate, for that reason, that Allen gives a virtuoso performance throughout, from the shallow, cynical marketing yuppie of the film's opening scenes all the way through to the jolly, dedicated symbol of the festive season that he eventually becomes. His well-judged mixture of incredulity and stroppiness is often highly entertaining. Allen seems to enjoy the more fantastical elements of the film as much as he does the more dramatic, emotional scenes which occur nearer the climax, appearing to take great delight in Scott's newly-found sweet tooth (especially his growing addiction to milk and cookies) as well as discovering the answer to a question which has no doubt troubled many a parent: exactly how Santa is able to visit homes which have no fireplace. (The solution may well be a great relief for the children who live in such homes, but in practical terms it does not prove to be such good news for Scott.) Allen had achieved huge fame thanks to his starring role as affable TV host Tim Taylor in ABC's *Home Improvement* (1991-99), which won him a Golden Globe Award (and four further Golden Globe nominations during the show's run), though he had made his cinematic debut some years earlier during a small part in Ciro Durán's dark thriller *Tropical Snow* (1988). The success of *The Santa Clause* was only to enhance his already prominent profile, as did his performance the following year as the voice of Buzz Lightyear in John Lasseter's smash hit *Toy Story* (1995). His prolific acting career has continued to the present day, and he has also worked as a producer, director and screenwriter.

While it is the strength of Allen's likeable performance which ensures the core appeal of *The Santa Clause*, to say nothing of his lightness of touch in his interpretation of the offbeat lead character, the film's supporting cast also do well with the material that they are given. Judge Reinhold is given the somewhat awkward task of taking Neil, a mildly neurotic shrink with a line in tasteless sweaters, and turning him into an engaging and sympathetic character. Though Neil inevitably comes off worst in his near-constant verbal sparring with Scott, Reinhold's naturally genial screen persona shines through in order to make the prissy psychologist as likeable as possible. Reinhold's acting career had enjoyed many successes throughout the eighties, with appearances in films such as Ivan Reitman's *Stripes* (1981), Amy Heckerling's *Fast Times at Ridgemont High* (1982), Joe Dante's *Gremlins* (1984), and most especially as Detective Billy Rosewood in Martin Brest's *Beverly Hills Cop* (1984) and its two sequels. He continued to appear in diverse films throughout the early nineties, with roles in features including Sam Pillsbury's romantic thriller *Zandalee* (1991) and Nick Mead's crime caper *Bank Robber* (1993), before his performance in *The Santa Clause*. He has also, in recent years, been active as a director and producer. His co-star, Wendy Crewson, also manages against the odds to make Laura a reasonably benevolent and concerned individual, bringing the character to life in ways that elevate her beyond the multi-purpose killjoy that she appears to be on paper. Crewson has, if anything, an even more difficult job than Reinhold, for Laura's protectiveness of Charlie seems to be more skewed towards resentment of Scott's desire to curry favour with his son instead of being borne entirely from an attempt to shield Charlie from Scott's seemingly-irrational behaviour. It is fortunate, therefore, that Crewson manages to inject the character with just enough poignancy to make Laura's concerns seem valid and justifiable, in order to avoid her ever seeming unsympathetic. Crewson had, in addition to prolific appearances on television, been working in the film industry since the early 1980s, her roles including parts in Ota Richter's *Skullduggery* (1983), Bruce Pittman's *Mark of Cain* (1985) and Francis Mankiewicz's short film *The Sight* (1985). Later to appear in a number of nineties features, such as Randa Haines's *The Doctor* (1991), Joseph Ruben's *The Good Son* (1993) and Jessie Nelson's *Corrina, Corrina* (1994), she has also more recently assumed production roles in both television and cinema.

Other performers worth looking out for throughout the film include industry veteran Peter Boyle – forever fondly remembered as The Monster in Mel Brooks's *Young Frankenstein* (1974) amongst the many other roles that he portrayed in his lifetime – as well as a spiky but sociable turn from the charismatic David Krumholtz, a well-regarded stage actor whose earlier film work had included appearances in James Lapine's *Life with Mikey* (1993) and Barry Sonnenfeld's *Addams Family Values* (1993). As Charlie, Eric Lloyd manages to tread a fine line between childhood wonder and obstreperous petulance, thankfully falling on the right side of the boundary almost all of the time. Given his significance to the central ensemble, this is vitally important, for it ensures that the film never spirals into a headlong nose-dive towards sentimentality even at the point of its emotional conclusion.

The Santa Clause generally performed well with the critics as well as in cinemas, even in spite of the fact that it faced stiff competition at the box-office in the form of Les Mayfield's *Miracle on 34th Street*, a popular John Hughes-produced remake of the perennial forties classic which was released during the holiday season in the same year.[3] Many commentators approved of *The Santa Clause*'s mix of contemporary invention and traditional charm[4], while others instead drew attention to the fact that Pasquin never allows the film's technical wizardry to detract from the underlying appeal and breezy goodwill of its core narrative.[5] While Tim Allen's lead performance garnered appreciation from many reviewers,[6] some considered that the main strength of his unconventional depiction of Santa Claus stemmed from the fact that the portrayal was so entertaining, it inadvertently obscured many of the film's perceived weaknesses.[7] These included, in the opinion of some critics, the storyline's occasional tendency to go astray into the realm of saccharine,[8] and rather too overtly mawkish performances from some of the supporting cast.[9] However, the overwhelming reception of the film was positive, and this critical response has continued into the present day with some recent appraisals of *The Santa Clause* citing it as being, in retrospect, a modern classic of its genre.[10]

The Santa Clause would also put in a strong performance at a number of industry awards ceremonies following its release, including nominations for Best Fantasy Film and Best Make-Up at the Saturn Awards, Best Breakthrough Performance and Best Comedic Performance for Tim Allen at the MTV Movie Awards, and Best Family Motion Picture (Comedy or Musical) and Best Performance by a Young Actor Co-Starring in a Motion Picture for Eric Lloyd at the Young Artists Awards. In addition to the above nominations, Michael Convertino was to win a BMI Film Music Award in 1995 for his original score for the film.

The considerable commercial success of *The Santa Clause* ultimately gave rise to two sequels in later years. Michael Lembeck's *The Santa Clause 2: The Mrs Clause* (2002) was to see the overwhelming majority of the original film's main and supporting cast returning for a light-hearted caper centring around Scott's discovery that he must observe another, hitherto-unrevealed clause. This mystical caveat states that he has to find himself a wife (the Mrs Clause of the title) no later than Christmas Eve, or else put the entire festive season at risk. Although the film's critical reception was significantly more mixed than that of the original, it performed very well at the box-office, paving the way for a second sequel in 2006. *The Santa Clause 3: The Escape Clause*, also directed by Michael Lembeck, mainly concerns the chaos which engulfs the North Pole due to the mischievous shenanigans of Jack Frost (a characteristically high-octane performance from Martin Short), who almost manages to derail the festivities of the holiday season if not for some quick thinking from Scott and his allies. Reviews were more hostile towards this third outing, with many commentators beginning to voice the opinion that the series was now running out of steam, but *The Santa Clause 3* nonetheless retained a healthy showing in cinemas over the festive period of its release.

There has rarely been a more literal interpretation of the transformative power of Christmas than was provided by *The Santa Clause*, and while the journey of its protagonist (from materialistic, corporate banality to altruistic kindness and geniality) is in line with other narratives expressed in festive cinema, it is in the deliberate broadening of the central familial sphere of influence that the film seems particularly interesting. Scott takes care, during the concluding scenes, to emphasise to Charlie that rather than his family being fractured, it has instead been enlarged – he will always have access to both of his parents, but will also have a stable home thanks to the bond between Neil and Laura. The film therefore exhibits a redemptive theme too, where Scott not only discovers a new and more fulfilling role for himself, becoming a more responsible father and rejecting the soullessly acquisitive nature of his corporate lifestyle, but he is also able to come to terms with the new and challenging family circumstances surrounding his son's relationship with his former wife and her new partner.[11] In so doing, *The Santa Clause* manages to fulfil a dual role, typifying many characteristic themes of established festive cinema whilst simultaneously broadening its appeal to encapsulate the changing social mores of the contemporary world.

The remainder of the nineties would see other commercially-successful Christmas fare appearing on cinema screens, particularly in the form of Brian Levant's *Jingle All the Way* (1998), a popular comedy surrounding a frantic pre-Christmas search for a (seemingly impossible to obtain) festive gift, starring a cast-against-type Arnold Schwarzenegger. George Gallo's *Trapped in Paradise* (1994) was also a noteworthy addition to the canon of festive movies, an entertaining variation on the Three Wise Men motif which playfully riffs on earlier entries in the subgenre such as *We're No Angels* and John Ford's *Three Godfathers* (1948). Other entries in the field during the latter half of the decade included Penny Marshall's *The Preacher's Wife* (1996), an all-star musical remake of *The Bishop's Wife*, animated entertainment in the form of William R. Kowalchuk Jr.'s *Rudolph the Red-Nosed Reindeer: The Movie* (1998), and festively-situated dramas such as *I'll Be Home for Christmas* (1998). However, the turn of the century was to bring about a sea-change in the commercial approach to festive film-making. Whereas the cinematic output of the eighties and nineties had been heavily influenced by particular key themes, whether in relation to materialism or domestic attitudes, the coming decade would see a major difference in the production of the Christmas film. Although the period of 2000-10 was to bear witness to a considerable expansion in the number of features being produced with intrinsic Christmas topicality or distinctively festive settings, this new proliferation of films would not share any one common thematic thread. While they would continue to draw upon the accepted tropes of film-making in the genre which had by now become instantly recognisable, they would also capitalise upon this audience familiarity to deconstruct and re-examine elements of the Christmas movie and question if, and why, they remained relevant to contemporary society. Audiences were about to enter the era of the thoroughly postmodern Christmas.

Historical Context

The Santa Clause was released in the United States on 11 November 1994. The other big cinematic debut on that day was Neil Jordan's *Interview with the Vampire: The Vampire Chronicles*, adapted by Anne Rice from her novel. Headlining the Billboard Hot 100 chart that week was Boyz II Men with their single 'I'll Make Love to You'. In current affairs at the time, George Foreman was declared boxing's oldest heavyweight champion, the chemical element Darmstadtium was discovered at the Gesellschaft für Schwerionenforschung in Wixhausen, and in the United States the Republican Party took control of both the House of Representatives and the Senate during the Midterm elections for Congress.

21

ELF (2003)

New Line Cinema/ Guy Walks into a Bar Productions

Director: Jon Favreau
Producers: Jon Berg, Todd Komarnicki and Shauna Robertson
Screenwriter: David Berenbaum

MAIN CAST

Will Ferrell	-	Buddy
James Caan	-	Walter
Bob Newhart	-	Papa Elf
Edward Asner	-	Santa
Zooey Deschanel	-	Jovie
Mary Steenburgen	-	Emily
Daniel Tay	-	Michael
Faizon Love	-	Manager at Gimbel's

The twenty-first century was to bring about a further renaissance in the fortunes of the Christmas film, albeit something of an unconventional one. The genre had proven to be a lasting box-office draw throughout the past two decades, and this commercial viability would not only continue throughout the first years of the new millennium but would also see a broadening of the appeal of festive film-making, such that it would become even more prolific in the period that was to follow. Just as this increase in the number of Christmas films took place from the year 2000 onwards, so too was there an augmentation of the variety of themes explored within the various features which saw release during this time. These included Ron Howard's *How the Grinch Stole Christmas* (2000), an elaborate live-action adaptation of the famous Dr Seuss tale, and Brett Ratner's *The Family Man* (2000), an innovative modern twist on the core concept of *It's a Wonderful Life*. Seth Kearsley's distinctive animated feature *Eight Crazy Nights* (2002) and LeVar Burton's festively-situated drama *Blizzard* (2003) were joined by more traditional Christmas fare such as John Shepphird's *I Saw Mommy Kissing Santa Claus* (2002) and Bill Ewing's *Christmas Child* (2003). Yet this modest increase in momentum at the beginning of the century would give little indication of the major commercial boom that was to accompany Christmas film throughout the rest of the decade, a trend which was to prove that the genre was more flexible and creatively abundant than ever before.

Into this melange of new interpretations on established festive tropes came *Elf*, a film which was to set the stage for one of the most prominent features of Christmas films in the noughties: the challenging and occasional destabilisation of long-held traditional thematic conventions into new, often subversive, configurations. Specifically, *Elf* was to present a very tongue-in-cheek variation on the exiled elf plot which had been imparted throughout *Santa Claus: The Movie*, depicting the chaos which results when an innocent denizen of Santa's workshop finds himself transplanted from the North Pole to modern-day New York. The result, however, is more than a simple culture-clash comedy of errors, for *Elf* is able – specifically because of its rejection of sentimental truisms and formula plotting – to posit an entirely new take on the traditionally established themes of Christmas film-making, upholding the virtues of the festive season at exactly the same time as it is gleefully poking fun at them.

Director Jon Favreau has been a successful actor on television and in film since the early nineties, his cinematic work including appearances in films such as Joel Schumacher's *Batman Forever* (1995), Doug Liman's *Swingers* (1996) (for which Favreau also provided the screenplay), George Hickenlooper's *Dogtown* (1996), and Mimi Leder's *Deep Impact* (1998), while his television roles encompassed series as diverse as *Seinfeld*, *Chicago Hope* and *The Larry Sanders Show*. He has also appeared in a number of made-for-television film productions, with a standout performance in the title role of Charles Winkler's boxing biopic *Rocky Marciano* (1999). Also an occasional screenwriter, Favreau's directorial career began in the late nineties with television feature *Bad Cop, Bad Cop* (1998), followed by comedies *Smog* (1999), *Made* (2001) and *Life on Parole* (2003). *Elf* was his cinematic directorial debut, and since that time his profile has continued to expand through later features which have included *Zathura: A Space Adventure* (2005), *Iron Man* (2008) and its sequel *Iron Man 2* (2010), and *Cowboys and Aliens* (2011). In 2005 Favreau was nominated for a Daytime Emmy in the Outstanding Non-Fiction Series Category for his acclaimed IFC talk show, *Dinner for Five* (2001), while his work on *Iron Man* would win him a Saturn Award from the Academy of Science Fiction, Fantasy & Horror Films in 2009. *Elf*, however, remains one of his best-loved and most memorable features, and was certainly one of the most instantly recognisable festive films of the earlier part of the decade.

Life is hard for an elf when he discovers that he doesn't fit in at Santa's North Pole workshop – especially considering that he's over six feet tall. Yet this is exactly the situation that is facing Buddy (Will Ferrell), a strapping man in his thirties who has lived his life believing that he is, in fact, an elf. Decades beforehand, during a gift-bearing visit to an orphanage one fateful Christmas Eve, Santa Claus (Edward Asner) unwittingly picked up a stowaway in his sleigh – an infant child with an insatiable sense of curiosity. Returning to the North Pole as usual, Santa is perplexed to discover the baby hiding away in an otherwise-empty gift sack, but Papa Elf (Bob Newhart), one of his most trusted assistants, offers to adopt the child and raise him as his own.

As the years progress, Buddy grows up blissfully unaware of his true origins, in spite of the fact that his adult height is more than twice that of his contemporaries. Much too tall to comfortably make his way around facilities designed with three-feet high individuals in mind, he is accepted by his peers even in spite of his distinct lack of toy-making talent – a difficult hurdle for an elf to overcome. Papa Elf takes Buddy as his apprentice, and explains that he will be assisting him in the maintenance of Santa's sleigh. However, as the reindeers' flight is powered by belief in the Christmas spirit, Buddy is dismayed to discover that festive cheer is in such short supply in the modern world that Papa Elf has had to fit the sleigh with a jet engine, by way of a backup plan.

Eventually assigned to the toy testing department, a dead-end position that no elf wants, Buddy is thunderstruck when he overhears two of his elf supervisors discussing his true heritage. The news comes as a complete shock to him. Distressed, he races home to consider the devastating news, but is met there by Papa Elf who finally explains the story of Buddy's origins. Having researched Buddy's life prior to his arrival in the orphanage, Papa Elf reveals a photo of his adoptive son's real parents, Walter Hobbs (James Caan) and Susan Welles (Jane Bradbury). He explains that his mother had passed away shortly after Buddy's birth, while his father – who lives in New York City – is unaware even of his son's existence. Still trying hard to absorb the enormity of this new information, Buddy goes wandering for a while in an attempt to decide on his next move. There, he encounters Leon the snowman (voice of Leon Redbone), who suggests that rather than facing a crisis of identity, Buddy's shock revelation may be just the opportunity he needs to find out who he really is.

Buddy decides that Leon is right, and prepares to head for New York. He seeks Santa's advice, and receives an abundance of homespun wisdom drawn from the many times that Father Christmas has visited the Big Apple. However, Santa is concerned about Buddy's sky-high expectations of meeting his father, and finds himself with no alternative but to reveal an unpalatable truth – Walter's name is on the wrong side of the 'naughty and nice' list. Buddy is aghast at this news, but Santa reassures him that perhaps a little infusion of Christmas cheer is all that is required to bring his father safely back onto the 'nice' column. Buoyed by this new purpose in life, Buddy leaves the comfort of Santa's workshop and sets sail on a glacier with the Empire State Building as his destination.

After a very long journey, Buddy finally makes it to rural North America, where he is confused to discover (after a rather violent encounter with a wild raccoon) that the animals are neither as civilised nor conversational as the ones that he has become accustomed to. Some time later, he manages to make his way into New York itself, emerging from the Lincoln Tunnel to find that the city is a rather different place from anywhere that he has experienced before. Things like revolving doors and subways are entirely new concepts to him, and even the rather aloof, self-contained attitudes of passing members of the public do little to dampen his enthusiasm for his new environment – especially when there is so much free candy (discarded chewing gum) lying around for him to enjoy.

Armed with a snowglobe showing a scene from the city – a gift from Papa Elf – Buddy is able to identify the Empire State Building and, upon reaching it, is awestruck by its sheer scale. Thoroughly baffled by the operation of the elevator, Buddy eventually (against the odds) makes it to Walter's office. There, he discovers that his father is a successful, straight-talking but ultimately rather mean-spirited senior editor for a city publisher who believes that Buddy is some kind of singing elf-o-gram who has been sent there as a prank. Walter is unmoved by Buddy's heartfelt insistence that he is the offspring that his curmudgeonly father never knew existed, believing him instead to be a rather creepy oddball. However, when Buddy mentions Susan Welles, Walter finds himself forced to consider the situation more carefully, though only for as long as it takes for him to have the luckless would-be elf ejected from the building.

Amazingly, Buddy's zeal is undiminished by his less than successful meeting with his father. With Christmas in full swing throughout New York, he decides to pay a visit to the nearby Gimbel's department store. After some difficulty traversing the escalator, he looks around in awe at the vast array of goods that are on display, but has little time to appreciate them before he is mistaken for one of the costumed elves in the shop's Christmas display by one of the store managers (Faizon Love). Believing that Buddy is bunking off during work time, the supervisor drags him into the store's Christmas area and 'back' to work. He also announces – much to Buddy's barely-contained amazement – that Santa will be present at Gimbel's the following day, to hear what the children of New York want for Christmas.

As he acclimatises to working in the lavish Christmas display, Buddy meets the beautiful but hard-edged Jovie (Zooey Deschanel), whose cynicism towards the holiday season leaves Buddy aghast. Believing first that Buddy is trying to provoke her, and then that he is a crank, Jovie eventually finds herself intrigued by his deadly earnestness towards the conventions of the festive season. Clearly concerned about Buddy's mental state, she seems relieved to hear the announcement that the store is due to close in ten minutes as it gives her the perfect excuse to withdraw. Buddy, however, has no intention of leaving – believing that the store's attempt at recreating the North Pole is nowhere near satisfactory for the impending arrival of Santa himself, he takes it upon himself to do a little extra decorating (even if he has to dodge several security guards in order to do it).

Back at his well-appointed city apartment, Walter appears to be more rattled by Buddy's claims about his parenthood than he had initially appeared. He puzzles his wife Emily (Mary Steenburgen) by avoiding his usual family dinner with her and their son Michael (Daniel Tay), instead retreating to his study to leaf through some old college yearbooks. Looking wistfully at his long-lost love from the age of flower power, he seems to become thoughtful about times gone by. The next day, Walter is making his way to work when he discovers Buddy sleeping in one of Gimbel's display windows. He remains as dumbfounded as ever by the wakening Buddy's steadfast (and very public) assertion that they are related. Buddy later attempts to deliver a wrapped gift to Walter, but is quickly intercepted and ejected by the security officers at the Empire State Building (not that his unceremonious departure dampens his enthusiasm much).

Before Gimbel's opens to the public, Buddy is intrigued to hear singing emanating from the women's washroom, and decides to investigate. There, he discovers Jovie in fine voice – much to his delight, as she had earlier told him that she hated the notion of giving a vocal performance in public. Jovie is shocked when she discovers that Buddy is directly outside her shower cubicle, however, and demands that he leave in no uncertain terms. Shortly after, the store opens to customers delighted by Buddy's astonishing new decorations for the Christmas section, which include a reproduction of an entire block of the city (including the Empire State Building) made entirely from Lego bricks, various ostentatious ornamental hangings – many of them illuminated – and even a picture-perfect rendering of Da Vinci's Mona Lisa on an Etch-a-Sketch. The manager is absolutely flabbergasted at the sight that meets him, though he explains it away by reasoning that the company's board of directors had presumably sent in a team of professional decorators overnight. While the manager worries that someone is aiming to unseat him from his post, Jovie confronts Buddy and asks him why he had followed her into the washroom that morning. Buddy seems oblivious to her assertions that he was spying on her for voyeuristic reasons, instead emphasising that he was only listening to her wonderful singing voice. In spite of her bemusement, his explanation is so guileless that Jovie actually seems to believe it.

Gimbel's Santa (Artie Lange) arrives and gives a hearty festive welcome to the assembled children, who are already queuing to meet him. Buddy is initially overjoyed to see his old friend again, but becomes suspicious when it is clear that they don't recognise each other. 'Santa' becomes increasingly irate as Buddy subjects him to repeated questioning, which comes to a climax when he tears off his fake beard, much to the distress of the assembled children. Having reached the end of his tether, 'Santa' becomes embroiled in a no-holds-barred brawl with

Buddy, the pair managing to destroy much of the store's Christmas section in the process. Only the manager's timely intervention manages to save Buddy's skin from the now-furious store Santa.

Back at the Empire State Building, Walter is opening his recently-delivered Christmas gift from Buddy with considerable trepidation. Inside is a home-made card which, to his surprise, contains a photo of Susan and himself from the sixties (the same shot which was featured in his college yearbook). He has little time to ponder this conundrum before his phone rings – the police have taken Buddy into custody following the debacle at Gimbel's. Walter heads to the station in order to bail out Buddy, but is growing increasingly frustrated at his inability to gain any meaningful answers from the strange man. Unwilling to accept Buddy's continued claims that they are related (not that Buddy's sincere assertion that he was given the photograph of his parents by his surrogate elf father does much to help his case), Walter takes him to the clinic of his family's medical doctor (Jon Favreau) in order to undertake a paternity test. Much to Walter's horror, his worst suspicions are revealed – Buddy is indeed his son. The doctor explains that it is possible that Buddy's erratic behaviour and eccentric manner can be explained by a reversion to a childlike state of mind, caused by his psychological reaction to encountering Walter, and recommends that he be introduced to Walter's family in the hope of allowing his mental state to return to normal over time.

To Walter's surprise, Emily is excited at the surprise news that he has another son and becomes eager to meet Buddy. Even Walter's earnest warning about Buddy's elf-like traits can't dampen her enthusiasm that is, until they open the door to their apartment and discover that Buddy has transformed it into another winter wonderland. Amidst the gingerbread treats and improvised decorations (including a festive cutlery chain), the family have dinner together. Concerned that Buddy is psychologically disturbed, Emily asks him to stay with them at their home so that they can support him in resolving the issues in his life. Walter is stupefied at her generosity of spirit, preferring instead that he and Buddy go their separate ways, but Emily reminds him that as his father, he has a responsibility for Buddy's welfare whether he likes it or not.

Buddy is elated at the chance to spend more time with Walter, although the Hobbs are having difficulty acclimatising to the new addition to their family (especially when Buddy is so keen to help around the apartment that he builds a rocking horse out of Walter and Emily's exclusive furniture). Walter is also less than impressed at Buddy's eagerness to keep him up to date with everything that is going on in his life – no matter how trivial – by means of mobile phone. Things don't improve when Walter gets to work and discovers that he is in trouble with his superiors; the company's sales figures are tanking, and he is charged with tracking down a guaranteed bestseller by Christmas Eve in order for the book to ship in the first quarter of the following year. Despite being unsure of how he is going to conjure up a children's book of such cast-iron quality, Walter knows that his professional future depends on his success in this onerous task.

Buddy makes an effort to get to know Michael better, though initially to his half-brother's disdain (being followed around by a grown man in an elf costume having the habit of leading to social death for a self-respecting adolescent). However, after Buddy manages to achieve a dazzling defence during a snowball fight, the two become fast friends. Buddy also learns that Michael is disenchanted with Walter, considering his father to be a self-obsessed workaholic who has little time for anything other than the accumulation and retention of money. They visit Gimbel's, where Buddy discovers that the manager of the Christmas section has been drafted in as a hasty replacement for the now-departed store Santa. Michael quickly notices that Buddy is entranced by Jovie, and encourages him to ask her out on a date. This he does, in his characteristically unconventional way, and to his amazement she agrees to meet him for dinner in a few days' time.

Walter is nonplussed when he discovers a massive fir tree being hoisted into position in his lounge, not least when he discovers that Buddy has chopped it down in Central Park in order to bring it to the apartment. Emily is enthused to see Michael having fun for once, but Walter worries about the influence that the seemingly-unhinged Buddy is having on their son. He suggests that Emily take him to work with her, thus keeping him from leading Michael astray, but Emily declines on account of a meeting that she can't extricate herself from. Instead, Walter decides that he has no choice but to bring Buddy with him to the offices of the publishing company instead. It takes little time there for Buddy to drive him to distraction, however, so Walter arranges to have him work in the mail room instead, thus giving him some peace to work out how to discover a sure-fire hit children's book. A couple of his regular writers suggest that he contact Miles Finch (Peter Dinklage), a legendary but notoriously prima-donnaish figure in children's literature who may just be able to save the day. Making a phone call to Finch, Walter manages – if only just – to arrange a meeting with him, though he very nearly loses the chance to discuss the project when Buddy inadvertently causes mayhem in the mail room, temporarily disrupting the call.

Buddy's date with Jovie arrives that night. She seems pleasantly surprised at Buddy's transformation since substituting his elf costume in favour of rather more conventional attire. He takes her on a whirlwind journey of his discoveries since arriving in New York, including the miracle of revolving doors and a whistlestop tour of the many Christmas trees that he has come across during his time there. Jovie finds herself won over by his ingenuous charm, and during some impromptu ice-skating they share a kiss (much to Buddy's amazement).

The following day is Christmas Eve, and the diminutive Miles Finch arrives at the publishing company for a strictly time-limited discussion with Walter and his creative team. He is brisk and remote but totally professional, and wastes no time in sketching out the kind of material that will create the bestseller that Walter's company is looking for. No sooner has the consultation begun, however, when Buddy bursts into the office to tell Walter about his romantic success with Jovie. Seeing Finch's slight physical stature, Buddy is convinced that he is an elf, but the touchy Finch naturally interprets this as a slight against his lack of height. Buddy's constant questioning, in spite of Walter's desperate attempts to get him out of the office, eventually enrages Finch, who enters into fisticuffs with Buddy before storming out of the building, taking his creative genius with him. Incensed that

Buddy has effectively wrecked any chance he might have had of ensuring a dependable hit book, Walter demands that he leave his office, his family and his life.

With only hours to go until the publishing company's board of directors meet to hear his pitch, Walter is despairing. Just as hope seems lost, one of his writers makes the surprise discovery that Finch has accidentally left his notebook in the conference room. Using one of the ideas that Finch has sketched out in note form, Walter sends the creative team to draw up storyboards before the meeting is convened. Their work is complete just in the nick of time, and Walter is ready to make his presentation when Michael comes racing into the boardroom, much to the annoyance of the gathered executives. His son has discovered a note from Buddy, explaining that the wayward elf – feeling that he now belongs nowhere – has gone for good. Afraid for Buddy's safety, Michael begs his father to help him search for his half-brother. But the company's CEO demands that Walter give the presentation immediately, sending Michael packing. Sensing the genuine urgency of his son's concerns, Walter regrets his earlier harsh words. Turning his back on the boardroom, he heads off to find Buddy, even in spite of the CEO's promise that his defiance has just cost Walter his job.

Dejected, Buddy is wandering New York late at night when he suddenly spots a bright light in the sky – Santa's sleigh, tumbling to the ground. He races to Central Park, where he is reunited with his old friend. Santa explains that due to a complete lack of Christmas spirit, his reindeer were robbed of the power of flight, and the sleigh's backup jet engine has misfired, leaving him stranded in Manhattan. He enlists Buddy's help in repairing the engine while there is still time. Although Buddy is reluctant, believing himself to be a truly substandard elf, Santa ensures him that his human heritage is no shortcoming – his attitude and enthusiasm make Buddy the most dedicated elf that Santa has ever known. Jubilant at feeling useful at last, Buddy races to find the detached engine (which has landed elsewhere in the park) and discovers that Michael and Walter have already stumbled upon it. Walter apologises to Buddy for his earlier treatment of him, and the pair enjoy a heartfelt rapprochement. But there is no time to lose – if Santa's sleigh isn't restored to flight soon, Christmas will be in jeopardy for everyone.

Walter is shocked to meet Santa, very much alive and well in the heart of New York. As Buddy works to reattach the jet engine to the sleigh, Santa presents Michael with his Christmas gift – a skateboard – which causes the sleigh to elevate due to his festive joy. But with the Central Park Rangers triangulating on the sleigh's position, time is running out for Buddy's repairs. Walter tries unsuccessfully to distract their approach, while Michael races to a nearby news team and reads out the contents of Santa's naughty and nice list, causing a new wave of belief in his existence when various viewers hear their names read out on live TV. This aids in powering up the sleigh although only temporarily. A glitch in the cameras' power supply causes the transmission to fail, meaning that the broadcast meets with an unexpectedly abrupt conclusion.

While Michael and Walter are reunited with Emily, who has been watching the events from the park on television, Jovie also appears in search of Buddy, unaware that he is currently trying desperately to reactivate the engine on Santa's sleigh as it makes a valiant attempt to escape the custody of the Rangers. Remembering Buddy's advice that Christmas songs are the best way of engendering festive spirit, Jovie overcomes her fear of public performance and starts to sing. Although the assembled crowd are initially rather puzzled at her seemingly-spontaneous recital, they soon join in, giving Santa the boost he needs to get his sleigh out of harm's way. With power restored to the TV cameras, people all across New York begin to join in with Jovie's song, meaning that Santa has easily enough power to return to his normal Christmas Eve duties with a little help from Buddy.

As the film concludes, it is revealed that Walter later establishes his own independent publishing company, enlisting the help of Buddy who pens a runaway success to start his business off with a bang – a 'fictional' account of his experiences during his journey from the North Pole to the Big Apple. As Buddy's writing career gains momentum, his relationship with Jovie deepens. They split their time between New York and Santa's workshop, where the film ends as the couple visit a doting Papa Elf just in time to introduce him to their new baby.

It is fair to say that it would have been all too easy for *Elf* to become a distinctly one-joke film. But while it is true that Will Ferrell's goofy, fish-out-of-water character – earnest and innocent in equal measure – causes an amusing display of havoc across New York through a very skilfully selected range of comedic situations, the narrative never becomes entirely dependent on the core absurdity of the film's outlandish premise in order to drive events. Indeed, it is to the immense credit of screenwriter David Berenbaum that *Elf* is never allowed to rely upon easy sight gags and slapstick: the underlying theme of the importance of the Christmas spirit, along with a cast of engaging supporting characters, elevates *Elf* far beyond the confines of a straightforward culture-clash comedy.

Although the elf-gone-astray plot is a variation on the events of *Santa Claus: The Movie*, if played much more knowingly (not least because it seems difficult to imagine Dudley Moore's character eating discarded gum from a subway entrance in the belief that it was free candy), the film's emphasis on unconventional family ties and the desire for belonging and a secure identity hearkens back to the concerns of nineties Christmas film-making. Yet Favreau and Berenbaum also draw interesting contrasts between the creative but guileless Buddy and the soul-sucking corporate blandness of the department store and upmarket publisher, a comparison which has more resonance with the anti-materialism themes of the eighties. Like many films since the turn of the century, *Elf* is a fascinating patchwork of established conventions and fresh approaches, making a resolute attempt to justify the key themes of the Christmas film in a way which is relevant to modern audiences. The notion of Buddy managing to engender Christmas spirit in the lives of world-weary New Yorkers is inspired (even if it does exhibit undeniable parallels with the climax of Ivan Reitman's *Ghostbusters II*, 1989), as is the rather pleasant notion that Buddy at the end of the film is more or less the same character that he had been at the beginning of it, uncorrupted by the cynicism of contemporary life and retaining both his innocence and an infectious enthusiasm.

The film benefits greatly from the inclusion of real New York locations and landmarks, especially the Empire State Building. The modern-day imagining of Gimbel's is effectively rendered too, a winning evocation of a grand department store from the city's past. Yet the fantasy sequences of *Elf*, set at the North Pole, are particularly full of charm, replete with stop-motion characters which range from anthropomorphic narwhals and Arctic puffins to decidedly chatty snowmen. It seems obvious that Favreau derives considerable amusement from the juxtaposition of the elves, who are in perfect scale to their environment, and Buddy, who is grossly oversized in relation to everything around him. Yet even this running gag is never overplayed.

It is no exaggeration to state that *Elf*'s effectiveness as a filmic experience depends very much on an appreciation of Will Ferrell's portrayal of Buddy. Ferrell delivers a dazzling performance throughout the film: an unrivalled, tireless exhibition of manic intensity interspersed with wide-eyed, childlike innocence. The interplay between the straight-faced Walter and his hyperactive, hitherto-unknown son is particularly well played, as is Buddy's outrage at Gimbel's ersatz Santa and his continual (if unintentional) aggravation of the department store's section manager. Ferrell quite simply never misses a beat in his performance, and succeeds right the way through in presenting a congenial (if undeniably strange) character whose wide-eyed innocence and frank openness are constantly at odds with the world around him. He also manages to walk a fine line in order to articulate Buddy's desire to fit in, and his sense of isolation, without ever allowing his efforts to come across as mawkish or unconvincing – not an easy task given the film's general tendency towards the outrageous and the tongue-in-cheek. Ferrell had been active as an actor both on American TV and in cinema since the mid-1990s. His best-known television work remains his long and well-received stint on *Saturday Night Live* (1995-2006), though he had also appeared in episodes of series as wide-ranging as *Grace Under Fire* (1995), *On Our Own* (1995), *Cow and Chicken* (1997) and *King of the Hill* (1999). His diverse range of film roles included a highly entertaining cameo appearance in Jay Roach's *Austin Powers: International Man of Mystery* (1997) and its sequel *Austin Powers: The Spy Who Shagged Me* (1999), and performances in features such as John Fortenberry's *A Night at the Roxbury* (1998), Donal Lardner Ward's *The Suburbans* (1999), Nick Gomez's *Drowning Mona* (2000), Reginald Hudlin's *The Ladies' Man* (2000), Kevin Smith's *Jay and Silent Bob Strike Back* (2001), Ben Stiller's *Zoolander* (2001) and Todd Phillips's *Old School* (2003), amongst many others. He is also an experienced producer and screenwriter. Since the release of *Elf*, the success of Ferrell's career has continued to grow, with Golden Globe Award nominations in the Best Performance by an Actor in a Supporting Role in a Motion Picture category in 2006 (for his appearance in Susan Stroman's *The Producers*, 2005), and in the Best Performance by an Actor in a Motion Picture (Musical or Comedy) category in 2007 (for his performance in Marc Forster's *Stranger Than Fiction*, 2006). He was also to be nominated for three MTV Movie Awards in 2005 for *Anchorman: The Legend of Ron Burgundy* (2004) and two further nominations in 2007 for his performance in Josh Gordon and Will

Speck's *Blades of Glory* (2007). Additionally, he was nominated for two Emmy Awards in 2009 for his television special, HBO's *You're Welcome America: A Final Night with George W. Bush* (2009), having previously been nominated for an Emmy in 2001 for his performance in a previous episode of *Saturday Night Live*.

Another masterstroke on Favreau's part was the casting of James Caan – immortalised in a number of hard-man roles throughout his career – as Buddy's constantly confounded father. Caan is, quite simply, the perfect foil for the naive, childlike Buddy, continually in awe of this bizarre elf-man and his strange customs. Many of the film's most entertaining sequences are based on the conflict between the tough, straight-talking New York publisher and his sugar plum-obsessed offspring. It is to Caan's considerable credit, then, that Walter's eventual acceptance of Buddy does actually feel like a natural progression, moving from hostility to grudging forebearance and eventually to tolerance and the acknowledgement of his paternity, especially when Buddy's unexpected interference in his life causes him to question the direction of his career and his future. One of the most prolific and accomplished American actors of his generation, Caan's career began with television appearances in the early sixties, in a number of famous TV shows which included *Naked City* (1961), *The Untouchables* (1962), *Dr Kildare* (1963), *Wagon Train* (1965) and *Get Smart* (1969). His cinematic roles included appearances in films such as Howard Hawks's *El Dorado* (1966), Robert Altman's *Countdown* (1968) and Jack Smight's *Rabbit, Run* (1970) before what is generally regarded as his breakthrough performance, that of Santino 'Sonny' Corleone in Francis Ford Coppola's *The Godfather* (1972) and its first sequel, *The Godfather: Part II* (1974). Since then, he has appeared in literally dozens of film roles which have encompassed everything from comedy drama to science fiction, among them being features which have included Herbert Ross's *Funny Lady* (1975), Norman Jewison's *Rollerball* (1975), Richard Attenborough's *A Bridge Too Far* (1977), Michael Mann's *Violent Streets* (1981), Graham Baker's *Alien Nation* (1988), Rob Reiner's *Misery* (1990), Chuck Russell's *Eraser* (1996) and Lars von Trier's *Dogville* (2003). Caan was nominated for the Best Actor in a Supporting Role Academy Award in 1973 for his performance in *The Godfather* (1972), and has also received nominations for Emmy Awards, Daytime Emmy Awards, and no less than four Golden Globe Award nominations.

The film's supporting cast is every bit as strong, beginning with a memorable performance from Zooey Deschanel as Buddy's unlikely love interest. Although the point is not laboured, Jovie clearly feels almost as isolated as Buddy, and in spite of her initial coldness towards him she quickly develops a sense of intrigue and even affection regarding this most unconventional of individuals. Deschanel's acting career began on television with roles in prominent TV series including episodes of *Veronica's Closet* (1998), *Frasier* (2002) and *Cracking Up* (2004). Her cinematic work began with an appearance in Lawrence Kasdan's *Mumford* (1999), a role which would be followed up by a number of different performances in films such as Cameron Crowe's *Almost Famous* (2000), Miguel Arteta's *The Good Girl* (2002), Ed Decter's *The New Guy* (2002), Amy Lippman's *House Hunting* (2003) and, perhaps most prominently, David Gordon Green's *All the Real Girls* (2003), a film which was to win her the Best Actress Award at the Mar del Plata Film Festival in 2003, and also a nomination for an Independent Spirit Award in the Best Female Lead category. She has continued to remain a successful and popular performer in American cinema since the release of *Elf*, often in quirky and intelligent roles, including appearances in films such as Garth Jennings's sci-fi adaptation *The Hitchhiker's Guide to the Galaxy* (2005), Gabor Csupo's fantasy adventure *Bridge to Terabithia* (2007), Andrew Dominik's historical drama *The Assassination of Jesse James by the Coward Robert Ford* (2007), and Marc Webb's offbeat romantic comedy *500 Days of Summer* (2009).

Also of note was the choice casting of Ed Asner, forever remembered by American TV audiences for his role as Lou Grant on CBS's *The Mary Tyler Moore Show* (1970-77). *Elf* was to present the fourth time that Asner had portrayed Santa Claus, after voice performances in two animated TV movies - Toby Bluth's *The Story of Santa Claus* (1996) and Steve Moore's *Olive, the Other Reindeer* (1999) - and also a live-action appearance in an episode of CBS's *The Ellen Show* (2001). He makes for an agreeably spiky Santa, possessing Christmas cheer and sardonic wit in roughly equal measure (clearly this is a Father Christmas who doesn't suffer fools gladly). Academy Award-winning actress Mary Steenburgen puts in a winning performance as Walter's warm-hearted wife Emily, and Peter Dinklage comes close to stealing the show for his cameo as the pompous, hot-tempered creative genius Miles Finch. Bob Newhart, instantly recognisable for his starring role in CBS's long-running TV series *The Bob Newhart Show* (1972–78) and *Newhart* (1982–90), is an inspired choice for Buddy's slightly careworn adoptive elf father, Papa Elf, also the narrator for the film's opening and conclusion. There are also some blink-and-you'll-miss-them cameos from Jon Favreau as Walter's doctor (also the voice of the North Pole narwhal), and screenwriter David Berenbaum as one of the office workers at Walter's publishing company. And last but not least, in the cameo role of Ming-Ming – one of the assembly line supervisor elves at Santa's workshop – is an uncredited Peter Billingsley, better known as *A Christmas Story*'s Ralphie Parker.

Elf was met with widespread enthusiasm from commentators when it was released into cinemas, with critics praising the film for its appeal to the whole family,[1] Jon Favreau's well-judged direction,[2] and David Berenbaum's astute, deftly-structured screenplay.[3] A majority of the reviewers' approval was reserved for Will Ferrell's central performance, which was commended for his perfect grasp of the film's fish-out-of-water premise,[4] his knowing depiction of Buddy's gullible ingenuousness,[5] and the innate sense of fun which is on display right throughout the duration of his portrayal.[6] Naturally, however, there were competing views with regard to the film's effectiveness. Some commentators questioned whether the film's calculating juxtaposition of cynicism and naïveté undermined the authenticity of its conclusion,[7] while others found Buddy's artlessness to be a little too saccharine to prove entirely bearable.[8] But in the eyes of many, the film epitomised a refreshing break from the increasing number of direct retreads over the past glories of festive cinema,[9] showing itself to be a feature that was unafraid to revel in its own preposterous situations with good humour and warm sentiment.[10]

Elf was recognised at awards ceremonies the year after its release, winning the Golden Trailer Award for Best Comedy as well as an ASCAP Award for John Debney's original score. Will Ferrell was nominated in the Best Comedic Performance category of the MTV Movie Awards, and was also given a nomination for Choice Movie Actor at the Teen Choice Awards, where the film itself was nominated in the Choice Movie: Comedy category. Additionally, the film was nominated for two awards at the Phoenix Film Critics Society Awards, in the Best Live Action Family Film category as well as for Best Use of Previously Published or Recorded Music.

Elf's continued popularity with audiences has recently been enhanced by a new stage musical which opened on Broadway in November 2010. With a score by Matthew Sklar and Beguelin, and the book adapted by Thomas Meehan and Bob Martin from David Berenbaum's original screenplay, *Elf: The Musical* retells Buddy's story in a new musical format, and has proven to be a major commercial success. The growing appeal of *Elf*, perhaps, lies not just in the charm of its characters and the entertaining absurdity of its situations, but also in its themes of redemption and enlightenment (Walter's emotional epiphany, Jovie's ebbing self-consciousness, and the positive changes in Michael's attitude) as well as Buddy's demonstration that the compelling attraction of festive goodwill can have a profound and lasting impact on people and communities even in a jaded and discontented world. Yet although *Elf* had managed to justify the efficacy of such traditional conventions in a thoroughly relevant setting, its rousing interpretation would prove to be far from the only innovative approach to Christmas themes as this creatively fruitful decade progressed.

Historical Context

Elf received its premiere at the Austin Film Festival on 9 October 2003, and was then released in cinemas across America on 7 November that year. Making their premieres on the same date were Casey Rodgers's *Hades Night*, Ben Ross's *Special Breakfast Eggroll: 99¢*, and Mark Sobel's *The Commission*. 'Baby Boy' by Beyoncé, featuring Sean Paul, was at number one on the Billboard Hot 100 chart that week. Appearing in current affairs at the time, the Harris Theatre opened in Chicago, Mexican President Vicente Fox began a three state trip to the United States, and NASA's famous Voyager 1 probe finally left the confines of the Earth's solar system.

22

BAD SANTA (2003)

Columbia Picture/ Dimension Films/ Triptych Pictures/ Blixa Zweite Film Produktion GmbH & Co. KG

Director: Terry Zwigoff
Producers: Sarah Aubrey, John Cameron and Bob Weinstein
Screenwriters: Glenn Ficarra and John Requa

MAIN CAST

Billy Bob Thornton	-	Willie B. Stokes
Tony Cox	-	Marcus
Brett Kelly	-	The Kid/ Thurman Merman
Lauren Graham	-	Sue
Lauren Tom	-	Lois
Bernie Mac	-	Gin Slagel
John Ritter	-	Bob Chipeska
Ethan Phillips	-	Roger Merman

If *Elf* had shown what was achievable when the comforting tropes of the traditional Christmas film were held up to the harsh light of modern life's cynicism and irony, then *Bad Santa* was to crank up the intensity of this subversiveness by at least a factor of ten. For where the protagonist of *Elf* had been a kindly innocent, unprepared for the misanthropy and perpetual scepticism of twenty-first century living, the central figure of *Bad Santa* was to prove to be the very antithesis of joy and goodwill. A direct and deliberately apparent subversion of *Miracle on 34th Street*'s Kris Kringle, this film was to present the world with a kind of anti-Santa figure, a character who was a miserable, unscrupulous criminal so devoid of moral integrity that presumably even Scrooge would have considered him to have gone a bit too far in his contempt for the festive season.

Bad Santa was directed by Terry Zwigoff, a noted director who has become best-known for the penetrating analysis of his documentary film work. A highly distinctive talent, Zwigoff's directorial career had encompassed diverse features which had included music documentary *Louie Bluie* (1985), art biopic *Crumb* (1994) and the surreal *Ghost World* (2001). In 2002 he was nominated for the Academy Award, along with his co-writer Daniel Clowes, in the Best Writing (Screenplay Based on Material Previously Produced or Published) category for his work on *Ghost World*. With *Bad Santa*, however, he was to make a dramatic departure from the tone of his earlier material, focusing his meticulous cultural scrutiny onto a narrative which would chew up and spit out many preconceptions about what would be possible – and push the boundaries of what was acceptable – in a Christmas film.

Willie B. Stokes (Billy Bob Thornton) is quite possibly the worst department store Santa imaginable. Stroppy and completely unenthusiastic, he has no love for Christmas and even less fondness for children. However, one thing that Willie does have (aside from a problem with alcoholism) is a talent for theft on a grand scale. Aided by his partner in crime Marcus (Tony Cox), who spends his days accompanying 'Santa' as one of his elves, Willie uses the festive season as a cover for highly lucrative robberies. The story opens as the pair subvert a Milwaukee store's burglar alarm system and crack its night-safe, making a getaway with stolen goods and thousands of dollars in cash.

Their ill-gotten gains safely stashed away, Marcus and Willie head to a bar for a celebratory drink. Marcus chides Willie for his sloppiness; his criminal skills are not what they once were, which is putting them both at risk. But Willie, summoning up the closest that he can get to sanguinity, tells his sidekick that there is no need to worry: he is planning to go straight and head for Miami, in the hope of starting a new life for himself. Having heard it all before, Marcus tells Willie that he'll believe this when he sees it. In his opinion, Willie will simply sink all of his money into purchasing booze, and will then end up returning to his usual criminal racket by the time Christmas has arrived the following year.

Sure enough, some time later Willie makes the move to Miami as planned, but winds up spending his time stealing drinks from bars and ogling beautiful women. With clearly no intention of turning his back on casual criminality, he purloins a set of car keys from a nearby valet parking lot, uses them to steal a flash car, and then (after a quick look at the documentation in the glove compartment to find an address) takes a drive back to the owner's lavish home. There, he avails himself of the luxious house's amenities before robbing its safe, eventually winding up in a sleazy strip club where he spends most of the stolen loot on scratch cards and yet more alcohol. However, Willie's aimless ennui comes to a temporary end when he discovers a message from Marcus on his answerphone, asking him to meet in Phoenix, Arizona.

Sure enough, Willie makes his way across the country for the resumption of their annual scam, but Marcus is becoming worried at his increasingly erratic behaviour. Mall manager Bob Chipeska (John Ritter) greets the pair, having been impressed by their speculative application for the Santa post, but a clearly inebriated Willie almost blows their chances of employment. Growing suspicious, Chipeska alerts the mall's head of security Gin Slagel (Bernie Mac) to keep an eye on the new arrivals. Things go from bad to worse when Willie, who still can't stop drinking, is on an even shorter fuse than usual during his first session at the mall's grotto. After racing through a seemingly neverending queue of excitable children eager to tell him their gift requests, Willie is faced by a somewhat off-putting kid (Brett Kelly) who – improbable though it may sound – believes the dishevelled drunkard to be the real Santa Claus. In spite of Willie's usual foul-mouthed tirade of cynicism, the overweight little boy seems absolutely convinced of his authenticity as jolly old Saint Nick. Finding himself thoroughly creeped out, Willie sends the kid packing at the first opportunity.

Although he remains in a state of extreme drunkenness at the end of his shift, Willie still decides to visit a nearby bar to drown his sorrows, unaware that he is still being watched by the mildly-disturbing little boy. There he meets bartender Sue (Lauren Graham), who reveals that she has a fetish for men in Santa Claus outfits. Too intoxicated to be puzzled by this revelation, Willie invites Sue to his car and soon finds that even Santa can receive an unexpected Christmas present. After they part, he is assaulted by a mentally-disturbed man (Ajay Naidu) in the parking lot. The assailant is hysterical, and cannot be reasoned with. He is in the process of molesting Willie when he is interrupted by the tubby kid from the mall, outraged that anyone would attack Santa. The kid's timely intervention sends the interloper running, much to Willie's relief.

Willie drives the boy home, though as a result of doing so he is forced to field an endless torrent of questions about Santa's sleigh and life at the North Pole (which he answers with characteristic bad grace). Eventually they reach the kid's home, though when he is informed that the boy's father is absent and his mother is dead – he is being cared for by his elderly grandmother – Willie wastes no time in donning a face mask, preparing to rob the place. However, to his surprise Willie faces no resistance to his criminal intentions: believing that he is helping Santa, the boy happily furnishes Willie with the location of the family safe and even hands over the keys to his father's car, which Willie wastes no time in commandeering.

The next day, Chipeska is doing his rounds of the mall when, to his shock, he discovers Willie spreading a little festive cheer in the ladies' changing room of a clothing store. He calls Willie and Marcus to his office and, in spite of Willie's steadfast denial of any wrongdoing, attempts to dismiss them both from their post. However, when Willie threatens him with a discrimination suit – and all of the subsequent bad press that would accompany it – Chipeska meekly backs down. But Marcus realises that their position is becoming ever more tenuous by the day. After later seeing Willie making a spectacularly unsubtle pass at a teenager (Briana Norton), he entreats him to keep a lower profile so that they do not attract any further unwanted attention.

Chipeska speaks to Gin again and fills him in with regard to his earlier encounter. Gin seems unimpressed with Chipeska's account, given that Willie's indiscretions are still vague enough to make a clear dismissal a risky strategy. Chipeska then asks Gin to watch the pair as closely as possible in the hope that he can uncover enough evidence of wrongdoing to allow Willie and Marcus to be fired for other reasons. Although apparently considering the whole situation to be mundane in the extreme, Gin agrees to keep his eyes peeled.

That evening, Willie gets back to the motel where he is staying only to discover a police officer rummaging through his room. He sidesteps a confrontation, knowing that he has stored no evidence of wrongdoing there, and instead heads back to the kid's home. The little boy is elated that the one and only Santa Claus has decided to spend some time with him (Willie explains that he will have to stay there for a while on account of trouble at the North Pole). Due to a combination of tiredness and inebriation, Willie finds that no amount of angry retorts will keep the kid's relentless line of questioning at bay – even when he takes a bath, the boy is bombarding him with queries about elves and reindeer. The kid is confused by the fact that Santa appears to be more fond of whisky than he is of milk and cookies; even an offer of sharing the chocolate from his Advent calendar is met with a less than enthusiastic response.

Back at the mall, Marcus is furious to learn that Willie is staying at the kid's home, believing that it will compromise their operation. Willie, naturally, couldn't care less about Marcus's concerns – or, indeed, anyone else's. He snaps at a woman and her child when he is interrupted during his lunch break, causing yet more unnecessary attention to his behaviour, little realising that Gin is already hard at work attempting to uncover concrete evidence of his wrongdoing.

Later, Willie is playing checkers with the kid, though he flies into a fit of outrage when he is easily beaten by the little boy. They are interrupted when Herb (Matt Walsh), one of the kid's neighbours, arrives to enlist their help with the street's Christmas decorations – a request which, to put it mildly, does not go down well with Willie. But remaining determined to make himself at home, Willie invites Sue over on the premise that he is renting the property while he's working in town. He seems blissfully unaware of the rather obvious fact that Sue seems keen to get to know him better than these superficial encounters between them allow, and her disappointment is palpable when he explains that he will only be in Arizona until Christmas, following which he and Marcus will be moving on.

Gin's investigations begin to pick up pace when a trace on Willie's stolen car reveals that it is registered to Roger Merman (Ethan Phillips), the kid's father, who is currently in jail due to a conviction for embezzlement. After a few questions with Roger during a visiting session at the prison, Gin quickly establishes that Willie is using the car without Roger's permission, and indeed that the incarcerated man has no knowledge that Willie is even staying at his house. Gin stalls Chipeska while his inspection of Willie's conduct continues, oblivious to the fact that Marcus and Willie are already beginning to smuggle equipment into the mall in preparation for their forthcoming raid.

Willie also finds himself – much in spite of his expectation – growing closer to the kid and his addled grandmother (Cloris Leachman). He ends up cooking dinner for them, repairs the little boy's beloved Advent calendar after tearing it apart while drunk, and tends to the kid when he accidentally cuts his hand. Later, during his time at work, Willie is visited by the boy again and finds that he has been set upon by bullies outside the mall. The boy asks Santa for a gorilla to protect him from harassment, but Willie explains that no amount of large hairy primates will be sufficient to defend himself – what he really needs to do is stand up for himself.

Gin approaches Marcus and Willie and reveals that their game is up. He explains that his investigation has turned up the fact that they have used the same robbery scam on seven separate occasions (on different years, and in different cities) to considerable success – so far. But rather than handing them over to the authorities, Gin instead decides to strike a lucrative deal. He will happily let them carry out their robbery, provided that they give him half of the proceeds. Once they have handed over the stolen cash, he will feign ignorance of their activities and leave them free to continue their criminal activities elsewhere. Willie is livid, but Marcus finds that he is unable to negotiate: Gin is holding all the cards. This leads Willie to drink himself to near oblivion, horrifying onlooking parents and children as he smashes up the mall's Christmas display in an inebriated stupor. Gin, who now has a stake in the success of Willie's operation, plans to square the wayward Santa's behaviour with Chipeska in order to avoid any danger of dismissal. But the conflict between Gin and Marcus is tangible.

Despairing, Willie goes to the kid's garage and attempts to asphyxiate himself by pumping carbon monoxide from the car's tailpipe into its interior. The boy interrupts his suicide bid, and Willie gives him an envelope containing a confession of his criminal activities, which he asks him to hand over to the police when his body is found. However, on noticing that the kid has suffered further bullying (he now has a black eye), Willie changes his mind and returns to the mall, where he beats up the teenaged ringleader of the gang (Max Van Ville) that has been harassing his young acquaintance. The other kids look on in awe as Santa wipes the floor with the sullen tormenter.

Willie is amazed at the feeling of self-worth that has resulted from helping out the kid, and enlists Marcus in helping him give the boy some boxing lessons. Unfortunately for all concerned, Willie's tuition proves to be very far from conventional defence training, and consequently nobody learns much of anything as a result. Later, while Willie is entertaining Sue at the kid's house, the boy makes an unexpected appearance and tells him that, as he will no doubt be off on his sleigh when Christmas Eve arrives, he wants to give him his Christmas gift early. He presents Willie with a carved wooden pickle, explaining that he had cut his hand earlier while making it himself. For the first time, Willie actually appears to be genuinely moved.

The following morning, the kid finds the thoroughly hung-over Willie in his kitchen and proudly shows him his school report card. Willie finds that he has little to say about the boy's average grades, but is bemused to finally discover his name, which is Thurman Merman. When Thurman asks Willie's opinion on his progress at school, Willie admits that he is doing better in third grade than he had ever done, which leads the kid to ask if that means that he will get a present for Christmas. After all, he adds, Santa has passed his house two years running without leaving any gifts. Exasperated by the boy's wide-eyed naïveté, Willie finally tells him that he isn't really Santa, just someone who is working in a mall. Betraying little disappointment, Thurman admits that he had realised this fact a long time ago – he just thought that as they had become acquaintances, he hoped that Willie would want to give him a gift for Christmas. Against all expectation, this gives Willie pause for thought.

Determined to keep Gin out of his scheme, Marcus follows the sleuth's car after work and – staging the breakdown of his van – asks him for a jump-start. As Gin attaches jump leads to the van's battery, Marcus's accomplice Lois (Lauren Tom) drives into him, breaking his ribs. Unsatisfied that the detective has been incapacitated thoroughly enough, Marcus then electrocutes him for good measure. Meanwhile, Sue joins Willie at Thurman's home and the pair spend time decorating the house for Christmas – albeit that their ornamentation does not exactly take the most traditional of approaches. Willie even, against all odds, provides the exterior decorations that the street's neighbourhood committee had requested. Knowing that it is Christmas Eve, Thurman offers to make Willie a sandwich, realising that he will soon be leaving. Willie promises him that as soon as his 'business' at the mall is complete, he will return to join him for Christmas dinner.

Right on schedule, Marcus smuggles himself into the duct system of the mall and disables the building's surveillance cameras before shutting down the alarm system. Willie finds, to his disgust, that the mall's safe is one of a select number of models which are considered uncrackable not that this deters him for long. Eventually gaining entry, he leaves Marcus to load up the abundant stacks of banknotes while he heads into the mall to pick up one final item – the stuffed toy elephant which is all that Thurman wants for Christmas. On retrieving it, however, Willie turns to see Marcus pointing a gun at him. Initially he believes the double-cross has been instigated because of Gin's demand for a cut of the money, but Marcus explains that the security chief is dead; the reason that he wants Willie out of the picture is because he has become so unreliable that he is a liability to their operation. He takes aim to fire, but is interrupted when they realise that they are surrounded by armed police officers. A desperate chase then ensues, with Marcus and the loot being pursued in one direction while Willie tears off in another, shotguns blasting all the way. More by luck than design, Willie reaches his stolen car and manages to drive through a police blockade near the mall, a sudden attack of conscience making him desperate to ensure that Thurman receives his much-wanted Christmas gift at all costs. Tailed by half a dozen police patrol cars, Willie finally manages to reach Thurman's home but is gunned down before he can reach the front door.

In an epilogue, Willie explains in a letter to Thurman that he now realises that the reason the police knew in advance about his operation at the mall was because the kid had handed over his letter of confession (written prior to Willie's earlier suicide attempt), tipping them off with regard to his whereabouts and intentions on Christmas Eve. However, as they wrongly believed that Willie was confessing in advance of the crime, he is being treated more favourably than Marcus and Lois, who have been convicted for their part in the raid. Willie arranges for Sue to be named as Thurman's legal guardian, to take care of him at his home until Willie (or indeed his father Roger) is released from prison. The kid, meanwhile, shows that Willie's mentoring had not been entirely in vain when he defends himself against the neighbourhood bully in a way that demonstrates that he had learned something from his earlier boxing lessons after all.

Central to the success of *Bad Santa* is the fact that it is a film which, just like its protagonist, takes great delight in breaking all the rules. Just as David Kitay's score regularly juxtaposes warmly evocative Christmas tunes and elegant classical music with Willie's wilfully profligate behaviour, so too does the film revel in setting up traditional festive scenes only to undermine them. The mall's brightly decorated Santa's grotto is the very image of jollity, until the drunken Willie sees fit to tear it apart with his bare hands. The sunny, arid Arizonan location is as far from a winter wonderland as it is possible to imagine. The expressions of wonder on the faces of children queued up to see Santa at the mall might be diminished by Willie's all-pervading disinterest in their festive glee, but somehow they never quite seem to be wiped away completely. And yet, in spite of Willie's charmless demeanour and permanently scruffy appearance, we still find ourselves siding with this maladjusted misanthrope over the likes of the prudish Chipeska, with his social awkwardness and hand-wringing political correctness. Willie may well be a criminal – and proud of the fact – but he is also undeniably his own man, his lack of respect spread equally around everyone who is unfortunate enough to cross his path. While these characteristics make him absolutely the worst candidate to embody the festive cheer personified by Santa Claus, they do undoubtedly provide the foundation for a highly entertaining comedy.

While *Bad Santa* is unmistakably *Miracle on 34th Street* viewed through a glass darkly (Thurman even gets to utter the iconic 'Leave Santa alone!' line), the film was also distinctive in its depiction of Santa Claus as a character diametrically opposed to his traditional role. While other evocations of Father Christmas shown throughout the noughties tended to correspond more closely with the established model of the character, as had been the case in films such as *Elf*, Robert Zemeckis's *The Polar Express* (2004) and David Dobkin's *Fred Claus* (2007), the radical nature of Terry Zwigoff's take on Santa could be matched only by the extreme subversions that had manifested themselves in horror parodies such as

Charles E. Sellier's *Silent Night, Deadly Night* (1984) and David Steiman's *Santa's Slay* (2005). Glenn Ficarra and John Requa's well-judged screenplay manages to identify the tolerable boundaries of taste in a Christmas film, and then proceeds to ignore them at every turn – to striking effect. If, in decades past, the secular approach to the festive season had been accused in some quarters of undermining the religious underpinnings of Christmas, then the postmodern age was clearly not above challenging even the notions that had come to define the very concept of Christmas. With *Bad Santa* the audience is presented with a Father Christmas who hates the festive season, who is massively promiscuous, who swears constantly, who drinks to excess and is often barely continent as a result. His comically unkempt red suit is permanently stained and soiled, his filthy off-white beard little more than an afterthought. Clearly, this was no *Santa Claus: The Movie*. In fact, *Bad Santa* has proven – at time of writing – to be almost certainly the most profane Christmas film of all time, with most fan websites agreeing on a total of around three hundred separate instances of bad language throughout the course of its running time. Yet the film doesn't stop there: the traditional festive connotations of family, home and hearth are lampooned by means of the effectively parentless Thurman Merman, socially maladjusted and with a resultingly skewed expectation of what exactly he should anticipate from Christmas and Santa. His grandmother, who spends much of the film appearing to be on the cusp of death, and his incarcerated embezzler father, are such ineffectual characters that it falls to the brazenly felonious Willie and his kinky bartender quasi-girlfriend to act as parent figures. Even the Christian symbolism of the season doesn't go unscathed, with a blindly inebriated Willie tearing model donkeys to pieces in Santa's grotto while a police officer in pursuit of the hapless criminal accidentally blows the head off Nativity figures with a shotgun. If there is any Christmas shibboleth that has not been shattered by Zwigoff at the time of the film's conclusion, it is difficult to imagine what it might be.

And yet, in spite of this all-guns-blazing assault on the sentimentality and conformity of traditional festive tropes, there is little doubt that *Bad Santa* does indeed have a heart: the fact that it doesn't expose itself until the climax, and even then only obliquely, adds greatly to the film's effectiveness. Willie's redemption is considerably underplayed, as unorthodox as it is astute, and manages to remain covert even longer than had been the case in that other hymn to cynicism at the holiday season, *Scrooged*. Zwigoff has to be commended for succeeding, even in the midst of such carnage and supreme bad taste, in still being able to deliver a happy ending in the grand tradition of the Christmas film genre without the gesture appearing mawkish or surplus to requirements. In the world of film, it seems, the festive season has retained the ability to alter and improve the character and disposition of individuals even in an age of postmodern deconstruction and moral uncertainty.

As had been the case in *Elf*, the other major Christmas film of 2003, much of the proficiency of *Bad Santa* can be attributed to the central performance of its lead actor. Billy Bob Thornton delivers a blisteringly spiky performance as Willie, brilliantly milking the character for every morose, antagonistic trait that he can muster.[1] That he can do so while still somehow making the character seem strangely likeable – albeit in a very circuitous manner – is nothing short of astonishing. (One particularly amusing example of Willie's shaky shift in character comes when he destroys Thurman's treasured Advent calendar while drunk and, later feeling bad about his actions, quickly repairs it with new improvised 'treats' which include Aspirin capsules.) An accomplished actor, writer, director and producer, Thornton has been active in film since the early eighties, appearing in features which included Robert C. Hughes's *Hunter's Blood* (1986), Mark Rezyka's *South of Reno* (1988) and Dan Hoskins's *Chrome Hearts* (1989) before hitting the big time with a prominent performance in Carl Franklin's *One False Move* (1992), a film which was also written by Thornton and Tom Epperson. His popularity increased throughout the nineties thanks to roles in high-profile films including Adrian Lyne's *Indecent Proposal* (1993), George P. Cosmatos's *Tombstone* (1993), Jim Jarmusch's *Dead Man* (1995), Oliver Stone's *U Turn* (1997) and Mike Nichols's *Primary Colors* (1998). Thornton won an Academy Award in 1997 in the Best Writing: Screenplay Based on Material from Another Medium category for his film *Sling Blade* (1996), also being nominated for the Best Actor in a Leading Role Oscar for his performance in the same film. Additionally, his role in Sam Raimi's *A Simple Plan* (1998) was to see him nominated for an Academy Award again, this time in the category of Best Actor in a Supporting Role. Among his many other plaudits have been a Daytime Emmy nomination in 2000, and Golden Globe nominations in 1999, 2000 and 2004.

Bad Santa's range of supporting players form an eclectic selection of talent, foremost among them Lauren Graham as Sue, a woman who is passionate about Christmas in more ways than one. Although their time together on-screen is brief, Graham and Thornton conjure up a touchingly believable chemistry, with the affectionate bartender clearly seeing something in the haggard Willie that is less than obvious to the world at large. Appearing on television and in cinema since the mid-nineties, Graham's profile benefited from roles in many high-profile TV series including *Third Rock from the Sun* (1996), *Caroline in the City* (1995-96), *Law and Order* (1997) and *Seinfeld* (1997), as well as films which included Ole Bornedal's *Nightwatch* (1997), Carl Franklin's *One True Thing* (1998) and Pat O'Connor's *Sweet November* (2001). Also a producer for television and in film, in 2002 Graham was nominated for a Golden Globe Award in the category of Best Performance by an Actress in a Television Series (Drama) for her appearances as Lorelai Gilmore in the Warner Brothers Television Network's long-running drama *Gilmore Girls* (2000). Also worthy of note is Bernie Mac as the intense, cheerfully duplicitous mall security operative Gin Slagel. With his highly distinctive dress sense and evident desire to make the most of his position as the arbiter of justice at the mall – when it suits him, at least – Gin is a memorable antagonist, his fierce verbal sparring with Marcus proving to be particularly entertaining. Mac's film appearances began in the nineties with roles in features such as Peter MacDonald's *Mo' Money* (1992), Ted Demme's *Who's the Man?* (1993), Preston A. Whitmore II's *The Walking Dead* (1995) and Paris Barclay's *Don't Be a Menace to South Central While Drinking Your Juice in the Hood* (1996). He was particularly well-known for his television series *The Bernie Mac Show* (2001–06), which saw him nominated for Emmy Awards in 2002 and 2003, and Golden Globe Award nominations in 2003 and 2004. From the turn of the century, he made a number of appearances in prominent films prior to the release of *Bad Santa*, which included Steven Soderbergh's *Ocean's Eleven* (2001), Sam Weisman's *What's the Worst That Could Happen?* (2001) and Chris Rock's *Head of State* (2003). His career also expanded in the latter years of his life, to include writing and production credits on a number of features for television.

Among the other members of the cast, Tony Cox puts in a full-blooded performance as the sarcastic Marcus, the long-suffering brains behind the film's criminal operations, while Lauren Tom is clearly having a great deal of fun as Lois, his glamorous but hard-nosed accomplice. Brett Kelly brings a touchingly affecting strain of weirdness to his role as the sandwich-obsessed Thurman Merman, while John Ritter steals every scene that he appears in as the strait-laced but ultimately weak-willed mall manager Bob Chipeska, a character with more hang-ups than the average cloakroom.

Although it may seem that *Bad Santa* is the kind of film that is almost tailor-made to divide audiences, it was actually to meet with high praise from many mainstream critics at the time of its release – though it must be noted that some reviewers were more fulsome in their commendation of the film than others. While many applauded *Bad Santa*'s unashamedly caustic wit,[2] for some it was the barefaced glorification of bad taste that made the film stand out from the crowd.[3] The gleefully excessive vulgarity of Billy Bob Thornton's performance was found to be of critical note too,[4] as was the fact that the film never once gives in to the emotional slushiness that is sometimes so typical of the season,[5] though some commentators did question whether the film's mould-breakingly unsentimental approach would be enough to guarantee it any degree of lasting appeal.[6]

Bad Santa was not forgotten at awards ceremonies throughout the year following its release, with Billy Bob Thornton receiving a nomination in the Best Performance by an Actor in a Motion Picture (Musical or Comedy) category at the Golden Globe Awards, and Bernie Mac being nominated for the Outstanding Supporting Actor in a Box Office Movie award at the BET Comedy Awards. Additionally, Mary Vernieu and Felicia Fasano were nominated for the Best Casting for Feature Film (Comedy) award by the Casting Society of America, while Brett Kelly won the award for Best Performance by a Youth in a Lead or Supporting Role (Male) at the Phoenix Film Critics Society Awards.

Following the theatrical release of *Bad Santa*, an 'unrated' version of the film was released on DVD in 2004. This release was seven minutes longer than the original cut of the film, and restored a number of sequences which had not been exhibited in the film's original cinematic run. Following this in 2006, the film was also to be released in a new director's cut,[7] which presented the feature as Terry Zwigoff had originally intended. The director's cut is a pacier and marginally more condensed experience, its duration slightly shorter than the original theatrical version of the film.

Bad Santa has earned its reputation as a thoroughly twenty-first century

Christmas film, being original and innovative while experimenting (at times rather drastically) with the apparatus of traditional festive conventions. Thanks to the cult success of its director, and indeed the fact that its executive producers were none other than the legendary Coen Brothers, the film remains of interest to movie buffs in general as much as it does to aficionados of Christmas cinema. It also re-emphasised the point that not only had festive flms proven to be surprisingly adaptable in terms of narrative and content, but also that subgenres of this category of flm were still being cross-pollinated to striking effect, producing features which were to explore the continuing relevance of established Christmas tropes in a rapidly-changing modern world.

Historical Context

Bad Santa made its cinematic premiere in American theatres in 26 November 2003. Also debuting in cinemas on that date were Rob Minkoff's *The Haunted Mansion* and Ron Howard's *The Missing*. Still at number one on the Billboard Hot 100 that week was 'Baby Boy' by Beyoncé, featuring Sean Paul; the song would remain at the top of the chart until 5 December that year. In the news during this week, American President George W. Bush made a surprise Thanksgiving Day trip to Baghdad to visit the American troops stationed there, Pakistan and India announced a ceasefire in the Kashmir region, and the British Columbia Railway was purchased from the British Columbia provincial government by the Canadian National Railway.

23

NOEL (2004)

Code Entertainment/ Red Rose Productions LLC

Director: Chazz Palminteri
Producers: Al Corley, Eugene Musso and Zvi Howard Rosenman
Screenwriter: David Hubbard

MAIN CAST

Susan Sarandon	-	Rose Harrison
Paul Walker	-	Mike Riley
Penélope Cruz	-	Nina Vasquez
Alan Arkin	-	Artie Venizelos
Marcus Thomas	-	Jules Calvert
Chazz Palminteri	-	Arizona
Sonny Marinelli	-	Dennis
Daniel Sunjata	-	Marco

Romance has long been a staple of Christmas films, even from the time of the genre's golden age with the blossoming of true love proving to be a key theme in such classic films as *It's a Wonderful Life*, *The Bishop's Wife* and *White Christmas*. But in the noughties, the subgenre of the romantic Christmas film (that is, a film where romance is the principal theme of the film, with traditional festive themes usually subordinate to the central love story) was to undergo something of a rebirth thanks to the success of Richard Curtis's *Love Actually* (2003). Curtis's movie was to give this category of film a welcome kick-start, leading to many subsequent Christmas romances later in the decade which included Nancy Meyer's *The Holiday* (2005) and Seth Gordon's *Four Christmases* (2008). But the factor which distinguished *Love Actually* from previous festive films dealing with romance was Curtis's skilful use of a large ensemble cast, the stories of each individual character woven tightly together to form a detailed narrative patchwork which explores many corresponding themes of love and affection.

While the ensemble Christmas tale was – in and of itself – a well established subgenre, particularly within the realm of TV movies, films such as Nora Ephron's *Mixed Nuts* (1994) had proven that it was a genus of storytelling which could be adapted effectively for the big screen. Curtis had proven, to much success, that such a format was compatible with the exploration of romantic themes, laying the groundwork for further multi-character romantic comedies and dramas set at Christmas. With *Noel*, Chazz Palminteri was to create a lively fusion of these different subgenres, bringing together a wide range of very dissimilar characters to explore the notion of love – and not simply love of a romantic nature – against the background of a snowy New York City during one fateful Christmas Eve. David Hubbard's screenplay for the flm was to carve an interesting niche for itself, reinventing the time-honoured format of the ensemble drama to explore the concerns and aspirations of several characters whose lives intersect at several key points of connection. The manner in which these individuals relate to each other, and the correlations that are drawn between the motivating power of the human spirit and the transformative influence of the festive season, were to make *Noel* one of the most offbeat and unconventional of Christmas films to appear in the decade of its release.

Noel was to be the cinematic directorial debut of Chazz Palminteri, who had previously helmed a made-for-televison film (the 2002 MGM Televison comedy *Women vs Men*) as well as an episode of TV series *Oz* in 1999. Also a producer and screenwriter, he is considerably better known for his accomplished acting career, which began in the eighties with appearances in films such as Stewart Bird's *Home Free All* (1984) and Michael Schultz's *The Last Dragon* (1985), and performances in episodes of television series including *Hill Street Blues* (1986), *Matlock* (1987) and *Dallas* (1989). In the nineties his profile was to increase with a range of well-received roles in films which included Robert De Niro's *A Bronx Tale* (1993), Lee Tamahori's *Mulholland Falls* (1996) and Harold Ramis's *Analyze This* (1999). In 1995 he was to receive an Academy Award nomination for Best Actor in a Supporting Role for his performance in Woody Allen's *Bullets Over Broadway* (1994), a role which also won him an Independent Spirit Award in the Best

Supporting Male category, while his portrayal of Dave Kujan in Bryan Singer's *The Usual Suspects* (1995) was to win him an NBR Award for Best Acting by an Ensemble from the National Board of Review, along with the rest of the film's main cast. With *Noel*, however, he was to enter new territory, both directing the feature in addition to appearing as one of its many characters.

It's Christmas Eve in Manhattan, and publishing editor Rose Harrison (Susan Sarandon) is out doing a little last-minute gift shopping. As she meanders around the stores, she bumps into old high school friend Debbie Carmichael (Donna Hanover). The pair seem stunned to have met each other after so many years. Debbie proudly tells Rose of her husband and four children, while Rose replies that she is also married, with twin daughters, but can't talk any longer as she has a Christmas dinner to prepare for no less than thirty-five guests. Debbie seems impressed to learn of her old acquaintance's fortunes.

In reality, however, Rose's festive plans are considerably more modest. After parting from Debbie, she heads from a local hospital where she visits her mother Helen (Una Kay), who is suffering from Alzheimer's disease. It soon becomes apparent that Rose has bought all of the gifts for her mother, but because her dementia is now at an advanced stage the older woman is totally unresponsive to Rose's conversation. Rose tries to tempt her to eat, but to no avail. She has also brought along festive decorations, but – spotting another patient across the hall who appears to be in a comatose state – she decides to hang one of her Christmas angels in his room instead. There, she is surprised to find a mysterious visitor in the room (an uncredited Robin Williams), who she has never encountered before. Rose mentions that she had never seen the man in the bed receiving visitors before now, but the enigmatic guest merely smiles and thanks her for the beautiful gift. After her time at the hospital is over, Rose meets her mother's affable physician Dr Mathew Baron (John Doman) as she is leaving, and inadvertently reveals that in spite of her earlier grandiose claims to Debbie about having an expansive family, she is in fact single and childless.

Elsewhere in the city, cop Mike Riley (Paul Walker) is driving in his patrol car when he spots his fiancée, paralegal Nina Vasquez (Penélope Cruz). Nina is on her lunch break, so he picks her up and they return to their apartment to spend some time together. They are obviously very much in love, and talk eagerly about their forthcoming wedding. Nina is keen to encourage Mike to practice dancing, though he is resistant to the notion – not least because he doesn't want to be late getting back to work. However, Nina's considerable charms mean that he eventually acquiesces, if only for a while.

At the publishing company where she works, Rose is feeling downbeat about Christmas. Her sister is unable to join her for Christmas Eve due to work commitments, her psychiatrist is away for the holidays, and her ex-husband and his new wife – and their children – have invited her to join them in Connecticut, an offer which does not enthuse her. Rose bemoans the fact that she never had offspring of her own (a sore point, given that she edits children's books), and that she seems bound to spend the holidays with only her incommunicative mother for company. Her secretary gently suggests that Rose has spent too much of her life caring for her mother, and her father before that, particularly given that it was her concern for her parents which ultimately led to the breakup of her marriage several years beforehand. In particular, she recommends that Rose should think about returning the advances of her amorous colleague Marco (Daniel Sunjata), who is obviously attracted to her, but the withdrawn Rose is not convinced that this would be a good idea. Later, however, the smooth-talking Marco drops by her office and summons the courage to ask her out on a date. Remembering her secretary's advice, Rose reluctantly agrees, which takes Marco aback – particularly as he had assumed that she would have been otherwise occupied on Christmas Eve. They arrange to meet after work.

Back in his car, Mike is dropping Nina off at the legal firm where she works. As she heads off, he notices that she is wearing a new pair of ear-rings and asks where she'd acquired them. Nina replied that a colleague in the firm had given them to her as a gift, making Mike immediately feel suspicious. She warns him that he has no need to feel mistrustful; it was, after all, merely an innocent present to mark the season. However, as he starts to drive away he notices her embracing someone at the door of the firm, causing him to stare after her in jealous anger.

At a nearby deli, Jules Calvert (Marcus Thomas) is explaining to his friend Glenn (Merwin Mondesir) that he has an unconventional plan for the holidays. Due to an injury when he was fourteen, when he had ended up in hospital due to a sledging accident, he was introduced to the only experience of his youth that had ever made him truly happy: a hospital Christmas party. He now intends to devise a plan to wind up with another injury, in the hope that he can get back into hospital and live the dream of his childhood nostalgia. Jules also arranges with Glenn to be introduced to the mysterious Arizona (Chazz Palminteri) in order to conduct some unexplained business. Glenn explains that money must change hands first, and arranges with Jules to meet at an old theatre later that night when the transaction will take place.

Mike arrives in the deli and meets with fellow officer Dennis (Sonny Marinelli), who is irate at the fact that Mike is meeting with him much later than planned. Mike brushes off the delay with talk of unexpected wedding preparations, and orders a cup of coffee. The member of staff serving the table, Artie Venizelos (Alan Arkin), arrives to take his order but immediately seems to recognise Mike, his speech becoming hesitant. Mike is puzzled by the older man's strange behaviour, having never seen him before. Dennis jokingly suggests that there is an attraction between them, which causes Mike to seek a confrontation with Artie, but Dennis quickly defuses the tension, warning him to calm his notoriously hot temper – especially while in uniform. Artie brings Mike the coffee as arranged, as well as a plate of cookies which transpire to be Mike's favourite variety. This deeply confuses Mike. While settling the bill, Artie asks Mike if they can meet after work. Mike, believing that Artie is making a pass at him, reacts angrily. Dennis sends Mike out to the car and then strongly suggests to Artie that he drop his overtures towards his colleague. Artie is confused, explaining that it has been such a long time since the last encounter between Mike and himself. But knowing that Mike has no recollection of ever meeting Artie, Dennis tells him that he should keep his distance from Mike or risk spending Christmas Eve locked up at the station.

That night, Rose and Marco meet for dinner as arranged. Rose discusses her concerns for the lone patient who is in the room opposite her mother's in the hospital, and Marco responds that he admires her concern for people other than herself. However, Rose finds Marco to be rather intense company and is uncomfortable with his obvious affection towards her. As the meal draws to a close, Marco suggests that they retire to her apartment for a drink. Rose is clearly unsettled by the notion, but Marco – who has worked with her for some time – eventually manages to convince her. They head for Rose's home, where Marco tries to get closer to her. But Rose feels that he is moving too fast and decides to end the date. Marco is disappointed, hoping that she would have reciprocated his advances to some degree, and agrees to leave. In parting, though, he reproaches her for being so uptight and standoffish, particularly as they have known each other (professionally, at least) for years. Thus Rose winds up alone on Christmas Eve after all.

Back at Nina and Mike's apartment, Nina is busy with an interior decorator friend – the unidentified man that Mike spotted at her legal firm earlier – who is setting up a Christmas tree in her lounge. Mike arrives back at the apartment earlier than expected and – seeing Nina on friendly terms with the decorator – immediately flies off the handle, attacking him and sending the man flying backwards into the tree that he has just dressed. Both tree and decorator topple to the ground, causing Nina to round angrily on Mike for his jealous nature. The tree was, after all, supposed to be a surprise for his return from work. Mike seems embarrassed at reacting so badly towards an entirely innocent situation, but tries to justify his actions by telling her that he had seen her earlier encounter with the decorator and had felt threatened by the lack of explanation. Sensing that Mike's lack of trust is getting out of control, Nina leaves him in do doubt about her feelings on the matter before she heads out of the apartment, leaving Mike with only a ruined tree and broken ornaments for company. In particular, he finds himself thoughtfully regarding a broken glass angel from the top of the tree.

Later, Mike is calling around some friends in the hope of tracking down Nina, who hasn't been back in touch since he caused her to storm out. While he is on the phone, he spots Artie waving to him from an alleyway across the street. Annoyed at having been pursued, Mike heads out into the night and confronts the older man, telling him that he has obviously confused him with another person and that he should leave immediately. But Artie implores Mike to give him just a few minutes of his time, which will allow him to explain why he has gone to all the trouble of tracking him down. Intrigued if wary, Mike invites Artie into his apartment to give the promised elucidation. Artie presents him with a boxed gift, although Mike – believing him to be either confused or unhinged – casually tosses it to one side. Still unnerved at Artie's apparent familiarity with him, Mike finally gives him the opportunity to explain who he is.

As the evening wears on, Rose is wandering the streets of the city. She stares enviously as she passes window after window of partying revellers, enjoying their

Christmas Eve while she remains cold and lonely outside. Stopping to open a door to allow some partygoers to enter a nearby house with a child's pushchair, Rose finds herself swept into the home accidentally. Hearing sobbing from an adjacent room, she enters to discover a stranger – Nina – crying next to a Christmas tree. Stopping to ask if she is alright, Rose listens as Nina explains that she believes that she has fallen pregnant, and that her fiancée doesn't yet know about it. Although she loves him deeply, she is growing ever more concerned about his inability to control his jealousy and hot temper. Rose and Nina form a bond, with Nina believing her to be a family friend from Pittsburgh who has been invited along to the party. Before Rose can correct her, she is invited to dinner with the rest of the family, much to her surprise. She allows herself to be swept along with the festive euphoria until she actually arrives in the dining room, and it becomes apparent that nobody has the foggiest clue who she is. Mortally embarrassed, Rose flees the house, but Nina pursues her and asks if she will reconsider joining them. Rose refuses point-blank to do so, and thus Nina suggests that they have a drink in a nearby bar that she knows instead.

Nina drowns her sorrows as Rose listens attentively. Apprehensive because her wedding to Mike is due to take place in just a week's time, Nina explains that she wishes that there was something she could do to mollify the excesses of Mike's overprotective behaviour. As if his possessiveness wasn't bad enough, there is the fact that as they both want to have children so badly, she must take into account his suitability as a father. Nina tells Rose that she has had difficulty becoming pregnant in the past, and is desperately hoping that she will be able to carry her baby to term. Later, after Nina has gone, Rose takes part in an open-mike session at the bar, where a prize is being offered for the patron who can give the best reason why they hate Christmas. Rose, unable to think of a suitably witty reposte, instead tearfully explains that she had given birth to a daughter many years ago, but that she was stillborn, meaning that her little girl had both been born and had died on Christmas Day. Though her tragic story is far from the amusing anecdotes that the small audience are expecting, it is easily the saddest tale of the night, winning her the piano-playing host's tiny Christmas tree by way of a prize.

Back at Mike's apartment, a tongue-tied Artie is just about to explain his presence there when he is interrupted by a knock at the door – Dennis has decided to pay an unexpected festive visit on his colleague, along with two friends named Holly and Merry (Rachelle Lefevre and Erika Rosenbaum). Dennis obviously plans for Mike to join them for a little fun on the town, but is stopped in his tracks when he spots Artie in the apartment. Mike manages to persuade the revellers to leave without him, but Dennis is concerned by Artie's presence and warns Mike that he has a bad feeling about the enigmatic deli waiter. Once they have gone, Artie explains – with a completely poker-faced delivery – that he believes that Mike is the reincarnation of his late wife, which is the reason why he found himself gravitating towards him earlier in the day. Now convinced that Artie is unbalanced, Mike wastes no time in throwing him out of the apartment.

After Artie has gone, Nina surprises Mike by returning to her home as abruptly as she left. Tearfully, she explains to him that although she adores him, she cannot deal any longer with his stifling jealousy. However, Mike manages to spectacularly miss the point and instead blames the men who show an interest in her for inflaming his temper. His love for her, he claims, is what fuels and drives his controlling nature. Nina is exasperated by Mike's inability to understand his failings, and finds herself compelled to head back out of the apartment again. Mike follows her, but he is distracted by a confrontation between Dennis and Artie on the sidewalk. Before leaving with his friends, Dennis had spotted Artie skulking in a nearby doorway and has decided to extract an explanation for his behaviour. In the confusion that ensues, Nina manages to leave in a yellow cab before Mike can prevent her from doing so. Furious, Mike blames Artie for her departure and knocks the older man over. This appears to trigger a heart attack in Artie, which leads to the two policemen calling for an ambulance.

At the abandoned theatre across town, Glenn leads Jules into a creepily-lit auditorium. There, he explains that Arizona – a squatter of some repute – will grant him a brief audience. Rather wary, Jules asks Arizona if the rumours are true: that the shadowy man has a rare skill when it comes to shattering the bones in people's hands. Arizona proudly confirms that this is indeed the case, and asks Jules whose hands he would like broken. He is rather surprised when Jules replies that his intended victim is himself.

Over at the hospital, Rose has decided to pay her mother a visit. Dr Baron explains that as Helen hasn't eaten in some days, the staff will need to insert a feeding tube soon if Rose can't convince her to ingest some nutrition. Rose speaks of her enduring love for her mother, and the doctor gently commends her devotion. After Baron leaves, Rose tries to encourage Helen to eat, but is frustrated at her continual failure to do so. Instead, she proudly presents her with the little Christmas tree that she won at the bar. But when its fairy lights fuse, Rose grows aggravated and throws it aside. Downcast, she quietly pays a visit on the comatose patient in the room across the corridor in order to calm her nerves. Watching the prone form on the bed in front of her, Rose quietly tells the forlorn man that she loves him, even although she knows that he has no way of responding.

Down in the emergency room, a rather subdued Jules – now with his hand encased in Plaster of Paris – is clearly a little saddened that his Christmas experience in hospital isn't exactly what he had anticipated. Far from the jolly atmosphere of his youthful visit, the waiting area is full of incoming emergencies and agitated crosstalk. He tries to strike up a conversation with Mike, who is waiting nearby, but the policeman is far more concerned with the fate of Artie. A medical receptionist refuses to give out any information due to the fact that Mike isn't related to Artie, but an orderly (Billy Porter) overhears the conversation and promises Mike that he'll look into Artie's condition for him.

Rose, who appears more despondent than ever, is walking along a lonely stretch of pier. As she quietly regards the water's edge, she is startled to discover that the strange man who she met at the hospital (the visitor who had come to see the comatose man earlier that day) is standing next to her. He introduces himself as Charlie Boyd and seems keen to chat, but Rose is suspicious of his motives –

and, in any sense, she is in no mood for conversation. But Charlie perseveres, and explains that until recently he was a priest but upon losing his faith had decided to leave the church a year earlier. He now feels isolated with neither a personal family nor his parishioners for company. Charlie suggests that they hail a taxi and go for a cup of coffee to talk further, an offer which Rose agrees to. However, their cab journey has barely begun when Charlie begins to suffer from crippling stomach pains. Concerned for his safety, Rose asks the driver to divert the journey to her apartment which is nearby.

Back at the hospital, Mike is surreptitiously given access to Artie's room. He is told that Artie's condition is now stable, though he remains unconscious. Dennis arrives and tells Mike that he has used police records to check out Artie's background. It transpires that many years earlier, Artie had returned home to find his wife spending time with an old friend. Drawing the wrong conclusions, he had flown into a rage and attacked the supposed interloper, accidentally killing him in the process. Artie's wife, rushing to flee the scene, ended up dying in a road crash shortly afterwards. Mike becomes emotional, seeing the clear parallels that lie between Artie's situation and his own. Dennis grows concerned for his friend and suggests that they leave and allow the hospital to care for Artie. But Mike, sensing that something profound is taking place, elects to stay at Artie's bedside instead.

Realising that the grim reality of Christmas in a hospital emergency room is never going to match the happy memories of his childhood, Jules has become desperate to leave. But as the staff suspect that his injuries are self-inflicted, they decide that they want to keep him admitted for observation and psychiatric assessment. Growing increasingly obstreperous, he eventually flies off the handle, forcing security guards to restrain him.

At Rose's apartment, Charlie appears to have got over the wave of abdominal pain that had been affecting him. They spend the night talking on Rose's couch, sharing their innermost thoughts. Charlie tells Rose that he is concerned that she spends so much time looking after the needs of other people that she has forgotten to focus on her own life. He also speaks candidly about his crisis of religious faith and the hopelessness that it has brought him, a subject which strikes a chord with the world-weary Rose.

Still sitting beside the unconscious Artie at the hospital, Mike expresses regret over his earlier treatment of him. He tells Artie that he had let his possessiveness towards Nina blind him to the damage that he risks inflicting on their treasured relationship, but that Artie's story has made him reconsider his attitude. Mike is interrupted by the arrival of Paul (Rob Daly), Artie's son. Confused by Mike's presence, Paul tells him that he will look after his father and that he is now free to go. As Mike leaves, Paul puts two and two together and asks if Artie had claimed that Mike had been the reincarnation of his dead wife, Paul's mother. When Mike indicates that this was indeed the case, Paul is amused, explaining that Artie does the same thing to a different stranger every year.

Some time later, Paul is surprised to find Mike still waiting outside the room. The two men talk, and Paul is astonished to discover that Mike knows the story behind his mother's death. He tells Mike that Artie has never been able to forgive himself for the events that took place that day, and that he still holds on to the glass angel that his wife had bought him as a surprise for the top of their Christmas tree. Mike is dumbfounded, remembering the glass angel that had been perched atop Nina's tree but which he had later broken in his fit of pique. Paul regrets that his father has never stopped looking for absolution, given the fact that as Artie's wife is now dead there is no way that he can ever truly find it.

Rose wakes up on the morning of Christmas Day to discover that Charlie is still in her apartment. Seeming much more resolute than before, Charlie thanks her for restoring his faith in God and in humanity. When Rose seems confused, he explains that he had heard her say 'I love you' in the hospital room, and that he realised that in his loneliness God had spoken to him through her voice. Rose is baffled, not realising that Charlie had been present when she had said those words the previous day. Charlie then tells Rose that her mother wants her to live her life, not spend it looking after Helen in hospital. Rose is indignant, telling Charlie that he has no idea what her mother would want, but Charlie calmly informs her that he is certain of his facts because Helen has given him the message herself. Now disturbed by Charlie's odd pronouncements, she tells him to leave her apartment. He does so, though before stepping through the door he stops to tell her that he loves her, too.

At the hospital, Jules is undergoing an assessment by psychiatrist Dr Batiste (Carmen Ejogo). She asks him if his hand injury was self-inflicted, and eventually he admits that this is indeed the case. When Batiste probes further, Jules explains that he was regularly subjected to physical abuse as a child and that when he was admitted to hospital for Christmas as a child, his injury didn't come from a sleighing accident but rather from a severe beating from his stepfather. What's more, when he was discharged from the hospital's care his mother never came to pick him up, following which Jules decided to disown them both. He reveals that his stepfather died some years beforehand, but that his mother is still alive – albeit that he hadn't heard anything from her since that fateful incident when he was fourteen. Batiste advises that Jules should consider contacting his mother again, suggesting that perhaps she was just as frightened of his stepfather as Jules himself had been. Jules is initially reluctant but, when Batiste leaves the office, he decides to throw caution to the wind and picks up the receiver of her office telephone.

Artie regains consciousness and is surprised to see that Mike is still sitting next to his bed. He thanks him for having stayed with him throughout his ordeal. Mike is relieved to see that Artie is now looking better, if still very weak, and tells him with complete sincerity that he is forgiven – Mike gives him his own personal pardon for all of the regrets that Artie has regarding his past actions. This gesture means more to Artie than he can express with words. Mike then withdraws as Paul comes back into the room, reassured to know that his father is awake again.

Back at her family home, Nina is checking the results of a pregnancy testing kit when Mike appears. He tells her that he now understands her concerns, but that it was not her who should have been frightened of his actions – it was Mike who was afraid because of his own sense of inadequacy. While Mike assures her that he does genuinely trust her, he admits that he is unable to trust himself, or to feel wholly sufficient as an individual when he compares himself to the high-flying lawyers that she associates with every day. Leaving her to draw her own conclusions, Mike parts by giving an assurance that Nina's happiness means more to him even than their relationship. Nina is so thunderstruck by his sudden turnaround in attitude that she is literally lost for words.

Rose, upon clearing up her apartment, discovers that Charlie has left his cross neckchain behind him. Carefully retrieving it, she heads for the hospital in the hope of returning it to him. However, on reaching the room where the comatose patient is situated, she is shocked when she gets a good look at the man for the first time and realises that it has been Charlie in the bed all along. A nurse (Ruth Chiang) is confused by Rose's line of questioning, explaining that Charlie has never had any visitors in all the time that he has been in hospital. Rose is therefore left in no doubt that the Charlie Boyd who she had spoken to over the course of the past day has been an apparition of the man who is lying unconscious in the bed next to her. Moved beyond measure, she takes his hand and tells him that he can let go now; they have changed each other's lives more than either can know. Showing faint signs of awareness, Charlie smiles at Rose's new understanding as he begins to slip away.

Mike returns home and finally opens Artie's package. Inside, he is taken aback when he discovers the glass angel that Paul had described. He carefully hangs it on the top of his tree just as Nina returns to the apartment. Forgiving Mike for his earlier behaviour, she has decided to trust in the turnaround of his mindset and announces, to his delight, that he will soon be a father. Jules, meanwhile, is emerging from hospital with his hand still in plaster, a new-found sense of purpose in his stride. And Rose returns to her mother's room to discover that she is eating at last, thanks to the kindly ministrations of Dr Baron. Baron is mortified when he discovers that Rose has overheard his one-sided conversation with Helen, as he had been telling his patient that he had been hoping to pluck up enough courage to ask Rose out on a dinner date. Rose finds this idea appealing and tells him so, much to the embarrassed doctor's intense satisfaction. As Baron leaves the two women alone, Rose comments that the doctor seems like a decent man, and Helen responds by squeezing her hand. Rose is stunned at her mother's unexpected awareness, realising that hope still remains in her life after all.

It seems reasonable to venture the opinion that *Noel* is among the least orthodox of Christmas films, even in a decade where traditional genre boundaries were being challenged and overlapped as never before. It is a film which blends dry comedy with moving pathos, and contrasts emotional drama with perceptive character observations. Linking each of the individual stories is an exploration of love, be it romantic (Nina and Mike, Rose and Dr Baron), familial (Artie and Paul, Rose and Helen), emotional (Charlie and Rose, Jules and his abandonment issues), or spiritual (Charlie and his faith). There are various motifs which connect these tales, most prominent among them angel ornaments – Mike breaks the glass angel on Nina's tree, which is replaced by Artie's, while Rose buys a renaissance angel for Helen and ends up presenting it as a gift to Charlie. Christmas trees also crop up regularly throughout the narrative; when Mike's temper causes him to wreck the tree that Nina has set up for him, he unwittingly mirrors the incident that derailed Artie's life in the seventies, while Nina makes her pregnancy relevation next to a decorated fir tree and Rose's maudlin open-mike performance causes her to win a rather sorry-looking plastic tree which she later gives her mother as an early Christmas present.

Of course, connecting all of the stories is a search for affirmation. Rose's devotion to her mother has caused her to isolate herself from almost everyone around her, while the subsequent failure of her marriage and the sadness that she feels about her lack of children has led her to question the direction of her life. Only the intervention of Charlie, who himself is attempting to reconnect with his sense of religious faith, can convince her to reach out and unite with the world again. Nina, who seeks the lasting love of Mike, first needs assurance that the relationship will not founder on account of his domineering behaviour, while Mike must find a way to strike a balance between his genuine affection for his fiancée and his deep-seated desire to control her every move. Artie cannot rest until he can somehow find a way of making amends for his earlier disastrous error of judgement, while Jules, who has been badly let down by his family, must first find his own peace of mind before he can seek rapprochement with his estranged mother. By the conclusion of the film, each of the characters have resolved their principal anxieties, as the ability of Christmas to change people's hearts and attitudes has given them all a new chance to move on with their lives – even if, in the case of Charlie, it means accepting that he has reached the end of his own journey.

For all its occasional moving charm, *Noel* is a film which contains many strange coincidences and rather odd leaps of logic. Sometimes these consistencies are minor, but others are less so. Having never seen him before that fateful day, how exactly does Artie manage to track down Mike's apartment in a city as massive as New York? Although Paul explains that Artie's revelation of his reincarnation story to a total stranger has become an annual event, nobody seems to question exactly why he takes this particular course of action instead of seeking a more direct route to redemption. Then there is the issue of Mike feverishly trying to track down the runaway Nina by telephone but neglecting the first and most obvious location, which is the home of her family where she has actually taken refuge. Perhaps most contentious of all is the issue of Charlie's 'ghost', who visits Rose between Christmas Eve and Christmas Day. While an allusion to the supernatural was hardly a revolutionary angle for a film of the festive season to take – Charles Dickens certainly had no issue with making use of it in *A Christmas Carol*, for instance – the device seems cumbersome and unexpected in a film which is as grounded in the modern world as *Noel*, though admittedly screenwriter Hubbard may be making the point that at Christmas, miracles can take place even in the most unlikely of places. Exactly how awkward the fit might be depends on the opinion of the individual viewer, but it does seem like a bit of a stretch to believe that Rose has been in and out of Charlie's hospital room on a number of occasions and yet doesn't once take a look at his face until the film's conclusion. Suspension of disbelief is by no means a new requirement in

Christmas cinema, but some of the creative choices that are made in *Noel* – particularly with Jules's story, which seems so oblique to the other narrative threads that the character almost seems to have wandered into the film by mistake – combine to make the film something of an acquired taste.

No matter how polarising its plot may seem, there is no denying that *Noel* certainly had an impressive pedigree when it came to its production. Director of Photography Russell Carpenter had won the Academy Award for Best Cinematography due to his work on James Cameron's *Titanic* (1997), and he certainly impresses with his evocation of a snowy and atmospheric New York. This seems even more impressive when, for all the evocative location shots of the Big Apple's famous skyline and distinctive street scenes, *Noel* was actually filmed in Montreal.[1] Composer Alan Menken had been nominated for many Academy Awards over the years, winning Oscars for the scores that he had provided for Disney productions including *The Little Mermaid* (1989), *Beauty and the Beast* (1991), *Aladdin* (1992) and *Pocahontas* (1995). His work on *Noel* was no less accomplished, creating a contemplative mood without ever venturing into the territory of the over-emotional. Special mention must also be paid to the film's well-judged set decoration by Frances Calder, Suzanne Cloutier and Marie-Claude Gosselin; their incredible attention to detail brings the film to life in effective and unexpected ways, with fine points such as the assorted framed family photographs bedecking the wall of Helen's hospital room and the eclectic selection of knick-knacks adorning Nina and Mike's apartment helping to accentuate the characters' individual personalities.

As is the convention for an ensemble drama, *Noel* carefully divides the screen time of its actors amongst a number of different story threads, and yet Rose's story – intersecting with the other characters to a greater degree than most – seems to take centre-stage most regularly. Susan Sarandon is well cast as the troubled Rose, a pleasant and friendly woman whose affable exterior conceals an aching emotional pain and a desire to connect with people which she herself is ultimately denying. It is testament to her skill as a performer that her eventual realisation that her life can still improve, in spite of the hand that fate has dealt her, is both touching and believable. Sarandon, winner of the Best Actress in a Leading Role Academy Award for her performance in Tim Robbins's *Dead Man Walking* (1995) – and a four-time Oscar nominee in the same category between 1982 and 1995 – has been a familiar face on American cinema screens since the late 1960s, both on television and in film. From her debut cinematic performance in John G. Avildsen's hard-hitting drama *Joe* (1969), she has developed a massively successful career which has featured cult hits like Jim Sharman's *The Rocky Horror Picture Show* (1975) to historical dramas such as George Roy Hill's *The Great Waldo Pepper* (1975) via romantic thrillers including Charles Jarrott's *The Other Side of Midnight* (1977), and covering almost every genre in-between. Sarandon continued to diversify throughout the eighties with well-received appearances in films such as Louis Malle's *Atlantic City* (1980), George Miller's *The Witches of Eastwick* (1987) and Ron Shelton's *Bull Durham* (1988). In the nineties she gave some of the finest performances of her career, in a variety of high-profile features which included

Ridley Scott's crime drama *Thelma and Louise* (1991), Tim Robbins's political satire *Bob Roberts* (1992), Joel Schumacher's legal thriller *The Client* (1994), and Chris Columbus's moving comedy-drama *Stepmom* (1998). Still greatly active in cinema throughout the past decade, she has appeared in many films which have included Cameron Crowe's *Elizabethtown* (2005) and Peter Jackson's *The Lovely Bones* (2009). Also involved in film production, during the course of her career she has been nominated for several BAFTA Awards, Emmy Awards, a Daytime Emmy Award, and has been nominated on no less than eight occasions for Golden Globe Awards.

The rest of the cast form a diverse range of actors, but Paul Walker stands out due to the strength of his performance as the mistrustful cop Mike. Walker deserves high praise for being able to take a character who is sometimes petulant, occasionally self-centred and often bordering on the emotionally self-destructive, and still managing to forge Mike into someone who is able to evoke some degree of sympathy in the audience. Though Mike's eventual relinquishment of his possessive nature towards Nina is well enough played, it is actually in the character's interaction with the troubled, enigmatic Artie that Walker's performance really shines. Walker has been active on television and in film since the mid-1980s. His TV roles included episodes of series such as *Highway to Heaven* (1985-86), *Who's the Boss?* (1991), *The Young and the Restless* (1993) and *Touched by an Angel* (1996), while he made his cinematic debut in 1986 with Bob Dahlin's horror parody *Monster in the Closet*. Since then, he has appeared in a wide range of different genres, with roles in films such as Gary Ross's *Pleasantville* (1998), Steve Boyum's *Meet the Deedles* (1998), Rob Cohen's *The Skulls* (2000), John Dahl's *Road Kill* (2001) and Richard Donner's *Timeline* (2003). More recently involved in film production, Walker has been the recipient of many awards, including an MTV Movie Award (and a further nomination) for his performance in Rob Cohen's *The Fast and the Furious* (2001), three nominations for Young Artist Awards, and two wins at the Young Hollywood Awards in 2000 and 2001.

Complimenting Walker's performance with great gusto is the ever-radiant Penélope Cruz, who brings considerable Latin passion to Nina along with great emotional sensitivity. She articulates well the two-pronged apprehension of losing Mike on one hand, but fearing the repercussions of his tempestuous personality on the other. There is a great deal of warmth to her portrayal of Nina, which helps to maintain viewer interest in the ups-and-downs of the character's relationship problems that play out throughout the film. Cruz first burst onto cinema screens with a winning performance in Bigas Luna's romantic drama *Jamon Jamon* (1992), and her fame and career diversity have continued to grow ever since. Throughout the nineties she was to appear in many films produced in her native Spain, including Rafael Alcázar's *El laberinto griego* (*The Greek Labyrinth*) (1993), Fernando Colomo's *Alegre ma non troppo* (*Glad, But Not Too Much*) (1994) and Pedro Almodóvar's *Carne trémula* (*Live Flesh*) (1997), alongside international productions such as Stephen Frears's *The Hi-Lo Country* (1998), Jacques Weber's *Don Juan* (1998) and Nick Hamm's *Talk of Angels* (1998). Since the turn of the century her star profile across the world has risen considerably due to successful roles in Ted Demme's *Blow* (2001), Cameron Crowe's *Vanilla Sky* (2001) and John Madden's *Captain Corelli's Mandolin* (2001). In 2009 she was to win the Best Performance by an Actress in a Supporting Role Academy Award for Woody Allen's *Vicky Cristina Barcelona* (2008), having been nominated for Oscars both previously (Best Performance by an Actress in a Leading Role for Pedro Almodóvar's *Volver*, 2006) and subsequently (Best Performance by an Actress in a Supporting Role for Rob Marshall's *Nine*, 2009). Her many other awards have included a win and nomination at the BAFTAs, the Best Actress Award at the 2006 Cannes Film Festival, two wins and five nominations at the European Film Awards, and three nominations for Golden Globe Awards.

There are many other performances worthy of note throughout the film, not least the curiously uncredited Robin Williams's brief but affecting appearance as Charlie, the troubled priest who – close to death – longs to rediscover and restore his lost faith in God. Williams had won the Academy Award in the Best Actor in a Supporting Role category for his performance in Gus Van Sant's *Good Will Hunting* (1997), and he is at his most restrained in *Noel*, teasing out the character's physical discomfort as well as his spiritual and emotional distress. Director Chazz Palminteri seems to be enjoying himself in his short cameo as the inscrutable Arizona, while Rob Daly puts in an effective performance as Paul, Artie's caring but practical son. Marcus Thomas's turn as the oddball Jules is both quirky and emotionally aware, making the character something more than the curious postscript that he sometimes appears to be. But almost certainly the most touching of all the film's performances is delivered by Alan Arkin, perhaps best known in recent years for his Academy Award-winning role in Jonathan Dayton and Valerie Faris's *Little Miss Sunshine* (2006). Arkin excels in lending an appealing conviviality to Artie, making the character seem amiable and responsive even while simultaneously – and carefully – stirring up the audience's suspicions about what the character's strange motivations might actually be.

Noel opened to a decidedly mixed response from the critics, with reactions which ranged from the hesitant to the hostile. Some commentators praised the film for its sense of emotional warmth,[2] while others disagreed completely, disapproving of what they considered to be a very deliberate, premeditated and rather obvious attempt to provoke a sentimental response from the audience.[3] The latter assessment was taken by a number of reviewers, who criticised *Noel* for taking a sugary and rather corny approach,[4] having a lacklustre and overly convoluted narrative,[5] and, at times, a profound lack of verisimilitude.[6] That said, not all criticism of the film was negative, for others were enthusiastic about the way that *Noel* managed to exhibit a slightly different attitude from other similar features of the time, finding hope and conviction in the human condition even given the cynicism of modern cultural mores.[7]

With its emphasis on the search for a sense of belonging, the importance of family and the need for individual redemption, *Noel* is a film which typifies many primary concerns of the Christmas film genre. And yet, with its overlapping stories and evocation of an urban mood during a thoroughly contemporary holiday season, it also employs the conventions of the ensemble drama to good effect, making the most of its diverse and impressive cast. Although *Noel*'s nonconformist approach has made it something of a curio amongst Christmas films since its release, it can be seen as part of a wider movement towards a more particular engagement with themes of love and redemption, utilising an ensemble framework, within a festively-situated narrative. Yet as the next chapter will explain, employment of the ensemble format in a Christmas film would not prove to be the exclusive province of romantic stories; in different configurations, the formal qualities in question were to prove themselves to be much more mutable and adaptive in their potential applications.

Historical Context

Noel was released in American cinemas on 12 November 2004. Don Mancini's *Seed of Chucky* was also appearing for the first time on that date in United States theatres, as was anthology film *Stories of Lost Souls*, directed by Illeana Douglas, Deborra-Lee Furness, William Garcia, Paul Holmes, Mark Palansky, Col Spector, Toa Stappard and Andrew Upton. At the top of the Billboard Hot 100 chart that week was 'My Boo' by Usher and Alicia Keys. Featuring in current affairs at the time was the death of Palestinian political leader Yasser Arafat, a large earthquake affecting northern Japan, and the first official release of Mozilla's now-famous Firefox open source web browser.

24

JOYEUX NOËL (2005)

Nord-Ouest Productions/ Senator Film Produktion/ The Bureau/ Artémis Productions/ Media Pro Pictures/ TF1 Films Production/ Les Productions de la Guéville

Director: Christian Carion
Producer: Christophe Rossignon
Screenwriter: Christian Carion

MAIN CAST

Diane Krüger	-	Anna Sörensen
Natalie Dessay	-	Singing Voice of Anna Sörensen
Benno Fürmann	-	Nikolaus Sprink
Rolando Villazón	-	Singing Voice of Nikolaus Sprink
Guillaume Canet	-	Audebert
Gary Lewis	-	Palmer
Dany Boon	-	Ponchel
Daniel Brühl	-	Horstmayer

Just as *Noel* had demonstrated an interesting synthesis of subgenres, fusing the ensemble drama and romantic story to create a highly distinctive festive tale, other films since the turn of the century have likewise shown considerable effectiveness in experimenting with different tropes of the Christmas movie, but few more successfully than Christian Carion's *Joyeux Noël*. The historical Christmas tale had been a relatively untapped field in cinema during the recent past (adaptations of *A Christmas Carol* notwithstanding), with films such as Anthony Harvey's *The Lion in Winter* (1968) and Milton H. Lehr's *The Juggler of Notre Dame* (1970) proving to be comparatively exceptional in terms of their choice of subject matter. Even during the prolific production of Christmas films throughout the noughties, the only other prominent historical feature aside from *Joyeux Noël* was to be Catherine Hardwicke's *The Nativity Story* (2006), a Biblical adaptation which remained very close to accepted convention where the retelling of the events leading up to Christ's birth was concerned. But with its deep scrutiny of Christmas in a rarefied and historically accurate setting, Carion's film was to achieve a kind of power and prevailing sense of plaintiveness which has, as yet, proven to be almost unique in the genre. *Joyeux Noël* was to show, beyond doubt, that a Christmas film did not need to principally concern itself with embracing modernity in order to prove deeply relevant to its audience.

The film features a fictionalised account of the famous Christmas Truce of 1914, one of the most extraordinary events in the history of the First World War. In the period immediately preceding Christmas, a number of combat zones along the Western Front were to be witness to an unprecedented (and unofficial) ceasefire, a remarkable situation given the carnage of trench warfare. During that brief time, there were documented accounts of soldiers from different nations emerging from their trenches to walk openly on No-Man's Land, exchanging pleasantries and even presents with both allied and enemy combatants. In a war of unspeakable horror and countless casualties, the Christmas Truce was an outstanding testament to the human spirit, where the festive season had produced the necessary conditions for a fleeting moment of peace to blossom in the most appalling conditions of warfare imaginable. But as *Joyeux Noël* would demonstrate, this unplanned armistice was eventually to produce harsh ramifications for those who had been involved in it.

French director and screenwriter Christian Carion has led a distinguished cinematic career which, although spanning only four features to date, has garnered him a considerable reputation in the world of film-making, most especially (but certainly not exclusively) in Europe. His short film *Monsieur le député* (*The Deputy*) (1999) was to lead him to the production of a full-length motion picture, the romantic comedy-drama *Une hirondelle a fait le printemps* (*The Girl from Paris*) (2001), which earned Carion the Gold Guild Film Award from the Guild of German Art House Cinemas, the John Schlesinger Award (Honorable Mention) at the Palm Springs International Film Festival, and a nomination in the Best First Work category at France's prestigious César Awards. Since the release of *Joyeux Noël*, Carion has gone on to direct one further film to date, espionage thriller *L'affaire Farewell* (*Farewell*) (2009), which was to feature several of the stars from his earlier Christmas drama. Carion has written the screenplays for all of his films thus far, and has performed as an actor in the latter three, whilst also making a brief appearance in Guillaume Canet's mystery thriller *Ne le dis à personne* (*Tell No One*) (2006). But in the eyes of many, *Joyeux Noël* remains the crowning achievement of his career to date.

It is the summer of 1914, and war has been declared in Europe. In a Scottish village, an Episcopal priest named Palmer (Gary Lewis) watches with detached concern as his assistant William (Robin Laing) is swept up in the patriotic fervour of his brother Jonathan (Steven Robertson), optimistic that the outbreak of hostilities will bring some excitement to their lives as they head for basic training in Glasgow. Knowing that this conflict will bring not high adventure but unspeakable horror, Palmer quietly weeps as the two younger men race away to make their preparations. Meanwhile, in the heart of Germany, Danish soprano Anna Sörensen (Diane Kruger) is performing at the Berlin Opera House with her partner – and lover – Nikolaus Sprink (Benno Fürmann), a talented tenor. Just as Sprink heads onto the stage, in full costume, to join Anna in an operatic performance, the pair are interrupted by the arrival of an armed forces recruitment officer (Peter Rühring) who disrupts the recital to read out an urgent request to the audience from Kaiser Wilhelm. As the officer proceeds to call up reserve troops to fight in the conflict that lies ahead, Sprink and Anna exchange a concerned glance, knowing only too well what must come next.

On the front lines, French officer Lieutenant Audebert (Guillaume Canet) is with the 26th Infantry as his troops prepare for an assault against a German emplacement. Clearly racked with anxiety, he snatches a glance at a photograph of his wife which is safely tucked away in his wallet before emerging into the trenches to address his soldiers. He informs them that their heavy guns have been firing on the German lines for an hour, in the hope of softening up the enemy defences before the allied assault. Adding that they will be receiving support from nearby Scottish troops, he tells the men that they must overwhelm the Germans' position and occupy the farm which lies beyond; reinforcements will be on their way later to buttress their advance. The troops seem sceptical, but Audebert adds that they all want the same thing: a brisk end to hostilities, and to return home to their families. If they fulfil their orders, he assures them, the conflict will all be over by Christmas.

Audebert leads his men over the top of the trench, where they are immediately met with machine-gun fire and a barrage of shelling. Simultaneous with the French advance, the Royal Scots Fusiliers are pushing against the German emplacements. William is shot by the enemy guns, and his brother Jonathan – who is fighting alongside him – has no option but to leave him to a death in No-Man's Land, a fact which haunts him afterwards. Both sides sustain heavy casualties during the assault. Palmer, who is now working as a stretcher-bearer, tries to console Jonathan's sense of grief and guilt, but has little time to converse before Lieutenant Gordon (Alex Ferns) calls the young soldier away to base, where they will await reinforcements. Hearing a call for help in No-Man's Land, Palmer desperately scrambles out of the trench in the hope that he can provide aid to the wounded, but only narrowly avoids being killed when a flare in the night sky reveals his position to the Germans, who immediately fire on him. In one of the German trenches, Sprink notes with disgust that their side have shot at a stretcher-bearer, but Lieutenant Horstmayer (Daniel Brühl) – commanding this division of the 93rd Infantry regiment – approves of the action, believing that there is no sense in taking any unnecessary risks. Horstmayer then orders Sprink to assist in the repairs; following the attack, their emplacements have taken major damage.

Back in the French trenches, Audebert is being upbraided by his father, a Major-General (Bernard Le Coq), for having retreated from the battlefield after only fifteen minutes. Audebert points out that his men were being cut to pieces by machine-gun fire, and that the odds against them were overwhelming – particularly when the Scots were forced to withdraw first. It transpires that Audebert's wife, who is pregnant, was last seen in the area of France that has been occupied by the Germans. The Major-General has been unable to track down her exact location, but adds that the German troops have thus far been conducting their affairs in line with international agreements; it is hoped that Audebert's wife and their unborn child have not been harmed. The Major-General adds that a new vacancy has opened up in an artillery division, which would provide Audebert with a faster track to promotion, and suggests that he take it. Audebert refuses, preferring to stay with his troops, but his father orders him to comply with the transfer; as soon as December is over, he is to report to Poitiers for new training. The Major-General tells Audebert to hold his troops' position for the next three days, and then advance back towards the farm again, in the hope that conditions will be quieter as Christmas approaches. Later, after his father's departure, Audebert is distraught to discover that he has lost his wallet on the battlefield; the photograph of his wife appears to be gone forever.

Back in Germany, Anna has approached a senior officer (Gilbert von Sohlern) to arrange to give a recital to the troops at Christmas in the hope of raising morale. The officer is disdainful of this request, telling Anna that the severity of the army's situation is such that the battlefield is no place for a vocal performance. But to his disgust, Anna has already gone over his head and appealed to the Crown Prince, who has agreed to allow her to perform at his headquarters. The officer's contempt is palpable, not least as he perceives that her apparent altruism is merely an attempt to reunite with Sprink. Anna knows that she will have the last laugh, however.

Snow has fallen on the front lines near the now-ruined farm, and the temperatures are plunging. In the Scottish trenches, a rather overbearing English Major (Christopher Fulford) is informing Gordon that reinforcements will be delayed – in the event of a German attack, the Fusiliers will have to defend their position as best they can. He then rounds on Palmer, reprimanding him for his attempt to save lives on the battlefield when the endeavour may have triggered a German assault. The men are unimpressed by the Major's pomposity however, particularly given Palmer's popularity among the ranks, and – as he eventually departs from the front line – one of the soldiers lets loose a shot, causing the

Major to momentarily panic and stumble into the latrines (much to the amusement of the rest of the troops).

Over in the German emplacements, the rogue shot has caused some consternation – Horstmayer is convinced that the British will stop at nothing to stage another attack, even at Christmas. The German troops are also bemused at the arrival of dozens of fir trees, part of an order from the top brass that a Christmas tree will be placed every five metres along the front line as an unexpected concession to the festive season. Horstmayer receives a missive from headquarters, requesting that Sprink be relieved from his duties for one night so that he can accompany Anna at the recital for the Crown Prince. It is clear that Horstmayer is contemptuous of Sprink and his apparent preferential treatment, preferring soldiers who have been drafted from what he regards as harder-working professions than performing artists. Sprink is unconcerned by the Lieutenant's disdain, even although it seems to be shared by some of his fellow troops.

At an occupied manor house, Anna arrives to prepare for her recital, but discovers that the once-wealthy French owners (Michel Serrault and Suzanne Flon) have had little perception of what's going on inside their own home since the Germans invaded several months beforehand and turned the building into their headquarters. She eventually tracks down Sprink, but finds him greatly changed from their last encounter; he is haunted by his gruesome experiences on the front lines, and is riddled with lice from the dreadful conditions there. As planned, the pair perform for the Crown Prince (Thomas Schmauser), though Sprink is unimpressed with the nobleman's empty platitudes and his naïve belief that they will all be back in Berlin by the spring of the following year. Sprink also discovers, to his distress, that his exquisite voice has been adversely affected by his time in the trenches. However, he quickly recovers in time to deliver a moving recital for the Crown Prince and his assembled generals, who listen with rapt attention.

Following the performance, Anna speaks to Sprink in private. Sprink is disgusted at the preening self-importance of the high-ranking officers at the headquarters, knowing all too well what the situation is like at the front line. He decides that the Crown Prince should not be the only one to enjoy a recital at Christmas, and determines that he will return to the trenches early in order to sing for his fellow troops. Sprink is horrified when Anna decides to accompany him, knowing that the blood-spattered Western Front holds untold misery that she cannot possibly conceive. But Anna is unwavering in her determination; having waited so long to be reunited with her lover, she is not willing to be separated again so quickly, even by war.

In the French trenches, Audebert reluctantly asks for a volunteer to scout the German positions – much to the aversion of his troops, given that it is Christmas Eve. A soldier named Gueusselin (Lucas Belvaux) eventually agrees to carry out the reconnaissance, albeit grudgingly. The task is not one that he undertakes lightly, knowing that if the Germans become aware of his presence it is likely to trigger a counterattack. Just as he begins to crawl gingerly across No-Man's Land, however, bagpipe music strikes up from the Scottish trenches as the Fusiliers sing along with as much enthusiasm as they can muster. This causes some degree of confusion to both the French and German soldiers, and triggers annoyance in Gueusselin who fears that it will compromise his position. Then Sprink and Anna arrive at the German front line, much to the consternation of Horstmayer who cannot believe that his subordinate would knowingly put his operatic partner in such mortal danger. When Sprink informs Horstmayer that he is there on the authority of the Crown Prince, however, the Lieutenant quickly consents to his request to perform a recital of Christmas carols for the assembled troops.

As the troops place fir trees up onto the lip of the German trench, much to Gueusselin's astonishment, Sprink bursts into a rousing rendition of 'Silent Night'. Thoroughly enchanted, the Scots listen with rapt attention to the beautifully performed carol, while the French worry that the Germans are using this apparent attempt at festive cheer as a front for more sinister motives. Then, to the amazement of the Germans, Palmer begins to play the bagpipes over in the Scots trenches to accompany Sprink's singing. Sprink continues, eventually standing over the top of the trench to the shock of Horstmayer, who fears that the allies will take a shot at him. But quite the opposite is true: instead, Sprink receives a standing ovation from the Scots when the heads of the Fusiliers begin to appear over their own trench. Palmer then begins to play 'Adeste Fidelis', which immediately prompts Sprink into another performance. This time, however, Sprink stuns everyone by grabbing one of the Christmas trees and heading out into No-Man's Land to place it in the heart of the battlefield. By all accounts, this gesture should have led to his instant demise, and yet nobody in the allied trenches fires a single shot. When the song has concluded, he wishes the Scots a good evening, which is reciprocated in good spirits.

Horstmayer follows Sprink out onto No-Man's Land and demands that he return to the trenches immediately. But before they can do so, they are joined on the battlefield by Gordon, who meets them on cordial terms. The French troops watch stunned from their trench, and Audebert, determined to find out what is going on, emerges to join his foreign counterparts. Gordon explains that he and Horstmayer have been discussing the idea of an unofficial truce for the duration of Christmas Eve. After all, he reasons, nobody is likely to censure them for seeking to treat each other with a bit of civility at this particular time of year. Audebert orders a bottle of champagne to be brought up from his personal quarters, and the three commanders – along with Sprink – toast the notion of their collective festive armistice. As they wish each other a Merry Christmas, a series of flares rise up from the German trenches in celebration of the ceasefire.

Then, slowly at first, troops from all three nations rise from their respective trenches to meet in No-Man's Land. They regard each other with a combination of festive goodwill and deeply-ingrained suspicion. Even the previously-concealed Gueusselin, his cover now well and truly blown, emerges from his hiding place in ill-disguised awe of what is going on around him. The soldiers congregate around their commanding officers at the centre of the battlefield, and the French and Scottish Lieutenants react with surprise when they are introduced to Anna; the beautiful soprano is the last person who they would have expected to face on this cold and frosty night in the combat zone. Some of the troops exchange gifts of chocolate and wine, and engage in a good-natured argument over the name of the sociable cat (who belongs to the wrecked farm) that regularly visits both the French and German trenches in search of food.

As the German soldiers try with little success to play the bagpipes, much to the hilarity of the assembled Scots, other troops are showing photos of their wives and girlfriends to their counterparts on the opposing sides, many of whom then happily return the favour. The officers are doing likewise, and Audebert notes that he is unable to show his own wife to Gordon and Horstmayer because of the fact that he has lost his only photo of her. Horstmayer realises that Audebert had dropped his wallet in the German trench on the night of the attack, and returns it to him – much to Audebert's relief. Audebert reveals that his wife was pregnant when he last saw her, and that he fears both for her safety and that of their child. Horstmayer notes with some irony that he had visited France only a few weeks before the breakout of hostilities, as he and his wife had been on holiday there.

Palmer leads a Mass service on the battlefield, which most of the soldiers join in. As he is conducting it in Latin, it is equally accessible to all present. While Palmer delivers this religious ritual, Jonathan is quietly tracing his way around No-Man's Land in search of his brother's body. He eventually finds William's frozen corpse and weeps over it. A wandering German soldier, who has little time for Palmer's Christian fervour, discovers Jonathan nearby and invites the Scot to join him in a cup of champagne. But Jonathan has no time for this courtesy, no matter how sincerely it is meant in the spirit of the season. Unresponsive to the miraculous scenes of festive goodwill that are breaking out around him, Jonathan returns to his brother while the rebuffed German continues on his way. Even Anna's impromptu, haunting rendition of 'Ave Maria', which enraptures the watching troops, leaves Jonathan in a state of total indifference.

Eventually the ceasefire ends, and the troops and officers return to their respective trenches. In the early hours of the following morning, however, Jonathan causes alarm when he returns to No-Man's Land and begins digging a grave for his dead brother. When they hear his spade in the ground, the Germans initially believe that he is planting mines on the battlefield. Palmer and Gordon race after Jonathan, and Gordon demands that he return to the trench at once. As they retreat, Horstmayer calls out to Gordon and requests a further summit meeting, for which they are once again joined by Audebert. Over coffee, they agree to an extension of their improvised Christmas armistice in order to give each other the opportunity to give their dead a respectful burial. The Germans will return the bodies of the fallen Scots and French soldiers, while the French agree to hand over any German cadavers from an assault which had taken place the previous month. Scenes of extraordinary co-operation then take place, as the different countries' troops work together to lay their dead to rest with mutual consideration. Palmer offers to deliver the Last Rites to soldiers of all nationalities as the burials take place.

Once all of the deceased have been interred, Anna wanders the makeshift graveyard and becomes emotional at the sheer number of soldiers who have lost their lives. She begs Sprink to desert the army and flee over the border to Holland with her, rather than await the inevitable death that will result by staying on the front line. But Sprink points out that there is no favouritism in warfare: if he is caught, his superiors will have no hesitation in executing him for fleeing the battlefield. Besides, he adds, the Netherlands are a long distance away on foot, and he would be caught without doubt on the way there. Desperate to find a workable solution, Anna then suggests that they cross the adjacent French border instead. Before Sprink can respond, they are interrupted by some other German soldiers who, over coffee, ask Anna to take letters back to their families when she returns to Berlin. This, they feel, will be a more reliable way of reaching their loved ones than trusting the notoriously-unreliable military postal service.

As the day continues, troops from the opposing sides join in a friendly game of football, while others engage in card games and sociable conversation. Horstmayer offers to deliver a letter to Audebert's wife, though Audebert is sceptical, knowing that if his German counterpart is caught in the act then it will likely lead to his court martial. Jonathan, meanwhile, has cut himself off from the co-operative spirit which exists around him, and is busy writing a letter to his mother in which he assures her that William is alive, well and still fighting by his side. In the German trench, Horstmayer reveals to Sprink that he has received a telephone call from headquarters. It has become clear that the top brass had no idea that Sprink had taken Anna to the front line, and have consequently come to the conclusion that he has deserted. They have thus sent a car to take Anna back to Germany, while Sprink will be placed under two weeks' arrest for disobeying orders. Sprink is contemptuous of this censure, particularly given the spirit of multilateral collaboration and benevolence that is going on around them, but Horstmayer warns him to hold his tongue and start complying with the requirements of his duties.

On Boxing Day, it is clear that the ceasefire is coming to an end. Horstmayer appears unexpectedly at the entrance to the French trench and warns Audebert that the German artillery are about to begin shelling their position. He suggests that the French and Scottish troops take shelter in the German trench until the bombardment is at an end. The shelling is particularly thorough, to the point that Gordon and Audebert know that they probably owe Horstmayer their lives. Audebert also decides to take Horstmayer up on his generous offer, and hands over a letter which is addressed to his wife in the occupied territories. Once the bombardment has concluded, Horstmayer suggests that the Scots and French soldiers return to their respective trenches, but Gordon instead recommends that the Germans accompany them due to the likelihood of a reciprocal burst of shelling. Sure enough, the German lines are showered with explosives – falling with just as much ferocity as before – while Horstmayer and his troops remain safe in the French trenches. They then realise that their paths must not cross again. Shaking hands, Horstmayer grimly reflects that under different circumstances, they may all have been friends rather than adversaries. Gordon's Fusiliers play a heartfelt interpretation of 'Auld Lang Syne' on the bagpipes as the

Germans return to their trenches for the final time.

Once the Germans have gone, one of Audebert's soldiers presents him with a detailed list of the enemy machine gun emplacements. Audebert pockets it, saddened that the grim reality of war has returned once again. No sooner has he returned to his quarters, he discovers Sprink and Anna, who request that he take them prisoner. Audebert is infuriated by their appeal, knowing that he has no reasonable way of explaining their presence in the French trenches, but Anna's empassioned supplication eventually convinces him to help the pair. He demands that they be sent under armed guard to a nearby village that is under Allied control.

Before they part, Sprink hands Audebert the bundle of German letters that had been given to Anna, asking him to pass them on to the Red Cross for distribution. Far from reaching the families for which they were intended, however, the letters quickly fall into the hands of Audebert's superiors. The majority of the correspondence provides evidence of the Christmas Truce, with much of the mail proving to be withering in its condemnation of the politicians and generals who have been responsible for igniting and waging the war.

Some time later, Palmer is ministering to injured troops at a field hospital when his Bishop (Ian Richardson) pays him a visit. Furious at his actions during the Christmas armistice, the Bishop informs Palmer that he is to return to his parish in Scotland, and that he no longer has any place on the front line. Palmer objects, telling the Bishop that he believes that he has a duty to provide spiritual support to the men fighting for the crown, and that he is also convinced that Christ Himself had led him to deliver the Mass service in No-Man's Land that fateful Christmas Day. But the Bishop is unmoved by Palmer's pious motivations, telling him that the regiment that he had supported is soon to be disbanded by Royal command as a mark of its disgrace, and that Palmer should consider his continuing suitability as a member of the clergy. Leaving the priest stunned in his wake, the Bishop then gives a sable-rattling sermon to an assembled gathering of newly-mobilised troops where he mangles Biblical scripture to present a fanatical call to arms, dehumanising the enemy by depicting them as demonic savages who have neither moral fibre or spiritual integrity. Knowing differently as a result of his own experiences on the front line, Palmer is disgusted by the Bishop's hypocrisy, pointedly leaving behind his cross and neckchain as he departs the hospital.

Back on the front line, the Fusiliers' Major has made an unwelcome return and is furious when he spots a German wandering out of an enemy trench in broad daylight only for the Scottish troops to leave their guns silent. He repeatedly orders them to shoot him, and the Scots give the rogue soldier every opportunity to withdraw – including intentionally missing him a number of times – before they eventually have no choice but to cut him down. However, it soon transpires that the 'German' is in fact French soldier Ponchel (Dany Boon) in disguise. Audebert races out of the French trenches to the man's aid, but it is already too late. Ponchel reveals that he had been smuggled across enemy lines in order to visit his mother, but that his plan has obviously gone horribly awry during the return journey. With his dying breath, he informs Audebert that his wife is well, and that the Lieutenant's child is safe – a son, named Henri. The Scots Major looks on aghast from the adjacent trench at the tearful exchange between the two Frenchmen.

Audebert returns to his quarters and is angrily confronted by his father. The Major-General is incandescent over the events of Christmas, and informs his son that the only thing that stands between him and a change of high treason is the fact that there is no way that the French authorities could execute Audebert and all of his men without attracting unwanted attention. Audebert is equally furious at his father's singular lack of understanding, and tells him that actually fighting a war is quite different to simply waging one. He had felt more camaraderie with his German front line counterparts than he could ever imagine experiencing with those who glorify war without experiencing it. The General informs Audebert that he and his men will be sent to Verdun, his transfer to an artillery unit (and, it is implied, any serious chance of future promotion) now at an end.

Horstmayer and his men are on a train carriage bound for the Eastern Front when they are visited by the Crown Prince. Aghast at their actions, he tells the gathering of troops that they will be transferred directly to East Prussia without any leave to contact relatives. Pouring scorn on Horstmayer to the extent that he belittles even the fact that he has been awarded the Iron Cross, the Crown Prince storms off. As he leaves, crushing the mouth-organ of one of the soldiers, Jörg (Frank Witter), in his wake, the men begin to defiantly hum one of the tunes that the Scottish troops had taught them over Christmas – 'I'm Dreaming of Home'. Sickened by their insolence, the Crown Prince retreats to his car as the train pulls away, taking Horstmayer and his soldiers to an almost certain death fighting the Russian Army.

Although Christmas films often promote notions such as joy, goodwill and the ability of the festive season to improve lives and foster better relations between human beings, *Joyeux Noël* presents a touching evocation of what can happen when these seemingly abstract concepts are brought to bear during a real-life historical situation, and to the most immediate effect. The fact that the film's events, though fictionalised, are based upon one of the single most extraordinary situations in the course of history's bloodiest conflict adds a further sense of poignancy to its narrative as it unfolds. Indeed, the simple observation that the peace and inspiration of the festive spirit could penetrate even the mass carnage of attritional trench warfare is what makes *Joyeux Noël* one of the single most affecting and humbling viewing experiences in the history of the Christmas film.

The realism of this cinematic experience is aided by the performers' authentic use of the English, French and German languages, subtitled for audiences, as is the employment of a large international cast. Yet what is perhaps the most effective factor of all in reflecting humanity in the grim conditions which are depicted is the way in which Carion effortlessly switches between the horrors of the conflict and the day-to-day interplay of its unwilling participants. Whereas on one hand we witness a poignant examination of Jonathan's mental fragility, psychologically unable to come to terms with the death of his brother in combat, we are also treated to the sociably chatty banter that takes place between

Audebert and his batman Ponchel, or the larking camaraderie of the Fusiliers. Likewise, the Bishop's denunciation of the entire wartime German nation as irredeemable, morally bankrupt fiends sits uneasily with the principled Horstmayer and the affable German soldier Jörg with his affectionate interactions shared with his adopted feline friend Felix (or Nestor, as the French troops name him). Perhaps the most profound contrast is drawn between the freezing, lice-ridden trenches and the refined surroundings enjoyed by the German generals, perfectly personified in the mincingly aristocratic, hopelessly out-of-touch Crown Prince. There is no doubt that *Joyeux Noël* is a film with the strongest of anti-war messages, but in Carion's hands it becomes much more than that. The delineation between the largely-reluctant people who have been drafted in to fight the Great War, and the privileged bureaucrats and noblemen who are instigating it from a safe distance, is made right throughout the film, most especially at its conclusion. Yet the remarkable events that take place during the Christmas Truce, we become aware, are uniquely linked to the nature of the festive season – its ability to enrich the life experience of individuals, to change attitudes, and to transform dispositions for the better.

Although the film is dramatised, many of the events have their grounding in historical reality. The soccer match which takes place on Christmas Day is based upon the most famous incident of the Christmas Armistice, though in reality the game is thought to have taken place between soldiers from the Saxon Infantry and the Royal Welsh Fusiliers. The dating of the match, however, is accurate – it is documented as having been played on the Christmas Day of 1914. Additionally, some have speculated that the Nikolaus Sprink character has its foundation in Walter Kirchhoff (1879-1951), a German tenor who had performed on the Western Front in support of troop morale during the war. Like Sprink, Kirchhoff's performance was so audible that it was heard by French troops in the enemy trenches, who applauded his recital. It must be noted that in the film, the singing voices of Nikolaus Sprink and Anna Sörensen were provided not by the actors portraying the characters, but by two leading international musical talents in the form of French coloratura soprano Natalie Dessay and Mexican-born tenor Rolando Villazón. Both deliver flawless performances throughout.

Joyeux Noël contains painstaking attention to period detail, from the lavish furnishings of the occupied French manor house being used as the German Army's headquarters on the Western Front to the frosty ambience of each nation's muddy, vermin-ridden trenches. Walther Vanden Ende's excellent cinematography is absolutely dead on beam, as is Alison Forbes-Meyler's faultless costume design – a vitally important detail in a film such as this, when the uniforms of several different countries' armed forces are on display throughout the entire duration of the film. Yet Philippe Rombi's original score is worthy of special praise, a work of restrained beauty and lingering, evocative poignancy.

Undoubtedly, one of the film's strongest characteristics is its outstanding international cast. Although the emphasis shifts regularly between characters from all three nations, there is special emphasis on the character of Sprink, who comes to embody the long-term effects of the conflict. Unwillingly drafted from his leading role at productions in the Berlin Opera House, Sprink quickly finds that his refined lifestyle and deferential entourage become distant memories when he is exposed to the lice, squalor and endless death on display in the trenches. Sprink's humanity is very effectively articulated by actor Benno Fürmann, who had become a familiar face both on German television and in European cinema at the time of the film's release. His cinematic debut performance was in Franziska Buch's *Die ungewisse Lage des Paradieses* (*In Search of Paradise*) (1992), following which he was to make many appearances in German-language features which included David Jazay's comedic horror *Küssen Sie mein blut* (*Kiss My Blood*) (1998), Stefan Ruzowitzky's medical thriller *Anatomie* (*Anatomy*) (2000) and Tom Tykwer's romantic mystery *Der Krieger und die Kaiserin* (*The Princess and the Warrior*) (2000), for which he was nominated for an Audience Award at the European Film Awards in 2001. Fürmann has also been the recipient of a German Television Award for Best Actor in a Movie Made for Television or Miniseries in 1999, a Bavarian Film Award in 2001, and an Adolf Grimme Award in Gold in 2005. Additionally, he has been nominated for the Best German Actor Award at 2005's Golden Camera Awards.

Fürmann is expertly complimented by Diane Kruger in the role of Anna Sörensen. As shrewd and talented as she is beautiful and graceful, Anna makes for a compelling female lead character, and Kruger develops her emotional and psychological qualities most adroitly. Anna's political nous and disdain for the widespread bloodshed that is spilling across Europe elevate the character far beyond the function of a simple romantic interest, and her determination to pull Sprink away from a situation of almost inevitable death in combat (both perceptive and prophetic, given the fate of the rest of his regiment) engages sympathy thanks to the credible on-screen chemistry that Kruger shares with Fürmann. Kruger had been active on television and film since 2002; following a strong debut performance in Jean-Pierre Roux's thriller *The Piano Player* (2002), she was to alternate between international cinematic features such as Cédric Klapisch's *Ni pour, ni contre: bien au contraire* (*Neither For, Nor Against: Quite to the Contrary*) (2002), Guillaume Canet's *Mon idole* (*Whatever You Say*) (2002) and Louis-Pascal Couvelaire's *Michel Vaillant* (2003), and also English-language films which included Wolfgang Petersen's *Troy* (2004), Paul McGuigan's *Wicker Park* (2004) and Jon Turteltaub's *National Treasure* (2004). In 2003 she was to win the Chopard Trophy at the Cannes Film Festival, and indeed her recognition within the film industry has continued in recent years, with her performance as Bridget von Hammersmark in Quentin Tarantino's *Inglourious Basterds* (2009) earning her a nomination for Outstanding Performance by a Female Actor in a Supporting Role at the Screen Actors Guild Awards, a Best Supporting Actress nomination at the Online Film Critics Society Awards, and the Best International Actress Award at Germany's Golden Camera Awards.

The film's expansive ensemble cast is uniformly strong, with a notable performance by French star Guillaume Canet, a winner and four-time nominee at the César Awards, who was at the time best-known to international audiences for his performance as Étienne in Danny Boyle's *The Beach* (2000). Also a director, producer and screenwriter, Canet is an acting personality of considerable stature in his native France, and his performance as Audebert is replete with his trademark sensitivity of character observation. Scottish actor Gary Lewis, who had previously appeared in films as diverse as Danny Boyle's *Shallow Grave* (1994), Stephen Daldry's *Billy Elliot* (2000) and Martin Scorsese's *Gangs of New York* (2002), also impresses as Palmer, the compassionate Episcopal Priest who finds that his strong Christian conscience is at odds with the official line of his superiors within the clergy. Dany Boon, known in his native France for performances in features which included Philippe Le Dem's *Paroles d'hommes* (*The Words of Men*) (1997), Olivier Doran's *Le déménagement* (*The Removal*) (1997) and Gabriel Aghion's *Pédale dure* (*The Last Pedal*) (2004), provides both pathos and occasional comic relief as Ponchel, the French barber turned infantryman who serves Audebert in the trenches (never knowingly separated from his beloved alarm clock). As Horstmayer, the upright German Lieutenant, Daniel Brühl was at the time perhaps best known for his appearances in Wolfgang Becker's *Goodbye Lenin!* (2003), Hans Weingartner's *Die fetten Jahre sind vorbei* (*The Edukators*) (2004), and Charles Dance's *Ladies in Lavender* (2004). And special mention is of course due to Ian Richardson, forever remembered for his BAFTA Award winning performance as the shady Parliamentarian Francis Urquhart in Paul Seed's TV miniseries *House of Cards* (1990), who delivers an absolutely glacial performance in his cameo appearance as the warmongering Bishop.

Upon its cinematic release, *Joyeux Noël* met with near-unanimous praise from commentators. Many reviewers were to commend the film's compelling narrative and attention to historical detail,[1] while others instead drew attention to the strong performances and weighty moral commentary.[2] Carion's uncompromising approach to a true chapter from one of history's bloodiest conflicts impressed a number of critics,[3] while the film's powerful message of hope and common humanity made a profound impact on some.[4] Approval was more muted in a few quarters however, with *Joyeux Noël*'s solemn moral intent being considered a potential drag on its momentum,[5] while others ventured the opinion that the overarching message of the film – by its very nature – led to a gloomy, relentlessly downbeat conclusion which was awkwardly unsubtle in the pursuit of its life-affirming objective.[6] Bridging these extremes of critical opinion was the perceptive and too often ignored observation that in addition to its worth as a record of a poignant historical event, the film's exploration of international warfare was also extremely topical in relation to the current affairs of the early twenty-first century.[7]

Joyeux Noël performed very favourably at awards ceremonies across the world, perhaps most notably receiving a nomination for the Best Foreign Language Film of the Year Oscar at the 2006 Academy Awards. The film was also nominated for Best Foreign Language Film at the Golden Globe Awards, Best Film at the European Film Awards, and Best Film Not in the English Language at the BAFTA Awards. Additionally, it received no less than six nominations at France's César Awards, in the categories of Best Film, Best Writing (Original), Best Supporting Actor, Best Music Written for a Film, Best Production Design and

Best Costume Design.

With *Joyeux Noël*, Carion had produced one of the most distinctive of all Christmas films – a motion picture which typified everything that makes the festive season a time of hope and benignity, and which celebrated the enduring power of the human spirit against the odds presented by entrenched hatred and organised conflict. Even in a decade which had seen a considerable increase in the number of festively-situated movies being commercially released in cinemas, *Joyeux Noël*'s emotive historical setting and innate relevance to audiences of all ages has led to it becoming one of the best-regarded of all recent films in the genre. But in a modern world which had so inherently linked the festive season with commercialism and preconceived notions of traditional conventions, *Joyeux Noël* remains a timely reminder of the true meaning of Christmas, offering a strident message of love, optimism and humanity for people of all nations.

Historical Context

Joyeux Noël premiered in the United States at the AFI Film Festival on 11 November 2005, following which it received a limited release on 3 March 2006. Other films debuting on that release date were Kevin Palys's *Flourish* and Kurt Wimmer's *Ultraviolet*. 'Check on It' by Beyoncé, featuring Slim Thug, was at number one on the Billboard Hot 100 that week. In the news, the United States signed an historic civilian nuclear pact with India during a visit to the country by President George W. Bush, the Facebook website was officially made accessible to the public for the first time, and the closing ceremony of the 2006 Winter Olympics in Turin, Italy took place.

25

A CHRISTMAS CAROL 3D (2009)

Walt Disney Pictures/ ImageMovers Digital

Director: Robert Zemeckis
Producers: Jack Rapke, Steve Starkey and Robert Zemeckis
Screenwriter: Robert Zemeckis, from the novel by Charles Dickens

MAIN CAST

Jim Carrey	-	Ebenezer Scrooge/ The Ghost of Christmas Past/ The Ghost of Christmas Present/ The Ghost of Christmas Yet to Come
Gary Oldman	-	Bob Cratchit/ Jacob Marley/ Tiny Tim
Colin Firth	-	Fred
Robin Wright Penn	-	Fan/ Belle
Bob Hoskins	-	Mr Fezziwig/ Old Joe
Cary Elwes	-	Portly Gentleman #1/ Dick Wilkins/ Mad Fiddler/ Guest #2/ Business Man #1
Julian Holloway	-	Fat Cook/ Portly Gentleman #2/ Business Man #3
Lesley Manville	-	Mrs Cratchit

The Christmas film genre was becoming an increasingly well-populated one as the noughties drew to a close, with entries in the field proving to be as varied as they were numerous. Among the many movies to see a release in the latter half of the decade were William C. Laufer's heartwarming drama *Christmas at Maxwell's* (2006), Greg Kiefer's tongue-in-cheek comedy *Stalking Santa* (2006), Preston A. Whitmore II's light-hearted romance *This Christmas* (2007), Brian Samuel Davis's knowing horror *Ornaments* (2008), Alfredo De Villa's urban family drama *Nothing Like the Holidays* (2008) and Debbie Isitt's partly-improvised comedy *Nativity!* (2009). This brief roll-call is but to scratch the surface of what was to be one of the most prolific periods for features in the genre, even within a decade which had seen the Christmas film increase its commercial profile as never before. Yet for all the diversity of subject matter on display as the decade neared its conclusion, with many features taking a highly innovative and sometimes very unconventional approach, perhaps the most high-status of all features in the genre during the latter half of the decade was to proceed from an unequivocally traditional foundation.

As we near the conclusion of this survey of festive film-making, it seems difficult to imagine how any director could possibly hope to discover a fresh approach to *A Christmas Carol* in the twenty-first century. Today's audiences are, of course, intimately familiar with the Dickensian fable in just about every possible permutation, from lavish musicals to modernised versions and everything in-between. Thus there was considerable intrigue amongst commentators and the general public in the latter years of the noughties when it was announced that the Walt Disney Company were planning to bring the story of Ebenezer Scrooge to the big screen in 3D for the first time, combining the ground-breaking effects work pioneered by film-maker Robert Zemeckis with the resurgence in popularity of 3D imaging in commercial cinematic productions. The result is one of the most fascinating adaptations of *A Christmas Carol* in recent years, albeit one which would ultimately divide critics straight down the middle at the time of its release.

A Christmas Carol 3D marked Disney's third engagement with Dickens's novella; the company had previously produced Burney Mattinson's acclaimed short animated film *Mickey's Christmas Carol* (1983), where Ebenezer's role was to be filled by Scrooge McDuck, the spendthrift Scottish uncle of Donald Duck, and of course Brian Henson's *The Muppet Christmas Carol* in 1992. This new production was to differ from these earlier films in one key characteristic, namely that it was the first Disney adaptation of *A Christmas Carol* where all of the characters were portrayed by well-known actors rather than being played by other pre-existing fictional figures (either Disney characters or Muppet performers). Although there had been numerous television versions of *A Christmas Carol* throughout the same decade, perhaps the most prominent cinematic adaptation in recent years had been Jimmy T. Murakami's *Christmas Carol: The Movie* (2001). A feature-length animated film which featured an all-star cast, including the voices of Simon Callow as Scrooge, Nicolas Cage as Jacob Marley and Kate Winslet as Belle, Murakami's adaptation was met with general critical indifference at the time of its release, leaving the field open for a new and fresh take on the story to suit the audiences of the new millennium.

Robert Zemeckis has long earned a deserved reputation as one of the most technologically innovative directors in the mainstream of American cinema. Also a prolific producer and screenwriter, Zemeckis's directorial career began in the late seventies with musical romantic comedy *I Wanna Hold Your Hand* (1978), followed soon after by madcap satire *Used Cars* (1980). His profile was considerably enhanced by the adventure comedy *Romancing the Stone* (1984), a film which received recognition at both the Academy Awards and the Golden Globes. However, his definitive breakthrough came in 1985 with the legendary time travel comedy *Back to the Future*, a film which accumulated many nominations at awards ceremonies and was to win the Oscar for Best Effects: Sound Effects Editing, as well as an Academy Award nomination for Best Writing (Screenplay Written Directly for the Screen) which was shared with his frequent writing collaborator Bob Gale. Zemeckis also directed two well-received sequels to the film, which were released in 1989 and 1990. With *Who Framed Roger Rabbit?* (1988), he created a pioneering feature which seamlessly combined animation with live action footage to celebrate the golden age of Hollywood and spoof the hard-boiled detective story, winning three Academy Awards for effects work and a further four Oscar nominations. The macabre, special effects-laden comedy *Death Becomes Her* (1992) was followed by one of the triumphs of Zemeckis's career, historical romantic comedy *Forrest Gump* (1994), an adaptation of Winston Groom's novel. *Forrest Gump* was to see Zemeckis receiving the Academy Award for Best Director, while the film won five other Oscars (including Best Actor for Tom Hanks) and an additional seven nominations. Amongst the film's most notable technical accomplishments was the flawless insertion of Hanks's eponymous protagonist into archive footage of real historical events, which added greatly to the authenticity of the film's compelling narrative. An adaptation of Carl Sagan's science fiction mystery *Contact* (1997) followed, as did the tense Hitchcockian thriller *What Lies Beneath* (2000) and emotional adventure drama *Cast Away* (2000).

However, it was in 2004 that Zemeckis was first to turn his hand to the production of a Christmas film, making a triumphant return to computer graphics technology with *The Polar Express* (2004), an interestingly-pitched adaptation of the Chris Van Allsburg book. Released both in conventional theatres and in IMAX 3D (the first animated film of feature length to be exhibited in this format), *The Polar Express*'s interesting combination of purely computer generated imagery and complex performance capture techniques, which allowed the expressions and gestures of human actors to be implemented into the animation of the onscreen characters, was to break new ground. Zemeckis refined this technology still further a few years later with *Beowulf* (2007), based upon the Old English heroic epic poem and similarly released in a 3D version. It was this leading edge approach that, as we shall see, he would hone to an even greater level of sophistication with *A Christmas Carol 3D*. In addition to his success at the Academy Awards, Zemeckis has also been a multiple winner and nominee at many other award ceremonies, among them being the Golden Globe Awards, Daytime Emmy Awards, BAFTA Awards, César Awards and Saturn

Awards, to name only a few.

It seems fair to assume that the time travel elements of *A Christmas Carol* could not have failed to appeal to the director of the *Back to the Future* trilogy, and indeed Zemeckis makes the most of Dickens's ability to appeal to the imagination as well as the sentiment of the audience. The cutting-edge special effects of the 3D *Christmas Carol* certainly exhibited a great deal of Zemeckis's justified reputation for technological refinement in film-making, with the opening sequences alone – which feature sweeping and highly detailed aerial views of Victorian London – managing to eclipse the CGI wizardry of his earlier feature *The Polar Express*. Yet it was not the imagery of the film in isolation that marked it out for interest amongst audiences, but rather Zemeckis's enthusiastic adoption of the RealD 3D system. *The Polar Express*, along with the revolutionary filming techniques of films such as James Cameron's *Ghosts of the Abyss* (2003), had been instrumental in the renaissance of 3D in mainstream cinema, a resurgence which has continued until time of writing. But even at a time when digital 3D was becoming increasingly commonplace in commercial film-making, *A Christmas Carol 3D* was to make exceptionally effective use of the process, achieving an outstanding sense of depth which – when combined with the clarity of vision achieved by the razor-sharp rendering of the film's computer-generated characters – was to create a very memorable cinematic experience.

Yet it must be noted that Zemeckis's script is pitched carefully to ensure that the film's special effects are used to articulate the key themes of Dickens's work, rather than to obscure or dominate them. Indeed, the screenplay remains very close to the word as well as the spirit of the novella, with most of the embellishments being reserved for the movie's conclusion. Whereas Scrooge's grim self-revelation proved to be the apex of his encounter with the Ghost of Christmas Yet to Come in Dickens's book, here we are presented with a breakneck race through the cobbled streets of London as a rapidly-shrinking Scrooge is pursued by the ominous spirit. But Zemeckis seems content to leave the fantastical embellishments to a minimum, and – by and large – the special effects are employed to enhance existing elements of the novella (such as an effectively-depicted interpretation of Scrooge's ethereal transition through different periods of his life) rather than to add entirely new incident to the narrative.

That said, Zemeckis proves he is not taking the experience so completely seriously that he is above scattering the occasional knowing in-joke throughout the film. The Cratchits have a portrait of none other than Charles Dickens hanging in their house, while the elated Scrooge hangs on to the back of a moving horse-drawn carriage in a clear visual reference to Marty McFly's skateboarding antics in *Back to the Future*. These touches of detail succeed in lightening the tone of what occasionally proves to be, in places, a rather intense filmic experience. Festive vivacity is further articulated by composer Alan Silvestri – himself well-known for the memorable original scores that he provided for all three *Back to the Future* films – who draws on many traditional Christmas carols throughout the course of the soundtrack, including the emotionally powerful overture which plays over the opening credits sequence. The score of *A Christmas Carol 3D* is concluded by

Andrea Bocceli's full-blooded recital of 'God Bless Us Everyone', a song performed to the film's main title theme following the climax of the narrative.

While any version of *A Christmas Carol* is largely dependent on the talents of its lead actor to ensure its success, this was even more true than usual of Zemeckis's adaptation due to the fact that Jim Carrey was not only to portray Ebenezer Scrooge, but all three Ghosts of Christmas into the bargain. His Scrooge is suitably curmudgeonly, harking back (as so many had done before him) to Alastair Sim's landmark performance from the fifties. In this sense, it is fortunate that Zemeckis had refined his performance capture technique to a further degree than had been possible with *The Polar Express*; some characters in the earlier film had occasionally seemed awkward or lifeless, their facial expressions too stiff or too flaccid to seem entirely convincing. But with *A Christmas Carol 3D*, the expressiveness of the main characters had improved dramatically, advancing to the point that not only did Scrooge's scrowls and incredulous gaping seem entirely believable, but so did the facial tics of the anthropomorphic flame that is The Spirit of Christmas Past. Although Carrey's interpretation of Scrooge is more than adequate in and of itself, there is a very real sense that he is deriving more enjoyment in portraying the various spirits who torment the hapless miser, especially the raucously ebullient Liverpudlian accent of The Spirit of Christmas Present. Carrey's acting career began on television with *The All-Night Show* (1980), and although his TV appearances continued throughout the eighties and nineties, he was soon to establish a presence in cinema with performances in comedy films such as David Mitchell's *Copper Mountain* (1983) and Anthony Kramreither's *All in Good Taste* (1983). His career diversified throughout the late eighties, with film appearances in a range of different genres including romantic fantasy (Francis Ford Coppola's *Peggy Sue Got Married*, 1986), sci-fi comedy (Julien Temple's *Earth Girls Are Easy*, 1988), and crime thriller (Buddy Van Horn's *The Dead Pool*, 1988). However, his profile was to escalate dramatically in the early nineties as a result of his starring roles in Tom Shadyac's *Ace Ventura: Pet Detective* (1994), Chuck Russell's *The Mask* (1994) and Peter Farrelly's *Dumb and Dumber* (1994). For the remainder of the decade he was to alternate between his trademark zany comedy and weightier, often more subtle dramatic roles in films which ranged from Joel Schumacher's *Batman Forever* (1995) and Ben Stiller's *The Cable Guy* (1996) to Peter Weir's *The Truman Show* (1998), by way of Tom Shadyac's fantasy comedy *Liar Liar* (1997) and Milos Forman's Andy Kaufman biopic *Man on the Moon* (1999). The turn of the century would see him in the lead role of Ron Howard's Dr Seuss adaptation *How the Grinch Stole Christmas* (2000) as well as Bobby and Peter Farrelly's zany *Me, Myself and Irene* (2000). As the new decade progressed, he continued to refine his career with many diverse roles, including Tom Shadyac's fantasy *Bruce Almighty* (2003), Michel Gondry's surreal *Eternal Sunshine of the Spotless Mind* (2004), and Brad Silberling's adaptation of Daniel Handler's childrens' adventure novel *Lemony Snicket's A Series of Unfortunate Events* (2004). Also well established as a screenwriter, Carrey is the winner of two Golden Globe Awards to date (for *The Truman Show* and *Man on the Moon*), and is a four-time Golden Globe nominee. Tribute to his continuing popularity as a performer, his many other accolades include MTV Movie Awards, People's Choice Awards and a London Critics Circle Film Award, as well as nominations for Screen Actors Guild Awards, Online Film Critics Society Awards, American Comedy Awards and the BAFTA Film Awards.

Just as Carrey had engaged with several different roles in the course of *A Christmas Carol 3D*, the same could also be said for the film's starry ensemble cast. Gary Oldman, star of films as diverse as Oliver Stone's *JFK* (1991), Francis Ford Coppola's *Dracula* (1992), Luc Besson's *The Fifth Element* (1997), and his own acclaimed film *Nil by Mouth* (1997), makes for a suitably tortured Jacob Marley, while he brings a nuanced approach to the put-upon Bob Cratchit and lends restrained poignancy to the clerk's son, Tiny Tim. The amiable Fred, Scrooge's Christmas-loving nephew, is brought to buoyant life by Colin Firth, known for his roles in films such as Anthony Minghella's *The English Patient* (1996) and John Madden's *Shakespeare in Love* (1998), who has since become even better regarded by audiences and critics thanks to performances in Peter Webber's *Girl with a Pearl Earring* (2003), Tom Ford's *A Single Man* (2009) and - more recently - Tom Hooper's *The King's Speech* (2010), for which he won the Best Actor Oscar at the 2011 Academy Awards. No less than five supporting roles are assumed by the charismatic Cary Elwes, versatile star of Rob Reiner's *The Princess Bride* (1987), Edward Zwick's *Glory* (1989), Gary Fleder's *Kiss the Girls* (1997) and Tim Robbins's *Cradle Will Rock* (1999), who is particularly memorable as Dick Wilkins and the Mad Fiddler. The film also gave Zemeckis the opportunity to collaborate with actors with whom he had worked in previous features, among them Bob Hoskins – star of *Who Framed Roger Rabbit?* (1988) – who proves to be good value for money as Scrooge's jovial old employer Fezziwig and the macabre Old Joe, while Robin Wright Penn (who had performed in both *Forrest Gump* and *Beowulf*) brings melancholic grace to Scrooge's fiancée Belle while also embuing the miser's younger sister Fan with a mixture of warm affection and childlike enthusiasm.

A Christmas Carol 3D was met with a definite sense of critical ambivalence upon its theatrical release, with a number of reviewers praising aspects of the film which would, in turn, become the focus of other commentators' censure. While the virtues of Zemeckis's ground-breaking special effects were extolled by many,[1] others considered the computer-generated imagery to be merely a façade for an ultimately rather soulless cinematic experience which did not fully engage on an emotional level.[2] Just as the film was commended for its fidelity to the source material, and the fact that the CGI characters were able to articulate the otherworldliness of Dickens's creations,[3] it also met with disparagement by those who felt that the non-human actors were unable to lend this version of *A Christmas Carol* the required sense of poignancy or gravitas.[4] The breakneck pace that is set by Zemeckis, while still retaining historical attention to detail and the retention of the spirit of Dickens's novella, was noted by some,[5] while others instead considered that the technical achievement on display throughout the film had the effect of subordinating the powerful moral resonance of the original story into a mere postscript to the action.[6] Yet in spite of the fact that the film was to divide critics so sharply, it was not forgotten during the following year's awards season. *A*

Christmas Carol 3D was nominated for the Best Animated Film Award at the 2010 Saturn Awards, and was also to see Jim Carrey winning the Blimp Award for Favorite Voice from an Animated Movie, also in 2010.

With its combination of the traditional and the modern, *A Christmas Carol 3D* forms a suitable end-point for the decade of its production, and indeed this examination of festive film-making. Although Zemeckis's film was to make full use of the most advanced imaging technology available, and has come to fit comfortably amongst the most effective of the current revival of 3D features, it is also an adaptation which never strays too far from the underlying intentions of Dickens's original text, retaining the stark warning against covetousness and contempt towards one's fellow human being at the same time as it celebrates the cheerful high spirits and transformative power of Christmas. Like so many of its contemporaries since the turn of the century, *A Christmas Carol 3D* was to prove that no matter how innovative or subversive an individual approach to the festively-situated narrative may prove to be, traditional themes remained as relevant and as significant to modern audiences as they had always been – even in spite of the fact (or, sometimes, because of the fact) that a film may proceed from the standpoint of seeking to challenge or even undermine such a theme. To set out with the intention of disputing the validity of an idea is, ultimately, still to engage directly with said idea, and it is in this sense that the underlying subject matter of the Christmas film has proven to be so versatile: even in situations where perennial themes of festive film-making are being forced to justify themselves, they remain adaptable enough to sustain reconfiguration in order to meet the expectations (and prove relevance to) audiences which are contemporary to a particular film's release. And yet with features like *A Christmas Carol 3D*, it can be seen that the converse is also true, namely that new techniques and approaches need not coincide with a contestation of existing genre tropes, but may rather be used to augment traditional themes and continue to ensure their consequence to modern viewers. It is this, perhaps, more than any other factor, which augurs well for the future of Christmas cinema and its fortunes at the box-office in the years that are to come.

Historical Context

A Christmas Carol 3D was released in cinemas across the United States on 6 November 2009. One other major film was to make its first appearance on that date: Wes Anderson's *Fantastic Mr Fox*. At the top of the Billboard Hot 100 chart during that week was 'Down' by Jay Sean, featuring Lil Wayne. Appearing in current affairs at the time were American voters going to the polls in the United States Congressional elections of 2009, two earthquakes occurring in southern Iran injuring approximately seven hundred people, and the plugging of an oil leak on the West Atlas oil rig in the Timor Sea.

CONCLUSION

As I hope this study has explored in some detail, the Christmas film has come to mean a great many things to a great many people over the years. For some it is the Nativity story, for others it is an account of Santa Claus, and for many it is the notion of peace, hope and goodwill to every man, woman and child or, at the very least, a heart-warming diversion to pass the cold winter months. But whatever specific element springs to mind when people think of festive movies, we have seen that this category of cinema has spanned a very wide variety of different genres over the years, from fantasy and horror to comedy and drama. Yet given how acutely Christmas films are concerned with the preservation of tradition, it is also interesting to note just how dynamic and adaptable the genre has proven to be as the decades have passed. Although the content of festive cinema has inevitably been affected by changing social attitudes, many aspects of it have tended to remain largely impervious to the influence of contemporary stylistic movements within the world of film; the genre has been inclined to march to its own drumbeat rather than being shaped by the development of other cinematic trends that were evolving around it. This has been due, at least in part, to the way in which many Christmas films encompass a certain nucleus of recurrent subject matter that are concerned with embracing certain archetypes and/ or mythological areas integral to the traditional festive season: the legend of Santa Claus, Christian symbolism and iconography, and the recognised customs of the modern Christmas (cards, gifts, decorated trees, etc.) which have been established since at least the nineteenth century.

Mentioned throughout this study has been the emergence of four prominent themes which have established themselves in Christmas films since the post-War period. Evident from the mid-1940s onwards, these key premises have been revisited time and again by the cinema of the festive season, surviving the prolonged period of creative paucity during the sixties and seventies when the genre had (in theatrical terms, if not on television) temporarily gone out of fashion with studios and film-makers. Yet even in the less conventional of Christmas films, such as the vigorous contemporisation of films such as *Scrooged* or the clever trope subversion of *Black Christmas*, these central themes have continued to surface – and to be engaged with – by directors and screenwriters in intelligent and innovative ways, even if only to examine or question their continued relevance to modern audiences.

Perhaps the most perennial of these key issues has been the well-established topic, evident at least from the time of *Miracle on 34th Street*, that society should avoid allowing commercial concerns to distract it from the true meaning of Christmas. It should be noted, of course, that while many Christmas films express some degree of scepticism about the increasing commercialism of the festive season, the vast majority focus their disapproval squarely upon greed and excess rather than any inherent flaw in the free market system. Capitalism is generally depicted as innocuous, or even advantageous, when engaged with responsibly and employed in moderation. It is shown favourably in films such as *Miracle on 34th Street* itself, where Kris Kringle sees no conflict between his benevolent role as Santa Claus and the use of the commercial sector to distribute presents, though he intervenes to ensure that shoppers are acquiring their gifts at the fairest and most reasonable price. Indeed, the notion is reinforced more fully in *Trading Places*, where Randolph and Mortimer Duke's malign machinations are only made possible by their wealth and social position, but where their comeuppance is ultimately brought about when the very economic system that they prize so much is used against them, ensuring that justice is done. The overriding message in most films of this type seems to be that there is no iniquity in using the festive season as a means to build an honest profit, but excessive material greed is incompatible with the spirit of giving that is embodied in the traditional Christmas tale.

In consideration of this theme there is, of course, no small amount of irony in the fact that Christmas films have often performed very well at the box-office, making them among the most commercially visible of all marketable commodities during the festive season. The end of December has, in recent decades, become well recognised as a boom-time for cinema takings in general, with the holiday season proving to be a perennial draw for moviegoers. This is, of course, true of audiences attending films of all genres over the Christmas period, but – as features such as *Home Alone* have shown – many Christmas films (which are, given their subject matter, naturally more inclined to see a theatrical release proximate to the festive season) have a proven ability to attract very considerable box-office revenue.

This issue of universality brings us to the second theme, namely the assertion made by Charles Dickens – through the immortal words of Ebenezer Scrooge – that the Christmas spirit can, and should, be preserved all the year round to the benefit of all. This topic is critical to the narrative of films such as *The Bells of St Mary's*, where the Christmas sequences are crucial to the development of the overall plot and illustrate the way in which character arcs are profoundly shaped by the indefinable redemptive power of the season, leading individuals to adapt their behaviour in ways that positively influence their actions throughout their lives at large. Naturally, this potential for emancipation and deliverance (moral, spiritual and/ or behavioural) is delineated succinctly in the many different adaptations of *A Christmas Carol* over the years, but even the modern trend in romantic films set within seasonal frameworks – such as Richard Curtis's *Love Actually* (2003) and Nancy Meyers's *The Holiday* (2005) – are obliquely evocative of the power of Christmas to profoundly restructure the lives of protagonists, using the blossoming of new relationships to symbolise a new beginning for individuals in a light which is affirmative, optimistic and constructive.

This topic dovetails neatly with the third key theme of festive film-making, namely that Christmas presents us with a chance to give something back to our community and to value the family unit. Over the years, of course, films have been forced to re-examine the basic concept of community, and to consider that the notion of family extends beyond blood ties, but this theme does remain both persistent and relevant. In part this is due to the community/ mutual collaboration theme being fundamental to many of the most popular Christmas films, including *It's a Wonderful Life* and *White Christmas*, while a preoccupation with familial ties has been especially crucial to many festive features from the early 1990s onwards, especially *Home Alone*, Jon Turteltaub's *While You Were Sleeping* (1995), Arlene Sanford's *I'll Be Home for Christmas* (1998) and Brett Ratner's *The Family Man* (2000).

Corresponding to this theme is a subordinate argument, but a persistent one nonetheless, that declares a universal belief that all human beings seek, at some level, a sense of acceptance and belonging, and that awareness of this need is intensified at the festive season. On one hand, this encompasses 'fish out of water' scenarios which examine Christmas from the point of view of unconventional outsider characters, such as *The Nightmare Before Christmas* or *Elf*, but in more subtle ways it can be witnessed in other films where protagonists are forced to re-evaluate their feelings toward the festive season. This is particularly relevant to films such as *We're No Angels*, where hardened criminals become the selfless (if somewhat edgy and eccentric) liberators of individuals in need, or even John Ford's *Three Godfathers* (1948), which playfully challenges Western genre conventions at the same time as it reconfigures well-known character archetypes in unexpected ways, in order to fit the needs of atypical narrative functions.

The fourth and final of these recurrent themes is that which states that those who celebrate Christmas should never forget the true reason which lies behind the festive season, irrespective of one's religious or cultural belief. The latter statement is particularly important, because this premise – which originated in films with an explicitly spiritual *modus operandi*, such as *The Bishop's Wife* and George More O'Ferrall's *The Holly and the Ivy* (1952) – soon moved away from unambiguously religious nuances with the cumulative secularisation of the fifties and sixties, eventually evolving instead into an assertion of traditional but non-spiritual values of Christmas: altruism, concern for others, and responsibility for the individual by the individual. This is, perhaps, the single most enduring of all four key themes in festive cinema, and one which can be seen in everything from the stalwart defence of traditionalism in *A Christmas Story* and *Santa Claus: The Movie* to the robust (and sometimes ingenious) defence of the virtues of festive season which is in evidence within films such as *National Lampoon's Christmas Vacation*, *Noel*, and Debbie Isitt's *Nativity!* (2009).

These four vital themes are, of course, supplemented by many other minor but recurrent motifs. These include unconventional variants on Nativity themes, such as the Virgin Birth (Joan Rivers's *Rabbit Test*, 1978) or the Three Wise Men (*We're No Angels*, and George Gallo's *Trapped in Paradise*, 1994); examinations of the origin and function of Santa Claus (*Santa Claus: The Movie*, *The Santa Clause*, and David Dobkin's *Fred Claus*, 2007), and subversions of traditional Christmas tropes which ultimately have the effect of reinforcing the very same key values that underpin the festive season (*Scrooged*, *Elf* and *Bad Santa*). There are also – as has been observed at length throughout this study – specific periods when one particular theme has predominated, such as the cautionary anti-materialism parables of the eighties and the staunch defence of family values throughout the course of the nineties, the latter being articulated via fundamentally enduring moral principles which remained at work even in a social climate which was changing and developing at an ever greater pace. (*Home Alone* may have celebrated the nuclear family while *The Santa Clause* later observed the rise of the constellation family, for instance, but the central concern remains largely the same.) This sharp contrast between traditionalism and modernity has been key to many Christmas narratives over the years, and remains compelling even today. Yet the fact that these pivotal approaches have proven to be both lasting and adaptive is particularly interesting, for it adds weight to the observation that the constant evolution of the Christmas film – necessary to meet the tastes of increasingly sophisticated audiences and complex demographics – continues to take into account the basic fundamentals of the genre which were laid down in the immediate post-War period, even if only to subvert, challenge or attempt to defy this established traditional methodology.

Further intricacy is contributed by the fact that, alongside interaction with these perennial topics throughout the development of the genre, other subgenres have evolved as by-products of the continued re-examination of festive customs within the Christmas film. These have included the boom in Christmas horror films from the early eighties, spurred on by the critical acclaim of the pioneering *Black Christmas* and the huge commercial success of Joe Dante's *Gremlins* (1984), which paved the way both for many similar 'creature features' within the mainstream horror genre as well as prominent cult entries set within the festive season such as Charles E. Sellier's *Silent Night, Deadly Night* (1984) and David Steiman's *Santa's Slay* (2005). Yet while categories such as comedies and fantasy features set during the festive season have featured constantly throughout the years, other subgenres of the Christmas film have had rather more sporadic periods of development, such as the Christmas romance. Romantic themes within the festive movie were prominent in the forties and fifties, featuring in everything from *Miracle on 34th Street* and *The Bishop's Wife* through to Don Hartman's *Holiday Affair* (1949), Frank Tashlin's *Susan Slept Here* (1954) and, of course, *White Christmas*. The frequency of romantic Christmas films tailed off in later years, often remaining in evidence if not as a major fixture of the genre, before re-emerging in the last decade as one of the single most prominent subgeneric trends: Mike Mitchell's *Surviving Christmas* (2004), Roger Kumble's *Just Friends* (2005) and Seth Gordon's *Four Christmases* (2008), to name but a few titles, all exhibited conspicuous romantic themes in this period.

So with such a multifaceted path of development over the past seven decades, what remains in store for the Christmas film? Certainly the commercial boom in the genre – over the past decade in particular – has proven that there remains a unique audience appeal surrounding the warmth and inviting nature of Christmas's comforting traditions and transformative capacity which has managed to largely transcend our current era of hard-edged, cynical postmodernity. Yet box-office success is, on its own, no guarantor of survival in the notoriously fickle world of film: the golden age of Christmas films in the 1940s and 50s created many highly lucrative productions (key among them the top-grossing *White Christmas*, which rocketed to the top of the cinematic charts in 1954), but this prolonged run of success was followed by a wilderness period of two decades where festive film-making became sporadic and largely out of fashion.

Whether the abundance of entries in the genre over the past decade has ultimately created an over-exposure of Christmas-themed features, which may risk heralding a decline in popularity over the coming years, is of course unclear at the present time. However, the Christmas film does appear to be well-served with regard to its long-term survival due to its undiminished ability to attract, rather than exclude, casual audience interest. It has, for several decades, largely but subtly distanced itself from engaging directly with the religion which is responsible for the celebration which forms its basis, thus pre-empting the increasing secularisation of modern society in a manner which has avoided alienating either believers or non-believers. This is because the genre remains flexible enough to accommodate the most spiritually traditional of Christmas narratives even in today's climate of agnosticism and multi-faith coexistence, such as Catherine Hardwicke's *The Nativity Story* (2006), while also expanding upon the non-religious Christmas mythos so extensively (the numerous competing Santa Claus origin stories which have appeared in recent years, for instance) that a wide-ranging sense of inclusiveness has developed over the years which has lent the genre a broad, inoffensive and lasting appeal. It must be noted that not all modern iterations of the Christmas film have entirely disavowed a connection with the religious underpinnings of the season, but it is fair to say that the Christian aspects of festive film-making rapidly developed into one single thematic node of the genre rather than informing the genre at large.

Inclusiveness and continuing relevance have proven to be vital to the ongoing success of the Christmas film, and the way that these two attributes have evolved are at the heart of what has brought such longevity to the genre. In a critical environment where realism and verisimilitude reign supreme, there is an almost carnivalesque quality to the cinema of the festive season: the joyful unleashing of a seasonal world of unabashed fantasy and frivolity has allowed an upbeat and optimistic approach to fiction quite unlike that of any other category of film. Yet the ability of the various subgenres of the Christmas film to constantly reinvent the approach to their subject matter, while remaining true to the invariable core themes of festive film-making, reflects another crucial aspect of their continuing attraction with audiences: the prominent characteristic of transformative self-improvement. Dramatic realism may attempt to reflect society as it actually is, but the whimsicality of the Christmas film presents us with an appealing projection of how we would ideally like things to be. The achievement of the beatific community life of Bedford Falls may seem like the most implausible of goals in a postmodern age riven with self-isolation and assertive self-interest, but that does not impede audiences from a genuine desire to believe that such a benevolent, unselfish and civilised existence remains possible and desirable. So too, as the world's societal and cultural norms continue to change with ever-greater rapidity, are we left with an irrepressible notion that there is undeniable comfort in a seasonal mythology full of reassuring invariants; where the ever-compassionate Santa Claus sets out to deliver his gifts every Christmas Eve in a flying-reindeer-driven sleigh, where a redemption that might otherwise seem impossible suddenly proves a reality, and where we are all presented with a chance to smile more easily and disseminate goodwill even if only for a few weeks in the year.

It seems certain that as long as there is a holiday celebration every December that there will also be a thriving market in Christmas flms: continuing commercial success and a persisting audience appetite for festive cinematic fare remain undiminished in the modern age, with viewer enthusiasm not lessened even by intimate familiarity with the time-honoured tropes of the genre. But while time alone will tell if Christmas films will ever again reach the heady heights of critical acclaim which saw the genre showered with Academy Award nominations in the 1940s during its silver screen heyday, the fact remains that the festive movie has proven to be one of cinema's great survivors, a category of film-making which has exhibited both endurance and adaptability. The Christmas film continues to appeal to the idealist in all of us, encouraging the hope that even in a world of uncompromising realities and unending moral complexity, there may yet be a chance for each of us to achieve a happier life and pursue a brighter tomorrow. And as the newly-reformed Scrooge once so eruditely put it, may that truly be said of us, and all of us.

ILLUSTRATIONS

The illustrations include one page for each of the following movies:

The Bells of St. Mary's (1945)
It's a Wonderful Life (1946)
Miracle on 34th Street (1947)
The Bishop's Wife (1947)
Scrooge: A Christmas Carol (1951)
White Christmas (1954)
We're No Angels (1955)
The Apartment (1960)
Santa Claus Conquers the Martians (1964)
Scrooge (1970)
Black Christmas (1974)
Trading Places (1983)
A Christmas Story (1983)
Santa Claus: The Movie (1985)
Scrooged (1988)
National Lampoon's Christmas Vacation (1989)
Home Alone (1990)
The Muppet Christmas Carol (1992)
The Nightmare Before Christmas (1993)
The Santa Clause (1994)
Elf (2003)
Bad Santa (2003)
Noel (2004)
Joyeux Noël (2005)
A Christmas Carol 3D (2009)

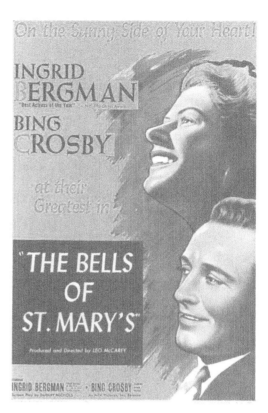

MAUREEN
O'HARA

JOHN
PAYNE
in

Miracle on
34th Street

EDMUND GWENN 20th CENTURY-FOX GEORGE SEATON
WILLIAM PERLBERG

SAMUEL GOLDWYN Presents
Cary GRANT
Loretta YOUNG
David NIVEN
in
"The BISHOP'S WIFE"
with
Monty Woolley
JAMES GLEASON · GLADYS COOPER
Directed by
HENRY KOSTER
RKO RADIO PICTURES, INC.

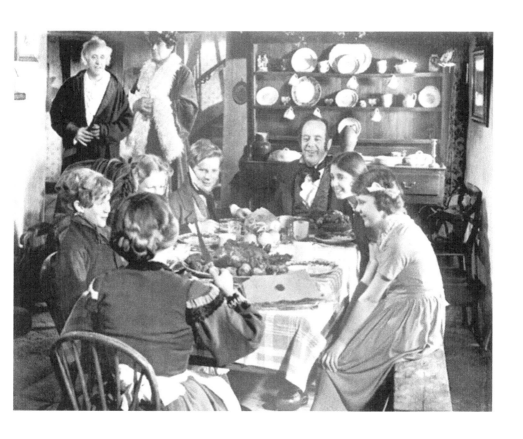

Dan Aykroyd   Eddie Murphy

They're not just getting rich... They're getting even.

TRADING PLACES

Some very funny business.

R

A Tribute to the Original,
Traditional, One-Hundred-Percent, Red-Blooded,
Two-Fisted, All-American Christmas...

A CHRISTMAS STORY

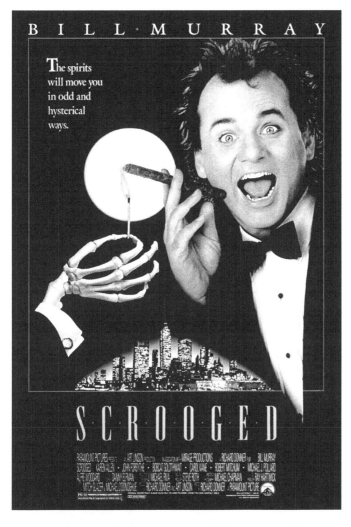

THIS HOLIDAY, DISCOVER YOUR INNER ELF.

WILL FERRELL   with JAMES CAAN

NOVEMBER 7

Penelope CRUZ
Susan SARANDON
Paul WALKER
Alan ARKIN
NOEL
Miracles are closer than you think

GOLDEN GLOBE® NOMINEE • BEST FOREIGN LANGUAGE FILM

Christmas Eve, 1914.

On a World War I battlefield, a Momentous Event
changed the lives of soldiers from France, Germany and England.

Based on a true story.

(OFFICIAL SELECTION
CANNES FILM FESTIVAL)   (OFFICIAL FRANCE ENTRY
ACADEMY AWARDS®
Best Foreign Language Film)

JOYEUX NOEL

(MERRY CHRISTMAS)

JIM CARREY

Disney's A
CHRISTMAS
CAROL

IN THEATRES, DISNEY DIGITAL 3D, AND IMAX 3D.
SEASON'S GREEDINGS NOV 6

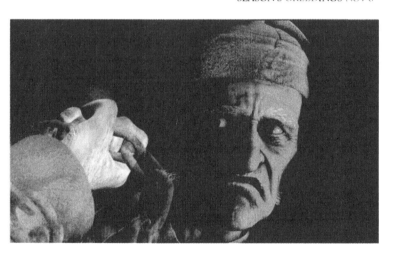

TIMELINE

A CONCISE TIMELINE OF CHRISTMAS FILMS

It would be next to impossible to provide a complete chronology of all Christmas films; so many motion pictures are set during the festive season, or at the very least have a tangential relationship with the Christmas period (while – in many cases – not actually engaging with the issues which derive from it), that a full and frank account of all movies with a festive association would fill many volumes of comparative size to this one. Therefore, what follows is a brief timeline of some of the most significant Christmas films to have been produced since the post-War period. The list is certainly not intended to be anything even close to exhaustive and, as has been the case with the rest of this book, it includes reference only to cinematic releases rather than features which were made specifically for television. It does, however, give an overview of some of the most prominent and influential movies which are concerned specifically with themes and issues deriving from Christmas (as opposed to merely being set during the festive season) from the mid-1940s until the present day.

The Bells of St. Marys (1945)
Rainbow Productions
Dir. Leo McCarey
Starring: Bing Crosby, Ingrid Bergman, Henry Travers.

Christmas in Connecticut (1945)
Warner Bros./ First National Pictures
Dir. Peter Godfrey
Starring: Barbara Stanwyck, Dennis Morgan, Sydney Greenstreet.

The Cheaters (1945)
Republic Pictures
Dir. Joseph Kane
Starring: Joseph Schildkraut, Billie Burke, Eugene Pallette.

It's a Wonderful Life (1946)
Liberty Films
Dir. Frank Capra
Starring: James Stewart, Donna Reed, Lionel Barrymore.

Miracle on 34th Street (1947)
Twentieth Century-Fox Film Corporation
Dir. George Seaton
Starring: Maureen OHara, John Payne, Edmund Gwenn.

The Bishops Wife (1947)
The Samuel Goldwyn Company
Dir. Henry Koster
Starring: Cary Grant, Loretta Young, David Niven.

Christmas Eve (1947)
Miracle Productions
Dir. Edwin L. Marin
Starring: George Raft, George Brent, Randolph Scott.

Bush Christmas (1947)
Ralph Smart Productions
Dir. Ralph Smart
Starring: Chips Rafferty, John Fernside, Helen Grieve.

Three Godfathers (1948)
Argosy Pictures Corporation
Dir. John Ford
Starring: John Wayne, Pedro Armendáriz, Harry Carey Jr.

Holiday Affair (1949)
RKO Radio Pictures
Dir. Don Hartman
Starring: Robert Mitchum, Janet Leigh, Wendell Corey.

The Great Rupert (1950)
Eagle Lion Productions
Dir. Irving Pichel
Starring: Jimmy Durante, Terry Moore, Tom Drake.

Scrooge (1951)
George Minter Productions
Dir. Brian Desmond Hurst
Starring: Alastair Sim, Kathleen Harrison, Mervyn Johns.

The Lemon Drop Kid (1951)
Paramount Pictures/ Hope Enterprises
Dir. Sidney Lanfield
Starring: Bob Hope, Marilyn Maxwell, Lloyd Nolan.

The Holly and the Ivy (1952)
London Film Productions/ De Grunwald Productions
Dir. George More O'Ferrall
Starring: Ralph Richardson, Celia Johnson, Margaret Leighton.

White Christmas (1954)
Paramount Pictures
Dir. Michael Curtiz
Starring: Bing Crosby, Danny Kaye, Rosemary Clooney.

Susan Slept Here (1954)
RKO Radio Pictures
Dir. Frank Tashlin
Starring: Dick Powell, Debbie Reynolds, Anne Francis.

We're No Angels (1955)
Paramount Pictures
Dir. Michael Curtiz
Starring: Humphrey Bogart, Aldo Ray, Peter Ustinov.

Bell, Book and Candle (1958)
Phoenix Productions Inc.
Dir. Richard Quine
Starring: James Stewart, Kim Novak, Jack Lemmon.

The Apartment (1960)
The Mirisch Corporation
Dir. Billy Wilder
Starring: Jack Lemmon, Shirley MacLaine, Fred MacMurray.

Santa Claus (1960)
Cinematográfica Calderón S.A.
Dir. Rene Cardona
Starring: José Elías Moreno, Cesáreo Quezadas, José Luis Aguirre.

Santa Claus Conquers the Martians (1964)
Jalor Productions
Dir. Nicholas Webster
Starring: John Call, Leonard Hicks, Vincent Beck.

The Lion in Winter (1968)
AVCO Embassy/ Haworth Productions
Dir. Anthony Harvey
Starring: Peter O'Toole, Katharine Hepburn, Anthony Hopkins.

The Christmas Tree (1969)
Jupiter Generale Cinematografica/ Les Films Corona/ Valoria Films
Dir. Terence Young
Starring: William Holden, Virna Lisi, Madeleine Damien.

The Juggler of Notre Dame (1970)
Lou Tillman Productions
Dir. Milton H. Lehr
Starring: Jessica Benton, Barry Dennen, Christopher Ellis.

Scrooge (1970)
Waterbury Films/ Cinema Center Films
Dir. Ronald Neame
Starring: Albert Finney, Edith Evans, Kenneth More.

Black Christmas (1974)
Film Funding Ltd./ Vision IV/ Canadian Film Development Corporation/ Famous Players
Dir. Bob Clark
Starring: Olivia Hussey, Keir Dullea, Margot Kidder.

Rabbit Test (1978)
Laugh or Die Productions
Dir. Joan Rivers
Starring: Billy Crystal, Alex Rocco, George Gobel.

Christmas Evil (1980)
Edward R. Pressman Productions
Dir. Lewis Jackson
Starring: Brandon Maggart, Jeffrey DeMunn, Dianne Hull.

To All a Good Night (1980)
Four Features Partners/ Intercontinental Releasing Corporation
Dir. David Hess
Starring: Buck West, Katherine Herington, Sam Shamshak.

Trading Places (1983)
Paramount Pictures/ Cinema Group Ventures
Dir. John Landis
Starring: Dan Aykroyd, Eddie Murphy, Denholm Elliott.

A Christmas Story (1983)
Metro-Goldwyn-Mayer/ Christmas Tree Films
Dir. Bob Clark
Starring: Melinda Dillon, Darren McGavin, Peter Billingsley.

Gremlins (1984)
Warner Bros./ Amblin Entertainment
Dir. Joe Dante
Starring: Zach Galligan, Phoebe Cates, Keye Luke.

Silent Night, Deadly Night (1984)
TriStar Pictures/ Slayride Productions
Dir. Charles E. Sellier
Starring: Robert Brian Wilson, Toni Nero, Lilyan Chauvin.

Don't Open Till Christmas (1984)
Spectacular Trading International
Dir. Edmund Purdom
Starring: Edmund Purdom, Alan Lake, Belinda Mayne.

One Magic Christmas (1985)
Walt Disney Pictures/ Silver Screen Partners/ Téléfilm Canada
Dir. Phillip Borsos
Starring: Mary Steenburgen, Gary Basaraba, Harry Dean Stanton.

Santa Claus: The Movie (1985)
TriStar Pictures/ Calash Corporation/ GGG Productions/ Santa Claus Ltd.
Dir. Jeannot Szwarc
Starring: Dudley Moore, John Lithgow, David Huddleston.

Scrooged (1988)
Paramount Pictures/ Mirage Productions
Dir. Richard Donner
Starring: Bill Murray, Karen Allen, John Forsythe.

Ernest Saves Christmas (1988)
Touchstone Pictures/ Silver Screen Partners
Dir. John R. Cherry III
Starring: Jim Varney, Douglas Seale, Oliver Clark.

National Lampoon's Christmas Vacation (1989)
Warner Bros./ Hughes Entertainment
Dir. Jeremiah S. Chechik
Starring: Chevy Chase, Beverly D'Angelo, Juliette Lewis.

Prancer (1989)
Cineplex-Odeon Films/ Nelson Entertainment/ Raffaella Productions
Dir. John D. Hancock
Starring: Sam Elliott, Cloris Leachman, Rutanya Alda.

Home Alone (1990)
Twentieth Century Fox Film Corporation/ Hughes Entertainment
Dir. Chris Columbus
Starring: Macaulay Culkin, Joe Pesci, Daniel Stern.

All I Want For Christmas (1991)
Paramount Pictures
Dir. Robert Lieberman
Starring: Harley Jane Kozak, Jamey Sheridan, Ethan Randall.

Home Alone 2: Lost in New York (1992)
Twentieth Century Fox Film Corporation/ Hughes Entertainment
Dir. Chris Columbus
Starring: Macaulay Culkin, Joe Pesci, Daniel Stern.

The Muppet Christmas Carol (1992)
The Jim Henson Company/ Walt Disney Pictures
Dir. Brian Henson
Starring: Michael Caine, Dave Goelz, Robin Weaver.

The Nightmare Before Christmas (1993)
Touchstone Pictures/ Skellington Productions Inc./ Tim Burton Productions
Dir. Henry Selick
Starring: Danny Elfman, Chris Sarandon, Catherine O'Hara.

Miracle on 34th Street (1994)
Hughes Entertainment/ Twentieth Century Fox
Dir. Les Mayfield
Starring: Richard Attenborough, Elizabeth Perkins, Dylan McDermott.

The Santa Clause (1994)
Walt Disney Pictures/ Hollywood Pictures/ Outlaw Productions
Dir. John Pasquin
Starring: Tim Allen, Wendy Crewson, Judge Reinhold.

Trapped in Paradise (1994)
Twentieth Century Fox Film Corporation
Dir. George Gallo
Starring: Nicolas Cage, Jon Lovitz, Dana Carvey.

Mixed Nuts (1994)
TriStar Pictures
Dir. Nora Ephron
Starring: Steve Martin, Madeleine Kahn, Anthony LaPaglia.

The Ref (1994)
Touchstone Pictures/ Don Simpson/ Jerry Bruckheimer Films
Dir. Ted Demme
Starring: Denis Leary, Judy Davis, Kevin Spacey.

While You Were Sleeping (1995)
Hollywood Pictures/ Caravan Pictures
Dir. Jon Turteltaub
Starring: Sandra Bullock, Bill Pullman, Peter Gallagher.

The Preacher's Wife (1996)
Touchstone Pictures/ Mundy Lane Entertainment/ Parkway Productions/ The Samuel Goldwyn Company
Dir. Penny Marshall
Starring: Denzel Washington, Whitney Houston, Courtney B. Vance.

Jingle All the Way (1996)
Twentieth Century Fox Film Corporation/ 1492 Pictures
Dir. Brian Levant
Starring: Arnold Schwarzenegger, Sinbad, Phil Hartman.

Rudolph the Red-Nosed Reindeer: The Movie (1998)
Cayre Brothers/ Goodtimes Entertainment/ Rudolph Productions/ Tundra Productions
Dir. William R. Kowalchuk Jr.
Starring: Eric Pospisil, Kathleen Barr, John Goodman.

I'll Be Home for Christmas (1998)
Walt Disney Pictures/ Leo Productions/ Mandeville Films
Dir. Arlene Sanford
Starring: Jonathan Taylor Thomas, Jessica Biel, Adam LaVorgna.

How the Grinch Stole Christmas (2000)
Imagine Entertainment/ LUNI Productions
Dir. Ron Howard
Starring: Jim Carrey, Taylor Momsen, Jeffrey Tambor.

The Family Man (2000)
Universal Pictures/ Beacon Pictures/ Riche-Ludwig Productions/ Howard Rosenman Productions/ Saturn Films
Dir. Brett Ratner
Starring: Nicolas Cage, Téa Leoni, Don Cheadle.

Christmas Carol: The Movie (2001)
MBP/ Scala/ The Film Consortium/ The Illuminated Film Company/ Film Council/ FilmFour
Dir. Jimmy T. Murakami
Starring: Simon Callow, Nicolas Cage, Kate Winslet.

I Saw Mommy Kissing Santa Claus (2002)
Regent Entertainment/ ACH/ Medien Capital Treuhand
Dir. John Shepphird
Starring: Connie Sellecca, Corbin Bernsen, Cole Sprouse.

Eight Crazy Nights (2002)
Happy Madison Productions/ Meatball Animation
Dir. Seth Kearsley
Starring: Adam Sandler, Jackie Titone, Austin Stout.

Elf (2003)
New Line Cinema/ Guy Walks into a Bar Productions
Dir. Jon Favreau
Starring: Will Ferrell, James Caan, Bob Newhart.

Christmas Child (2003)
Impact Productions
Dir. Bill Ewing
Starring: William R. Moses/ Tonya Bordeaux/ Steven Curtis Chapman.

Bad Santa (2003)
Columbia Pictures/ Dimension Films/ Triptych Pictures/ Blixa Zweite Film Produktion
Dir. Terry Zwigoff
Starring: Billy Bob Thornton, Tony Cox, Brett Kelly.

Blizzard (2003)
Knightscove Entertainment/ Holedigger Films/ Ralph Winter Productions
Dir. LeVar Burton
Starring: Paul Bates, Brenda Blethyn, Brittany Bristow.

Love Actually (2003)
Universal Pictures/ StudioCanal/ Working Title/ DNA Films
Dir. Richard Curtis
Starring: Bill Nighy, Colin Firth, Liam Neeson.

Surviving Christmas (2004)
DreamWorks Pictures/ Tall Trees Productions/ LivePlanet
Dir. Mike Mitchell
Starring: Ben Affleck, James Gandolfini, Christina Applegate.

Christmas with the Kranks (2004)
Revolution Studios/ 1492 Pictures
Dir. Joe Roth
Starring: Tim Allen, Jamie Lee Curtis, Dan Aykroyd.

Noel (2004)
Code Entertainment/ Red Rose Productions LLC
Dir. Chazz Palminteri
Starring: Susan Sarandon, Paul Walker, Penélope Cruz.

The Polar Express (2004)
Warner Bros./ Castle Rock Entertainment/ Shangri-La Entertainment/ Playtone/ ImageMovers/ Golden Mean/ Universal CGI
Dir. Robert Zemeckis

Starring: Tom Hanks, Leslie Zemeckis, Eddie Deezen.

The Family Stone (2005)
Fox 2000 Pictures/ The Family Stone Productions/ Michael London Productions
Dir. Thomas Bezucha
Starring: Claire Danes, Diane Keaton, Rachel McAdams.

The Ice Harvest (2005)
Bona Fide Productions/ Focus Features
Dir. Harold Ramis
Starring: John Cusack, Billy Bob Thornton, Lara Phillips.

Just Friends (2005)
Inferno Distribution/ Cinerenta/ BenderSpink/ Cinezeta/ Infinity Media/ Just Friends Productions
Dir. Roger Kumble
Starring: Ryan Reynolds, Amy Smart, Anna Faris.

The 12 Dogs of Christmas (2005)
Alchemist Productions/ Ken Kragen Productions
Dir. Kieth Merrill
Starring: Jordan-Claire Green, Tom Kemp, Susan Wood.

Joyeux Noël (2005)
Nord-Ouest Productions/ Senator Film Produktion/ The Bureau/ Artémis Productions/ Media Pro Pictures/ TF1 Films Production/ Les Productions de la Guéville
Dir. Christian Carion
Starring: Diane Kruger, Natalie Dessay, Benno Fürmann.

Santa's Slay (2005)
Media 8 Entertainment/ Rat Entertainment/ M8 Production 1/ VIP 1 Medienfonds/ VIP 2 Medienfonds
Dir. David Steiman
Starring: Bill Goldberg, Douglas Smith, Emilie de Ravin.

The Holiday (2005)
Columbia Pictures/ Universal Pictures/ Relativity Media/ Waverly Films
Dir. Nancy Meyers
Starring: Cameron Diaz, Kate Winslet, Jack Black.

Deck the Halls (2006)
Regency Enterprises/ New Regency Pictures/ Corduroy Films/ All Lit Up Productions
Dir. John Whitesell
Starring: Danny DeVito, Matthew Broderick, Kristin Davis.

Christmas at Maxwell's (2006)
LauferFilm
Dir. William C. Laufer
Starring: Andrew May, Jack Hourigan, Helen Welch.

Stalking Santa (2006)
Cosmic Pictures
Dir. Greg Kiefer
Starring: Chris Clark, Daryn Tufts, Lisa Clark.

The Nativity Story (2006)
New Line Cinema/ Sound for Film Productions
Dir. Catherine Hardwicke
Starring: Keisha Castle-Hughes, Oscar Isaac, Hiam Abbass.

Unaccompanied Minors (2006)
Warner Bros./ Donners' Company/ Village Roadshow Pictures
Dir. Paul Feig
Starring: Lewis Black, Wilmer Valderrama, Tyler James Williams.

Fred Claus (2007)
Warner Bros. Pictures/ Silver Pictures/ David Dobkin Productions/ Jessie Nelson
Productions
Dir. David Dobkin
Starring: Vince Vaughn, Paul Giamatti, John Michael Higgins.

This Christmas (2007)
Facilitator Films/ Rainforest Films/ Screen Gems
Dir. Preston A. Whitmore II
Starring: Delroy Lindo, Idris Elba, Loretta Devine.

Four Christmases (2008)
New Line Cinema/ Spyglass Entertainment/ Birnbaum/ Barber/ Wild West Picture
Show Productions/ Type A Films/ Ott Medien
Dir. Seth Gordon
Starring: Vince Vaughn, Reese Witherspoon, Robert Duvall.

Nothing Like the Holidays (2008)
2DS Productions/ Overture Films/ State Street Pictures
Dir. Alfredo De Villa
Starring: Alfred Molina, Elizabeth Peña, Freddy Rodríguez.

Ornaments (2008)
Apple Cart Productions/ Maven Design House
Dir. Brian Samuel Davis
Starring: Angela Dawe, Romel Jamison, Brian Samuel Davis.

Nativity! (2009)
BBC Films/ Mirrorball Films/ Screen West Midlands
Dir. Debbie Isitt
Starring: Martin Freeman, Ashley Jensen, Pam Ferris.

A Christmas Carol (2009)
Walt Disney Pictures/ ImageMovers Digital
Dir. Robert Zemeckis
Starring: Jim Carrey, Gary Oldman, Bob Hoskins.

ɴoᴛes ᴀɴᴅ
ʀefeʀeɴces

INTRODUCTION

1. Fred Guida, 'A Christmas Carol' and Its Adaptations: A Critical Examination of Dickens' Story and Its Productions on Stage, Screen and Television (Jefferson: McFarland, 2000).

2. Frank Thompson, *American Movie Classics' Great Christmas Movies* (Dallas: Taylor, 1998).

3. Gary J.Svehla, and Susan Svehla, *It's Christmas Time at the Movies* (Baltimore: Midnight Marquee Press, 1998).

THE BELLS OF ST MARY'S (1945)

1. Anthony Burke Smith, 'America's Favorite Priest: *Going My Way* (1944)' in *Catholics in the Movies*, ed. by Colleen McDannell (New York: Oxford University Press US, 2008), pp.107-126.

2. Bruce Babington and Peter William Evans, 'Theorising the Biblical Epic', in *Biblical Epics: Sacred Narrative in the Hollywood Cinema* (Manchester: Manchester University Press, 1993), pp.18-20.

3. Kristine Butler Carlson, '1945: Movies and the March Home', in *American Cinema of the 1940s: Themes and Variations*, ed. by Wheeler Winston Dixon (Piscataway: Rutgers University Press, 2006), pp.158-60.

4. Both radio adaptations of the film were broadcast as part of *The Screen Guild Theater* radio program. The airdates were 26 August 1946 and 6 October 1947. Additionally, Bing Crosby had earlier performed as Father O'Malley, along with Barry Fitzgerald and Paul Lukas, in an adaptation of *Going My Way* which was broadcast on radio under *The Screen Guild Theater* banner on 8 January 1945.

IT'S A WONDERFUL LIFE (1946)

1. Frank Thompson, *American Movie Classics' Great Christmas Movies* (Dallas: Taylor, 1998), p.149.

2. Gary J.Svehla and Susan Svehla, *It's Christmas Time at the Movies* (Baltimore: Midnight

Marquee Press, 1998), pp.150-51.

3. For a fuller discussion of possible socialistic themes which can be discerned in *It's a Wonderful Life*, particularly with regard to the negative portrayal of banker Mr Potter, the following text is of value: John A. Noakes, 'Official Frames in Social Movement Theory: The FBI, HUAC, and the Communist Threat in Hollywood', in *Frames of Protest: Social Movements and the Framing Perspective*, ed. by Hank Johnston and John A. Noakes (Oxford: Rowman and Littlefield, 2005), pp.95-101.

4. Eamonn McCusker, '*It's a Wonderful Life*', in *DVD Times*, 20 November 2008. <http:// www.dvdtimes.co.uk/ content/ id/ 69440/ itswonderful-life.html>

5. For a full and frank discussion of the politics of *It's a Wonderful Life*, please consider: Patrick McGee, *Cinema, Theory, and Political Responsibility in Contemporary Culture* (Cambridge: Cambridge University Press, 1997), pp.7-11.

6. Raymond Carney, *American Vision: The Films of Frank Capra* (Cambridge: Cambridge University Press, 1986), p.379.

7. Brian Geoffrey Rose, *An Examination of Narrative Structure in Four Films of Frank Capra* (New York: Arno Press, 1980) [1976], p.181.

8. Leonard Quart and Albert Auster, *American Film and Society Since 1945*, 3rd edn (Westport: Greenwood Publishing Group, 2002), pp.22-23.

9. For a discussion of the film's significance to audiences, see: Michael Willian, *The Essential Its a Wonderful Life: A Scene-by-Scene Guide to the Classic Film* (Chicago: Chicago Review Press, 2006), p.ix.

10. Stephen Cox, 'On a Wing and a Prayer', in *The Los Angeles Times*, 23 December 2006.

11. Originally broadcast on 12 February 1995.

12. Originally broadcast on 19 December 1995.

13. Originally broadcast on 11 December 1977.

14. Originally broadcast on 21 December 1980.

MIRACLE ON 34th STREET (1947)

1. Glen O. Gabbard and Krin Gabbard, *Psychiatry and the Cinema*, 2nd edn (Washington D.C.: American Psychiatric Press, 1999), p.337.

2. Ross D. Levi, *The Celluloid Courtroom: A History of Legal Cinema* (Westport: Greenwood Publishing Group, 2005), p.147.

3. Originally broadcast on 14 December 1955.

4. Originally broadcast on 27 November 1959.

5. Originally broadcast on 14 December 1973.

6. A radio adaptation of *Miracle on 34th Street* was broadcast by Lux Radio Theater on 20 December 1948, with Edmund Gwenn reprising his role of Kris Kringle. This one-hour version of the play was later adapted into a thirty minute edition, also starring Gwenn, which would feature as part of the Screen Director's Playhouse.

7. Hal Hinson, '*Miracle on 34th Street*', in *The Washington Post*, 18 November 1994.

8. An example of the negative criticism directed at Les Mayfield's remake can be found at: Zachary Woodruff, '*Miracle on 34th Street*', in *Tucson Weekly*, 5 January 1995. <http:// www.filmvault.com/ filmvault/ tw/ m/ miracleon34thstreet.html> For a contrasting opinion, consider: Roger Ebert, '*Miracle on 34th Street*', in *The Chicago Sun-Times*, 18 November 1994.

9. Noel Murray, '*Miracle on 34th Street*', in *The Onion A.V. Club*, 13 December 2006. <http:// www.avclub.com/ articles/ miracle-on-34th-street,8045/>

10. Ace Collins, *Stories Behind the Great Traditions of Christmas* (Grand Rapids: Zondervan,

2003), pp.132-33.

THE BISHOP'S WIFE (1947)

1. John Howard Reid, *Movies Magnificent: 150 Must-See Cinema Classics* (Morrisville: Lulu.com, 2005), p.23.

2. ibid., p.23.

3. Karin J. Fowler, *David Niven: A Bio-Bibliography* (Westport: Greenwood Publishing Group, 1995), pp.103-04.

4. Greg Garrett, *The Gospel According to Hollywood* (Louisville: Westminster John Knox Press, 2007), p.6.

5. Ken D. Jones, Arthur F. McClure and Alfred E. Twomey, *Character People* (New York: A.S. Barnes, 1977), p.208.

6. See, for example: Anon., 'Movie of the Week: *The Bishops Wife*', in *Life*, 12 January 1948, pp.71-72.

7. Originally broadcast on 1 March 1948.

8. Originally broadcast on 19 December 1949.

9. Originally broadcast on 11 May 1953.

10. Originally broadcast on 1 March 1955.

SCROOGE: A CHRISTMAS CAROL (1951)

1. Fred Guida, *'A Christmas Carol' and Its Adaptations: A Critical Examination of Dickens' Story and Its Productions on Stage, Screen and Television* (Jefferson: McFarland, 2000), pp.103-09.

2. Phyllis Strupp, *The Richest of Fare: Seeking Spiritual Security in the Sonoran Desert* (Scottsdale: Sonoran Cross Press, 2004), pp.177-79.

3. Thomas M. Leitch, *Film Adaptation and Its Discontents: From* Gone With the Wind *to* The Passion of the Christ (Baltimore: Johns Hopkins University Press, 2007), pp.74-75.

4. Kate Carnell Watt and Kathleen C. Lonsdale, 'Dickens Composed: Film and Television Adaptations 1897-2001', in *Dickens On Screen*, ed. by John Glavin (Cambridge: Cambridge University Press, 2003), p.206.

5. Sue Harper, 'Bonnie Prince Charlie Revisited: British Costume Film in the 1950s', in *The British Cinema Book*, 2nd edn, ed. by Robert Murphy (London: British Film Institute, 2001), p.129.

6. Anon., 'Cinema: Import: *A Christmas Carol*', in *Time*, 3 December 1951.

7. Richard Michael Kelly, 'Introduction', in Charles Dickens, *A Christmas Carol* (Peterborough: Broadview Press, 2003) [1843], p.28.

See also Anon., 'Top 10 Classic Christmas Movies', in *The Coventry Evening Telegraph*, 23 October 2009.

8. Richard McBrien, 'Angels and Spirituality: Comfort, Help of Angels May Hover Close at Hand', in *The National Catholic Reporter*, 4 March 1994.

WHITE CHRISTMAS (1954)

1. Peter Lev, *Transforming the Screen: 1950-1959* (Berkeley: University of California Press, 2003), pp.120-21.

2. Steven Cohan, 'Introduction: Musicals of the Studio Era', in *Hollywood Musicals: The Film Reader*, ed. by Steven Cohan (London: Routledge, 2002), p.12.

3. David A. Jasen, *Tin Pan Alley: An Encyclopedia of the Golden Age of the American Song* (New York: Routledge, 2003), p.33.

4. James C. Robertson, *The Casablanca Man: The Cinema of Michael Curtiz* (London: Routledge, 1993), p.118.

5. ibid.

6. Karal Ann Marling, *Merry Christmas!: Celebrating Americas Greatest Holiday* (Cambridge: Harvard University Press, 2000), pp.321-31.

7. Eric Michael Mazur, 'Going My Way?: Crosby and Catholicism on the Road to America', in *Going My Way: Bing Crosby and American Culture*, ed. by Ruth Prigozy and Walter Raubicheck (Rochester: University of Rochester Press, 2007), p.28.

8. Ray B. Browne and Glenn J. Browne, *Laws of Our Fathers: Popular Culture and the U.S. Constitution* (Bowling Green: Bowling Green State University Popular Press, 1986), pp.163-64.

See also: Marshall W. Fishwick, *Popular Culture in a New Age* (Binghampton: Haworth Press, 2002), pp.165-66.

9. Anon., 'Bingle All the Way: Crosby and Kaye Celebrate an Early *White Christmas*', in *Life*, 11 October 1954, pp.158-61.

10. Don Tyler, *Music of the Postwar Era* (Westport: Greenwood Publishing Group, 2008), p.125.

11. Stanley Green, *Hollywood Musicals Year by Year*, 2nd edn. rev. by Elaine Schmidt (Milwaukee: Hal Leonard, 1999), p.186.

12. John Howard Reid, *Hollywood Movie Musicals: Great, Good and Glamorous* (Morrisville: Lulu.com, 2006), pp.218-20.

13. Robertson, p.118.

WE'RE NO ANGELS (1955)

1. John Reid, *Movies Magnificent: 150 Must-See Cinema Classics* (Morrisville: Lulu.com, 2005), pp.220-22.

2. Paul Peterson, 'Michael Curtiz: The Mystery-Man Director of *Casablanca*' in *Political Philosophy Comes to Rick's: Casablanca and American Civic Culture*, ed. by James F. Pontuso (Lanham: Lexington Books, 2005), p.149.

3. James C. Robertson, *The Casablanca Man: The Cinema of Michael Curtiz* (London: Routledge, 1993), p.119.

4. Barbara Paulding, *Suzanne Schwalb and Mara Conlon, A Century of Christmas Memories 1900-1999* (New York: Peter Pauper Press, 2009), p.74.

5. Maria Pramaggiore, *Neil Jordan* (Champaign: University of Illinois Press, 2008), p.3.

THE APARTMENT (1960)

1. Wilder discusses the genesis of *The Apartment* in his own words in: The American Film Institute, 'Dialogue on Film: Billy Wilder and I.A.L. Diamond', in *Billy Wilder: Interviews*, ed. by Peter Brunette (Jackson: University Press of Mississippi, 2001), pp.110-31.

See also: Anon., 'The Wilder Touch: The director explains his zany method for relaxing actors', in *Life*, 30 May 1960, pp.41-42.

2. Daniel J. Leab, 'A Walk on the Wilder Side: *The Apartment* as Social Commentary', in *Windows on the Sixties: Exploring Key Texts of Media and Culture*, ed. by Anthony Aldgate, James Chapman and Arthur Marwick (London: I.B. Tauris, 2000), pp.1-18.

3. Peter Bradshaw, '*The Apartment*', in *The Guardian*, 11 July 2008.

4. Christopher Deacy, *Faith in Film: Religious Themes in Contemporary Cinema* (Aldershot: Ashgate Publishing, 2005), pp.58-61.

5. Roger Ebert, 'Great Movies: *The Apartment*', in *The Chicago Sun-Times*, 22 July 2001.

<http:// rogerebert.suntimes.com/ apps/ pbcs.dll/ article?AID=/ 20010722/ REVIEWS08/ 107220301/ 1023>

6. Glenn Hopp, *Billy Wilder: The Complete Films* (Köln: Taschen Books, 2003), pp.146-47.

7. Gene D. Phillips, *Some Like It Wilder: The Controversial Films of Billy Wilder* (Lexington: University Press of Kentucky, 2010), pp.244-45.

8. *Variety* Staff, '*The Apartment*', in Variety, 18 May 1960.

9. Richard Armstrong, *Billy Wilder: American Film Realist* (Jefferson: McFarland and Company, 2000), pp.106-07.

10. Sam Adams, 'Screen Picks: *The Apartment*', in *The Philadelphia City Paper*, 5-12 July 2001.

11. *Promises, Promises* received its Broadway premiere at the Shubert Theater on Sunday 1 December 1968.

SANTA CLAUS CONQUERS THE MARTIANS (1964)

1. More details of Nicholas Webster's biography can be found at: Anon, 'Reflections', in *Masters of Imaging*, 2010. <http:// www.mastersofimaging.net/ Reflections.html>

2. Gary J. Svehla, and Susan Svehla, *It's Christmas Time at the Movies* (Baltimore: Midnight Marquee Press, 1998), p.219.

3. Originally broadcast on 21 December 1991.

4. See, for example: Bruce Felton, *What Were They Thinking?: Really Bad Ideas Throughout History*, rev. edn. (Guilford: Lyons Press, 2007), p.101.

5. H. Paul Jeffers, *Legends of Santa Claus* (Minneapolis: Lerner Publishing Group, 2001), pp.87-88.

6. Floyd Conner, *Hollywood's Most Wanted: The top 10 book of lucky breaks, prima donnas, box office bombs, and other oddities* (Virginia: Brassey's, 2002), p.208.

7. Gary J. Svehla and Susan Svehla, p.215.

8. Tim Healey, *The World's Worst Movies* (London: Octopus Books, 1986), pp.58-59.

9. Richard Crouse, *The 100 Best Movies You've Never Seen* (Toronto: ECW Press, 2003), pp.188-91.

10. Stephen D. Hales, 'Putting Claus Back into Christmas', in *Christmas: Philosophy for Everyone*, ed. by Scott C. Lowe (Chichester: Blackwell, 2010), p.168.

11. Anon., 'Singles Reviews: Christmas Highlights', in *Billboard*, 21 November 1964, p.18.

SCROOGE (1970)

1. Fred Guida, '*A Christmas Carol*' and Its Adaptations: A Critical Examination of Dickens' Story and Its Productions on Stage, Screen and Television* (Jefferson: McFarland, 2000), pp.110-15.

2. *Life* Magazine ran a photographic showcase of some of the film's costumes just prior to its release:
Marie Cosindas, 'Gallery', in *Life*, 27 November 1970, pp.8-11.

3. Richard Schickel, 'Critic's Roundup', in *Life*, 18 December 1970, p.6.

4. Judith Crist, 'Cinema', in *New York Magazine*, 23 November 1970, p.77.

5. Roger Ebert, '*Scrooge*', in *The Chicago Sun-Times*, 1 January 1970.

6. Ace Collins, *Stories Behind the Great Traditions of Christmas* (Grand Rapids: Zondervan, 2003), p.132.

7. James Chapman, 'God Bless Us, Every One: *Movie Adaptations of A Christmas Carol*', in *Christmas at the Movies*, ed. by Mark Connelly (London: I.B. Tauris, 2000), pp.25-27.

8. David C. Cook, *The Inspirational Christmas Almanac: Heartwarming Traditions, Trivia,*

Stories, and Recipes for the Holidays (Colorado Springs: Honor Books, 2006), p.103.

9. Robert Shail, *British Film Directors: A Critical Guide* (Edinburgh: Edinburgh University Press, 2007), p.153.

BLACK CHRISTMAS (1974)

1. Wyndham Wise, '*Black Christmas*', in *Take One's Essential Guide to Canadian Film*, ed. by Wyndham Wise (Toronto: University of Toronto Press, 2001), pp.21-22.

2. Ian Cooper, 'Bob Clark', in *Contemporary North American Film Directors: A Wallflower Critical Guide*, ed. by Yoram Allon, Del Cullen and Hannah Patterson (London: Wallflower Press, 2000), pp.85-86.

3. Gary J. Svehla and Susan Svehla, *It's Christmas Time at the Movies* (Baltimore: Midnight Marquee Press, 1998), pp.297-98.

4. Adam Rockoff, *Going to Pieces: The Rise and Fall of the Slasher Film, 1978-1986* (Jefferson: McFarland and Company, 2002), pp.42-44.

5. Jim Harper, *Legacy of Blood: A Comprehensive Guide to Slasher Movies* (Manchester: Headpress/ Critical Vision, 2004), pp.66-67.

6. Reviews of *Black Christmas* sometimes appeared under the film's alternative titles of *Silent Night, Evil Night* and *Stranger in the House*. See, for example: Edward Jones, 'Horror Cliches: Up From the Dead, and Still Fun', in *The Free Lance-Star*, 14 July 1975, p.14.

7. Noel Murray, '*Black Christmas*', in *The Onion A.V. Club*, 13 December 2006.
<http:// www.avclub.com/ articles/ black-christmas,8046/>

8. Peter Bradshaw, '*Black Christmas*', in *The Guardian*, 15 December 2006.
See also: Peter Hartlaub, 'Partridges, Pear Trees... And Deadly Icicles', in *The San Francisco Chronicle*, 27 December 2006.

9. Sam Adams, '*Black Christmas*', in *The Los Angeles Times*, 26 December 2006.

10. The influential and very comprehensive website for *Black Christmas* can be found at: <http:// www.itsmebilly.com/>

11. Bartlomiej Paszylk, *The Pleasure and Pain of Cult Horror Films: An Historical Survey* (Jefferson: McFarland and Company, 2009), p.135-36.

12. Andrew Patrick Nelson, 'Todorov's Fantastic and the Uncanny Slasher Remake', in *American Horror Film: The Genre at the Turn of the Millennium*, ed. by Steffen Hantke (Jackson: University Press of Mississippi, 2010), p.111-12.

TRADING PLACES (1983)

1. Gary J.Svehla and Susan Svehla, *It's Christmas Time at the Movies* (Baltimore: Midnight Marquee Press, 1998), p.112.

2. Larry Elliott and Dan Atkinson, *The Age of Insecurity* (London: Verso, 1999) [1998], pp.147-48.

3. Alan Nadel, 'Movies and Reaganism', in *American Cinema of the 1980s: Themes and Variations*, ed. by Stephen Prince (Chapel Hill: Rutgers University Press, 2007), pp.84-86.

4. David Denby, 'Supply-Side Hero', in *New York Magazine*, 22 August 1983, pp.62-63.

5. Roger Ebert, '*Trading Places*', in *The Chicago Sun-Times*, 9 June 1983.

6. Jay Carr, '*Trading Places*', in *The Boston Globe*, 9 June 1983.

7. Matthew Fraser, '*Trading Places*', in *The Toronto Globe and Mail*, 10 June 1983.

8. Martin Flanagan, 'John Landis', in *Contemporary North American Film Directors: A Wallflower Critical Guide*, ed. by Yoram Allon, Del Cullen and Hannah Patterson (London: Wallflower Press, 2002), pp.310-12.

A CHRISTMAS STORY (1983)

1. Greg Metcalf, '"Its (Christmas) Morning in America": Christmas Conventions of American Films in the 1980s', in *Beyond the Stars: Plot Conventions in American Popular Film*, ed. by Paul Loukides and Linda K. Fuller (Bowling Green: Bowling Green State University Popular Press, 1991), p.105.

2. David J. Mansour, *From Abba to Zoom: A Pop Culture Encyclopedia of the Late 20th Century* (Kansas City: Andrews McMeel Publishing, 2005), p.310.

3. Roger Ebert, '*A Christmas Story*', in *The Chicago Sun-Times*, 15 December 1983.

4. Vincent Canby, '*Christmas Story*, Indiana Tale', in *The New York Times*, 18 November 1983.

5. David C. Cook, *The Inspirational Christmas Almanac: Heartwarming Traditions, Trivia, Stories, and Recipes for the Holidays* (Colorado Springs: Honor Books, 2006), p.103.

6. Noel Murray, '*A Christmas Story*', in *The Onion A.V. Club*, 9 December 2003.
<http:// www.avclub.com/ articles/ a-christmas-story-dvd,11656/>

7. Brian W. Fairbanks, *I Saw That Movie, Too: Selected Film Reviews*, 2nd edn (Morrisville: Lulu.com, 2008), pp.84-85.

8. Diane Werts, *Christmas On Television* (Westport: Greenwood Press, 2006), pp.15-16.

9. Donato Totaro, 'Bob Clark', in *Guide to the Cinema(s) of Canada*, ed. by Peter Harry Rist (Westport: Greenwood Press, 2001), pp.38-39.

SANTA CLAUS: THE MOVIE (1985)

1. Jack Santino, *All Around the Year: Holidays and Celebrations in American Life* (Champaign: University of Illinois Press, 1994) [1985], pp.189-90.

2. Nathan Rabin, 'My Year of Flops: Case File #96: *Santa Claus: The Movie*', in *The Onion A.V. Club*, 25 December 2007.
<http:// www.avclub.com/ articles/ my-year-of-flops-case-file-96-santa-claus-the-movi,10128/>

3. Daniel Miller, *Consumption: Critical Concepts in the Social Sciences, Volume IV: Objects, Subjects and Mediations in Consumption* (London: Routledge, 2001), pp.324-25.

4. Jack Santino, *New Old-Fashioned Ways: Holidays and Popular Culture* (Knoxville: University of Tennessee Press, 1996), pp.143-44.

5. Mark Connelly, 'Santa Claus: The Movie', in *Christmas at the Movies*, ed. by Mark Connelly (London: I.B. Tauris, 2000), p.123.

6. Anon, 'Brief Movie Reviews: *Santa Claus: The Movie*', in *New York Magazine*, 16 December 1985.

7. Roger Ebert, '*Santa Claus: The Movie*', in *The Chicago Sun-Times*, 27 November 1985.

8. *Variety* Staff, '*Santa Claus: The Movie*', in *Variety*, 27 November 1985.

9. H. Paul Jeffers, *Legends of Santa Claus* (Minneapolis: Lerner Publishing Group, 2001), p.88-89.

10. Norman Short, '*Santa Claus: The Movie*', in *DVD Verdict*, 12 October 2000.
<http:// www.dvdverdict.com/ reviews/ santaclaus.php>

11. Anthony Nield, '*Santa Claus: The Movie*', in *DVD Times*, 16 November 2005.
<http:// homecinema.thedigitalfix.co.uk/ content.php?contentid=59246>

12. Budgetary data from the Internet Movie Database.
<http:// uk.imdb.com/ title/ tt0089961/ business>

13. Box-office data from BoxOfficeMojo.com.
<http:// www.boxofficemojo.com/ movies/ ?id=santaclausthemovie.htm>

SCROOGED (1988)

1. Thomas M. Leitch, *Film Adaptation and Its Discontents: From* Gone with the Wind *to* The Passion of the Christ (Baltimore: Johns Hopkins University Press, 2007), pp.84-86.

2. Fred Guida, *'A Christmas Carol' and Its Adaptations: A Critical Examination of Dickens' Story and Its Productions on Stage, Screen and Television* (Jefferson: McFarland, 2000), p.220.

3. James Chapman, 'God Bless Us, Every One: Movie Adaptations of *A Christmas Carol*', in *Christmas at the Movies: Images of Christmas in American, British and European Cinema*, ed. by Mark Connelly (London: I.B. Tauris, 2000), pp.29-30.

4. Murray Baumgarten, 'Bill Murray's Christmas Carols', in *Dickens on Screen*, ed. by John Glavin (Cambridge: Cambridge University Press, 2003), pp.61-63.

5. David Denby, 'Holiday Horror', in *New York Magazine*, 5 December 1988, p.178-80.

6. Vincent Canby, 'Bill Murray in *Scrooged*: Meanness's Outer Limits', in *The New York Times*, 23 November 1988.

7. Roger Ebert, '*Scrooged*', in *The Chicago Sun-Times*, 23 November 1998.

8. Jay Carr, '*Scrooged*', in *The Boston Globe*, 23 November 1988, p.21.

9. Gene Siskel, '*Scrooged*', in *The Chicago Tribune*, 25 November 1988.

10. Mick LaSalle, '*Scrooged*', in *The San Francisco Chronicle*, 23 November 1988.

11. Hal Hinson, '*Scrooged*', in *The Washington Post*, 23 November 1988.

12. *Variety* Staff, '*Scrooged*', in *Variety*, 25 November 1988.

13. Jeffrey M. Anderson, '*Scrooged*', in *Combustible Celluloid*, 10 December 2008. <http:// www.combustiblecelluloid.com/ archive/ scrooged.shtml>

14. Christopher Null, '*Scrooged*', in *FilmCritic.com*, 2 January 2006. <http:// www.filmcritic.com/ reviews/ 1988/ scrooged/ ?OpenDocument>

15. Gary Panton, '*Scrooged*', in *Movie Gazette*, 23 December 2003. <http:// www.movie-gazette.com/ 572>

NATIONAL LAMPOON'S CHRISTMAS VACATION (1989)

1. Roger Ebert, '*National Lampoon's Christmas Vacation*', in *The Chicago Sun-Times*, 1 December 1989.

2. Janet Maslin, 'On *Vacation* Once Again', in *The New York Times*, 1 December 1989.

3. Rita Kempley, '*National Lampoon's Christmas Vacation*', in *The Washington Post*, 1 December 1989.

4. *Variety* Staff, '*National Lampoon's Christmas Vacation*', in *Variety*, 1 December 1989.

5. Chris Hicks, '*National Lampoon's Christmas Vacation*', in *The Deseret News*, 16 December 2002.

6. Patrick Naugle, '*National Lampoon's Christmas Vacation*: Special Edition', in *DVD Verdict*, 16 October 2003. <http:// www.dvdverdict.com/ reviews/ christmasvacationse.php>

7. Daniel Stephens, '*National Lampoon's Christmas Vacation*', in *DVD Times*, 17 November 2003. <http:// www.dvdtimes.co.uk/ content.php?contentid=6068>

8. Ryan Arthur, '*National Lampoon's Christmas Vacation*', in *eFilmCritic.com*, 15 October 1998. <http:// efilmcritic.com/ review.php?movie=1116>

HOME ALONE (1990)

1. Hal Hinson, '*Home Alone*', in *The Washington Post*, 16 November 1990.

2. Monica Bohm-Duchen, *The Private Life of a Masterpiece* (Berkeley: University of California Press, 2001), p.151.

3. Budgetary and box-office data from the Internet Movie Database.

<http:// uk.imdb.com/ title/ tt0099785/ business>

4. Box-office data from BoxOfficeMojo.com.

<http:// www.boxofficemojo.com/ movies/ ?id=homealone.htm>

5. Rowana Agajanian, '"Peace on Earth, Goodwill to All Men": The Depiction of Christmas in Modern Hollywood Films', in *Christmas at the Movies: Images of Christmas in American, British and European Cinema*, ed. by Mark Connelly (London: I.B. Tauris, 2000), p.149.

6. Jeanne Cooper, '*Home Alone*', in *The Washington Post*, 16 November 1990.

7. Marc Savlov, '*Home Alone*', in *The Austin Chronicle*, 11 January 1991.

8. Roger Ebert, '*Home Alone*', in *The Chicago Sun-Times*, 16 November 1990.

9. David Packard, '*Home Alone: Family Fun Edition*', in *DVD Verdict*, 1 January 2007.

<http:// www.dvdverdict.com/ reviews/ homealonese.php>

See also: Michael Mackenzie, '*Home Alone*', in *DVD Times*, 25 December 2004.

<http:// homecinema.thedigitalfix.co.uk/ content.php?contentid=55627>

10. Chris Hicks, '*Home Alone*', in *The Deseret News*, 21 November 2000. For a contrasting view, consider: Owen Gleiberman, '*Home Alone*', in *Entertainment Weekly*, 25 July 2007.

11. Noel Murray, '*Home Alone*', in *The Onion A.V. Club*, 13 December 2006.

<http:// www.avclub.com/ articles/ home-alone,8044/>

12. Chris Jordan, *Movies and the Reagan Presidency: Success and Ethics* (Westport: Greenwood Publishing Group, 2003), pp.156-57.

THE MUPPET CHRISTMAS CAROL (1992)

1. Thomas M. Leitch, *Film Adaptation and Its Discontents: From* Gone With the Wind *to* The Passion of the Christ (Baltimore: Johns Hopkins University Press, 2007), pp.91-92.

2. Hugh H. Davis, 'A Weirdo, A Rat, and A Humbug: The Literary Qualities of *The Muppet Christmas Carol*', in *Studies in Popular Culture*, 21:3, 1999.

<http:// pcasacas.org/ SiPC/ 21.3/ hdavis.htm>

3. James Chapman, 'God Bless Us, Every One: Movie Adaptations of *A Christmas Carol*', in *Christmas at the Movies*, ed. by Mark Connelly (London: I.B. Tauris, 2000), pp.31-32.

4. Ginger Stelle, '"Starring Kermit the Frog as Bob Cratchit": Muppets as Actors', in *Kermit Culture: Critical Perspectives on Jim Henson's Muppets*, ed. by Jennifer C. Garlen and Anissa M. Graham (Jefferson: McFarland and Company, 2009), pp.94-101.

5. Roger Ebert, '*The Muppet Christmas Carol*', in *The Chicago Sun-Times*, 11 December 1992.

6. Desson Howe, '*The Muppet Christmas Carol*', in *The Washington Post*, 11 December 1992.

7. Janet Maslin, '*The Muppet Christmas Carol*: Kermit, Etc. Do Dickens Up Green', in *The New York Times*, 11 December 1992.

See also: *Variety* Staff, '*The Muppet Christmas Carol*', in *Variety*, 11 December 1992.

8. Jonathan Romney, '*The Muppet Christmas Carol*', in *The New Statesman*, December 1992-January 1993.

9. Jeffrey M. Anderson, '*The Muppet Christmas Carol*: Never Eat Singing Food', in *Combustible Celluloid*, 25 December 2005.

<http:// www.combustiblecelluloid.com/ classic/ muppchris.shtml>

10. Gary J.Svehla and Susan Svehla, *It's Christmas Time at the Movies* (Baltimore: Midnight Marquee Press, 1998).pp.197-99.

11. Christopher Null, '*The Muppet Christmas Carol*', in *FilmCritic.com*, 20 November 2005.

<http:// www.filmcritic.com/ reviews/ 1992/ the-muppet-christmas-carol/>

12. John J. Puccio, '*The Muppet Christmas Carol*: Kermit's 50th Anniversary Edition', in *DVD Town*, 30 November 2005.

<http:// www.dvdtown.com/ review/ muppet-christmas-carol/ dvd/ 3295/ 2>

THE NIGHTMARE BEFORE CHRISTMAS (1993)

1. Tim Burton speaks at length about the film's production in the following interview, which was conducted during the production of *The Nightmare Before Christmas*: Mimi Avins, 'Ghoul World', in *Tim Burton: Interviews*, ed. by Kristian Fraga (Jackson: University Press of Mississippi, 2005), pp.95-102.

2. The artistic merits of the film's stop-motion techniques are discussed in detail in the following book: Barry J.C. Purves, *Stop Motion: Passion, Process and Performance* (Oxford: Elsevier, 2008), p.299.

3. The skilful way that Burton strikes a contrast between the cultural values of Christmas Town and Halloween Town is explored by M. Keith Booker in the text below:

M. Keith Booker, D*isney, Pixar, and the Hidden Messages of Children's Films* (Santa Barbara: Praeger, 2010), pp.120-22.

4. Roger Ebert, 'Tim Burton's *The Nightmare Before Christmas*', in *The Chicago Sun-Times*, 22 October 1993.

5. Richard Harrington, '*The Nightmare Before Christmas*', in *The Washington Post*, 22 October 1993.

6. Todd McCarthy, '*The Nightmare Before Christmas*', in *Variety*, 7 October 1993.

7. Desson Howe, '*The Nightmare Before Christmas*', in *The Washington Post*, 22 October 1993.

8. Allan Neuwirth, *Makin' Toons: Inside the Most Popular Animated TV Shows and Movies* (New York: Allworth Press, 2003), pp.9-10.

9. Kristin Munson, '*The Nightmare Before Christmas*: Collector's Edition', in *DVD Verdict*, 26 August 2008. <http:// www.dvdverdict.com/ reviews/ nightmareb4ce.php>

10. Keith Phipps, '*The Nightmare Before Christmas*', in *The Onion A.V. Club*, 29 March 2002. <http:// www.avclub.com/ articles/ the-nightmare-before-christmas,20203/>

11. For an example of a contrary viewpoint to the film's general approval amongst commentators, see: Peter Bradshaw, 'Tim Burton's *The Nightmare Before Christmas 3D*', in *The Guardian*, 17 November 2006.

THE SANTA CLAUSE (1994)

1. The film's depiction of Santa Claus in the guise of a modern everyman is discussed by Mark Connelly, in relation to other films centring on the figure of Father Christmas, in: Mark Connelly, 'Santa Claus: The Movie', in *Christmas at the Movies*, ed. by Mark Connelly (London: I.B. Tauris, 2000), pp.116-17.

2. John Pasquin and Tim Allen discuss changes in the film's tone during its production process in the following book: Frank Thompson, *American Movie Classics' Great Christmas Movies* (Dallas: Taylor, 1998), pp.208-12.

3. The skilful marketing strategy which lay behind the cinematic release of *The Santa Clause* is discussed in: Frank Roost, 'Synergy City: How Times Square and Celebration Are Integrated Into Disney's Marketing Cycle', in *Rethinking Disney: Private Control, Public Dimensions*, ed. by Mike Budd and Max H. Kirsch (Middletown: Wesleyan University Press, 2005), pp.265-66.

4. Roger Ebert, '*The Santa Clause*', in *The Chicago Sun-Times*, 11 November 1994.

5. Leonard Klady, '*The Santa Clause*', in *Variety*, 10 November 1994.

6. Desson Howe, '*The Santa Clause*', in *The Washington Post*, 11 November 1994.

See also: Chris Hicks, '*The Santa Clause*', in *The Deseret News*, 16 December 2004.

7. Zachary Woodruff, 'The Santa Clause', in Tucson Weekly, 12 January 1995.
<http:// www.filmvault.com/ filmvault/ tw/ s/ santaclausethe.html>

8. Rita Kempley, 'The Santa Clause', in The Washington Post, 11 November 1994.

9. Hollis Chacona, 'The Santa Clause', in The Austin Chronicle, 18 November 1994.

10. John J. Puccio, 'The Santa Clause: Special Edition', in DVD Town, 7 December 2003.
<http:// www.dvdtown.com/ review/ Santa_Clause_The_Special_Editi/ 11496/ 1871/>

11. Jay Mechling, 'Rethinking (and Reteaching) the Civil Religion in Post-Nationalist American Studies', in Post-Nationalist American Studies, ed. by John Carlos Rowe (Berkeley: University of California Press, 2000), p.76.

ELF (2003)

1. Mark Sells, 'Elf', in The Oregon Herald, November 2003.
<http:// www.oregonherald.com/ reviews/ mark-sells/ reviews/ elf.html>

2. Mick LaSalle, 'Ferrell magical in sardonic, sweet Elf', in The San Francisco Chronicle, 7 November 2003.

3. Stephanie Zacharek, 'Elf', in Salon.com, 7 November 2003. <http:// www.salon.com/ entertainment/ movies/ review/ 2003/ 11/ 07/ elf/ index.html?CP=IMD&DN=110>

4. Ed Park, 'The Elfin Man Takes Manhattan, Faces the Wrath of Caan', in The Village Voice, 4 November 2003.

5. David Rooney, 'Elf', in Variety, 25 October 2003.

6. Peter Travers, 'Elf', in Rolling Stone, 7 November 2003.

7. Sam Adams, 'Little Big Man', in The Philadelphia City Paper, 6-12 November 2003. See also: Scott Tobias, 'Elf', in The Onion A.V. Club, 4 November 2003.
<http:// www.avclub.com/ articles/ elf,5362/>

8. Claudia Puig, 'Ferrell is a bit too cutesy for comfort in Elf', in USA Today, 7 November 2003.

9. Roger Ebert, 'Elf', in The Chicago Sun-Times, 7 November 2003.

10. Marjorie Baumgarten, 'Elf', in The Austin Chronicle, 7 November 2003.

BAD SANTA (2003)

1. Billy Bob Thornton talks at length about his approach to the character of Willie in the following interview: John Patterson, 'Black Christmas', in The Guardian, 29 October 2004.

2. Mike Clark, 'Bad is dreaming of a blight Christmas', in USA Today, 25 November 2003. See also: Roger Ebert, 'Bad Santa', in The Chicago Sun-Times, 26 November 2003.

3. Stephanie Zacharek, 'Bad Santa', in Salon.com, 26 November 2003.
<http:// www.salon.com/ entertainment/ movies/ review/ 2003/ 11/ 26/ bad_santa/ index.html?CP=IMD&DN=110>

4. Peter Travers, 'Bad Santa', in Rolling Stone, 20 November 2003.

5. C.W. Nevius, 'A not-so-jolly old elf with a dark past, holiday hangover', in The San Francisco Chronicle, 26 November 2003.

6. Dennis Harvey, 'Bad Santa', in Variety, 17 November 2003.

7. The merits of the director's cut of the film are discussed in: J. Hoberman, 'Bah, Humbug!: Bad Santa, as it was intended', in The Village Voice, 11 December 2007.

NOEL (2004)

1. Army Archerd, 'Chazz touts *Noel*'s good charms', in *Variety*, 17 December 2003.
2. Ed Gonzalez, '*Noel*', in *Slant Magazine*, 29 October 2004.
3. Roger Ebert, '*Noel*', in *The Chicago Sun-Times*, 12 November 2004.
4. Andrew Pulver, '*Noel*', in *The Guardian*, 25 November 2005.
5. Todd McCarthy, '*Noel*', in *Variety*, 19 September 2004.
6. Noel Murray, '*Noel*', in *The Onion A.V. Club*, 8 November 2004. <http:// www.avclub.com/ articles/ noel,4824/>
7. J.R. Jones, '*Noel*', in *The Chicago Reader*, 5 November 2005.
<http:// www.chicagoreader.com/ chicago/ noel/ Film?oid=1057506>

JOYEUX NOËL (2005)

1. Lisa Nesselson, 'Merry Christmas: *Joyeux Noël*', in *Variety*, 16 May 2005.
2. Andrew O'Hehir, 'Beyond the Multiplex', in *Salon.com*, 2 March 2006.
<http:// www.salon.com/ entertainment/ movies/ review/ 2006/ 03/ 02/ btm/ index2.html?CP=IMD&DN=110>
See also: Jessica Winter, '*Joyeux Noël (Merry Christmas)*', in *The Village Voice*, 21 February 2006.
3. Mick LaSalle, 'When troops called a truce for a day', in *The San Francisco Chronicle*, 10 March 2006.
4. Roger Ebert, '*Joyeux Noël*', in *The Chicago Sun-Times*, 10 March 2006.
5. Peter Bradshaw, '*Merry Christmas*', in *The Guardian*, 16 December 2005.
6. Nathan Rabin, '*Joyeux Noël*', in *The Onion A.V. Club*, 28 February 2006.
<http:// avclub.com/ articles/ joyeux-noel,4065/>
7. Marrit Ingman, '*Joyeux Noël*', in *The Austin Chronicle*, 31 March 2006.

A CHRISTMAS CAROL 3D (2009)

1. Roger Ebert, 'Disney's *A Christmas Carol*', in *The Chicago Sun-Times*, 5 November 2009.
2. Mary Elizabeth Williams, 'Disney's *A Christmas Carol*: Bah, humbug!', in *Salon.com*, 5 November 2009 <http:// www.salon.com/ entertainment/ movies/ review/ 2009/ 11/ 05/ christmas_carol/ index.html?CP=IMD&DN=110>
See also: Nick Schager, '*A Christmas Carol*', in *Slant Magazine*, 3 November 2009.
3. Amy Biancolli, 'Disney's *A Christmas Carol*', in *The San Francisco Chronicle*, 6 November 2009.
4. Claudia Puig, '*Christmas Carol* lost in 3-D interpretation', in *USA Today*, 6 November 2009. See also: Ella Taylor, 'Jim Carrey and Robert Zemeckis' Very CGI *Christmas Carol*', in *The Village Voice*, 3 November 2009.
5. Rene Rodriguez, 'Disney's *A Christmas Carol*', in *The Miami Herald*, 3 November 2009.
6. Marjorie Baumgarten, 'Disney's *A Christmas Carol*', in *The Austin Chronicle*, 6 November 2009.
See also: Matt Pais, 'Disney's *A Christmas Carol*', in *Chicago Metromix*, 5 November 2009.
<http:// chicago.metromix.com/ movies/ movie_review/ disneys-a-christmas-carol/ 1582551/ content>

CHRONOLOGICAL FILMOGRAPHY

1. THE BELLS OF ST MARY'S (1945)

Production Company: Rainbow Productions.
Distributor: RKO Radio Pictures.
Director: Leo McCarey.
Producer: Leo McCarey.
Screenplay: Dudley Nichols, from a story by Leo McCarey.
Original Score: Robert Emmett Dolan.
Director of Photography: George Barnes.
Film Editing: Harry Marker.
Art Direction: William Flannery.
Set Decoration: Darrell Silvera.
Costume Design: Edith Head.
Running Time: 126 minutes.
Main Cast: Bing Crosby (Father Chuck O'Malley), Ingrid Bergman (Sister Mary Benedict), Henry Travers (Horace P. Bogardus), William Gargan (Joe Gallagher), Ruth Donnelly (Sister Michael), Joan Carroll (Patricia 'Patsy' Gallagher), Martha Sleeper (Mary Gallagher), Rhys Williams (Dr McKay), Dickie Tyler (Eddie Breen), Una O'Connor (Mrs. Breen).

2. IT'S A WONDERFUL LIFE (1946)

Production Company: Liberty Pictures.
Distributor: RKO Radio Pictures.
Director: Frank Capra.
Producer: Frank Capra.
Screenplay: Frances Goodrich, Albert Hackett and Frank Capra, with additional scenes by Jo Swerling, from a story by Philip Van Doren Stern.
Original Score: Dimitri Tiomkin.

Director of Photography: Joseph Biroc and Joseph Walker.
Film Editing: William Hornbeck.
Art Direction: Jack Okey.
Set Decoration: Emile Kuri.
Costume Design: Edward Stevenson.
Running Time: 130 minutes.
Main Cast: James Stewart (George Bailey), Donna Reed (Mary Hatch), Lionel Barrymore (Mr Potter), Thomas Mitchell (Uncle Billy), Henry Travers (Clarence), Beulah Bondi (Mrs Bailey), Frank Faylen (Ernie), Ward Bond (Bert), Gloria Grahame (Violet), H.B. Warner (Mr Gower), Frank Albertson (Sam Wainwright), Todd Karns (Harry Bailey), Samuel S. Hinds (Pa Bailey), Mary Treen (Cousin Tilly), Virginia Patton (Ruth Dakin), Charles Williams (Cousin Eustace), Sara Edwards (Mrs Hatch), Bill Edmunds (Mr Martini), Lillian Randolph (Annie), Argentina Brunetti (Mrs Martini), Bobbie Anderson (Little George), Ronnie Ralph (Little Sam), Jean Gale (Little Mary), Jeanine Ann Roose (Little Violet), Danny Mummert (Little Marty Hatch), Georgie Nokes (Little Harry Bailey), Sheldon Leonard (Nick), Frank Hagney (Potter's Bodyguard), Ray Walker (Joe from the Luggage Shop), Charlie Lane (Real Estate Salesman), Edward Kean (Tom from the Building and Loan), Carol Coomes (Janie Bailey), Karolyn Grimes (Zuzu Bailey), Larry Simms (Pete Bailey), Jimmy Hawkins (Tommy Bailey).

3. MIRACLE ON 34TH STREET (1947)

Production Company: Twentieth Century-Fox Film Corporation.
Distributor: Twentieth Century-Fox Film Corporation.
Director: George Seaton.
Producer: William Perlberg.
Screenplay: George Seaton, from a story by Valentine Davies.
Original Score: Cyril Mockridge.
Director of Photography: Lloyd Ahern and Charles Clarke.
Film Editing: Robert Simpson.
Art Direction: Richard Day and Richard Irvine.
Set Decoration: Ernest Lansing and Thomas Little.
Costume Design: Kay Nelson.
Running Time: 96 minutes.
Main Cast: Maureen O'Hara (Doris Walker), John Payne (Fred Gailey), Edmund Gwenn (Kris Kringle), Gene Lockhart (Judge Henry X. Harper), Natalie Wood (Susan Walker), Porter Hall (Granville Sawyer), William Frawley (Charlie Halloran), Jerome Cowan (District Attorney Thomas Mara), Philip Tonge (Julian Shellhammer).

4. THE BISHOP'S WIFE (1947)

Production Company: The Samuel Goldwyn Company.
Distributor: RKO Radio Pictures.
Director: Henry Koster.
Producer: Samuel Goldwyn.
Screenplay: Leonardo Bercovici and Robert E. Sherwood, from the novel by Robert Nathan.
Original Score: Hugo Friedhofer, Emil Newman and Herbert W. Spencer.

Cinematography: Gregg Toland.
Film Editing: Monica Collingwood.
Art Direction: Perry Ferguson and George Jenkins.
Set Decoration: Julia Heron.
Costume Design: Irene Sharaff.
Running Time: 109 minutes.
Main Cast: Cary Grant (Dudley), Loretta Young (Julia Brougham), David Niven (Bishop Henry Brougham), Monty Woolley (Professor Wutheridge), James Gleason (Sylvester), Gladys Cooper (Mrs Hamilton), Elsa Lanchester (Matilda), Sara Haden (Mildred Cassaway), Karolyn Grimes (Debby Brougham), Tito Vuolo (Mr Maggenti), Regis Toomey (Mr Miller), Sarah Edwards (Mrs Duffy), Margaret McWade (Miss Trumbull), Anne O'Neal (Mrs Ward), Ben Erway (Mr Perry), Erville Alderson (Stevens), Bobby Anderson (Defense Captain), Teddy Infuhr (Attack Captain), Eugene Borden (Michel).

5. SCROOGE: A CHRISTMAS CAROL (1951)

Production Company: George Minter Productions.
Distributor: Renown Pictures Corporation/ United Artists.
Director: Brian Desmond Hurst.
Producer: Brian Desmond Hurst.
Associate Producer: Stanley Haynes.
Screenplay: Noel Langley, from the novella by Charles Dickens.
Original Score: Richard Addinsell.
Cinematography: C. Pennington-Richards.
Film Editing: Clive Donner.
Art Direction: Ralph Brinton.
Costume Design: Constance Da Finna and Doris Lee.
Casting Director: Maude Spector.
Running Time: 86 minutes.
Main Cast: Alastair Sim (Ebenezer Scrooge), Kathleen Harrison (Mrs Dilber), Mervyn Johns (Bob Cratchit), Hermione Baddeley (Mrs Cratchit), Michael Hordern (Jacob Marley/ Marley's Ghost), George Cole (Young Ebenezer Scrooge), John Charlesworth (Peter Cratchit), Francis de Wolff (Spirit of Christmas Present), Rona Anderson (Alice), Carol Marsh (Fan Scrooge), Brian Worth (Fred), Miles Malleson (Old Joe), Ernest Thesiger (The Undertaker), Glyn Dearman (Tiny Tim), Michael Dolan (Spirit of Christmas Past), Olga Edwardes (Fred's Wife), Roddy Hughes (Fezziwig), Hattie Jacques (Mrs. Fezziwig), Eleanor Summerfield (Miss Flora), Louise Hampton (Laundress), C. Konarski (Spirit of Christmas Yet to Come), Eliot Makeham (Mr Snedrig), Peter Bull (First Businessman/ Narrator), Douglas Muir (Second Businessman), Noel Howlett (First Collector), Fred Johnson (Second Collector), Henry Hewitt (Mr Rosehed), Hugh Dempster (Mr Groper), Maire O'Neill (Alice's Patient), Richard Pearson (Mr Tupper), Patrick MacNee (Young Jacob Marley), Clifford Mollison (Samuel Wilkins), Jack Warner (Mr Jorkin).

6. WHITE CHRISTMAS (1954)

Production Company: Paramount Pictures.
Distributor: Paramount Pictures.
Director: Michael Curtiz.
Producer: Robert Emmett Dolan.
Screenplay: Norman Krasna, Norman Panama and Melvin Frank.
Lyrics and Music: Irving Berlin.
Cinematography: Loyal Griggs.
Film Editing: Frank Bracht.
Art Direction: Roland Anderson and Hal Pereira.
Set Decoration: Sam Comer and Grace Gregory.
Costume Design: Edith Head.
Casting Director: Maude Spector.
Running Time: 120 minutes.
Main Cast: Bing Crosby (Bob Wallace), Danny Kaye (Phil Davis), Rosemary Clooney (Betty Haynes), Vera Ellen (Judy Haynes), Dean Jagger (Major General Thomas F. Waverly), Mary Wickes (Emma Allen), John Brascia (John), Anne Whitfield (Susan Waverly).

7. WE'RE NO ANGELS (1955)

Production Company: Paramount Pictures.
Distributor: Paramount Pictures.
Director: Michael Curtiz.
Producer: Pat Duggan.
Screenplay: Ranald MacDougall, from the play *La Cuisine de Anges* by Albert Husson.
Original Music: Frederick Hollander.
Cinematography: Loyal Griggs.
Film Editing: Arthur Schmidt.
Art Direction: Roland Anderson and Hal Pereira.
Set Decoration: Sam Comer and Grace Gregory.
Costume Design: Mary Grant.
Running Time: 106 minutes.
Main Cast: Humphrey Bogart (Joseph), Aldo Ray (Albert), Peter Ustinov (Jules), Joan Bennett (Amelie Ducotel), Basil Rathbone (Andre Trochard), Leo G. Carroll (Felix Ducotel), John Baer (Paul Trochard), Gloria Talbott (Isabelle Ducotel), Lea Penman (Madame Parole), John Smith (Medical Officer Arnaud).

8. THE APARTMENT (1960)

Production Company: The Mirisch Corporation.
Distributor: United Artists.
Director: Billy Wilder.
Producer: Billy Wilder.
Associate Producers: Doane Harrison and I.A.L. Diamond.
Screenplay: Billy Wilder and I.A.L. Diamond.
Original Music: Adolph Deutsch.

Cinematography: Joseph LaShelle.
Film Editing: Daniel Mandell.
Art Direction: Alexander Trauner.
Set Decoration: Edward G. Boyle.
Running Time: 125 minutes.
Main Cast: Jack Lemmon (C.C. 'Bud' Baxter), Shirley MacLaine (Fran Kubelik), Fred MacMurray (Jeff D. Sheldrake), Ray Walston (Joe Dobisch), Jack Kruschen (Dr Dreyfuss), David Lewis (Al Kirkeby), Hope Holiday (Mrs Margie MacDougall), Joan Shawlee (Sylvia), Naomi Stevens (Mrs Mildred Dreyfuss), Johnny Seven (Karl Matuschka), Joyce Jameson (The Blonde), Willard Waterman (Mr Vanderhoff), David White (Mr Eichelberger), Edie Adams (Miss Olsen).

9. SANTA CLAUS CONQUERS THE MARTIANS (1964)

Production Company: Jalor Productions.
Distributor: Embassy Pictures Corporation.
Director: Nicholas Webster.
Producer: Paul L. Jacobson.
Associate Producer: Arnold Leeds.
Executive Producer: Joseph E. Levine.
Screenplay: Glenville Mareth, based on a story by Paul L. Jacobson.
Original Music: Milton DeLugg.
Director of Photography: David L. Quaid.
Film Editing: Bill Henry.
Art Direction: Maurice Gordon.
Set Decoration: John K. Wright III.
Costume Design: Ramsey Mostoller.
Running Time: 81 minutes.
Main Cast: John Call (Santa Claus), Leonard Hicks (Kimar), Vincent Beck (Voldar), Bill McCutcheon (Dropo), Victor Stiles (Billy), Donna Conforti (Betty), Chris Month (Bomar), Pia Zadora (Girmar), Leila Martin (Momar), Charles Renn (Hargo), James Cahill (Rigna), Ned Wertimer (Andy Henderson), Doris Rich (Mrs Claus), Carl Don (Chochem/ Von Green), Ivor Bodin (Winky), Al Nesor (Stobo), Joe Elic (Shim), Jim Bishop (Lomas), Lin Thurmond (Children's TV Announcer), Don Blair (TV News Announcer), Tony Ross (Santa's Helper), Scott Aronesty (Santa's Helper), Ronnie Rotholz (Santa's Helper), Glenn Schaffer (Santa's Helper).

10. SCROOGE (1970)

Production Company: Waterbury Films/ Cinema Center Films.
Distributor: Twentieth Century Fox Film Company/ National General Pictures.
Director: Ronald Neame.
Producer: Robert H. Solo.
Associate Producer: David W. Orton.
Executive Producer: Leslie Bricusse.
Screenplay: Leslie Bricusse, based on a story by Charles Dickens.
Original Music: Leslie Bricusse.
Cinematography: Oswald Morris.

Film Editing: Peter Weatherley.
Art Direction: Bob Cartwright.
Production Design: Terry Marsh.
Costume Design: Margaret Furse.
Running Time: 113 minutes.
Main Cast: Albert Finney (Ebenezer Scrooge), Alec Guinness (Ghost of Jacob Marley), Edith Evans (Ghost of Christmas Past), Kenneth More (Ghost of Christmas Present), Paddy Stone (Ghost of Christmas Yet to Come), David Collings (Bob Cratchit), Frances Cuka (Ethel Cratchit), Richard Beaumont (Tiny Tim), Karen Scargill (Kathy Cratchit), Michael Medwin (Harry, Scrooge's Nephew), Mary Peach (Harry's Wife), Gordon Jackson (Tom, Harry's Friend), Laurence Naismith (Mr Fezziwig), Kay Walsh (Mrs Fezziwig), Suzanne Neve (Isabel Fezziwig), Anton Rodgers (Tom Jenkins), Geoffrey Bayldon (Pringle, the Toyshop Owner), Reg Lever (Punch and Judy Man), Keith March (Well Wisher), Marianne Stone (Party Guest), Derek Francis (Charity Collector #1), Roy Kinnear (Charity Collector #2), Molly Weir (Debtor #1), Helena Gloag (Debtor #2), Nicholas Locise (Goose Boy), Peter Lock (Urchin #1), Clive Moss (Urchin #2).

11. BLACK CHRISTMAS (1974)

Production Company: Film Funding/ Vision IV.
Distributor: Warner Brothers Pictures/ EMI Distribution.
Director: Bob Clark.
Producer: Bob Clark.
Co-Producer: Gerry Arbeid.
Associate Producer: Richard Schouten.
Executive Producer: Findlay Quinn.
Screenplay: Roy Moore.
Original Music: Carl Zittrer.
Director of Photography: Reg Morris.
Film Editing: Stan Cole.
Art Direction: Karen Bromley.
Running Time: 98 minutes.
Main Cast: Olivia Hussey (Jess), Keir Dullea (Peter), Margot Kidder (Barb), John Saxon (Lieutenant Fuller), Marian Waldman (Mrs Mac), Andrea Martin (Phyl), James Edmond (Mr Harrison), Douglas McGrath (Sergeant Nash), Art Hindle (Chris), Lynne Griffin (Clare), Michael Rapport (Patrick), Les Carlson (Bill Graham), Martha Gibson (Mrs Quaife), John Rutter (Laughing Detective), Robert Warner (Doctor), Syd Brown (Farmer), Jack Van Evera (Search Party), Les Rubie (Search Party), Marcia Diamond (Woman), Pam Barney (Jean), Robert Hawkins (Wes), Dave Clement (Cogan), Julian Reed (Jennings), Dave Mann (Cop), John Stoneham (Cop), Danny Gain (Cop), Tom Foreman (Cop).

12. TRADING PLACES (1983)

Production Company: Paramount Pictures/ Cinema Group Ventures.
Distributor: Paramount Pictures.
Director: John Landis.
Producer: Aaron Russo.

Associate Producers: Irwin Russo and Sam Williams.
Executive Producer: George Folsey Jr.
Screenplay: Timothy Harris and Herschel Weingrod.
Original Music: Elmer Bernstein.
Director of Photography: Robert Paynter.
Film Editing: Malcolm Campbell.
Casting: Bonnie Timmermann.
Production Design: Gene Rudolf.
Set Decoration: George DeTitta and George DeTitta Jr.
Costume Design: Deborah Nadoolman.
Running Time: 118 minutes.
Main Cast: Dan Aykroyd (Louis Winthorpe III), Eddie Murphy (Billy Ray Valentine), Jamie Lee Curtis (Ophelia), Denholm Elliott (Coleman), Ralph Bellamy (Randolph Duke), Don Ameche (Mortimer Duke), Kristin Holby (Penelope Witherspoon), Paul Gleason (Clarence Beeks), Avon Long (Ezra), Tom Mardirosian (Officer Pantuzzi), Charles Brown (Officer Reynolds), Robert Curtis-Brown (Todd), Nicholas Guest (Harry), John Bedford-Lloyd (Andrew), Tony Sherer (Philip), Clint Smith (Doo Rag Lenny), Gwyllum Evans (President of Heritage Club), Jacques Sandulescu (Creepy Man), W.B. Brydon (Bank Manager), Kelly Curtis (Muffy), Tracy K. Shaffer (Constance), Susan Fallender (Bunny), Alfred Drake (President of Exchange), Lucianne Buchanan (President's Mistress), Jimmy Raitt (Ophelia's Client), James Belushi (Harvey), Deborah Reagan (Harvey's Girlfriend), Al Franken (Baggage Handler #1), Tom Davis (Baggage Handler #2), Don McLeod (Gorilla), Richard Hunt (Wilson), Maurice D. Copeland (Secretary of Agriculture), Shelly Chee Chee Hall (Monica), Donna Palmer (Gladys), Barry Dennen (Demitri).

13. A CHRISTMAS STORY (1983)

Production Company: Metro-Goldwyn-Mayer/ Christmas Tree Films.
Distributor: MGM/ UA Entertainment Company.
Director: Bob Clark.
Producers: Bob Clark and René Dupont.
Associate Producer: Gary Goch.
Screenplay: Jean Shepherd, Leigh Brown and Bob Clark, from Jean Shepherd's novel *In God We Trust, All Others Pay Cash*.
Original Music: Paul Zaza and Carl Zittrer.
Cinematography: Reginald H. Morris.
Film Editing: Stan Cole.
Casting: Jane Feinberg, Mike Fenton, Karen Hazzard and Marci Liroff.
Production Design: Reuben Freed.
Art Direction: Gavin Mitchell.
Set Decoration: Mark S. Freeborn.
Costume Design: Mary E. McLeod.
Running Time: 94 minutes.
Main Cast: Melinda Dillon (Mrs Parker), Darren McGavin (The Old Man/ Mr Parker), Peter Billingsley (Ralphie Parker), Ian Petrella (Randy Parker), Scott Schwartz (Flick), R.D. Robb (Schwartz), Tedde Moore (Miss Shields), Yano Anaya (Grover Dill), Zack Ward (Scut Farkus), Jeff Gillen (Santa Claus), Les Carlson (Tree Man), Jim Hunter (Freight Man), Patty Johnson (Head Elf), Drew Hocevar (Male Elf), David Svoboda (Goggles), Dwayne McLean

(Black Bart), Helen E. Kaider (Wicked Witch), John Wong (Chop Suey Palace Owner), Johan Sebastian Wong (Waiter #1), Fred Lee (Waiter #2), Dan Ma (Waiter #3), Rocco Bellusci (Street Kid), Tommy Wallace (Boy in School), Jean Shepherd (Narrator/ Adult Ralphie/ Man Waiting in Line for Santa/ Santa Claus).

14. SANTA CLAUS: THE MOVIE (1985)

Production Company: TriStar Pictures/ Calash Corporation/ GGG/ Santa Claus Ltd.
Distributor: TriStar Pictures.
Director: Jeannot Szwarc.
Producers: Ilya Salkind and Pierre Spengler.
Associate Producer: Robert Simmonds.
Screenplay: David Newman, from a story by Leslie Newman and David Newman.
Original Music: Henry Mancini.
Cinematography: Arthur Ibbetson.
Film Editing: Peter Hollywood.
Casting: Lynn Stalmaster.
Production Design: Anthony Pratt.
Supervising Art Director: Tim Hutchinson.
Art Direction: Don Dossett, John Hoesli and Malcolm Stone.
Set Decoration: Stephanie McMillan.
Costume Design: Bob Ringwood.
Running Time: 107 minutes.
Main Cast: Dudley Moore (Patch), John Lithgow (B.Z.), David Huddleston (Santa Claus), Burgess Meredith (Ancient Elf), Judy Cornwell (Anya Claus), Jeffrey Kramer (Dr Eric Towzer), Christian Fitzpatrick (Joe), Carrie Kei Heim (Cornelia), John Barrard (Dooley), Anthony O'Donnell (Puffy), Melvyn Hayes (Goober), Don Estelle (Groot), Tim Stern (Boog), Peter O'Farrell (Honka), Christopher Ryan (Vout), Dickie Arnold (Goobler), Aimée Delamain (Storyteller), Dorothea Phillips (Miss Tucker), John Hallam (Grizzard), Judith Morse (Miss Abruzzi), Jerry Harte (Senate Chairman), Paul Aspland (Reporter #1), Sally Cranfield (Reporter #2), Michael Drew (Reporter #3), John Cassady (Wino), Ronald Fernee (Policeman #1), Michael Ross (Policeman #2), Walter Goodman (Street Corner Santa).

15. SCROOGED (1988)

Production Company: Paramount Pictures/ Mirage Productions.
Distributor: Paramount Pictures.
Director: Richard Donner.
Producers: Richard Donner and Art Linson.
Co-Producer: Ray Hartwick.
Associate Producer: Jennie Lew Tugend.
Executive Producer: Steve Roth.
Screenplay: Mitch Glazer and Michael O'Donoghue.
Original Music: Danny Elfman.
Cinematography: Michael Chapman.
Film Editing: Fredric Steinkamp and William Steinkamp.
Casting: David Rubin.

Production Design: J. Michael Riva.
Art Direction: Virginia L. Randolph.
Set Decoration: Linda DeScenna.
Costume Design: Wayne Finkelman.
Running Time: 101 minutes.
Main Cast: Bill Murray (Frank Cross), Karen Allen (Claire Phillips), John Forsythe (Lew Hayward), John Glover (Brice Cummings), Bobcat Goldthwait (Eliot Loudermilk), David Johansen (Ghost of Christmas Past), Carol Kane (Ghost of Christmas Present), Robert Mitchum (Preston Rhinelander), Nicholas Phillips (Calvin Cooley), Michael J. Pollard (Herman), Alfre Woodard (Grace Cooley), Mabel King (Gramma), John Murray (James Cross), Jamie Farr (Jacob Marley), Robert Goulet (Himself), Buddy Hackett (Scrooge), John Houseman (Himself), Lee Majors (Himself), Pat McCormick (TV Ghost of Christmas Past), Brian Doyle Murray (Earl Cross), Mary Lou Retton (Herself), Al 'Red Dog' Weber (Santa Claus), Jean Speegle Howard (Mrs Claus), June Chandler (June Cleaver), Michael Eidam (Wally Cleaver), Mary Ellen Trainor (Ted), Bruce Jarchow (Wayne), Sanford Jensen (IBC Executive #1), Jeffrey Joseph (IBC Executive #2), Dick Blasucci (IBC Executive #3), Peter Bromilow (Archbishop), Damon Hines (Steven Cooley), Tamika McCollum (Shasta Cooley), Koren McCollum (Randee Cooley), Reina King (Lanell Cooley), Paul Tuerpé (Stage Manager), Lester Wilson (Choreographer), Ron Strang (Art Director), Kate McGregor-Stewart (Lady Censor), Ralph Gervais (Mouse Wrangler), Lisa Mende (Doris Cross), Ryan Todd (Frank as a Child), Rebeca Arthur (Tina), Roy Brocksmith (Mike the Mailman), Stella Hall (Lew Hayward's Secretary), Sachi Parker (Belle), Delores Hall (Hazel), Wendie Malick (Wendie Cross), Chaz Conner Jr (TV Ghost of Christmas Future), Maria Riva (Mrs Rhinelander), Michael O'Donoghue (Priest), Winfred Tennison (Marvin).

16. NATIONAL LAMPOON'S CHRISTMAS VACATION (1989)

Production Company: Hughes Entertainment/ Warner Brothers.
Distributor: Warner Brothers.
Director: Jeremiah Chechik.
Producers: John Hughes and Tom Jacobson.
Associate Producers: William S. Beasley, Mauri Syd Gayton and Ramey E. Ward.
Executive Producer: Matty Simmons.
Screenplay: John Hughes.
Film Editor: Jerry Greenberg and Michael Stevenson.
Director of Photography: Thomas Ackerman.
Unit Production Manager: William S. Beasley.
Original Score: Angelo Badalamenti.
Production Design: Stephen Marsh.
Casting: Risa Bramon, Billy Hopkins and Heidi Levitt.
Art Direction: Beala B. Neel.
Set Decoration: Lisa Fischer.
Costume Design: Michael Kaplan.
Running Time: 97 minutes.
Main Cast: Chevy Chase (Clark Griswold), Beverly D'Angelo (Ellen Griswold), Juliette Lewis (Audrey Griswold), Johnny Galecki (Russell 'Rusty' Griswold), John Randolph (Clark Wilhelm Griswold Sr), Diane Ladd (Nora Griswold), E.G. Marshall (Art Smith), Doris Roberts (Frances Smith), Randy Quaid (Cousin Eddie Johnson), Miriam Flynn (Cousin Catherine Johnson), Cody Burger (Cousin Rocky Johnson), Ellen Hamilton Latzen (Cousin

Ruby Sue Johnson), William Hickey (Uncle Lewis), Mae Questel (Aunt Bethany), Sam McMurray (Bill), Nicholas Guest (Todd Chester), Julia Louis-Dreyfus (Margo Chester), Nicolette Scorsese (Mary), Keith MacKechnie (Delivery Boy), Brian Doyle Murray (Frank Shirley), Natalia Nogulich (Helen Shirley), Michael Kaufman (Young Executive).

17. HOME ALONE (1990)

Production Company: Hughes Entertainment/ Twentieth Century Fox Film Corporation.
Distributor: Twentieth Century Fox Film Corporation.
Director: Chris Columbus.
Producer: John Hughes.
Associate Producer: Mark Radcliffe.
Executive Producers: Tarquin Gotch, Mark Levinson and Scott M. Rosenfelt.
Screenplay: John Hughes.
Cinematography: Julio Macat.
Film Editing: Raja Gosnell.
Original Score: John Williams.
Production Design: John Muto.
Casting: Janet Hirshenson and Jane Jenkins.
Art Direction: Dan Webster.
Set Decoration: Eve Cauley and Dan Clancy.
Costume Design: Jay Hurley.
Running Time: 103 minutes.
Main Cast: Macaulay Culkin (Kevin McCallister), Joe Pesci (Harry Lyme), Daniel Stern (Marv Merchants), John Heard (Peter McCallister), Roberts Blossom (Marley), Catherine O'Hara (Kate McCallister), Angela Goethals (Linnie), Devin Ratray (Buzz), Gerry Bamman (Uncle Frank), Hillary Wolf (Megan), John Candy (Gus Polinski), Larry Hankin (Officer Balzak), Michael C. Maronna (Jeff), Kristin Minter (Heather), Daiana Campeanu (Sondra), Jedidiah Cohen (Rod), Kieran Culkin (Fuller), Senta Moses (Tracy), Anna Slotky (Brooke), Terrie Snell (Aunt Leslie), Jeffrey Wiseman (Mitch Murphy), Virginia Smith (Georgette), Matt Doherty (Steffan), Ralph Foody (Johnny/ Gangster #1), Michael Guido (Snakes/ Gangster #2), Ray Toler (Uncle Rob), Billie Bird (Woman in Airport), Bill Erwin (Man in Airport), Gerry Becker (Officer #1), Victor Cole (Officer #2), Porscha Radcliffe (Cousin), Brittany Radcliffe (Cousin), Clarke Devereux (Officer Devereux), Dan Charles Zukoski (Pizza Boy), Lynn Mansbach (French Woman), Peter Siragusa (Lineman), Alan Wilder (Scranton Ticket Agent), Hope Davis (French Ticket Agent), Dianne B. Shaw (Airline Counter Person), Tracy J. Connor (Check Out Girl), Jim Ryan (Stock Boy), Ken Hudson Campbell (Santa), Sandra Macat (Santa's Elf).

18. THE MUPPET CHRISTMAS CAROL (1992)

Production Company: Jim Henson Productions/ The Jim Henson Company/ Walt Disney Pictures.
Distributor: Buena Vista Pictures.
Director: Brian Henson.
Producers: Brian Henson and Martin G. Baker.
Co-Producer: Jerry Juhl.
Line Producer: David Barron.

Executive Producer: Frank Oz.
Screenplay: Jerry Juhl, from the novella by Charles Dickens.
Director of Photography: John Fenner.
Film Editing: Michael Jablow.
Original Score: Miles Goodman.
Music and Lyrics: Paul Williams.
Production Design: Val Strazovec.
Casting: Mike Fenton, Gilly Poole and Suzanne Crowley.
Art Direction: Dennis Bosher.
Supervising Art Director: Alan Cassie.
Set Decoration: Michael Ford.
Costume Design: Ann Hollowood and Polly Smith.
Running Time: 85 minutes.
Main Cast: Michael Caine (Ebenezer Scrooge), Dave Goelz (The Great Gonzo as Charles Dickens/ Waldorf as Robert Marley/ Dr Bunsen Honeydew as Charity Collector #1/ Bettina Cratchit/ Rat/ Voice of Zoot), Steve Whitmire (Kermit the Frog as Bob Cratchit/ Rizzo the Rat/ Beaker as Charity Collector #2/ Bean Bunny/ Belinda Cratchit/ Beetle/ Sprocket the Dog), Frank Oz (Miss Piggy as Emily Cratchit/ Fozzie Bear as Fozziewig/ Sam the Eagle as Headmaster of Junior High School Graduates/ Animal/ George the Janitor), Louise Gold (Mrs Dilber/ Spider), Jerry Nelson (Statler as Jacob Marley/ Ma Bear/ Lew Zealand/ Mouse/ Penguin/ Mr Applegate/ Pig Gentleman/ Pops), David Rudman (Peter Cratchit/ Swedish Chef), Steven Mackintosh (Fred, Scrooge's Nephew), Robin Weaver (Clara), Meredith Braun (Belle), Kristopher Milnes (Young Scrooge), Russell Martin (Young Scrooge), Raymond Coulthard (Young Scrooge), Edward Sanders (Young Scrooge), Theo Sanders (Young Scrooge), Anthony Hamblin (Boy #1), Fergus Brazier (Boy #2), Jessica Fox (Voice of Ghost of Christmas Past), Karen Prell (Ghost of Christmas Past (Muppet Performer)/ Voice of Additional Muppets), Robert Tygner (Ghost of Christmas Yet to Come (Muppet Performer)/ Ghost of Christmas Past (Muppet Performer)/ Turkey), William Todd Jones (Ghost of Christmas Past/ Additional Muppets), Donald Austen (Ghost of Christmas Present (Muppet Performer)/ Ghost of Christmas Yet to Come (Muppet Performer)), Mike Quinn (Pig Gentleman/ Voice of Undertaker), David Shaw Parker (Voice of Old Joe), Marcus Clarke (Voice of Puppeteer), David Barclay (Additional Muppet Performer), Robbie Barnett (Additional Muppet Performer), Sue Dacre (Additional Muppet Performer), Geoff Felix (Additional Muppet Performer), Nigel Plaskitt (Additional Muppet Performer), Simon Williamson (Additional Muppet Performer), Tim Rose (Additional Muppet Performer).

19. THE NIGHTMARE BEFORE CHRISTMAS (1993)

Production Company: Touchstone Pictures/ Skellington Productions Inc.
Distributor: Buena Vista Pictures.
Director: Henry Selick.
Producers: Tim Burton and Denise Di Novi.
Co-Producer: Kathleen Gavin.
Associate Producers: Danny Elfman, Jill Jacobs, Diane Minter and Philip Lofaro.
Screenplay: Caroline Thompson, based on a story and characters by Tim Burton.
Director of Photography: Pete Kozachik.
Film Editing: Stan Webb.
Original Score: Danny Elfman.

Production Manager: Philip Lofaro.
Casting: Mary Gail Artz and Barbara Cohen.
Art Direction: Deane Taylor.
Running Time: 76 minutes.
Main Cast: Chris Sarandon (Voice of Jack Skellington), Danny Elfman (Singing Voice of Jack Skellington/ Voice of Barrel/ Voice of Clown with the Tear Away Face), Catherine O'Hara (Voice of Sally/ Voice of Shock), William Hickey (Voice of Dr Finklestein), Glenn Shadix (Voice of Mayor), Paul Reubens (Voice of Lock), Ken Page (Voice of Oogie Boogie), Ed Ivory (Voice of Santa), Susan McBride (Voice of Big Witch/ Voice of WWD), Debi Durst (Voice of Corpse Kid/ Voice of Corpse Mom/ Voice of Small Witch), Gregory Proops (Voice of Harlequin Demon/ Voice of Devil/ Voice of Sax Player), Kerry Katz (Voice of Man Under Stairs/ Voice of Vampire/ Voice of Corpse Dad), Randy Crenshaw (Voice of Mr Hyde/ Voice of Behemoth/ Voice of Vampire), Sherwood Ball (Voice of Mummy/ Voice of Vampire), Carmen Twillie (Voice of Undersea Gal/ Voice of Man Under the Stairs), Glenn Walters (Voice of Wolfman), Mia Brown (Additional Voice), L. Peter Callender (Additional Voice), Ann Fraser (Additional Voice), Jennifer Levey (Additional Voice), Jesse McClurg (Additional Voice), John Morris (Additional Voice), Robert Olague (Additional Voice), Bobbi Page (Additional Voice), Elena Praskin (Additional Voice), Trampas Warman (Additional Voice), Judi Durand (Additional Voice), Doris Hess (Additional Voice), Daamen Krall (Additional Voice), Christina MacGregor (Additional Voice), David McCharen (Additional Voice), Gary Raff (Additional Voice), David J. Randolph (Additional Voice), Gary Schwartz (Additional Voice).

20. THE SANTA CLAUSE (1994)

Production Company: Walt Disney Pictures/ Outlaw Productions/ Hollywood Pictures.
Distributor: Buena Vista Pictures.
Director: John Pasquin.
Producers: Brian Reilly, Robert Newmyer and Jeffrey Silver.
Co-Producers: Caroline Baron and William W. Wilson III.
Associate Producers: Jennifer Billings and Susan E. Novick.
Executive Producers: Richard Baker, Rick Messina and James Miller.
Screenplay: Leo Benvenuti and Steve Rudnick.
Cinematography: Walt Lloyd.
Film Editing: Larry Bock.
Original Score: Michael Convertino.
Production Design: Carol Spier.
Casting: Renée Rousselot.
Art Direction: James McAteer.
Set Decoration: Elinor Rose Galbraith.
Costume Design: Carol Ramsey.
Running Time: 97 minutes.
Main Cast: Tim Allen (Scott Calvin/ Santa Claus), Judge Reinhold (Dr Neil Miller), Wendy Crewson (Laura Calvin Miller), Eric Lloyd (Charlie Calvin), David Krumholtz (Bernard the Elf), Larry Brandenburg (Detective Nunzio), Mary Gross (Miss Daniels), Paige Tamada (Judy the Elf), Peter Boyle (Mr Whittle), Judith Scott (Susan Perry), Jayne Eastwood (Judy the Waitress), Melissa King (Sarah the Little Girl), Bradley Wentworth (Elf at North Pole), Azura Bates (Elf in Hangar), Joshua Satok (Larry the Elf), Joyce Guy (Principal Compton), Jesse Collins (Ad Executive), Steve Vinovich (Dr Pete Novos), Aimee

McIntyre (Ruth), Tabitha Lupie (Future Ballet Girl), Dennis O'Connor (Mailman), David Sparrow (Bobby's Dad), Ron Hartmann (Judge G. Whelan), Nic Knight (Quintin), Scott Wickware (Officer Malone), Gene Mack (Officer Newman).

21. ELF (2003)

Production Company: New Line Cinema/ Guy Walks into a Bar Productions.
Distributor: New Line Cinema.
Director: Jon Favreau.
Producers: Jon Berg and Todd Komarnicki.
Co-Producer: David Householter.
Executive Producers: Kent Alterman, Cale Boyter, Toby Emmerich, Jimmy Miller and Julie Wixson Darmody.
Screenplay: David Berenbaum.
Director of Photography: Greg Gardiner.
Film Editing: Dan Lebental.
Original Score: John Debney.
Production Design: Rusty Smith.
Casting: Susie Farris.
Art Direction: Kelvin Humenny.
Set Decoration: Johanne Hubert.
Costume Design: Laura Jean Shannon.
Running Time: 97 minutes.
Main Cast: Will Ferrell (Buddy), James Caan (Walter), Bob Newhart (Papa Elf), Edward Asner (Santa), Mary Steenburgen (Emily), Zooey Deschanel (Jovie), Daniel Tay (Michael), Faizon Love (Gimbel's Manager), Peter Dinklage (Miles Finch), Amy Sedaris (Deb), Michael Lerner (Fulton), Andy Richter (Morris), Kyle Gass (Eugene), Artie Lange (Gimbel's Santa), Leon Redbone (Voice of Leon the Snowman), Ray Harryhausen (Voice of Polar Bear Cub), Claire Lautier (NY1 Reporter), Ted Friend (NY1 Anchor), Patrick Ferrell (Security Guard), Patrick McCartney (Security Guard), Jon Favreau (Doctor), Annie Brebner (Elf Student), Lydia Lawson-Baird (Carolyn), Brenda MacDonald (Nun).

22. BAD SANTA (2003)

Production Company: Columbia Pictures/ Dimension Films/ Triptych Pictures/ Blixa Zweite Film Produktion GmbH & Co. KG.
Distributor: Dimension Films.
Director: Terry Zwigoff.
Producers: Sarah Aubrey, John Cameron and Bob Weinstein.
Co-Producer: David Crockett.
Executive Producers: Ethan Coen and Joel Coen.
Co-Executive Producers: Harvey Weinstein and Brad Weston.
Screenplay: Glenn Ficarra and John Requa.
Director of Photography: Jamie Anderson.
Film Editing: Robert Hoffman.
Original Score: David Kitay.
Production Design: Sharon Seymour.
Casting: Felicia Fasano and Mary Vernieu.

Art Direction: Peter Borck.
Set Decoration: Robert Greenfield Jr.
Costume Design: Wendy Chuck.
Running Time: 91 minutes.
Main Cast: Billy Bob Thornton (Willie), Tony Cox (Marcus), Brett Kelly (The Kid), Lauren Graham (Sue), Lauren Tom (Lois), Bernie Mac (Gin), John Ritter (Bob Chipeska), Ajay Naidu (Troublemaker), Lorna Scott (Milwaukee Mother), Harrison Bieker (Milwaukee Boy), Alex Borstein (Milwaukee Mom with Photo), Alexandra Korhan (Girl on Santa's Lap), Dylan Charles (Milwaukee Bratty Boy), Billy Gardell (Milwaukee Security Guard), Lisa Ross (Milwaukee Bartender), Bryan Callen (Miami Bartender), Tom McGowan (Harrison), Grace Calderon (Big Booty Woman), Christine Pichardo (Photo Elf), Georgia Eskew (Barbie Girl), Hayden Bromberg (Fraggle-Stick Boy), Max Van Ville (Skateboard Bully), Briana Norton (Pinball Girl), Octavia L. Spencer (Opal).

23. NOEL (2004)

Production Company: Code Entertainment/ Red Rose Productions LLC.
Distributor: Red Rose Productions LLC/ Screen Media Films.
Director: Chazz Palminteri.
Producers: Al Corley, Eugene Musso, Bart Rosenblatt and Zvi Howard Rosenman.
Co-Producers: Matt Luber and James Mulay.
Line Producer: Micheline Garant.
Associate Producers: Michael Klastorin and Kim Olsen.
Executive Producers: Daniel Adler, Jeff Arnold and Jonathan Dana.
Screenplay: David Hubbard.
Director of Photography: Russell Carpenter.
Film Editing: Susan E. Morse.
Original Score: Alan Menken.
Production Design: Carol Spier.
Casting: Nadia Rona.
Art Direction: André Chamberland.
Key Decorator: Frances Calder.
Set Decoration: Suzanne Cloutier and Marie-Claude Gosselin.
Costume Design: Renée April.
Running Time: 96 minutes.
Main Cast: Susan Sarandon (Rose Harrison), Paul Walker (Mike Riley), Penélope Cruz (Nina Vasquez), Alan Arkin (Artie Venizelos), Marcus Thomas (Jules Calvert), Sonny Marinelli (Dennis), Daniel Sunjata (Marco), Chazz Palminteri (Arizona), Rob Daly (Paul), John Doman (Dr Matthew Baron), Billy Porter (Randy), Carmen Ejogo (Dr Batiste), Donna Hanover (Debbie Carmichael), Merwin Mondesir (Glenn), Una Kay (Helen), Sonia Benezra (Aunt Sonya), Marcia Bennett (Nurse Stein), Howard Rosenstein (E.R. Doctor), Jane Wheeler (Karen), David Hirsh (Barton), Marguerite Kinh (Mrs Lee), Arthur Holden (Piano Player), Maurizio Terrazzano (Tom), Rachelle Lefevre (Holly), Erika Rosenbaum (Merry), Charles Rosenbaum (Coffee Vendor), Victoria Sanchez (Young Mother), Scott Faulconbridge (Man in Front Row), Budd Mishkin (NY1 Reporter), Carmen Echeverria (Young Girl), Gianpaolo Venuta (Young Guy), Nicholas Haze (Waiter), Ruth Chiang (Nurse Woo), Kevin Ryder (Bartender), Andy Bradshaw (Security Guard #1), Robert Newton Brown (Security Guard #2), Bill Corday (Meek Man), Jennifer Seguin (Young Woman).

24. JOYEUX NOËL (2005)

Production Company: Nord-Ouest Productions, in co-production with Senator Film Produktion/ The Bureau/ Artémis Productions/ Media Pro Pictures/ TF1 Films Production/ Les Productions de la Guéville.
Distributor: Sony Pictures Classics.
Director: Christian Carion.
Producer: Christophe Rossignon.
Co-Producers: Andrei Boncea, Christopher Borgmann, Bertrand Faivre, Soledad Gatti-Pascual, Benjamin Herrmann, Kate Ogborn and Patrick Quinet.
Associate Producers: Philippe Boeffard and Alexandre Lippens.
Assistant Producer: Marielle Duigou.
Screenplay: Christian Carion.
Director of Photography: Walther Vanden Ende.
Film Editing: Judith Rivière Kawa and Andrea Sedláčková.
Original Score: Philippe Rombi.
Production Design: Jean-Michel Simonet.
Casting: Susie Figgis and Sabine Schroth.
Executive Art Director: Ève Machuel.
Art Direction: Vraciu Eduard Daniel and Anina Diener.
Set Decoration: Patrick Colpaert.
Costume Design: Alison Forbes-Meyler.
Running Time: 116 minutes.
Main Cast: Diane Kruger (Anna Sorensen), Natalie Dessay (Singing Voice of Anna Sorensen), Benno Fürmann (Nikolaus Sprink), Rolando Villazón (Singing Voice of Nikolaus Sprink), Guillaume Canet (Audebert), Gary Lewis (Palmer), Dany Boon (Ponchel), Daniel Brühl (Horstmayer), Lucas Belvaux (Gueusselin), Alex Ferns (Gordon), Steven Robertson (Jonathan), Frank Witter (Jörg), Bernard Le Coq (General), Ian Richardson (Bishop), Thomas Schmauser (The Crown Prince), Joachim Bissmeier (Zimmermann), Robin Laing (William), Michel Serrault (Squire), Suzanne Flon (Lady of the Manor), Calum Anthony Beaton (Scottish Bagpipe Player), Philippe Beautier (Morallec), Steffen Bielig (Markus), Nicholas Biggam (English Youngster), David Bruce (Scottish Bagpipe Player), Christian Carion (Nurse), France Corbet (Madeleine), Micky Dedaj (Dressmaker), Steven Duffy (Stretcher Bearer), Markus Friedmann (German Staff Officer), Christopher Fulford (Major).

25. A CHRISTMAS CAROL 3D (2009)

Production Company: Walt Disney Pictures/ ImageMovers Digital.
Distributor: Walt Disney Studios Motion Pictures.
Director: Robert Zemeckis.
Producers: Jack Rapke, Steve Starkey and Robert Zemeckis.
Co-Producer: Steven J. Boyd.
Line Producer: Peter M. Tobyansen.
Associate Producers: Heather Kelton and Katherine C. Concepcion.
Executive Producer: Mark L. Rosen.
Screenplay: Robert Zemeckis, from the novel by Charles Dickens.
Cinematography: Robert Presley.
Film Editing: Jeremiah O'Driscoll.

Original Score: Alan Silvestri.

Production Design: Doug Chiang.

Casting: Scot Boland, Victoria Burrows and Nina Gold.

Art Direction: Brian Flora, Marc Gabbana, Norman Newberry and Mike Stassi.

Set Decoration: Karen O'Hara.

Running Time: 96 minutes.

Main Cast: Jim Carrey (Voice of Scrooge/ Ghost of Christmas Past/ Scrooge as a Young Boy/ Scrooge as a Teenage Boy/ Scrooge as a Young Man/ Scrooge as a Middle-Aged Man/ Ghost of Christmas Present/ Ghost of Christmas Yet to Come), Steve Valentine (Voice of Funerary Undertaker/ Topper), Daryl Sabara (Voice of Undertaker's Apprentice/ Tattered Caroler/ Beggar Boy/ Peter Cratchit/ Well-Dressed Caroler), Sage Ryan (Voice of Tattered Caroler), Amber Gainey Meade (Voice of Tattered Caroler/ Well-Dressed Caroler), Ryan Ochoa (Voice of Tattered Caroler/ Beggar Boy/ Young Cratchit Boy/ Ignorance Boy/ Young Boy with Sleigh/ Tiny Tim), Bobbi Page (Voice of Tattered Caroler/ Well-Dressed Caroler), Ron Bottitta (Voice of Tattered Caroler/ Well-Dressed Caroler), Sammi Hanratty (Voice of Beggar Boy/ Young Cratchit Girl/ Want Girl), Julian Holloway (Voice of Fat Cook/ Portly Gentleman #2/ Business Man #3), Gary Oldman (Voice of Bob Cratchit/ Marley/ Tiny Tim), Colin Firth (Voice of Fred), Cary Elwes (Voice of Portly Gentleman #1/ Dick Wilkins/ Mad Fiddler/ Guest #2/ Business Man #1), Robin Wright Penn (Voice of Fan/ Belle), Bob Hoskins (Voice of Mr Fezziwig/ Old Joe), Jacquie Barnbrook (Voice of Mrs Fezziwig/ Fred's Sister-in-Law/ Well-Dressed Caroler), Lesley Manville (Voice of Mrs Cratchit), Molly C. Quinn (Voice of Belinda Cratchit), Fay Masterson (Voice of Martha Cratchit/ Guest #1/ Caroline), Leslie Zemeckis (Voice of Fred's Wife), Paul Blackthorne (Voice of Guest #3/ Business Man #2), Michael Hyland (Voice of Guest #4), Kerry Hoyt (Voice of Adult Ignorance), Julene Renee (Voice of Adult Want), Fionnula Flanagan (Voice of Mrs Dilber), Raymond Ochoa (Voice of Caroline's Child), Callum Blue (Voice of Caroline's Husband), Matthew Henerson (Voice of Poulterer), Aaron Rapke (Voice of Well-Dressed Caroler), Sonje Fortag (Voice of Well-Dressed Caroler/ Fred's Housemaid).

SELECT BIBLIOGRAPHY

Adams, Sam, '*Black Christmas*', in *The Los Angeles Times*, 26 December 2006.

—. 'Little Big Man', in *The Philadelphia City Paper*, 6-12 November 2003.

—. 'Screen Picks: *The Apartment*', in *The Philadelphia City Paper*, 5-12 July 2001.

Agajanian, Rowana, '"Peace on Earth, Goodwill to All Men": The Depiction of Christmas in Modern Hollywood Films', in *Christmas at the Movies: Images of Christmas in American, British and European Cinema*, ed. by Mark Connelly (London: I.B. Tauris, 2000).

Aldgate, Anthony, and Jeffrey Richards, *Best of British: Cinema and Society from 1930 to the Present* (London: I.B. Tauris, 2002).

Aldgate, Anthony, James Chapman and Arthur Marwick, eds, *Windows on the Sixties: Exploring Key Texts of Media and Culture* (London: I.B. Tauris, 2000).

Allon, Yoram, Del Cullen and Hannah Patterson, eds, *Contemporary North American Film Directors: A Wallflower Critical Guide* (London: Wallflower Press, 2000).

American Film Institute, The, 'Dialogue on Film: Billy Wilder and I.A.L. Diamond', in *Billy Wilder: Interviews*, ed. by Peter Brunette (Jackson: University Press of Mississippi, 2001).

Anderson, Jeffrey M., '*Scrooged*', in *Combustible Celluloid*, 10 December 2008.
<http://www.combustiblecelluloid.com/archive/scrooged.shtml>

—. '*The Muppet Christmas Carol*: Never Eat Singing Food', in *Combustible Celluloid*, 25 December 2005.
<http://www.combustiblecelluloid.com/classic/muppchris.shtml>

Anon., 'Bingle All the Way: Crosby and Kaye Celebrate an Early *White Christmas*', in *Life*, 11 October 1954.

Anon, 'Brief Movie Reviews: *Santa Claus: The Movie*', in *New York Magazine*, 16 December 1985.

Anon., 'Cinema: Import: *A Christmas Carol*', in *Time*, 3 December 1951.

Anon., 'Movie of the Week: *The Bishop's Wife*', in *Life*, 12 January 1948.

Anon, 'Reflections', in *Masters of Imaging*, 2010.
<http://www.mastersofimaging.net/Reflections.html>

Anon., 'Singles Reviews: Christmas Highlights', in *Billboard*, 21 November 1964.

Anon., 'The Wilder Touch: The director explains his zany method for relaxing actors', in *Life*, 30 May 1960.

Anon., 'Top 10 Classic Christmas Movies', in *The Coventry Evening Telegraph*, 23 October 2009.

Archerd, Army, 'Chazz touts *Noel*'s good charms', in *Variety*, 17 December 2003.

Armstrong, Richard, *Billy Wilder: American Film Realist* (Jefferson: McFarland and Company, 2000).

Arthur, Ryan, '*National Lampoon's Christmas Vacation*', in *eFilmCritic.com*, 15 October 1998. <http:// efilmcritic.com/ review.php?movie=1116>

Ashby, Justine, and Andrew Higson, eds., *British Cinema, Past and Present* (London: Routledge, 2000).

Austin, Joe, and Michael Nevin Willard, eds, *Generations of Youth: Youth Cultures and History in Twentieth-Century America* (New York: NYU Press, 1998).

Avins, Mimi, 'Ghoul World', in *Tim Burton: Interviews*, ed. by Kristian Fraga (Jackson: University Press of Mississippi, 2005).

Babington, Bruce, and Peter William Evans, *Biblical Epics: Sacred Narrative in the Hollywood Cinema* (Manchester: Manchester University Press, 1993).

Basinger, Jeanine, Frances Goodrich and Leonard Maltin, eds, *The* It's a Wonderful Life *Book* (New York: Alfred A. Knopf, 1986).

Batchelor, Bob, and Scott Stoddart, *The 1980s* (Westport: Greenwood Publishing Group, 2006).

Base, Ron, and David Haslam, *The Movies of the Eighties* (London: Portland, 1990).

Baumgarten, Marjorie, 'Disney's *A Christmas Carol*', in *The Austin Chronicle*, 6 November 2009.

—. '*Elf*', in *The Austin Chronicle*, 7 November 2003.

Baumgarten, Murray, 'Bill Murray's Christmas Carols', in *Dickens on Screen*, ed. by John Glavin (Cambridge: Cambridge University Press, 2003).

Biancolli, Amy, 'Disney's *A Christmas Carol*', in *The San Francisco Chronicle*, 6 November 2009.

Bohm-Duchen, Monica, *The Private Life of a Masterpiece* (Berkeley: University of California Press, 2001).

Booker, M. Keith, *Disney, Pixar, and the Hidden Messages of Children's Films* (Santa Barbara: Praeger, 2010).

Bookman, Milica, and Aleksandra S. Bookman, *Economics in Film and Fiction* (Plymouth: Rowman and Littlefield Education, 2009).

Bradshaw, Peter, '*Black Christmas*', in *The Guardian*, 15 December 2006.

—., '*Merry Christmas*', in *The Guardian*, 16 December 2005.

—. '*The Apartment*', in *The Guardian*, 11 July 2008.

—. '*Tim Burton's The Nightmare Before Christmas 3D*', in *The Guardian*, 17 November 2006.

Breznican, Anthony, 'It's already beginning to look a lot like Christmas at theaters', in *USA Today*, 4 November 2009.

Brown, Joe, '*Scrooged*', in *The Washington Post*, 25 November 1988.

Browne, Ray B., and Glenn J. Browne, *Laws of Our Fathers: Popular Culture and the U.S. Constitution* (Bowling Green: Bowling Green State University Popular Press, 1986).

Browne, Ray B., and Pat Browne, *The Guide to United States Popular Culture* (Madison: University of Wisconsin Press, 2001).

Brunette, Peter, ed., *Billy Wilder: Interviews* (Jackson: University Press of Mississippi, 2001).

Budd, Mike, and Max H. Kirsch, eds, *Rethinking Disney: Private Control, Public Dimensions* (Middletown: Wesleyan University Press, 2005).

Canby, Vincent, 'Bill Murray in *Scrooged*: Meanness's Outer Limits', in *The New York Times*, 23 November 1988.

—. '*Christmas Story*, Indiana Tale', in *The New York Times*, 18 November 1983.

Carlson, Kristine Butler, '1945: Movies and the March Home', in *American Cinema of the*

1940s: Themes and Variations, ed. by Wheeler Winston Dixon (Piscataway: Rutgers University Press, 2006).

Carney, Raymond, *American Vision: The Films of Frank Capra* (Cambridge: Cambridge University Press, 1986).

Carr, Jay, '*Scrooged*', in *The Boston Globe*, 23 November 1988.

—. '*Trading Places*', in *The Boston Globe*, 9 June 1983.

Chacona, Hollis, '*The Santa Clause*', in *The Austin Chronicle*, 18 November 1994.

Chapman, James, 'God Bless Us, Every One: Movie Adaptations of *A Christmas Carol*', in *Christmas at the Movies*, ed. by Mark Connelly (London: I.B. Tauris, 2000).

Clark, Mike, '*Bad* is dreaming of a blight Christmas', in *USA Today*, 25 November 2003.

Cohan, Steven, 'Introduction: Musicals of the Studio Era', in *Hollywood Musicals: The Film Reader*, ed. by Steven Cohan (London: Routledge, 2002).

—. ed., *Hollywood Musicals: The Film Reader* (London: Routledge, 2002).

Collins, Ace, *Stories Behind the Great Traditions of Christmas* (Grand Rapids: Zondervan, 2003).

Connelly, Mark, ed., *Christmas at the Movies* (London: I.B. Tauris, 2000).

—. 'Santa Claus: The Movie', in *Christmas at the Movies*, ed. by Mark Connelly (London: I.B. Tauris, 2000).

Conner, Floyd, *Hollywood's Most Wanted: The Top 10 Book of Lucky Breaks, Prima Donnas, Box Office Bombs, and Other Oddities* (Virginia: Brassey's, 2002).

Connolly, Joseph, 'Personally speaking *It's a Wonderful Life* spotting all the gaffes', in *The Sunday Telegraph*, 23 December 2007.

Cook, David C., *The Inspirational Christmas Almanac: Heartwarming Traditions, Trivia, Stories, and Recipes for the Holidays* (Colorado Springs: Honor Books, 2006).

Cooper, Ian, 'Bob Clark', in *Contemporary North American Film Directors: A Wallflower Critical Guide*, ed. by Yoram Allon, Del Cullen and Hannah Patterson (London: Wallflower Press, 2000).

Cooper, Jeanne, '*Home Alone*', in *The Washington Post*, 16 November 1990.

Cosindas, Marie, 'Gallery', in *Life*, 27 November 1970.

Cox, Stephen, *It's a Wonderful Life: A Memory Book* (Nashville: Cumberland House Publishing, 2005).

—. 'On a Wing and a Prayer', in *The Los Angeles Times*, 23 December 2006.

Crist, Judith, 'Cinema', in *New York Magazine*, 23 November 1970.

Crouse, Richard, *The 100 Best Movies You've Never Seen* (Toronto: ECW Press, 2003).

Davis, Hugh H., 'A Weirdo, A Rat, and A Humbug: The Literary Qualities of *The Muppet Christmas Carol*', in *Studies in Popular Culture*, 21:3, 1999.
   <http:// pcasacas.org/ SiPC/ 21.3/ hdavis.htm>

Deacy, Christopher, *Faith in Film: Religious Themes in Contemporary Cinema* (Aldershot: Ashgate Publishing, 2005).

Denby, David, 'Holiday Horror', in *New York Magazine*, 5 December 1988.

—. 'Supply-Side Hero', in *New York Magazine*, 22 August 1983.

Detora, Lisa M., ed., *Heroes of Film, Comics and American Culture: Essays on Real and Fictional Defenders of Home* (Jefferson: McFarland, 2009).

Dickens, Charles, *A Christmas Carol* (Peterborough: Broadview Press, 2003) [1843].

—. *The Christmas Books* (Ware: Wordsworth Editions, 1995) [1852].

Dixon, Wheeler Winston, ed., *American Cinema of the 1940s: Themes and Variations* (Piscataway: Rutgers University Press, 2006).

Docker, John, *Postmodernism and Popular Culture: A Cultural History* (Cambridge: Cambridge University Press, 1994).

Ebert, Roger, '*A Christmas Story*', in *The Chicago Sun-Times*, 15 December 1983.

—. '*Bad Santa*', in *The Chicago Sun-Times*, 26 November 2003.

—. 'Disney's *A Christmas Carol*', in *The Chicago Sun-Times*, 5 November 2009.

—. '*Elf*', in *The Chicago Sun-Times*, 7 November 2003.

—. 'Great Movies: *The Apartment*', in *The Chicago Sun-Times Online*, 22 July 2001. <http:// rogerebert.suntimes.com/ apps/ pbcs.dll/ article?AID=/ 20010722/ REVIEWS08/ 107220301/ 1023>

—. '*Home Alone*', in *The Chicago Sun-Times*, 16 November 1990.

—. '*Joyeux Noël*', in *The Chicago Sun-Times*, 10 March 2006.

—. '*Miracle on 34th Street*', in *The Chicago Sun-Times*, 18 November 1994.

—. '*National Lampoon's Christmas Vacation*', in *The Chicago Sun-Times*, 1 December 1989.

—. '*Noel*', in *The Chicago Sun-Times*, 12 November 2004.

—. '*Santa Claus: The Movie*', in *The Chicago Sun-Times*, 27 November 1985.

—. '*Scrooge*', in *The Chicago Sun-Times*, 1 January 1970.

—. '*Scrooged*', in *The Chicago Sun-Times*, 23 November 1998.

—. '*The Muppet Christmas Carol*', in *The Chicago Sun-Times*, 11 December 1992.

—. '*The Santa Clause*', in *The Chicago Sun-Times*, 11 November 1994.

—. '*Tim Burton's The Nightmare Before Christmas*', in *The Chicago Sun-Times*, 22 October 1993.

—. '*Trading Places*', in *The Chicago Sun-Times*, 9 June 1983.

Elliott, Larry, and Dan Atkinson, *The Age of Insecurity* (London: Verso, 1999) [1998].

Ellis, John, *Visible Fictions: Cinema, Television, Video* (London: Routledge, 1989) [1982].

Everett, William A., and Paul R. Laird, eds., *The Cambridge Companion to the Musical* (Cambridge: Cambridge University Press, 2008).

Fairbanks, Brian W., *I Saw That Movie, Too: Selected Film Reviews*, 2nd edn (Morrisville: Lulu.com, 2008).

Fairclough, Norman, *Critical Discourse Analysis: The Critical Study of Language* (Harlow, Longman: 1995).

Felton, Bruce, *What Were They Thinking?: Really Bad Ideas Throughout History*, rev. edn. (Guilford: Lyons Press, 2007).

Fishwick, Marshall W., *Popular Culture in a New Age* (Binghampton: Haworth Press, 2002).

Flanagan, Martin, 'John Landis', in *Contemporary North American Film Directors: A Wallflower Critical Guide*, ed. by Yoram Allon, Del Cullen and Hannah Patterson (London: Wallflower Press, 2002).

Forbes, Bruce David, *Christmas: A Candid History* (Berkeley: University of California Press, 2007).

Fowler, Karin J., *David Niven: A Bio-Bibliography* (Westport: Greenwood Publishing Group, 1995).

Fraga, Kristian, ed., *Tim Burton: Interviews* (Jackson: University Press of Mississippi, 2005).

Fraser, Matthew, '*Trading Places*', in *The Toronto Globe and Mail*, 10 June 1983.

French, Philip, '*The Apartment*', in *The Observer*, 13 July 2008.

Frow, John, *Genre* (London: Routledge, 2006).

Gabbard, Glen O., and Krin Gabbard, *Psychiatry and the Cinema*, 2nd edn (Washington D.C.: American Psychiatric Press, 1999).

Garlen, Jennifer C., and Anissa M. Graham, eds, *Kermit Culture: Critical Perspectives on Jim Henson's Muppets* (Jefferson: McFarland and Company, 2009).

Garrett, Eddie, *I Saw Stars in the 40's and 50's* (Victoria: Trafford Publishing, 2005).

Garrett, Greg, *The Gospel According to Hollywood* (Louisville: Westminster John Knox Press, 2007).

Giddings, Robert, and Erica Sheen, eds, *The Classic Novel: From Page to Screen* (Manchester: Manchester University Press, 2000).

Glavin, John, ed., *Dickens On Screen* (Cambridge: Cambridge University Press, 2003).

Gleiberman, Owen, '*Home Alone*', in *Entertainment Weekly*, 25 July 2007.

Gonzalez, Ed, '*Noel*', in *Slant Magazine*, 29 October 2004.

Green, Stanley, *Hollywood Musicals Year by Year*, 2nd edn. rev. by Elaine Schmidt (Milwaukee: Hal Leonard, 1999).

Guida, Fred, *'A Christmas Carol' and Its Adaptations: A Critical Examination of Dickens' Story and Its Productions on Stage, Screen and Television* (Jefferson: McFarland, 2000).

Hales, Stephen D., 'Putting Claus Back into Christmas', in *Christmas: Philosophy for Everyone*, ed. by Scott C. Lowe (Chichester: Blackwell, 2010).

Hantke, Steffen, ed., *American Horror Film: The Genre at the Turn of the Millennium* (Jackson: University Press of Mississippi, 2010).

Hardy, Phil, ed., *The Aurum Film Encyclopedia: Science Fiction* (London: Aurum Press, 1995).

Harper, Jim, *Legacy of Blood: A Comprehensive Guide to Slasher Movies* (Manchester: Headpress/ Critical Vision, 2004).

Harper, Sue, 'Bonnie Prince Charlie Revisited: British Costume Film in the 1950s', in *The British Cinema Book*, 2nd edn, ed. by Robert Murphy (London: British Film Institute, 2001).

Harrington, Richard, '*The Nightmare Before Christmas*', in *The Washington Post*, 22 October 1993.

Hart, B.H. Liddell, *History of the First World War* (London: Papermac, 1997) [1930].

Hartlaub, Peter, 'Partridges, Pear Trees… And Deadly Icicles', in *The San Francisco Chronicle*, 27 December 2006.

Harvey, Dennis, '*Bad Santa*', in *Variety*, 17 November 2003.

Healey, Tim, *The World's Worst Movies* (London: Octopus Books, 1986).

Hicks, Chris, '*Home Alone*', in *The Deseret News*, 21 November 2000.

—. '*National Lampoon's Christmas Vacation*', in *The Deseret News*, 16 December 2002.

—. '*The Santa Clause*', in *The Deseret News*, 16 December 2004.

Hill, John, and Pamela Church Gibson, eds, *The Oxford Guide to Film Studies* (Oxford: Oxford University Press, 1998).

Hinson, Hal, '*Home Alone*', in *The Washington Post*, 16 November 1990.

—. '*Miracle on 34th Street*', in *The Washington Post*, 18 November 1994.

—. '*Scrooged*', in *The Washington Post*, 23 November 1988.

Hoberman, J., 'Bah, Humbug!: *Bad Santa*, as it was intended', in *The Village Voice*, 11 December 2007.

Hoffman, Robert C., *Postcards from Santa Claus: Sights and Sentiments from the Last Century* (New York: Square One Publishers, 2002).

Hollows, Joanne, and Mark Jancovich, eds, *Approaches to Popular Film* (Manchester: Manchester University Press, 1995).

Hopp, Glenn, *Billy Wilder: The Complete Films* (Köln: Taschen Books, 2003).

Howard, Michael, *The First World War: A Very Short Introduction* (Oxford: Oxford University Press, 2002).

Howe, Desson, '*The Muppet Christmas Carol*', in *The Washington Post*, 11 December 1992.

—. '*The Nightmare Before Christmas*', in *The Washington Post*, 22 October 1993.

—. '*The Santa Clause*', in *The Washington Post*, 11 November 1994.

Hunter, Allan, ed., *The Wordsworth Book of Movie Classics* (Ware: Wordsworth, 1996) [1992].

Ingman, Marrit, '*Joyeux Noël*', in *The Austin Chronicle*, 31 March 2006.

Jasen, David A., *Tin Pan Alley: An Encyclopedia of the Golden Age of the American Song* (New York: Routledge, 2003).

Jeffers, H. Paul, *Legends of Santa Claus* (Minneapolis: Lerner Publishing Group, 2001).

Johnston, Hank, and John A. Noakes, eds, *Frames of Protest: Social Movements and the Framing Perspective* (Oxford: Rowman and Littlefield, 2005).

Jones, Edward, 'Horror Cliches: Up From the Dead, and Still Fun', in *The Free Lance-Star*,

14 July 1975

Jones, J.R., 'Noel', in *The Chicago Reader*, 5 November 2005.
<http://www.chicagoreader.com/chicago/noel/Film?oid=1057506>

Jones, Ken D., Arthur F. McClure and Alfred E. Twomey, *Character People* (New York: A.S. Barnes, 1977).

Jordan, Chris, *Movies and the Reagan Presidency: Success and Ethics* (Westport: Greenwood Publishing Group, 2003).

Kelly, Richard Michael, 'Introduction', in Charles Dickens, *A Christmas Carol* (Peterborough: Broadview Press, 2003).

Kempley, Rita, '*National Lampoon's Christmas Vacation*', in *The Washington Post*, 1 December 1989.

—. '*The Muppet Christmas Carol*', in *The Washington Post*, 14 December 1992.

—. '*The Santa Clause*', in *The Washington Post*, 11 November 1994.

Klady, Leonard, '*The Santa Clause*', in *Variety*, 10 November 1994.

LaSalle, Mick, 'Ferrell magical in sardonic, sweet *Elf*', in *The San Francisco Chronicle*, 7 November 2003.

—. '*Scrooged*', in *The San Francisco Chronicle*, 23 November 1988.

—. 'When troops called a truce for a day', in *The San Francisco Chronicle*, 10 March 2006.

Leab, Daniel J., 'A Walk on the Wilder Side: *The Apartment* as Social Commentary', in *Windows on the Sixties: Exploring Key Texts of Media and Culture*, ed. by Anthony Aldgate, James Chapman and Arthur Marwick (London: I.B. Tauris, 2000).

Leitch, Thomas M., *Film Adaptation and Its Discontents: From* Gone With the Wind *to* The Passion of the Christ (Baltimore: Johns Hopkins University Press, 2007).

Lester, Meera, *Why Does Santa Wear Red? ...and 100 Other Christmas Curiosities Unwrapped* (Avon: Adams Media, 2007).

Lev, Peter, *Transforming the Screen: 1950-1959* (Berkeley: University of California Press, 2003).

Levi, Ross D., *The Celluloid Courtroom: A History of Legal Cinema* (Westport: Greenwood Publishing Group, 2005).

Loukides, Paul, and Linda K. Fuller, eds, *Beyond the Stars: Plot Conventions in American Popular Film* (Bowling Green: Bowling Green State University Popular Press, 1991).

Loukides, Paul, and Linda K. Fuller, eds, *Beyond the Stars: Studies in American Popular Film Volume 5: Themes and Ideologies in American Popular Film* (Madison: Popular Press, 1996).

Lowe, Scott C., ed., *Christmas: Philosophy for Everyone* (Chichester: Blackwell, 2010).

Mackenzie, Michael, '*Home Alone*', in *DVD Times*, 25 December 2004.
<http://homecinema.thedigitalfix.co.uk/content.php?contentid=55627>

Mansour, David J., *From Abba to Zoom: A Pop Culture Encyclopedia of the Late 20th Century* (Kansas City: Andrews McMeel Publishing, 2005).

Marling, Karal Ann, *Merry Christmas!: Celebrating America's Greatest Holiday* (Cambridge: Harvard University Press, 2000).

Maslin, Janet, 'On *Vacation* Once Again', in *The New York Times*, 1 December 1989.

—. '*The Muppet Christmas Carol*: Kermit, Etc. Do Dickens Up Green', in *The New York Times*, 11 December 1992.

Mazur, Eric Michael, 'Going My Way?: Crosby and Catholicism on the Road to America', in *Going My Way: Bing Crosby and American Culture*, ed. by Ruth Prigozy and Walter Raubicheck (Rochester: University of Rochester Press, 2007).

McBrien, Richard, 'Angels and Spirituality: Comfort, Help of Angels May Hover Close at Hand', in *The National Catholic Reporter*, 4 March 1994.

McCarthy, Todd, '*Noel*', in *Variety*, 19 September 2004.

—. '*The Nightmare Before Christmas*', in *Variety*, 7 October 1993.

McCusker, Eamonn, '*It's a Wonderful Life*', in *DVD Times*, 20 November 2008.
  <http:// www.dvdtimes.co.uk/ content/ id/ 69440/ itswonderful-life.html>

McDannell, Colleen, ed., *Catholics in the Movies* (New York: Oxford University Press US, 2008).

McGee, Patrick, *Cinema, Theory, and Political Responsibility in Contemporary Culture* (Cambridge: Cambridge University Press, 1997).

Mechling, Jay, 'Rethinking (and Reteaching) the Civil Religion in Post-Nationalist American Studies', in *Post-Nationalist American Studies*, ed. by John Carlos Rowe (Berkeley: University of California Press, 2000).

Metcalf, Greg, '"It's (Christmas) Morning in America": Christmas Conventions of American Films in the 1980s', in *Beyond the Stars: Plot Conventions in American Popular Film*, ed. by Paul Loukides and Linda K. Fuller (Bowling Green: Bowling Green State University Popular Press, 1991).

Miller, Daniel, *Consumption: Critical Concepts in the Social Sciences, Volume IV: Objects, Subjects and Mediations in Consumption* (London: Routledge, 2001).

Miller, Toby, and Robert Stam, eds., *A Companion to Film Theory* (Oxford: Blackwell, 2004) [1999].

Mitchell, Jeremy, and Richard Maidment, eds., *The United States in the Twentieth Century: Culture* (London: Hodder and Stoughton, 1994).

Moore, Kenneth, *The Magic of 'Santa Claus': More Than Just a Red Suit!* (Martinez: Ken Moore Productions, 2006).

Müller, Jürgen, *Movies of the 80s* (Köln: Taschen Books, 2002).

Munson, Kristin, '*The Nightmare Before Christmas: Collector's Edition*', in *DVD Verdict*, 26 August 2008.
  <http:// www.dvdverdict.com/ reviews/ nightmareb4ce.php>

Murphy, Robert, ed., *The British Cinema Book*, 2nd edn (London: British Film Institute, 2001).

Murray, Noel, '*A Christmas Story*', in *The Onion A.V. Club*, 9 December 2003.
  <http:// www.avclub.com/ articles/ a-christmas-story-dvd,11656/>

—. '*Black Christmas*', in *The Onion A.V. Club*, 13 December 2006.
  <http:// www.avclub.com/ articles/ black-christmas,8046/>

—. '*Home Alone*', in *The Onion A.V. Club*, 13 December 2006.
  <http:// www.avclub.com/ articles/ home-alone,8044/>

—. '*Miracle on 34th Street*', in *The Onion A.V. Club*, 13 December 2006.
  <http:// www.avclub.com/ articles/ miracle-on-34th-street,8045/>

—. '*Noel*', in *The Onion A.V. Club*, 8 November 2004.
  <http:// www.avclub.com/ articles/ noel,4824/>

Nadel, Alan, 'Movies and Reaganism', in *American Cinema of the 1980s: Themes and Variations*, ed. by Stephen Prince (Chapel Hill: Rutgers University Press, 2007).

Natale, Richard, '"*Disclosure*" Edges Out "*Santa*" at the Box Office: Movies: Much-hyped sexual-harassment drama pushes aside the Tim Allen heavyweight', in *The L.A. Times*, 12 December 1994.

Naugle, Patrick, '*National Lampoon's Christmas Vacation: Special Edition*', in *DVD Verdict*, 16 October 2003.
  <http:// www.dvdverdict.com/ reviews/ christmasvacationse.php>

Neale, Steve, *Genre and Hollywood* (London: Routledge, 2000).

Neff, Alan, *Movies, Movie Stars, and Me* (Bloomington: AuthorHouse, 2008).

Nelson, Andrew Patrick, 'Todorov's Fantastic and the Uncanny Slasher Remake', in *American Horror Film: The Genre at the Turn of the Millennium*, ed. by Steffen Hantke (Jackson: University Press of Mississippi, 2010).

Nesselson, Lisa, 'Merry Christmas: *Joyeux Noël*', in *Variety*, 16 May 2005.

Neuwirth, Allan, *Makin' Toons: Inside the Most Popular Animated TV Shows and Movies* (New York: Allworth Press, 2003).

Nevius, C.W., 'A not-so-jolly old elf with a dark past, holiday hangover', in *The San Francisco Chronicle*, 26 November 2003.

Nield, Anthony, '*Santa Claus: The Movie*', in *DVD Times*, 16 November 2005. <http:// homecinema.thedigitalfix.co.uk/ content.php?contentid=59246>

Noakes, John A., 'Official Frames in Social Movement Theory: The FBI, HUAC, and the Communist Threat in Hollywood', in *Frames of Protest: Social Movements and the Framing Perspective*, ed. by Hank Johnston and John A. Noakes (Oxford: Rowman and Littlefield, 2005).

Null, Christopher, '*Scrooged*', in *FilmCritic.com*, 2 January 2006. <http:// www.filmcritic.com/ reviews/ 1988/ scrooged/ ?OpenDocument>

—. '*The Muppet Christmas Carol*', in *FilmCritic.com*, 20 November 2005. <http:// www.filmcritic.com/ reviews/ 1992/ the-muppet-christmas-carol/>

—. '*The Santa Clause*', in *FilmCritic.com*, 13 April 2002. <http:// www.filmcritic.com/ reviews/ 1994/ the-santa-clause/>

O'Hehir, Andrew, 'Beyond the Multiplex', in *Salon.com*, 2 March 2006. <http:// www.salon.com/ entertainment/ movies/ review/ 2006/ 03/ 02/ btm/ index2.html?CP=IMD&DN=110>

Packard, David, '*Home Alone*: Family Fun Edition', in *DVD Verdict*, 1 January 2007. <http:// www.dvdverdict.com/ reviews/ homealonese.php>

Pais, Matt, 'Disney's *A Christmas Carol*', in *Chicago Metromix*, 5 November 2009. <http:// chicago.metromix.com/ movies/ movie_review/ disneys-a-christmas-carol/ 1582551/ content>

Palmer, William J., *The Films of the Eighties: A Social History* (Carbondale: Southern Illinois University Press, 1993).

Panton, Gary, '*Scrooged*', in *Movie Gazette*, 23 December 2003. <http:// www.movie-gazette.com/ 572>

Paszylk, Bartlomiej, *The Pleasure and Pain of Cult Horror Films: An Historical Survey* (Jefferson: McFarland and Company, 2009).

Park, Ed, 'The *Elf*in Man Takes Manhattan, Faces the Wrath of Caan', in *The Village Voice*, 4 November 2003.

Patel, Sonja, *The Christmas Companion* (London: Think Books, 2008).

Patterson, John, 'Black Christmas', in *The Guardian*, 29 October 2004.

Paulding, Barbara, Suzanne Schwalb and Mara Conlon, *A Century of Christmas Memories 1900-1999* (New York: Peter Pauper Press, 2009).

Peterson, Paul, 'Michael Curtiz: The Mystery-Man Director of *Casablanca*' in *Political Philosophy Comes to Rick's: Casablanca and American Civic Culture*, ed. by James F. Pontuso (Lanham: Lexington Books, 2005).

Phillips, Gene D., *Some Like It Wilder: The Controversial Films of Billy Wilder* (Lexington: University Press of Kentucky, 2010).

Phipps, Keith, '*The Nightmare Before Christmas*', in *The Onion A.V. Club*, 29 March 2002. <http:// www.avclub.com/ articles/ the-nightmare-before-christmas,20203/>

Pontuso, James F., ed., *Political Philosophy Comes to Rick's: Casablanca and American Civic Culture* (Lanham: Lexington Books, 2005).

Pramaggiore, Maria, *Neil Jordan* (Champaign: University of Illinois Press, 2008)

Prigozy, Ruth, and Walter Raubicheck, eds., *Going My Way: Bing Crosby and American Culture* (Rochester: University of Rochester Press, 2007).

Prince, Stephen, ed., *American Cinema of the 1980s: Themes and Variations* (Chapel Hill:

Rutgers University Press, 2007).

Puccio, John J., '*The Muppet Christmas Carol*: Kermit's 50th Anniversary Edition', in *DVD Town*, 30 November 2005.
<http:// www.dvdtown.com/ review/ muppet-christmas-carol/ dvd/ 3295/ 2>

—. '*The Santa Clause*: Special Edition', in *DVD Town*, 7 December 2003.
<http:// www.dvdtown.com/ review/ Santa_Clause_The_Special_Editi/ 11496/ 1871/>

Puig, Claudia, '*Christmas Carol* lost in 3-D interpretation', in *USA Today*, 6 November 2009.

—. 'Ferrell is a bit too cutesy for comfort in *Elf*', in *USA Today*, 7 November 2003.

Pulver, Andrew, '*Noël*', in *The Guardian*, 25 November 2005.

Purves, Barry J.C., *Stop Motion: Passion, Process and Performance* (Oxford: Elsevier, 2008).

Quart, Leonard, and Albert Auster, *American Film and Society Since 1945*, 3rd edn (Westport: Greenwood Publishing Group, 2002).

Rabin, Nathan, '*Joyeux Noël*', in *The Onion A.V. Club*, 28 February 2006.
<http:// avclub.com/ articles/ joyeux-noel,4065/>

—. 'My Year of Flops: Case File #96: *Santa Claus: The Movie*', in *The Onion A.V. Club*, 25 December 2007.
<http:// www.avclub.com/ articles/ my-year-of-flops-case-file-96-santa-claus-the-movi,10128/>

Reid, John Howard, *Hollywood Movie Musicals: Great, Good and Glamorous* (Morrisville: Lulu.com, 2006).

—. *Movies Magnificent: 150 Must-See Cinema Classics* (Morrisville: Lulu.com, 2005).

Richards, Jeffrey, *Films and British National Identity: From Dickens to Dad's Army* (Manchester: Manchester University Press, 1997).

Rist, Peter Harry, ed., *Guide to the Cinema(s) of Canada* (Westport: Greenwood Press, 2001).

Robertson, James C., *The Casablanca Man: The Cinema of Michael Curtiz* (London: Routledge, 1993).

Rockoff, Adam, *Going to Pieces: The Rise and Fall of the Slasher Film, 1978-1986* (Jefferson: McFarland and Company, 2002).

Rodriguez, Rene, 'Disney's *A Christmas Carol*', in *The Miami Herald*, 3 November 2009.

Romney, Jonathan, '*The Muppet Christmas Carol*', in *The New Statesman*, December 1992-January 1993.

Rooney, David, '*Elf*', in *Variety*, 25 October 2003.

Roost, Frank, 'Synergy City: How Times Square and Celebration Are Integrated Into Disney's Marketing Cycle', in *Rethinking Disney: Private Control, Public Dimensions*, ed. by Mike Budd and Max H. Kirsch (Middletown: Wesleyan University Press, 2005), pp.265-66.

Rose, Brian Geoffrey, *An Examination of Narrative Structure in Four Films of Frank Capra* (New York: Arno Press, 1980) [1976].

Rowe, John Carlos, ed., *Post-Nationalist American Studies* (Berkeley: University of California Press, 2000).

Ryan, Michael, and Douglas Kellner, *Camera Politica: The Politics and Ideology of Contemporary Hollywood* (Indianapolis: Indiana University Press, 1988).

Santino, Jack, *All Around the Year: Holidays and Celebrations in American Life* (Champaign: University of Illinois Press, 1994) [1985].

—. *New Old-Fashioned Ways: Holidays and Popular Culture* (Knoxville: University of Tennessee Press, 1996).

Savlov, Marc, '*Home Alone*', in *The Austin Chronicle*, 11 January 1991.

Schager, Nick, '*A Christmas Carol*', in *Slant Magazine*, 3 November 2009.

Schickel, Richard, 'Critic's Roundup', in *Life*, 18 December 1970.

Sells, Mark, 'Elf', in The Oregon Herald, November 2003.
    <http:// www.oregonherald.com/ reviews/ mark-sells/ reviews/ elf.html>
Shail, Robert, British Film Directors: A Critical Guide (Edinburgh: Edinburgh University Press, 2007).
Short, Norman, 'Santa Claus: The Movie', in DVD Verdict, 12 October 2000.
    <http:// www.dvdverdict.com/ reviews/ santaclaus.php>
Simpson, Paul, ed., The Rough Guide to Cult Movies (London: Haymarket Customer Publishing, 2001).
Siskel, Gene, 'Scrooged', in The Chicago Tribune, 25 November 1988.
Smith, Anthony Burke, 'America's Favorite Priest: Going My Way (1944)' in Catholics in the Movies, ed. by Colleen McDannell (New York: Oxford University Press US, 2008).
Staiger, Janet, Perverse Spectators: The Practices of Film Reception (New York: New York University Press, 2000).
Stelle, Ginger, '"Starring Kermit the Frog as Bob Cratchit": Muppets as Actors', in Kermit Culture: Critical Perspectives on Jim Henson's Muppets, ed. by Jennifer C. Garlen and Anissa M. Graham (Jefferson: McFarland and Company, 2009).
Stephens, Daniel, 'National Lampoon's Christmas Vacation', in DVD Times, 17 November 2003.
    <http:// www.dvdtimes.co.uk/ content.php?contentid=6068>
Strupp, Phyllis, The Richest of Fare: Seeking Spiritual Security in the Sonoran Desert (Scottsdale: Sonoran Cross Press, 2004).
Sullivan, Daniel J., 'Sentimental Hogwash?: On Capra's It's a Wonderful Life', in Humanitas, Vol. XVIII, Nos. 1 and 2, 2005.
Svehla, Gary J., and Susan Svehla, It's Christmas Time at the Movies (Baltimore: Midnight Marquee Press, 1998).
Taylor, Ella, 'Jim Carrey and Robert Zemeckis' Very CGI Christmas Carol', in The Village Voice, 3 November 2009.
Thomas, Tony, A Smidgeon of Religion (Bloomington: AuthorHouse, 2007).
Thompson, Frank, American Movie Classics' Great Christmas Movies (Dallas: Taylor, 1998).
Tobias, Scott, 'Elf', in The Onion A.V. Club, 4 November 2003.
    <http:// www.avclub.com/ articles/ elf,5362/>
Totaro, Donato, 'Bob Clark', in Guide to the Cinema(s) of Canada, ed. by Peter Harry Rist (Westport: Greenwood Press, 2001).
Travers, Peter, 'Bad Santa', in Rolling Stone, 20 November 2003.
—. 'Elf', in Rolling Stone, 7 November 2003.
Turner, Graeme, Film as Social Practice (London: Routledge, 1999).
Tyler, Don, Music of the Postwar Era (Westport: Greenwood Publishing Group, 2008).
Variety Staff, 'National Lampoon's Christmas Vacation', in Variety, 1 December 1989.
Variety Staff, 'Santa Claus: The Movie', in Variety, 27 November 1985.
Variety Staff, 'Scrooged', in Variety, 25 November 1988.
Variety Staff, 'The Apartment', in Variety, 18 May 1960.
Variety Staff, 'The Muppet Christmas Carol', in Variety, 11 December 1992.
Watt, Kate Carnell, and Kathleen C. Lonsdale, 'Dickens Composed: Film and Television Adaptations 1897-2001', in Dickens On Screen, ed. by John Glavin (Cambridge: Cambridge University Press, 2003).
Werts, Diane, Christmas On Television (Westport: Greenwood Press, 2006).
Williams, Mary Elizabeth, 'Disney's A Christmas Carol: Bah, humbug!', in Salon.com, 5 November 2009.
    <http:// www.salon.com/ entertainment/ movies/ review/ 2009/ 11/ 05/ christmas_carol/ index.html?CP=IMD&DN=110>
Willian, Michael, The Essential It's a Wonderful Life: A Scene-by-Scene Guide to the Classic Film

(Chicago: Chicago Review Press, 2006).

Wilson, Richard, *Scrooge's Guide to Christmas: A Survival Manual for the Festively Challenged* (London: Hodder and Stoughton, 1997).

Winter, Jessica, '*Joyeux Noël (Merry Christmas)*', in *The Village Voice*, 21 February 2006.

Wise, Wyndham, '*Black Christmas*', in *Take One's Essential Guide to Canadian Film*, ed. by Wyndham Wise (Toronto: University of Toronto Press, 2001).

—. ed., *Take One's Essential Guide to Canadian Film* (Toronto: University of Toronto Press, 2001).

Woodruff, Zachary, '*Miracle on 34th Street*', in *Tucson Weekly*, 5 January 1995.
<http:// www.filmvault.com/ filmvault/ tw/ m/ miracleon34thstreet.html>

—. '*The Santa Clause*', in *Tucson Weekly*, 12 January 1995.
<http:// www.filmvault.com/ filmvault/ tw/ s/ santaclausethe.html>

Zacharek, Stephanie, '*Bad Santa*', in *Salon.com*, 26 November 2003.
<http:// www.salon.com/ entertainment/ movies/ review/ 2003/ 11/ 26/ bad_santa/ index.html?CP=IMD&DN=110>

—. '*Elf*', in *Salon.com*, 7 November 2003.
<http:// www.salon.com/ entertainment/ movies/ review/ 2003/ 11/ 07/ elf/ index.html?CP=IMD&DN=110>

IMAGE CREDITS

The Bells of St. Mary's (1945)
Rainbow Productions/ Republic Pictures/ Worldvision Enterprises
It's a Wonderful Life (1946)
Liberty Films/ Paramount Pictures
Miracle on 34th Street (1947)
Twentieth Century-Fox Film Corporation
The Bishop's Wife (1947)
The Samuel Goldwyn Company/ MGM/ UA
Scrooge: A Christmas Carol (1951)
George Minter Productions/ United Artists
White Christmas (1954)
Paramount Pictures
We're No Angels (1955)
Paramount Pictures
The Apartment (1960)
The Mirisch Corporation/ MGM/ UA
Santa Claus Conquers the Martians (1964)
Jalor Productions/ Reel Media International
Scrooge (1970)
Waterbury Films/ Cinema Center Films/ Paramount Pictures
Black Christmas (1974)
Vision IV/ Warner Brothers
Trading Places (1983)
Cinema Group Ventures/ Paramount Pictures
A Christmas Story (1983)
Christmas Tree Films/ MGM/ UA Entertainment Company
Santa Claus: The Movie (1985)
Calash Corporation/ GGG/ Santa Claus Ltd./ TriStar Pictures
Scrooged (1988)
Mirage Productions/ Paramount Pictures
National Lampoon's Christmas Vacation (1989)
Hughes Entertainment/ Warner Brothers
Home Alone (1990)
Hughes Entertainment/ Twentieth Century-Fox Film Corporation
The Muppet Christmas Carol (1992)
Jim Henson Productions/ The Jim Henson Company/ Walt Disney Pictures
The Nightmare Before Christmas (1993)
Skellington Productions Inc./ Touchstone Pictures
The Santa Clause (1994)
Walt Disney Pictures/ Hollywood Pictures/ Outlaw Productions
Elf (2003)
Guy Walks into a Bar Productions/ New Line Cinema
Bad Santa (2003)
Dimension Films/ Triptych Pictures/ Blixa Zweite Film Produktion GmbH & Co. KG
Noel (2004)
Neverland Films/ Red Rose Productions LLC
Joyeux Noël (2005)

Nord-Ouest Productions
A Christmas Carol 3D (2009)
Walt Disney Pictures/ ImageMovers Digital

CRESCENT MOON PUBLISHING

ARTS, PAINTING, SCULPTURE

The Art of Andy Goldsworthy: Complete Works
Andy Goldsworthy: Touching Nature
Andy Goldsworthy in Close-Up
Andy Goldsworthy: Pocket Guide
Andy Goldsworthy In America

Land Art: A Complete Guide
Richard Long: The Art of Walking
The Art of Richard Long: Complete Works
Richard Long in Close-Up
Richard Long: Pocket Guide
Land Art In the UK
Land Art in Close-Up
Land Art In the U.S.A.
Land Art: Pocket Guide

Installation Art in Close-Up
Minimal Art and Artists In the 1960s and After
Colourfield Painting

Land Art DVD, TV documentary
Andy Goldsworthy DVD, TV documentary
The Erotic Object: Sexuality in Sculpture From Prehistory to the Present Day
Sex in Art: Pornography and Pleasure in Painting and Sculpture
Postwar Art
Sacred Gardens: The Garden in Myth, Religion and Art
Glorification: Religious Abstraction in Renaissance and 20th Century Art
Early Netherlandish Painting
Leonardo da Vinci
Piero della Francesca
Giovanni Bellini

Fra Angelico: Art and Religion in the Renaissance
Mark Rothko: The Art of Transcendence
Frank Stella: American Abstract Artist
Jasper Johns: Painting By Numbers

Brice Marden
Alison Wilding: The Embrace of Sculpture
Vincent van Gogh: Visionary Landscapes
Eric Gill: Nuptials of God
Constantin Brancusi: Sculpting the Essence of Things
Max Beckmann

Caravaggio
Gustave Moreau
Egon Schiele: Sex and Death In Purple Stockings
Delizioso Fotografico Fervore: Works In Process 1
Sacro Cuore: Works In Process 2
The Light Eternal: J.M.W. Turner
The Madonna Glorified: Karen Arthurs

MEDIA, CINEMA, FEMINISM and CULTURAL STUDIES

J.R.R. Tolkien: The Books, The Films, The Whole Cultural Phenomenon
J.R.R. Tolkien: Pocket Guide
The *Lord of the Rings* Movies: Pocket Guide
The Ghost Dance: The Origins of Religion
Cixous, Irigaray, Kristeva: The *Jouissance* of French Feminism
Julia Kristeva: Art, Love, Melancholy, Philosophy, Semiotics and Psychoanalysis
Luce Irigaray: Lips, Kissing, and the Politics of Sexual Difference
Hélene Cixous I Love You: The *Jouissance* of Writing
Andrea Dworkin
'Cosmo Woman': The World of Women's Magazines
Women in Pop Music
Discovering the Goddess (Geoffrey Ashe)
The Poetry of Cinema
The Sacred Cinema of Andrei Tarkovsky
Andrei Tarkovsky: Pocket Guide
Andrei Tarkovsky: *Mirror*: Pocket Movie Guide
Andrei Tarkovsky: *The Sacrifice*: Pocket Movie Guide
Walerian Borowczyk: Cinema of Erotic Dreams
Jean-Luc Godard: The Passion of Cinema
John Hughes and Eighties Cinema
Ferris Bueller's Day Off: Pocket Movie Guide
Jean-Luc Godard: Pocket Guide
The Cinema of Richard Linklater
Liv Tyler: Star In Ascendance
Blade Runner and the Films of Philip K. Dick
Paul Bowles and Bernardo Bertolucci
Media Hell: Radio, TV and the Press
An Open Letter to the BBC
Detonation Britain: Nuclear War in the UK
Feminism and Shakespeare
Wild Zones: Pornography, Art and Feminism
Sex in Art: Pornography and Pleasure in Painting and Sculpture
Sexing Hardy: Thomas Hardy and Feminism

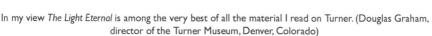

In my view *The Light Eternal* is among the very best of all the material I read on Turner. (Douglas Graham, director of the Turner Museum, Denver, Colorado)

The Light Eternal is a model monograph, an exemplary job. The subject matter of the book is beautifully organised and dead on beam. (Lawrence Durrell)

It is amazing for me to see my work treated with such passion and respect. (Andrea Dworkin)

Sex-Magic-Poetry-Cornwall is a very rich essay... It is like a brightly-lighted box. (Peter Redgrove)

CRESCENT MOON PUBLISHING
P.O. Box 393, Maidstone, Kent, ME14 5XU, United Kingdom. www.crmoon.com

Lightning Source UK Ltd.
Milton Keynes UK
UKOW06f1611040816

279970UK00005B/161/P

9 781861 713346